IN ... CE

"His attack on elitism and despair is impressive, his factual evidence undeniable."
Rt. Hon. David Blunkett MP

"A geographer maps the injustices of Selfish Capitalism with scholarly detachment."
Oliver James, author of *Affluenza*

"Beliefs which serve privilege, elitism and inequality infect our minds like computer viruses. But now Dorling provides the brain-cleaning software we need to begin creating a happier society."
Richard Wilkinson, Emeritus Professor of Social Epidemiology and author of *The Spirit Level*

"A powerful and passionate book. Useful contribution to the policy debate."
Diane Coyle, *Enlightened Economist blog*

"An impassioned and informed plea for greater social justice."
Peder Clark, *Public Health Today*

"This is a high content, high value book, to be recommended to anyone interested or involved in anything to do with poverty, inequality and injustice and attempts to redress them."
Edward Harkins, *Scotregen*

"Dorling's analysis is quietly, devastatingly persuasive. Once you've read him you have to reassess how you live."
Peter Florence, Director of the Hay Festival

"It occupies a place on my bookshelf where I can reach it easily, looking for the many neat arguments which carry the egalitarian cause forward."
Don Flynn in *Chartist*

"An indictment of our political classes and their neglect of the disadvantaged in contemporary Britain."
Diane Reay, Professor of Education (*Blackwells online review*)

"Witty, well-researched, well-intentioned and brimful of facts."
Jonathan Wright, *Geographical*

"Like the recent work of writers such as Richard Wilkinson, Kate Pickett and Oliver James, [Dorling] provides valuable ammunition for attacking the ideas of our rulers and his book deserves a wide readership."
Iain Ferguson, *Socialist Review*

"Engaged and angry."
New Left Review

"Essential reading for everyone concerned with social justice."
Morning Star

"One of the foremost thinkers on the issue of social inequality today."
Labour briefing

"The original edition of *Injustice* stands out as a masterpiece. This updated edition is perhaps even more important today."
Henry Parkyn-Smith, *Counterfire*

"Dorling's unsettling account makes it clear that inequity and inequality is less about 'ideology' and more about the self-serving interests of the powerful. His book is a passionate call for change."
Aniko Horvath, King's College London

"A must-read for those seeking to dispel the naturalness of injustice while reckoning with the fallout of the past five years of surging, post-recession inequality."
Geoffrey DeVerteuil, Cardiff University

This book is an extensively revised and updated edition of *Injustice: Why social inequality persists*, first published in 2010.

Other related titles from Danny Dorling with Policy Press

Ballas, D., Dorling, D. and Hennig, B.D. (2014) *The Social Atlas of Europe*

Dorling, D. (2013) *Unequal Health: The scandal of our times*
Extracts available as three ebooks:
1. *Public Health – Cholera to coalition*
2. *Social Medicine – Polarisation and perspectives*
3. *Health Inequalities – From Titanic to the crash*

Dorling, D. (2012) *Fair Play: A Daniel Dorling reader on social justice*

Dorling, D. and Thomas, B. (2011) *Bankrupt Britain: An atlas of social change*

Shaw, M., Davey Smith, G., Thomas, B. and Dorling, D. (2008) *The Grim Reaper's road map: An atlas of mortality in Britain*

Thomas, B. and Dorling, D. (2007) *Identity in Britain: A cradle-to-grave atlas*

Dorling, D., Rigby, J., Wheeler, B., Ballas, D., Thomas, B., Fahmy, E., Gordon, D. and Lupton, R. (2007) *Poverty, wealth and place in Britain, 1968 to 2005*

Wheeler, B., Shaw, M., Mitchell, R. and Dorling, D. (2005) *Life in Britain: Using Millennial Census data to understand poverty, inequality and place: Ten summary reports and a technical report*

Dorling, D. and Thomas, B. (2004) *People and places: A 2001 Census atlas of the UK*

Davey Smith, G., Dorling, D. and Shaw, M. (eds) (2001) *Poverty, inequality and health: 1800–2000 – A reader*

Mitchell, R., Dorling, D. and Shaw, M. (2000) *Inequalities in life and death: What if Britain were more equal?*

Shaw, M., Dorling, D., Gordon, D. and Davey Smith, G. (1999, 2000) *The widening gap: Health inequalities and policy in Britain*

Gordon, D., Davey Smith, G., Dorling, D. and Shaw, M. (eds) (1999) *Inequalities in health: The evidence presented to the Independent Inquiry into Inequalities in Health, chaired by Sir Donald Acheson*

INJUSTICE

WHY SOCIAL INEQUALITY STILL PERSISTS

REVISED EDITION

DANNY DORLING

This edition first published in Great Britain in 2015 by

Policy Press
University of Bristol
1-9 Old Park Hill
Bristol BS8 1SD
UK
t: +44 (0)117 954 5940
pp-info@bristol.ac.uk
www.policypress.co.uk

North American office:
The Policy Press
c/o The University of Chicago Press
1427 East 60th Street
Chicago, IL 60637, USA
t: +1 773 702 7700
f: +1 773 702 9756
sales@press.uchicago.edu
www.press.uchicago.edu

British Library Cataloguing in Publication Data
A catalogue record for this book is available from the British Library

Library of Congress Cataloging-in-Publication Data
A catalog record for this book has been requested

ISBN 978-1-4473-2075-3 [paperback]
ISBN 978-1-4473-2077-7 [ePub]
ISBN 978-1-4473-2078-4 [Kindle]

Cover design by Soapbox Design.
Printed and bound in Great Britain by TJ International, Padstow
Policy Press uses environmentally responsible print partners.

MIX
Paper from responsible sources
FSC www.fsc.org FSC® C013056

Rakaia Bridge, New Zealand, as first mentioned on page 60

To my parents,

Bronwen and David Dorling

Contents

List of figures

Acknowledgements

Alison Shaw at Policy Press revised the structure of this book and very tactfully persuaded me to at least try to be less self-indulgent and wordy; I am very grateful to her, to three anonymous reviewers for their critical comments on an early draft, to Jo Morton, who oversaw the production of the book, to Dave Worth, for typesetting it and to Margaret Vaudrey (first edition) and Caroline Wilding (second edition) for compiling the index. Dawn Rushen copy-edited both editions of the book and convinced me to stop repeating myself so much. Paul Coles at the University of Sheffield redrew all the figures, and then Ailsa Allen of the University of Oxford redrew them again as I updated the data for this edition. Thank you all.

Dimitris Ballas, John Bibby, Stacy Hewitt, Bob Hughes, Steve Kidd, Bill Lodge, Charles Pattie, Kate Pickett, Molly Scott Cato, Ludi Simpson, Judith Watson and Richard Wilkinson also commented constructively on all or parts of earlier versions. The British Academy and the Leverhulme Trust funded most of the time out needed to begin and end the work, and I am very grateful to them. My colleagues in the School of Geography and the Environment at the University of Oxford, and at the Departments of Geography at both the University of Sheffield and the University of Canterbury in New Zealand (where the book began) were also extremely understanding. In particular, this book draws on the experiences of working with the Social and Spatial Inequalities Group at Sheffield, with colleagues from the Department of Social Medicine at the University of Bristol, with many other colleagues who have been producing reports on poverty and wealth for the Joseph Rowntree Foundation and the UK government, and with those with whom I have carried out work internationally on inequality, often as a result of the Worldmapper project (www.worldmapper.org).

Dave Gordon of the University of Bristol kindly provided the original statistics on poverty used in Chapter 4, and I am grateful to Dan Vale of The Young Foundation who did me a similar service as regards the statistics on mental health used in Chapter 7. Helena Tunstall, now at the University of Edinburgh, helped draw up Figure 21 and pointed me to the original source. Jon Minton, now at the University of Glasgow, introduced me to the interdisciplinary literature combining social evil, social control and war. Tomoki Nakaya of Ritsumeikan University introduced me to social statistics on Japan, and Kjartan Sveinsson, then of the Runnymede Trust, kindly pointed me to information on Iceland I would not otherwise have found, as also did Ben Hennig on Germany. I am also grateful to Dimitris Ballas, Anna Barford, Ben Hennig, John Pritchard, Mark Ramsden, Jan Rigby, Bethan Thomas, Dan Vickers and Ben Wheeler for their collaboration over the years, which is reflected in this book. Half a dozen former PhD students feature in these lists; I have almost certainly learnt more from them (and others I have 'taught') than they have learnt from me: thank you.

Finally I need to thank those people without whom there would be no book. Bronwen Dorling and Alison Dorling both helped turn my initial dyslexic encodings into more readable text. Bronwen, my mother, began trying to teach me to read when I was eight years old and finished trying to teach me how to write when I was 38. This second edition could not have been created without an enormous amount of help from David Dorling, my father, who retrieved the text from old files, corrected it, searched out new data and then meticulously commented on and corrected my revisions. This book is dedicated to my mother and father because they did so much more to help create it than authors' parents usually do!

Danny Dorling
Marston, Oxford
March 2015

The original bibliography, open source versions of all the figures, data tables not shown in this edition and the Excel spreadsheets that were used to create both the old and the revised figures in this book, and in its first edition, are available on the Injustice web pages at www.policypress.co.uk and via www.dannydorling.org

Letter from America: commentary by Sam Pizzigati

We live in a trickle-down world, or so insist our world's richest and those who cheer them on. The enormous fortunes our rich are amassing, their story goes, eventually trickle down and benefit us all.

Danny Dorling agrees – to a point. We do live, as he relates in these remarkable pages, in a trickle-down world. But what's trickling down brings us no benefits. The reason? Wealth isn't trickling down from above. Myths are. Myths that rationalise our young century's colossal concentration of riches and power. Myths – Danny calls them the 'ideologies of inequality' – that aim to justify injustice.

This injustice envelops us today and assaults us from every direction. We can't escape it. Injustice lurks everywhere we look, everywhere we click. Week by week, only the particulars change.

These particulars just happened to cross my computer screen over the last several days.

In California's plush Beverly Hills, one news report informs us, enterprising developers now have under construction six luxury homes they plan to offer at an astounding $100 million each. In nearby Bel Air, another new home will soon go on the market at a projected $200 million. This impressive manse sports its own IMAX theatre and a master bedroom suite that spans 7,000 square feet, about triple the size of the average American home.

The average American family, meanwhile, can no longer afford to live in the nation's choicest cities. To buy a home in San Francisco, a family currently needs an annual income of at least $140,000, nearly triple the nation's median household take-home pay. With homes so expensive, rents in San Francisco have soared. A typical one-bedroom apartment now lets for $3,460 per month.

Not all landlords, to be sure, can cash in on these soaring rents. Some have long-time tenants still covered by San Francisco's rent-control restrictions. But those restrictions have a loophole. Landlords can legally raise the rents they charge by 3 per cent a year. The greediest among them are storing up these allowable annual rate hikes, then hitting tenants with one huge rent increase that incorporates multiple years. The blindsided tenants can't afford this 'legal' rent increase. They have to move out.

On paper, theft in the United States never rates as 'legal' — unless, apparently, you already have a great deal and attempt to steal a great deal more. Consider billionaire Ira Rennert. He diverted the proceeds from bonds one of his companies issued into a slush fund to build a 29-bedroom mansion in the Hamptons, the summer watering hole for Wall Street's deepest pockets. A federal grand jury found Rennert guilty of looting. His penalty? A judge has just ruled he has to pay back $213 million.

Rennert currently sits on a personal fortune worth $6.1 billion. Given merely a modest return on his annual investments, he should be able to pay off that $213 million 'penalty' and still end up this year with a higher net worth than he held when the year started.

But Rennert may still feel personally aggrieved when he contemplates the 'justice' just meted out to Conrad Hughes Hilton III, the great-grandson of the founder of the Hilton hotel corporate empire. The 21-year-old Hilton faced felony charges from a July 2014 incident that saw him threaten to kill the crew and pilot of a British Airways flight. Seems that Hilton, after getting caught smoking tobacco and marijuana in the plane's lavatory, unleashed what news reports have described as 'a series of profanity-laced tirades' and accused the flight crew of 'taking the peasants' side'. Hilton originally faced 22 years in prison on felony charges. Prosecutors instead have settled for a single misdemeanor charge. Poor kids in America who disrespect authority regularly get shot. For viciously disrespectful young Hilton, prosecutors accepted probation.

How can society keep young people like Conrad Hilton on the straight and narrow? The Florida billionaire William Koch has a character-building activity that he's promoting as a solution. Polo!

The Oxbridge Academy, an elite private school in Palm Beach County that Koch spent $60 million to create, is launching a polo team to ensure students 'a positive, life-changing opportunity'. This particular life-changing opportunity doesn't come cheap. Oxbridge is supplying students with horse-riding lessons worth $250 an hour and $500 helmets. Students have to supply their own polo pants and $500-per-pair paddock boots.

Elsewhere in America, harried educators and parents aren't thinking horse-riding lessons. In Pennsylvania, the state with the widest per-student spending gap between poor and rich school districts, budget cuts are decimating educational offerings. In the city of Pittsburgh, Jessie Ramey's son sits in a classroom stuffed with 39 other students. The school's music, arts, and tutoring programmes have all been axed.

"Just about everything that isn't nailed down," says Ramey, "has been lost."

Lawmakers in Congress could, of course, tax the rich to help end the budget squeeze in America's public schools. Instead they're busy passing legislation that repeals what remains of the estate tax, the only federal level on grand fortunes like the $3 billion that William Koch sits atop.

This move to make all inherited wealth tax-free will cost the federal government $250 billion dollars in lost revenue over the next ten years. The same lawmakers who blessed this move have also voted to cut food stamps for America's poorest families by $125 billion.

What will future generations think about these sorts of injustices – and about us? Will they wonder how civilised societies could accept realities this grotesque? Will they even us consider us civilised?

Taxes, the great American jurist Oliver Wendell Holmes once noted, represent the price we pay for civilisation. In the United States and Britain, the developed world's two most unequal major nations, elites have been unwilling to pay this price. The rich grab as much and as furiously as they can. Virtually untaxed, the wealth they grab multiplies and metastasises – into a cancer on our culture.

Danny Dorling labels our staggeringly unequal distribution of income and wealth the 'disease behind injustice', a disease that binds the elitism, exclusion, prejudice, greed, and despair that define our epoch. But why do we let inequality define us? And that brings us full-circle back to the trickle-down essence of our contemporary age: we have simply imbibed too many myths from those who lord over us.

A century ago, amid the struggle for social insurance to protect workers injured on the job, men of wealth and power argued that workers insured against disability would cut off their own limbs to reap the rewards disability protection would provide. Today's rich and their hired hands seldom get that crude. They spin more sophisticated myths. Danny Dorling examines – and exposes – them all in the pages that follow. Sometimes with figures and charts. Sometimes with history. Sometimes with unrelenting logic.

Some words of warning about this second edition of *Injustice* for my fellow American readers: this noble work invites you – indeed, expects you — to take a leap out of your book-reading comfort zone.

We Americans have a reputation for not paying much attention to the lives people beyond our shores live – and even less attention to the lessons these lives may have for us. Danny Dorling and the good folks who have published this book have fixed on the notion that this reputation may be undeserved. This second *Injustice* edition does add a bountiful amount of material about the United States. But these pages also abound with stories and stats from the UK, that proverbial 'other side of the pond'.

Dorling and his fellow Brits are, in effect, betting that we Americans can learn as much from their experience as they can learn from ours. To me, that sounds like a fairly reasonable proposition.

But go ahead and decide for yourself. Read this book with an open mind. Let Danny Dorling, a social geographer by trade, guide you through our unequal, unjust world. You may never be the same. And if enough of us read and take inspiration from these pages, maybe that world will never be the same either.

Sam Pizzigati edits Too Much, a commentary on excess and inequality published by the Washington, DC-based Institute for Policy Studies. His most recent book is: *The rich don't always win: The forgotten triumph over plutocracy that created the American middle class, 1900–1970.*

Foreword by Richard Wilkinson and Kate Pickett

Money exists objectively as coins and bank notes. But it only works as money, as a medium of exchange and store of wealth, while people have confidence in its value and other people's willingness to accept it as payment. Without that subjective element, coins, banknotes and cheques are nothing more than a collection of metal discs or piles of paper. The same is true of the social structure and functioning of our society. Our society has an objective, physical reality – the existence of rich and poor, living in larger or smaller houses, the different schools their children go to, the towns and villages, police, hospitals, judicial systems, prisons, and so on. What holds them all in place, like the mortar between bricks, and gives each society its particular character, is the subjective collective beliefs and behaviour of the people in that society.

What Danny Dorling has done in this book is to show that these subjective elements – the beliefs and conceptions which justify the wealth differences, elitism and structure of inequality in our modern society – are based on falsehoods. He has, in effect, shown that the bricks of society are held in place not with proper mortar containing cement, but with wet sand. It is, for instance, false to think that we have to go on paying the rich huge salaries and bonuses because they have rare talents which we will not be able to replace if they emigrate. It is false to think that their greed somehow benefits the rest of society. It is false to think that elitist societies which stigmatise a large proportion of the population as inferior are more efficient. And it is false to think that people's position in the social hierarchy reflects how they have been sorted according to genetic differences in ability. How could we have fallen for a set of such improbable stories so obviously promulgated to justify and support privilege?

As individuals we tend to understand ourselves, and to explain our actions to others, in ways which are self-justifying. We try to present ourselves in a good light, as if to recruit people to a personal supporters club. The same thing happens at a societal scale. The dominant ideology always favours beliefs, conceptions and interpretations of reality which justify the system of social organisation and the position of the privileged. Societal ideologies typically suggest that their structure is a reflection of human nature, and so could not be other than it is.

But the truth is that human beings have lived in every kind of society, from the most egalitarian to the most tyrannical and we are equipped to behave in different ways according to the social context. The assumption that modern societies are a direct expression of human nature reflects a remarkable ignorance of the fact that, throughout at least 90 per cent of the time that humans have existed as 'anatomically modern', they lived in remarkably egalitarian societies, based on food sharing and gift exchange with little or no sign of differences in rank. The modern pattern of inequality was largely absent among hunters and gatherers and began to develop only with the beginnings of agriculture. In some parts of the world agriculture dates back around 10,000 years, but in most places it is very much more recent – just a moment in human existence.

We do of course have characteristics which have enabled us to adapt to living in highly unequal, stratified, societies, but these are almost certainly pre-human in origin. Dominance hierarchies, like animal ranking systems and pecking orders, are, in an important sense, a throwback to an evolved psychological and behavioural repertoire which has pre-human – or subhuman – foundations. Social relationships in animal ranking systems are little more than hierarchies based on who is strong enough to bully whom – the strongest animal ends up at the top and the weakest at the bottom. Disputes about status are resolved by trials of strength which continue until one of the combatants backs off, accepting inferiority.

With an impressive body of evidence, Christopher Boehm shows in his book, *Moral Origins: The evolution of virtue, altruism and shame* (2012), that it was only as humans started to hunt big game that assertively egalitarian societies, with a fully human social morality – respecting the needs of the weak as well as the strong – began to replace dominance hierarchies and their 'might is right' social structure.

The contrast between the behavioural logic of dominance hierarchies and of egalitarian societies could hardly be greater. The core of the difference is whether we are all rivals, in competition with each other, or whether we recognise each other's needs and cooperate. Dominance hierarchies are about self-advancement, everyone out for themselves – regardless of the needs of others. But greater equality is about sharing, cooperation and reciprocity. The fundamental issue is whether we compete for scarce resources, the strongest getting the lion's share, or whether we cooperate and share more equally. Because, as members of the same species, we all have the same needs, there is always the potential for conflict over access to scarce resources. The Hobbesian 'war of each against all' reflects our potential to compete like animals for access to food, sexual partners, territories, nesting sites and so on. But unlike animals, we not only have the potential to be each other's worst rivals; we can also be each other's best source of cooperation, assistance, love and learning. Other people can be the best or the worst, depending on the nature of our relationships.

The structure of social relations has always been so fundamental to human wellbeing that we have evolved an extraordinary sensitivity to their quality – to hierarchy and social status on the one hand and to friendship and equality on the other. That is why study after study shows that friendship is highly protective of health and happiness while social status differentiation and low social status are damaging. The nature of social relationships has always been of paramount importance and it all hinges on whether we recognise each other's needs or whether we pursue our own interests regardless of others. That is why, in the words of the anthropologist, Marshall Sahlins: 'Friends make gifts and gifts make friends'. The gift is the most concrete symbol that we recognise each other's needs and will not fight for possession. It is also why to refuse a gift is, in some societies, tantamount to a declaration of war. The ancient truth of the link between the nature of social relations and whether or not we share access to scarce resources is spelt out in words like 'companion' (combining '*com*' meaning together and '*panis*' meaning bread) which reminds us that our friends are those with whom we share food. The religious symbolism of the communion and the fact that we still eat meals together both reflect the importance of sharing access to the necessities of life.

Rather than social behaviour being based either wholly on equality and sharing or wholly on self-advancement and status competition, every society contains a mixture of both, but the balance between the two differs radically according to the level of inequality and the way it appears to rank us according to degrees of apparent superiority and inferiority. What is crucial is whether we find ourselves in a world in which we depend on cooperation and reciprocity, in which empathy is important, or in a world where we have to fend for ourselves, in which some people appear supremely important and others almost worthless, in which we feel our outward wealth is taken as the marker of our inner 'worth' and we all become highly sensitive to being put down and disrespected.

As a result, greater inequality brings out the worst in us. Research repeatedly shows that more unequal societies suffer more violence, community life weakens, bullying is more common in schools, people trust each other less, mental health suffers, standards of child wellbeing are lower, people are less willing to help each other, the penal system is harsher, there is more status anxiety and people spend more of their incomes on the rivalry of conspicuous consumption that fuels consumerism.

As we become more aware of the forces which shape human social behaviour and of the key role of inequality, we realise that we have, as never before, the possibility of creating a society better for all of us. Injustice is not only the stuff of which large-scale inequality is built, it is also a major obstacle to sustainability. With this book Danny Dorling has struck a powerful blow against it and taken us towards a better future.

Richard Wilkinson is Emeritus Professor at the University of Nottingham Medical School and **Kate Pickett** is Professor of Epidemiology in the Department of Health Sciences at the University of York. They are co-authors of *The spirit level: Why more equal societies almost always do better* (Allen Lane, 2009).

1

Introduction

> Injustice is sustained by many things. One is a sense of inevitability: that it's just one of those ugly, painful things life throws at you. Another is resignation: the mantra of 'there is no alternative', a general lack of hope that things could be different. And then there's intimidation: that the powerful are too strong to be overcome....[1]

The human world is changing at a greater rate than it has ever changed before. All kinds of peaks of consumption are being climbed. Global population growth has passed its maximum, with populations predicted soon to be falling, and most likely within the lifetimes of today's infants. Worldwide, we had our greatest ever number of babies as long ago as 1990.[2] There are more young adults alive today than there have ever been before, and possibly more than there will ever be again given the decline in fertility, and the stabilisation of world population.[3] Ask the young today why things are as bad as they currently are, why inequality is at its most pronounced and they may respond that there is little alternative. To be optimistic, they will need to think several moves ahead. Our current injustices are unsustainable. They will be overcome, but how?

Although few would say that they agree with injustice, we nonetheless live in an unjust world. In the world's richest countries, injustice is caused less and less by having too few resources to share around fairly. Rather, it is increasingly maintained by widespread adherence to beliefs that propagate injustice and waste. And although these beliefs are often presented as natural and long-standing, in fact, they are mostly modern creations. What appears fair and normal today will often be seen as unjust and wasteful tomorrow. It is our modern-day beliefs that are upholding current injustices.

This book aims to help redefine *injustice*. While no one claims to be on the side of injustice, without the continued spread of beliefs that actually support injustice, it would not survive long in its present form. Now that we have enough resources for all to be well fed, clothed, schooled, housed, cared for and employed, much that was previously seen as simply unfortunate has instead become unjust and, in some ways, unsustainable. We are doomed if we continue along our present trajectory, as thousands of scientists know, and as many activists, such as Naomi Klein, explain more and more forcefully.[4] What is far less often explained, however, is what underpins the current injustices that sustain our now increasingly unsustainable lifestyles.

Five years ago, in the first edition of this book, I suggested that the five tenets of injustice were as follows: *elitism is efficient*, *exclusion is necessary*, *prejudice is natural*, *greed is good* and *despair is inevitable*. Because of widespread and growing opposition to these five key unjust beliefs, including the acceptance that so many should now be 'losers', most of those who, in effect, advocate injustice, are becoming ever more careful with their words. And although attitudes are turning away from injustice, the majority of those in power in most rich countries still believe in these tenets of injustice.[5]

Although those in power may want to make the conditions of life a little less painful for others, they do not necessarily believe that there is a cure for modern social ills for everyone. Rather, they believe that just a few children are sufficiently able to be fully and properly educated, and only a few of those are then able to govern; the rest must be led. They believe that the poor will always be with us, no matter how well we organise our lives. Enough have also come to believe that most others are naturally inferior to them, and so deserve less. Many of this small group believe that their friends' greed and their own is helping the rest of humanity. They are convinced that to argue against such a counsel of despair is unrealistic and foolhardy.

This book brings together evidence showing that the beliefs sustaining our current injustices are unfounded. The evidence also shows how people who end up in power come so easily to hold these beliefs, or become converted to them, and how their beliefs provide false justification for those who benefit most from injustice. Five years ago, many of the links were less clear to see, and the economic crash had only just taken place. Today, in 2015, the connections between social inequality and environmental damage are far more obvious, as is the growing outrage of so many people faced with the realisation that the system of a few holding most of the wealth and consequently having the most power is not actually in the interests of the majority.

1.1 The beliefs that uphold injustice

Within affluent countries, especially the more economically unequal of affluent countries,[6] social injustices are now being recreated, renewed and supported by the five broad sets of unjust beliefs. They have old origins, but have taken on a modern relevance. Although these beliefs have now been publicly condemned as wrong, and they are beliefs that most individuals claim not to support, the acceptance of these beliefs by just a few, and the reluctance of many others to confront those few, is crucial to maintaining injustice in our times and our lands of plenty. World population is stabilising for the first time in two hundred years. It is because of this that we know there will be enough to go round.

This book brings together and updates many of the arguments against upholding these five broad beliefs. It suggests that if injustices are to be reduced for all, it is important not merely to claim that you do not hold these beliefs, but to positively reject them. Simply saying that you reject the labels attached to these beliefs (elitism, exclusion, prejudice, greed and despair) is not sufficient to reduce injustice. And so one aim of this book is to help readers to reject the often subtle propagation of these beliefs by so many of those currently in power, including politicians, the wealthiest 1 per cent, and much of the media they control.

The beliefs that uphold injustice in its contemporary form have been given many names and been categorised in many ways,[7] but most of the categorisations come within the following five beliefs: elitism is efficient, exclusion is necessary, prejudice is natural, greed is good and despair is inevitable. Each belief also creates a distinct set of victims – the delinquents, the debarred, the discarded, the debtors and the depressed. Those who uphold these beliefs find it hard to see possibilities beyond the current situation, which they see as inevitable; they are, in effect, advocates for the continuation of injustice, arguing that the victims will always be with us, in large numbers – 'that's just how it is', they say.

It is a sign of the duplicity of our times that institutions that often claim they are against elitism do much to promote it; that governments that say they aim to reduce social exclusion actually create it; that movements that pretend not to be prejudiced foster hate; that academic disciplines where the orthodoxy is to advocate greed (referred to as sound economics) cannot say so explicitly; and that many experts argue that the best that most can hope for is a life of which they themselves would despair. They do not, of course, say this explicitly, but it is implied in their accusation that those who argue against them are being 'utopian'. When some may say that in general people are only saved from despair by unrealistic optimism, then promoting unrealistic optimism becomes the only remedy: 'Go buy a lottery ticket'.

I am not a utopian. I was a mapmaker, someone who draws pictures of what is and what has been, not what could be. I began studying society by drawing detailed images of the UK, initially using largely social data concerning the 1970s and 1980s. I drew these images when we were first able to use microcomputers as a kind of social microscope.[8] However, I would say that cartography, exploration and utopia have always been romantically linked.[9] Drawing patterns to social structure has made me question how those patterns were formed and have been sustained.

It took me two decades to move from trying to find better ways to describe the shape of society to trying to describe better what sustains and alters its form. First, I relied on data, and then on reading and collecting others' data and ideas. I was searching for the beliefs that make the current levels of inequality and injustice possible. Here, the evidence that those beliefs exist is brought together. I, along with many others, realised that the beliefs that uphold injustice can be demonstrated to be unfounded, and that greater justice is only achievable if there is widespread rejection of them.

What has irritated me about the whole direction of politics since 1979 is that it has always prioritised individualism. People seem to have forgotten about the collectivist society; to have been convinced that there is only themselves and their families to consider. Does anyone else count? Does anyone else matter? The short answer to this is, yes, and we need to change our approach. This is the means of changing the trend towards ever-growing inequality. If you can change the approach, you really need to influence beliefs close to the heart and soul. While influencing heart and soul is the method, the object is to reduce injustice.[10]

As those with most power continue to promote elitism, exclusion, prejudice, greed and despair, injustice will not be reduced. Injustice is described as inevitable and as pragmatic politics, however it is only in the most unequal of rich nations that those with power can explicitly say that they believe there is good in the inequalities sustained by this injustice. Elsewhere in the rich world, most who favour injustice are more circumspect, but as the examples in this book go on to show, the powerful have been effective in many countries where life chances are now less fair than they were just a few decades ago. The good news, though, is that as time passes, those who support injustice are increasingly being opposed and exposed, and social movements are gathering momentum to challenge their views.

Because belief in the five tenets of injustice is so widespread among people in power, these beliefs are then propagated through what those people control. For instance, many of those who fund and manage educational institutions encourage teachers to present these beliefs as truths. Governments, whose departments for social security increasingly label the poor as wanting, feckless, immoral and criminal, also propagate the beliefs. They are supported by the media, where stories that some people are less deserving are common, where wealthy city businessmen (and a few businesswomen) are lauded as superheroes, and where immigrants looking to work for a crumb of the City's bonuses are seen as 'scroungers'.

The core beliefs of injustice are supported by a politics whose mantra is that without greed, there would be no growth, and without growth, we would all be doomed.[11] These beliefs are supported by industries, whose spokespeople say we must continue to consume more and more, and which now manufacture pharmaceutical treatments to cope with the consequent despair on a mass scale – within rich countries and worldwide. Mental distress and despair is the largest growth sector for pharmaceutical companies and front-line medical practitioners.[12] So in various ways academia, government, the media, politics and industry, each is a key element in promoting the tenets of injustice.

1.2 The five faces of social inequality

This book is concerned mainly with injustice in affluent countries, but it does touch on wider debates concerning worldwide inequalities. If you had to choose one word to epitomise the nature of human society as it is currently arranged worldwide, there is no better word than 'injustice'. Across all walks of life, between continents, and over the decades, injustice has been constantly prevalent. Hundreds of maps can be found online revealing inequality and injustice.[13]

Chapter 2 provides a summary of the recent history and current extent of injustice in general in affluent countries, before Chapters 3–7 go on to examine the domains most affected by each facet of inequality, starting with education. Chapter 8 concludes the argument, discussing what has changed since the first edition of this book was published in 2009.

'Elitism is efficient'

The origins of the ideas that currently constitute the core beliefs of injustice can be traced back to when we last lived in times as unequal as today, during the last 'gilded age', which began at the end of the American Civil War in 1865, and ended in 1914 in Europe, and in many ways continued to the late 1920s in the US.[14] Chapter 3 suggests that elite prizes such as those established by Alfred Nobel came about when they did, along with the first intelligence (IQ) tests, because it was only at that point that there were spoils great enough to be shared out more widely in rich countries, and those who had gained most needed to justify their positions in newly created hierarchies. Nobel Prizes were first awarded in 1901 in a time of such wealth concentration that it was unimaginable that there would not be a 'natural' elite.

The statistics produced by some international bodies, such as the Programme for International Student Assessment (PISA) of the Organisation for Economic Co-operation and Development (OECD), suggest that many such bodies still continue the tradition of trying to defend elitism as natural, but these bodies are now far more coy about their intent than those in the 1890s that first used social statistics to suggest that paupers mainly bred more paupers. That coyness suggests that in recent years some progress against rising elitism has been made, because elitists now know to hide their core beliefs about the distribution of human ability in obscure technical notes.

Although elitist views still underlie the beliefs of many in power, they have also now been institutionalised in the form of bodies such as the OECD. Those destined to be paupers today are labelled children 'limited in their ability' – a staggering seventh of all children born in the richest of countries are given this label today.[15] Almost 70 years ago in the UK, William Beveridge named 'ignorance' as one of his five social evils, but as ignorance has been overcome across the rich world, widespread elitism has taken its place, and children who would have appeared of normal ability in the 1940s are now called 'limited' today.

'Exclusion is necessary'

The most terrible result of elitism is that it can be used to justify the exclusion of so many people from normal social activity. Chapter 4 suggests that it was in the most affluent of countries only just over a century ago that the supposed scientific theories defending inequality began to be drawn up. The modern origins of exclusion can be traced to an academic paper of 1895, when data were first presented that showed the geographical distribution of English and Welsh paupers in a way that was designed to suggest that pauperisation was some kind of natural phenomenon.[16] The timing of this was no coincidence – this was the first time under a market system that such an abundance of wealth had emerged, the first time that leaving some people destitute became so obviously an option – a choice – and not inevitable.

It was only in the 19th century that it became necessary to try to update feudal justifications for the unequal distribution of that wealth, and to explain why so many should have to live with so little. The new justifications became dominant beliefs between the 1890s and the 1930s, but were then rejected for a generation before gaining ground again, as social exclusion rose from the late 1960s onwards, alongside the great growth in personal debt. Today, debts are often first taken out to keep up appearances, credit now being viewed as normal – something you have to take out just to study at university. The old social evil described by Beveridge as 'want' was cut down in size, but has now been replaced by an increased reliance on debt to finance the necessities of life: food rent, clothes, repairs to the car or to the hot water boiler, or any other unexpected expense that cannot be afforded.

The cycles of 'good luck' and then 'bad luck' through which people fell into exclusion due to having too little were first established as we currently see them only in the 1960s.[17] Before then, to be truly rich was to be landed.[18] To be poor was, for many, normal. Today, one in six of all households in rich countries are again excluded from social norms due to poverty, and are poor in at least two of the ways of assessing poverty.[19] What now makes those households poor are the effects of the riches of others.

'Prejudice is natural'

Elitism and exclusion have further causes and corollaries, and chief among these is prejudice. As elitism and inequality rise, and as more people become socially excluded, or are able to exclude themselves by using their wealth to avoid mixing, those at the top more often look down on others with ever greater disdain and, at the same time, with fear, as evidenced by growing social segregation.[20] Those at the bottom are also less likely to trust others, and more likely to become fearful in a society that so clearly values them so little. Racism rises in just these kinds of circumstances, and a wider form of racism – a new social Darwinism – quietly spreads.[21] Lack of respect for people seen as beneath you and as above you is widespread, and the banker with his high salary and the cleaner with her low one are both despised.

Chapter 5 documents the process by which prejudice grows. It shows how, over time, inequalities in wealth and health and the widespread acceptance of bigoted views all shrank from their height in the 1920s to reach minima in the early 1970s, before rising up again in that fateful decade of oil shock, inflation and overseas intervention (that is, war). As Owen Jones highlighted in the popular book *Chavs*, and as the rhetoric of 'scroungers' and 'skivers' made clear, it is not hard to make many people scared of those who have the least, who are the least powerful and the least dangerous.

Just as one in seven have been marked as 'limited' by elitist labels, and one in six are labelled as 'poor' by the economic circumstances of exclusion, as a result of new prejudices about how it is acceptable to treat others (which has overtaken the old social evil of 'idleness' in importance and effect), an even higher proportion of one in five households in rich countries were only just managing to get by with great difficulty, even before the financial crash of 2008. Chapter 5 outlines the material mechanism through which prejudice is transmitted between generations, how it is maintained by inherited wealth, and the deep social polarisation that results.

'Greed is good'

The rise of elitism, exclusion and prejudice were all precursors of the age of greed, ushered in during the 1980s, seen as good, and not questioned seriously until 2008. Chapter 6 shows how at least a quarter of households are now disregarded in what is considered access to normal infrastructure, whether it be simply the ability to own and drive a car, or having the means to access the internet.

In the US not to have a car these days is not to live as a 'normal' human being.[22] But in the UK almost half of the children of lone parents have no access to a car.[23] Many people who need a car, because they have young children or find it hard to walk or no longer live near shops, have no car, but many of the car journeys made by others are non-essential, and the majority of cars contain only one person, the driver. There are actually enough cars currently owned for all those who need a car to have one.

Mass car driving is the simplest example of what happens when greed begins to be valued in its own right. When you next look at a congested street, with cars jostling to move a few metres forward, pedestrians dodging in between, cyclists weaving dangerously around them, children walking past at the level of exhaust fumes, no one getting anywhere fast, and all those petrol engines continuously running, this is both the symbolic but also the very real collective outcome of individual greed encouraged to grow by the mantra of personal freedom.

'Despair is inevitable'

Unsurprisingly, growing despair is the result for those living in the most elitist of affluent societies, where inequalities are allowed and encouraged to rise untrammelled, where more and more are excluded or live partly in fear of becoming ostracised if they slip down the social ladder, where prejudice towards the 'lower orders' begins again to become normal, and where greed is commonly referred to implicitly (if not often explicitly) as good. Chapter 7 recounts how in the 1990s the fastest rise in despair occurred. This rise was not just in the growing use of prescription medicines, but also in the growth of feelings that there must be more to life.[24] Even children were hit with a feeling of despair, with the fastest increases in adolescent depression being recorded in North America in the 1990s, a rise found not to be due to changing diagnostic practice.[25]

In the UK growing despair appeared to reach new maxima by 2006 when it was reported that a third of families had at least one family member who was suffering from depression or a chronic anxiety disorder.[26] By 2014, more than one in six adults in Scotland were being prescribed anti-depressants each year, the highest number ever recorded.[27] The despair was also public, as shown by the publication of so many books criticising modern trends, the rise of the green movement and of new forms of social protest. Across Europe the majority of best-selling books on subjects such as economics were not business manuals, but alternative treatises on the woes of capitalism.

As early as 2004, anti-globalisation books were almost the only books on business or economics that sold well in Europe.[28] The US was slower to catch on to that trend, but in 2008 voted in a president on a very different ticket from the usual. The UK coalition government of 2010 also acted as if it had a very different ticket.[29] By 2015, austerity had reached such depths in the UK that the paperback edition of Mary O'Hara's *Austerity bites*[30] had to begin by apologising for under-estimating the growing extent of the crisis a year earlier. Over in the US, President Obama's second term in office was concluding to the sound of protestors chanting "Black lives matter".

Chapter 8 brings this book's argument to a conclusion. It concentrates on the 2000s, on how we stumbled into a crisis that no one now denies was of our own making. It then looks at the events of the 2010s. Events matter, but they are moments that reflect an underlying momentum. In Chapters 3–7 questions are asked as to *who*, *why*, *where*, *what* and *when* each new injustice hit, while Chapter 8 instead just asks *how* it is possible to be optimistic in the face of rising social injustices, a financial crash, and its aftermath. It concentrates on what is now different, on what we now know, and on how many more people are now involved in the arguments about what happens next.

Out of the many things that are now different, the increase in access to education is the most important, with a majority of young people in the world being literate, and majorities or near majorities in more equitable rich countries now attending university. Compared with the end of the last gilded age, it is now much harder to see who or what there is left to exploit, and how much harder it will be to fool so many better informed people this time round. Although the subtitle of this second edition has had the word 'still' added, to read 'why social inequality *still* persists', the conclusion is not pessimistic.

1.3 A pocket full of posies

With injustice, all is connected. From the depicting of 19th-century paupers, to the awarding of 20th-century peace prizes, and the mapping of 21st-century global income distributions, injustice is the common denominator. The same patterns of gross inequality are seen again and again. They appear when health inequalities are calculated and wealth inequalities are tabulated. Within rich countries, the artificial portrayal of children's abilities as lying along bell curves (as if these are natural things) is unjust.

In response to growing inequalities and unsustainability, the consequent curving upwards of rates of depression and anxiety is closely connected to how children are treated, how they are ranked, and how they expect to be treated later, when they are adults. Portraying large groups of adults as inferior is similarly unjust, as is promoting unprecedented greed among a few as some kind of benefit to the many, or seeing the distress of so many as a reflection of their imputed failings. Injustice has always survived because of its support by the powerful. The same is true today, but never have the powerful had so little of real substance to use as the basis to defend their huge wealth.

Arguments against injustice used to be rare treatises. A single essay against slavery written in 1785 could be held up high as a shining example of such work two centuries later,[31] but it has largely only been within living memory that we have started to learn that it was not the essays of aristocrats that made differences in the past – it was just that their contributions were far more often recorded and preserved.

Slaves made slavery uneconomic by not adapting willingly to slavery; they revolted. Even the science of management and business studies, which began with the study of slavery, could not make slavery work.[32] Similarly, it is only within the last century that the lives of the 'great men' of science, politics and business – men who are still so often put on pedestals – have been re-examined and found not to produce biographies of awe.[33] Their fallibilities, failings and most importantly, their luck, are all being revealed more frequently. In case after case it transpires that they are remembered for an achievement that was always just about to be made because of the circumstances or the actions of others around them, now mostly forgotten.

It is a misplaced belief that a few great people themselves standing on the shoulders of giants achieve human advancement. There are no giants and there are no superhuman people, and to say that they exist – to say that some people are that different – is unjust.[34] There are always some people who are a little ahead of the game, but who they are is changing. As Paul Mason explained in late 2014: 'Among the young, leftist clientele of the cafés in Exarchia, the famous bohemian district of Athens, they are thinking several moves ahead.'[35] There have never been more young adults in the world than there are now, and there may never be again. These young people need to think ahead, but they also need to look back.

Men still pay homage to other men. And men are far more often published and quoted, as the selection, mostly of the words of men, used in this chapter makes clear. But those ever quoted are themselves a tiny subset of all people. While the vast majority of that tiny group of humans who have had their histories recorded have been male, a new generation of men and women is beginning to realise how it is both unjust and unrealistic to claim more than an immeasurably small impact as their personal contribution.

One scholar, Elvin Wyly, who was among the early group to document how sub-prime lending was unsustainable in the US, wrote of his writings recently that all he had done was to have '… gathered a posie of other men's flowers, and only the thread that binds them is my own'.[36] Even that phrase was not his own, he admitted. It was attributed to the title page of one of Peter Gould's books on medical geography. Peter, in turn, was quoting from the title page of a book of poems collected during the Second World War, the author of which was, in turn, was quoting from.…

The earliest recorded version of the 'posie' acknowledgement dates from over 400 years ago, and reads: 'I have here only made a nosegay of culled flowers, and have brought nothing of my own but the thread that ties them together.'[37] The only reason that this was the first recording is that printing had only just been invented then. The idea that we do little more than collect the flowers of others' ideas and simply tie them together in slightly different ways will have begun with the first picking of flowers, long before it could be recorded on paper.

Several years' careful research across many academic disciplines, and the consequent documentation of many others' ideas and comments have come together in this book, which is the bringing together of others' posies with a few of my own thoughts to add to the call for greater levels of social justice. Another year has been spent updating this second edition, using new facts and arguments produced by yet hundreds more people. But the conclusion remains the same – true social justice will both create and require much greater equality than is as yet widely accepted to be possible.[38] However, in recent years we have begun to change what we are prepared to accept more rapidly than before. And, if not now, when?

2

Inequality, the antecedent and outcome of injustice

> In contrast to previous periods in American history, nearly all of the new income and wealth generated over the last decades has gone to the richest Americans. From 2009 to 2012, the incomes of the top 1% grew by 31.4%, whereas the incomes of the bottom 99% grew only by 0.4%....[1]

Social inequality within rich countries persists because of a continued belief in the tenets of injustice. Something is deeply wrong with much of the ideological fabric of the society we live in. Just as those whose families once owned slave plantations will have seen slave ownership as natural in a time of slavery, and just as not allowing women to vote was once portrayed as 'nature's way', so, too, the great injustices of our times are, for many, simply part of the landscape of normality.

It is still accepted and seen as acceptable today that there should be a few Ivy League universities for those with the 'greatest minds' to study at. Below these, prestigious institutions form the next tier, lesser institutions the next tier, intermediate training for the next, school certificates for those below, and possibly prison for those below them. All this is justified because of what is thought to be inherent within people – their apparently limited potential, needs and deserts. What matters most is not only just how persistent these beliefs of inherited difference remain, but how coded the language we now use to talk of them is, and how many who do not superficially think of themselves as elitist clearly believe in elitism.

Books on injustice, of which there have been many, usually begin by listing the books' antecedents: the great thinkers who have gone before, works that have inspired. And this book similarly makes no claim to be visionary or novel; it pulls together a collection from a large array of mostly very recent writing about a greater argument, the case for which is slowly becoming more widely accepted. This is the case about the nature of, and widespread harm caused by, the injustice of new social evils, and of the rising inequality that both results from old injustices and also underlies the rise of new forms or injustice.

In recent years the clamour calling for new social evils to be identified has grown much louder, and the language being used to condemn those who support injustice harder-edged. We no longer talk just about 'social evils' but about the 'structural evils' that support continued injustice. In 2014, black religious leaders in both the US and the UK began to use the phrase 'structural evil'. Although this book does not make a religious case to suggest that injustices should be reduced, it is worth noting that most of the world's major religions began at a time and in places of high inequality, and all partly had the goal of reducing those injustices.[2]

Following the shooting of yet more unarmed black men and children in the US in 2014, one Baptist preacher explained: 'Overcoming unjust systems through personal success and hard work (which has become the cornerstone of much white, evangelical theology) is not God's main desire: transforming structural evil is',[3] a thought echoed by a UK religious leader on BBC Radio 4's 'Thought for the day', who also used the phrase 'structural evil', although such a thought could only be voiced on the BBC on the only day that this programme was edited by someone who was also not white.[4] Calls to be more vocal and direct based on the legacy of accumulating injustices are spreading, but now being made by a wider and wider circle of advocates; and they are being aired to an ever better informed public. Supporting unjust inequality is now seen as profoundly immoral, wicked even, but what of supporting the processes that underlie the growth in inequality?

It has already been well established that maximising profits through dividing labour into smaller and smaller tasks minimises wages, generates monotony and makes just a few rich.[5] We also know that the world has enough for everyone's needs, but not for their greed.[6] There is no utopian revelation here because we are no longer living in a world where the people arguing for justice are in a tiny minority.[7] Most great utopian visions came about during times when far fewer people were permitted to voice opinions, and most who were so permitted believed that the day would never come when it would be held as a self-evident truth that all people are created equal (or they thought it would only come in some afterlife).

Most of us now say that we mostly believe that 'all people are created equal'[8] and do not see particular groups as inferior or superior, but, as I pull evidence together in what follows, I demonstrate that those with power increasingly do not really mean it when they say it, because such belief is inconsistent with what else they say they believe about other people and about themselves. Stated beliefs in equality and justice are often mere platitudes or refer to a very limited definition of the concepts.

The new injustices in affluent countries have several things in common: all are aspects of rising social inequalities; all have arisen from a surplus of riches; and all suggest that so far we have come up with the wrong answer to the question of what we should do now that we are so rich. In rich countries, other than in the US, we are almost all well off compared with our parents. On a worldwide level we would all be well off today if only we could share the surplus.[9] Being well off is not to be rich – it is to have enough.[10] But today, a few are obscenely rich, and many are consequently poor.

2.1 Inevitability of change: what we do now we could all have enough?

We now know that we have enough for everyone's needs, as we know with some precision how many of us there are on the planet, and we have a good idea of how many of us there soon will be – the 2003 central projection of the United Nations' (UN's) world population estimates showed that human population growth is coming to an end within the lifetime of most people alive today.[11] Projections released in 2011 and 2013 suggested the maxima might take a little longer to arrive, but they may well be underestimating the extent of falling fertility rates.[12] Stability and population decline will come not from pandemic or war, but simply because most women today have been having no more than three offspring, and most of their daughters are expected to have no more than two.

As we become fewer in rich countries, many are now arguing that further increases in our wealth are not necessarily producing greater happiness, longer healthy lives, a better- informed population or a freer society.[13] We live in times when we are now told very different stories about our history as a species and our 'progress' than those told to our parents. Across Europe today there is mass youth unemployment despite there being relatively fewer young people alive on the continent than ever before.[14] We are not using our riches well, even in the richest of places.

Today we now know that we are only just regaining the average heights of humans 13,000 years ago because we are at last again able to eat a wide enough variety of nutrients (with enough reliability of supply) for our bodies to grow to full height. The malnutrition began when we first farmed, diets became less varied and harvests periodically failed – past skeletons show this. We then shrank in stature even further due to the privations and famines that came with early industrialisation and lives increasingly lived on factory floors, in slums or as impoverished peasants in the countryside.

In 1992 it was claimed, using the examples of ancient skeletons found in what is now Greece and Turkey, that modern Greeks and Turks had still not regained the average heights of our hunter-gatherer ancestors due to average nutritional levels still not being as good as those found *before* antiquity. The heights to be re-attained were 5'10" (178cm) for men and 5'6" (168cm) for women.[15] These average heights had fallen by 7 and 5 inches respectively when agriculture was introduced.[16] By 2004, however, the average height of people living in Greece and Turkey had grown, although women were still an inch behind the average heights of those alive 13,000 years earlier.[17] Only in the most recent generation have Greek men finally regained the average height that our ancestors routinely reached.[18]

We can be optimistic about the possibility of significant change within our lifetimes because today we are living in very different circumstances compared with even just one generation ago. Only one generation ago, even the middle classes were mostly slightly stunted, as were the upper classes a generation before that, and the richest countries of the world lost a tenth of their infants to disease, because these infants were not as well fed or as well cared for medically as many much poorer people in more equitable rich countries are today. All these very rapid improvements are connected through better health, nutrition and sanitation.[19]

If you wrote about injustice in 1910 or in 1960, you were writing in remarkably different times. *As you write now, for the first time in human history, a majority of people worldwide are able to read what you write.* Five out of every six children in the world are now taught to read and write to a degree that only a minority of their parents were, and a majority of their children will probably have internet access.[20] More than one hundred million young adults worldwide now study at university each year.[21] Education may still be hugely unjust in how it is distributed, but there are many more people alive in the world today who have been given the freedom to learn, right through to college. This is not just many more than before, it is many more than the sum total of all those who ever went to university before.

Although university degrees are wonderful things, the ranking of them by hierarchy of institution is problematic, because then, people may be tempted to study for the label, for the university brand, rather than to actually learn. Because there were so few of them, the forerunners of today's university graduates almost all became part of a tiny elite, governing others and receiving riches as a result. Because there are so many more graduates now, only a very small minority of today's university graduates will become rich at the expense of others. This also applies to the most elite of universities as well as the rest. The majority of their graduates will not be able to join future elites as things stand: the elite has become too small, less than 1 per cent, and the graduates too many. The status quo is not even in the selfish interests of the majority of graduates of our most prestigious universities in the richest of our nations, but it can be hard to see why.

In the first edition of this book I included a complicated table[22] showing the categorisation of injustices used here, and how they related to categorisations made in 1942, and various subsequent attempts to update them made in 1983, 2007 and 2008. The table also included 10 examples of social woes that respond most closely to social inequalities listed in 2009 under the headline of 'Inequality: mother of all evils', as reported from the book *The spirit level*.[23] These were: increased or higher than average levels of mental illness, imprisonment, teenage pregnancies, poor literacy and numeracy, infant mortality, obesity, homicide, lack of trust, lower life expectancy and wider income gaps.

There is now widespread acceptance that old forms of injustice, once tackled, can rapidly morph into new ones. Updating that table now, to include all the new work that has been published since 2010 on the categorisation of injustice, would make it completely unreadable.[24] What matters is to appreciate that there has not been a sudden change in what we see as 'evil'. That evils have gradually transformed, and more of us now call injustices evil, not merely unfortunate. Today, far more people are concerned about the evils underpinning injustice and ensuring that social inequalities persist. The old social evils were: lack of education (ignorance), lack of money (want), lack of work (idleness), lack of comfort (squalor), and lack of health (disease). The new injustices have arisen out of a glut of: education (elitism), money (exclusion), scorn (prejudice), wealth (greed) and worry (despair).

Thus these five forms of injustice that form the basis of this work are each, in turn, amalgams of others' lists of concerns and perils. For simplicity, each new injustice can be said to have arisen most strongly a decade after the last (in the 1950s, 1960s, 1970s, 1980s and 1990s respectively), and out of the ashes of past evils that have largely been overcome in material terms. Tolerance and acceptance of (even advocating) the new injustices is at the heart of social injustice in rich countries today.

Poor countries remain bedevilled by the old social evils and in danger of being infected by the new, not because they are on some developmental ladder waiting for their problems to become problems of riches, but increasingly because of the ignorance, want, idleness, squalor and disease caused in most of the poor world as a side effect of the elitism, exclusion, prejudice, greed and despair now endemic within rich countries.

2.2 Injustice rising out of the ashes of social evils

'Elitism is efficient'

Well-meaning attempts to eliminate very poor education have had the unintended by-product of fuelling the rise of a new injustice, by beginning to promote the widespread acceptance of elitism. This has occurred over many years, through providing the most extra educational resources to those whose parents had generally themselves received the most. In the UK this took place through the provision of more grammar schools, then sixth form colleges, new and expanded universities, and now a multitude of new postgraduate degrees. All these extra resources were provided following the introduction of secondary education for all, and then, comprehensive education for most.

Those whose families had in the past secured slight educational advantages were now able to secure much greater advantages through amassing more and more qualifications within selective awarding institutions. In 1942 a tiny minority of adults had a university degree, and it was normal to have no formal qualifications. Now, although many young adults still have no or few formal qualifications, there are also many who hold a long list of school and university certificates. Pick two young people at random, and they are far more likely to be qualified to very different levels today, compared to any point in the past.

The mass schooling of children through to their late teens in rich countries marked an end to the acceptance of relative illiteracy as normal. This school movement grew in strength right through the gilded age, through the crash and depression, and came out of the Second World War with a victory for children, especially for girls, who became seen as educable throughout secondary school age. However, almost immediately after the war, in the beginnings of the Cold War and in an era of vehement anti-communism, many men were feeling threatened by capable women.

Women had shown that they could do men's jobs. This was combined with the well-off feeling threatened by the poor who had shown that, if taught, they, too, could be educated. The injustice of elitism began to be propagated. Michael Young rallied against this elitist trend in 1958 when he published *The rise of the meritocracy*, but he was mostly misunderstood.[25] Elitism after 1950 was more pernicious than previous class, religion, 'race' and gender bars to advancement because it was claimed that the elite should rule and be differently rewarded because they were most able to rule due to their advanced knowledge and skill, rather than because of some feudal tradition (because their fathers were part of the elite too). Their degrees and qualifications from the right places justified their elite status. Elitism became a new excuse for inequality.

Before the 1950s there was no need to argue for elitism. Women were rarely admitted to college, and girls very often left school earlier than boys. It was often said that girls were a different breed – in fact, everyone was a different breed from the few actually allowed to talk about 'breeds' of human then.[26] However, by the 1980s, the fact that people were paid differentially according to perceived differences in their skills and supposed abilities had been identified as a new social evil.[27] A quarter of a century after that, contemporary philosophers listed people not being encouraged to use their imagination or being unable to express emotion as threats to wellbeing, which could easily be placed under this same heading.

The rapid changes in what is considered to be an injustice illustrate just how quickly our demands, our human rights, can be raised, such as including being denied the opportunity to use imagination and to express emotion as a social evil. There are many 'bad' jobs where these disadvantages prevail.[28] However, when surveyed,[29] the public of recent years talked less of this as being an evil, and more of a fall in compassion and respect, and of problems emerging for young people caused by poor parenting, which resulted in seeing some as grossly inferior, and very few being part of 'the elite'. In affluent nations that have become even more unequal, following the rise of elitist thinking in the 1950s, people came to be socially segregated more and more by educational outcome.

Elitist thinking not only determines children's life chances, but also has an effect on everything that is seen as decent or acceptable in a society. In future, if there is progress, we are very likely to see people being denied the opportunity to use imagination and express emotion widely accepted as an evil. We will see this as an evil when it is denied to any person whatever their status, not just those nearest and dearest to us, and we will consider such a denial as being on a par with much that we currently consider to be far more serious – if there is progress, that is.

'Exclusion is necessary'

Where elitist thinking was allowed to grow most strongly, social exclusion became more widespread. Social exclusion was the name given to a new face of injustice that grew out of the general eradication of the bulk of an old social evil, 'want', going hungry, wanting for clothes and other basic possessions, warmth and other essentials. It was in the 1960s that the widespread eradication of old wants, which came with near full employment, pensions and more decent social security benefits, inadvertently resulted in new forms of exclusion, such as trying to exclude people for 'not being like us'; this was seen most clearly in rising racism, which increased during the 1970s.[30]

By the 1980s, the categories of new injustices included 'the exploitation of those who work'. Those in work were almost all able to eat enough, but as wages at the bottom declined in relation to those above, although those with no work did worst, many families of people in work but in bad jobs also began to become excluded from the norms of society, such as not having an annual holiday, or children not always getting breakfast before going to school. Being excluded from the norms of society was first suggested as a definition of poverty in the 1960s by the sociologist Peter Townsend.

As income inequalities grew, the numbers excluded because they had too little also grew. The numbers who could afford to exclude themselves from the norms of society, who didn't have to mix with the 'hoi polloi' because they were so rich, grew slightly too. Those who categorised injustices in 2006 saw how such exclusions threatened people's wellbeing, their bodily integrity and their ability to play, to relax and to take holidays.[31] The public defined the problems of social exclusion as being caused by individualism and consumerism, which had then led to more problems of drugs and alcohol corroding society.[32] To look at the wider context, in the rich countries that have become more consumerist, many poor people have been made even poorer by getting into debt just trying 'to keep up with the Joneses'.

The tendency for the affluent in rich countries to exclude themselves from social norms results in ever-greater consumption, both as these people buy more, and as they raise the expectations of others. That, in turn, causes want to rise elsewhere, including the old evil of the most basic of wants rising as peasants are made into paupers in poor countries. This occurs when poor countries are impoverished to satisfy the desires for wealth within rich nations. Many now see pauperisation as the direct end result of massive economic polarisation on a world scale,[33] and part of this pauperisation is the conscious de-linking of a few countries, such as North Korea and Myanmar, from the world economy in attempts to evade such polarisation.[34]

'Prejudice is natural'

Prejudice grows like mould, based on elitist myths in times of exclusion.[35] As inequalities began to fall after the pre-First World War gilded age, it became radical and then acceptable to argue in the 1930s that 'It is the mark of a civilised society to aim at eliminating such inequalities as have their source, not in individual differences, but in its own organisation.'[36] What was unforeseen in such arguments was that 40 years later, as the trend in inequality swung upward once again in the 1970s, creating the antecedents for what would later be a new gilded age, the argument would be reversed and some people would begin to preach that inequalities were simply reflections of individual differences in ability; if inequalities grew wider, well, that was just a clearer expression of those inherent differences.

By the 1990s prejudice had reached such heights that it had to be more clearly explained, by those opposed to elitism, that human beings were not born with huge inherent differences. Rather, people were born with plasticity – unlike many other species, human infants have very few of their '... neural pathways already committed'[37] at birth; they are then able (and have) to adapt to the conditions they find themselves born into. Those human beings born with fixed inherent traits would have been less likely to survive through the rapidly changing environments that they found themselves in over the course of human history.

We evolved to be more flexible. We inherited the ability not to inherit particular abilities! Those now born into times of scarcity and brutality are malleable infants who quickly learn to be selfish and to grab what they can, or they do so if that is what they learn from watching the actions of others. Born into times, or just into families, of good organisation and plenty, infants are capable of growing up to be cooperative and altruistic. But born into times of free market organisation and plenty, infants often just learn to want more and more and more. And there are also people able to present us with more and more to want.

Our inherent flexibility allows newborn infants to learn in a few years one of thousands of possible languages, and in most of the world, because most children are bilingual, two or more languages. It also allows newborns to adapt to thousands of different cultures, where survival remains best protected by new members quickly learning to behave in a way that fits their social and cultural environment.

Because so few of our neural pathways are committed at birth, we respond well to being nurtured, whether that nurturing is brutal or caring. Where nurturing is caring, growing up to care too has become a more cherished trait. More survive when there is wider caring, and so caring survives by being among the most appropriate behaviours to be taught and to evolve. This evolution includes evolution beyond our genes, cultural evolution. Humans pass on what it means to be human through their stories, libraries, museums, theatres, universities and, only so very recently, the ever-exploding internet.

It is the very fact that human societies can change in collective behaviour over extremely short periods of time that suggests that our destinies are not in our genes. We can move in just a few generations from being feudal or cooperative, to being competitive or totalitarian. We move within lifetimes from seeing large groups of people persuaded to take part in wars and not resisting conscription, to marching and singing for others' rights.

Prejudices rise and fall as people preach to promote them or teach against them. Prejudice is nurtured, a product of environments of fear, which is easily stoked up and takes years to quench. One manifestation of prejudice is that when great numbers are seen as less deserving, whether as slaves, paupers, or just 'average', a minority can describe their own behaviour not as greed, but as simply receiving higher rewards because they are different kinds of human beings, who deserve to be put on a pedestal above those whom they view with prejudice and look down on.

'Greed is good'

Our genes can sway parts of our destinies, although the environment will usually mitigate their influence and alter their expression. Greed has been excused as a side effect of otherwise beneficial evolutionary traits. This suggests that just as our hunter-gatherer desire to store calories by stuffing ourselves with fats and sugars was at one time usually beneficial, so, too, was our 'cave fire' interest in the stories of others and what they have and do, reflecting a then vital desire to understand the minds of all those around us. Unfortunately these traits of obsessing over what others nearby have and what they are doing, while beneficial in times of scarcity, can lead to greed where and when there is abundance.

A preoccupation with the minutiae of others' lives helped us to survive in small groups, but has now gone awry as we 'max out' on celebrity watching, gorging on, and, in a million small ways, mimicking soap operas.[38] Similarly, our genes trap us into perceiving our apparent status as crucially important. Slights to our status cause hurt that possibly has evolutionary origins because they cause us to fear that we are about to lose our position in ancient rank orders, with devastating effect. The status syndrome may well have preserved sustainable, if claustrophobic, patriarchal and matriarchal village hierarchies, where everyone knew their place and fitted like cogs in a machine.

Outside early village life, status importance causes misery and not equilibrium, but this misery gives us a reason to see why it would be to the greater good for all of us to behave justly and to minimise status hierarchies, which we may otherwise have a natural inclination to exacerbate.[39] Biologically we come programmed for tribal and village life, alongside our plasticity. This is rare in mammals. Socially, compared to other apes, we can appear more similar to particular kinds of East African rats and other animals that did not evolve in the forest but in places of more frequent scarcity.[40] Over time we evolved from being tribal to being feudal, but the village was still the key social entity.

As feudalism ended, our acute abilities to notice slights and our innate fear of being ostracised led, in the new worlds of cities and strangers, to a few seeking to rise ever upwards to be 'the big man', and to many feeling abandoned (feeling anomie), as if they had been placed outside the village to die. It is common to see these traits in turn coming from pre-human ranking systems common in mammals that live in groups.[41] However, stories conjured up through musing over evolutionary biology only take us so far, and are of themselves evidence that all is far from genetic, given how we only recently thought up these stories.[42]

Discovering our genes was a product of our cultures. Cultures developed not just to reward work, exploration and discovery, but also to protect leisure time through inventing Sabbaths and to prevent the hoarding of wealth; these inventions are as old as cave fires and village hearths. In contrast, it took the early spread of city living before many of our cultures developed enough to see usury, the taking of interest on others' debts, as a sin.[43] Now usury is seen as good business practice and the basis of capitalism.

People have been making their own history for quite some time, despite repeatedly lamenting that they find themselves in circumstances not of their choosing.[44] And our way of life is made collectively – we collectively now gorge on shopping and on soap operas. Status paranoia is reinforced as our people-watching is now done through watching television and surfing the internet. Being greedy is offered to us collectively through advertising deliberately creating envy and wants. "Work harder!" is the advertisers' implicit message, if you want more, but greed divides people as a result of unequal remuneration.

The rich in greedy societies did not become happier as greed came to be seen again as so good by so many in the 1980s.[45] We easily forget that the phrase 'greed is good' was evoked in resistance to the prevailing mantra that greed really was thought of as good, as 'wealth creating', and that everyone should strive to get more! Even Hollywood took part in the attempts to resist, constructing a different history, to tell a different story, to get a different future. The greedy do not gain happiness, but they do fuel others' misery by reducing everyone's sense of adequacy.

The rise again of greed was the unforeseen outcome of victory over squalor. Greed and squalor have coexisted for centuries, but it was with the widespread eradication of the worst aspects of material squalor in affluent nations that basic checks and balances on greed were lost. The rise in greed occurred not just because a few might be a little more programmed to be greedy; a tiny number have always been scurrilous enough to do better in business and then hoard gains. Greed rose because the circumstances were right; what had been in place to control greed had been removed in attempting to eradicate squalor. Poor living conditions were replaced by over-consumption.

We pumped out oil to drive cars so we no longer needed to live on streets full of horse manure. We pumped oil to make plastics to wrap around food and slow down its rotting. We pumped oil to make fertilisers to grow enough crops to feed millions of animals because we were greedy for meat. We mass-produced chickens and refrigerators, so that we could eat in a way we thought was better, eating meat almost every day as a result.

We ushered in mass consumption, removed the Sabbath and other high-days, declared usury a virtue, and then found there were almost no limits to individual desire for more cars, for more chicken, for more fridges and for more loans. We ended up with more than people could possibly need in any one home and, for those who could afford them, more homes than they could possibly use, containing yet more fridges, more cars, eating more meat, all initially seen as signs of success. And we ended up with widespread quiet despair.[46]

'Despair is inevitable'

Despair is the final injustice of the five new faces of inequality, mutating from the old social evil of widespread physical disease to mental illness. Health services now exist that effectively treat and contain most physical disease in affluent countries. However, while so many physical maladies are now well treated, with high-quality care in all but the most unequal of these rich countries, mental illness (including a form of 'affluenza') has been rising across the rich world.[47] In the UK depression is the most common cause of long-term sickness (followed by a bad back),[48] and clinical depression has been growing most quickly among adolescents (see Figures 21 and 25, Chapter 7).

Corporate profiteering and the strengthening of systems of competition, instead of cooperation, have both been shown to have influenced this rise, and to cause worldwide inequalities in health to be rising, as life expectancy is lower everywhere where economic inequalities are greater.[49] A more general malaise of despair has also settled over the populations of rich countries as elitism has strengthened, exclusion has grown, prejudice has been raised a level and greed has expanded. This is despair for the future, a despair that was felt throughout what were seen as the best of economic times, the late 1990s boom, despair which is now very much more palpable since those times have ended.[50]

2.3 So where do we go from here?

It can be annoying to read a book with the expectation that it will end in one way, only to find that it ends in an altogether different way. Having our expectations satisfied is part of what makes life good. So you should know now, that the main argument at the end of this book is that recognising the problem is actually the solution.

Elitism

No amount of affirmative action schemes, good schooling, money for computers or textbooks, different curricula or improved parenting methods are going to help improve how we are educated and think, if, in our heart of hearts, those who do most of the deciding as to how the rest get to learn harbour elitist pretensions. We should not expect to see any reduction in the numbers of children labelled as 'modern-day delinquents' wherever enough of the people who have more control over how others are treated still believe strongly enough that they themselves and their offspring are a little more inherently able than most, that they are different.[51]

If you think that you are somehow much more than simply the product of your upbringing and the environment into which the little plastic (flexible), neurally uncommitted you was thrust, that you might carry some inherited trait that makes you special (not just having a few idiosyncrasies, a favouring of maths, a disinclination for sprinting), then you, too, are part of the problem. Of course, because of differences in upbringing, environment and individual idiosyncrasies, different people do become better suited to doing different jobs by the time they are adults, and they need different training. However, even acknowledging this, it is very hard to justify the extent of educational apartheid we currently tolerate, and we could easily reduce differences dramatically among children if fewer were excluded, at the point of birth or before, from what is normal life for most. Society in countries with gross inequality is structured so that many, perhaps most, are predestined to relative if not absolute failure.

Exclusion

Social exclusion cannot be ended by complex schemes of tax credits, child benefits and local area funding, when those with the most are allowed to accrue even more. In the more unequal of rich countries, as long as we are happy to tolerate wide inequalities in income and wealth, there will always be large numbers of poor people. However, it is not easy to take the step of accepting this fact. We know this because it has not happened. Instead, it is easy to divide those with the least into two groups: one you think might be deserving of just a little more, and the other undeserving.

Infants born into poverty almost always feature in the 'deserving of a little more' group, unless they were born in the back of a lorry crossing from France to Britain, or Mexico to the US. The lone, young, feckless woman, sleeping around, stealing and injecting herself with heroin to escape reality, is almost always put in the undeserving category. In most cases it is women in her position who give birth to the infants who will have some of the worst chances in life, and whose deaths cause the greatest outcry when the circumstances of their deaths are revealed in court. However, understanding that child poverty will not end while we tolerate poverty for anyone is far from simple, otherwise we would have eradicated child poverty by now.

Becoming truly rich is not a matter of money, but of belief. Eradicating poverty is cheap because a little money goes a long way when you are poor. Poverty, as defined by social exclusion, is a relative measure; people are poor because they cannot afford to take part in the norms of society, and these norms only become unaffordable because the better-off have been allowed to become even better off. This happens, for example, when taxes are reduced, as taxes provide a source of redistribution from rich to poor, but much more important than that, they deter the greedy from trying to take such an unfair share.

What is most costly is maintaining a small group of extremely wealthy people who are able to exclude themselves from the norms of society at great expense, and this is what we do manage to do, despite the huge costs to everyone else. During 2014 it became clear that the richest 0.1 per cent of people in the US were hoarding a substantial part of their wealth in offshore tax havens. As a result, that tiny one thousandth of the population probably held about 23.5 per cent of all US wealth in 2012.[52] We allow illegal tax evasion and immoral tax avoidance activities to continue as long as we continue to be convinced that these people are somehow especially worthy of so much wealth. At the end of the last gilded age, following the 1920s excesses, the last time we stopped being so convinced we started to spread out what we all had more fairly, and we did not stop spreading it for two more generations, right through to the swinging and highly equitable sixties.

By the 1960s and through to 1978 poverty was far from eradicated, but people could at least appreciate each other's fears, concerns and lives more than many generations had before and any have done since. In the US, the UK and a few similarly rich countries, we then did the opposite for the next 30 years, and allowed the rich to take more each year than they had before.[53] We need to understand this history before considering what might be sufficient to reverse this growth of injustice.

Prejudice

The argument in this book does not end with a suggestion of how prejudice can be ended; it is not the kind of map of utopia that says 'turn left at hill marked "recognise institutional racism", then march up the valley of "reducing the gender gap", following the "gay and lesbian rights" river to find the "nirvana" mountain'. What I try to show is how the kinds of prejudices that were previously applied to fairly specific groups of people said to be different from 'us' have recently become expanded to a much wider populace who are now 'not like us', as 'us' has again shrunk for the better-off to a small group of winners who excuse their winning as being a mixture of their extra hard work, innate superior ability and the inherent failings of others. In 2014, Thomas Piketty termed this new excuse for inequality 'extreme meritocracy'.

The poor in particular are now subject to a widespread prejudice whereby it is often implied that they must have something wrong with them if they are not able to work their way out of poverty. In the end, the rich have to believe there is something nasty about ordinary people in order for them to believe that it is essential for their children not to have to live like ordinary people, and that it is fair to leave so much of their money to just their own few children rather than do something more useful with it. Historically, most people have inherited very little because their parents had very little to leave. To see inheritance as normal we have to have the mindset and beliefs about other people that only the aristocracy once had.

You can love your children and desperately want to spare them hardship, but in aggregate, you do not make their world safer if you are rich and leave your money to them as inheritance. Wealth is a measure of inequality, and most wealth in the world is amassed through inheritance and usury, not through work.[54] This is wealth that has not been earned by those who inherit, and almost all of it was not fairly earned by those who give it. The tiny amount that was originally collected through the sweat of the holder's own labour is only a minuscule fraction of the wealth of the world.

Most wealth comes from routes such as former plantation (slave) holdings that cascaded down to families in the US, or from parents finding their home had increased in value because it was located in London, and London contained the bankers who had found a new way of making money, which, for a time, indirectly increased house prices there. Relying on wealth indirectly amassing through the guile of bankers is not a good way to live.

Greed

Most inheritance of great wealth is justified on the basis of prejudice, of rich people believing that their children have a special right to more because it is somehow their 'duty' to be set up to be above others, and they are expected to do the same for their children. In this book I argue that it is a myth that the wealthy are the children of those who work hard, take risks, make money and just want to leave it to their family. Not too long ago only a small minority believed this myth about the wealthy. What is new today is how that belief has spread to the middle classes and to many of the poor who (especially in the US) would also repeal inheritance tax laws, not in case they win the lottery, but because they have swallowed the myth that hard work and a little risk-taking makes you wealthy.

Fear has grown as wealth inequalities have grown, resulting in heightened prejudice in deciding who marries whom, how much we collectively care, and who now dies youngest in times of plenty. However, often the children of the very rich (through drug overdoses, transport crashes and sporting accidents) suffer high mortality rates even in countries we currently see as quite equitable,[55] although if you try to argue today that children would be better off not with inherited money but if society as a whole provided better support for all, there will usually be disbelief. It was easier in the past to argue against inheritance, to have the great houses made accessible to the public, and to secure land reform around much of the globe.

Unlike in the 1940s, many people in affluent countries today are told that they have riches, that their houses are worth a great deal, or they believe that they will have money gained from some other source to inherit. If you point to other societies that are more equal – to Japan, to most of Western and Northern Europe, even to much of Canada and a few US states – and show the outcomes to be better, commentators may suggest that those nation-states or US states are more equal due to special historical circumstances that cannot easily be replicated in their more unequal country.[56] They say that they cannot replicate the kind of land redistribution that occurred in Japan after the Second World War, or the stronger sense of trust and belonging that exist in most affluent nations – but why not? All that is required to redistribute land is a significant land value tax, and we now know that trust rises in societies that become more equal. Attitudes change remarkably quickly in the aftermath of a rise in equality. What appeared to be impossible becomes common sense.

We have to say again and again that there are no beneficial side effects of one man's greed. It does not create worthwhile work for others,[57] it is not efficient, it does not curtail waste – in fact, it causes huge amounts to be wasted. Greed also corrupts thinking, as those who take most simultaneously argue that they fund state services the most through those taxes they cannot avoid. Greed must be seen as an injustice before it is even possible to imagine reining it in, as it has been reined in before. A recurrent theme in the saga of human history is the story of constraining greed, learning to store grain collectively, preaching against usury, cooperating more. We last did this when we benefited from contracting inequalities in wealth, as occurred from 1929 to 1978 across the rich world. However, this time, the circumstances are different.

Whenever greed has been reined in before, it has later found a new outlet, exploiting some foreign land, creating a monopoly or a cartel, or some other way in which exploitation and dominance could rise again. This time every last piece of land has already been colonised in one way or another. There are very few left to have their days brought into the paid labour market, or to be told that they are unemployed or a 'carer'; there are no more schemes where you whizz money around the world and pretend more exists in transit than at any one location (as was occurring at the point the global banking system crashed in 2008). That was only possible when so many were still illiterate and innumerate.

Today, it is harder than it has been for many years to sell dodgy home loans, which start off cheap but where interest payments rise greatly later. We have better-educated consumers, because so many were burnt before. That is why such loans could only be sold in large numbers in the most unequal of rich countries in the US to people who were most desperate in the 'sub-prime' sector. In that part of the US, according to Richard Wilkinson and Kate Pickett's 2009 book *The spirit level*, there lived the worst educated and most desperate of consumers. There should be fewer dupes next time, but there need not be a next time – another boom to lead to bust in future. What we have right now in the rich world is slow or no growth. An anathema to the financial markets, no or low growth could be our planet's salvation. From reducing carbon emissions to not buying so much food we throw some away and purchasing so many goods we don't actually need. Slow growth could help create a better future. It is precisely to ward off forgetting and being duped again that so many write, and say, and shout, and argue, and cry so much today that another future is possible. That a conserving, recycling, sharing counter-culture of our recent past is now presented as a preferable general culture to consumerism, competition, exploitation and greed.

Despair

Lastly, what solution is there to despair? Again, simply recognising that there is a problem is the first step. Count the pills, measure the anxiety, the alcohol consumption, the nervousness, the thoughts in the middle of the night when it doesn't all seem possible. Look at the mental state of children today in rich countries and compare that to the recent past, to your mental state as a child, and then ask yourself if this is the progress you had hoped for. Look at levels of self-harm. You may be lucky yourself, fortunate with your friends or family, your uncomplicated life or your high degree of self-confidence. But if you are not, or your children or friends and relatives are not, and if despite that you just say 'it isn't that bad', 'get a grip', 'pull yourself together' and claim 'we had tougher skins in our day and kept a stiff upper lip', if you don't look at what is wrong in your life and in society now and see how things have changed, but just try to tackle the symptoms of those wrongs, to wash away the worries, then there is no solution to despair.

There are many facets to despair: anxiety, fear, mistrust, anger, not quite knowing what might happen to you if you do not perform well enough or fit in neatly enough. How secure do you feel? You either have to have had a remarkably tranquil life by modern standards, a close and highly supportive set of friends and family, or a very high level of self-belief not to worry, not to often feel under strain. There are sets of standard questions routinely asked of people to see if they might be suffering from depression in affluent countries.[58] It is an interesting exercise to de-personalise these questions and ask them of those around you, or personalise them again and ask them of yourself.

Are the people where you live, the people who run your country, and those not as well off as you, able to concentrate on whatever they are doing? Do they lose much sleep through worry? Do they think they are playing a useful part in things? Are most capable of making decisions about things? Do most feel constantly under strain? Do they often feel that they cannot overcome their difficulties? Are they able to enjoy their normal day-to-day activities? Are they able to face up to their problems? Have they been feeling unhappy and depressed? Are they losing confidence in themselves? Do some see themselves as worthless? Have most been feeling reasonably happy, all things considered? Or not?

As a sign of the times, and certainly a cause for despair, the precise wording of the questionnaire that these questions are derived from is subject to copyright conditions and cannot be reproduced here, because a corporation wants to profit from these words.[59] Nor am I able to reproduce the scoring system that lets you decide if you are depressed. The owning of copyright on a test for depression is yet another of those facets of modern society that our recent ancestors could not have made up as a sick joke. Future generations may find it hard to understand that we ever tolerated this. Nevertheless, although the scoring system cannot be revealed, it is unlikely that, if you knew them well, you would describe the lives of many around you as being particularly happy and fulfilled. It is only because we do not know each other well that we can imagine that most around us do appear happier and (at a superficial glance) many appear fulfilled. It is, after all, often because everyone else around you appears to be having so much fun, especially those who live and smile on the television screen, that you blame yourself for not being as apparently fulfilled as them. But do you admit it to others?

In more unequal affluent countries, when asked a single question about their mental condition, most people say they are doing fine, even great, 'never been better'. In contrast, it is in those more equitable affluent countries where people live the longest, where social conditions are most favourable, that people are most likely to admit to not feeling so great all the time, because they can afford to admit to it.[60] In the most unequal of countries, admitting to yourself that you are down is the beginning of a journey on a slippery slope where you can expect little help other than 'therapy' at a high financial price, and where your 'therapist' has no financial incentive for you to quickly recover. The start of the solution to living in places and times of despair is to collectively and publicly admit to despair. The worst thing you and those around you can do is to pretend that all is fine. This just perpetuates injustice.

This book has no great single solution save 'the impossible', to offer a map of part of a route to end the injustices of elitism, exclusion, prejudice, greed and despair as the latest incarnations of rising inequality. No suggestion is made for a global jubilee where, not just between countries but also within them, debt is written off and the rich are helped to agree to end their claims on so much of the lives of so many of the poor. Such events are absolutely impossible, at least until the moment they happen. However, the last time a gilded age ended many people worked hard to reduce social inequalities and to secure more justice, so the 'impossible' has happened before, and it will happen again. All we can strive to do is alter when that might next be. It doesn't matter that we do not know when the tide will turn. Those who last turned it had no idea they were doing so. If they were lucky they were young and lived long enough to find out much later the part they had played.

3

'Elitism is efficient': new educational divisions

> Debrett's: This definitive guide to Britain's meritocracy is the major biographical study of the UK's most influential and successful people.[1]

In the richest, most unequal of countries in the world, pretence is made that only the most able, on merit, have got to the top. However, most of those who do make it up there come from affluent backgrounds. In contrast, people in poorer parts of the world today may easily be the first in their family to have graduated from a secondary school. At the same time, many children still rarely attend a primary school, let alone persevere through what is considered in rich countries to be a basic education. And university education is only for the very rich. In contrast, the affluent world is characterised by long-standing and ever-improving compulsory primary and secondary education for all children, with rates of university access rising almost continuously. Despite this, many young people are not presented as well educated in most affluent nations, but as failing to reach official targets. This chapter brings together evidence which shows how particular groups are increasingly seen as 'not fit' for advanced education, as being limited in their abilities, as requiring less of an education than the supposedly more gifted and talented.

The amassing of riches in affluent countries, the riches that allowed so much to be spent on education, has not resulted in an increased sense of satisfaction in terms of how young people are being taught and are learning. Instead, it has allowed an education system to be created which now expresses ever-increasing anxiety over how pupils perform, in which it has become common to divide up groups of children by so-called ability at younger and younger ages to try to coach them to reach 'appropriate' targets. This has a cumulative effect, with adolescents becoming more anxious as a result. In this environment, the children of 'aspirational families' are especially susceptible to rising anxiety.[2]

Despite the abandonment of the former grammar school system in Britain children are still being divided among and within schools. This is also evident in the US, but in Britain it is more covert. Parents have been moving house in order to get their children into their chosen state school, they may pretend to be religious to gain access to faith schools, and slightly more of them were paying for private education by 2007 than had done so before. As more resources are concentrated on a minority, the (perceived) capabilities of the majority are implicitly criticised.

In this chapter evidence is brought together to show how the myths of huge inherent difference have been sustained and reinforced by placing a minority on pedestals for others to look up to. Such attitudes vary in degree among affluent nations, but accelerated in intensity during the 1950s (to be later temporarily reversed in the 1960s and 1970s). In the 1950s, in countries like Britain, the state enthusiastically sponsored the division of children into 'types', with the amounts spent per head on grammar school children being much higher than on those at the alternative secondary moderns. Such segregationist policies are still pursued, and pursued with most determination in the more unequal rich countries. More equitable countries such as Finland, and the more equitable parts of unequal countries (such as Scotland and Wales in the UK), have pushed back most against this tide of elitism since it rose so high in the 1950s.

Until very recently, too few children even in affluent countries were educated for any length of time. All children are still at risk of being labelled as 'inadequate' despite the fact that the resources are there to teach them, of being told that they are simply not up to learning what the world now demands of them. All will fail at some hurdle in an education system where examination has become so dominant.

Those who are elevated also suffer. To give an example I am very familiar with, in universities, professors, using elitist rhetoric, try to tell others that the world is incredibly complicated and only they are able to understand or make sense of it; they will let you see a glimpse, they say, if you listen, but you cannot expect to understand; it takes years of immersion in academia, they claim; complex words and notions are essential, and they see understandable accounts as 'one-dimensional'.[3]

Occasionally there is no alternative to a complex account of how part of the world appears to work, but often a complex account is simply a muddled account. Professors often say that an aspect of the world is too complex for them to describe – because they themselves cannot describe it in a clear way, not because it cannot be described clearly. Suggesting such widespread complexity justifies the existence of academia because elitism forces those it puts on pedestals to pretend to greatness, but if you talk to academics, it thankfully becomes clear that most are, to some extent, aware of this pretence. They are aware, like the Wizard of Oz, of how humdrum they really are.

People are remarkably similar in ability. However, you can find a few people, especially in politics, celebrity (now a field of work) or business, who appear to truly believe they are especially gifted, that they are a gift to others who should be grateful for their talents and who should reward them appropriately. These people are just as much victims of elitism as those who are told they are, in effect, congenitally stupid, fit for little but taking orders and performing menial toil, despite having been required to spend over a decade in school. Under elitism education is less about learning and more about dividing people, sorting out the supposed wheat from the chaff, and conferring high status upon a minority.

The old evil of ignorance harmed poorer people in particular because they could not read and write and were thus easily controlled, finding it harder to organise and to understand what was going on (especially before radio broadcasts). What differentiates most clearly the new social injustice of elitism from the old evil of ignorance is that elitism damages people from the very top to the very bottom of society, rather than just being an affliction of the poor. Those at the top suffer because the less affluent and the poor have their abilities denounced to such an extent that fewer people end up becoming qualified in ways that would also improve the lives of the rich. For example, if more people were taught well enough to become medical researchers, then conditions that the rich may die of could be made less painful, or perhaps even cured, prolonging their lives. If more are taught badly at school – because it is labourers and servants that the rich think they lack – then cures for illnesses may not be discovered as quickly.

The British education system has been described as 'learning to labour' for good reason. It is the poorest who are still most clearly damaged by elitism, by the shame that comes with being told that their ability borders on illiteracy, that there is something wrong with them because of who they are, that they are poor because they have inadequate ability to be anything else.

3.1 The 'new delinquents': those most harmed by elitism, a seventh of all children

Although nobody officially labels a seventh of children as 'delinquent', they might just as well because that is the stigmatising effect of the modern labels that are applied to children seen as the 'least able'. A century ago delinquency was an obsession and thought to lead to criminality; education was the proffered antidote. However, it was not lack of education that caused criminality in the young; it was most often necessity. Today it is money for phone credits more often than food, as the nature of the need has changed, but old labels such as 'delinquent' are retained in the popular press, and a new form of what can still best be described as 'delinquency' has arisen.

Increased educational provision that has been increasingly unequally distributed has led to the rise of this new elitism. Where once there had been the castle on the hill and the poor at the gates, the castle grounds became subdivided into sections, places up and down the hill, neatly ordered by some supposed merit.[4] Today, an even neater ordering of people has been achieved – to demarcate social position and occupation, all now have numbers and scores, exam passes, credit ratings, postcodes and loyalty cards, rather than simply titles and surnames.

Scoring all individuals in affluent societies is a recent affair. Giving all children numbers and grades throughout their schooling and yet more grades afterwards (at university or college) was simply not affordable before the Second World War, in even the most affluent of countries. It was a luxury confined to the old grammar schools and universities. At that time, most children would simply be given a certificate when they left school to say that they had attended. This system changed when compulsory secondary education for all swept the affluent world following the war, although with the belief that all could be educated came the caveat that most of those who believed this did not see all the children that they were about to allow through to secondary school as equal in potential ability.

Ranking children according to 'ability'

Some of the best evidence of policy makers seeing different groups of children as very different comes from the work of educational economists. Half a century ago the rich countries created the Organisation for Economic Co-operation and Development (OECD), which was effectively a 'rich country' club that is now dominated by economists. The rise in power of orthodox or neoclassical economists, those who created and belonged to clubs like the OECD, contributed to the spread of elitism and the beliefs behind it. It is the OECD that published the figures used to draw Figure 1 (below), figures that suggest that one in seven children growing up in one particular rich country today (the Netherlands) have either no or very limited knowledge.[5]

Two things have changed between 2007 and 2014 in the educational statistics of the Netherlands. First, the proportion of children assessed to have no or very limited knowledge has increased from 13 to 14 per cent. Second, the OECD now no longer uses those terms so overtly, perhaps due to the widespread criticism it has received in the intervening seven years. But there is little evidence that that organisation has changed how it views and measures children and the implicit messages this creates.

We used to see the fate of children as being governed by chance, with perhaps even the day of their birth influencing their future life. Rewriting the old rhyme, the OECD would say of children today (in the Netherlands) that they can be divided into seven differently sized groups by their supposed talents and future prospects:

> The educational ode of the OECD (by Danny Dorling, age 41½)
> Monday's child has limited knowledge,
> Tuesday's child won't go to college,
> Wednesday's child is a simple soul,
> Thursday's child has far to go,

> Friday's child can reflect on her actions,
> Saturday's child integrates explanations,
> But the child that is born on the Sabbath day
> Has critical insight and so gets the most say.

The OECD economists and writers do not put it as crudely as this, however. It is through their publications (from which I have extracted the labels that follow)[6] that they say in effect that there is now a place where a seventh of children are labelled as failures by the time they reach their 15th birthday.

Using OECD data, if we divide children into seven unequally sized groups by the days of the week, and start with those most lowly ordered, then the first group are Monday's children (from Figure 1, 11%+3%=14%). They are those who have been tested and found to have, at most, only 'very limited knowledge'. Tuesday's children (20%) are deemed to have acquired only 'barely adequate knowledge' to get by in life. Wednesday and Thursday's children (28%) are labelled as being just up to coping with 'simple concepts'. Friday and Saturday's children (25%) are assessed as having what is called 'effective knowledge', enough to be able to reflect on their actions using scientific evidence, perhaps even to bring some of that evidence together, to integrate it.

The remaining children (11%+2%=13%), one in every seven again, are found by the testers to be able to do more than that, to be able to use well-'developed inquiry abilities', to link knowledge appropriately and to bring 'critical insights' to situations. But although these children may appear to be doing all right, even they are not all destined for greatness. According to the testers they will usually not become truly 'advanced thinkers'. It is just one in seven of the Sabbath children (100%÷7%÷7%=2%) who is found to be truly special. Apparently only one in fifty children have superior brains. Only these children will (it is decreed in the science section of the OECD description of each little proto-adult) clearly and consistently demonstrate 'advanced scientific thinking and reasoning', will be able to demonstrate a willingness to use scientific understanding 'in support of recommendations and decisions that centre on personal, socioeconomic, or global situations.' This child and the few like them, it is implied, are destined to be our future leaders.

Figure 1 shows the proportions of children in the Netherlands assigned to each ability label, from 'none' clockwise round to 'advanced'. The Netherlands is a place you might not have realised had brought up over 60 per cent of its children to have only a simple, barely adequate, limited education, or even no effective education at all (according to OECD statistics released in 2014). And that proportion is said by those same statistics to have risen slightly since 2006.

Fixing the results to a bell curve

The OECD, it is worth reiterating, is an organisation of economists, and not teachers, which now tells countries how well or badly educated their children are. According to these economists, the Netherlands is the country which best approximates to the 1:2:3:2:1 distribution of children having what is called limited, barely adequate, simple, effective and developed knowledge, by having reached the OECD's international testing levels 1a+1b, 2, 3, 4 and 5+6 respectively.

The distribution shown in Figure 1 is not how children in the Netherlands actually are, or how they appear to any group but the OECD; it is not how the majority of their parents think of them; it is not even how their teachers, school inspectors or government rank them. It is how the children of the Netherlands, and all other children in the richer countries of the world, have slowly come to be seen by those who carry out these large-scale official international comparisons. Large-scale international comparisons can be great studies, but should not be used to propagate elitist beliefs.

Given this damning description of their children, it may surprise you to learn that the Netherlands fares particularly well compared with other countries. Only half a dozen countries out of over 50 surveyed did significantly better when compared in 2006. More children in the UK were awarded the more damning levels of 1, 2 and 3 – 'limited', 'barely adequate' and 'simple', and even more by 2012. In the US, both Monday and Tuesday's children were found to be limited, and only half of Sunday's children were 'developed' – just half the Netherlands' proportion. Even that small share shrank in the six years to 2012 (see Figure 2).

Do the best of the richest countries in the world really educate only just under a seventh (13 per cent) of their children to a good level, and just

Figure 1: Children in the Netherlands ranked by ability (%) according to the OECD, 2012 (showing changes since 2006)

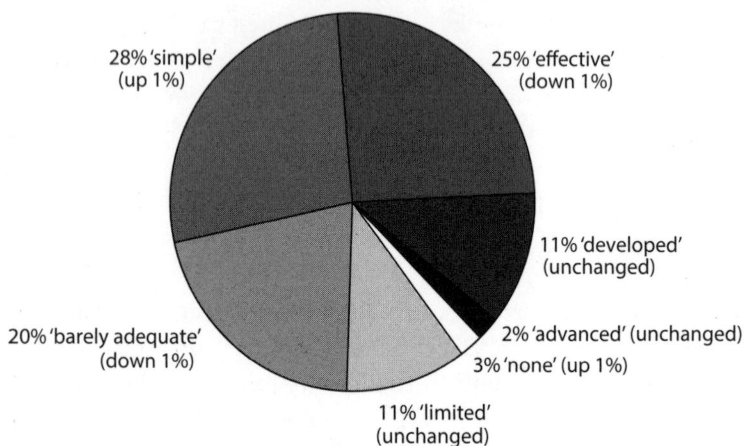

Notes: 'None' implies none as can be measured. 'Limited' implies possessing very limited knowledge. 'Barely adequate' stands for barely adequate knowledge in the view of the assessors. 'Simple' means understanding only simple concepts. 'Effective' is a little less damning. 'Developed' is better again; but only those rated as 'Advanced' are said to be capable of the kind of thinking that might include 'critical insight'.
Note that in the PISA 2012 update these words are no longer used and three scores have to be summed. The OECD PISA assessments put children in 7 levels by ability. The adjectives used here are extracted from PISA's own 2006 descriptions of what these bands represented as published in OECD (2007) *The Programme for International Student Assessment (PISA), OECD's latest PISA study of learning skills among 15-year-olds*, Paris: OECD, derived from figures in table 1, p 20: Updated using data from 2012 that is available here:
http://nces.ed.gov/pubs2014/2014024_tables.pdf
for "mathematics literacy scale" descriptions Exhibit M1, figures Table M1
for "science literacy scale" descriptions Exhibit S1, figures Table S1
for "reading literacy scale" descriptions Exhibit R1, figures Table R1

Source: (OECD 2012) (derived from figures in table below)

Label	Netherlands 2012	Math-ematics	Science	Literacy	Netherlands 2006	*Change*
3% 'none'	3.2	3.8	3.1	2.8	2.3	*0.9*
11% 'limited'	10.5	11	10.1	10.3	10.7	*-0.2*
20% 'barely adequate'	19.7	17.9	20.1	21	21.1	*-1.4*
28% 'simple'	27.6	24.2	29.1	29.2	26.9	*0.7*
25% 'effective'	25.3	23.8	25.8	26.1	25.8	*-0.5*
11% 'developed'	11.5	14.9	10.5	9	11.5	*0.0*
2% 'advanced'	2.2	4.4	1.3	0.8	1.7	*0.5*
	100.0	100.0	100.0	99.2	100.0	*0.0*

a seventh of those (2 per cent) to a level where they show real promise? Are just 2 per cent of children able, as the OECD definition puts it, to achieve 'level 6', 'to use scientific knowledge and develop arguments in support of recommendations and decisions that centre on personal, socioeconomic, or global situations'? In Finland and New Zealand, this 'genius strand' in 2006 was apparently 4 per cent, in the UK and Australia 3 per cent, in Germany and the Netherlands 2 per cent, in the US and Sweden 1 per cent, and in Portugal and Italy it was nearer to 0 per cent. The figures are very volatile, with the UK losing a third of those with apparent 'real promise' in just the six years to 2012.[8]

The level 6 are children who, according to the educational economists (usually adherents of the so-called orthodox school of economics), show real promise. They are the children who have been trained in techniques to answer exam questions in the ways the examiners would most like them to be answered. The proportions are so low because the international test results are graded so that the results are distributed around a 'bell curve'. This is a bell curve with smoothly tapering tails, cut off (internationally and intentionally) so that 1.3 per cent are labelled potential genii and 5.2 per cent as know-almost-nothings (see Figure 2 below).

Engineering competition in place of cooperation

OECD economists, former physicists and mathematicians[9] have used the results of their international comparative exercises for the purpose of making claims, such as '… having a larger number of schools that compete for students was associated with better results'.[10] Many of the people who work for organisations such as the OECD feel they have a duty to suggest that competition between countries, schools and pupils is good, and to encourage it as much as they can.[11]

According to this way of thinking, science education, which is usually extended to include technology, engineering, maths and (quietly) economics,[12] is the most important education of all.

Supporting such science education, its promotion and grading in these ways, is seen as working in support of recommendations and decisions that centre on best improving personal, socioeconomic and global situations, to engineer the best of all possible worlds. This imagined world is a utopia, with all benefiting from increased competition, from being labelled by their apparent competencies. This is a world where it is imagined that the good of the many is most enhanced by promoting the ability of the few.

Although the OECD tables, and almost all other similar performance tables, are presented explicitly as being helpful to those towards the bottom of their leagues, as being produced to help pull up those at the bottom, that is rarely what they achieve. Educational gaps have not narrowed in most places where such tables have been drawn up. This is partly because they suggest how little hope most have of ever being really competent; 'leave competency to the top 2 per cent' is the implicit message, for, unless you are at the very least in the top seventh, you cannot hope to have a chance of succeeding, where success means to lead. Even when standards improve and most level 1 children are replaced by level 2, level 2 by 3, and so on, the knowledge which is judged to matter will also have changed and become ever more complex. If we accept this thinking, the bell curves will be forever with us.

This bell curve thinking (illustrated by Figure 2) suggests that right across the rich world children are distributed by skill in such a way that there is a tiny tail of truly gifted young people, and a bulk of know-nothings, or limited, or barely able, or just 'simple' young people. It is no great jump from believing in the bell curve to thinking that, given the narrative of a shortage of truly gifted children, then as young working adults those children will be able to name their price and will respond well to high financial reward, that they need high incentives to work on what is most valuable – such as running investment schemes (managing the money of the very rich very well).

In contrast, the less able are so numerous they will need to be cajoled to work. These masses of children, the large majority, will not be up to doing any interesting work, and to get people to do uninteresting work requires the threat of suffering. This argument quickly turns then to suggest that the bulk of children will respond best to financial rewards sufficiently low as to force them to labour. It is best to keep them occupied through hours of drudgery, it has been argued, admittedly more vocally in the past than now – although we hear far more labelling of people as skivers and shirkers today than we did a generation ago.

But what of those in between, of Friday and Saturday's children, with effective but not well-developed knowledge – what is to be done with them? Offer them a little more, an average wage for work, a wage that is not so demeaning, and then expect them to stand between the rest of weekday children and those of the Sabbath, a place half-way up the hill. Give them enough money for a rest now and again, one big holiday a year, money to run a couple of cars, enough to be able to struggle to help their children get a mortgage – the middle-class aspiration to be allowed to take on a great debt.

Most of Friday and Saturday's children now go to university. When surveyed, they are increasingly likely to say that others shouldn't follow them on that route, except, of course, their own children. Only 10 per cent of working-class people believe that the numbers studying at university should be reduced in the UK compared to 26 per cent of the middle classes. Those most keen on reducing the numbers who can go to university have been educated in a private school. Again, it is not their own children who they think should not go.[13] So why do a large minority think that others' children should get less?

Nature or nurture, or neither?

Many people think there are some groups of children who are simply born less able than others, or made so by the way they have been brought up in their earlier years. There are obvious examples. Most commonly these are infants starved of oxygen in the womb or during birth, or denied basic nutrients during infancy. Such privations occur early on in the lives of many of the world's poorest children. But this physical damage, mostly preventable, and due in most cases to absolute poverty, now rarely occurs in North America, affluent East Asia or Europe.

When serious neglect does occur, the results are so obvious in the outcomes for the children that they clearly stand out. The only recent European group of children treated systematically in this way were babies given almost no human contact, semi-starved and confined to their cots in Romanian orphanages. Some have been found to have had their fate damaged irreparably. Medical scanning discovered that a part of their brain did not fully develop during the first few years of their lives, and their story is now told as potential evidence of how vital human nurturing is to development.[14]

Two generations earlier than the Romanian orphanages, some of the most telling stories of the effects that different kinds of nurturing can have on later behaviour come from Germany and Austria. There are worse things you can do to children than neglect them. It is worth remembering the wartime carnage that resulted in the creation of institutions for international solidarity. We easily now forget where the idea that there should be economic cooperation in place of competition came from. The most studied single small groups of individuals were those who came to run Germany from the mid-1930s through to the end of the Second World War. To understand why the word 'co-operation' remains in the title of the OECD, it is worth looking back at the Nazis (and their elitist and eugenicist beliefs) when we consider what we have created in the long period of reconstruction after that carnage.

The childhood upbringings of the men who later became leading members of the Nazi party have been reconstructed and studied as carefully as possible. Those studies found that as children these men were usually brought up with much discipline, very strictly, and often with cruelty. They were not born Nazis – the national social environment and their home environment both had to be particularly warped to make them so.

Equally out of the ordinary, it has been found, were the typical home environments of those equally rare German and Austrian children who grew up at the same time and in the same places but who went on to rescue Jewish people from the Nazi regime. Their national social environment was identical. And their home environment also tended to revolve around high standards and expectations, but standards about caring for others differed. The home was rarely strict, and as far as we know, never cruel. It was '... virtually the exact opposite of the upbringing of the leading Nazis'.[15] Further studies have found that many of the rescuers felt that they had no choice but to help, that understanding having been instilled in them from an early age: 'They would not be able to go on living if they failed to defend the lives of others.'[16]

Across Europe in the 1940s there were too few rescuers, and most Jews targeted for persecution were killed. The fact that people in mainland Europe[17] were largely complicit in the killing, and are still reluctant to accept this truth, is claimed as part of the reason for current silences about 'race'; it remains '... an embarrassment'.[18] However, out of that war came a desire to cooperate better internationally, and a widespread realisation that labelling large groups of people as sub-human is evil.

A particular kind of knowledge

The OECD, later so widely criticised as a rich nations club, was not set up to preserve privilege, reinforce stereotypes and encourage hierarchy. Originally called the Organisation for European Economic Co-operation (OEEC), it was established to administer US and Canadian aid to war-ravaged Europe. That thinking changed in the 1950s, and it was renamed the Organisation for Economic Co-operation and Development in 1961. Its remit gradually gravitated towards concentrating on what was called improving efficiency, honing market systems, expanding free trade and encouraging competition (much more than cooperation).

By 2008, in words penned just before the great financial crash, the OECD was being described in at least one textbook as a '... crude, lumbering think-tank of the most wealthy nations, bulldozing over human dignity without pause for thought. Its tracks, crushed into the barren dereliction left behind, spell "global free market".'[19] The organisation describes its future a little differently, as '... looking ahead to a post-industrial age in which it aims to tightly weave OECD economies into a yet more prosperous and increasingly knowledge-based world economy'.[20] Ever most prosperous is not necessarily ever more knowing.

The knowledge base that the OECD refers to is a particular kind of knowledge that comes from a particular way of valuing people, of seeing the world, a way that came to dominate the thinking of those appointed to high office in the rich world by the start of the 21st century. From the late 1970s onwards, if you did not think in this particular way, you would be quite unlikely to be appointed to work for bodies such as the OECD, or to rise high within any government in one of the more unequal affluent nations, even less likely to do well in business. This way of thinking sees only large amounts of money as bringing dignity, sees children as being of greatly varying abilities, and sees its own educational testers as knowing all the correct answers to its battery of questions, which include questions for which there is clearly no international agreement over the correct answers.[21] It is not hard to devise a set of questions and a marking scheme that results in those you test appearing to be distributed along a bell curve. But to do this, you have to construct the world as being like this in your mind. It is not revealed as such by observation.

Constructing and measuring intelligence

What observation reveals is that ever since we have been trying to measure 'intelligence', we have found it has been rising dramatically.[22] This is true across almost all countries in which we have tried to measure it.[23] The average child in 1900 measured by today's standards would appear to be an imbecile, 'mentally retarded' (a term used in the past), a 'virtual automaton'.[24] When we measure our intelligence in this way, it appears so much greater than our parents' intelligence, that you would think they would have marvelled at how clever their children were. Often they didn't because the change that comes with educating so more so rapidly was shocking and disconcerting for the old.[25]

In affluent countries over the course of the last century we have become better educated in the kind of scientific thinking that scores highly in intelligence tests. More of us have been brought up in small households, and therefore given more attention than older generations could have been given. We have been better fed and clothed. Parenting did improve in general, but we were also expected to compete more and perform better at those particular tasks measured by intelligence tests. What it means to be clever changes over time and between places.

If our grandparents had been the 'imbeciles' their test results would (by today's standards) now suggest, they would not have been able to cooperate to survive. Although today's young people have been trained to think in abstract ways and to solve theoretical problems on the spot – it would be surprising if they could not, given how many now go on to university – there are other things they cannot do which their grandparents could. Their grandparents could get by easily without air conditioning and central heating, and many grew their own food, while their grandchildren often do not know how to mend things and do other more practical work.

Our grandparents might not have had as much 'critical acumen' on average, but they were not exposed to the kind of mental pollution that dulls acumen such as television advertising, with all the misleading messages it imparts. Observation tells us that intelligence merely reflects environment, and is only one small part of what it means to be clever. Despite this, 'critical acumen', the one small highly malleable part of thinking that has become so much more common over the course of recent generations, has mistakenly come to be seen both as all important and as very unequally distributed within just one generation.

We are very fortunate that in the recent past, those who believed that children each carry very different genetic endowments for the potential to learn were in a minority. If they had won the argument when it was nascent in the 19th century, when less than half the population were literate, they would no doubt have said that literacy is beyond the genetic ability of the majority. Then they would have advocated that most people should only be taught to labour, not to read or write. Underlying the battle for education has been a battle to be considered fully human.[26] And that battle is still under way.

3.2 IQism: the underlying rationale for the growth of elitism

A new way of thinking, a theory, was needed to describe a world in which just a few would be destined to have minds capable of leading the rest, and in which all could be ordered along a scale of ability. That way of thinking has come to be called 'IQism'. This is a belief in the validity of the intelligence quotient (IQ), and in the related testing of children resulting in their being described as having ability strung along a series of remarkably similar-looking bell curves, as shown in Figure 2. The merits of thinking of intelligence as having a quotient were pushed forward fastest in the 1950s, when many young children and teenagers were put through intelligence tests.

In the UK almost all 11-year-olds were subjected to testing (the '11 plus'), which included similar 'intelligence' tests, to determine which kind of secondary school they would be sent to. Although such sorting of children is no longer so blatantly undertaken, the beliefs that led to this discrimination against the majority are now the mainstream beliefs of those who currently make recommendations over how affluent economies are run.

Just as we no longer divide children so crudely by subjecting them to just one test, the educational economists are now careful not to draw graphs of the figures they publish – this would present a miserable picture of the futures of those for whom the bell curves toll. There are no histograms of these results in the OECD report in which the data used here are presented.

If children had a particular upper limit to their intellectual abilities, an IQ, and that limit was distributed along a bell curve, then it would be fair to ascribe each to a particular level, to suggest that perhaps in some countries children were not quite performing at the levels they could be. But is it really true that in no country do more than 4 per cent of children show signs of being truly able?[27]

Graphs that arouse suspicion

Almost identical curves could be drawn for different countries if human ability were greatly limited, such as those curves shown in Figure 2. This is drawn from data released by the OECD in 2014 in a publication that included many graphs ranking countries, but none showing the supposed distribution of measured inequality within any country.[28] Similarly, but earlier, the key findings of the 2007 OECD report included six graphs. None of those graphs showed a single bell curve.

Figure 2 reveals how the OECD economists think ability is distributed among its member countries, and in three particular places. It is possible that the OECD economists were themselves reluctant to draw the graphs because they knew they would rightly arouse suspicion. However, it is far from easy to guess at motive. What it is possible, if extremely tedious, to do is to read the technical manual and find hidden, after 144 pages of equations and procedures, the fact that those releasing this data, when calibrating the results (adjusting the scores before release), '… assumed that students have been sampled from a multivariate normal distribution.'[29] Given this assumption, almost no matter how the students had 'performed', the curves in Figure 2 would have been bell-shaped. The data were made, and are still made, to fit the curve.

There is very little room under one end of a bell curve to be at the top. Bell-curved distributions suggest that, at best, if most were destined to have their abilities lifted, the vast majority (even if they improved) would remain 'limited', or barely 'adequate', or just able to understand 'simple things'. The implication of ability being strung out like this is that even following educational gain, the many would always have to be

Figure 2: Distribution of children by ability, according to the OECD, 2012 (%)

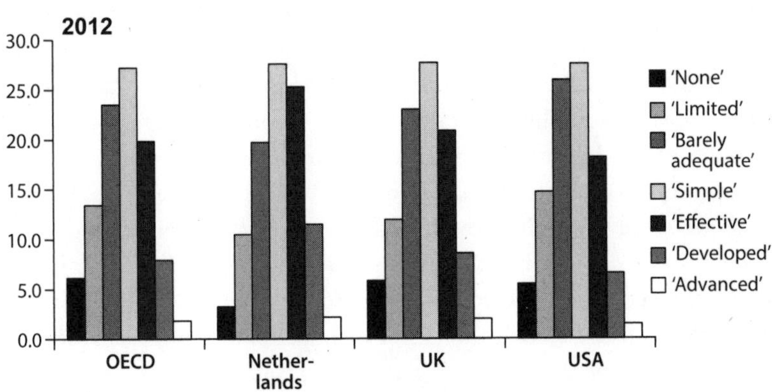

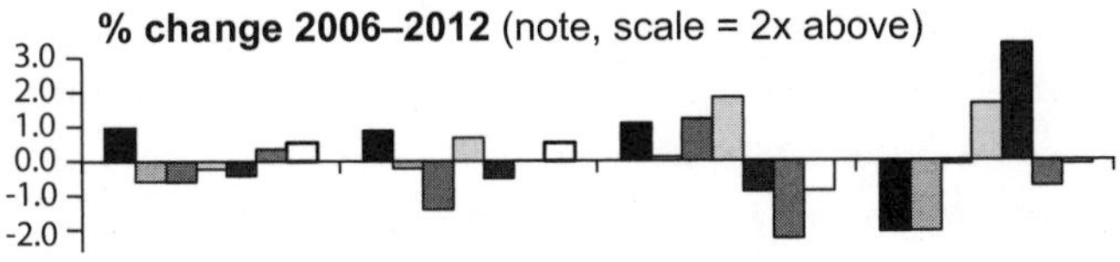

Source: Data originally given in OECD (2007) *The Programme for International Student Assessment (PISA), OECD's latest PISA study of learning skills among 15-year-olds, Paris:* OECD, derived from figures in table 1, p20. Updated using http://nces.ed.gov/pubs2014/2014024_tables.pdf (see Figure 1 notes)

Label	OECD	Nether-lands	UK	USA
'None'	1.0	0.9	1.1	-2.1
'Limited'	-0.6	-0.2	0.1	-2.1
'Barely adequate'	-0.6	-1.4	1.2	-0.1
'Simple'	-0.2	0.7	1.8	1.7
'Effective'	-0.4	-0.5	-0.9	3.4
'Developed'	0.2	0.0	-2.3	-0.9
'Advanced'	0.5	0.5	-0.9	-0.1
	0.00	0.00	0.00	0.00

governed by the few, the elite, 'the advanced'. If this testing is producing scores with any kind of validity concerning underlying ability, then only a very few children will ever grow up to understand what is going on. If this is not the case, if there is not just a tiny minority of truly able children, then to describe children in this way, and to offer prescriptions given such a description (and the subsequent outcomes), is deeply unjust.

Those people who believe in IQ have been thinking and writing about it for only a century. It is not an old idea. The concept was first proposed in 1912 with the German name *Intelligenz-Quotient*, derived from testing that occurred just a few years earlier in 1905 in France, but testing that did not, initially, assume a limit. Those with a taste for testing later developed the concept of assuming a limit to children's intellectual potential. The assumption was that intellectual ability was limited physically, like height. Different children would grow to different heights, which tended to be related to their parents' heights, but also to the wider social environment that influenced their nutrition, their exercise and their wellbeing.

The idea that intellectual ability is distributed like height was proposed within just a few years of the bell curve itself first being described mathematically. Subsequently, at any one time, only 27 per cent of the population can have an IQ of 110 or higher, 11 per cent 120 or higher and 0.6 per cent 140 or higher, by definition. It is now easy to see how it could have been imagined, why the idea of IQ and the concept of its hereditability came to flourish. Most people who were told of the idea were also told that their IQ was high. People who propagated the idea thought that their IQs were even higher. People enjoy flattery – it makes us feel safe and valued. But tragically, in the round, the concept of IQ made no individuals actually safer or more valued for who they really were. As the old-fashioned social evil of illiteracy is largely overcome in affluent nations, IQism is growing again as an ideological source for injustice.

Those recognised as making progress in the study of education suggest that thinking is as much like height as singing is like weight. You can think on your own, but you are best learning to think with others. Education does not unfold from within but is almost all '… induction from without.'[30] There are no real 'know-nothings'; they could not function. Children are not limited, or barely able, or simple. We are all occasionally stupid, especially when we have not had enough sleep, or feel anxious and 'don't think'.

Using singing as a metaphor for education, we are similarly all capable of singing or not singing, of singing better or worse. What is seen as good singing is remarkably culturally specific, varying greatly by time and place. Work hard at your singing in a particular time and place, and people will say you sing well if you sing as you are supposed to. It is possible to rank singing, to grade it, and to believe that some singing is truly awful and other singing exquisite, but the truth of that is as much in the culture and ears of the listener as it is in the vocal cords of the performer. Joseph Schumpeter proposed[31] that human beings have singing limits that are distributed along a bell-shaped curve.[32] After all is said, despite the fact that we are all capable of being stupid, the bell curve of singing ability did not catch on. We are not as vain about how good we are at yodelling in the shower as we are about being told we are especially clever. We can all sing, we can all be stupid, we can all be clever, we can all learn without limits.

Learning without limits

It is only recently that it has been possible to make the claim that almost all children in rich countries are capable of learning without limits. The same was not true of many of their parents and of even fewer of their grandparents. And the same is not true of almost a tenth of children worldwide, some 200 million five-year-olds. These children are the real 'failures', failing to develop all their basic cognitive functions due to iodine or iron deficiency, or malnutrition in general leading to stunting of the brain as well as the body, and/or having received inadequate stimulation from others when very young.[33] Children need to be well fed and cared for, both to learn to think well and to be physically able enough to think well, just as they do to be able to sing well. But well-fed and loved, there is no subsequent physical limiting factor other than what is around them. If you grow up in a community where people do not sing, it is unlikely that you will sing. If you grow up where singing is the norm, you are likely to partake.

Much of what we do now our recent ancestors never did. They did not drive cars, work on computers, few practised the violin, and hardly any played football, so why do we talk of a violinist or a footballer having innate talent? Human beings did not slowly evolve in a world where those whose keyboard skills were not quite up to scratch were a little less successful at mating than the more nimble-fingered. We learn all these things; we were not born to them, but we are born elastic enough to learn. How we subsequently perform in tests almost entirely reflects the environment we grew up in, not differences in the structures of our brains.[34] However, there remains a widespread misconception that ability, and especially particular abilities, are innate, that they unfold from within, and are distributed very unevenly, with just a few being truly talented, having been given a gift and having the potential to unfold that gift within them, hence the term 'gifted'.

The misconception of the existence of the gifted grew out of beliefs that talents were bestowed by the gods, who each originally had their own special gifts, of speed, art or drinking (in the case of Dionysus). This misconception was useful for explaining away the odd serf who could not be suppressed in ancient times, or the few poor boys who rose in rank a century ago. But then that skewed distribution of envisaged talent was reshaped as bell-curved. The results of IQ tests were made into a bell-curved graph by design, but people were told (what turned out to be) the lie that the curve somehow emerged naturally.[35]

Apply an IQ test to a population for which that test was not designed specifically, and most people will either do very badly or very well at that test, rather than perform in a way that produces a 'bell curve' distribution. Tests have to be designed and calibrated to result in such an outcome. The bell curve as a general description of the population became popular as more were required to rise in subsequent decades to fill social functions that had not existed in such abundance before: engine operator, teacher, tester. Today, educators are arguing to change the shape of the perceived curve of ability again, to have the vast majority of results skewed to the right, put in the region marked 'success', as all begin to appear so equally able. The conclusions of those currently arguing against the idea of there being especially gifted children make clear how '… categorizing some children as innately talented is discriminatory ... unfair ... wasteful ... [and] unjustified …'.[36] It contributes to the injustice whereby social inequality persists.

The gifted, the talented and the ugly

Although we are now almost all fed well enough not to have our cognitive capabilities limited physically through the effects of malnutrition on the brain, and more and more children are better nurtured and cared for as infants in affluent countries, and although we are now rich enough to afford for almost all to be allowed to learn in ways our parents and grandparents were mostly not allowed, we hold back from giving all children that encouragement and instead, tell most from a very early age that they are not up to the level of 'the best in the class', and never can be. We do this in numerous ways, including where we make children sit at school, usually on a table sorted by ability, if primary school teachers are following Ofsted guidance. Within our families all our children are special, but outside the family cocoon they are quickly ranked, told that to sing they need to enter talent shows that only a tiny proportion can win, told that to learn they need to work harder than the rest and, more importantly, that they need to be 'gifted' if they are to do very well.

It is now commonly said that children need to be 'gifted' to become Sunday's well-developed 'level 5' child. They need to be 'especially gifted' to be that seventh of a seventh who reach 'level 6', and it is harder still to win a rung on the places stacked above that scale. Most are told that even if they work hard, they can at best only expect to rise one level or two, to hope to be simple rather than know-nothings, or to have effective knowledge, to be a useful cog in a machine, rather than just being a 'simpleton'.

Aspiring to more than one grade above your lot in life is seen as fanciful. Arguing that there is not a mass of largely limited children out there is portrayed as misguided fancy. Most say this quietly, but I have collected some of their musings here, and I give many examples later in this book to demonstrate this; occasionally a few actually say what they think in public: '"Middle-class children have better genes," says former schools chief, "and we just have to accept it"'.[37] Such public outbursts are not the isolated musings of a few discredited former schools' inspectors or other mavericks. Instead, they reveal what is generally believed by the kinds of people who run governments that appoint such people to be schools' inspectors. It is just that elitist politicians tend to have more sense than to tell their electorate that they believe most of them to be so limited in ability.

You might think that what the OECD educationalists are doing is trying to move societies from extreme inequality in education, through a bell curve of current outcome, to a world of much greater equality. However, the envisaged distribution of ability is not progressively changing shape from left-skewed, to bell-shaped, to right-skewed uniformly across the affluent world. In countries such as the Netherlands, Finland, Japan and Canada, people choose to teach more children what they need to know to reach higher levels. In those countries it is less common to present a story of children having innate differences. In other countries, such as the UK, Portugal, Mexico and the US, more are allowed to learn very little, and children are more often talked about as coming from 'different stock'.[38] The position of each country on the scale of how elitist their education systems are has also varied over time.

Looking at changes in IQ test results, when older tests and calibrations are applied to younger cohorts, it becomes possible to monitor how different groups are treated differently within countries at different times. This evidence shows that these tests measure how well children have been taught in order to pass tests. So the generation you are born into matters in determining IQ. Intelligence tests have almost nothing to do with anything innate.[39] Take two identical twins separated at birth, and you will find that their physical similarities alone are enough for them to be similarly treated in their schools, given, in effect, similar environments to each other, in a way that accounts for almost all later similarities in how they perform in IQ tests. If both are tall and good-looking, for instance, they are more likely to become more confident, receive a little more attention from their teachers, a little more praise at their performance from their adoptive parents, a little more tolerance from their peers; they will tend to do better at school.[40] These effects have been shown to be enough by themselves to account for the findings in studies of identical twins who have been separated at birth, but usually brought up in the same country, and who follow such similar trajectories. The trajectories also tend to be so similar because, of course, the twins are brought up over exactly the same time span.[41]

Many rivers to cross

In the US, the 'IQ' gap between black and white Americans fell from the 1940s to the 1970s, but rose subsequently back to the 1940s levels of inequality by the start of the 21st century. This move away from elitism and then back occurred in tandem with how the social position and relative deprivation of black versus white Americans changed.[42] From the 1940s to the 1970s, black Americans won progressively higher status, won the right to be integrated more into what had become normal economic expectations, and wages equalised a little. Then, from the 1970s onwards, the wage gap grew; segregation increased again; civil rights victories were followed by the mass incarceration of young black men – no other country locks up as many of its own people as the US. In 1940 *10 times* fewer were locked up in jail in the US as now, and 70 per cent of the two million now imprisoned are black.[43] This huge rise in imprisonment in the US, and its acceptance as normal partly because of who is now most often imprisoned, is perhaps the starkest outcome of the growth of elitism in any single rich country.

Treating a few people as especially able inevitably entails treating others as especially unable. If you treat people like dirt, you can watch them become more stupid before your eyes, or at least through their answers to your multiple-choice questions in public examinations. From the 1970s onwards, poor Americans, and especially poor black Americans, were progressively treated more and more like dirt. Literally just a few were allowed to sing.[44] To a lesser extent similar trends occurred in many other parts of the affluent world, in all those rich countries in which income inequalities grew. And they grew most where IQism became most accepted.

IQism can be a self-fulfilling prophecy. If you believe that only a few children are especially able, then you concentrate your resources on those children, and subsequently they will tend to appear to do well. They will certainly pass your tests, as the tests are designed for a certain number to pass, and the children you selected will have been chosen and then taught to pass such tests. Young people respond well to praise and get smarter as a result. They respond badly to disrespect, which reduces their motivation to learn, so they perform badly in tests. People, and especially children, crave recognition and respect. Telling children they rank low in a class is a way of telling them that they have not earned respect. Children are not particularly discerning about what they are taught. They will try to do well at IQ tests if you train them to try to do well at IQ tests. Almost everyone wants to fit in, to be praised, not to rank towards the bottom, not to be seen as a liability, as those at the bottom are seen.

There is a river in New Zealand called the Rakaia that is spanned by a suspension bridge of novel design. (A photograph of it is included on page vii.) There is a notice by the bridge that tells its history and that of the ford that existed before the bridge. The river is wide and fierce, draining water from the Southern Alps. The notice says that before the bridge was built, the Maori would cross the river in groups, each group holding a long pole placed horizontally on the surface of the water so that the weakest would not be swept off their feet. The people who came after the Maori, who knew how to build a bridge of iron supported from beneath, but who did not understand why a group of people would cross a river with a pole, wrote the notice. Crossing together was, in fact, not to protect the weakest, but to protect the entire group. Any individual trying to ford a fast-flowing river draining glacial waters runs a great risk. If you hold onto a long horizontal pole with others, you are at much lower risk. The concept of 'from each according to his abilities, to each according to his needs' was a concept that took shape in places and times when it was better understood that all benefited as a result. When crossing a freezing river with a pole, you need as many others holding onto that pole with you as can fit.

All children are different. They grow up to be adults with differing idiosyncrasies, traits (often mistaken as talents or natural endowments) both peculiar to them and to the types of societies they are raised in. Some will turn out to be considered great singers, others to sing well in choirs, if brought up where it is normal to sing. Some of these idiosyncrasies are related to physical features – taller people may have held on better to that pole, for example. Because of what was allowed at the time, and not any genetic trait, it will almost certainly have been a man, but it will not necessarily have been an especially tall man who grew up to think of suspending a bridge across the Rakaia.

Almost every adult who thinks of building a suspension bridge was a child who had seen it done before, and almost none of the children who have never seen a bridge made that way will work out how to do so without prompting by someone who has. No one had the 'unique' idea in the first place. Or, to put it another way, every slight change that was made, from the earliest tree-trunk bridge to the latest design, was 'unique', as are all our thoughts.

We are, none of us, superhuman. We are not like the gods with their gifts. We can all be stupid. We hold onto the pole to cross the river having faith in the strength of others. This is a much safer way to proceed than having a few carried by others who are not joined together. If, in the short term, you value being dry above solidarity, or if you are led to believe that you are destined to carry others who are your superiors, then all are at greater risk of drowning.

3.3 Apartheid schooling: from garaging to hot-housing

Before we had suspension bridges, many people drowned crossing rivers. And many also died in the process of building the bridges. Suspension bridges were first built using huge amounts of manual labour to dig out the ironstone needed, and the coal to forge the iron, to construct the girders and rivet everything in place. Almost everything was originally made by hand, and even the job of constructing each rivet, as in Adam Smith's idealised pin factory, was initially done by dividing the process into as many small processes as possible, and then giving responsibility for a particular part of the work, the flattening of the head of the rivet, say, to a particular man, woman or child labourer.

When pin factories were first created; they initially mostly employed adult men – it did not take much schooling to teach a man how to squash a hot rivet in a vice so that its head was flattened. It took even less schooling to teach the woman who fed him at night how to cook the extremely limited rations available to those who first worked in factories. But it took a little more schooling to teach the foreman in charge of the factory how to fill in ledgers to process orders. It took even more schooling to train the engineer who decided just how many rivets were needed to make the bridge safe.

If you could look at the bridge currently spanning the gorge of the Rakaia River, you would see that whoever made that decision erred on the side of caution – there tend to be a lot of rivets in old bridges. A lot of rivets meant a lot of rivet makers. If reasonably fed, then rivet makers and their wives had many children, little future rivet makers, almost none of whom, living in the towns where rivets were made, grew their own food, and so there were a great many new hungry mouths to feed and not enough time or people to spare to teach most of the little ones, who, after all, were destined to make yet more rivets for yet more bridges. But incrementally, a surplus of wealth was amassed, and a small part of that surplus was used to build schools, especially in the countries to where most of the surplus came, such as Britain.

A good age for education

Slowly, a little more time was found, won and forged out of lives of great drudgery. Women gained a little power, managed to say 'no' a little more, and have six children each rather than eight. By 1850 in a country like the UK, most children attended some kind of school, often only Sunday school. By the 1870s it became law that all children should attend school until the age of 10; that age was ratcheted up steadily until the 1970s, after which there was a hiatus. By the 1970s, women in Britain were having on average two children with the help both of the pill and of not insignificant liberation (just a century earlier people had been imprisoned for teaching about condoms). Educational equality rose, ignorance was slowly abated, and (as fertility fell) there were fewer children to teach, and it was increasingly felt that there was more to teach to all of them. But that trend of increased equality came to an end in the 1970s as 1950s elitism began to outweigh earlier progress.

The latter half of Figure 3 shows, as far as university entry is concerned, a curtailing of hope and opportunity as the belief that we did not all inherently have the same potential gained sustenance from arguments over IQ and aspects of intellectual 'potential'. Mostly recently, however, as the very final years in the figure show, those elitist arguments have been partly lost concerning school-leaving age in at least one unequal rich country – all will now be in education until the age of 18 in Britain, although whether all, if not in the 'top streams', will be thought educable till then and treated with respect in schools is a battle still being fought. By autumn 2014 it became clear that the numbers entering universities were dropping, possibly permanently. In 2014, statisticians who dealt with university applications reported that: 'English 18 year olds became

Figure 3: School-leaving age (years) and university entry (%), Britain, 1876–2013

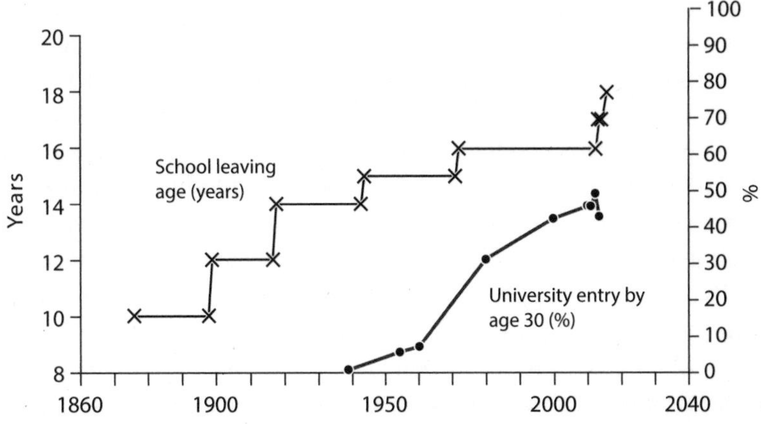

Sources: BBC (2007) 'School leaving age set to be 18', report, 12 January; Meikle, J. (2007) 'Education dropouts at 16 will face sanctions', *The Guardian*, 23 March; Timmins, N. (2001) *The five giants: A biography of the welfare state* (new edn), London: HarperCollins, pp 2, 73, 198 and 200); and latest official estimates, see Higher Education Funding Council for England website on widening participation of local areas: www.hefce.ac.uk/Widen/polar/ Figures respectively are:

Year	University entry per 100	
	By age 30	By any age
1938	1	1
1954	5	7
1959	7	10
1980	31	47
2000	42	63
2010	46	
2011	46	
2012	49	
2013	43	

Year	School leaving age
1876	10
1898	10
1899	12
1917	12
1918	14
1943	14
1944	15
1971	15
1972	16
2012	16
2013	17
2014	17
2015	18

Updated figures 2006/7 to 2012/13 available at https://www.gov.uk/government/statistics/participation-rates-in-higher-education-2006-to-2013 which suggests that university entry rose to 49% in 2011/12 but fell back to 43% in 2012/13. The fall was due to students not deferring entry to avoid having to pay £9,000 a year fees and was thought to be temporary. The prediction for 2014 entry is '46%'.

less likely to apply to higher education in 2012.... The preceding trend had been for cycle-on-cycle increases. Against this trend, the fall in 2012 represented a proportional reduction in demand of over 5 per cent. The pattern of changes across the UK makes it very likely that this reduction was largely due to the increase in annual tuition fees from around £3,000 to close to £9,000.'[45] That fall in applications in 2012 resulted in the first drop in student numbers in 2013.

Increased elitist thinking can tolerate raising the school-leaving age to 18, but it is not commensurate with provision of further education for all after that. Furthermore, increased segregation by educational establishment from the age of 16 is now English government policy. Schools that have become academies can deny entry to children from age 16 who live within the catchment if their overall exam grades are not deemed good enough. New 'university technical colleges' are being built across the country partly to take children from ages 14 to 19 who are rejected from what until recently were comprehensive schools. Comprehensive meant taking everyone; despite the use of the word 'university' in university technical colleges, these are schools for children who mostly won't be going to university.

In contrast to the recent acceleration in school-leaving age, the rapid rise in university entry that peaked around the late 1960s is now decelerating, and decelerated most quickly in the most recent decade, as Figure 3 makes clear. Any further increases in school-leaving age would require compulsory university attendance, as tertiary education would be provided for all, just as secondary education was to current students' grandparents. Comprehensive universities would be as different to current universities as comprehensive schools are to grammar schools. Such a thing is hard to imagine today, but no harder than it was to imagine compulsory secondary school attendance just one lifetime ago, and a welfare state to go with it. That welfare state was first created in New Zealand.

Progress and rationing

Eventually all the great gorges in New Zealand had been spanned, even as far south in the world as the Rakaia River. Roads were built, agriculture further mechanised. Food was preserved, chilled, shipped abroad; mouths in Europe were fed; money from Europe was returned (with 'interest'); and so much of this within just a decade of the first IQ test being christened on the other side of the planet. Rivet making was automated. The requirement for all children in rich countries to attend an elementary school until the age of 14 was finally fully enforced, occurring less than the length of a human lifetime ago (see Figure 3). That requirement was extended to compulsory secondary education for girls as well as boys, in all affluent nations.

In early 1950s Britain, food was still limited by rationing, even though the war had ended. It was then that IQ tests were initially used to decide, to 'ration', which kind of secondary school children would be allowed to go to. Although food and education were not directly related, the ideas of how you could rationally plan the allocation of both had arisen during wartime. For education, the future rationing of what were then scarce resources (graduate teachers) was based on how those children performed on one day with pen and paper at a desk around the time of their 11th birthday.

For some involved, the intention was altruistic, to secure the best for the 'brightest' of whatever background, but the result was gross injustice. Similar injustices occurred in most other newly affluent nations. These injustices were resisted, seen as segregation by 'race' in the US, and by social class in Britain, and within just another couple of decades, almost all children went to their nearest school, with no continuing distinction between grammar and secondary modern.

The phenomenon of almost all children going to their nearest secondary school, to the same school as their neighbours' children, had occurred hardly anywhere in the world before the 1970s. When all local children go to the same neighbourhood state school, it is called a 'comprehensive' school because it has to provide a comprehensive education for all. In Britain, the main alternatives to genuine state comprehensive schools include selective state schools (often called 'grammar schools'), a surviving relic from the education system that prevailed until the 1970s when, in effect, most children were selected to go to a school for 'rejects' (called 'secondary moderns'), and only a few were admitted to schools for those not rejected by a test. Grammar schools still award places according to rank order of performance in their entrance tests. However, very few areas in the UK still retain a selective grammar school system today, Before there was a change to the system, three quarters of children would typically be relegated to those secondary moderns. In Britain in 1965, 8 per cent of all children of secondary school age attended a comprehensive school, 12 per cent in 1966, 40 per cent in 1970, 50 per cent in 1973, 80 per cent by 1977 and 83 per cent by 1981.[46] Today, from the age of 16 to begin with, we are starting to see a return to such segregation.

It was under the Conservative administration led by Margaret Thatcher that the final cull of over a third of the 315 remaining grammar schools still functioning in 1979 was undertaken, with 130 becoming comprehensives by 1982.[47] However, the Conservative government then introduced 'assisted places' in 1979, the scheme whereby they began to sponsor a small group of children chosen by private schools. And so, just at the time when it looked as if divisive state education was ending, the state itself sponsored an increase in division, which was the first major increase in private school entry in Britain in decades. And Britain was not alone in seeing such elitism rise.

In 1979 Britain was following events that had first had their immediate impact elsewhere. In California, where Ronald Reagan was governor until 1975 (later becoming US President in 1980), private school entry first rose rapidly after years of decline. Between 1975 and 1982, in just seven years, the proportion of children attending private schools in California rose, from 8.5 to 11.6 per cent.[48] This occurred when, as a result of Ronald Reagan's decision not to properly fund the poorest of schools, the state reduced the funding of all maintained schools to a level near that of the lowest funded school, following a Californian Supreme Court ruling of 1976. The ruling stated that it was unconstitutional to fund state schools variably between areas in relation to the levels of local property taxes. Before the court ruling, state schools in affluent areas were better funded than state schools in poorer parts of California.

Before the abolition of almost all selective grammar schools in Britain, affluent parents whose children were much more likely to attend such schools had seen much higher state funding of their children's education compared with that of the majority. In both the US and Britain, the advent of much greater educational equality was accompanied by a significant growth in the numbers of parents choosing to pay so that their children would not have to be taught alongside certain others, nor given the same resources as those others.

The rise in private school places occurred with the fall in grammar school places in Britain, and was much greater in the US with the equalising down of state education resources in California. In Britain the greatest concentration of private school expansion occurred in and on the outskirts of the most affluent cities such as London, Oxford and Bristol – not where local schools did worse, but where a higher proportion of parents had higher incomes. Educational inequalities had been reduced to a historic minimum by the 1970s in the US, just as income inequalities had. In education this trend was turned around by the reaction to the notorious[49] *Serrano v Priest* California court cases of 1971, 1976 and 1977.

In Britain, half of all school children were attending non-selective secondary schools by 1973; again, educational inequalities fell fastest when income inequalities became most narrow. These were crucial years where issues of equality between rich and poor were being fought over worldwide as well as between local schools. Internationally, poorer countries that controlled the supply of oil worked together to raise the price of oil dramatically in that same turbulent year (during the October Yom Kippur war). International inequalities in wealth fell to their lowest recorded levels; worldwide inequalities in health reached a minimum a few years later.[50] Within Britain and the US, such health and wealth inequalities had reached their lowest recorded levels a little earlier, around the start of the 1970s.[51] This was a wonderful time for people in affluent countries, who had never had it so good. Wages had never been as high; even the US minimum wage was at what would later turn out to be its historic maximum.[52]

Before the jobs went at the end of the decade, before insecurity rose, it was a great time to be ordinary, or to be average, or even above average, but the early 1970s were a disconcerting time if you were affluent. Inflation was high; if you were well off enough to have savings, then those savings were being eroded. People began to realise that their children were not going to be as cushioned as they were by so much relative wealth, by going to different schools.

When politicians said that they were going to eradicate the evil of ignorance by educating all children in Britain, or that they were going to have a 'Great Society' in the US, they did not mention that this would reduce the apparent advantages of some children. Equal rights for black children, a level playing field for poor children – these can be seen as threats if you belong to a group that wants to be viewed and treated as elite. More appear to be competing in a race where proportionately fewer and fewer can win. But it is only a race if you view it as one – better education need not be a race any more than securing better health.

Because you're worth it?

In 2009, the OECD revealed (through its routine statistical publications) that Britain diverted a larger share of its school education spending (23 per cent) to a tiny proportion of privately educated children (7 per cent) than almost any other rich nation. That inequality had been much less 30 years earlier. In 2014, OECD statistics revealed that UK universities had become 70 per cent privately funded by 2011, representing the fastest rise across all of the OECD, up from 30 per cent in 2000. Only Chile and Korea now spend a lower share of public money on state education compared to private spending.[53]

It is not hard for most people to know that they are not very special. Even affluent people, if they are not delusional, know in their heart of hearts that they are not very special; most know that they are members of what some call the 'lucky sperm club', born to the right parents in their turn, or just lucky, or perhaps both lucky and a little ruthless.[54] However, you don't carry on winning in races that have relatively fewer and fewer winners if you don't have a high opinion of yourself. Only those who maintain the strongest of narcissistic tendencies are sure that they became affluent because they were more able. A few of those who couple such tendencies with eugenicist beliefs think that their children will be likely to inherit their supposed acumen and do well in whatever circumstances they face. The rest, the vast majority of the rich, who are not so cocksure, had a choice when equality appeared on the horizon. They could throw in their lot with the masses, send their children to the local school, see their comparative wealth evaporate with inflation, and join the party, or they could try to defend their corner, pay for their children to be segregated from others, look for better ways to maintain their advantages than leaving their savings to the ravages of inflation, vote and fund into power politicians who shared their concerns, and encourage others to vote for them too. They encouraged others to support them by playing on their fears, through making donations to right-wing parties' advertising campaigns (see Section 5.1, later). Advertising works and propaganda, especially in newspapers owned by the super-rich, works. Opinions can be swayed. They convinced enough voters that the centre-left had been a shambles in both the US and the UK. The opposition to the right-wing parties was too weak, campaign funding too low, and in 1979 in Britain and 1980 in the US, the right wing won.

Although not as rare as the wartime rescuers of the 1940s, the effective left-wing idealists of the 1970s were too few and far between, although there were more of these idealists in some countries than in others. In Sweden, Norway and Finland, left-wing idealists won, but society also held together in Japan, Germany, Austria, Denmark, Belgium, the Netherlands and France, in Spain after Franco, in Canada, to an extent in Greece (once the generals were overthrown), in Switzerland and in Ireland.

It was principally in the US, but also in Britain, Australia and New Zealand, Portugal and Singapore, that those who were rich had the greatest fears, and the greatest influence. It was there that the political parties and idealists of the rich fared best. There, more than elsewhere, most who had riches and other advantages looked to hold on to them. They donated money to right-wing political parties and helped them become powerful again. They donated because they were afraid of greater equality; not because they believed that most people would benefit from their actions by becoming more equal, but because they thought that the greater good would be achieved by promoting inequality. By behaving in this way, they began to sponsor a renewed elitism.

One effect of right-wing parties winning power was that they attacked trade unions. And as unions declined in strength, left-wing parties were forced to look for other sources of finance. Having seen the power of funding politics on the right, the affluent could more easily be cajoled to begin to sponsor formerly left-wing and middle-of-the-road political parties and to influence them, not least to give more consideration to the interests of the rich, and because they knew right-wing parties could not carry on winning throughout the 1990s. The rich spent their money in these ways, with their donations becoming ever more effective from the early 1960s onwards.[55]

In hindsight it is not hard to see how the Democrats in the US and later New Labour in Britain began similarly to rely so completely on the sponsorship of a few rich individuals and businesses. Once it became common for the affluent to seek to influence politicians with money, and occasionally to receive political honours from the politicians they sponsored as a result, there was no need to limit financial sponsorship to just the right wing.

In those few very unequal affluent countries, where the self-serving mantra of 'because you're worth it' was repeated most often, part of what it meant to be in the elite came more and more from the 1970s onwards to be seen as someone who gave money to 'good' causes, to charities, and to political parties who do the same 'good' works, while not altering the status quo, not reducing their own status and not reducing inequality. Inequality can be made politically popular.

An equality worth fighting for

In the southern states of the US, the ending of slavery brought the fear of equality. Initially this was translated politically into votes for the Democratic Party and the suppression of civil rights there through to at least the 1960s, including the right for children to go to the same school as their neighbours. In South Africa in the late 1940s, apartheid was introduced with popular political support from poorer whites who felt threatened as other former African colonies were beginning to claim their freedom from white rule.[56] Again, segregation began at school.

When Nelson Mandela was put on trial in 1963, and facing a possible death sentence, in his concluding court statement he defined, as an equality worth fighting for, the right of children to be treated equally in education, and for them to be taught that Africans and Europeans were equal and merited equal attention. At that time the South African government spent 12 times as much on educating each European child as on each African child. Nelson Mandela was released from prison in 1990. In that year children in inner-city schools in the US, such as those in Chicago, were having half as much spent on their state secondary education as children in the more affluent suburbs to the north, and 12 times less than was spent on the most elite private school education.

By 2003, almost nine out of ten of the US inner-city children were black or Hispanic, and inequalities in state school spending in America had risen four-fold. Inequalities rose even further if private schools are also considered, and were still growing by 2006 as private school fees rose quickly (at the extreme exponentially) while the numbers of private school places increased much more slowly.[57] By 2014, it was being reported that at the very top of the Chicago education system the pay of just eight senior staff at the University of Chicago, including the university president, provost and vice president, had increased by $7.6 million. But '… because a majority of the University of Chicago's trustees appoint future trustees, change is only likely to come through public outrage, then informal, inefficient mechanisms like faculty votes, online petitions, and withdrawal of alumni donations'.[58] It is likely that part of the reason those at the top of the US education system took such large salary increases was to be able to ensure their own children did not need to get into debt just to gain a university degree.

Admissions to private schools rose slowly and steadily in countries like the US and the UK from the 1970s onwards. They rose slowly because few could afford the ever-rising fees, and because some held out against segregating their children. They rose steadily because, despite the cost and inconvenience of having to drive children past the schools to which they could have gone, parents' fears rose at a greater rate. Rising inequalities in incomes between families from the 1970s onwards have tended to accompany increased use of private educational provision in those countries where income inequalities have increased. Rising income inequalities also increase fear for children's futures, as it is easier to be seen as failing in a country where more are paid less. It is much harder to appear to succeed where only a few are paid more, especially when that few are paid much more.

Just as anti-colonialism and the abolition of slavery fostered unforeseen new injustices, the success of civil rights for black children in the US and working-class children in Europe in the 1960s fostered the rise of new injustices of elitism, increased educational segregation and the creation of different kinds of schools for children seen increasingly as different, who might otherwise have been taught together.

By 2002, in many inner-city state schools in the US a new militaristic curriculum was being introduced, described as a curriculum of fear, according to a leading magazine of the affluent, *Harpers*. Not a single noise is tolerated in these schools; Nazi-style salutes are used to greet teachers; specific children are specified as 'best workers' and, according to a headmaster administering the 'rote-and-drill curricula' in one Chicago school, the aim was to turn these children into tax-paying automata who will 'never burglarize your home…'.[59]

In 2009, President Barack Obama promoted Arne Duncan, the man who had been responsible for education policy in Chicago at this time, to be put in charge of education policy for the nation. He could have learned from what are now widely regarded as mistakes, but instead, he propagated them across the country, transforming 'schools from a public investment to a private good, answerable not to the demands and values of a democratic society but to the imperatives of the market place'.[60] By 2014, he was roundly accused of both meddling too much and leaving too much to the will of an increasingly privatised education market, which was quite an achievement.[61]

In Britain, children placed towards the bottom of the increasingly elitist education hierarchy are not 'rote-and-drill' conditioned so explicitly, but are instead now 'garaged', kept quiet in classes that do not stretch them, by teachers who understandably have little hope for them, or sent to those new university technical colleges, out of sight. These children and young adults are made to retake examinations at the ages of 16–19 to keep them in the system and in education, but they are not being educated. The elitist beliefs that have been spread are that if just a few children are gifted, but most are destined for a banal future, then providing the majority with education in art, music, languages, history, even athletics, can be viewed as profligate, while such things are presented as essential for the able minority.

It is not that progress was reversed in the 1970s but that, as has so often happened before, with every two steps taken forward towards greater justice, one step is taken backwards. Ending formal slavery in the southern US saw formal segregation established, an injustice far more minor than slavery, but one that came to be seen as equally great. As the end of direct colonial rule was achieved across Africa, apartheid was established in the south, once again more minor, but colonialism at home, within a country. As segregation of children between state secondary schools in Britain was abolished during the 1970s, in the South East there was a boom in private sector education, and now a plethora of academies and free schools, colleges and school specialising in particular subjects are emerging – as many varieties of school as of a well-known brand of baked beans. Variety can be the spice of life, but variety in an era of growing elitism tends towards a hierarchy.

As each great injustice was overcome, a more minor injustice was erected in its place, to be overcome again in turn, as was segregation after slavery, as was apartheid after colonialism, as elitism probably will be after the latest British school reorganisation (based on renewed IQist beliefs) is abolished. In every case, what had been considered normal behaviour came to be considered abhorrent: slave holding, suggesting Africans were not capable of self-rule, proposing separate but far from equal lives. Separate lives are hard to justify, from the black woman forced to sit at the back of the bus to the children who are told that the only place for them is in a sink school. Separation is not very palatable once carefully thought about.

By 2007, in some parts of the UK there were hopeful signs of a move away from seeing children as units of production to be repeatedly tested, but the English school system had become a market system, where schools competed for money and for children. The introduction of 57 varieties of state school saw to that, as did the expansion of private schools, which saw their intake rise to 7 per cent while the children in these schools obtained a quarter of top grade A-level results and gained over half the places in the 'top' universities.[62] Almost all the remaining elite places in these universities go to children in the better funded of the 57 varieties of state school, or to those who had some other advantage at home. Elitist systems claim to be meritocracies, but in such systems almost no one gets to where they are placed on merit, not when we are all so inherently equal. In more equitable societies numerous '... studies reveal the overwhelming educational and socializing value of integrated schooling for children of all backgrounds.'[63]

3.4 Putting on a pedestal: superhuman myths

Every injustice can be paired with a human failing. The failing that pairs best with elitism, given its 1950s' high point, is chauvinism. This is typically a prejudiced belief in the inherent superiority of men, in particular, a small selected group of men. To see chauvinism in action when it comes to elitism, all you need do is look to the top, and at the top in the field of academia is the Nobel Prize (although not all Nobel Prizes concern academia, most do). Out of almost 848 people awarded Nobel laureates by the end of 2014, only 46 of them were women, a staggeringly low 5.4 per cent! But a rapid improvement on 4.4 per cent achieved by 2008. Either women had recently become much more able, or the nominating committees were becoming more sensitive to how they might be viewed.

Overall, more prizes were given for work in medicine to men and women jointly than for work in any other single subject. In medicine, teamwork often involving subordination is more common, thus a significant handful of women were included among the medical laureates. Physics has lower but similar numbers of prizewinners compared with medicine, but only two women have ever been awarded the Nobel Prize for physics. While chemistry is fractionally more welcoming, literature is much more female-friendly, with women being awarded just over a tenth of all the prizes handed out. But given how many women are authors today, is there really only one great woman author for every 10 men? Peace is similarly seen as more of a female domain – women were possibly even in the majority as members of some of the 20 organisations awarded the peace prize over the years. But they were in a small minority of actual named winners. As Figure 4 shows, prizes are largely a macho domain.

The table in the figure shows the percentage increase in the number of prizes awarded to men and women in each subject area since the data for first edition of this book collected in 2008. In the years 2009–14 there has been a 31 per cent increase in the number of prizes awarded to women, but only an 8 per cent increase in the number awarded to men (as compared to the number women and men had respectively received in the 1901-2008 period). As prizes are now almost always given in every subject every year, these percentages have to rise, but the difference between men and women shows a remarkable change taking

Figure 4: Male and female Nobel (and economics) laureates, by subject, 1901–2014 (change since 2008)

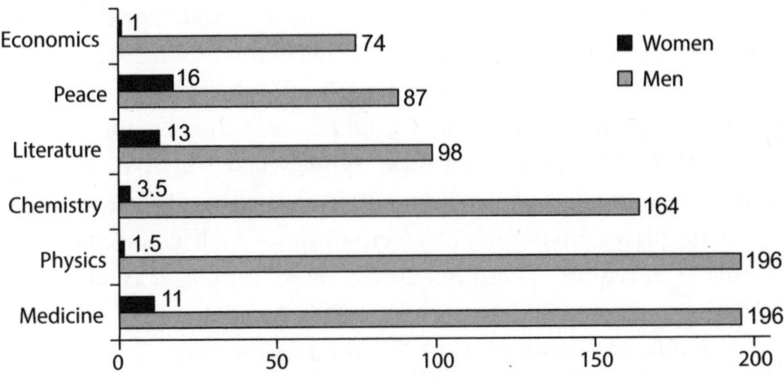

Note: Marie Curie is split between physics and chemistry (0.5/0.5); John Bardeen (Physics twice) and Fred Sanger (Chemistry twice) are counted only once. After this graph was first published in 2009 five women were prize winners in just one year.
Source: http://nobelprize.org/index.html
Specifically: http://stats.areppim.com/stats/stats_nobel_sexxcat.htm

Increase in the number of prizes awarded in 2009-2014 compared to 1901-2008 (%)

	Medicine	Physics	Chemistry	Literature	Peace	Economics	Total
Change, men	7%	9%	10%	4%	4%	19%	8%
Change, women	38%	0%	40%	18%	33%	Infinite	31%

Women awarded a Nobel prize 1901–2014

Physics
1903 – Marie Curie
1963 – Maria Goeppert-Mayer

Chemistry
1911 – Marie Curie
1935 – Irène Joliot-Curie
1964 – Dorothy Crowfoot Hodgkin

Physiology or Medicine
1947 – Gerty Cori
1977 – Rosalyn Yalow
1983 – Barbara McClintock
1986 – Rita Levi-Montalcini
1988 – Gertrude B Elion
1995 – Christiane Nüsslein-Volhard
2004 – Linda B Buck
2008 – Françoise Barré-Sinoussi
2014 – May-Britt Moser

Peace
1905 – Bertha von Suttner
1931 – Jane Addams
1946 – Emily Greene Balch
1976 – Mairead Corrigan
1976 – Betty Williams
1979 – Mother Teresa
1982 – Alva Myrdal
1991 – Aung San Suu Kyi
1992 – Rigoberta Menchú Tum
1997 – Jody Williams
2003 – Shirin Ebadi
2004 – Wangari Maathai
2011 – Ellen Johnson Sirleaf
2011 – Leymah Gbowee
2011 – Tawakel Karman
2014 – Malala Yousafzai

Literature
1909 – Selma Lagerlöf
1926 – Grazia Deledda
1928 – Sigrid Undset
1938 – Pearl Buck
1945 – Gabriela Mistral
1966 – Nelly Sachs
1991 – Nadine Gordimer
1993 – Toni Morrison
1996 – Wislawa Szymborska
2004 – Elfriede Jelinek
2007 – Doris Lessing
2013 – Alice Munro

Prizes awarded to women in 2009
Elizabeth Blackburn – Medicine
Carol Greider – Medicine
Ada Yonath – Chemistry
Herta Müller – Literature
Elinor Ostrom – Economics

place, other than in physics, where no woman has recently been part of any team wining a prize. The number of prizes awarded to women in 2009 was unprecedented, so they are separately tabulated in the figure.

We know most people in the world are labelled as in some way 'stupid' or 'backward', 'limited' or having only 'simple' ability when tested by international examination (see the 'OECD' histogram in Figure 2, above). What is less well known is that those not labelled 'stupid' have to live out lies which increase in magnitude the more elevated their status. At the top are placed mythical supermen, those of such genius, talent or potential as to require special nurturing, an education set aside. Within this set they are arranged into another pyramid, and so on, up until only a few handfuls are identified, lauded and further sorted.

Until the most recent generation, elite education has almost exclusively been set aside for men. In the rare cases that women were recognised as having contributed, they were often initially written out of the story, as in the now notorious case of Rosalind Franklin who contributed to discovering the shape of the double helix within which genes are carried. Rosalind was not recognised when the Nobel Prize was awarded to James Watson and Francis Crick.[64]

'People who have to deal with black employees'

Nobel Prizes in science are the ultimate way of putting people on pedestals, and provide wonderful examples of inherent *equality* when it comes to our universal predisposition to be stupid. In his later years, James Watson provided the press with a series of astounding examples of this, saying, for instance (it is claimed), that he had hoped everyone was equal but that '… people who have to deal with black employees find this not true.'[65] This is no one-off case of prejudice among prizewinners. Around the time that Watson was being given his laureate for double helix identification, a physics laureate of a few years earlier, William Shockley, was advocating injecting girls with a sterilising capsule that could later be activated if they were subsequently deemed to be substandard in intelligence, in order to prevent reproduction.[66] Francis Crick's own controversial support for the oddly named 'positive eugenics' was also well recorded by 2003, if not so widely known and reported in the popular press.[67]

James Watson's work was mainly undertaken at the University of Cambridge, and William Shockley ended up working at Stanford University in California. Perhaps we should not be surprised that men with backgrounds in the sciences who were educated and closeted in such places as Cambridge or Stanford should come to hold the view that so many not like them are inferior. Why should someone who examines things down microscopes or who studies X-rays know much about people? Surely, you might think, those who *might* have been awarded a Nobel Prize in social sciences, the arts or the humanities might be a little more enlightened, and so the academics in these areas often appear to be, but perhaps only because in these fields there are no such prizes, and so no such prize holders to be put on pedestals from which to confidently pontificate.[68]

Telling someone that they are very able at one thing, such as passing a test or winning a prize, can easily make them think they are more likely to be right about other things, such as the morality of sterilising women. Fortunately, at least in order for this experiment in putting people on pedestals to continue, one social science was later treated differently, and the results were telling. In 1969, Sveriges Riksbank, Sweden's central bank, created a special prize in economics. Over the subsequent 40 years up to 2008, all the 60-odd prizes, some joint, were, *without exception*, given to men (eventually, in 2009, one was awarded to a woman, Elinor Ostrøm, but she was followed by 11 more men).

Maybe only men are able to be good economists, and maybe there is such a thing as an especially good economist, one especially able to understand the monetary workings of society, to uncover the truth as to how there is some underlying logic to resource allocation by individual decision making other than the obvious. Maybe just a chosen few are able to glimpse these truths and reveal them to the small minority of the most able of the rest of us, the masses who are barely able to understand. Alternatively, maybe we have had here a group of men awarding each other prizes if they *fitted in*. Evidence that the latter is the case, and that these men are no more able or less stupid than other people, abounds.[69]

It is not just through the statements of a few on issues such as what they think about black employees that we know that prizewinners are so flawed. When you begin to search, you find that top economists are often involved in what, from a distance, appear as childish spats with one another.[70] Given the passing of a few years, their theories often do not look very clever, do not appear to apply well to today's world, or they appear to be simply the next logical step in a line of thinking that is, as a whole, too complex to be the work of just one mind, no matter how beautiful.

Examination upon examination

Some of the worst consequences of elitism in education are seen in what happens to those deemed to be the elite. In New York City, one of the twin hearts of the world financial system, live some of the richest people on earth. By 2008, the most affluent paid around $25,000 a year per child for a pre-school place in an exclusive nursery.[71] By 2013 in the UK, top nursery fees had reached £42,000 a year.[72] Such pre-schooling is thought to lead to what looks like exam success in each year that follows.

The children sent to elite nurseries are far more likely than any other children to end up as college students at the Russell Group (UK) or Ivy League (US) universities, those universities that pay the highest salaries, partly to be able to employ the most Nobel laureates. Does this mean that these children will also exhibit great intellectual abilities? George W. Bush attended Yale and Harvard, while David Cameron attended Oxford. Or will they appear later in life a little more like especially spoilt (but cajoled) adolescents who have been given little choice over their upbringing, who suffer from being repeatedly told how gifted they are, and from believing the people who tell them this?

Examination upon examination, exclusive school after exclusive school, and then exclusive university, all the time being told you are special. And the only way out is down. Given this type of an education, it is hard not to come to believe you are special, hard not to start to look down on the 'little people', hard to understand that you are not so clever. That initial $25,000 or £42,000 down-payment may be followed by up to a million dollars' or pounds' worth of 'investment' in each child of the super-rich, as their way is paid through school and exclusive college. Fees, designer clothes, exclusive cars and the cash and credit cards needed to stay on the social circuit all increase in cost far faster than average commodities. An elite education tends to be a very expensive education.

Rising inequalities in income and wealth within the US were closely followed by increases in inequalities in educational outcome over the course of the last quarter-century.[73] Rich children appeared to be doing much better, a large part of that rise in educational inequality being their apparent advancement rather than increased illiteracy among the poor. However, what the affluent were becoming better at was passing examinations, not necessarily otherwise useful learning.

In Britain, it has only been from the 1970s that the most exclusive private boarding schools took conditioning their young ladies and gentlemen to pass examinations seriously. Before then, if they did not become scholars, access through old boys' networks to jobs in the City of London,[74] or to high-ranking positions in the armed forces, was still common, and the girls simply had to marry well. At the same time the poor were being given access to comprehensive secondary education, and a chance, as compared with the no-chance future of being sent to a secondary modern, that led to the very richest of all being forced to 'swot'. They did not become wiser or cleverer as a result, just more able to pass a particular examination on a particular day, aided by a little more help each year from their tutors with the coursework.

People who have taught the children of the wealthier classes at the universities they go to see the result of the growth in elitism. These children have been educationally force-fed enough facts to obtain strings of A grades, but they are no more genii than anyone else. There is a tragedy in making young people pretend to superhuman mental abilities which neither they nor anyone else possess. To justify their situation they have to swallow and repeat the lie being told more and more often, that only a few are especially able, and that those few are disproportionately found among these high social classes. The pill is sweetened by living in a context where much of the assumption and perception of social status is taken for granted. High private school fees are paid as much to ensure this context as to secure high grades and a place in a prestigious university. The most prestigious universities of all, with their ivy and their towers, also provide a comfortable sheltered context to continue to believe that you are especially able. Why else would you be there, you might ask.

The 'IQ gene'

In recent years, in the more unequal of affluent countries like Britain and the US, it has become a little more common for the elite to suggest among themselves that children born to working-class or black parents simply have less natural ability than those born to higher-class or white parents.[75] In contrast, they claim that there has been a 'growth in hedge funds run by "super-intelligent" human beings'.[76] The people who tend to say this are not being particularly original; they are just a little more boldly and openly echoing claims made commonly, if discreetly, by the class they were born into or (in a few cases) have joined. They often go on to quietly suggest that children of different class backgrounds tend to do better or worse in school on account of some '… complex interplay of sociocultural and genetic factors'.[77] It may sound subtle to include the words 'complex' and 'sociocultural', but once 'genetic factors' are brought into the equation, all subtlety is lost. 'Genetic factors' could be used to defend arguments that women are inherently less able than men, black people in essence less able than white. Slip 'genetic factors' into your argument, and you cross a line.

The best evidence we have that genetic factors influence school results is that there is more chance of your star sign or month of birth influencing your mental abilities than there is of your genes so doing.[78] Being young for your year in school does put you at a disadvantage, although a tiny one compared to being poor in your school. The possible genome-wide effects that have been detected in ability for children aged 11–14 are very small: 'these differences approximate to a tenth of that seen across the sexes for performance in English at this age.'[79] Girls do better than boys at these ages, but better-off boys perform much better than poorer girls. Any genetic influences are all but drowned out in these contexts.

It is the country and century you are born into, how you are raised, and how much is spent on your schooling that all actually matter. Star signs matter slightly in that they indicate when in the year you were born and hence how physically developed you were when you first entered school. It does not matter whether you were born on a Monday; it matters only a little whether you are a Capricorn; and 'the IQ gene' does not exist: 'the hunt for "genes for" this or that behaviour becomes even more embarrassingly vacuous. Heritability estimates become a way of applying a useless quantity to a socially constructed phenotype and thus apparently scientizing it – a clear-cut case of Garbage In, Garbage Out.'[80]

Sadly, it is belief in things like the IQ gene or equivalent that results in teachers being asked around the rich world to *identify* children who may become especially 'gifted and talented'.[81] The finding of weak genome-wide associations with geeky-ness is picked on all too quickly as important, whereas the actual implications are trivial.[82] We may well be born with varying 'idiosyncrasies', blue eyes or brown eyes, distinct chins or no chins, but these no more imply that the upper classes have superior genes than that Sunday's children are more likely to be born 'bonny and blithe, and good and gay'.

Putting people on pedestals is not always dangerous as long as those placed there are greatly embarrassed by the process. Researchers have found that different children can grow up to be differently able in ways other than through the fiction of inherent intelligence. Some children grow up to be adults who appear far more able to help others in a crisis, the most celebrated of these adults in recent European history being those very few who helped rescue and shelter Jewish people in occupied Europe. It is worth repeating that when the rescuers' backgrounds were looked into, it was commonly found that their parents had set high standards for them as children, high standards as to how they should view others, and their parents did not treat them as if there were limits to their abilities, nor did they tell them that others were limited. If you see others as inherently inferior, then inequality will always be with you. Childhood upbringings akin to those of the rescuers are now much more common than they were in the 1920s and 1930s. Far fewer young adults would blithely obey orders and fight for their countries now than agreed to then. However, it is still just as possible to train people to follow orders now. There is no inevitability to progress. But it is harder to cajole those who have been taught, while young, that others are equal and deserving of respect to behave in a way they find abhorrent. And it is just as hard to convince those brought up to think of themselves as superior that there is no natural unlevel playing field of inherent ability.

Figure 5: Female Nobel laureates (%), by decade, worldwide, 1901–2014

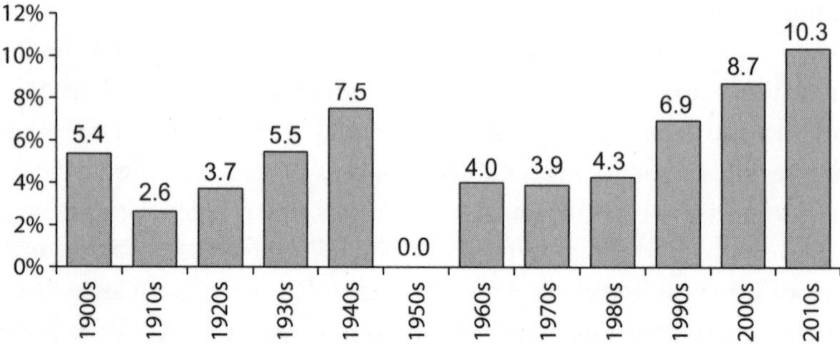

Notes: Since the 1950s almost all the prizes for women have been in literature or peace, and only a few in medicine. Nobel prizes for 2014 have been included. In most of the cells below, fewer than five women were expected to receive a Nobel prize because these were awarded so rarely to women in the past. It is not possible to estimate an indirect test of independence, but the 1950s and 2000s were clearly very unusual.

Source: http://nobelprize.org/index.html

Original data, including the calculations (right) used to try to determine how unusual the trend was up to 2009

Decade	Women	Total	Women (%)
1900s	3	56	5.4
1910s	1	38	2.6
1920s	2	54	3.7
1930s	3	55	5.5
1940s	3	40	7.5
1950s	0	71	0
1960s	3	75	4.0
1970s	4	103	3.9
1980s	4	94	4.3
1990s	7	101	6.9
2000s	10	115	8.7
2010s	6	58	10.3

Decade	$(O-E)^2/E$*
1900s	0.0153
1910s	0.4229
1920s	0.1785
1930s	0.0241
1940s	0.5063
1950s	3.5411
1960s	0.1466
1970s	0.2517
1980s	0.1010
1990s	0.7646
2000s	3.1704

*$(O-E)^2/E$ = Test statistic indicating if decade is unusual (O = observed, E = expected). A high number indicates an unusual decade; the 2010s are not yet concluded.

3.5 The 1950s: from ignorance to arrogance

The way in which women currently are and previously have been treated provides clear testament to the arbitrary nature of discrimination based on presumption of inherent difference. The development of gender roles also highlights how progress is far from inevitable. Figure 5 suggests that had you been observing the Nobel Prizes tally in 1950, you might have felt (optimistically) that by the end of the century a quarter of prizes would have been won by women, or even half if you hoped for a little acceleration reflecting the rapid promotion of women into secondary education, universities and beyond. However, by the end of the 1950s, you would have been shocked to find that *not a single prize* had been awarded to a woman that decade. Had you lived to September 2009, you would be perhaps saddened to find that the 1940s tally of 7.5 per cent had never been matched again. However, so many prizes were then awarded to women in 2009 and subsequent years that the 2000's decadal tally rose from 6 to 8.7 per cent in just two years, and by late 2014, the 2010s tally stood at 10.3 per cent of all prizes in the 'teens' having been awarded to women, and rising.

The awarding of no Nobel Prizes to women in the 1950s, and so many from 2009 onwards, did not occur by chance; it is too unlikely an event for that.[83] These trends also did not occur from conspiracy; they are too glaring an outcome for that.

Conspiracy between the committees would have ensured at least one single woman selected during the 1950s decade, as a token gesture. Women had been given prizes in every previous decade, so it did not occur because of how few women had been in 'top jobs'. It occurred because those who awarded the prizes and made the initial nominations were reflecting the times they were living through. The prizes had begun to matter greatly, not for their cash value, but for the prestige that they carried and the message that their awarding gave. Women were still nominated during the 1950s, of course. For the peace prize, nominations included educationalist Maria Montessori in 1951, birth control campaigner Margaret Sanger in both 1953 and 1955, and Helen Keller in 1954 for her work on disability and ability. As I write, nominations for the peace prize up to 1963[84] can easily be accessed online, and these show that although a few women were nominated, such as those three, increasingly it was men, especially anti-communists, who were pushed forward, nominations flooding in on their behalf from groups of various MPs who appeared to lobby the peace prize awarding committees most effectively. Other committees appear to have been even more strongly influenced by their times: Winston Churchill was awarded the prize for literature in 1953, Ernest Hemingway in 1954, and Boris Pasternak in 1958.

We easily forget that as soon as the Second World War ended, a new Cold War started. In affluent countries this became a war on enemies imagined to be within, on communists and their sympathisers. We similarly easily forget that with the great steps taken forward to secure basic social security, education, housing, employment and healthcare for most in the 1940s and early 1950s came the counter-force of a renewed interest in being elitist. The two were connected. It was, after all, communists who most loudly proclaimed the virtues of various equalities.

That no woman was awarded any of the highest of international prizes between 1947 and 1966 was because of the social changes at that time, not due to any lack of achievement. That such an unprecedentedly large number of women were awarded prizes between 2009 and 2014 may illustrate changing attitudes among nominating and selecting groups following the 2008 economic crash as much as individual achievements. Global events alter collective thinking.

Fear of communism was first seriously fuelled when the 1917 Revolution in Russia could not be overcome by foreign invasion and did not collapse in on itself, nor transform quickly enough back to market competition. Before it became clear that other ways of organising societies were possible, there appeared to be less at stake, no obvious route through which greater equality might quickly come, and no need to defend unequal societies by claiming that those at the top were of greater ability.

Although arguments that inequality is natural began in the gilded age, the alternative of communism in practice added a great impetus to those who would argue that different people were destined for different futures because they were of differing ability. In 1922 it was said (by Walter Lippmann, an oft-quoted early advocate of testing) that if it became thought that these 'ability' tests measured anything like intelligence, and revealed predestined ability, then it would be a thousand times better if both the testers and their tests were 'sunk at sea and lost without trace'.[85]

The opposite transpired; the tests did come to be seen as revealing predestined ability. Testing became all-pervasive in education in many affluent countries, and especially in the most unequal.

Testing became all-pervasive partly as a defence of privilege in response to greater equality being won by the poor in affluent nations, and partly because of the perceived threat from poorer nations, from communism and from former colonies winning independence. It is clear today that latent inequalities in individual talent did not and do not exist, and thus that categorising some children as innately talented discriminates on an essentially racist basis.[86] But to understand the fear that leads to such renewed and expansive racism requires an understanding of the erosion of status position that was felt by those who had been placed at the peaks of society following the Second World War. Understanding the changes that have taken place since 2008, from subjects as disparate as Nobel Prizes awarded to women, or the respect given to the orthodox understanding of economics, requires understanding what we have been through and how it has not resulted in a safer world run by those men with supposed great ability.

From IQism to league tables

After the Second World War the worldwide testing industry took off with a vengeance. There was no great legacy of mass testing and labelling of children around ages 11 or 15 before then. Only since the war have most children still been in school at 15, and then only in affluent countries. Mass testing of children is a symptom of affluence. It is an unintended by-product of riches, where to be seen as insufficiently clever, insufficiently scientific, is to err. Today's children's parents were taught to try to ensure they were not innumerate, their grandparents were taught to ensure they were not illiterate. Future children and grandchildren will in turn face different hurdles, but will not necessarily be strung up along a bell curve as today's children are by our current obsession to test.

As described earlier, the bell curve of supposed ability came to be used most perniciously in countries like Britain as a model immediately after the Second World War. Children were tested at age 11 and had their future roles, through future 'choice' of schools, allocated on the basis of that test result. The tests had taken 40 years to develop from their

French origins at the start of the century. It took a further 40 years for the tests to be removed from the lives of most young children, so that by the early 1980s, most were going to the same schools as others in their neighbourhood and had not had their futures predetermined by one test. For most, this was the ending of a kind of racism in education, of institutionalised ignorance. A few still went to selective schools, including private schools, but until the late 1980s, that proportion was dropping.

The tide turned back towards elitism during the 1980s. To continue with the British example, in the very early 1980s in England, the number of selective secondary (grammar) schools was cut to its minimum of just under 200 by 1982,[87] but the Conservative government that made that final cut had plans for new educational segregation. These plans were far subtler than the 1940s plan for each large town to have one selective grammar school for those deemed able, and several secondary moderns for those deemed less able. The new plans were to create a market in education, an economic curve, a continuum of supply differentiated by quality to cater for an imagined distribution of demand for education, from those whose needs were seen as least to those who, it was claimed, merited most attention. Every child was now to be educated,[88] but some educated in very different ways from others. Most crass were the assisted places introduced to subsidise the private school fees of children with especially pushy parents but with fewer financial resources. Much more subtle was the introduction of school league tables.

It took until the early 1990s for league tables to be introduced across Britain. Often it was a little later in similar countries, while in more egalitarian countries such as Germany, they don't yet exist. These tables created a market for state school places with parents paying through their house price to access more selective state schools. Before owner-occupation had reached its early 1980s peak, a spatial market in education could not easily operate in this way. Then, as higher and higher proportions of young adult incomes were spent on housing, a spiral of spatial educational discrimination set in. The same occurred in the US, but with even more emphasis on private provision in universities. The result there was that, from 1980 to the turn of the millennium, '... public expenditure on prisons increased six times as fast as public expenditure on education, and a number of states have now reached a point where they are spending as much public money on prisons as on higher education'.[89] This change in provision resulted in more prisoners than college students coming from many residential areas in states such as California. Americans put up with this because they had been taught to be optimistic.

Very few people look at their newborn baby boy and say that he'll probably have been in prison at least once by the time he is 30. Many people look, and hope that he'll go to college. If few go to college from the area where they live, then they hope, they dream, that he'll be the one, their baby will be the exception. A watered-down version of these dreams led parents in many of the few parts of England where the couple of hundred overtly selective state schools remain to vote in recent years to keep selective state schooling, a majority locally believing that their children were in the top fifth of some ability range of all state-educated children who lived nearby.

To believe that your children are in the top fifth requires first, to believe that there is a top fifth. At any one time you can subject a group of children to testing and a fifth can be singled out as doing best. That fifth will be slightly more likely than their peers to rank in the top fifth in any other related test, but that does not mean that there is an actual top fifth that is waiting to be identified. Across all of the OECD countries, under a fifth of children (16.2 per cent) gain a top mark when tested in science, reading or maths, and only 4.4 per cent in all three.[90]

The higher the correlations between different tests, the more the same children come to be selected in that top fifth under different test regimes. The more this happens, the more they will have been coached to perform well, the more likely they will be to live in a society that takes the idea of such testing seriously, a society, from government to classroom, that implicitly accepts the idea of inherent differences in ability. It is the smallest of steps from that position to accept that what you think is inherent is inherited.

From putting prizewinners on pedestals to putting whole populations in prisons, how we treat each other reveals how we see each other. We no longer view it as acceptable to make black people sit together at the back of the bus, but we still think it acceptable to sit 'slow' children together at the back of the class. IQism has become the current dominant unquestioned underlying belief of most educational policy makers in the more unequal of affluent nations.[91] Thinking that you and your children are special and are likely to climb to the top is a very dangerous way to think.

The steeper the slope to the top, the fewer the places on the pinnacle, the more likely your dreams are to be dashed. Taking such thinking to an extreme means that in a majority of schools in the US where a minority of pupils are white, armed police are now permanently stationed in the school. Schools in poorer areas of the US now routinely identify and exclude students they consider being on the 'criminal justice track'[92] (meaning on the way to prison). By doing this they cause these children to start along a route that makes such predictions a near certainty.

From prison to privilege

Britain and similar countries follow in North America's wake in penal and education policy, and are not as far behind as you might think. Over the course of a decade, around the start of this century, the rate of imprisoning children in Britain increased ten-fold, despite no significant increase in criminality.[93] Increased permanent exclusion from ever more competitive schools contributed. Most adults imprisoned are barely out of childhood; their biggest mistake is not their crime, but having been born at the wrong time, to the wrong family, in the wrong place, in the wrong country.

There is nothing inherently evil within North Americans that means they are much more likely to commit crimes than any other group of people in the world. The overall US incarceration rate has become so high that worldwide it is on a par only with the imprisonment that followed the criminal actions of Rwandans during the genocide there.[94] The US imprisons more of its own people than any other country because of what it has become. Because of the extent of the elitism that has taken hold in the US, people are finally waking up to realise that the American dream is only a dream, a dream of a memory. That elitism now raises a few dozen young celebrities to stardom, a few hundred young entrepreneurs to great riches, and projects a few thousand young people sent to Ivy League colleges to totter high on unstable pedestals while condemning millions of other children to criminal alternatives. Most who become rich started rich – 70 per cent of the sons of the top 1 per cent start off working in the already well-established family business despite going to university to broaden their horizons.[95]

In life what was previously seen as fair, or at least fair enough for each generation, becomes unjust, from slavery being justified, to denying votes to the poor, preventing equal rights for women, discriminating over disability, paying poverty wages – all become unpalatable. But the extension of freedoms also triggers counteractions. On a small scale at first, and only at the very pinnacles of power, the witch hunts for communists and the macho politics of the 1950s reflected the fact that more powerful people were feeling a little more out of control. By the 1960s across Europe and especially in North America, that feeling was spreading. In the 1970s people who generally thought of themselves as affluent became yet more frightened of what they saw as threats from within. They did not have quite enough of the advantages which they thought were due to them, and to their children. Poor countries appeared to be gaining more power as oil and other prices rose in rich countries; most poor countries did not have oil, and many became poorer.

Within affluent countries it appeared to the rich that poor people were being given more and more. There was a reaction. In the subsequent decades, the affluent ensured indirectly through their political gains that almost every additional university place, especially in the more prestigious institutions, was offered first to their offspring. They did this not through conspiracy but by individually working to secure advantages that they had taken for granted in the past, securing their children college places in a way that might not have been necessary in earlier years. But once all the university places were filled, once all their children went to college, what next? Do you begin to think of paying for postgraduate education for your children? Perhaps buying them PhDs? Per year these are cheaper than enrolling them in a one-year postgraduate degree in Financial Mathematics at £31,000 (for home and EU students).[96] Or is it easier to talk about maintaining standards and voting for and funding political parties who support charging more and excluding more from entering their hallowed halls? You can even begin to see how your child's position of relative advantage can be maintained if you argue for more prisons to house other people's children once they grow up, rather than seeing other people's children as like yours. But great problems can arise from placing offspring on pedestals. This occurs most frequently when they fail to perform as expected.

Throughout the 1980s and 1990s, the rich did not talk about those of their children who did not succeed on their terms, as that might be embarrassing. A misinformed few might even have thought that such talk would reflect badly on their genes. Instead, they voted for and funded politicians who had an agenda that implicitly included limiting additional access to universities to exclude the poor, minimising subsidised access to 'elite' universities, cutting affirmative action (also called 'positive discrimination'). This was no conspiracy. It was simply referred to as 'practical politics'.

Governments claimed that their policies were slightly widening access, even as it actually narrowed. They may even have thought that access *was* widening, as the overall numbers going to university increased and the numbers from poorer areas also rose. However, more affluent children took up almost all the extra places being taken up in universities in countries like Britain, especially, and more enduringly, in the more elite universities.[97] More obtusely, the affluent tended to be opposed to those who would raise their taxes to fund educational changes to lower the barriers to others' children. Did their own children thank them for this? Occasionally, in those years, you might have heard a young adult say how grateful they were for the 'sacrifices' their parents had made in sending them to a fee-paying school, but you heard such stories less and less over time as it became more obvious that being able to afford to make such a 'sacrifice' was hardly a state of privation. It also became more and more obvious that where you got to began again to depend more on how rich your parents were, or how unethically they were willing to behave ('entrepreneurially' making as much money as they could) – such 'a privilege' was becoming less of a thing to boast about.

From competition to capabilities

In the more unequal affluent nations, educational discrimination rose during the 1980s and 1990s, but just as the rich children of the 1960s had not appeared particularly grateful to their parents or respectful of their views, so again, privileged children did not necessarily embrace the elitism that their parents had fostered. The age of elitism did not produce a particularly happy or knowledgeable generation of affluent young people, despite all the money spent on their learning. Being taught that for most of your life you will have to compete to keep your place, that beneath you is a seething mass of competitors a little less deserving than you but just waiting to take your place, is hardly comforting.

Being taught that if you fall at any point it is your fault, and that it will reflect badly on your family, does not provide a good environment in which to learn. *Being taught that you learn in order to secure your social position is no education.* The affluent could no longer learn more by studying further under such conditions, but became obliged to 'swot', to appear to study, to send their children to study, to justify their even more exalted future positions. They were no longer becoming more content as a result of greater wealth because they already had enough for their needs. Nor were they becoming more engaged in their work, but were working to maintain and increase their wealth. As they lived longer lives, they lived into extreme frailty at rates that had been rare before. They were not made happier by additional material possessions, because you can only drive one car at a time, sleep in one bed, wear one set of clothes.

There comes a time when enough is enough, when you no longer feel driven to maintain your comparative advantage by holding others down, by denying others education, inclusion, respect, health and happiness. Injustice begins with education, its denial, its mutation, its mutilation. *Good, fair, just education is not provided in societies where the accepted belief is that different children have different capacities, where it is presumed that most people are always destined to struggle, and that each has a low limit to what they can be expected to achieve.* At times, such assumptions are made explicit, such as in the official proposals to change English education law in 2005 in which it was claimed that 'we must make sure that every pupil – gifted and talented, struggling or just average – reaches the *limits* of their capability.'[98] In England, the idea that different children have different limits has for so long been part of the social landscape that, despite the best efforts and advice, it still underlies key thinking. In 2013, Dominic Cummings, the special adviser to the then Secretary of State for Education, self-published his personal thesis claiming that the richest 1 per cent constituted half the supposed geniuses in the US, and implied that this was the case in the UK, too, that we were ruled by our betters.[99]

English policy makers were often brought up on childhood stories written by authors during the dying days of the empire, where a hierarchy of characters was presented to the minds of young readers, often with subservient ones being depicted as animals. The stoats and the weasels in the book *Wind in the Willows* had limits and needed to be kept in their places; so, too, with the great ordering of creatures in the *Narnia Chronicles*; and it was the unruly subservient class getting above its station in life that threatened to wreck 'the Shire' and the natural order of a fictitious world (looking remarkably like Europe) in *Lord of the Rings.* Thus, in the most fictional of children's fantasy tales in hierarchical societies, hierarchy is defended, suggested as being under threat and in need of reinforcement. The same can be said of old stories of trains and tank engines with 'bolshie' buses and pliant (female) trucks, or of cabals of privileged 'famous fives', or 'secret sevens' rounding up criminals from the lower orders. But these are old stories. The new stories are different.

Children's stories and the stories we tell our children are changing. They might still contain fantastic animals that speak, and echoes of the society in which they are written, but less and less do they so overtly defend hierarchy. For younger children, the typical plot of illustrated stories now concerns such issues as how sharing makes you happier (*Rainbow Fish*). Underdogs are increasingly being portrayed as eventual victors (*Harry Potter*); hierarchy and authority as bad (*His Dark Materials*). The villain in children's stories became, by 2007, the banker figure of '… a businessman in a grey suit who never smiled and told lies all the time'.[100] By 2014, the last of the *Hunger Games* trilogy was being filmed, in which children are made to compete to the death by adults. The settings might still be gothic boarding schools, Oxford colleges or imaginary lands, but the tales within those settings are no longer the same. With imaginations differently fired, and underlying assumptions not so strongly set, tomorrow's policy makers are likely to think quite differently.

From dissent to hope

Already in the US there are the beginnings of a 'detracking movement', advocating not grouping children into classes and sets by 'ability', not sitting the 'slow' ones together in class. There are subversive cartoons undermining what have been only recently promoted as traditional US values of selfishness. Even the pre-school children's book *Rainbow Fish* has been turned into a 26-episode series which has been shown on the Home Box Office (HBO) television channel since the year 2000 (causing many cries of socialist subversion!).

As the counter-culture grows, there is also more formal rebellion. In Britain, calls not to set children into school classes grouped by ability are becoming clearer, not to have gifted and talented ghettos which in turn simply end up being reflected by a more distinct set of bottom sets in schools for those destined for criminality.[101] In 2006, official but concealed education statistics were leaked to the press revealing that, on average, a black school child in Britain was five times less likely to be officially registered as either 'gifted' or 'talented' compared with a white school child.[102] In 2014, evidence was published showing that streaming children by supposed ability was harmful overall.[103] The labelling of children into so many groupings was a stupid idea, but often stupid ideas have had to have been played out for the stupidity to be fully recognised. If children in Britain were not so badly educated, and those categorised as 'the top' did not so often grow up to become such elitist adults, then ideas such as the official targeting of the so-called gifted would be laughed off long before becoming policy.

In the US, the 'no child left behind' policy of testing children repeatedly, including those who speak Spanish as a first language being tested (and humiliated) in English, is increasingly drawing criticism for its inherent racism. The results of such testing demoralise the majority and stoke up arrogance in a minority, while everyday interactions at home and school can reinforce these unfortunate outcomes. We have also only very recently come to learn that there are alternative strategies that could have fortunate outcomes as long as children are able to feel confident that they can succeed:

> We learn best in stimulating environments when we feel sure we can succeed. When we feel happy or confident our brains benefit from the release of dopamine, the reward chemical, which also helps with memory, attention and problem solving. We also benefit from serotonin which improves mood, and from adrenaline which helps us to perform at our best. When we feel threatened, helpless and stressed, our bodies are flooded by the hormone cortisol which

> inhibits our thinking and memory. So inequalities, in society and in our schools, have a direct effect on our brains, on our learning and educational achievement.[104]

Aspects of this kind of thinking are slowly creeping into policy, but only just getting in through the cracks not policed by those who favour inequality, or, as it is more often called, *competition*. Just two years after the Education Act that talked of children having limits, in the British government's *Children's plan* of 2007, a recommendation appeared that group setting of children be abolished (hidden on page 69). Everywhere there are signs of dissent. The higher up the hierarchy you travel, the more such dissent is hidden, but it is there.

In 2008, a key government adviser in Britain, Jonathan Adair Turner, was asked to tackle the issues of either drugs or pensions. He said that his belief was that drugs should be decriminalised – so he was given the pensions remit, and then the problem of climate change, to solve![105] His background was in banking, as was that of so many key advisers to British governments recently. Banking had become the most celebrated occupation, and so it was thought he could understand anything, such as drugs, or pensions, or climate. But, as Adair demonstrated, even with bankers it is becoming harder to identify people to give these posts to, who can be guaranteed to sing sweetly from a set-belief hymn sheet.

Elitism is partly sustained because people are unlikely to seek high office, or feel able to remain there, if they do not have a high view of themselves and of their abilities. But it is also sustained because we tolerate such arrogance, and accept so readily the idea of there being just a few great minds, of there being just a few who should aspire to great positions of power, who are able to advise, lead and lecture. We rarely question why we have so few positions of great power, so few judges, ministers and other leaders. But if you took every top post and created two jobs, each on half the salary, you would do a great deal to reduce privilege. It is harder to lord it over others when your pay is made more similar to theirs.

The social evil of ignorance was the old injustice of too few receiving even the most basic education in affluent countries. The injustice of widespread elitism is revealed through the production today of a surfeit, an excess, of many more apparent qualifications bestowed on those who already have most. This leads to others' abilities being often now labelled as inadequate to excuse growing inequality in many aspects of life.

But there is hope. In 2005, Larry Summers, economist and then president of Harvard University, stated that part of the gender gap in academic appointments could well be due to differences in innate aptitude, with women simply being less able than men.[106] Within a year he was forced to resign. In 2013, he lost out on becoming chair of the Federal Reserve to, Janet Yellen, the first woman to hold the position and someone who appears not to suffer Summers' faults as much. His critics list these as having '… a limited understanding of empathy, holds his friends to a lower bar, and does not know how to admit mistakes'.[107] Those at the very top of our elite hierarchies are now more likely to be taken to task for their failings than has ever before been the case.

All that is required to overcome elitism in education is not to believe in the myths of superhuman ability, not to be in awe of those who are placed on pedestals. All that is required is to argue that we all deserve a little more education and we should not concentrate resources on just a few. It was difficult initially to suggest that all children had a right to education, and then that all should have that right extended through to their late teenage years. Both of these propositions were said to be impossible to achieve and unwarranted, until the point at which they were achieved.

If we are to stop such elitism we need universal tertiary education. Universities in rich countries must become more comprehensive in their outlook and behaviour, must teach across the board, not concentrating on a few antiquated subjects, and teach at the ages when people want to learn. We could start to argue for slow learning in place of the fast 'get-qualification-quick' education marketplace of today: more rights to learn again later in life, and no special credit given for chalking up qualifications in ever greater numbers, ever more quickly.

From babies to battles

One day, in the near future, most likely when all children and young adults in affluent countries are given the right by law to be educated up to the age of 21, or to return later for free if they left earlier, a declaration will be made. It will be announced that for the first time in human history, not as a result of pandemic, famine or plague, but simply because of what we have become and how we now behave, the number of human beings on the planet has fallen, as it already is doing in most rich countries were it not for immigration. People are choosing to have fewer children.[108] On that day people will still squabble about what kind of education they are to receive and who receives most, but we will hopefully no longer consign six out of every seven children to categories of failure, and consign six out of every seven who are seen to be good to positions where they play purely supporting roles to their 'genius' betters. It is unlikely we will again allow so few to stand so high above the rest, as we did in the 20th century.

Outside the rich world, children will become more precious simply because their numbers are declining. Almost all children will routinely complete their secondary school education. The world will be a little more equal, partly because it cannot get much more unequal, but also because the vast majority of those who lose out from growing inequality can no longer be presumed to be ignorant, and be ignored. But the 21st century will be no utopia. There will still be Nobel Prizes and women will be awarded far less than half of them; there will be sexism and racism, prejudice, bigotry and pomposity, but a little less of each, and all a little less tolerated. Change can occur suddenly and unexpectedly. From 1900 to 2008, only 12 women had ever been awarded a Nobel Prize in science. Then, in 2009, three women, one based in Hong Kong, were awarded science prizes, along with a male scientist of Indian origin; a woman writer from Germany won the literature prize and, least remarkably of all in this changing context, Barack Obama was awarded the peace prize for deeds yet to be done.

In just one week in October 2009, the Nobel Prize-giving committees upturned a century of predictability. The change to Figure 5 took the first decade of the 21st century from being mediocre to off-the-scale: 9 per cent of prizewinners in the decade being female once that week in 2009 was included, the highest ever proportion, with women receiving a third of all the prizes in that one year. Then, on Monday, 12 October 2009, as if to confirm that the times really were changing, the economics committee awarded one of their prizes, for the first time ever, to a woman, Elinor Ostrøm. In the five years that followed, another six women were awarded prizes, over 10 per cent of the total, breaking through another very low glass ceiling.

All manner of other trinkets and tokens will be awarded in future, and there is nothing wrong in that. It is not hard to stamp more medals, to print more certificates. Many primary school children in rich countries already receive hundreds of prizes a year telling them 'well done' for all forms of achievements. It is not hard to imagine our schools changing to encourage children more and to test them less. And when will these things come about? Although they make no claims about school-leaving age, success, failure, prizes or inequality, those who come together in the UN do prophesy one part of this story with growing certainty. The year in which the day will dawn with one less human being than the day before will be some time between 2050 and 2100.[109] This will be simply because we have learned to have fewer babies, not due to the public actions of an elite, but through billions of private and very personal decisions, made mainly by the group which has been treated as stupid for longest: women. Human population growth has been curtailed by the billions of decisions of mostly poor and only very cheaply educated women, not by any elite group. These women learned that they held the power among themselves. Even in China, fertility was falling rapidly before the state-introduced compulsion.[110]

We become more able through learning, and we learn collectively. That is how we have come to control our numbers. It is through learning together that we will come to understand that if performing at a uniform level in tests of a particular kind of logic were an important trait for humans to possess, then we would almost all possess it, just as we almost all have binocular vision and an opposable thumb.[111] There is so much more that is vital to being human, to working together, than being good at tests that simply involve manipulating numbers. There are no *important* genetic differences in ability that elitists can use to justify their elitism. The sun did not shine differently or the soil vary from place to place in a way that made it imperative that some groups of humans became better suited to later solving Sudoku puzzles than others. We are all human, but no one is superhuman. We work and live better if we are together rather than divided by caste, class or classroom. All this we are still learning.

All children have ability, not potential, capacity or capability. We can learn without limits, given the right to a good education based on access rather than segregation. The coming battle in affluent countries will concern access to universal comprehensive tertiary education. The coming battle worldwide will focus on the right to be seen as equally able. These battles will be fought against elitism.

4

'Exclusion is necessary': excluding people from society

> It is neither the council's or the Government's responsibility that people die due to policies. If they die, they die. (Comments attributed to a local councillor on hearing of a suicide resulting from welfare cuts, 2014)[1]

The Resolution Foundation predict that in the UK, as 2015 draws to a close, 'almost 7.1 million of the nation's 13 million youngsters will be in homes with incomes judged to be less than the minimum necessary for a decent standard of living'.[2] Increases in VAT and other indirect taxes and essential charges such as fuel and food, declines in wages, in tax credits, and in other welfare payments will have combined so that a majority of children in the country will be living in households with resources below what is now seen as a minimally acceptable standard. To be living on not enough has become normal for children in Britain. A growing number of those with less than that are very poor and extremely poor. British politics has become '... a system that only "sees" what it needs to perpetuate itself, and that simply doesn't include disadvantaged young people'.[3]

Politicians try very hard today not to see poverty in all its forms. In 2014, the findings of a group of University of Manchester researchers were released showing that in political and media debates, food bank users have been variously described as: 'opportunists', 'not able to cook or budget' and 'living like animals'. However, the main reason for referring a person to a food bank was a delay in benefit payments. At the extreme, food bank users report turning to them as an alternative to turning to prostitution to feed their children. They also talk of the shame: 'It throws your pride out of the window.... I am doing it for my kids, I am not going to make my kids suffer just because of my pride.'[4]

Just as the post-Second World War surfeit of resources in affluent nations was initially directed at targets such as eliminating ignorance, but came through time to be focused more on education spending that supported elitism, so the old social evil of want, of poverty, of having too little, was initially the direct target of spending in many postwar states. Additional resources for extra personal expenditure, through social security benefits, were initially aimed at the elimination of want, but then, when the worst of want was seen to have been eliminated, public monies and state attention moved elsewhere in a way that supported growing exclusion. Tax rates were reduced for the rich, benefit levels tagged to inflation (or less) for the poorest. Furthermore, inflation for the poorest has been much higher than in general because the goods the poorest have to spend most of their money on rise faster in price. Had this been taken into account, 300,000 more people would have been recognised as being poor in the UK by 2014.[5]

The income of the rich moved further away from that of average earners, who in turn, saw their incomes increase faster than those on welfare benefits. The initial contraction (reduction of the spread) of income distributions that came with the introduction of social security in many affluent nations, and the taxation needed to fund it, was reversed most quickly in those countries that become most unequal. High social security spending was not essential for high levels of social inclusion, but low levels of income inequality were. Thus, relatively few people would describe themselves as poor and needing to take out loans 'just to get by' in countries as diverse as Japan and the Netherlands, whereas in Britain and the US, relative and now absolute rates of poverty have grown greatly in recent decades, simply because inequality has grown.[6]

Poverty that mostly results from inequality comes in the form of a new kind of exclusion: exclusion from the lives, the understanding and the caring of others. This is through social norms becoming stretched out along such a wide continuum, as most additional income becomes awarded to the most affluent, more of that left to the next most affluent and so on. The elimination of the worst of early 20th-century poverty, coupled with the tales of elitists who believed that those who were poorer were inferior, reduced the power of the argument of groups that had previously succeeded in bringing down inequalities in resources between families and classes within many affluent societies. It is slowly becoming clear that growing financial inequality results in large and slowly growing numbers of people being excluded from the norms of society, and creates an expanding and increasingly differentiated social class suffering a new kind of poverty: the new poor, the indebted, the excluded.

In 2013, *Forbes Magazine* published an article titled: 'America's poor still live better than most of the rest of humanity'.[7] What the magazine meant is that, despite the huge widening of inequalities in the US, America's poor still received more dollars a day to live off than people in most of the rest of the world when taking a simple measure of cost of living into account – they even received more than in many countries in Europe. What the magazine did not add is that it is much harder to live without having a car in the US and without having ready money to pay for medical treatment. Often there are no pavements, little is within walking distance, and there is no national health service. The real costs of living in the US are far higher for the poor there than for the poor in Europe.

For the very poorest of the poor, the US government calculated that without $4.50 a day, a person could not sustain enough nutritional intake to survive unless they ate out of bins. An income of $10 a day is needed to clothe, clean and (with great difficulty) transport oneself. If that level is adopted worldwide, then nearly 80 per cent of the people in the world are poor, and that percentage is rising. Poverty worldwide can only be shown to be falling with a great deal of statistical manipulation. When groups such as The World Bank and the UN Millennium Campaign suggest that poverty has been reduced worldwide, London School of Economics (LSE) academics were forced to explain how they are lying.[8] When they suggest inequality is falling worldwide, senior analysts at Oxfam unpick The World Bank reports to show the errors they make, but at least The World Bank now worries about inequality.[9] In affluent countries, where poverty and inequality have been measured consistently for longer, it is harder to get away with blatant lies.

The new poor (by various means of counting) now constitute at least a sixth of households in countries like Britain, and a higher proportion in the US. However, these are very different kinds of households from those that lived through immediate postwar poverty. What the poor mostly had in common by the end of the 20th century were debts they could not easily handle, debts that they felt, due to social pressures, they could not avoid acquiring, and debts that were almost impossible to escape from. They might have a little income, but they often also held negative wealth.

Just short steps above the poor in the status hierarchy, fewer and fewer were living average 'normal' lives. The numbers of those who had a little wealth had also increased, but even many of them felt the financial strain of 'keeping up'. Above the only-just-wealthy, the numbers of those who were so well off they could afford to exclude themselves from social norms were hardly growing at all, although their wealth was growing greatly. Much of this wealth came indirectly from the rest of the population, through rising housing costs and the cost of credit, especially for the poorest.

4.1 Indebted: those most harmed by exclusion, a sixth of all people

There are many ways of defining a person or household as poor in a rich society. All sensible ways relate to social norms and expectations, but because the expectations as to what it is reasonable to possess have diverged under rising inequality, poverty definitions have become increasingly contentious over time. In the most unequal of large affluent nations, the US, it is very hard to define people as poor as so many have been taught to define 'the poor' as those who do not try hard enough not to be poor.[10] Similarly, growing elitism has increased support for arguments that blame the poor for their poverty due to their apparent inadequacies, and there has been growing support for turning the definition of the poor into being 'that group which is unable or unwilling to try hard enough'.

The suggestion that at least a sixth of people live in poverty in some affluent nations results from arguments made in cross-country comparisons which suggest that a robust way of defining people as poor is to say that they are poor if they appear poor on at least two out of three different measures.[11] These three measures are: first, do the people concerned (subjectively) describe themselves as poor? Second, do they lack what is needed (necessities) to be included in society as generally understood by people in their country? And third, are they income-poor as commonly understood (low income)? It is currently solely through low income that poverty is officially defined, in Europe in relative terms and within the US in absolute terms. In 2014 in Latin America, UNICEF implemented a wider definition of poverty for children who were said to be poor when deprived of the material, spiritual and emotional resources needed to survive, develop and thrive, and when unable to enjoy their human rights and to participate as an equal member in society.[12] Europe and the US now lag behind.

A household can have a low income but not be otherwise poor, as in the case of pensioners who have accrued savings that they can draw on. Similarly, a household can have an income over the poverty threshold but be unable to afford to pay for the things seen as essential by most people, such as a holiday for themselves and their children once a year, or Christmas presents or a birthday party. A family that cannot afford such things is likely to be expenditure (or necessities) poor, and very likely to feel subjectively poor even if they are just above the official income poverty line.

In Britain, around 5.6 per cent of households appear poor on all three measures (subjectively, by expenditure and by income), some 16.3 per cent on all three or any two (see Figure 6). It should be clear that any household, person or family which is poor on at least two of these criteria is likely to be excluded from the norms of society in some significant way, hence a sixth is a safe lower band to quote when asked how many people are truly poor. Figure 6 shows how that sixth was constituted in Britain at the turn of the millennium. Since then, poverty has risen, so that by 2014, one in six of all adults in paid work are now classified as poor in the UK; the proportion of all households that are poor will be greater than this, and the proportion of all children who are poor will be greater again.[13]

In other similarly unequal affluent countries, and in Britain in other years, these proportions would be higher or lower and made up of differing combinations of the three constituent groups. They change year on year in all countries and vary for different groups in the population. They reduced a little for families with children in Britain in the early years of the 21st century through tax credits, but then increased greatly for all groups as the economic crash was met with policies resulting in widening differentials. This was felt in three ways: *subjectively* when people

Figure 6: Proportion of poor households by different measures (%), Britain, 1999

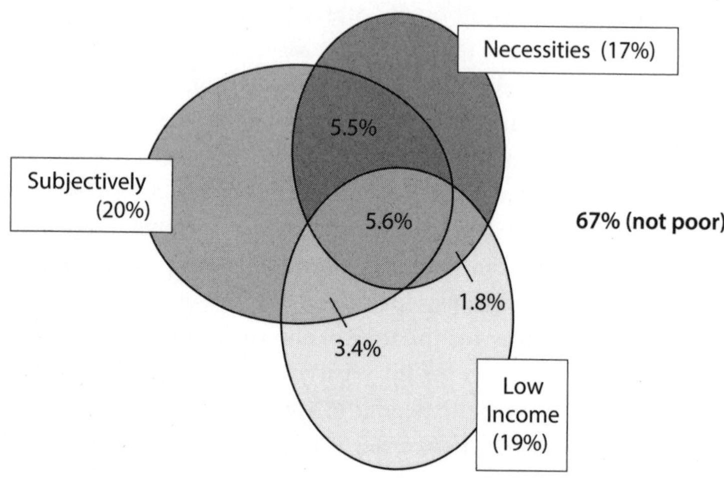

Notes: The sixth who are poor on at least two criteria are shown in the areas with percentages labelled in them (5.5%+3.4%+1.8%+5.6% = 16.3%). There are no recent figures for all three groups. Over the 30 years to 2014 the proportion who are 'necessities poor' has risen from 14% to 33%. The 17% shown here is therefore relatively low. See: http://www.poverty.ac.uk/editorial/pse-team-calls-government-tackle-rising-deprivation

Source: Drawn from figures given in table 6 of the original study: Bradshaw, J. and Finch, N. (2003), 'Overlaps in dimensions of poverty', *Journal of Social Policy,* vol 32, no 4, pp 513-25.

Share of households falling within each group, 1999

Group number	Necessities poor	Subjectively poor	Low income poor	Proportion (%)
1	Yes	Yes	Yes	5.6
2	Yes	Yes	No	5.5
3	Yes	No	No	4.0
4	No	Yes	Yes	3.4
5	No	No	Yes	7.7
6	No	Yes	No	5.0
7	Yes	No	Yes	1.8
8	No	No	No	67.0
	16.9	19.5	18.5	100.0

compare their lives to their recent past; through *necessities* becoming harder to acquire, and by falls in real *incomes*.

Necessities, worries and strife

In Britain by the start of the 21st century, almost as many households were poor because they lacked the necessities required to be socially included and because their constituent members knew they were poor (5.5 per cent) as were poor because they fell into all three poverty categories (5.6 per cent). When the population was surveyed as to what items were necessities and what were luxuries, the two key essential expenditures that the current poverty line pivoted on were, first, an ability to make small savings each month (£10 in the case of Britain); and second, to be able to have an annual holiday away from home and the wider family. These were the two items that a majority of people in Britain thought others should, as a minimum, be able to afford, and which the largest numbers could not afford.[14]

In the 15 years since the data used to draw Figure 6 was recorded, poverty has risen greatly. For the bottom 10 per cent, their incomes to 2007 grew by only 17 per cent in a decade, while spending grew by 43 per cent because prices, rent and fuel costs grew. The bottom 10 per cent are most frugal, but to get by, they have been forced to get into more and more debt. Fewer people can save just £10 a week.[15] The situation has become much worse since 2007. Between 2007 and 2012, the proportion of children in Britain unable to have a week's holiday away from home with their family rose from 32 to 37 per cent.[16] If that rate were to continue, then no British child will have a holiday by 2075. The British are seeing a rise in poverty in the midst of affluence that was unprecedented in their history.

The injustice of social exclusion had, by the 21st century, debt at its heart. Debt replaced joblessness, destitution and old age that were the key drivers of 'want' when today's pensioners were born. It is now debt that prevents most poor people from being able to afford necessities – you cannot save each month if you have debts to pay off, and holidays are affordable to almost anyone except those with too much unsecured debt. As debt grew in importance over time, the link between low income and low expenditure on necessities weakened slightly, with the smallest overlap in Figure 6 being between those two poverty measures. This is because low income does not initially prevent the purchase of necessities if there is access to debt.

In countries where inequality is higher, debts are accrued to pay for holidays, and to allow the newly income-poor, those who lose their jobs, divorce or see their spouse die, to be (for a little while at least) less expenditure-poor. The effect in Britain of the increased necessity of falling back on debt and of keeping up appearances, in what has become one of the most unequal countries in Western Europe, was that half of the 2006 mountain of all credit card debt in all of Western Europe was held by British citizens.[17] By 2013, that proportion had fallen as lenders became more careful, but four times as many people had credit card debts in the UK as in Germany, and in the European Union (EU) only Romanians were more likely to be borrowing on cards.[18]

A not insignificant proportion of the 2006 debt had been amassed to finance going on holiday. People were taking holidays more than ever before, because in Britain, being able to take a holiday had become the marker of social acceptability, just as being able to wear a suit to church had been in a previous era, and just as being able to afford to run a car if you had children became a social norm not long after that. In the US, another significant purchase, a second car for a family of four or more, serves the same purpose of establishing yourself as someone currently coping rather than not. It is not the object itself, but what it signifies and makes possible that matters. The US built suburbs without pavements. The UK built up the idea that those who worked hard would be rewarded with holidays. Tony Blair used to take his holidays very publicly, alongside (Sir) Cliff Richard, the man who made millions singing about holidays in 1963 at a time when most people could neither afford an annual holiday nor choose to borrow to take one.[19]

Holidays matter now in most rich countries because they have become such a clear marker separating those who are just getting by from those who are doing all right from those who are doing well or very well. 'Where did you go on holiday?' is now an extremely intimate question to ask of another adult; the answers divide parents picking up children from school into groups; they divide work colleagues into camps; they divide pensioners by their employment history as it is that history that determines their pensions and hence their holidays. In 2007, 21 per cent of people were unable to afford a holiday in the UK, but by 2011, that had risen to 30 per cent of the population.[20]

Rest days and Sabbath days, festive seasons and taboos on working at certain times have all been built into human cultures to ensure that we take holidays. Relaxation is vital, but today's holidays are often not greatly satisfying, family holidays having the most minor of net effects on reported subjective happiness compared with almost anything else that occurs of significance in people's lives.[21] Perhaps it was always thus, but it is hard to believe that those who first won the right to an annual holiday did not usually greatly enjoy that time off. Those who do not get a week's holiday today are almost all those who are rewarded the least during the rest of the year.

In an age where holidays are common, people mostly take holidays because other people take holidays. It has become an expectation, and as a result, holiday making in affluent countries is remarkably similar within each country as compared to between countries. Most people in Japan take only a few days' holiday a year, but household working weeks and working lives are not excessively long. In contrast, the two-week 'summer holiday' and one-week 'winter break' have become standard in parts of Europe. In contrast again, only minimal holidays are common in the US, where holiday pay is still rare.

Everyone needs a rest, but whether that rest comes in the form of an annual holiday depends on when and where you are. Holidays became the marker of social inclusion in affluent European societies by the start of the current century because they were the marginal item in virtual shopping baskets, that commodity which could be afforded if there was money to spare, but which had to be forgone in hard times.

Safeguarding social standing

In any society with even the slightest surplus there is always a marginal commodity. It has been through observing behaviour historically in relation to those marginal commodities that the unwritten rules of societies were initially unravelled. The necessity of having furniture, televisions, cars and holidays came long after it was observed that workers needed good quality shirts and shoes (first recognised in 1759), that in order to have self-respect they should not have to live in a 'hovel' (observed by 1847), and that it was not unreasonable to ask to be able to afford a postage stamp (affirmed in 1901).[22] Mill-loom woven shirts, brick-built terraced houses, postage stamps, all became necessities less than a lifetime after the mass production of looms and large-scale brick making and the introduction of the Penny Post in Britain and equivalents in many similar countries. Within just one more lifetime, the mechanisation of looms, automation of brick making and later of letter sorting had made shirts, brick-built homes and postage stamps parts of life that all could enjoy, no longer marginal items that the poor had to go without. Slowly a pattern was emerging.

Towards the end of the Second World War it was becoming clear to Karl Polanyi, in his studies of male-dominated society, that the '... outstanding discovery of recent historical and anthropological research is that man's economy, as a rule, is submerged in his social relationships. He does not act so as to safeguard his individual interest in the possession of material goods; he acts so as to safeguard his social standing, his social claims, his social assets.'[23] However, what was far from clear in 1944 (when Karl published *The great transformation*) was in what ways, as men's and then women's individual interests in material goods – their basic needs – were better met, people would need to act differently to maintain their social standing.

Pecking orders and rank do not simply disappear in an abundance of goods. For men, social standing had largely been secured through earning enough to safeguard their family, enough to be able to afford to put a good shirt on their own back, enough to feel they were not living in a hovel. Occasionally a man might have spent the excess on trinkets such as a postage stamp for a letter to a lover, and much more often beer, the poorest of men and women drinking themselves to death on cheap gin. However, from the 1960s onwards, those times began to fade in memory, as mass consumption followed mass production. For example, it was mass production of pre-rolled cigarettes that made widespread smoking possible, initially in richer countries, shortly before the First World War (and initially mostly for men). In 1955, almost 80 per cent of high-income men in Norway smoked; 50 years later, it had become poorer women in poorer countries who were increasingly likely to smoke.[24]

Mass consumption often consists of what appear to be trinkets and trivia, of more clothes than people possibly need, no longer one good linen shirt, or of more shoes than can easily be stored, no longer just one good pair, of houses with more rooms than can easily be kept clean, and – in place of that postage stamp – junk mail. However, trinkets, trivia and fecklessness only appear as such to those who *can choose* not to buy them. From the trading of shells in ancient Polynesian societies, to curvier cars in 1950s America, we have long purchased with our social status foremost in mind.

Trinkets have always held great social importance, and mechanisation did not decrease this. Mass-produced trinkets, such as jewellery in place of shells, and production-line cars, soon came to no longer signify high standing; that requires scarcity. Mass-produced goods become necessities with normal life reorganised around them, for example, from letters to the telephone to the internet. In Europe in 1950, to be without a car was normal; 50 years later it is a marker of poverty. In Europe in 1950, most people did not take a holiday; 50 years later not taking a holiday has become a marker of poverty (and holidays can now easily cost more than second-hand cars). Being able to afford to smoke tobacco used to be a sign of wealth; now it is an indicator of poverty to smoke.

Since the 1950s most of the increase in debt has been accrued by people in work. Of those debts not secured on property (mortgages), most have been accrued by people in low-paid work. Work alone no longer confers enough status and respect, not if it is poorly paid. People working on poverty wages, which in Europe is defined as three fifths of national median wages (which itself is well below the arithmetical mean average wage in countries with high inequality), tend to be most commonly employed in the private sector, then in the voluntary sector, and most rarely in the state sector.[25] This is still true despite recent below inflation increases for lower-paid public sector workers. The private sector takes advantage of high levels of unemployment with schemes such as no fixed hours contracts, and relies on the benefit system to cope with the inadequate wages it so frequently pays.

Overall, the private sector pays higher (on arithmetical but not median average) because those in charge of themselves, with little accountability to others, tend to pay themselves very well. By doing so they reinforce the idea that the more valuable a person you are, the more money you should have. It takes only a small but illogical jump from that to the fiction that the more money you happen to have, the more valuable a person you are. The state sector pays its managers less because there is a little more self-control levied when accountability is greater, although most people are amazed when they do hear what some public sector managers earn. Even in the state sector the belief is widespread that the more someone requests to be paid, the more they must be worth. People are not paid according to their value, but to their ability or lack of ability to bargain for their pay.

In the absence of accountability, people in the state sector are just as capable of transgressing, as state-employed members of the UK Parliament illustrated when many of their actions were revealed in the expenses scandal of 2008/09. What they bought with those expenses illustrated what they had come to see as acceptable purchases and as their right in an age of high and rising inequality. The voluntary sector is a mix of these two extremes. God or the charity commissioners might be omnipresent in theory, but in practice, some still take what they can get away with or misguidedly believe they are worth, misusing charitable donations rather than government money.

In all sectors if you find yourself at the bottom of each pyramid and look up, the pyramids are becoming steeper, harder to climb and easier to slide down (should you rise a few steps up). To then value your intrinsic self when others are so materialistic requires either great and unusual tenacity, or alternatively borrowing just a little extra money to supplement your pay. You borrow it to buy things which others like you have because 'you're worth it', and you want to believe you are like them, not inferior to them. The rich suggest that the poor should live with hardly any possessions, while showing hardly any restraint themselves.

Mortification and empathy

If you have been led to believe that a valuable person is a well-paid person, then it becomes especially important to accrue debt when your income is falling in order to maintain your self-esteem, to avert what even hard-nosed economists, from Adam Smith onwards, have identified as the mortifying effect of social downgrading.[26] People spend and get into debt to maintain their social position, not out of envy of the rich, but out of the necessity to maintain self-respect.[27]

Social downgrading has a physical effect on human bodies – being disgraced or shamed in public makes you feel sick. Humans are conditioned, and have almost certainly evolved, to fit in, to be social animals, to feel pain, concern and anxiety which prevents them from acting in ways likely to lead to their being ostracised by their friends, family and co-workers, by their small social group. We have recently come to realise that it is not just our own social pain that we feel, but through possessing 'mirror neurons' we physically feel the pain of others, as empathy appears to be '... automatic and embedded'[28] in our brains.

We now know some of the physical reasons why most of us react instantly to others' hurt, social hurt as well as physical. If you see someone hit on the head, you wince. If you see someone shamed, you too feel his or her shame physically. If social standing is linked to financial reward, it becomes necessary to accrue and to spend more and more in order to stay still. The alternative, of not seeing financial reward as reflecting social standing, is a modern-day heresy.

It is possible to be a heretic, to not play the game, to not consume so much, to not be so concerned with material goods, but it is not easy. If it were easy to be a heretic, there would be far more heretics; they would form a new religion and we would no longer recognise them as heretics. To reject contemporary materialism you would have to give others (including children) presents only in the quantities that your grandparents were given, own as many clothes as they did, quantities which were adequate when two could share one wardrobe; you are no heretic if you only consume a little less than others currently around you and recycle a little more. It is partly because we consume so much more than our grandparents that we now get into such debt.

For some, the alternative to getting into debt is not to take a holiday. Even at the height of the worldwide economic boom in 2001, in the most expensive city to be housed in on the planet, one child in every five in London had no annual holiday because their parents could not afford one. By 2011, 60 per cent of all children in lower-income London households took no annual holiday away from home or family.[29] Research shows that poor children in London are more likely to be living in overcrowded homes than poor children nationally, less likely to be able to afford to go swimming, to own a bicycle, have somewhere to play outdoors, have friends round to tea (even just once a fortnight), have a hobby, be able to afford to go to a playground once a week, go on a school trip once a term or celebrate an occasion like a birthday. The cost of so many of these things is higher in London than elsewhere, especially after paying for housing.[30]

By 2011, the parents of 60 per cent of London's lower-income children could not even afford the cheapest week's holiday a year. Very few of the parents of those children will have chosen for their child not to have had a holiday that year because they saw package holidays as a con, or hiring a caravan for a week as an unnecessary luxury. Of the children being looked after by a single parent in London, the original 2001 survey of recreational norms showed that most had no annual holiday then, and that 44 per cent of those single-parent families could not afford other things commonly assumed to be essentials, such as household insurance. Since 2001, living standards have fallen fastest for the children of single parents.[31]

Household insurance is hardly an extravagance. In 2001, 8 per cent of households were uninsured, but by 2012, that had risen to 12 per cent.[32] Insurance makes it possible to replace the material goods amassed over a lifetime, goods you could mostly live without physically, but not socially. It is the families of the poorest of children who are most likely to suffer from theft and the aftermath of theft, or fire or flooding, because they more often live where burglary is more common, where house fires are more likely, and where homes are cheaper because they are built lower down the hill where they are at greater risk of flooding. So, for them, avoiding paying insurance is not a sensible saving.

While a few people get very rich running the firms that sell insurance, this does not mean that it is sensible to avoid buying insurance altogether. The less you have to start with, the more you may need what you do have. If you are not insured, the only way to cope with insurable events may be to get further into debt. It is often the sort of shocks that better-off families might insure against that plunge poorer families into long-lasting debt, but rising debt is also a product of rising lending. And all this is as true internationally as it is in the homes of Britain's poor.

Corruption and usury

Just as there is money to be made by those working in finance out of the poor who live in the shadows of Canary Wharf and Manhattan, as long as many are ripped off, just a little each, so too, but on a far greater scale, is there money to be made from the poor abroad. Commentators from rich countries, especially national leaders, often boast about various aspects of the roughly $100 billion a year which their countries donate as aid (or spend on debt write-offs) for people in poor countries. They rarely comment on how, for every one of those dollars in, another ten flow out in the opposite direction, siphoned to rich countries from poor countries, mainly by traders who buy cheap and sell dear.

The estimates that have been made[33] suggest that major corporations are responsible for the majority of a trillion-dollar-a-year flow of illicit funds to a few people in rich nations using webs of financial trusts, nominee bank accounts, numerous methods to avoid tax and simple mispricing. The firms most prominently featuring in many accounts are oil, mining and other commodity trading firms. Direct bribery and corruption within poor countries account for only 3 per cent of this total exploitation sum. Despite this, when corruption is considered, it is almost always that kind of corruption and not the other 97 per cent, the corruption of very rich Western bankers and businessmen (and a handful of businesswomen), that is being considered. This corruption is orchestrated from places such as those gleaming financial towers of London's banking centre, from New York, and from a plethora of well-connected tax havens.

Between 1981 and 2001, only 1.3 per cent of worldwide growth in income was in some way directed towards reducing the dollar-a-day poverty that the poorest billion live with. In contrast, a majority of all the global growth in income during the 1990s was secured by the richest 10 per cent of the planet's population.[34] During the noughties, according to the bank Credit Suisse, global growth in wealth became most concentrated among the 1 per cent richest people on the planet who saw their wealth rise to almost 50 per cent of the global total by 2014. Among them it was the very richest of all who took the most after the financial crash, with the number of billionaires more than doubling in the five years after 2009, to stand at 1,646 by 2014. When this news was released, Andy Haldane, Chief Economist and Executive Director at the Bank of England, said such extreme inequality was not in 'the wider collective interest.'[35]

Most of the recent growth in income for the rich has been growth in the value of the stocks and shares that were traded by people like those bankers with few morals. The introduction of 'quantitative easing' after the financial crash increased their value. However, for the richest in the world, the returns from these were not enough, and they invested millions at a time in hedge funds run by yet more private bankers, who worked in less obvious edifices than skyscrapers. It is the monies that these people hold that have come to give them a right, they say, to 'earn' more money. Ultimately, those extra monies have to come from somewhere, and so are conjured up from others as debt 'interest' (as more is lent). The richer the rich become, the greater the debt of others, both worldwide and in the shadows of the bankers' own homes. The financial crisis showed how debt worked, but has not yet resulted in anything other than attempts to try to curtail the chances of such a sudden crash occurring again, soon. The problem was that the very rich became too rich.

To be very rich is to be able to call on the labour and goods of others, and to be able to pass on those rights to your children, in theory, in perpetuity. The justification of such a bizarre arrangement requires equally bizarre theories. Traditionally, rich monarchs, abbots of monasteries and Medici-type bankers (and merchants) believed it was God's will that they should have wealth and others be poor. As monarchies crumbled and monasteries were razed, it became clear that many more families could become mini Medicis. That those who did so was due to the will of God became a less convincing theory, although we did create Protestantism, partly to justify the making of riches on earth.

Instead of transforming religions that preached piety in order to celebrate greed, those who felt the need to justify inequality turned to science. Once seen as heresy, science is often now described as the new religion of our times. More specifically, those searching to find new stories to justify inequality turned to the new political and economic science of the Enlightenment,[36] then to emerging natural sciences, in particular to biology, and finally to new forms of mathematics itself. Those such as Tony Blair and Michael Gove, who talk of 'God-given genes', or Bill Clinton, who said of the genome 'we are learning the language in which God created life', often mix up this science with older religions, but with genes there is now a surer way to suggest that most are destined not to be rich.

4.2 Geneticism: the theories that exacerbate social exclusion

If most people in affluent nations believed that all human beings were alike, then it would not be possible under affluent conditions to justify the exclusion of so many from so many social norms. The majority would find it abhorrent that a large minority should be allowed to live in poverty if they saw that minority as the same sort of people as themselves. And the majority would be appalled that above them a much smaller minority should be allowed to exclude themselves through their wealth.

It is only because the majority of people in many affluent societies have come to be taught, and then to believe, that a few are especially able and hence apparently deserving, and others particularly unable and hence undeserving, that current inequalities can be maintained. Inequalities cannot be reduced while enough people believe that such inequalities are natural, and a few even suggest that inequalities are beneficial.

In the course of the last century, theories of inherent differences among the whole population became widespread. Before then it was largely believed that the gods ordained only the chosen few to be inherently different, those who should be favoured, the monarchs and the priests. In those times, before fossil fuels were harnessed to replace manual labour, there were simply not enough resources for the vast majority to live anything other than a life of frequent want. But the spoils that came from new energy sources mostly went to those who started off with most.

When more widespread inequalities in income and wealth began to grow under 19th-century industrialisation, theories (stories) attempting to justify these new inequalities as natural were widely promulgated. Out of evolutionary theory came the idea that there were a few great families which passed on superior abilities to their offspring and, in contrast, a residuum of inferior but similarly interbreeding humans who were much greater in number. Often these people, the residuum, came to rely on various Poor Laws for their survival, and were labelled 'paupers'. Between these two extremes was the mass of humanity in the newly industrialising countries, people labelled as capable of hard working but incapable of great thinking.

Inequality as 'variation'

Scientific diagrams were produced to support the geneticist beliefs that emerged during industrialisation. One, redrawn here as Figure 7, purports to show that the 1891 geographical distribution of recorded paupers in England and Wales followed a natural pattern, a result, it was presumed, of breeding. These paupers were people recorded as receiving what was called 'outdoor relief', the most basic of poverty relief which did not force the recipient to enter a workhouse. Such relief ranged in prevalence between geographical areas from about 0.5 per cent of the population, to highs of around 8.5 per cent (not at all unlike the variation in the rates of people claiming unemployment benefits in those two countries a century later).

Figure 7 shows two statistical curves plotted on the original diagram by its original author, Karl Pearson. Karl drew the curves to show how they fitted the data closely. These were the binomial (Bernouli) and normal (bell curve) distributions. The reason the curves were fitted was to further Karl's attempt to imply that variation in numbers of paupers between areas followed some kind of 'natural' distribution. Around this time the normal distribution was being proposed to describe the distribution of intelligence. Later an Intelligence Quotient (IQ) was defined as having a normal distribution. A world in which people were of different classes was being transformed into one in which all were seen as having a place along an ordered scale, but that place depended on your pedigree.

Hereditary thinking would have it that some areas had more paupers because more genetically inferior people had come to cluster there and had interbred; other areas were spared such pauperisation presumably due to the inherent superiority of the local populace, through the driving away of paupers or through their 'extinction' through the workhouse or starvation. The close fit of the two curves to the actual data was implicitly being put forward as proof that there was an underlying natural process determining the numbers identified as being in this separate, implicitly sub-human, group. This 'truth' was apparently revealed when all human

Figure 7: Geographical distribution of paupers, England and Wales, 1891

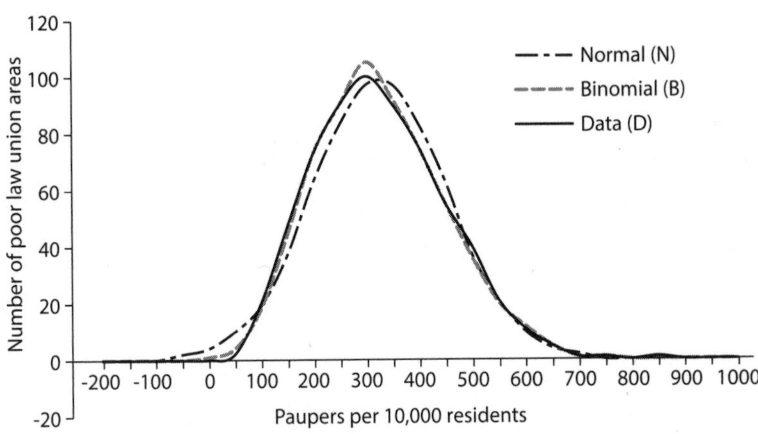

Note: This graph was drawn to try to suggest there was something natural and inevitable about the distribution of poverty in 1891. In fact, using a method developed by the statistician who presented these figures to the Royal Society, it can be shown that it is highly unlikely these figures have not been fiddled because the fit is too good to be true. The details of this proof were given in the first edition of *Injustice*.

Source: Redrawn from the original: Pearson, K (1895) 'Contributions to the mathematical theory of evolution. II. Skew variation in homogeneous material', *Philosophical Transactions of the Royal Society of London, Series A, Mathematical,* vol 186, pp 343-414, Figure 17, plate 13).

Paupers (P)*	Normal (N)	Binomial (B)	Data (D)	B-D	$(B-D)^2$	$(B-D)^2/B$
100	19	18	20	1	1	0.043
150	37	44	47	-3	9	0.205
200	63	73	73	0	0	0
250	83	90	90	0	0	0
300	97	105	100	5	25	0.238
350	97	92	90	2	4	0.043
400	83	75	75	0	0	0
450	63	55	55	0	0	0
500	37	36	40	-4	16	0.444
550	21	20	21	-1	1	0.05
600	10	12	11	1	1	0.083
Total	632	632	632			1.250

*Per 10,000 residents

subjects were separated into some 632 Poor Law union areas and the paupers' proportions calculated. The graph was published in 1895.

Figure 7 is important because it is a reproduction of one of the first attempts to use a graph to apply a statistical description to groups of people, and to demonstrate to others that the outcome, what is observed, reflects a process that cannot be seen without that graph but which must be happening to result in such a distribution. Millions of similar bell curves have been drawn since of supposed human variation in ability. The apparent smoothness of the data curve and closeness of the fit is key to the implication and strength of the claim that some natural law is being uncovered here. At the time the distribution in Figure 7 was drawn, the normal (then called Gaussian or Laplacian) statistical distribution being applied to a probability was well known among scientists, but the idea of it being seen as biologically 'normal' was less than a couple of decades old.[37] Originally 'normal' had a technical meaning of orthogonal rather than 'usual', and was only later interpreted as somehow 'natural', as 'normal'. Just at the time, in fact, that it came to be used to describe people.

When it comes to categorising human ability, the process by which a distribution comes to take on the appearance of a bell-shaped curve is far more likely to reflect the forces acting on those who count than those who are counted. Nowadays, many exam results are graded in such a way that the distribution of grades that students receive tends to form just such a shape.[38] It is always possible to set grade boundaries that suggest that your students are distributed by ability along a normal curve, or any other curve you fancy. For instance, if you want to suggest that almost none of your students are lazy, almost all are especially able, then you do not subdivide second degree classes in your university (or award hardly any marks low enough to result in lower second class degrees being awarded any more).

It is important to remember that random social processes, such as noting in which areas more winning lottery tickets are sold, having taken into account the total number of tickets sold, will reflect a normal distribution if there are enough places and enough winners. Thus, if the marking of university degrees was largely a random process, we would expect a normal distribution to emerge. With any set of measurements there is always a lowest and a highest (except theoretically in a truly normal distribution), with the majority usually not being at the extremes.

What is interesting is the occasion when the data fit so closely to such a distribution that it is unlikely that such a good fit would have happened by chance. This, it turns out, is what happens in Figure 7.

Fixing the figures

In 1891 there was great pressure on Poor Law unions not to give too much 'relief'. Unemployment, a new term only recently invented, had hit different areas with different effects. Different places had had bad harvests; different industries had been differently hurt by the recession of the late 1880s; Poor Law union officials did not want to look out of line and tried to curtail their spending, so no surprising outliers were found; almost every district had a workhouse and some monies for outdoor relief (not requiring institutionalisation) so that a small number would always be provided for. Almost the very last people to have an individual impact on the shape of the distribution were the paupers themselves, but just as it is not the unemployed today who choose to be unemployed, or who carry some inherited propensity to unemployment, the paupers of yesterday had little say over what was said about them or whether they became paupers.

Today we largely recognise that in rich countries unemployment is mostly the product of being born at the wrong time in the wrong place and can strike us all, although with greatly varying probabilities depending on our precise circumstances,[39] but we live in danger of forgetting this and of reverting to the late 19th-century thinking of eugenics, the 'science' of drawing ability distributions from outcome events, of which Figure 7 is the world's first ever geographical example. In the past, more examples were explicitly explained this way; today, people often try to hide their prejudices a little more carefully.

Like today's unemployed, the paupers of 1891 did have a small role to play in their distribution as many moved around the country. With little support, people tend not to stay for long in a place with no work and move towards jobs. Outdoor relief was supposed to be available only to local people in order to reduce such migrations, but if there was a single process whereby the actions of individuals were helping to form the shape of the curve, it was through their get-up-and-go, not their recidivism. However, it was recidivism for which the drawer of the curves was looking.

It would prove very little were the statistical curves in Figure 7 found to be good fits to the data. However, the fit of the curves to the data presented in Figure 7 is so very close it is implausibly good. In the first edition of this book I applied Pearson's test to his data, and suggested that it is entirely possible (although very unlikely) that results as close fitting as this could have been drawn from the binomial distribution.[40] In other words there is a very good chance that Pearson altered his data to fit his model.

A new religion

An unusually high number of those who find playing with numbers, mathematical probabilities and statistics not to be very difficult have found understanding people to be extremely tricky. When reading others' accounts of him, it does cross your mind that one of these people might have been Karl Pearson.[41] It is possible that Pearson's thoughts about people led him, perhaps unconsciously, to draw those two curves, and then alter the data to fit them so closely together on that graph paper so many years ago.

How could that close fit occur unless the figures were fiddled or, implausibly, the commissioners of the Poor Law unions arranged for the relief to be distributed geographically according to the binomial distribution? Even if most Poor Law authorities were following the herd in the amount of relief they offered, a few being more generous than most, and a few more constrained, due to random variation, the fit should not be that close to the binomial curve. Pearson was labouring under the belief that the poor were a curse and were in danger of over-breeding. It is when such beliefs become articles of faith that figures are fiddled and graphs are drawn with curves that fit as closely and as improbably as Figure 7 suggests. It is when people become convinced that they know a great truth, the underpinnings of what might soon almost become a new religion, that the normal questioning and conventions are abandoned.

Just seven years after drawing his curves of the geography of paupers, Karl Pearson, who came to be seen as one of the founders of the science of eugenics, proclaimed (in 1902) that his belief would prevail and become widespread 'twenty years hence'.[42] He was right in that at least. Eugenics had become almost a religion by the 1920s, it being an article of faith that some were more able than others, and that those differences were strongly influenced by inherited acumen. During the First World War, Michael Sadler, Master of University College Oxford, complained that 'German education makes good use of all second grade ability which in England is far too much a waste product.'[43] Presumably he said this to try to explain why the war was taking so long and so many lives. Sadly the English elite tends to maintain this view of ability today.

It was not just among the earlier lovers of the new science of statistics that the eugenic religion took hold. These ideas were particularly attractive to male mathematicians, natural scientists and economists.[44] It really was almost as if there was an innate predisposition to be attracted to eugenists' ideas among those men who found numbers easy but empathising with others a little more difficult. The chance of men being likely to find such communication difficult is four to five times higher than for women,[45] although there were several key women in the early eugenics movement. However, the dominance of men among those few who still argue for eugenics today is intriguing. Is it their nature, or their nurture, that leads men more often to such folly?

Women who knew him wrote that Pearson found women tricky. He was far from alone among Victorian men in either this or in believing in eugenics, but there were a few prominent people who offered different views and who were not so much products of their time as Karl. For instance, although not all early feminists spoke with one voice, the fledging women's movement did argue against eugenicist ideas and specifically Karl Pearson's suggestion that women's primary function was reproduction of the 'race', and that women who resisted his arguments were asexual, in search of an equality with men that was not possible, and that such women were '... a temporary aberration in the race'.[46]

In the years prior to the First World War, the myth was first spread that progress for the specific 'races' (mythical racessuch as the supposed Aryan and Nordic races and even a British race) relied on the identification and empowering of men '... of exceptional talent from the mass ... the mass is, almost invariably, feminized'.[47] If geneticist thinking saw races as fundamentally different, sexes were even more riven apart by biological deterministic theories of gender difference.[48]

It was partly the immediate reaction of horror to the genocide of the Second World War, but also the experience of working together as a nation in that war, and the later realisation that generation and environment mattered so much more than all else over how well children performed in tests, that led to eugenics later being shunned. Hitler's preference for eugenics helped in this. Ideas such as universal health services being made available on an equal basis to all arose as practical possibilities because of the rejection of eugenics.[49] That wartime experience also had the unforeseen result of a much wider acceptance of the idea that, at least, all people within one country were in some ways of equal value. It would appear that even mild eugenicists, such as William Beveridge in Britain, exorcised their policy recommendations of eugenicist thinking as they became aware of the genocide being perpetrated early on during the war. And so, in the aftermath of genocide, at the heights of postwar anti-communism, eugenics floundered. Its means and ends were too illiberal. As a result, eugenics as denial of freedom became linked then with fascism, and that kept its popularity down.

Crypto-eugenics

By the time of the Soviet invasion of Hungary in 1956, eugenics had to be practised in secret as it had become associated with the totalitarianism of communists as well as fascists. At that time the idea's dwindling supporters used the term 'crypto-eugenics', largely in secret.[50] Many of these covert eugenicists actively supported family planning services, abortion and voluntary sterilisation, not for the benefit to the individual, but for the imagined benefit to society if targeted at the 'less desirable'. By the mid-1970s it was acknowledged that not a single *reputable* scientific study had been undertaken that suggested with any authority that inheritable intelligence existed.[51] By the early 1980s, those few eugenicists still out in the open were easy targets for ridicule.[52] And, while taught how to use his tests, university undergraduates studying statistics were taught nothing of Pearson's past and the murky origins of his subject of study. That eugenic past was being forgotten.

In the latter half of the 20th century, partly in reaction to the achievement of greater equalities, and as the passing of time resulted in forgetting the social miseries of 1920s inequality, the economic despair of 1930s depression, the moral outrage of 1940s atrocity, and 1950s social contracts to counter communism, growing inequalities were again foisted on populations, and attempts at trying to justify social inequalities crept out of the shadows. At the forefront of the resurgence of the 'eugenic-like' argument was the oft-criticised, simultaneously both dreary and revolting literature on supposedly innate racial differences, literature that so clearly '... compound[s] folly with malice'.[53] But in the background was more subtle writing, almost all by men put in positions of power trying to justify the pedestals they stood on. A few examples follow. In those justifications they reached back to that early mixing of genetic theory and human social distribution. And so the too-good-to-be-true fit of two curves drawn by hand and reproduced in the few surviving copies of a dusty old journal of 1895 still matter. The first curves matter because the documents they appear in betray the follies in the founding tenets of geneticism. They matter because the greatest danger is to forget.

Contemporary work on epigenetics explicitly steers away from saying genetic make-up determines the social destiny of humans along an ability continuum.[54] In contrast, geneticism is the current version of the belief that not only do people differ in their inherent abilities, but that our 'ability' is to a large part inherited from our parents. Despite such obvious differences between siblings, this belief is now again widely held among many of those who advise some of the most powerful governments of the world in the early years of the current century.

Eugenicism has arisen again, just over a century after Figure 7 was drawn, but now goes by a different name and appears in a new form. It is now hiding behind a vastly more complex biological cloak. For example, David Miller, a University of Oxford professor who was an adviser to the notionally left-wing New Labour government in Britain, suggested (in a book supposed to be concerned with 'fairness') that '... there is a significant correlation between the measured intelligence of parents and their children. ... Equality of opportunity does not aim to defeat biology, but to ensure equal chances for those with similar ability and motivation.'[55] There are, of course, numerous possible reasons for this correlation apart from 'biology'.

Contrast the view of some in the English elite, including those who introduced very high university fees, with that of Dorothee Stapelfeldt, senator for science in Hamburg, who explained why her federal state scrapped all university charges in 2012. Dorothee explained: 'Tuition fees are socially unjust. They particularly discourage young people who do not have a traditional academic family background from taking up studies. It is a core task of politics to ensure that young women and men can study with a high quality standard free of charge in Germany.'[56] By 2014, no federal state in Germany charged university tuition fees – because of how Germans now view other Germans.

Intelligence is not like wealth. Wealth is mostly passed on rather than amassed. Wealth is inherited. Intelligence, in contrast, is held in common. Intelligence, the capacity to acquire and apply knowledge, is not an individual attribute that people are born with, but rather, it is built through learning. No single individual has the capacity to read more than a minuscule fraction of the books in a modern library, and no single individual has the capacity to acquire and apply much more than a tiny fraction of what humans have collectively come to understand. But despite such obvious individual limitations on us all, we act and behave as if there are a few great men with encyclopaedic minds able to comprehend the cosmos; we assume that most of us are of lower intelligence than them, and we presume that many humans are of much lower ability than us.

In truth, the great men are just as fallible as the lower orders; there are no discernible innate differences in most people's capacity to learn. Learning for all is far from easy, which is why it is so easy for some educators to confuse a high correlation between test results of parents and their offspring with evidence of inherited biological limits. It is as wrong to confuse that as it was wrong to believe that there was some special meaning to the fact that the geographical pattern in pauper statistics of 1891 appeared to form a curve. Human beings cannot be divided into sub-groups from birth with similar inherent abilities and motivations; there is no biological distinction between those destined to be paupers and those set to rule over them.[57]

There is a correlation between the geography of those today who make hereditarian claims, and their propensity to reveal their beliefs. Today's hereditarians appear to come disproportionately from elite institutions. In Britain, the elite university for the humanities is located in Oxford.[58] To give a second example, several University of Oxford sociologists and their colleagues suggested that there was the possibility '... that children born to working-class parents simply have less natural ability than those born to higher-class parents'.[59] In saying that the possibility of an inherited 'natural ability' process was at work, these academics were only parroting what is commonly believed in such places, oft-repeated by colleagues within their colleges.

Here is a third example, from yet another University of Oxford professor, John Goldthorpe, who claims that: '... children of different class backgrounds tend to do better or worse in school – on account, one may suppose, of a complex interplay of sociocultural and genetic factors'.[60] It would be a dreary exercise to trawl through the works of many more contemporary academics at the very pinnacles of the career ladders in countries like Britain and in places like Oxford, to draw yet more examples of what 'one may suppose'. While these are only examples drawn from a small group, all three of the professors quoted had and still have access to the ears of government ministers and even prime ministers.

Tony Blair was the British Prime Minister during the time that the examples referenced above were published. He had clearly come to believe in a geneticism of the kind they promoted, as revealed in his speeches that used phrases such as 'God-given potential'.[61] He is unlikely to have formed such beliefs as a child. Whether he came to his views while he was studying at university as an undergraduate, or later, through the influence of advisers, who were, in turn, influenced by academics (similar to the three quoted above), is unclear. What is clear is that by the 1990s, geneticist theories were being widely discussed in circles of power.

Should you wish to search for further examples, there is now a literature that suggests we should link theories on behavioural genetics with public policy.[62] In 2014, the Joseph Rowntree Foundation produced a strategy for tackling poverty in the UK that suggested that we needed to consider '... whether people are able to reach their potential, for example at school and at work'.[63] The implication is that everyone has a limit to their potential that can be foreseen, and a benign government only has to aim to help each move towards their internal ceiling of ability. How did particular groups and clusters of people come to hold such views?

We should recognise the disadvantages of working in a place like the University of Oxford when it comes to studying human societies. It is there and in similar places (Harvard and Heidelberg are usually cited) that misconceptions about the nature of society and of other humans can so easily form. This is due to the staggering and strange social, geographical and economic separation of the supposed crème de la crème of society into such enclaves. The elite universities in Paris could be added to a roll call of centres of delusion. They were not in the original listing of a few towns because it was in Paris that the man making that initial list, Pierre Bourdieu, ended up working.[64] And there is much more to Paris than its universities, but that is also true of Oxford, Boston and Heidelberg.

4.3 Segregation: of community from community

It is easier to grow up in Boston or Oxford and know nothing of life on the other side of your city than is the case in Paris or Heidelberg. This is because social inequality in the US and the UK is greater than in France or Germany. Maintaining high levels of inequality within a country results in rising social exclusion. Exclusion occurs even without increases in income inequality. Simply by holding inequalities at a sufficiently high level, the sense of failure of most is maintained long enough to force people to spend highly and to get into further debt just to maintain their social position.

One effect of living in an affluent society under conditions of high inequality is that social polarisation increases between areas. Geographically, with each year that passes, where you live becomes more important than it was last year. As the repercussions of rising social exclusion grow, the differences between the educational outcomes of children going to different schools become ever more apparent; buying property with mortgage debt in more expensive areas appears to become a better long-term 'investment' opportunity. As the difficulties of living in poverty under inequality increase, living away from the poorer people becomes ever more attractive, and for most people, only marginally obtainable.

Poverty surveys

The social experiment of holding inequality levels in Britain high during the economic boom, which coincided with Tony Blair's 1997–2007 premiership, has allowed the effects of such policies to be monitored by comparing surveys of poverty undertaken at around the start of the period with those undertaken towards the end.[65] Among British adults during the Blair years, the proportion unable to make regular savings rose from 25 to 27 per cent; the number unable to afford an annual holiday away from home rose from 18 to 24 per cent; and the national proportion who could not afford to insure the contents of their home climbed a percentage point, from 8 to 9 per cent. However, these national proportions conceal the way in which the rising exclusion has hit particular groups especially hard, not least a group that the Blair government had said it would help above all others: children living in poverty.

The comparison of poverty surveys taken towards the start and end of Tony Blair's time in office found that, of all children, the proportion living in a family that could not afford to take a holiday away from home (other than staying with family relations) rose between 1999 and 2005, from 25 to 32 per cent. This occurred even as the real incomes of most of the poorest rose, but rose more for the affluent. In consequence, as housing became more unequally distributed, the number of children of school age who had to share their bedroom with an adult or sibling over the age of 10 and of the opposite sex rose from 8 to 15 per cent nationally. Rising housing costs cancelled out the benefits of rising incomes.

It was in London that such overcrowding became most acute, and where sharing rooms rose most quickly. Keeping up appearances for the poor in London was much harder than in Britain as a whole,[66] not simply because London had less space, but because within London, other children were so often very wealthy. Even among children going to the same school, the incomes of their parents had diverged, and consequently, standards of living and expectations of the norm did too. Who do you have round for tea from school when you are ashamed of your home because (as a teenage girl) you do not want to admit to sharing a bedroom with your older brother? Nationally, the proportion of those who said their parent(s) could not afford to let them have friends round for tea doubled, from 4 to 8 per cent. The proportion of children who could not afford to pursue a hobby or other leisure activity also rose, from 5 to 7 per cent, and the proportion who could not afford to go on a school trip at least once a term doubled, from 3 to 6 per cent. For children aged below five, the proportion whose parents could not afford to take their young children to playgroup each week also doubled under the Blair government, from 3 to 6 per cent. And then, after the economic crash of 2007/08, the situation worsened, so that by 2012, 4 million children in Britain were going without at least two everyday necessities, up from 2 million in 1999,[67] and parents were resorting to more and more debt to try to protect their children.

For those who do not have to cope with debts, it becomes easier to imagine why you might go further into debt when that debt allows you, for example, to have the money to pay a pound to attend a playgroup rather than sit another day at home with your toddler. Taking out a little more debt helps pay another couple of pounds so that your school-age child can go on a school trip and not have to pretend to be ill that day. Concealing poverty becomes ever more difficult in an age of consumption. When you are asked at school where you went on holiday, or what you got for Christmas, a very active imagination helps in making up a plausible lie. Living in a consumerist society means living with the underlying message that you do not get to go on holiday or get presents like other children because you have not been good enough, because your family are not good enough.

The most expensive of all consumption items are housing costs – rent or mortgage – and these have also diverged as income inequalities have increased. Having to move to a poorer area, or being unable to move out of one, is the geographical reality of social exclusion. People get into further debt to avoid this. But usually debt simply delays the day you have to move, and makes even deeper the depth of the hole you then move into. The second most expensive consumer item is a car (until recently, cars were more costly than home buying in aggregate). This is why so many people buy cars through hire purchase, or 'on tick', as it used to be called in Britain, or 'with finance' as the euphemism now is. The combined expense and necessity of car ownership is the reason why not having a car is, for many, a contemporary mark of social failure. It is also closely connected to why so many car firms were badly hit so early on in the crash of 2008, as they were selling debt as much as selling cars with their finance arrangements.

Poverty cycles

Snap-shots of figures from comparative social surveys reveal the direction of social change, but underplay the extent to which poverty is experienced over time, because many more families and individuals experience poverty than are poor at any one time. The figures on the growth of social exclusion under the New Labour government often surprise people in Britain, because they are told repeatedly how hard that government had worked to try to help the poor, and there were a lot of policies.[68] What these policies did achieve was to put a floor under how bad things could get for most, but not all, people, by introducing a low minimum wage and a higher minimum income for families with children through complex tax credits plus a huge range of benefits-in-kind 'delivered' through various programmes, although the minimums were not enough to enable many families to live in a 'respectable' way.

Up until 2008, New Labour had been seriously relaxed about financial regulation, and also about the wealth of the super-rich. More benevolent social policies might have put a slightly higher limit on how far down it was possible to fall if you had children, but they did nothing to narrow the range of inequalities in incomes and wealth overall, nothing to reduce the number of people who ended up falling down into a cycle of deprivation, or the increasing amount of money that ended up pouring into the pockets of a few.

Figure 8 illustrates the cycle of exclusion and inclusion in societies like Britain.[69] Each circle in the figure represents the economic position of a household at one fixed instance; the arrows show the prevailing direction in which most households move socially, and the boxes show how these households can be categorised at any point in time.[70] Starting bottom right, as a household's income rises when a job is gained or a partnership is formed, expenditure and standard of living also rise, but a little later. It is that expenditure that allows the household to become better socially included, to afford a little saving, to have an annual holiday. A few households, usually dual earner, see their incomes rise even further, experience no financial knocks, no redundancies, little illness, no divorce, and begin to be able to save more, take a few more holidays a year, move to a 'better' area, send their children to a private school. If all still goes well, they typically take out private health insurance and move into the top right box, where they are excluded from the norms of society by being above them. This group grew slightly in size under Margaret Thatcher's government in the 1980s and again since 1997, as the incomes of those already paid most were allowed to rise most quickly.

Figure 8: Circling from exclusion to inclusion and back again (model)

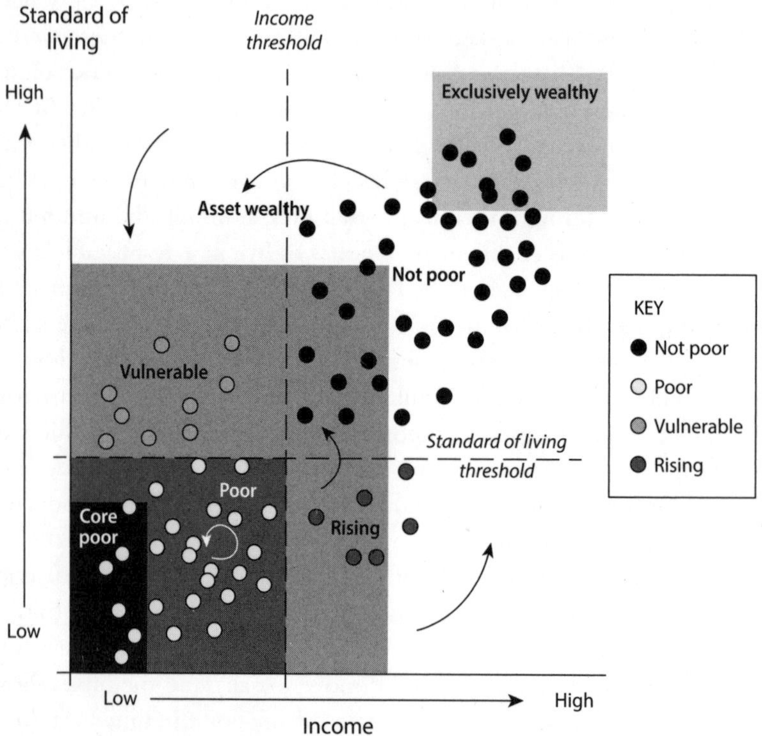

Note: It is because a change in income usually precedes changes in standard of living, that we tend to spiral anti-cockwise within this figure, sometimes just in small eddies.

Source: Adapted from David Gordon's original and much replicated drawing. See publication details of various of the works (where earlier versions appear) at the Townsend Centre for International Poverty Research, University of Bristol (www.bris.ac.uk/poverty/).

However, most people whose incomes rose in countries such as the US and Britain did not receive enough extra to be able to enter this box, and many who did fell out, again through divorce, downgrading at work or simply through falling ill.

When a financial knock comes, households are hardly ever in a position to immediately decrease their outgoings in line with their decreased income. Instead, they move across the diagram in Figure 8, from right to left, from being exclusively wealthy to being normal; from being normal to being vulnerable, exhausting savings and getting into debt to avoid having to reduce expenditure as rapidly as their income necessitates. They do this to avoid having to take no holidays at all, after they have become used to having several a year. They think they are being frugal, but they are spending more than is coming in because, as the width and the height of the cycle becomes larger with growing inequality, it becomes harder to learn how to live like others live. Households cut back, but rarely in direct proportion to the cuts in their income, largely because they feel they have to maintain their dignity and social standing. In the same way, they rarely increase expenditure directly in line with any windfall; given a lot of money, most people do not know what to do with it at first.

It is because of our commitments and burdens that socially we spiral anti-clockwise around Figure 8, often in small circles in just part of the realm of possibilities, not too near the bottom if we are lucky, spinning round over larger cycles, or trapped in the bottom left-hand corner if less fortunate. After misfortune, those lucky enough to find another partner with a good income following divorce, lucky enough to quickly get another job, or to quickly recover from the illness that had led to their troubles, can cycle round again, but many are not so lucky, and drop down the left-hand side of the cycle, down to poverty and social exclusion of various degrees of acuteness, and most stay there for considerable lengths of time.

Poverty choices

As expenditure is (over the long term) clearly constrained by income, the higher the income inequalities a society tolerates, the greater inequalities in standards of living and expenditure its people will experience, and the wider and higher will be both axes of possibility, shown in Figure 8. Very few households cycle from the extremes of top-right to bottom-left. Instead, there are many separate eddies and currents within those extremes.

The rich live in fear of being 'normal' and in hope of being ever more rich, but have little concept of what poverty really is. The richer they get, the more they rely on interest 'earned' from their savings to fund their expenditure. Much of that income is derived from their banks lending those savings to the poor. Sub-prime mortgages were especially fashionable because they were aimed at the poor from whom the greatest profit is usually made by lenders, through higher interest rates being charged.

Without the poor paying interest on debt, and the average paying instalments on mortgages, the rich could not have so many holidays, could not spiral around in their own worlds as easily. Each rich saver requires the additional charges on debt payment of many dozens of average and poor people to generate the interest payments that their much larger savings accrue (or did before interest rates were slashed worldwide over the course of 2008). Thus, there are only a few households that can ever get to the top right-hand corner of Figure 8; the rich can only ever be a small and very expensive minority.

For each affluent country in the world, in each different decade, a different version of Figure 8 can be drawn. In some countries the range along the bottom is much shorter than in others, and as a consequence, the range of expenditures along the side is shorter; far fewer families fall down into poverty, and slightly fewer families move up into the box marked 'exclusively wealthy'. This was true of Britain and the US half a century ago; it is true of Japan and France today.

We choose the shape that Figure 8 takes, or we allow others to choose to shape it, to stretch it, to make the eddies small and smooth or larger and more violent. Insecurity rises when it becomes easier to spin around, or reduces when we reduce inequalities or when we suppress the mixing such as when rank and race are made more permanent attributes and the cycle is a picture of many smaller eddies. In different countries, different social battles have different outcomes; different decisions have been taken by, or were taken for, the people there.

Those countries on the losing side of the Second World War, including Germany, Japan and Italy, had in some cases great equality thrust on them through the eradication of the remaining wealth of their old aristocracies by occupying forces, and by the introduction of land reform resulting in wealth becoming much more equally spread out by the 1950s and 1960s. That land reform occurred under postwar military occupation. American military intervention in Korea and also the establishing of a presence (at one time) in Iceland, ironically also partly contributed to the rise of equality in those countries. The redistribution of land was seen as one way to avert the rise of communism by US planners working overseas after the war.

Figure 8 is drawn to represent the extent of inequalities and the exclusion that results, as experienced in Britain by the early years of the current century. The simplest and most telling way in which that inequality can best be described is to understand that, by 2005, the poorest fifth of households in Britain had each to rely on just a seventh of the income of the best-off fifth of households. A fifth of people had to work for seven days, to receive what another fifth earned in one day. Imagine working Monday, Tuesday, Wednesday, Thursday, Friday and Monday and Tuesday again, to get what another receives for just one day of work, that single day's work almost always being less arduous, more fulfilling, more enjoyable, and of higher status, than your seven. Well-paid work is almost certainly a far more luxurious pastime than seven days spent surviving on the dole, or on a state pension. Well-paid work is almost always non-manual, undertaken in well-heated or air-conditioned premises, sitting in comfortable chairs, doing interesting things, meeting people, travelling. People gaining well-paid work acclimatise extremely quickly to their lot and rarely count their blessings. The affluent are not paid more because their work is more arduous, but because of the kind of society they live in.

International comparisons of the quintile ranges of income inequality are some of the most telling comparisons that can be made between countries. The best current estimate of UK income inequality on this measure is that the best-off fifth received 7.2 times more income on average than the worst-off fifth by 2005.[71] Even after equalising for household size, the poorest fifth of households in the UK were still the poorest in Western Europe by 2014.[72] According to the tables in the UN Development Programme's annual report, the most widely used source, that ratio is around 6.1 to 1 in Ireland, in France it is 5.6 to 1, in Sweden it is 4.0 to 1 and in Japan it is 3.4 to 1. By contrast, in the US, that same ratio of inequality is 8.5 to 1.

The lowest quintile usually live on very similar incomes within that quintile; this is not the case for the highest quintile, so the ratio of the income of the highest paid to the lowest paid individual in any organisation is dramatically higher. Campaigners for reduced inequality argue for 8:1 ratios between the very highest paid person and the very lowest paid in any workplace.[73] In 2010, David Cameron proposed a maximum 20:1 wage ratio for the UK public service, but it has not been implemented. Although a small group of people, presumably at the top, in any organisation must be approving of their wage structure, few organisations publish or fully explain it.

To reiterate, in a country like Japan where, if you are at the bottom of the heap, you need 'only' work Monday, Tuesday, Wednesday and Thursday morning, to gain what those at the top are awarded for working just on Monday, low-paid work is not so bad; although the figures are disputed, and although all is far from utopia in Japan, that extent of equality has actually been achieved. Want to find a country where people of different social strata live more often in similar neighbourhoods than they do in Europe? Visit Japan. In contrast, in the US, you need to labour for the number of days the worst-off (day labourers) work in Japan and a whole additional five-day working week to achieve the same reward, the same money, as the best-off fifth earn in a single day. If you want to find a country with far less mixed neighbourhoods than in Europe, visit the US.

Economists based in New York find it hard to explain how those at the top in Japan can be paid so much less than in the US. They put it down to internal promotion being more important than poaching 'top talent' there. Similarly, they can't explain why there was 'essentially no change in the level of CEO compensation during 1936–1970'.[74] It actually fell despite firms growing in size. And their models, published in 2008, that equated chief executive officer (CEO) pay with firm size, failed to predict that in the years that followed publication, CEO remuneration continued to rise as firm sizes fell. A single chief investment officer (CIO) could be paid a $290 million bonus in one year even when his fund had seen $64 billion pulled out of it by investors in a year. This happened to Bill Gross in 2014, and he was far from the highest paid. The four highest paid US financiers in 2013 each received between $3.5 billion and $2.2 billion in just one year.[75]

4.4 Escapism: of the rich behind walls

The human failing most closely associated with exclusion is a particular kind of bigotry, a lack of respect for those seen both as above and as beneath you. This lack of respect varies greatly between different affluent countries, and appears to reflect how unequal each is. Where there is great inequality, it is possible to hire armies of cleaners and to set them to work each night, making office blocks appear immaculate in the morning. And it is not just the cleaners, but also many more people who need to wake up in the early hours to undertake the long commute to work in those countries compared with more equitable ones. Commuting times are shorter, there is better public transport, and even the trains run to time more often in more equal affluent countries.

Many more people try to hold down several jobs at once in unequal countries because they need the extra money. Many more are on zero hours contracts, never sure when they will be working, or how much they will earn. More are day labourers, regularly looking for new piecework, often spending days without paid work hanging around where they might be picked up to do a cash-in-hand labouring job. Of those with a work contract in unequal countries, many more have to work long hours; holiday, maternity and sickness pay is often worse than in most OECD countries, or even non-existent.[76]

In fact, the situation in the UK and the US is so bad that researchers studying whether there might be a connection between genetics and political attitude have suggested that for those who might appear to be more clever: 'In more inegalitarian and market-oriented countries such as the United States or the United Kingdom, we should instead expect individuals higher in cognitive ability to more often embrace similar leftist political attitudes in the economic realm.'[77] These researchers are arguing that supposedly clever people in the UK and the US should be better placed to see what outliers those two countries are. However, there is not much evidence that they do, which might imply that those who are so often said to be the most able in the UK and the US are not as able as they often suppose.

Inequality and personal relationships

Children are far more often put into day care in countries where wages and benefits are more unequal. More inequality also results in more nannies, day care for the children of the affluent. With greater inequality, the cost of day care in general is less for the wealthy as the wages of the carers are relatively lower and more 'affordable', but the need for two adults to earn in affluent families is greater in unequal countries as even affluent couples tend not to think they have enough coming in when wide inequalities are normal. Those who are affluent do not compare themselves and their lives with the lives of those who care for their children or who clean their workplaces. They compare themselves with other couples they see as like themselves, and other couples with just a little bit more. In more unequal affluent countries, when couples split up, which they do more frequently, they become new smaller households with lower incomes, and so often drop down the sharply differentiated social scale. It is not just because of the awkwardness of the split that they lose so many of their 'friends'. It is because friendship in more unequal countries is more often about mostly mixing with those of your circumscribed class, a small group of people who are deemed to be like you.

People live far more similar (and often simpler) lives in affluent countries where incomes, expenditure and expectations are more equal. For instance, what they eat at breakfast will be similar to what others eat, and they are all more likely to be eating breakfast, not having to skip that meal for the commute, or sending their children to school hungry to save a little money.

In more equal countries, children are much more likely to travel to the nearest school to learn, so the lengths of journeys to school are shorter and far fewer children need to be driven. They are more likely to eat with their parents before school, and are more likely to still have two parents at home. Their friends will more often be drawn from nearby, and from much more of a cross-section of society than in more unequal countries. And that wider cross-section will not vary as much by income, standard of living and expectations.

In more unequal countries, parents feel the need to be more careful in monitoring who their child's friends are and even who their own friends are. If they are rich, then more often they drive their children to visit friends past the homes of nearby children considered less suitable to be their offspring's acquaintances, driving from affluent enclave to affluent enclave. If very rich, they even have another adult do that driving. But the most effective way for parents in an affluent unequal country to monitor with whom their offspring might mix is through segregating them from others by where they choose to live and which school they go to. Parents do this not because they are callous, but because they are insecure, more afraid, more ignorant of others, and less trustful, in more unequal countries. In 2009, The Equality Trust produced evidence that levels of trust are higher in more equal countries.[78]

Insecurity and mistrust

Insecurity and mistrust rise as inequality rises. Those with resources have to look a longer way down to see where they might end up should anything go seriously wrong in their lives. Depression, unemployment and divorce feature highly as personal failings to be feared; fears of pandemics and atrocities, worldwide recession and large-scale immigration are more widely held fears that can be more easily stoked the more unequal the world as a whole becomes. If you cannot trust others around you in normal times, how do you think people might react if many are made redundant in your neighbourhood, or following some other disaster? Will people help each other out if there is flooding? Or will the National Guard or Territorial Army be sent in with guns to (supposedly) prevent looting, as happened in New Orleans in 2005? It did not happen in Japan in 2011 where, in that much more equal country, the disaster of a tsunami was not further exacerbated by mass mistrust. As inequality rises, people begin to treat others less and less as people, and begin to behave towards some people (those that we say *don't count*) as if they are a different species.

The higher inequality is in an affluent country, the more the poor over-estimate the security that wealth provides,[79] the more striving to become rich becomes an end in itself. Social status becomes the measure that most determines how strangers interact when they meet in unequal societies. Eye contact is avoided more often the more inequality grows in a society. We look more towards the feet rather than the faces of those above us, having ascertained their superior status from clues of dress and behaviour, and from other status cues such as the homes they live in and the cars they drive.[80] As social status rises as the measure of apparent worth, it becomes seen as more important to spend, and for the very rich to spend on schooling that leads to particular behaviour patterns, manners and values, and cues, including everything from wearing the right shoes, carrying the correct handbag, to appearing to be confident and self-assured: the apparently effortless superiority engendered by a private school and Oxbridge education.

In London in 2014, a book was published which described the effect of gentrification in London as an influx of 'high-quality' people who would have an '... effect on the productivity of those already there, because increasing the scale of this dense and effective agglomeration of high-quality people will raise everyone's game'. The book's author stated that London schools were doing well '[i]n spite of the ethnic mix'.[81] Labelling some people as being of higher quality than others and talking of an ethnic mix as a problem for a school are assumptions that can only be made in places and times of great inequality, and so are not queried by copy-editors or proof-readers. Some people thought like this in the recent more equitable past, but they did not get to express such thoughts in print so often.

We become used to living in unequal worlds, to avoiding eye contact and worrying about our appearances, even having our hair cut at far greater expense and more often than our parents or grandparents did. It is a great shock to suddenly be cast into a more equal society, to be viewed for what you might be, not for which level you might appear to be at. In 1936, while George Orwell was in Barcelona during the Spanish civil war, he found that, for the first time in his life, waiters in cafes looked him in the eye. It was a shock. It was only when what had been normal was removed that he realised how strange normality had been, how odd it was not to look others in the eye, how much better people treated one another when there were no 'better people', when all the cars were taken away and all travelled alike.[82]

Experiments in living under widespread social equality in affluent countries have been rare. Fascists in Spain wiped out George Orwell's example with support from fascists abroad, just a few months after he wrote about Barcelona. Experiments in equality were transformed a little more slowly to terror elsewhere in the Soviet Union, then China, then across Latin America. The pressure from abroad for most overt experiments in increased equality to fail was enormous. But even without outside interference, dictatorship is never benign. Just as attempts to promote equality were usually crushed from abroad, imposing and sustaining inequality was often supported from abroad: apartheid in

South Africa, dictatorships in South America, and totalitarianism all across much of the rest of Asia and even into southern Europe received tacit and sometimes explicit endorsement from many of the most affluent in the world's richest countries. The rich supported dictators in Greece and Chile, in Vietnam, Iran and South Africa, because they were afraid of what they saw as the potentially evil outcomes of greater equality in each country. The affluent have come to justify themselves through attempts to justify inequality more widely. If it is right that a few should have so much, then it must also be right that just a few should govern over the many.

Valuing money multiplicatively

Multiplicatively is a strange word that describes a very strange phenomenon that is poorly understood, despite its widespread acceptance in, among other places, pay negotiations. When pay rises are negotiated, it is normal to agree an *x* per cent pay rise across the board. Hardly ever is the suggestion made of having a £*y* pay rise agreed across the board, irrespective of the effect on the total wage bill. Multiplication is used instead of addition, money is valued multiplicatively and how much it is worth depends on how rich you are. The world distribution of income inequality only appears to have a bell-shaped curve when incomes are compared on a logarithmic scale that depicts the difference between existing on $1 dollar a day and on $10 a day as being the same, one ten times the other, as the difference between living on $100 and on $1,000 a day. Figure 9 shows that curve, and within it four more curves, all bell-shaped again, but of four very different continental income distributions. By using purchase power parity US dollars, these incomes have been adjusted so that they refer to amounts of money that can buy similar amounts of goods, whether chickens or trousers or medicines, regardless of the currency exchange rate and whether they are cheaper in poorer countries.

Even adjusting for costs of living, annual modal family income in Africa around the year 2000 was still only equivalent to around $4 a day ($1,500 a year); in Europe modal annual family income was nearer $30,000 ($80 a day). A logarithmic scale is used here because it shows how it is possible to make the distribution of income look natural, and to

Figure 9: Distribution of income inequality, worldwide, 2000

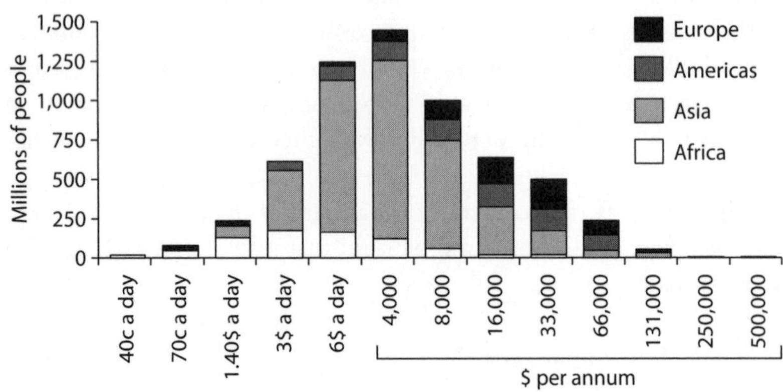

Note: X-axis shows a continuous log scale of annual income in comparable dollars, Y-axis shows millions of people living in families supported by such incomes.

Source: Figures (in purchase power parity, US$) derived from estimates by Angus Maddison, from version produced in spreadsheets given in www.worldmapper.org, based in turn on UNDP income inequality estimates for each country; derivation shown below.

Millions of people living in households by minimum annual income (US$ppp) by Worldmapper Region (www.worldmapper.org)

GDP /capita	Central Africa	South-eastern Africa	Northern Africa	Southern Asia	Asia Pacific	Middle East	Eastern Asia	South America	Eastern Europe	North America	Western Europe	Japan	Total
32	0.2	0.2	0.6	0.0	0.0	0.0	0.0	0.0	0.0	0.0	0.0	0.0	1.0
64	0.9	1.1	2.6	0.0	0.0	0.0	0.0	0.3	0.0	0.0	0.0	0.0	4.9
128	4.2	5.9	9.9	0.0	0.5	0.1	0.3	1.4	0.0	0.1	0.0	0.0	22.4
256	12.8	22.6	27.3	1.3	4.1	1.6	3.6	5.9	0.1	0.4	0.0	0.0	79.6
512	23.3	59.2	54.1	23.0	18.9	8.8	26.7	18.3	0.7	1.8	0.0	0.0	234.7
1024	27.0	80.3	80.9	173.7	61.8	28.8	112.9	42.9	3.4	5.9	0.0	0.0	617.5
2048	19.3	51.5	98.5	496.3	138.9	61.6	274.9	74.2	16.6	14.0	0.2	0.0	1246.1
4096	8.0	25.2	91.9	502.8	167.8	85.9	385.6	94.4	58.0	25.8	3.3	0.0	1448.7
8192	2.6	15.3	53.2	172.1	102.4	90.3	317.1	87.6	87.3	46.8	25.4	0.4	1000.6
16384	0.8	9.9	16.8	19.1	42.7	61.9	163.5	59.3	62.1	86.8	99.4	18.6	641.1
32768	0.3	5.5	2.9	0.7	19.3	26.9	55.2	29.4	20.9	115.4	160.7	76.7	513.8
65536	0.1	2.3	0.3	0.0	7.7	7.2	10.8	10.7	2.3	86.0	85.8	30.7	243.9
131072	0.0	0.7	0.0	0.0	1.8	1.1	1.2	2.9	0.1	33.9	15.4	1.1	58.2
262144	0.0	0.2	0.0	0.0	0.2	0.1	0.1	0.6	0.0	7.1	1.2	0.0	9.5
524288	0.0	0.0	0.0	0.0	0.0	0.0	0.0	0.1	0.0	0.8	0.0	0.0	1.0
1048576	0.0	0.0	0.0	0.0	0.0	0.0	0.0	0.0	0.0	0.0	0.0	0.0	0.1
Total	99.4	280.1	439.0	1389.2	566.3	374.3	1351.9	427.9	251.4	424.6	391.5	127.5	6123.1

add justification to income scales where people are judged to be worth many times other people. In each column people live on twice as much a day as in the previous column, but only half what the next column have. Pay rises are not in dollars but in percentages. What matters is not how much you can afford, but how many times your income exceeds another. The value of money is becoming multiplicative rather than additive.

Multiplicative beliefs in the value of money suggest that the actual value people have come to put on money only makes sense if you take into account expectations. Multiplicative beliefs become stronger in affluent and more unequal countries. Money is not valued for what it can buy, but for the status it confirms. Goods are not bought for what they can do, but more and more for the status they bestow on those who buy them. Clothes must look good rather than keep you warm. What matters about decoration, kitchenware, furniture, cars, homes, even holidays, is what you think others might think of you should they compare their possessions with yours, their consumption with your consumption, their lives with yours. Unions demand salary rises in terms of percentages of incomes; bonuses for bosses become even greater multiples of some measure; only the increases in the incomes of the poorest, state pensioners and others reliant on benefit or the minimum wage are described in pounds (although the increases are often in pence), dollars, euros or yen.

Only for the poorest is money additive. Only for the poorest does one and one mean two; for others it means loose change, too little to give as a tip. For the very rich it means a sum not worth fishing down the back of the sofa for. In societies that have come to value money in multiplicative ways, conventional economic thinking makes absolutely no sense because the basic mathematical metric of reasoning has been transformed. In a multiplicative-thinking country you cannot redistribute from a few rich people and make everyone better off, not when a majority dream of having riches, of having multiplicatively more, not just a little additional income.

For the majority in poor countries, money remains additive. An extra few cents means much the same to most people in the world, an actual improvement in their standards of living, filling a hunger in their stomach, or a genuine material need, buying a pair of shoes that loosely fit a child's feet. It is only once consumption goes beyond basic needs that money becomes multiplicative.

A shilling in places like England used to mean the same thing to most people, which is why units of currency are mentioned in old novels. Today, units of currency are rarely mentioned in books or films, not just due to the effects of inflation, but because there is far less of a common conception of what a reasonable amount of, say, pocket money for a child might be, of how much a pint of beer might cost in a pub, or how much you might spend on a raincoat. People reading a novel in the mid-19th century would understand what could be bought with a sum of money no matter which decade they were reading in. Thomas Piketty commented on this in 2014 when also pointing out how Jane Austen and Honoré de Balzac also repeatedly mentioned the sums of money required to secure an adequate income from wealth.[83]

Although inflation rose during and following the First World War, because incomes became more equal, people watching television in the mid-20th century were more similar to each other than audiences are today. In the 1980s and 1990s in England, there was even a game show on television where contestants had to guess the market value of goods. That format failed to work when it was revived in 2006 and 2007 as the market value now varies by consumer niche.[84] In poorer countries there remains much of the uniformity of values that used to exist in affluent countries. At the bottom, so many are struggling to get by, they value things similarly, but the market for films or novels for the poor is small and so prices are again not mentioned. In most of the world the poor really need the vast majority of what they purchase.

Dreaming of being normal

There are a few poor countries such as Costa Rica and Cuba, and a few states within countries, such as Kerala in India, or New Hampshire in the US, which are more equitable than the global norm, but their impact on the global distribution is cancelled out by much greater than average inequality in places such as Brazil and South Africa. When there is a global pattern that is mirrored in local patterns, it is usually the case that a common process is at work. This is how trees come to grow so similarly twisted, and how coastlines wiggle to the same extent, whether viewed by eye or from space. This was why Karl Pearson wanted to show that paupers in Britain were strung along a bell curve by area. Income distribution curves tend to appear similar even when viewed for very different groups in different parts of the world. However, it is no natural process that results in the fractal nature of world income inequality, just a very human process that, by 2000, had become near universal: a move from reality to a kind of fantasy, escapism.

Escapism is one way of describing the process whereby family incomes have become, over time, strung along a curve so skewed that it makes little sense to talk of social groups with different levels of income, such as talking of those living on $100, $200, $300, $400, $500, $600 or $700 a day, but instead different orders of magnitude are discussed: $20, $50, $100, $250, $500, $1,000, $2,000 a day. Escapism becomes the dominant determinant of income distribution once the majority of income is no longer being used to satisfy basic needs, but is instead being used to signify social status.

There is no dignity in simply satisfying basic needs; just getting by is very little to be proud of in a place where that is no longer the norm. There was a great loss of dignity in not being able to buy a postage stamp to send a letter in York in 1900, just as there was loss of dignity in not being able to afford a computer to connect to the internet in New York in 2000. That computer is now the equivalent of the stamp when it comes to the means we use to communicate. Dignity is about having what others have, what is considered normal. The importance of dignity is so strongly felt that we quickly confuse what we want with what we need, because we feel strongly that we need these things to protect our dignity.

When basic needs cannot be met, where hunger remains, everyone is extremely thankful for an extra dollar a day, whether they are living on just one dollar a day, or two, or ten. However, offer that extra dollar a day to a person on an annual salary of $30,000, and they may well be insulted by what is, in effect, a 1 per cent pay rise. They might say that inflation is higher than 1 per cent or, more likely, that other groups are receiving greater rises and an additional $365 a year is an insult. It represents a drop in status when those already receiving more each year receive even greater annual increases. It represents a demotion if some from below are receiving proportionately bigger increases, even if smaller amounts. We resent the effects of multiplicativity on those earning more than us, and insist on it with those earning less.

The poorest tenth of the world's population regularly go hungry. The richest tenth cannot remember a time of hunger in their family's history. The poorest tenth can only secure the most basic education for their children; among the richest tenth are many who pay high school fees to ensure that their children do not mix with poorer children. The poorest tenth almost all live in places where there is no social security, no unemployment benefit. The richest tenth cannot imagine themselves ever having to try to live on those benefits. The poorest tenth can only secure day work in town, or are peasants in rural areas; the richest tenth cannot imagine not having a secure monthly salary. Above them, the top fraction, the very richest, cannot imagine surviving on a salary rather than on the income coming from the interest that their wealth generates.

A wealthy man on television recently explained, in an attempt to show he was 'decent', that he would be happy for a daughter of his to become a nurse, and would gladly pay her an annual income from her inheritance to make that possible (as living off a nurse's income was clearly not conceivable to him). He said he didn't want to spoil his children by just giving them his money; he only wanted to do that if they did something 'good'.[85] So taking a 'normal' job becomes 'doing good'. That attitude, out of place still in Britain, is not unusual in the US, the most unequal large rich country in the world, where the poorest tenth have no access to healthcare,[86] and the richest tenth shun the healthcare provided to most in their country, usually opting to pay much more to secure what they are told is better treatment.

The gulfs between our worlds are so wide that comparisons are rarely made between the lives of the richest and poorest on the planet. Worldwide, the poorest tenth will die having hardly left a scratch on the earth. The richest tenth will each individually consume more oil through travel, and minerals through gadgets, than dozens of previous generations of their own families ever did, at least six times more each than their already affluent parents, and in doing so, they consume the vast majority of all those resources that are consumed worldwide.[87] People are illiberal when they claim there are too many humans on earth with no recognition that almost all consumption and pollution is down to a tiny affluent minority. And those who want to appear liberal say they will sponsor their daughters to be nurses!

If an affluent family in a rich country were to behave as their parents behaved, they would be labelled as deep-green environmentalists. This would involve cutting down to a single car, very rarely travelling by air, not heating their home so often, owning just a couple of pairs of shoes per person, a few changes of clothes, rarely going out to eat, not eating meat very often, taking just one holiday a year. It is precisely because it has become normal in affluent countries to consume, to want so much more than our parents had, especially if our parents were rich, that escapism has taken hold. In summer 2014, the UN published a report that showed that 'The two-way relationship between inequality and climate change aggravates both: inequality contributes to climate change, whose impacts in turn tend to increase inequality.'[88]

The reality of worldwide inequalities, of injustice, is so great that the rich try not to think of it and of others too much; for this, they need escapism to a fantasy world where there is injustice in how they see themselves treated. It is an easy fantasy to sustain. The very rich often do not notice average people in the same way that average people often do not notice those who clean and do the other very lowliest of tasks around them. In this fantasy the rich are over-taxed, much maligned and misunderstood. It is hard to remember to be satisfied with what you have when you cannot remember not having most of what you wanted, let alone what you needed. The cravings to satisfy basic needs transformed into cravings to satisfy ever-growing wants soon after the needs were mostly met. Consumerism, particularly of cars, in the US in the 1950s is often identified as an early example of such cravings being created.

But what do you do when you have all your televisions, cars and holidays, when your home is full of possessions that cost such huge amounts? The answer is: you begin to live in fear. You move to what you conceive of as safer and safer environments. Eventually, you can end up with a home in a gated estate, a gilded cage for the new gilded age. Visitors have to check in with guards before they can get to your door. Your children are too afraid to go outside the gates to play. They watch television; maybe they dream of being nurses. And you live in fear that they might just do that, and your grandchildren or great-grandchildren will be poor, or just average.

4.5 The 1960s: the turning point from inclusion to exclusion

Only a minority of North Americans got to satisfy the newly stoked-up craving for the trappings of wealth in the 1950s, trappings such as big fast cars and large homes, but with ever-growing access to television, a more equitable distribution of incomes, low unemployment and an ever more cleverly constructed advertising, that minority became the consuming majority in the US during the 1960s. Collective craving created consumerism, which drove the demand for domestic production. Within the US, production peaked during the 1960s, and mostly moved abroad in the decades following. Despite many remaining in poverty, and the need for a 'Great Society' programme to tackle that, these were years of relative equality in the US. However, they were also the years in which the rich became sufficiently frightened for some of them to start to act. They were frightened that such novel equality was unsustainable. They acted to insulate themselves from any downturn to come, to reduce the effects of inflation eating into their wealth, and to take more again from those who had the least so that they could 'save'. Others who could have stopped them had become complacent and placated enough not to see what was coming.

Consumerism rose in Europe later and in Japan a little later still. Figure 10 shows that 10-year growth in the economy of the US (and by association, during those more equitable times, the median average growth for all the Americas), which peaked at 30 per cent in the decade to 1968, fell, then stumbled back up a fraction higher to 31 per cent by 1973, before crumbling down to below 20 per cent, occasionally below 10 per cent, equating to average annual growth rates of around 2 per cent then 1 per cent. This was nothing like the crashes of 1929 or 2008, but enough of a shock for those who also had to get used to being more like others within each of those countries.

When the rich countries of the world are combined, their average annual growth rates between 1965 and 1979 were 3.5 per cent; these more than halved by 1998, and halved again between 2007 and 2010. For the poor countries of the world, the combined rates were 2.4 per cent in the early period, falling to an average growth of zero by 1998, but then rising during the noughties.[89]

Figure 10: Real growth per decade in GDP (%), per person, by continent, 1955–2010

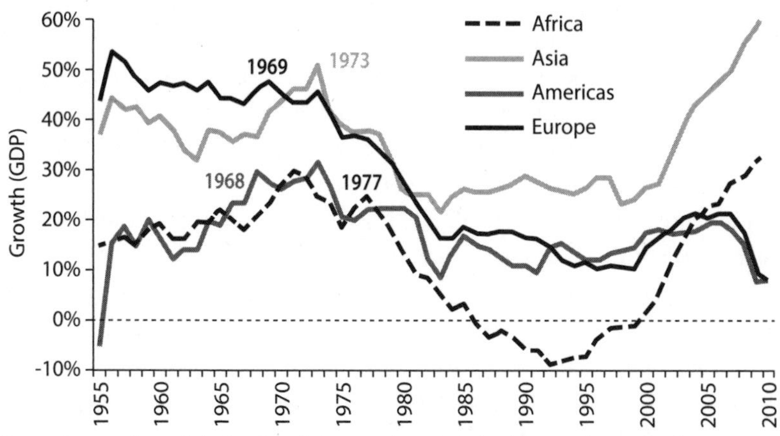

Source: Figures (growth in the decade to year shown) derived from estimates by Angus Maddison. Updated using figures provided by the Maddison Project: http://www.ggdc.net/maddison/maddison-project/home.htm

Change in GDP (US$ppp) per person over the decade to the year shown 1991-2010

	Africa	Asia	Americas	Europe
1991	-6%	28%	9%	16%
1992	-9%	26%	15%	15%
1993	-8%	26%	15%	12%
1994	-8%	25%	14%	11%
1995	-7%	26%	12%	11%
1996	-4%	29%	12%	10%
1997	-2%	28%	13%	11%
1998	-2%	23%	14%	11%
1999	-1%	24%	14%	10%
2000	1%	26%	18%	14%
2001	5%	27%	18%	17%
2002	11%	32%	17%	18%
2003	16%	39%	18%	20%
2004	20%	43%	18%	21%
2005	23%	45%	19%	20%
2006	24%	48%	20%	21%
2007	27%	50%	18%	21%
2008	29%	55%	15%	17%
2009	32%	59%	8%	10%
2010	34%	64%	8%	8%

Note: These figures are 10 times larger than annual changes.

Gross domestic product (GDP) estimates are some of the oddest social statistics that have ever been created. Although the word 'domestic' appears in their title, they are as much a measure of success in international trade as of any kind of ingenuity at home. They are also a measure of how well a country avoids being exploited by others. They are an estimate of the value of goods and services that are produced. The great assumption in their calculation is that value can be calculated from the amount people have to pay for those goods and services.

The short-cut route to calculating GDP is to sum national wages, salaries and profit, as it is stated that those wages, salaries and profits reflect the value of the goods and services that people produce. The theory goes on to suggest that, over time, due to innovation, people produce more and more valuable goods, become individually more productive, and so their combined product rises. If that is the case, then the question Figure 10 poses is: why, following the 1960s, did production per person fall so consistently worldwide? And what will happen given the bifurcation of the noughties?

Unsustainable growth

From the decade 1945–55, through to the end of the 1960s, production per person in the world was rising by between 2 and 4 per cent a year, between 22 and 48 per cent a decade (the scale shown in the graph in Figure 10 is of change over the previous decade). This is, on average, a doubling of global living standards in just one generation: 1945–68. But the doubling of already high living standards across rich countries had very different effects compared to the doubling of very low living standards in poor countries. It took a hugely greater proportion of global income to double the incomes of the rich compared to doubling the living standards of the poor.

At the continental extremes of comparing North America with Africa, ten times as many resources were needed to double living standards in the former as in the latter areas, despite Africa's much greater population. The continuation of that kind of growth following the 1960s was unsustainable. Growth from 1945 to 1968 could partly only be so great because postwar productivity was initially so low. It was impossible to repeat that growth from 1968 to 1991. Had the rich world carried on growing at those high earlier rates, we would have run out of places just to store the rubbish created. Not enough goods could have been made quickly enough for consumers with all that new money in rich countries to consume. China and India could grow, but they were growing from decimated economic beginnings.

Instead of further worldwide growth, there were three global economic slumps in the 24 years after 1968, and inflation initially soared. Inflation need not have followed the initial late 1960s price rises; the prices only rose because enough people in rich countries still had the incomes to pay the higher prices. They still had high enough incomes because, when the choice had to be made, at the end of the 1960s and into the early 1970s, as to how to manage a fall in resources, those with more did not choose to limit their own consumption but to curtail the consumption of those with less. That was when the collective and partly subconscious choice was made. It took many more years for the effect of the choice to be clear.

The curtailment of the rise in the living standards of the poor was not the snappy phrase used to explain the choice that was made, and it was not how those making the choice saw the choice they had made. Instead they called it 'anti-communism'. Anti-communism peaked in bloodshed during the 1960s and early 1970s. This was seen with British military interventions in the Middle East in the mid-1960s, in the support of Western right-wing governments for the Greek military coup of 1967, across to the 1968 peak of the US invasion of Vietnam, through to interventions across much of the rest of Asia, much of Africa and Latin America. The bloodshed was also genocidal within communist countries.

Genocide rarely occurs without the cloak of secrecy that comes with war or the threat of war and invasion. That genocide bolstered anti-communism, but there is a coincidence in the timing of the peaks of anti-communist action and the slump in apparent productivity that gives a hint as to how thousands of small decisions, soon to become a doctrine gaining in strength, arguing for inequality, became one great decision. The most significant point in that coincidence was when Richard Nixon unilaterally cancelled the Bretton Woods agreement and ended the direct convertibility of the US dollar into gold in 1971. He did not want to do it but was forced to due to the costs of the Vietnam War, and it may well be coincidence that productivity fell from then on, and debt rose unchecked (look again at Figure 10). The decision to behave in this way was not taken by Richard Nixon alone – it was a great collective decision that was taken by many people who each had a little bit of power and quite a lot of wealth. It was taken through the results of many thousands of individual decisions taken under the newly forming doctrine that inequality was good.

Inequality, it was suggested by the right in the 1970s, led to competition, to people working harder; there would be more for all in the long term; a tide would come and all the boats would rise (as Ronald Reagan used to misquote John Kennedy). Equality led (the right wing thought and still think) to complacency, to inefficient decisions being made, to a levelling down, eventually to communism, misery for all and the denial of liberty. If a country turned communist, its resources would not so easily be made available for exploitation (called trade). Their corrupt leaders might choose to try to maximise the production that stayed within their country, and 'free' trade would be limited. As it began to become harder to secure more resources in general, particularly with the oil price rises of 1973, the great decision was finalised that the greatest sacrifice should be made by the poor, in concert, but not as a conspiracy.

The sacrifice of the poor

The poorest of the poor lost out most in the post-1960s swing to market-dominated economies. Figure 10 shows how the entire average income growth of the African continent went into free fall in the 1970s, and then became negative by the mid-1980s and throughout the 1990s. That little dotted curve at the bottom of Figure 10 is the simplest visual summary of abandonment of a continent in the name of the doctrine of inequality. However, although resources from African countries could be squandered throughout these decades (cheap oil extracted from Nigeria with kick-backs to dictators, diamonds extracted from the Congo while exploiting miners on starvation wages), the amount of income that could be saved globally by giving Africans an unfairly low return for their product was very small. This was because they had been given so little to begin with. It took until 2003 for GDP per capita to again exceed what had been reached in 1980, but after the crash of 2008, incomes per person in Africa rose while they fell across Europe and the Americas. After 2008, business was no longer continued 'as usual'.

It was from denying fair terms of trade to most countries in Asia and a few elsewhere that more monies came to be amassed in the rich countries, again until the years just prior to and especially after the 2008 crash. Above all, it was from denying the continued internal spreading out of those gains within affluent countries that the rich within some of the richest of countries managed to not only retain the growth in their living standards, as living standards worldwide stood still or fell, but to increase the rate of growth of their own wealth. And that is how they came later, as a group, in the 1980s, to see their living standards rise more rapidly than any other group anywhere in the world. After the 2008 crash, the richest people in the most unequal of rich countries, the US and the UK, continued to take more and more, but now more to the detriment of those just beneath them in their own countries.[90]

Reaction to the end of 1950s growth resulted in a few more affluent people, especially affluent North Americans, funding a new spate of right-wing think-tanks which promoted inequality. This was not a great conspiracy but something far more dangerous and difficult to prevent, which resulted in a turning point occurring in the 1960s. It is the fact that it took thousands of smaller decisions to cumulate in a result of such significance that should be of concern. It was the everyday politics of the envy within the rich and fear of those who had come to know a little luxury, who wanted much more as a result, and who lived in constant uneasy fear of it being taken away.

The turning point came in the 1960s not just because those who might have opposed it did not try hard enough, or because of effective arguments from a particularly influential economist or two. It had to come then; what had gone before, a rapidly growing but relatively (proportionately) equitable sharing out of more and more economic spoils, year on year on year, had to end. The postwar boom ended simply because it had run out of resources. With only one planet, the easy gains had been made, the easy oil had been drilled, the easiest mass distribution of pesticides accomplished, the easiest industrialisation undertaken. What was occurring globally was way beyond the comprehension of any individual or group at the time. It took decades of time and thousands of writers and thinkers to figure it out. As the 1960s ended, the US landed on the moon and found it to be no great resource substitute, no consolation for having only one planet. Savings had to be found elsewhere. Although the 1960s were the turning point, it took all of the 1970s before it became clear to those at the top from where most of the savings they wanted to make would come.

The slowdown in the rise in incomes in affluent countries from the late 1970s onwards was handled very differently in different countries. In the US, when the population was sorted into five equal-sized groups, quintiles, annual incomes were found to have risen from poorest to richest between 1949 and 1979 by 2.6, 2.3, 2.5, 2.6 and 2.3 per cent respectively. Rather like the global trend over a similar period, all had benefited with a slight equalisation over time at the upper extreme. However, between 1979 and 2003, under Reagan, Clinton and the Bushes, the respective annual growth rates diverged, those five rates respectively from poorest to richest quintile being 0.2, 0.6, 0.9, 1.4 and 2.7 per cent.[91] In the later years of George W. Bush leading up to the financial crisis, these inequalities grew even faster, and the median group even saw their incomes fall by over $1,000 a year.[92] At the extremes, in the US, even average incomes finally had to fall to finance the wealth grabs of the super-rich in what became the heights of excess of a new gilded age. By the Obama years, the statistic that almost all the gains that were being made by anyone were being made by just the top 1 per cent became so well known that it does not need referencing here, being the inevitable end point of a longer-term trend in that direction.

In Britain, by poorest to richest quintile of the population, annual increases in incomes from 1979 to 1990 to the nearest percentile were respectively 0.5, 1, 2, 3 and 4 per cent,[93] with the incomes of those who had most to begin with being allowed to continue to increase at historically rare rates, with all the sacrifice being made by those who had the least to sacrifice. During 1979–90, Margaret Thatcher's Conservative Party was elected three times to government; her own party rather than the electorate finally deposed her. John Major replaced her as Prime Minister, and from 1990 to 1997 there was no further increase in inequality, rather a slight decrease as the richest quintile's income rose annually by only 0.5 per cent while the poorest's rose at three times that rate, by 1.5 per cent.[94] This showed a slight reduction in inequality but hardly dented the effects of those earlier 11 years. Then, under Tony Blair's government, income inequalities were almost perfectly preserved from 1997 to at least 2007, with initially all quintiles seeing annual growth of 2.5 per cent.[95] However, high and sustained income inequalities led to rising social exclusion and increasing inequalities in wealth. When, 18 years after Mrs Thatcher was forced to resign by her own party, Tony Blair was forced out by his, the richest fifth still received 42 per cent of all income in Britain, the same proportion in 2007 as in 1991.[96] However, it was only the top half of the best-off fifth that had seen any increase, and then only until 2007. The bottom half of the best-off fifth received just 15 per cent of all income, 'only' 50 per cent more than absolute equality would have given them. Then, under the premierships of Gordon Brown and David Cameron, the top 1 per cent alone moved away, leaving the rest of the top 10 per cent falling behind.[97]

Inequalities almost stopped rising 40 years after the 1960s turning point, not because of any great conversion to a belief in the merits of equality by British or US governments, but because there was little left to squeeze from the poor, and average rises in national and global incomes were still slowing. Attempts were made to cut further. The Adam Smith Institute advocated decentralising welfare support so that what you received, if destitute, depended on the whims of those in power where you lived. And everyone who could work should be forced to work, for free, if they were to receive any benefits at all: 'no work, no benefits'.[98] The Adam Smith Institute's recommendations were adopted by the 2010 Coalition, and local government was handed more and more discretion of whether to pay certain housing benefits or not, while its funding was savagely cut.

Profligacy and promiscuity

In Britain, the 1960s' turning point mirrored an earlier one, just prior to the 1880s, when the original gilded age began. Inequalities in incomes between the best-off tenth of skilled men in full-time manual employment in Britain and the worst-off slowly rose during the original gilded age, from the best-off tenth being paid 2.09 times as much as the worst-off tenth in 1886, to 2.36 times as much by 1906. It was not just an economic crash but political agitation that brought the discrepancy down to 2.07 by 1938, and slowly fractionally further down to 2.06 by 1960. But soon after that it rose quickly to 2.19 by 1970, fell again to 2.07 by 1976, but then rose rapidly, peaking at 2.37 in 1986 (above even 1906 inequalities), and then soared to 2.55 by 1996.[99] Since then, inequalities by these decile measures have held up around this British historical maximum, before peaking again just a fraction higher in 2008.[100] By 2013, just over 5 per cent of all employees were earning over £55,000 a year (or £30 an hour), and the same were earning the then minimum wage of just over £6 an hour (£11,000 a year), or less. By 2013, the worst-off 10 per cent receiving the London living wage of £8.55 an hour were receiving a third of the £25 an hour that had become typical of the top tenth.[101]

The increasing concentration of income and wealth among a few within countries like Britain and the US from 1980 onwards was mirrored internationally by a growing reluctance to see monies flowing out of rich countries in any form other than investments, financial instruments designed to secure that yet more money would flow back in. In 1980, some half a per cent of annual national income in Britain was spent on international aid. This was cut by a third in 1983, then by more in 1984, and overall was halved by 1994 to reach a low of just a quarter of a per cent.[102] It has since risen slightly, and stands at just over half a per cent again, but the fact that this is still argued over illustrates how monies were being clawed in from all directions to keep up the share going to the very richest of people in the richest of countries. A great deal of the overseas aid money is now used for activities such as promoting British businesses, including arms sales.[103]

In Conservative writing and talk, the 1960s have come to be seen as the era of great evils of a different kind. They are not seen as the time when all those little decisions arising from fear of the poor among the rich resulted in the unconscious group-think decision being made to begin to penalise the poor, but as a time when the poor and the young were first allowed in large numbers to behave badly, as a time of emerging new social evils of immorality. Chief among these supposed evils was more freedom over sexual behaviour due to the introduction of the contraceptive pill. The pill became blamed for all manner of social ills, for destroying the 'cultural norm'. According to one commentator from New Zealand, Alan Gibbs, it supposedly '… relaxed the pressures that mothers put on their daughters to hold this cultural norm together.'[104] The pressure being talked about here was the pressure not to have sex before marriage, for fear of becoming pregnant and because of the huge social stigma that was then usually associated with the birth of an illegitimate child. There was also the risk involved, childbirth still being the greatest killer of young women worldwide today, and there was a lack of legal access to abortion at the start of the 1960s in most rich countries; law enforced motherhood following conception. Fifty years later, the situation is much better, but still the government's 'broken Britain Tsar', Louise Casey, wants mothers with large families taken to see the doctor for contraceptive advice.[105] Louise doesn't understand that people choose to have fewer children in more equitable countries. She bases her beliefs on "what I see" and what she thinks people are telling her, and she puts these facts in the public domain when thinking she is making a rational case for what she is doing.[106] This is nothing new.

Those who complain of birth control creating immorality forget that it was initially promoted to control the reproduction of the poor by elitist eugenicists who also believed in the need for the rich to breed more in order to improve the 'stock' of humanity. They also forget, or never knew, that it was the introduction of the pill coupled with the winning of other basic educational rights for women around the world that has been mainly responsible for the rapid slowdown in population growth since the early 1960s, so that today – and it is worth saying this again and again – worldwide, the average family is made up of two adults and fewer than three children, and those children are projected to form families of – on average – just two children, ending worldwide population growth, possibly within 42 years' time, for the first time since possibly as long ago as the Black Death, or perhaps for the first time since the spreading of old world diseases to the Americas. The majority of the growth to come to a world population of 10 billion is predicted to come from more of us being around for longer to be counted at any one time, not from more births.[107]

The monsters our fears create

The expected end of net natural global population growth within current lifetimes is hardly ever celebrated as a great human achievement in self-control and collective decision making gone well. All those men, from Adam Smith to the Reverend Thomas Malthus, to modern-day orthodox economists[108] who were so concerned about lust and temptation being uncontrollable, need not have worried. The fact that world population growth is ending due to the actions of women demonstrates that there is no need for billions of individual human decisions to end up with a bad result. It should also be seen as a reason why we should be less concerned about the global slowdown in estimated production per person; we are slowly and steadily, but ever so surely, producing less of ourselves, fewer in need of being provided for.

A great deal of production prior to the 1960s was work being carried out to prepare for the large generation to come, the children of the generation born shortly after the war, who had their own baby-producing boom in affluent countries in the mid-1960s. Homes had to be built for all the additional families being formed, highways constructed to link the homes, industries forged to provide for growing demand. All those increases are ending, but we still lament the ending of the postwar period of great prosperity that mainly employed people in building and preparing for the age to come.

Sadly and mistakenly, many still talk of the 1960s as being the advent of new evils. Their forebears, such as Ronald Reagan, talked of 'welfare queens', of the poor as having become sexually promiscuous, irresponsible and dependent since those days. In talking in this old way, modern Conservatives try to change the terms of the debate as to why so many are now excluded from society, to imply that it is somehow the result of supposedly timeless forces of nature and biology. 'The poor will always be with us because of their genes' is the current manifestation of this theory, but its antecedents were seen in places like Britain much further back, from the introduction of the Poor Law and before.[109]

In 2014, Arnold Abbott, a 90-year-old charity worker in Fort Lauderdale, Florida, was threatened with 60 days in jail if he insisted on continuing to feed homeless people with a team of church volunteers. The city authorities did not want homeless people on their streets, and so had passed a law saying that 'do-gooders' would not be permitted to help prevent them from starving because: 'Economic development and tourism don't mesh well with homeless folks and the agencies that serve them.'[110] Those interested in promoting tourists would rather the homeless were elsewhere, possibly even dead. To achieve this it is no longer enough to 'simply' criminalise the poor; now those who try to help the poor are also criminalised.

We remain haunted by old ghosts, prejudices and the monsters that our fears have created over the course of centuries. These fears have come in recent decades to dictate the way in which those with more have come to view those with less. These are the fears that support racism, which underpin the idea of social exclusion as acceptable; they are the fears behind elitism. They are the fears that underlie the argument which says that since it is natural biological forces which have resulted in different groups of human beings living in such widely varying circumstances around the globe, then, as a result, there must be something natural, almost biologically preordained, about the unequal situations in which people find themselves.

It is a highly prejudiced view to suggest that human beings are ordered into different castes, races, classes and groups with destinies which vary naturally and in line with their supposed talents, resulting not in unfair exclusion, but in segregation, both worldwide and local, that is natural and good. This leads to an acceptance of a world where the wheat is sorted from the chaff, the sheep from the goats, the leaders from the people who make up their markets; this view has many faces but no common name. It is akin to a widening of racism, but for now, let us just call it: prejudice. And it is becoming more widely recognised. In 2014, one of the world's most influential writers on economics, Martin Wolf, said of the huge growth in inequality: 'It is increasingly recognised that, beyond a certain point, inequality will be a source of significant ills.... The costs to society of rising inequality go further. To my mind the greatest costs are the erosion of the republican ideal of shared citizenship.'[111] He was talking about the concepts and prejudice that results in the loss of a sense of the common good that can lead to actual exclusion, which in its turn, fosters more prejudice.

5

'Prejudice is natural': a wider racism

> **Antipoverty programs have been increasingly oriented around rewarding and encouraging work …** Despite concerns that antipoverty programs may discourage employment, the best research suggests that work disincentive effects are small or non-existent for most programs.[1]

In 2014 in the US, a council of the most esteemed men of the land advised their leader that people needed to be virtually forced to work (workfare). Their words, quoted above, were chosen to attempt to reduce concerns that many Americans would not work if anti-poverty programmes were too generous. The economic advisers do not say this of themselves; they say it of others, of those beneath them and thus – indirectly – especially of African Americans who are far more likely to rely on anti-poverty programmes than white Americans. They even gave credence to such 'concerns' when drafting a report for a Black president.

In the UK, poverty is less widespread and less extreme than in the US, and yet, by the time they had reached the age of 11, half of all the children born in the UK in the year 2000 had faced poverty at some point in their lives.[2] Of the parents of those children, one in four is unfairly treated, is bullied, threatened, and intimated or abused at work, and many, if not most, people in work have a sense of meaninglessness about the actual value of what they are being asked to do.[3]

It is more likely that non-white workers will be badly treated, or made to do the most mindless work, to guard doors or clean floors. In a society that cared more there would simply be less need for people to employ guards or house cleaners: people would clean their own houses (with fewer spare rooms) and there would be less risk and fear of burglary with fewer low-paid jobs. In the UK, just as in the US, there is a sense of prejudice about the value of those 'beneath' that is both wider than racism and – in many ways – a wider racism. Racism remains but is transforming its shape, as Paul Gilroy so carefully clarifies: 'Long after racism is supposed to have faded away, racial abuse, like racialized inequality, remains.'[4]

Why did racism become so strong again in affluent countries in the 1970s? Why was it that postwar racist killing in Western Europe became most common then: the stabbing of Asian men by white men, the kicking to death of black youths?[5] Why, from then on, was 'race' such a crucial determinant of the shape of the US political map, with whites in the South switching at that time in huge numbers to the Republican Party, later ensuring Ronald's Reagan's victory in the presidential election of 1980?[6] Was it just a backlash reaction after the winning by blacks of a few, albeit important, civil rights in the 1960s?

Why across Europe did far-right parties start to form and grow again, so often in the late 1970s?[7] Had it been a sufficiently long time after the war? Why were the 1970s the decade of the greatest visible growth in racist graffiti, with swastikas appearing in support of the far-right National Front in Britain?[8] Why at that time did skinhead thugs reappear across Europe? Was it discontent and racist votes that were enough to tip the balance and allow Margaret Thatcher not just victory but a large majority in Britain in 1979?[9] Was this just a backlash, a reaction to recent increases in immigration, and to seeing a few more black and brown faces on the streets?

Did the same recurrence of racism emerge in Japan when, from the early 1970s onwards, a few Filipino migrants were allowed in to do the 'dirty', 'dangerous' and 'difficult' jobs that the Japanese would no longer do; in Japanese: *kitanai*, *kiken* and *kitsui*, the '3k' jobs?[10] For some reason, in almost all the richest countries, prejudice towards others resurged strongly at this time. In the US this was for people doing the lowly '5f' jobs. These were 'food' – fast-food outlets, cafes, restaurants; 'filth' – cleaning in the streets, hotels and offices; 'folding' – laundry work; 'fetching' – messenger work; and 'filing' – low-level office work.[11] In Britain, the fascist National Front became popular as it became harder to secure skilled employment, followed in the 1980s by the British National Party (BNP) and most recently by the UK Independence Party (UKIP), which copied the mainland European model of inflaming fear of 'foreigners', especially those seen to be of different races.

Racism has a long history in all affluent countries, although it became briefly less acceptable to express anti-Semitic racist opinion publicly following the Second World War. However, in all these countries, as governments also sought to minimise idleness and unemployment, the great evil of xenophobia used so effectively by fascists before the war shrank. Racism was still rife in everyday life, especially as it affected the Irish in Britain and black people in the US, but as we forgot fascism (and as rank began to matter more again), in place of xenophobia, crude race-hate and old-fashioned jingoism, a space was created for new versions of prejudice to grow.

It was not just in Japan that the young sought harder to avoid dirty, dangerous and difficult work, but also across all rich nations. The mass unemployment of the 1930s had resulted in far fewer children being born in these countries at that time. The postwar baby boom was only a boom seen against the backdrop of rapidly declining fertility within rich nations. People were individually becoming more precious in both their attitudes and their rarity. By the 1960s, for the first time in human history, a majority could say no to low-paid work that they did not want to do. But that majority also began to demand new services that required the work of more people than ever before: more health services, more public transport, more shops. The demand for labour grew rapidly.

Within rich nations in the 1950s and 1960s, the demand for labour that was not satisfied internally was partly met by immigration, facilitated, for example, by the slight relaxing of incredibly strict immigration laws in places like Japan. In Europe, the demand was met and not curtailed until the late 1960s. Forewarned, many people came to the UK just before restrictions were increased there in 1965, and others stayed in the UK for fear of not later being allowed to return if they left.[12] Immigration was greatest in the US, where the winning of more civil rights by some black people partly led to the importing of new waves of non-white people to fill in the void that a little emancipation had created, to do the jobs black Americans no longer had to do.

Immigration rates in the US '... began to pick up in the late 1960s, and soared after 1980'.[13] One reason for the soaring migration was rapidly rising inequality within the US which creates many more jobs at the very bottom servicing the rich, cleaning their homes and hotels, caring for their children and elderly; in so many different kinds of ways, being servants. In more equitable rich countries there are far fewer jobs at the bottom to attract in poorer migrants, and those that there are tend to be far better paid and respected so that locals are much happier to carry them out, as can be seen when interviewing office cleaners in Japan, but racism can be stoked up even at times and in places when economic inequalities are low.

In countries like those that make up the UK, anxiety over the arrival of people seen as new, coupled with the growth in want and exclusion for so many who saw themselves as 'indigenous white', was stirred up by racist agitators to incite racist prejudice, particularly from the late 1970s onwards. That agitation is traced back to different times in different places. In Britain in the West Midlands, Conservative MP Enoch Powell made a speech in 1968, since called the 'rivers of blood' speech, in relation to immigration. He said he could see rivers foaming with blood as the British nation heaped 'up its own funeral pyre' by allowing immigration. At the heart of this racism was a bizarre rationalisation of why others should labour in your place, but only just enough others labouring near you to meet what you saw as your personal needs. It was fine for immigrants to run your local corner shop (no one else wanted to work those hours), or be nurses in your local hospital that couldn't function without them. The problem, apparently, was not those immigrants on your doorstep, but the ones running wild in your imagination.

Racism can be an extension of the old rationalisation used by aristocrats to justify their luxurious existence when almost everyone else had to toil. The difference is that a few families were not just applying the justification, but entire social groups began behaving like aristocracy. These groups consist of people who had been taught to think of themselves *as being of* an ethnicity, class, nationality, religion and culture which allow them to feel superior to others. For instance, ideas such as those of Enoch Powell were more favoured by people who were white, upper-working class, Anglo-Saxon,[14] male, English, middle-aged and Protestant.

Enoch Powell had aimed to become Viceroy of all India, and failed. He held aristocratic pretensions.[15] Before his era, the new aristocracy of the first gilded age in the late 19th century had selfishly corralled most of the wealth of an entire empire to be used by just a small proportion of rich families. Their rationalisation that had trickled down from even older aristocratic ideals was as follows: there are different types of people; some are best motivated by being given higher salaries; they deserve good pensions and good health insurance, and their children need expensive education. The highest caste of all requires and deserves the very highest remuneration, including the right to live in luxury in old age, instant attention when ill, the most exclusive schools for its offspring, who in turn are also destined for wonderful futures. Lower castes, this warped logic would suggest, are best motivated by fear. It is essential they be threatened with poverty, or even with the threat of repatriation to poor 'homelands', to ensure that they work hard and do not complain. Such repatriation or deportation could occur if people were found guilty of a criminal offence, for instance, as happens now and as was so often used in the past such as when the Tolpuddle labourers were deported to Australia. How else, aristocrats argued, are we to get people to undertake dirty, dangerous or difficult work and not to unite in common cause?

In the 1970s, the relationship between 'us' and 'them' was questioned much more often than before, but the language that was used was far older. The claims that are made about 'them' are that these lower castes do not need high incomes and the promise of pensions to make them work hard; instead, they only respond to fear; and their children do not need good education because they are not destined for great things. They do not deserve good healthcare when ill, because they are dispensable.

The old social evil of idleness, of mass unemployment in the 1930s, had been used to incite prejudice in Europe earlier. This new injustice was being incited without such dire economic conditions, although unemployment rose again in the 1970s, and the social costs were recognised as being far greater than the economic costs.[16] Living standards for most were still rising, but rose more at the top than the bottom, so that social rank grew again in importance. In this way the overcoming of mass idleness partly precipitated the great postwar rise in prejudice. The most vocal expressions of that prejudice were dampened down after the 1970s. Racist violence, especially murder, was at its peak in the 1960s in the US and in the 1970s in Europe, but is less common now.

High proportions of younger people unequivocally express revulsion at racism today. The older members of the population of affluent nations have been slower to change than the younger, but all are now changing their collective view from the time when prejudice peaked. In the US in 1978, 54 per cent of people said they disapproved of marriages between blacks and whites, some 36 per cent approved and 10 per cent would not say or had no view. By 1991, some 48 per cent approved; by 2002, 65 per cent; by 2007, 77 per cent,[17] and by 2012, 86 per cent.[18] Prejudice rises easily, like anger, but can be dampened down over time. The proportion of North Americans in future who will be found to disapprove of the kind of marriages that resulted in their current president being born will be a telling statistic. But prejudice today is changing; it is less about skin colour and more about suspicions and feelings that there are biological and psychological differences between groups, differences that are more than skin deep. Prejudice is now more about genes than pigment.

5.1 Indenture: labour for miserable reward, a fifth of all adults

How would you answer the following question that is occasionally asked in social surveys: 'Which of these phrases would you say comes closest to your feelings about your household's income these days: Living comfortably, coping, finding it difficult to manage, or finding it very difficult to manage on present income?' Excluding those who responded 'don't know' or who did not answer, Figure 11 shows the typical response to such a question as recorded over the course of about two decades. On average, around a fifth of the population (21 per cent) routinely find it either difficult or very difficult to get by on their incomes. This particular proportion is the figure for Britain; the proportion would almost certainly be higher in the US and much lower in Japan. International statistics are hard to compare, however, as language and meaning varies so greatly. 'Finding it difficult to manage' is a very British euphemism for not managing. Among those doing better than this, almost half the population in Britain described their situation as coping but would not go as far as to say they were living comfortably.

In all affluent countries, governments do not like to admit how hard most households find it to 'get by'. Members of the governing party in Britain took great pride in pointing out how, just before the economic collapse, the share who appeared to be finding managing most

Figure 11: Households' ability to get by on their income in Britain, two decades before the crash, 1984–2004

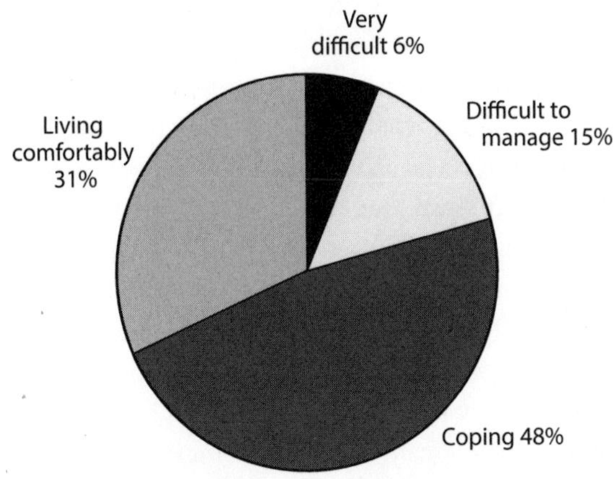

Note: Respondents were asked 'Which of the (above) phrases comes closest to your feelings about your household's income these days?'. Excludes those who did not answer.

Source: Derived from ONS (2006) *Social Trends (No 36)*, London: Palgrave Macmillan, table 5.15, p 78, mean of 1984, 1994 and 2004 surveys.

Perceptions of the economic climate after the crash, in 2009, by income, UK (%)

	Less than £20,000	£20k-£40k	£40k-£60k	£60k-£100k	£100k+	All individuals
The economic situation in the world:						
Good or very good	6	3	2	1	0	4
Neither good or bad	17	18	12	8	8	16
Bad or very bad	77	79	85	91	92	80
The economic situation in the UK:						
Good or very good	8	5	4	4	0	6
Neither good or bad	17	15	13	4	11	15
Bad or very bad	76	80	83	92	89	80
The financial situation in your household:						
Good or very good	28	44	54	64	63	40
Neither good or bad	47	42	35	36	34	43
Bad or very bad	25	14	11	1	3	18

Source: 2009 Survey of Public Attitudes and Behaviours towards the Environment, Department for Environment, Food and Rural Affairs – collected February–March, ONS 2012, *Social Trends 41*, *Income and Wealth*, Table 1.

difficult was falling, and the number of those who said they were living comfortably was rising.[19] These figures were published in 2006 in the official publication *Social Trends* (No 36). The following year *Social Trends* (No 37) showed how those gains had been achieved by borrowing. Total lending in Britain had, we later found out, peaked in 2004 (Figure 6.13 in *Social Trends*, No 37). Personal insolvencies were rising exponentially by 2004 (Figure 6.14 in *Social Trends*, No 37). The next year, *Social Trends* (No 38) revealed that even the wealthiest, those who had property they could borrow against, had managed to be comfortable by often borrowing yet more money against their property. This was then called 'equity withdrawal' and it was responsible for over 8 per cent of all personal income in Britain by 2004 (according to Figure 6.14, *Social Trends*, No 38)! Again, the peak had been in 2004, but it was not obvious until 2008 that even the wealthy had been increasing their borrowing to maintain their comfortable lifestyles. In hindsight, even the minority who said they were living comfortably were often doing so partly by borrowing more.

The last printed edition of *Social Trends,* the 40th, was published in 2010 – the incoming coalition government cut its funding. An online version of the 41st, cut-back, report was produced, however, which revealed that 80 per cent of people thought the economic situation in the UK was bad or very bad, while 18 per cent thought their own was that bad and only 40 per cent of people in the UK described their household's financial situation as good or very good. Of households with an income of over £100,000 a year, only 63 per cent described their own financial situation as good or very good! Households earning between £60,000 and £99,000 a year were more likely to say they were doing well and three times *less likely* to say that things were hard as compared to the richest as revealed by the statistics in the table below Figure 11).[20]

By 2014, the Joseph Rowntree Foundation was reporting that the UK labour market had 'completely changed' in a very short period of time. Many people were doing any job they could do. The employment rate for women had never been higher, and for men it was nearly the highest it had ever been, probably because: 'Average weekly earnings have risen more slowly than prices every month since 2010',[21] and benefits were now so low. People were becoming desperate. The proportion of British households who owed at least £5,000 more than the combined value of all the assets they had rose from 9 to 12 per cent between 2008 and 2012.[22] By 2014, we no longer asked people if they were living comfortably or coping in the UK in government surveys.

No rest

Borrowing money to maintain a comfortable lifestyle is far from good, but that luxury is not even imaginable for those who are finding it difficult or very difficult to get by, those who are doing worse than just coping. For the fifth that are not managing, debt is a necessity just in order to keep going, not as a means to maintain living in even mild luxury. It is this fifth who have the fewest real choices in life in Britain and similar countries. They have few choices over what kind of work they do, and usually take any job they can get. Having to do a job that you can get but would not choose to do is as demoralising as being indentured to labour for a fixed term to pay off debts (although in the latter case, at least the term of indenture tends to be known). In the past, indentured labour was usually reserved for people thought of as being a different racial group to those who employed them. Today we tolerate the equivalent of indenture, many people having no choice over what job, or type of job, they can get, no choice over how much they can earn and over getting into debt, because enough of us still see others as sufficiently different, akin to racially different, to not deserve anything better. In rich countries, for a fifth of the population to be failing to manage is unjust. It is unnecessary to have less than a third able to say that they are living comfortably.

Being unable to manage in 21st-century Britain usually involves being unable to 'rest', including being unable to have an annual holiday. Rest has meant different things at different times. From ancient times, where Abrahamic religions dominate, a day of rest has been called a Sabbath, and it occurs every seven days. Outside that world, rest days and feast days have been just as plentiful if a little differently spaced out. For instance, the ancient Chinese week was 10 days long.[23]

Weeks were invented when rest had to be scheduled in. Now, in much of the rich world, a fifth of households are unable to take a rest day. That is, they cannot take the modern-day Sabbath, a seventh day of rest. This has very little to do with not working on Sundays, but has a lot to do with having a day off a week from worry, shopping, household maintenance and work-related stress. It is still essential to be able to rest, relax, not to be worried all the time about 'getting by'. Those who cannot rest in their minds can be seen not just through the proportions who say they cannot manage, but as overlapping greatly with the fifth of people highlighted in Chapter 4 of this volume, who have to toil and struggle, for seven days, to receive what another fifth are awarded for just a single day's labour. Given the contemporary cultural dominance worldwide of the seven-day week, it is now at the precise point where that seventh day has to be sacrificed, cannot be enjoyed and cannot be used for rest, that basic common choices in life disappear most clearly.

From country to country, the proportion of households that cannot afford a seventh day of rest varies. In Britain, it is the worst-off fifth that must get by on only a seventh of the income of the best-off fifth. In the US, even more of the population live such lives. In mainland Europe, fewer people have to toil so long; and in Japan, even less. The overall rich world average can be assumed to be about a fifth being unable to mentally rest because they are finding it difficult or very difficult to get by. Invariably people in this fifth will be much more likely to be identified as members of those racial groups that are most discriminated against: more will be women; children are disproportionately born into households in this fifth; and adults more often fall into this fifth on having children. These become households whose time and labour are now, for all real purposes, indentured. This indenture is not just of those able to sell their labour, but also of those whose labour in caring for children or others is given no employment value, or those too old or sick to work whose labour is in looking after themselves but who still cannot manage to get by despite qualifying for a pension or an allowance. By 2014, the OECD was reporting that within most of its 34 member states, inequalities had grown so that the best-off tenth of individuals now receive on average 9.5 times what the poorest tenth received in any country; 30 years earlier that individual level ratio had been 7:1. That ratio is now as high at 16:1 in the US, 27:1 in Mexico and 30:1 in Chile.[24]

False promises

In the past, indentured debt might have been the cost of passage to the Americas, or the supposed cost of forcible deportation to Australia, in the case of convicts. The indentured are by definition not free to stop working, but also by definition, their children will not be indentured, and so they differ from slaves in this respect. They themselves were told that after a number of years they would be free, and usually they were freed on time. Today's indentured labourers are more fortunate in that the alternative to work is not starvation or the workhouse, but they are not so fortunate in other ways. They are given a more vague promise of future emancipation for good behaviour. They are led to believe that they will be free eventually from their irksome existence, and that if their life is lived with little in the way of choice or hope – on benefits or in low-paid work – the lives of their children will be more fortunate as a result of their pliant behaviour. This is turning out to have been a false promise.

Today's indentured labourers in affluent countries are not described as such and are not formally indentured; often they are not even in paid employment but indentured to benefits. They are, however, often in debt. What sets them apart is that their choices in life are so limited. Those in work have not chosen their work but are compelled to work out of fear of poverty. Similarly, those reliant on social security do not, as is sometimes fictionally portrayed, choose such a life willingly. There is no great mass of feckless people who want to be living on the basics of social security, or in very lowly paid work in preference to having choices. No one rationally chooses to live on the miserliness of sickness benefits because they see it as a good living. All these people are in a variety of ways indentured because they have little or no choice, and they are not happy with their fate.

Young mothers do not become pregnant because the social security benefits are so wonderful. Teenage pregnancies are highest in those affluent countries where benefit rates are lowest, where inequalities are greatest, where there is less money to 'be made' from having a baby.[25] Teenagers and other mothers, often young ones, are most likely to have to give their children up for adoption in those affluent countries where social benefits are worse.[26] Elsewhere, teenagers and young adults simply choose, and are better placed to be able to choose, to have children less often. Teenage pregnancy rates are lowest in the most equal of rich nations, such as Japan, Sweden, the Netherlands, Denmark, Spain, Finland, Belgium, France, Norway, Germany and Austria. These are also places where getting a university degree is simply getting a degree – not about amassing great debt or worrying about the status of where you study In the more equitable countries of the rich world, who has babies young and who doesn't is far less predictable by class, and overall, far fewer from any social group will become young parents.[27]

What today's indentured have is a curtailment of all kinds of choices. The majority who work have little choice over the work they do, or whether to work. Within indentured households, most of those who do not work are children, the sick, carers, or pensioners. The indentured have very little choice over where they live, which city they inhabit, even the home they occupy. In countries with social housing they are allocated their place in a block; in countries without such housing the free market directs them towards 'skid row'. Their children then usually have no choice over their education. They have to go to school where others choose not to – choice for some reduces choice for others.

Contemporary indentured labourers in affluent societies owe their debts to car loans, clothing catalogues and other credit companies and to those debt-collectors to whom debts are sold on following initial defaulting. The indentured may be in arrears on their rent, on their mortgage, on paying their utility bills, on the taxes they owe local government, on loans arranged through banks that up until 2008 were more and more relaxed over lending, with poorly regulated payday loans and illegal loan sharks for the poorest. These indentured are often in default on hire purchase agreements, even on court orders to pay a fine for not having a licence to watch their television. They have all manner of ways in which they can be in debt, no longer owing to a single creditor, but usually owing to numerous faceless creditors. They owe because their incomes are insufficient to support their outgoings, outgoings needed to preserve basic dignity in the countries where they live, countries where it has become acceptable to string people out along a widening and ever more skewed curve of reward, creating many losers towards the bottom. Many losers are required to pay for (and service) every new winner given a place at the top, and winners are expensive to support.

The indentured are treated so badly because a powerful minority have come to believe that these are people who do not deserve more. Just as women were allowed to vote only when a majority of powerful enough people came to believe that they should vote and deserved the vote, just as slavery was only formally abolished when the majority of the powerful minority deemed it right, just as children and older people were not required to work once such enforced labour was deemed wrong, so, too, modern indenture, people having to undertake work with no other option, will continue to be tolerated, even justified, until it is seen as intolerable. The various justifications begin by suggesting that if ending slavery, or introducing female emancipation, or reducing child labour, or introducing pensions, begins in one place, then that place will suffer economic loss. It simply isn't 'economic', such an argument claims, for there not to be slaves, for people not to be forced to undertake work they would otherwise not choose to do. When it is suggested that all could be paid a living wage in affluent countries, so that only those who freely chose to undertake undesirable work do so,[28] perhaps by being paid more to carry out unpopular work, the question of economic expense is raised to make such a prospect appear impossible, just as the idea of paying slaves was once an anathema.

To defend it, modern indenture requires more than just an appeal to strange notions of affordability. Something becomes easily more unaffordable when it does not apply to you personally. Slavery is defensible only when slaves can be painted as racially different;[29] this included Celts in Icelandic antiquity, blacks in recent American history, some indigenous Indians in Brazil today, and women almost everywhere until very recently. The denial of women's liberties is only possible if you can persuade men that their mothers, sisters and daughters are less deserving than their fathers, brothers and sons. Child and old age labour requires us to forget our beginnings and not to try to imagine our dotage. Modern indenture requires us to see having no choice over what work is on offer as being the fate of others in our affluent countries, those whom we imagine have less ability.

The undeserving

A myth of our times is that people fall to the bottom because they are undeserving (lazy), and that they probably also lack the inherent ability to ever do much better. This myth is being questioned. People now know not to express such thoughts out loud in polite company, but they express them instead indirectly, in ways that clearly betray their prejudice. The clues can be found in what they expect others to do for them that they would not do in return. This is the prejudice of believing that you and yours are so special that you deserve greatness, and that greatness will by default necessitate the indenture of others to provide the kinds of services and lifestyle that you and yours 'deserve'. The social security benefits of others have to be kept low to keep them in fear of not toiling, so as not to reward sloth, and because you and your family supposedly deserve so much and do not want to be taxed more.

It is always hard to draw the line at what is an unreasonable request to make of others, but everyone has a line in their mind. Few believe that royal butlers should be required to dress the heir to the throne each morning, as Prince Charles apparently is dressed. Such behaviour comes from a different era, but what about more common 'services'? The kinds of service those who are prejudiced may believe they deserve range from the making of the beds they sleep in, to having their children looked after by others, to having drinks made for them and served on a silver tray. Almost everyone is capable of making their own bed, childcare is done best when shared among the parents of children, and serving family and friends with drink yourself is far more fun and less likely to result in over-indulgence than taking glasses from the tray of a waiter at some 'function'. In the past, most children did the same work as their parents, but one of the very few occupations that children rarely followed their parents into was working in service. If former chambermaids, nannies and butlers impressed one thing on their own offspring, it was not to follow them into serving others in the same way.

Spending time with children and with your older relatives can be the best of times, although you often do not realise it until they are gone.[30] Privatise child and elderly care, and then time spent with children and the elderly becomes seen as a burden. Care workers for older people are the largest least well-paid group in most affluent societies, because we don't value caring as a skill, and we don't generally like to be reminded of our own mortality. Carers are taught through their hours, wages and conditions of labour how little in turn we value older people. Most care workers do not choose to end up working in old age care homes; they simply cannot get any other work. When it was suggested that immigration controls in Britain be tightened after the economic crash so that care workers could only be imported if they were subsequently paid wages higher than the minimum, the care home owners lamented that they would never find enough willing staff locally who could live off the minimum wage, even under conditions of mass unemployment. Few people bring up their children in rich countries today to hope that one day they might grow up to be able to work in an old age care home.

It need not be like this. Care work could be a respected job, an admired job, a well-paid job in a rich country. The rich choose for that not to be. They want many of these jobs done, but they want them done on the cheap, and they don't respect those who do them. They talk of efficiency savings. However, it is grossly inefficient to have people so well-off that they buy goods and services that they don't need; it is not efficient to have many people permanently exhausted and demoralised because they are paid so little and end up working such long hours when added to the hours of unpaid work that many of those care workers have to do when they get home.

In a grossly unequal society there are many jobs that most people would never believe their children would be lucky enough to hold. These are jobs that most people are told that their children are not capable of aspiring to. Remarkably, these very same 'unachievable' jobs are, from even higher perches of privilege, seen as far too lowly to undertake. Thus, the dream jobs of some are the nightmare drudgery of others. In Britain, the former Prime Minister, Tony Blair, is said by Robin Cook to have sent his children to selective schools because he did not want them *merely* to become school headteachers or university professors, jobs he considered unworthy of his progeny.[31] These were the kinds of jobs secured by the offspring of another former Labour Prime Minister, Harold Wilson. Tony Blair thought his children were deserving of, capable of, entitled to, more. When people like Tony Blair think like this, and ensure that low wages remain low by not raising the minimum wage sufficiently, it is hardly surprising that the message percolates down, that to work in a care home for older people is to have failed. The message also percolates up, that if a Labour Prime Minister can act like this, then when a Liberal Democrat or Conservative leader behaves in a similar way, they are simply behaving 'normally'. It becomes normal to be elitist.

Work harder!

Across the rich world, at the end of the last gilded age, aristocratic dynasties slowly crumbled in Europe following all the deaths of the First World War; robber baron[32] wealth in the US was decimated in the 1930s and began to be redistributed in the 1940s; aristocracy was dismantled in Japan following the Second World War; social rank and religious caste slowly and steadily fell in importance over the entire period from 1929 through to 1973. From 1950 to 1973 across all OECD nations, the length of the average working week fell by half a day, so those at the bottom were permitted to toil less; their fears of poverty were reduced as social security was improved and it became possible to take more rest; all became slightly more equal.[33] Then, with a little help from renewed prejudices, most of the economic gains began to be reversed from around 1973,[34] and by 2007 people were again working longer hours than they had been working in 1950. However, they have not produced as much in those hours in recent years. Just as slavery and exploiting women, children and older people have been found to have been inefficient in the past as a means of creating a good life – even for the few – so too is indenture inefficient today.

US productivity per worker hour fell by half between 1973 and the mid-1990s,[35] not because people were working fewer hours, but because more were working longer hours less effectively at more demeaning, dirty, often more pointless and sometimes simply more dangerous and difficult jobs, such as 'security', which had been so much less prevalent in the past. And all for lower real wages than most of their parents had worked for. They had become, in all but name, indentured.

Workers could be more often indentured by the 1990s because compared with the 1970s they were so much more looked down on. Often workloads were increased with no extra pay. This was called efficiency savings, their jobs were devalued, and simultaneously they became less respected and lost status. With high levels of unemployment and reduced trade union muscle, the workers could do little about it. Although needed, many found themselves despised at work and struggling to cope at home. The new prejudice had created vast new gross injustices.

The new prejudice against the poor grew slowly in the early 1970s. The early symptoms of rising prejudice can be seen in both the Adam Smith Institute in Britain and the Heritage Foundation in the US, both created in 1973 with donations from rich individuals and remits to promote policies which have, in hindsight, been seen to have fostered prejudice against the poor so effectively that it became normalised. Those rich donors only donated when they did because they thought the wider public were becoming too keen on ideals of equality – what they saw as market 'solutions' were being squeezed out. They were so successful that ideas of elitism and a new tolerance of exclusion flourished. It grew strong enough for what they proclaimed, what appeared at first to be unjustified, to quickly begin to appear justifiable again. By 2011, it became possible for Owen Jones to pen a bestseller about the process: *Chavs: The demonization of the working class*. Owen himself was then constantly ridiculed by the right wing, but he fought back with arguments full of facts and passion and then, in 2014, published an exposé, *The establishment: And how they get away with it.*

The new injustices that result from a rise in prejudice did not fall solely on the poorest in rich societies. In the US, the greatest increase in hours worked has been for those married couple households where both adults had a university degree.[36] Between 1968 and 2000 in the US, the average weekly number of hours spent in paid work by parents in households with children rose from 53 to 64.[37] Similarly in Britain, working hours increased most for some of the more highly paid. All those in work laboured (on mean average) an additional 130 minutes a week by 2001 compared with 1991.[38] Comparing 1981 and 1998, there was an increase of some 7.6 weeks paid work a year in households where at least one adult was in employment.[39] In the US in the 2000s, some two to three months more time in paid employment a year was being spent by adults compared with the 1960s, and people were, overall, worse off! A large part of this increase was due to more women being in paid work without any great reduction in the number of men in paid work. Fewer women 'staying at home', although partly due to emancipation, was largely due to the felt need for a second wage earner. Few of the new jobs were so desirable that you would do them even if you didn't need the money.

When a fifth face modern indenture, many more than a fifth face a curtailing of their choices, such as the choice to work fewer hours. They work harder to attempt to avoid indenture. People begin to complain of not being able to work more hours, of having part-time work or zero hours contracts, because so much work now pays so badly. Only 1 in 40 of the net increase of supposedly a million jobs created in the UK between 2008 and 2014 were full-time, 24 out of 40 were self-employed work, the rest were part-time.[40] A majority of people do not do the extra work they are now engaged in out of choice. They are not indentured, they have some choices and crucially, they are not finding it 'difficult' or 'very difficult' to get by when asked, but they are less free.

Most jobs remain mundane and boring. Most jobs held by people with university degrees now involve much drudgery, such as too much 'paperwork'. People today work longer hours in rich countries because they feel they have to. The poor have to because the minimum wage in countries like the US fell in real terms so sharply from the end of the 1960s that they became indentured. The more affluent feel they have to work longer hours than their parents did because as the poor become indentured, it becomes ever more important not to have to live like or live near the poor, and that costs money.

In the US, where the need to labour just to survive is greatest, over a quarter of the young elderly, people aged 65–69, undertake paid work simply to get by, as do a sixth of those aged 70–74. In the EU, less than a tenth of the young elderly continued to work before 2008, and few aged 70–74 worked, but the numbers have risen since the great recession took hold.

Because opportunities for tertiary education for the poor are so curtailed and benefits so low (or non-existent) in many US states, less qualified people will take any job offered; almost half of young adults aged 15–24 are in paid employment in the US, compared with less than a third of that group in the EU, even now when the definition is expanded to include most of Eastern Europe.[41] In Japan, the proportions in work as young adults or when elderly are much lower again. Different groups of affluent countries have chosen different courses to take; within each, different prejudices have been allowed to rise while others have been curtailed. And on top of all this, all affluent nations have been adversely affected by the crash that has most damaged the prospects and circumstances of the young.

5.2 Darwinism: thinking that different incentives are needed

When we compare with today the apparent freedom that people in rich countries had to work fewer hours in the 1960s, the freedom to 'tell their boss to shove it' (US) or 'pack their job in' (UK) if they did not like it and take another under conditions of near *real* full employment and choice, it is easy to see why modern indenture has increased. The choices of most have been reduced and the choices of a few constrained to almost no choice. This required a change in what we collectively came to believe was possible. We did not lose that world of choice overnight, and it was largely a world of choice only for men. But from almost all walks of life men could have a choice as to how they laboured in the 1960s in affluent countries. The main exceptions to this were the grandchildren of slaves in the US, where the legacy of slavery and the prejudice that legacy carried meant that more options were curtailed if you were black.

It is very simple to show that the choices of all but a tiny few have been curtailed, with that curtailment rising from the early 1970s onwards. Increasingly, choice comes in a simple form, money; it tends to be coloured green if printed on paper, silver or gold if minted, but more and more frequently the ticket that allows choice is a small piece of plastic that, if affluent, you pass to the waiter at the end of your meal, the plastic which, for instance, you use to pay for your hotel room and the right to have others clean up after you, the plastic that pays for holidays, the new car, the new kitchen and for those weekends of shopping. As incomes and wealth have polarised, so, too, has choice. Increasing the affluence of rich people means more nights that can be spent away from home in a hotel, as more hotels are built. But it is impossible to have more hotel beds without more bed makers, room cleaners, and even wine waiters.

As a small group of very rich people becomes even richer, each such affluent household buys more luxury objects such as more expensive new cars that require far greater labour than cheaper cars to make. These have to be made, serviced and cleaned, and so more production line workers, mechanics and valets are required. A luxury lifestyle implies wanting more servants, wanting more people to do jobs you would not want your children to do, and wanting them to be paid as little as possible to do them. A luxury lifestyle creates poverty. If the affluent replace their kitchens more often, they require more joiners, electricians and plasterers, and more rubbish collectors to take away the old kitchen. In the recent past you might have acquired a new cooker, but the concept of getting a new kitchen had not been invented – as far as most people in rich countries were concerned, you incrementally improved the old one.

Huge numbers of extra shop assistants are required if much more shopping is to be possible, more shelf stackers, shop security guards and so on. One economist estimates that by 2005, one in four Americans were employed purely to guard the wealth of the rich in one way or another: 'America employs more private security guards than high-school teachers.'[42] But it did not have to be quite this way, and in most other affluent countries most people get to use their labour for a slightly greater good than most in the US or the UK. There are fewer demeaning jobs and fewer low-paid workers in Japan, Norway, Germany, Denmark, Switzerland and the Netherlands.

The curtailing of choices that came with rising income and wealth inequalities also resulted in the revival of old ways of justifying such inequalities. When social inequalities were high in Victorian Britain, Charles Darwin's novel ideas of evolution were drawn on to try to justify the enormous wealth gaps. The rich were painted as the 'fittest', people who had survived most successfully, their pedigrees outlined on family trees that stretched back at least to the Plantagenets in the case of the few who owned the most land. These were those few families mostly descended (via the Angevin dynasties and the Houses of Anjou) from the Normans who seized land in England after 1066 and still held a tenth of all land in Britain by 2006. Many may have married into the new rich of Victorian industrial families to maintain their status, but it was not those sides of their families which were most celebrated when family trees of human 'pedigree' were being drawn up, documents proving how they came from 'good stock', from royal blood or from some of the families which are more established and ancient than the royal family itself.

Opposing multiculturalism

After the Second World War and the holocaust, racism was denounced, as in the UNESCO's anti-racist statement in 1950: 'For all practical social purposes "race" is not so much a biological phenomenon as a social myth. The myth of "race" has created an enormous amount of human and social damage. In recent years, it has taken a heavy toll in human lives, and caused untold suffering.'[43] However, across Europe and the Americas and throughout Japan, from the 1970s onwards, scientific racism rose again. When the rich once again became very rich, joined by a few newcomers, but mostly from the old families, the old ideas of survival, self-advancement and supremacy of the supposed fittest again rose to power, and the opposition to the growth of racism from those in power became muted in the 1970s.

It was not just because Margaret Thatcher wanted to deny the National Front votes that she used the term 'swamping' in relation to immigrants on television in 1978; it is that she believed then what she said, that: '… we must hold out the clear prospect of an end to immigration … [because] … We are a British nation with British characteristics.'[44] That racism, and its new wider face of prejudice, fitted the revived Darwinian rhetoric too well to be too strongly opposed.

The racism that arose newly emboldened in the 1970s came with a nationalist twist, which was to see countries as natural units and to suggest that those which were supposedly home to a single racial group tended to be happy places to live, where people got on with one another. Those portrayed as having had groups brought together, new groups brought in, tended more often to be places of strife, mistrust and inequality. Opponents of multiculturalism suggested that inequality was the natural consequence of trying to mix people together who do not easily mix. By this way of thinking, the social problems of the US became the problems of dealing with black people. The US could never aim to be as equal as Europe, to have the kind of healthcare systems Europeans have, to have such widespread and respected state schooling as Europeans, because (so this misguided argument goes) the US is not a naturally homogeneous society – the US, by this prejudicial way of thinking, is said to lack 'ethnic homogeneity'. This way of thinking and of describing the world is now said to hardly deserve a response by people who look into others' psychological flaws.[45] But it is worth thinking about where this thinking came from, and what it leads to, especially as such thinking is at the core of much current racist ideology.

To be able to describe a country or a city as ethnically heterogeneous requires thinking of the different residents of that place as belonging to a myriad of different ethnic/racial groups. It is possible to describe almost any place as being made up of a myriad of different racial groups. A university campus can often by typified in this way, but it isn't, because the students have more in common as students than they have differences due to ethnic background. You could describe the people of a major city in a country like Greece as coming from a huge variety of backgrounds because it is near the crossroads of continents, but national identity and a national orthodox religion are often stressed, rather than the huge variety of hair and skin tones of the population – these are usually simply not remarked on. A similar situation occurs in London where a majority of the mothers of newborn infants were themselves born abroad, but where this great mix of people also have a huge amount in common. When people have much in common, they are described using a common term, such as being all 'students', or all 'Greeks', or even all 'Londoners'. Where identity is less shared, lives less similar, opportunities and outcomes far more constrained by skin tone or family history, then the people in that place are more often called, for example, white, Hispanic, black or Asian, broken down into ethnic classifications.

A homogeneous ethnicity, the idea of a common identity, is created by how aspirations and beliefs are described. In 2014 in the UK, despite a long-term fall in racism, there was a 55 per cent increase in religious hate crimes in that year as the politics of identity turned nasty.[46] It is remarkably simple to turn politics nasty by 'playing the race card', as occurred across Europe at that time,[47] and remarkably easy to also forget how different politics can be. Ten years earlier, in 2004, one of the Swedish political parties wrote in its election material that '… everyone is fragile at some point in time. All Swedes need each other. All live their lives in the here and now, together with others, caught up in the midst of change. All will be richer if all of us are allowed to participate and nobody is left out. All will be stronger if there is security for everybody and not only for a few.'[48] Of course, there is much racism in Sweden, however; where some people are not recognised as Swedes and the far right Swedish

'Democrat' Party secured one in seven seats in Parliament in the 2014 parliamentary elections.

Elsewhere in Scandinavia, in Denmark, in an argument that is as much about countering racism directed towards Muslims as it is about class, it is suggested that the population cannot afford not to be egalitarian, not just out of idealism, but because securing continuous improvement in human lives and ability is vital to the economy. Minimisation of poverty and insecurity is a precondition for effective social investment. A commitment to social citizenship, pooling risks collectively, is essential to successful 21st-century living.[49] A group of people comes to have a common ethnicity not just by having an identity thrust on them, but by also creating one through working for a common identity.

If those working for solidarity within Scandinavian countries win, then the homogeneous ethnic image of Scandinavia that is presented will change, become a little less white, more homogeneous. If they lose, then it will be said that there are distinct different and separate ethnicities there, heterogeneity. However, whatever transpires, neither scenario will completely encapsulate the case. In 2014, the far-right Danish People's Party secured over a quarter of the vote in the European elections and entered an alliance with the far-right British Conservatives. The UK Conservatives were themselves facing new competition from the even further right-wing UKIP, a party bolstered by fears of what they called immigration, by which they meant 'people not like you'.

Both ethnic heterogeneity and homogeneity are myths. Heterogeneity as a useful concept is a myth because we almost all live in heterogeneous communities; it is just that we often do not recognise that. Our communities are also not ethnically homogeneous because people are not more predisposed to mix better with others of similar skin tone or hairstyle. People are predisposed to mix better with those who society has made them most likely to mix with. Thus university students will mix on campus with other university students far more readily than they will tend to mix with poorer local young adults, even of their exact age and exact skin tone.

One reason some university students, and especially postgraduate students, don't mix with those who don't go to university is money. Former undergraduates tend to earn much more in the jobs they secure than people who did not go to university, and former postgraduates even more, but that is now likely to quickly change. By 2013, it was estimated that in the UK, 'Somebody with a Master's can on average expect to earn £5,500 more a year – or £200,000 over a 40 year working life – than someone only holding a Bachelor's degree. In the US, the annual premium is almost twice as high – $16,500 (£10,300).'[50] Of course that will not be the case in the future, as so many more young people will have postgraduate qualifications, but it was the case until recently, and that helps explain the lack of mixing by class and education.[51] It is money, not skin colour, which separates us.

Two people in a city in Greece will mix, regardless of their skin tone and hair colour, and even religion, more easily if their families are of similar social status, as in Greece, as elsewhere in the rich world, people tend to marry within social classes more even than within religious groups. There is more division between rich and poor than between Orthodox and Catholic, Christian and Muslim, Abrahamic and Dharmic. Where income, wealth and class differences are narrower, such as in Greece (when compared with, say, Portugal), people are a little freer to marry whom they like, because more are of a similar social class.

It is in countries of great income and wealth inequalities that there is more disapproval of certain groups within that country marrying: whites and blacks in the US, Christians and Muslims in Singapore, Dalits and Brahmins in India. In countries with far lower inequalities, membership of an ethnic, religious or caste group is much less of an issue, and also less likely. It is less likely because in more equitable countries more ethnic mixing has already happened, religion is less prescribed, the people have become less clearly defined, and castes cannot mean so much.

Racial purity

Children will mix with other children who live nearby if allowed out of their homes to do so. They will live near a greater mix of children in those countries where people are less scared of each other. In a country that is far more tolerant of what is seen as inter-racial mixing, there will be far more inter-racial mixing. This is far from obvious when, as often happens in such countries, almost everyone comes to be defined as of a single race and most as of a single class (such as the Japanese middle class). In a very different country, like the US, where such mixing was until recent generations proclaimed as evil, in schools, in bed, even on the same seats on buses, there will be less mixing still.

Mixing of those seen as different occurs most where people have been given a huge variety of racial and ethnic labels and have been put in very close proximity to each other at relatively young ages, especially in a place where housing is so expensive, and commuting so tricky that people have to live in whatever home they can afford, which is as near to their commuter routes as possible. Thus London is a good place for mixing. Londoners call themselves Londoners, often in preference to British, and certainly in preference to English, because no other word describes the mix. It is not solely because they live in London.[52] A Parisian is more likely to say they are French than identify first with Paris, and the English word for someone from Tokyo is so rarely used that you are unlikely to have ever heard it. But you know a New Yorker when you meet one (or you soon get to know they are from New York)! Thus a place defined as heterogeneous, like London or New York, is homogeneous.

Ethnic homogeneity is almost always a myth that is easily exposed. The supposedly homogeneous group can be found, after a little digging, to have a wide variety of origins, being made up of a collection of people with a far wider range of backgrounds than the myth would suggest. Scandinavian stories of the good of the many outweighing the selfish intent of the few can sometimes come also with the downside of invoking the myth of ethnic homogeneity, and then suffering from the danger of excluding those seen as outsiders, those less Scandinavian than others.

Iceland is a good example of homogenising Norse mythology, a far flung island where the myth of the supposed purity of its Nordic race, the descendants of Vikings, gained credence over generations of morale-boosting storytelling in an otherwise very beautiful but very cold, desolate and, until recently, extremely poor place. Genetic testing of the ethnic origins of Icelanders reveals that the Viking past of their island resulted in a somewhat less pure Nordic bloodline than the stories suggest. The Vikings were generally successful at what they did. That is why they are remembered. A large part of what they did was to take slaves from places like Britain, mainly Celtic slaves. And, like all groups who take slaves, they mixed with their slaves, but this wasn't talked of in their stories. We know they mixed because the evidence is in their, as it turns out, very heterogeneous genes.[53]

A similar story to the Scandinavian homogeneity myths can be told anywhere where such claims are made other than for the most isolated of Amazonian tribes. The more preposterous claims are rarely entertained nowadays, such as the claim that the Greeks of today are largely the direct descendants of the Greeks of antiquity. A few Greeks will, of course, be descended from an Ancient Greek man who is still remembered today, but they will also be the descendants of many more former slaves than that one famous man (let's call him Aristotle), and most people in Greece are descended mostly from people who lived outside Greece. It is worth remembering that just seven generations back, less than 200 years, you have over a hundred ancestors, and each one of them will have.... Of course, your ancestry is very mixed.

In contrast to Greece, in places where people have been more physically isolated by oceans from others, it has been easier to sustain myths of racial homogeneity, as in the case of Iceland. Some claim that being part of a small population aids homogeneity, but large populations can also be presented as homogeneous. Population size is no barrier to myth making. For instance, the Japanese population is usually presented to itself as at least as ethnically homogeneous as the Icelandic population. Immigration from the Philippines, Korea, China and elsewhere, past and present, is seen as minor and to have somehow disappeared without effect. Internal identities such as those of the *Yanato*, *Ainu* and the *Uchinan-chu* (the islanders of Okinawa), or of those living within the enclaves of Tokyo and Osaka, the differences you can see if you wish to imagine them in people's faces, are all rendered imaginary by the myth of the homogeneity of the Japanese.

The reason why it is possible to promulgate myths of racial homogeneity on islands such as those of Japan and Iceland is that in both, income inequalities and hence social differences are among the lowest in the rich world. On each island the poorest fifth receive just under a third of what the richest fifth receive in income a year.[54] In contrast, on islands such as Singapore, New Zealand and Britain, where inequalities are much wider, ethnicity is seen to matter much more. You might say that the visual indicators of ethnicity are clearer on these other islands, but what constitutes a difference to your eye depends on what you see as a difference in your mind, and that depends on what you have been brought up to view as a significant visual difference. Do singer Björk

Guðmundsdóttir and presenter Magnús Magnússon appear especially visually similar to you, or former Prime Minister Junichiro Koizumi and artist Yoko Ono? I have not picked these pairs because they look so different. I have picked them because they are probably among the best-known faces from the islands they were born in. Of course they look no more similar or dissimilar than any pair of famous Malay or Chinese faces from Singapore, *Maori* or *Pakeha* from New Zealand.

Survival of the fittest

What is common to both homogeneity and heterogeneity myths are new forms of social Darwinism. Social Darwinism grew strong about a century ago, suggesting that in humans there is a survival of the individually fittest, that this is a good thing, and that it can be accelerated for the common good. The truth is that there is no such natural process occurring with every single generation, although there is an enhanced potential for survival of the most sociable in normal times of sociability, and of the most selfish only in times of extreme scarcity and anarchy. Species occasionally mutate, but human beings are a very young species and remarkably genetically similar to each other as a result. Mainly other factors affect the numbers who die at younger ages. For humans, being ostracised by society is usually deadly – humans survive and prosper best in groups. The awful situations where only the 'fittest', or to describe them more accurately, the 'fortunate', survive are massacres, famines or genocide, such as the huge death toll that occurred during the mass transportation of slaves from Africa to the Americas.

Belief in social Darwinism and its precursors resulted in killing and ending bloodlines, not just through genocide, but also in the imposition of sterilisation on huge numbers of people. You usually only sterilise people you see as not being like you, but looking at who has been sterilised in human history you can see where and when ideas of social Darwinism took hold most strongly. Most large-scale genocide and almost all mass sterilisations in human history have occurred within living memory. Between the 1930s and 1970s, some 60,000 legal but coerced sterilisations were carried out in the US of 'undesirables'; over the same time span, 600,000 were carried out in Germany, mostly at the start of this period, of 'the unfit'.[55] Poorer Indians were the targets of the bulk of postwar sterilisation when millions were sterilised with bribes financed by monies coming mostly from the US and the UK;[56] at the time of writing (this second edition in 2014), the most recent reports of sterilisation are from Kenya within the last decade, and cases of 300,000 women being coerced into sterilisation in Peru in the 1990s are also only now emerging.[57]

Coerced sterilisation was not uncommon in the post-Second World War rich world. In Sweden and Japan in particular, both places suffering from the homogeneity myth, such sterilisation was common right through to the 1970s. By then it was mainly forced on those considered 'undesirable', people seen as 'mentally retarded' or suffering epilepsy, for instance; elsewhere in the world the targeting was wider, and the purpose more overt. In the 1980s in Singapore, an island that had become newly rich, a sterilisation scheme was introduced where the poor, mostly identified with one ethnic group, were offered money to be sterilised, while the rich, from another group, were offered tax breaks to have children.[58] Worldwide rates of sterilisation did not peak until 1983, when 20 million people, mostly women, were sterilised in China. At the heart of sterilisation was the rise of new wider prejudices.

Geographer Ruthie Gilmore has suggested that any deliberate human act that ultimately results in the premature deaths of groups of others can be defined as racism.[59] Racism curtails the length of life by inflicting insults ranging from high chances of imprisonment, to lower chances of being treated with respect at school, through to almost any form of discrimination affecting health.[60] All this is racist by Ruthie Gilmore's wider definition. But it is the racist actions that lead to death that are most shocking.

In the 1990s, two children were found dead in the undercarriage of an aeroplane that landed at Brussels. One carried a note which read 'Excellencies, gentlemen – members and those responsible in Europe, it is to your solidarity and generosity that we appeal for your help in Africa. If you see that we have sacrificed ourselves and lost our lives, it is because we suffer too much in Africa and need your help to struggle against poverty and wars. Please excuse us very much for daring to write a letter.'[61] The children were aged 15 and 16. These children were just two of thousands who died trying to enter Europe each year from the 1970s onwards, attempting to evade immigration controls; which were essentially controls of those not of the same 'stock'. Immigration restrictions are essentially racist. Children seen as of the same 'stock' are much more likely to be welcomed in, although, as economic inequalities rise, first Eastern European, then Southern Europeans, then all mainland Europeans have come to be seen as more foreign and talk spreads of controlling their migration and mobility too. Ironically, the greatest concentration of immigrant children living in Britain is of those born in the US, resident, with their families, a seventh of all children found near the heart of London are American.[62]

Stoking fear

Almost no distinction is made between refugees and those who are labelled as immigrants in the UK and the US. Often the term 'immigrants' excludes 'acceptable' migrants who don't count, such as well-off Americans in the UK, but includes many people who are not immigrants, having been born in the country where they reside. Fears of immigration vary dramatically between countries and over time, and such fears can only be kept high by being constantly stoked. When asked whether it is immigration that most worries people, it was reported as the main concern of 8 per cent of Germans, 11 per cent of Swedes, 12 per cent of the Dutch, 13 per cent of the French, 21 per cent of Australians, 28 per cent of Italians, a third of the citizens of the US, and there are almost as many fearful Spaniards as there are fearful Brits, some 46 per cent in 2007.[63] Since 2007, fear of immigrants has grown significantly in the UK despite there being more UK citizens claiming benefits elsewhere in the EU than other EU citizens claiming benefits in the UK.[64] And since 2012 more people have actually been leaving Spain than arriving there.

Although there are many Brits living in Spain, the rates of fear bear no resemblance to the proportions of immigrants in each country, or any effect these immigrants may have; they simply reflect how well those who want to stir up the fear and suffering are doing. In much of mainland Europe the term 'immigration' is more rarely used; instead people talk of a mobile population, and the press is less anti-migrant. It is said that people get the press they deserve, but that press is also thrust more on them in unequal countries where a few rich men often own much of the media. Note who controls much of the press in Australia,

Italy, the US and Britain, and look again at the list of countries above. Fears and belief systems are built up and altered through many media, but the national press is vital in this. When the press criticises immigrants and bolsters celebrities as deserving of riches, it is clear which systems of belief it is promulgating.

The press does not promulgate prejudice simply because it sells more papers and gains more viewers in fearful times, however. It also takes its lead from the actions of politicians. For example, in 2004 the British government passed an Asylum and Immigration Act, section 9 of which gave landlords, including local authorities, the power to evict from their homes families with children who refused to return voluntarily to their country of origin when not given a right to remain in Britain. These families with young children would thus be made homeless. At the time the legislation was described as 'one of the more overt aspects of cruelty within a system premised on cruelty.'[65] The political party system in Britain requires certain apparatchiks to be appointed as 'whips' to tell elected representatives how to vote, what the 'party line' is. Many MPs may simply not have been thinking, just following the whips' orders, but enough appeared to not see these children as quite as human as their own, to not see these adults as people much like themselves, to be able to support this Act and to make it law.

The opposite of a celebrity is 'an unknown', the unknown hundred million who were never born due to the sterilisation of their potential parents; the mostly unknown 10 million a year who die before their fifth birthday due to poverty; the largely unknown million (as a minimum) who die each year as adults due to wars, massacres or genocide; the single dead baby, name unknown, found in storage in a lorry travelling into Britain from France, smuggled in with parents in search of a better life. The unknown baby is, in this case, a fictional baby, invoked by an MP who asked, in the British Parliament, how a new law would work that would fine lorry drivers found to have smuggled people concealed in their vehicles. When queried whether the fine would still apply if the smuggled person was a baby, the minister replied 'yes'. When queried whether the fine would be applied if the baby was dead, the minister said it would, but only if the baby had died on the British side of the channel. The minister did not appear to view the baby as all that human, just as a problem if it was still breathing.[66] The tale of the unknown dead baby

Figure 12: Inequalities in chances of living to age 65 by geographical area in Britain, 1920–2006

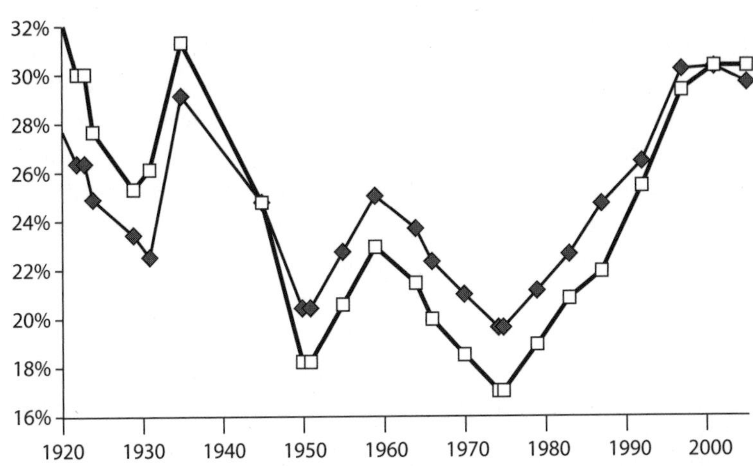

Note: The line marked by white squares shows how much *lower* the age-sex standardised under-age-65 mortality rate in the 10% of geographical areas (wards) with the lowest mortality is compared to the average. The line marked by dark diamonds shows how much *higher* that of the worst 30% is than the average.

Source: Dorling, D. and Thomas, B. (2009) 'Geographical inequalities in health over the last century', in H. Graham (ed) *Understanding Health Inequalities*: Oxford University Press, pp 66-83, derived from Table 4.3, with interpolation between five-year rates in some circumstances.

Standardised Mortality Ratio 0-64 (1921–2006) Decile 1 are the areas of the country containing the 10% of the population with the worst health outcomes at each time

RII	Ratio	Decile	1	10	Worst off 30%	Best off 10%
2.64	2.02	**1921-25**	141	70	0.263	0.300
2.41	1.83	**1926-30**	137	75	0.234	0.253
2.35	1.83	**1931-35**	136	74	0.225	0.261
2.89	2.25	**1936-39**	155	69	0.291	0.313
1.96	1.6	**1950-53**	131	82	0.204	0.182
2.25	1.76	**1959-63**	136	77	0.250	0.229
1.92	1.58	**1969-73**	131	83	0.196	0.170
2.12	1.7	**1981-85**	135	79	0.226	0.208
2.22	1.78	**1986-89**	139	78	0.247	0.219
2.49	1.93	**1990-92**	144	75	0.264	0.254
2.64	2.06	**1993-95**	149	72	0.280	0.277
2.8	2.16	**1996-97**	153	71	0.302	0.293
2.85	2.17	**1999-2001**	151	70	0.303	0.303
2.83	2.14	**2002-04**	150	70	0.299	0.298
2.84	2.14	**2004-06**	149	70	0.296	0.303

Note: RII is the Relative Index of Inequality, a measure of the overall level of inequality.

in storage, not worth a fine if it died, but not on British soil, is where the story of how policies based on social Darwinism and the values it puts on human life ultimately ends – in bizarre, uncaring legalistic behaviour, and in deaths that need not have been premature, in needless deaths.

According to Ruthie Gilmore, premature death caused by human harm, including indifference, provides evidence of the wider extent of racism in a society. It is worth looking at trends in premature mortality as indicative of trends in racist behaviour when racism is viewed more widely. Premature mortality rises above expected international norms when inequality rises, but what is more telling is how these life and death chances vary between different groups. Figure 12 shows how the rate of inequalities in premature mortality has changed in Britain over the period 1920–2006. It shows that inequalities in mortality fell throughout the 1920s, but rose again in the Great Depression as lives again became cheap. You almost certainly would not think of this as resulting from a form of racism, but one class of people had to look a long way down on another class of people, living in different parts of the country, to allow this to happen in the 1930s. This dominant class lost power in the 1940s, and these health inequalities plummeted thereafter before rising slightly again, following the remarkable equality achieved immediately after the Second World War, and probably during it too.

The attitudes of the rich to the poor had been changed by revolution, economic depression, war and rebuilding, although there was not always progress. Health inequalities between areas increased in the 1950s, but fell throughout the 1960s and early 1970s, to reach a minimum around 1969–73, when the best-off 10 per cent could 'only' expect about 18 per cent lower than average chance of dying before their 65th birthday any year, and the excess mortality of the worst-off 30 per cent was 'just' 20 per cent higher than the average. After that time, as prejudice grew, so did inequalities in premature death. Today, far more of the people living in the poorest of areas are not white. At the start of the period shown in the graph, more were Jewish or Irish. What mattered most at both times was that these groups were more likely to be seen as (and treated as) poor and less valuable. By 2014, it became evident that for some poorer groups in poorer areas, mortality rates were rising absolutely. For women, the ONS recently reported that between 2001–03 and 2008–10: 'Increases in mortality were observed in the Intermediate; Lower Supervisory and Technical; and the Semi-routine classes in several regions.'[67]

5.3 Polarisation: of the economic performance of regions

Prejudice, and the consequent rise in inequalities in income and wealth that accompanies its acceptance, does not just divide groups of people but also the places in which they live. Rising prejudice can encourage policies that increase the economic polarisation of regions, making it acceptable that certain areas and people are abandoned, while other places and groups are seen as vital and to be supported economically, come what may. In 2009, the then Labour government began to make great cuts to the regional growth budget to divert money into supporting the housing market in the South East of England, when it appeared to be under threat. The 2010–15 coalition government that followed spent more money on holding up that housing market than on any other single project.[68]

At the micro-regional level, when it comes to choosing where to live, the rich are even more constrained in options than the poor. Entire towns and cities can lack almost any very rich people, whereas almost no town or city lacks poor neighbourhoods. The super-rich are even more constrained in their choice of residential location than the very rich. There are just not that many multi-million pound/dollar/euro and billion yen properties on the market. The super-rich could build a house almost anywhere, but they need more than a home – they need other super-rich people with whom to socialise, to identify with, to share their prejudices with, and they are very afraid of the poor. Because of all this they cluster in their enclaves, in particular regions, in particular cities in those regions, and in particular streets in those cities. When we talk of rising segregation, it is often the segregation of ethnic or religious groups that is being imagined, but it is the rich who are most geographically segregated and who have been becoming more so in those countries that have been becoming more unequal.

Rising social prejudice is accompanied by growing social inequalities between neighbourhoods within cities, between cities within regions, and between regions within countries. The super-rich are surrounded, geographically as well as when out socially, by the slightly less rich. The place where these affluent households mostly settle becomes what is seen as the neighbourhood of choice. If a city has no such neighbourhoods, it is shunned more widely.

When inequalities are increasing, the city around and within which most of the rich settle becomes progressively richer and richer over time, even as it also attracts a greater number of poorer people to serve those affluent families. This is because each affluent family adds a great deal to the overall measure of the wealth of the city, whereas each poor family adds only a small number to the overall population that such wealth is divided by. The wealth is less and less well divided in practice, but statisticians divide it ever so smoothly to calculate the per capita income rates through which cities and regions are ranked, and whereby GDP is estimated. A city with a high GDP, such as the city of Luxembourg or New York, will tend not to be a place where most people are very well off, but a place that contains larger affluent enclaves than most similarly sized cities.

Within Europe, at least until recently, the London region was the richest when wealth was measured per person. This was despite London containing one of the greatest concentrations of poor people in Europe. London is one of those places where, beginning in the 1980s, the super-rich of the world find that they have to have a home if they are to fit into global super-rich social circles. One result has been that finding homes for the rest of Londoners who do not have multiple domiciles has been far from easy in recent years. For most of the previous 100 years London was declining in population and it was becoming easier to house families in the capital, without them being grossly overcrowded as a result.

The story in New York has been similar to London – population decline in central New York City continued right through to the 1970s. Other financial centres also declined in population, and then saw fresh people crowd in. Thus, from 1970 to 2000, the population of Luxembourg also rose dramatically (by over a third). A small part of that increase came because, from the 1970s onwards, the rich were settling in greater numbers in these places as their numbers declined elsewhere. In small town North America, in the outlying provinces of Britain, and in the more remote rural villages of Europe, in almost all of Japan except Tokyo, the children of the affluent migrated to richer enclaves or their vicinity. In those societies that became more polarised, as social polarisation increased, the rich felt more and more at home surrounded by 'their own'.

Not all countries saw such a concentration of the affluent in so few locations, however. In Japan, although particular districts of Tokyo did become synonymous with wealth, and many more with youth, the dividing of areas between rich and poor did not occur nationally with anything like the speed with which such processes were seen to operate in the US. The young moved to Tokyo, but the wealthy and poor did not polarise as much. In Japan, mixed neighbourhoods are the norm – houses are squeezed between apartment blocks, and school children usually walk to school rather than being driven. Extreme geographical polarisation by wealth is the exception in affluent countries, not the rule.

In Europe, although Luxembourg became a pole of attraction for the rich (and some notorious very rich companies), as did other small states with low taxes, across much of the rest of the continent there was no great abandonment of particular districts by the affluent, and a squeezing of the majority of the rich into just a few districts by a process ironically called 'choice'. Wealthier people used to be dispersed more widely in countries like Britain. When polarisation occurred, all that began to matter when determining how well a city or region appeared to fare was how near it was to London. Train travel times from London provided the best guide to how well cities did in terms of seeing their residents' incomes rise, jobless rates fall, education levels increase, and even health improve.[69]

Moving apart

Within countries, geographical, social and economic polarisation tends to take place slowly and steadily. You have to look at data over a long time period to see this clearly, partly because we come to accept the divides we currently live with. These forms of polarisation themselves cause beliefs to become more polarised. As polarisation rises, more people come to believe that others living elsewhere are less deserving than themselves.

Within a country like Britain, the changing extent of the social divide is perhaps most simply illustrated politically by considering changes in how concentrated the votes have been by area for the main political party of government in the 20th century – the Conservative Party. Figure 13 shows how – beginning just after the First World War and continuing right through to the 1960s – Conservative voters became far less spatially concentrated. It depicts a measure of the minimum proportion of such voters who would have to be transferred between a fixed set of parliamentary constituencies if each constituency was to have the same proportion of Conservative voters as nationally at each general election.

By the time of the 1960s general elections, just moving some 6 per cent of the national total of Conservative voters from some of the most Conservative seats to some of the least Conservative seats would have had the effect of making the share of the vote that the Conservatives secured in all seats the same. By 2005 that proportion had reached 15.7 per cent, higher than at any time since just before the 1920s. This is not evidence of just social polarisation, but of a geographical polarisation in underlying beliefs. In the 2010 General Election the proportion rose even further, to 16.4 per cent. The Conservatives were unable to form an overall majority because their votes were so geographically concentrated, and so many of those votes were wasted in seats where they were already doing well.

Political parties do not want their support either to be too geographically concentrated or too spread out. In the 1960s, when the Conservatives were unpopular, their core vote was spread out. By the late 1990s, when again unpopular, their core vote had become geographically concentrated. A great deal had changed in between in the lives of people living in different places in Britain. By 2015, unprecedented numbers were considering voting for none of the three main parties. It is possible that the Conservative vote will have polarised further, if support for that party falls where it is perceived to be weakest, with more perhaps voting for UKIP, and rises even further where it is already most strong. These changes do not only result from people with particular views tending to move house to particular localities, but also from people changing their minds, perhaps swayed by what are presented to them as the prevailing opinions, perhaps by choosing to buy the newspaper everyone else is reading in order to fit in.

Figure 13 is reminiscent of Figure 12, of trends in health inequalities, and as is shown below, this also reflects the trends in income inequalities in Figure 14. When trends appear similar it can help to check the likelihood that such similarity might arise from chance. Such checks provide no proof of a causal link, but they are helpful in the search for coincidences on which to speculate. For both simplicity and a little historical reparation,

Figure 13: Concentration of Conservative votes, British general elections, 1918–2010

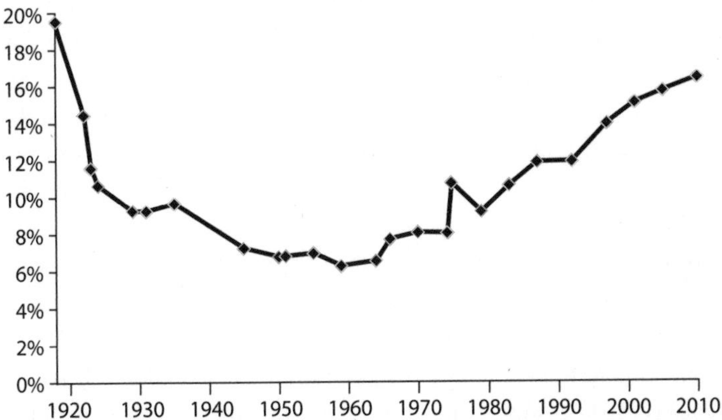

Note: The statistic being measured is the segregation index of Conservative votes across all British seats at each general election. The proportion is the minimum number of voters who would have to be moved across constituency boundaries to ensure that within each parliamentary constituency the Conservatives received exactly the same share of the vote.

Source: Drawn initially in Dorling, D. (2006) 'Class alignment renewal': *The Journal of Labour Politics*, vol 41, no 1, p 849, showing the spatial segregation index. Updated in Dorling, D. (2013) Crises and turning points: the pivots of history, *Renewal*, 21, 4, pp11-20.

The Segregation Index of Conservative voters in Britain*, 1885–2010

Election	Concentration	Election	Concentration
1885	7.11%	1951	6.77%
1886	5.53%	1955	6.93%
1892	5.81%	1959	6.24%
1895	4.70%	1964	6.51%
1900	4.39%	1966	7.69%
1906	6.67%	1970	8.04%
1910 Dec	6.24%	1974 Feb	8.01%
1910 Jan	7.91%	1974 Oct	10.72%
1918	19.30%	1979	9.17%
1922	14.44%	1983	10.59%
1923	11.57%	1987	11.84%
1924	10.62%	1992	11.88%
1929	9.24%	1997	13.94%
1931	9.23%	2001	15.05%
1935	9.65%	2005	15.69%
1945	7.21%	2010	16.40%
1950	6.74%	*2015*	*Unknown*

*Northern Irish seats are not included.

the first edition of this book used statistical tests associated with that great advocate of inequality, Karl Pearson. The Pearson product-moment correlation coefficient is named after him although often attributed to Charles Darwin's cousin Francis Galton, whom Pearson worked with and who was a far more unpleasant advocate of inequality and eugenics. Table 5 of the first edition of this book is available on this book's website, and shows that the correlation coefficients are 0.72 and 0.75 between the trend shown in Figure 13 and the two trends shown in Figure 12. The probability or chance that the concentration of voting is unrelated to the proportion of premature deaths occurring among the worst-off in society is less than one in 10,000, and there is a less than a one in 100,000 chance that the concentration of voting is unrelated to the health advantage of the best-off 10 per cent of society. This clearly does not mean that one causes the other, just that these two great falls and rises in inequality follow a similar periodicity. Something else might be causing both. However, both trends do almost certainly influence each other in several ways, for example, people who live longer being more likely to vote Conservative when, on average, Conservative voters get to vote in one more general election in their lifetimes than Labour voters because better-off people tend to live a little longer. Mortality and politics influenced and were influenced by much else, and are part of a more general greater trend.

Figure 13 shows the fall and then the rise in the *geographical concentration* of right-wing voting in Britain, as represented by the Conservative Party. Throughout the 20th century the Conservative Party was the party of old-fashioned views, often holding bigoted ideas, quietly accepting racism at whatever level it could be proclaimed in the polite society of the times, moving as slowly as possible towards, and often retreating from, a fairer future. Inequalities in health rose postwar when the Conservatives were in power in the 1950s, 1980s and 1990s, and only under New Labour when it appeared to behave, in terms of statistical correlation with inequalities in income rising, as a Conservative Party, following the 1997 General Election. During the 20th century people who were persuaded to vote for representatives of the Conservative Party initially became both less in number and less spatially concentrated. This clearly occurred from 1918 onwards. There were still Conservatives everywhere, but there were fewer and fewer of them, and fewer self-reinforcing clusters of them. However, in hindsight, by the early 1970s, it became clear that Conservative sympathies were about to begin to be newly created, increasingly concentrating spatially again, and growing in number.

The tipping point

Although Figure 13 shows the slow rise beginning in 1966 and continuing through to 1974, the decisive point is probably autumn 1974. Following the oil price shocks of 1973, in the February general election of that year voter segregation held steady, at 8 per cent. It was only in the October election that segregation rose, and rose abruptly. It was almost as if the country, to treat it like some individual, and the Conservative Party in particular, paused for a moment to decide which way to turn. It could choose between the collective path, where all would take a hit together, accept that oil prices had risen, accept that standards of living could not be so high again, that the empire had gone, and that the inequalities of the world should be reduced. Or it could turn the other way, make Britain supposedly 'great' again, concentrate on making money, exploit the rest of the world, abandon those parts of the country seen as unproductive, take away financial rules so that banks could make more and more profit out of individuals at home and overseas, and ensure that a few people could get increasingly rich.

By late 1974, the Conservative Party had still not converted fully to individualism – it was still 'one-nation Tory', but it was the most right-wing alternative available. In October 1974, in the South of England, there was a decisive swing in votes towards a more selfish alternative, not enough votes to win the election for the Conservatives, but enough to give the signal that set the country steadily on a new route towards more than four decades of rising political, economic and social polarisation. A year later, the grandees of the Conservative Party chose Margaret Thatcher to be their new leader. Less than four years after that, as their popular vote in the South East and the Midlands swelled, the Conservative Party reaped the benefit of having made that choice, and won a landslide victory.

The decision taken by so many voters in October 1974 and 1979, and not reversed with sufficient enthusiasm thereafter, meant that by 2004, Britain had become more socially divided than it had been in 1934 in terms of differences between areas in life expectancy (as shown in

Figure 12), income (Figure 14), votes (Figure 13), housing, education, wealth, and in much more of the fabric of life than just these basics. Britain, however, was not leading those parts of the world that made this choice; it was following closely behind the world leader in the slide towards selfishness and rising prejudice, the world leader being the US.

Follow the leader

The US, for all its anti-communist rhetoric at home and wars overseas, was a remarkably equitable place in 1974. It had a minimum wage it was possible to live on, worth more than twice as much as the minimum wage a generation later, in 2008, when measured in real terms. In other words, people at the bottom of US society were much better off in the 1970s than they were by the noughties. People in the middle saw their own position decline, as only a few at the top became much richer. By the current decade, this growing inequality had stirred up great anger. It is what had made the election of Barack Obama in 2008 possible. Obama then attempted to curb this economic trend, but slowly, and often not successfully.

Proposals to raise the minimum wage to $10.10 an hour were debated in 2014 but not enacted – even mean 'real' average wages were higher in the US in the 1970s than today. New civil rights and women's rights legislation was changing the face and feelings of North American society, and young people protested over war in a way that their parents could not have even imagined themselves doing, and their children might find difficult, during a 'war on terror'.

Higher wages for the poor in the 1970s and the slow and, for the rich, steady loss of their wealth, social position and power, angered many of those older white men with more money. As in Britain, where racism was used to bolster the 1979 Conservative vote, the US Republican Party (that these men supported) used and continues to use racist rhetoric. That rhetoric created anger among poorer white people who were becoming poor still after the heights of the 1970s, so great that Ronald Reagan's speeches about 'black welfare queens' helped him secure victory in 1980 with the support of unprecedented numbers of southern whites. It was 35 years before President Obama rebuked President Reagan's divisiveness head on in one of the finest State of the Union addresses ever spoken, which early on asked, 'Will we allow ourselves to be sorted into factions and turned against one another – or will we recapture the sense of common purpose that has always propelled America forward?'[70]

The rally towards increased prejudice had begun a little earlier in the US than the UK, but the US is a larger country, and it took right-wing North Americans a year longer to win their most important national election and to secure the presidency for Ronald Reagan in 1980. However, he was quicker to change rules, regulations and regimes to raise inequality when he is now compared to Mrs Thatcher. He may have left office in 1988, but his legacy and the legacy of those who supported him – or opposed him, but failed to reverse his impact – returned the US economy by 2005 not to inequalities last realised in the 1930s, but to levels not seen since the early 1920s! When those inequalities continued to rise and the best-off 1 per cent took more than 20 per cent of all income after 2012, the US became more unequal than it had been at any time since modern records began, in 1913.

In both the early 1920s and 2005, the best-off 1 per cent living in the US received 17 per cent of all income, and the highest 'compensated' 10 per cent received some 44 per cent of all US income. All the years in between (1925–2005) were more equal. The trend followed that same U-shaped distribution which is seen in this chapter's graphs of Britain (Figures 12–14). It is also worth noting that inequalities became so unequal that most of the rich did not feel very rich in 1925 or 2005. The average household within the top 10th, but excluding the top 100th, was almost six times worse off than the average within that top 1 per cent.[71] Income inequalities between the top percentile group and fifth percentile were also as great as between those placed 10th and 90th in the US income parades of both 1925 and 2005.

Although the Conservatives in Britain in 1979 and the Republicans in the US in 1980 had secured the largest number of votes to put them in power of those who could be persuaded to vote at all, there was only a turnout of 76 per cent turnout in the UK in 1979, and 53 per cent in the US in 1980. Both figures were low for the times. More of the poor had stopped voting. These victorious parties then both moved even further to the right and so they did not improve the living conditions of even most of those who voted for them, just those of the more affluent of their supporters. Thus, in the US, if people in most of the top tenth of society looked up, they saw the top 1 per cent flying away from them. When they looked down, they looked in fear to see ghettos forming and neighbourhoods being abandoned, entire rust belt regions forming, and the old industrial heartlands of the US being consigned to the scrap heap. Because of this, for a long time they could be persuaded to continue to vote in support of the selfishness of the rich in what looked like protection from being completely, not just partially, abandoned themselves.

The implicit threat, that if you don't vote for the party that opposes scroungers, migrants and skivers, was so powerful that it resulted in the Democrat and Labour Parties mirroring right-wing policy and trying to become electable through harnessing fear rather than hope. So when the Democrats in the US and Labour in the UK came to power in the most unequal of rich countries, these former opposition parties made no discernible impact on the kind of graphs shown in this chapter. Try to spot the break in slope in Figures 12, 13 or 14, when the party in power changed. You can't, because when it came to life and death issues, such as inequalities in health or wealth, it was as if nothing happened when the people voted into office what was supposed to have been 'the opposition'.

As with Ronald Reagan, the legacy of Margaret Thatcher and those who brought her to power continued long after she lost office. People living in areas that voted Conservative in 1997 in Britain saw greater improvements to their life expectancy and living standards over the course of the next 10 years than those experienced in Labour voting areas, despite Labour being in power all that time, and similar trends occurred in the US, under President Clinton.[72] However, it is possible that without Labour and the Democrats, the present would be far worse, that inequalities by 2008 would have surpassed that 1918 maximum. Alternatively, inequalities might just have risen higher earlier and somewhat faster, and then the financial markets would have failed a little earlier than 2008.

People do not happily polarise, but when unhappy, their voting and behaviour will polarise out of fear. When there appears to be no alternative to abandoning poorer areas and poorer people to keep average living standards stable, otherwise well-meaning people can be persuaded to act selfishly. They do this both at the ballot box, and in exercising what little choice they have over where they live. They will panic over what schools their children might go to. In the 1970s, most white families in both the US and Britain were much freer to choose different residential locations than they are now. As private housing later became more expensive, freedom to choose where to live for those who could afford private housing declined, even though the supply increased. The increased supply allowed a small group to buy several homes each and to become private landlords.

As the supply of social housing was reduced, the small amount of freedom of choice that had existed there was also reduced. In both the US and the UK, most families began to spend higher and higher proportions of their incomes to pay to live away from other people, often away from black and poor people, especially as prices rose in the mid-1980s and later 1990s. But hardly anyone would ever say that they bought a home in the suburbs of Chicago or Birmingham (England) to get away from blacks or the poor. They talked about the schools, or the air, or the décor, but their actions betrayed their beliefs, their rising prejudice. The evidence was to be found in higher and higher prices being paid for otherwise identical homes in posh areas compared with average areas, compared with poor areas; it was in the mantra that began in the 1970s and became a loud chant by the 1990s, that what mattered most in determining price was: 'location, location, location'.

Polarisation and cohesion

Once a process of economic polarisation begins, it is very hard to turn it around. Attitudes harden, fear grows on fear; as people polarise geographically, they begin to know less and less of each other, and become more fearful and more distrusting of each other.[73] Free market rhetoric stops being ridiculed as it was in the 1950s, when economists described events in the late 1920s as free market madness.[74] It is only under rising prejudice that it becomes acceptable again to have many people looking for work all the time, and changing jobs frequently, as the workless become seen as part of the 'oil' that makes the whole machine work smoothly. It takes a long time again for people to realise that jobs being lost and gained around the world, or relocated, results in huge gross turnover of human lives for small net increases in apparent productivity.

The turnover change and precarity is what most affects individual lives: insecurity, feeling worthless, being made redundant, being made redundant again and again, having to take whatever work is on offer. In

2011, Guy Standing published *The precariat: The new dangerous class*. He argued that this group were invariably working below their capabilities precisely because they have no other option. And they are dangerous because they know they have no other option as things stand. Standing himself cites graffiti written on a wall in Madrid in recent years as indicative of how this group thinks about transformation. The graffiti read: 'The worst thing would be to return to the old normal.'[75]

The precariat do not celebrate the net increases in numbers of people in paid employment, which is how government economists measure success when selfishness has become the norm. More people in paid work than ever before occurs when there is coercion for everyone who can work to have to do that work. Despite the prevailing rhetoric, it is not necessary that we all labour. Much non-renumerated work is valuable. Neither do we live in a zero-sum world, where jobs have to be lost in rich countries for them to be gained in poor ones and consequently that exchange will somehow make the world a more equitable place. If that were the case, globally, we would be so much more equal by now. Instead, areas are abandoned, other places become overcrowded, labour is casualised and spaces congested; the poorer people are, the more they are exploited. But economic statistics do not usually assess exploitation; just aggregate measures like growth.

During the 1980s in Britain, the motorway system was greatly extended, which allowed people to commute much further and more frequently by car than before. This aided spatial polarisation between areas, as you could live further away from the city centres in which you worked. Seen more widely, road building was part of a longer-term change in transportation to encourage individualism, although different affluent countries chose to undertake different levels of road building and of more collectivist and efficient railway building.

Road building and social polarisation in Britain led to more road use. The motorways became even more congested than before, despite more being built and more lanes added to the existing roads. It was because more cars were on the road due to more motorways having been built, and more people choosing to live in the suburbs, that the roads actually became even more congested. Conversely, while trams and urban railways had created the outer suburbs as residential possibilities, the car made commuter villages attractive.

Now in many cities, the rich have returned to the very centre to avoid congestion and the nearby initially affluent inner suburbs have been suffering decline. This pattern is found in many European cities, across the US and in Australasia – recent changes in the larger cities, such as Sydney, typify this pattern.[76] There are, however, some huge differences between what is normal in different rich countries in terms of how people travel and arrange their housing (see Figure 26 in Chapter 8, this volume). In general, the more economically equal people are within a country, the more often they have engineered their public transport systems to work well, and have arranged workplaces to be near enough to homes to avoid having to use cars all the time. Between 2005 and 2009 in the US, only 3.5 per cent of all journeys to work were by cycling or walking; in Australia, that proportion was 6 per cent, in Canada, 12 per cent, in France, 25 per cent, in Finland, 31 per cent, in Sweden, 32 per cent, in Denmark, 34 per cent and in the Netherlands, 51 per cent. Australia and the US chose to build sprawling car-dependent cities, they did not have to, but now their population have problems exercising as they spend many more hours getting to work behind a wheel rather than in healthy exercise.[77]

In different parts of the world, at different times, different parts of cities fare better than others. When in Europe and North America the poor became concentrated in the centres and the rich were spun out to the suburbs, the opposite pattern was found in poorer countries. There, the rich were initially spun into the centre. In poorer countries local taxes tend to be low or non-existent. In rich countries the affluent often initially moved out of city centres to avoid being taxed at city rates, thus avoiding having to help support the poor within their city, and avoiding having to live too near them. In richer countries they moved further out to create an outer ring of commuter towns.[78] In the most unequal of all rich countries, the most affluent ensure that local taxes are low and they have at least two homes, one in the city centre and one often even further out, so maybe one in Chelsea and the Cotswolds, or one in Manhattan and Maine.

And some of those with homes in more than one community complain of a general lack of community cohesion! Both the Conservative leader, and later Prime Minister, David Cameron and the 2008 Republican presidential nominee John McCain were unsure when asked on the campaign trail how many homes they owned.[79] It isn't possible to know all your neighbours when you own three, four, five, six or more homes. While community cohesion might be low where the most affluent live, these uncohesive areas tend not to experience many riots.

The phrase 'community cohesion' was not used before 2001. It is a strangely manufactured lament reflecting some old concerns associated with city living and migration, but perhaps also a new fear of the affluent who do not want to be blamed for causing others' woes by their own accumulation of riches. It is in the countries that have become more split apart by greed, in which the richest live as far away from the poor as they can, that you most often hear the lament that in poor areas people occasionally riot. Although the areas where the riots occur are almost always poor, reports on riots in recent years have not made the links between rioting and poverty made by earlier reports. Compare official reports on riots in places like Bradford in 2001 or London in 2011 with reports in the 1980s, including the Scarman report on the Brixton riots in London, or the 1960s California gubernatorial commission's findings on the Watts riots in Los Angeles.

It is now more common to hear that poverty is '*not* an excuse', that the fact that those areas have been disinvested in should *not* have led to disturbance (as so much has somehow been 'invested' through 'regeneration' schemes). But in the areas in which most rioters live, young people are given so little compared with most young people that they know they have little to lose. Instead of rioting, minor public order offences and what is called general anti-social behaviour are now more often blamed on supposed racial tension and on different groups of people labelled by skin colour and religion apparently not mixing much. Almost always these are groups that have mixed well in poor areas, as compared with the way the rich, despite flocking together, do not mix well with each other, let alone with the poor. The segregation and lack of community cohesion of the affluent is ignored, as is their lack of general community spirit, which harms the majority so much. Richard Wilkinson and Kate Pickett's *The Spirit Level* depressingly documents the decline in trust that occurs as inequality increases, encouraging the people with most to try to acquire yet more to protect themselves from those they then trust less and less, and consequently impoverish.

5.4 Inheritance: the mechanism of prejudice

Until recently in the US, the myth that all could become rich was so strong that even a majority of the very poorest voters were in favour of abolishing inheritance tax, called 'estate tax'. This was despite the fact that less than 1 per cent ever pay such taxes.[80] With US wealth falling after the economic crash it is becoming harder to sell the American dream as something to hang on to, and more and more vital to find sources of income to simply maintain the basic running of the US. Taxing the inheritance of the rich is the most obvious source of that income. Even Bill Gates, the richest single American in 2014 with $81 billion at stake, is in favour of it. However, the greatest obstacle to keeping, expanding and raising inheritance tax is racism. Inheritance tax is now seen as transferring money from white to black Americans, but it was not always so. Andrew Carnegie argued that inheritance tax was the only way to prevent a permanent aristocracy of the wealthy, which could have been prevented had the tax been maintained; instead, North America got that aristocracy, the aristocracy of the descendants of robber barons and bloated bankers. And the social group who take kinship and inheritance most seriously are the very richest of all, where even those who marry into the family can be described as 'outsiders'.

The human failing most closely associated with the injustice of prejudice is racism. It is racist to believe that we are inherently different. The idea that mental ability and other 'gifts' are inherited, and the concept of giving material and social advantage to your offspring, coupled with preventing them from apparently squandering their inheritances by urging them to marry from among a narrow class of partners, are the mechanisms through which prejudice is maintained over time. Where such behaviours over inheritance remain powerful, social inequalities remain high, and social solidarity tends to be low. A belief in inheritance both creates and maintains the ideas of racial groups and racial difference.[81] What separates white and black people most in the US is wealth. When people are free to consort with whomever they wish in a society, that society quickly becomes seen as racially homogeneous. This occurred in Iceland as it came out of abject poverty and almost all were seen as alike, or in Japan, following land reform that made all more equal and hence more alike. As a result, most people in Japan and Iceland are viewed as being of the same race.

The creation of race

We have not always belonged, and do not always belong, to particular ethnic groups. When there are restrictions on mixing, either legally imposed or through the creation of a tradition, then races become created and begin to take on huge importance in connection with life chances. A race can be made in a flicker of time, and one such flicker occurred in 1770.

On 22 April 1770 there were no indigenous Australians, no natives, no black people in Australia, there was no Australia; there were just a great many people who had lived in a very large land for a very long time. They belonged to many groupings, although these were constantly reforming and far from all-encompassing.

Of the people spread all across that huge continent, not one of them was called 'aboriginal'. In a flicker of time all that changed; all the nuances of kin groups, kingdoms and respect went when James Cook, initially apprenticed by Quakers in the Yorkshire seaside village of Whitby, claimed Australia for the English Crown.

If it hadn't been James Cook, it would have quickly been another sea captain who would have, at a stroke, turned the oldest great collection of continuously surviving human civilisations in the world into what within a few years would become one of the poorest racial minorities on the planet. He did this simply by claiming that Australia was, from then on, part of the inheritance of the British.[82] The British themselves were a manufactured race, who, from 1603 to 1714, had mostly been subjects of a Scottish monarchy, the Stuarts.

There were no British people in 1700; they were only 'made' to exist long after the successors of another James, King of Scotland from 1567, inherited the crowns of both Ireland and England in 1603.[83] These were times when the nationalities that people were given, their religions, and the languages they were expected to speak, depended greatly on the whims of princes and kings. And the prince or king you got depended entirely on when and where you were born.

Like nations, religions and ethnicities, races are created. They are manufactured from acts of royal marriage and infertility, exploration, discovery, colonisation, imperialism and expropriation. And races can also be dissolved. They are dissolved by inter-marriage and when no one considers them any longer as a race. Often religious groups are synonymous with racial groups, especially when persecuted, as in the cases of Jews, the Huguenots and Rastafarians.

The Quakers were one such group that was greatly persecuted, much as more accepted races were, and that could easily have become a mainstream race. There was a time when Quakers mostly married other Quakers, gave birth to children who in turn became Quakers, and were seen in countries like Britain as a group apart. When barred from the few universities that existed, a few of their oldest sons instead established what would later become great industries, and they were given a little space to allow that. In England in 1753, the Marriage Act of Parliament contained an exception to allow Quakers and Jews to follow their own traditions.

Just 17 years before James Cook landed on the Australian East coast, English law depicted Quakers on a par with Jews, and also as a 'race'/religion to be respected and tolerated. If respect and toleration last long enough, however, a race disappears. The Quakers received respect and toleration in most of the places where they lived, although the Jews often did not. When respect and tolerance are absent, race is all-pervasive, and races are maintained through oppression and persecution. Oppression and persecution occur most frequently where there is great economic inequality.

Race is often proposed as the reason '… for the absence of an American welfare state'.[84] The US does have a cut-down version of a welfare state, but properly functioning welfare states require a degree of mutual trust and understanding, greater than that which has been common in the US. When trust is absent, it is very hard to establish widespread support for a system where those who have fallen on hard times through sickness or worklessness will be supported until they are better, or back in work, or both. You have to see your fellow humans as like you in order to support such a system.

If you see other people around you as a different kind of human being, following different kinds of motivation, perhaps as lazier than you, not as clever as you think you are, or as upright or as moral, then you may be less likely to back systems of mutual support. Seeing groups of others as generally lazy, immoral and stupid is usually social status-related – it is part of seeing them as beneath you. The great injustice of the lack of a well-functioning welfare state in the US is the direct result of the tolerance, maintenance and even encouragement of racism.

Racism is everywhere, but found in each place to differing degrees. In most of Western Europe racism has been kept subservient enough to permit the establishment of a series of welfare states. These welfare states were brought in most solidly after the Second World War, partly to curtail dissent among poor people over continued social inequalities, but also because social solidarity and equality were then high enough to make welfare possible. It was possible even earlier in New Zealand, as the welfare state there was established in the 1930s.

Not all people in Western European countries have been subject to the protection of welfare states – the reasons for excluding a group are usually racist. Guest workers, non-EU tourists, illegal immigrants – these are all groups who can be excluded from medical care and rights to social security that would protect them during times of worklessness. In Japan, for example, guest workers are encouraged to leave when they fall ill or out of employment. In the UK in early 2015, the Prime Minister advocated restrictions on tax credits being available to some European migrants.

Within Europe the right to move freely for those with citizenship is yet another example of races dissolving, as Europeans come to be seen to have more in common with each other, to have common rights and expectations to be treated similarly – a common European inheritance. This is a constructed, not a natural, pan-European inheritance. How it is constructed is well illustrated by recent tensions over migration from Eastern Europe. This common inheritance and the fights on citizenship within Europe are also used, like the ideas of US citizenship and Japanese nationality, as a reason to exclude others, others not fortunate enough to have inherited through accident of birthplace the right to a protected life.

If you are born in one of the three rich regions of the world you should never go really hungry, never expect to fall ill and die on the street without healthcare; your children will have a right to education; your basic dignity will be respected. These are all things you have inherited because they are your inheritance as a citizen, through the accident of your birth. However, rather than admit this, it can be easier to suggest that in the past, people in these areas were specially endowed to become richer, and that superiority both existed and somehow justifies the current fortunes of their descendants, including almost everyone reading this book. Did the 'British race' come to rule an empire of many other 'races' that had its greatest extent in 1919 because 'the British' were especially able? This would be both a justification based on an identification of races and a racist argument.

It is hard to overplay the importance of how just being born in a wealthy country provides you with an inheritance that ends up marking you as different from others. This inheritance is not simply of systems of social organisations that are efficient at keeping people healthy and (usually) well fed, occupied and educated. It is also of the physical infrastructure that makes all this possible, of roads and railways built decades ago from profits often made from trade – trade that was often imposed on others.

Good health is maintained partly by the inheritance of sewer systems and health systems, and partly the product of being born to parents who, in their turn, will have been better fed and cared for than most other people in the world. However, being born in an affluent country also results in inheriting the right to have payments made indirectly to you in the form of interest on the loans your forefathers made to people in poorer countries. More generally, you inherit being at the right end of a mechanism that ensures that over time, you pay less and less for what is made and grown elsewhere, while those in poorer countries pay more and more.

By 2006, the UN Department of Economic and Social Affairs valued that transfer at $500 billion (net) moving from poor to rich countries annually.[85] All you need do to qualify for a share in these profits is simply ensure that you are born to the right parents in the right place at the right time. This is luck, not skill. Thus most of your pay packet, if you live and work in a rich country, reflects your luck in having been born there, not your skill at work. By 2014, that same department had identified that it was the rich within the most inequitable of the richest countries of the world who were polluting the most through carbon emissions, to the detriment of everyone else.[86]

Privilege and prejudice

Taxes, including inheritance tax, should be transfers of wealth from rich to poor. Protecting inheritance is all about maintaining unfairness. Inheritance preserves privilege and prejudice, and without it there would be precious little privilege or prejudice based simply on accruing power from accumulating money. No doubt new forms of privilege and prejudice would emerge, but they could not be based on looking down at others whose parents, for instance, could not afford, due to the cost of the school fees or of living in the right locality, to send their children to similar schools as yours, if you were more wealthy.

When someone says they have been privileged to have had a good education, that often means that they *think* that they were lucky because others were not given what they preserve as their social advantages. No one in a country where state schools were as well equipped as private schools would say that they had been privileged to have been educated privately; they would say they had been duped if someone had made a charge for what was theirs of right. Rarely are those who mention privilege talking about an education where they were *actually* taught well, extensively or widely. It is fear of losing these inheritances, these advantages that have little to do with useful learning, that keeps people behaving in particular ways. Often private schools have (privately marked) entrance exams so that only those children who are likely to find the next set of public exams relatively easy are allowed in, giving a false sense of the quality of the education they provide. These schools also teach children to conform and not to question their parents' choices for them.

Rights to pensions in old age, healthcare then and before, out-of-work and educational benefits, all help keep a population pliant and reduce the incentive for emigration. The recent experiences of people leaving Eastern Europe for Western Europe, or leaving Mexico for the US, or of some Koreans moving to Japan, all show how easily places can lose their people when there appears less and less to inherit at home, and more of a chance for a better life abroad. These included some 68,631 unaccompanied children who were apprehended trying to cross from Mexico to the US in the financial year to 2014.[87]

Passports and border controls were only necessary once it began to be appreciated that much inheritance was simply the result of being in a place. Emigration controls, having to apply for permission to leave many countries in Western Europe and a few other jurisdictions, only ended just over a century ago, when enough reasons to stay had begun to be put in place.

Unless you are seen as highly skilled, one of the few legal ways to move from the poor world to the rich world now, without relatives in the latter, is to gain rich relatives, by marrying. Immigration through marriage is permitted partly because the unwritten rules on marriage are so well adhered to that marriage across social classes remains rare. If people married whoever they wished to marry, their choices not influenced by tradition or another social direction, the world would become a dramatically more equitable place within just a few generations. However, recently in the UK, in a bid to keep poorer people out, prospective immigrants who are the spouses of people who are not well off may now not be allowed to join their husband or wife within the UK.

It is only through the most careful selection of who we marry that inequality is maintained over time, and this careful selection is largely carried out unconsciously. Geographical proximity to potential partners is not just controlled by practical considerations of travel, but also closely curtailed through monitoring by family and society over where young people travel and when. The extent of that control is reflected by the rates at which people marry those from families not like themselves, poorer or richer, black or white, not by what clothes young people are allowed to wear or by what time they have to be home.

Two centuries ago, the question of whom to marry became the staple of contemporary fiction in the English novel, dominating the market from shortly after James Cook returned to England and Jane Austen's writing gained favour, through to Catherine Cookson becoming the most widely read novelist in England by the time of her death in 1998. We now use terms like 'gender' and 'ethnicity' to refer to when people choose their partner's sex or race, but the extent of our actual choices is remarkably limited by how others view us. At the same time as there has been an increased freedom to be gay and much less tolerance of explicit racism, freedom to mix with those who have more or less has been curtailed.

'Assortative mating' is just one of the terms used to describe the myriad processes employed by varying human societies to ensure that like marry like. 'Homogamy' is another obscure word for the same thing. The fact that these terms are so obscure illustrates just how embedded the process is. It is not that some people practice assortative mating and others do not, or that a very sizeable majority follow homogamy; it is that these behaviours are so much the norm that these terms are not needed. When people married out of their economic class, it used to be a great scandal.

It was a scandal in 1960 when the prosecuting counsel in a well-known English obscenity trial asked the jury, 'Is it a book you would wish your wife or servants to read?' Because the prosecuting counsel was a man from the upper classes who had married a woman from the upper classes, inherited property and employed servants, he had assumed the jurors were in the same position and that they all had servants! Homogamy promotes and maintains such prejudices.

The subject of the infamous 1960 trial, *Lady Chatterley's lover*, was a book written by D.H. Lawrence in 1928 about a woman who had sex with her gamekeeper, a servant. It was immediately banned from publication until the trial collapsed in 1960, which was indicative of how prejudice had been reduced between 1928 and 1960. The trial had been held in order to try to stop the publisher (Penguin) in its attempt to produce a cheap paperback copy. The particular timing, the talk of servants and of lovers, is all worth bearing in mind when considering Figure 14.

Although banning books on subjects such as sex between social classes became seen as absurdly old-fashioned by 1960, marriage (if not so much sex) beneath one's station, especially for a woman, still carried great stigma; it still does, as evidenced by its continued rarity and patriarchy's continued dominance (at least at older ages). That stigma may be rising in countries where social mobility is falling. And social mobility falls when income inequality rises.[88]

The richest percentile

Figure 14 charts the share in annual incomes received by the richest single percentile of Britons as recorded between 1918 and 2010, both pre- and post-tax. The richest percentile of people in Britain usually receive some of their income from earnings, but a great deal also from interest on wealth, rent payments, dividends and shares, and returns on investments made in stocks.

Figure 14: Share of all income received by the richest 1% in Britain, 1918–2010

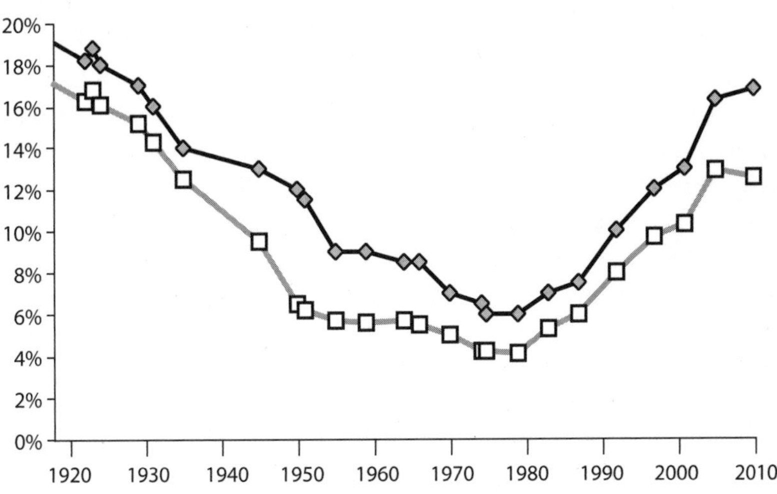

Note: Lower line is the share of all income after tax has been deducted.

Source: Atkinson, A.B. (2003) 'Top incomes in the United Kingdom over the twentieth century', Nuffield College Working Papers, Oxford (http://www.nuff.ox.ac.uk/Economics/History/Paper43/43atkinson.pdf), figures 2 and 3; from 1922 to 1935 the 0.1% rate was used to estimate the 1% when the 1% rate was missing, and for 2005 the data source was Brewer, M., Sibieta, L. and Wren-Lewis, L. (2008) *Racing away? Income inequality and the evolution of high incomes,* London: Institute for Fiscal Studies, p11; the 2005 post-tax rate of 12.9% is interpolated using the 2001 ratio. The 2010 figure comes from the World Top Incomes database which suggests that incomes are reduced by 25.10% for the top 1% due to income tax and that the post-tax share of adults in the top 1% was 12.55% in 2010.

Annual income share of the best-off 1%, 1918–2010, % of all income:

	Pre-tax (%)	Post-tax (%)
1918	19.1	17.1
1922	18.2	16.3
1923	18.8	16.8
1924	18.0	16.1
1929	17.0	15.2
1931	16.0	14.3
1935	14.0	12.5
1945	13.0	9.5
1950	12.0	6.5
1951	11.5	6.2
1955	9.0	5.7
1959	9.0	5.6
1964	8.5	5.7

	Pre-tax (%)	Post-tax (%)
1966	8.5	5.5
1970	7.0	5.0
1974 Feb	6.5	4.2
1974 Oct	6.0	4.2
1979	6.0	4.1
1983	7.0	5.3
1987	7.5	6.0
1992	10.0	8.0
1997	12.0	9.7
2001	13.0	10.3
2005	16.3	12.9
2010	16.8	12.6

At the end of the First World War, the richest one in every 100 people lived in total on about a sixth of the national income, 17 or 18 times more than the average family, 100 times more money than the poorest tenth saw in a year. The rich all had servants then, including gamekeepers, just like the one D.H. Lawrence wrote about in 1928. From 1918 through the 1920s, 1930s, 1940s, 1950s and 1960s, the share of national income received each year by the rich fell. Many of the heirs to great estates had died in the Great War, the government taxed the aristocratic families, but just as crucially, the 'great' families became a little more lax over whom they slept with, and subsequently married. There were far fewer groundsmen, gamekeepers or (paid) gardeners in the 1960s as a result.

The arithmetic of homogamy is simple. If you were a member of a family in the top percentile of income earners in 1918, you might expect to receive around £150,000 a year in today's money, 18 times the average individual income. If you were careful and ignored 99 potential life partners in every 100, you might, in theory, have met and only chosen from the one percentile like yourself. Because social networks were so limited, it was not hard to avoid at least 90 of the other 99, or to meet them only as servants, but the other nine, you had to tell yourself, were beneath you when you did meet. Then, as a couple, and later possibly as a family, you would remain in that top 1 per cent of earners. However, if you found a young man or woman from the bottom of that top decile more attractive, or caring, or more understanding, then as a pair, you would drop out of the top percentile. Another couple or individual would enter it, but they would not have been as well off as you (or else they would have been in that group already), and so the average income of the best-off falls.

Figure 14 shows a combination of many things, but it also includes the effect of the social equalising process of marrying outside of your class at work, gaining in strength right through to the 1970s. Note that this is especially true for the very rich, as a large proportion of the income of the richest 1 per cent is interest earnings from holding wealth, and high wealth is thus largely maintained over generations by marrying 'correctly'. Young women in particular were told that they should 'marry well'.

In England, debutantes (young aristocratic or upper-class girls) were presented at court at the start of each social season, right up until 1958. They were presented to make it clear that they were available for marriage into the correct families. After 1958 it became progressively harder to know so exactly who was the most 'respectable'. The process carries on today, however, especially in the US (and, ironically, Russia), at various huge 'charity' balls, but is less overtly state-sponsored than when the most suitable of young ladies were regularly presented to the Queen of England at court, just half a century ago.

The rich did not willingly give up their income and wealth. In 1951, William Rees-Mogg, then president of the Oxford Union and later editor of *The Times*, wrote that: 'For a quarter of a century the rich have been getting poorer and the standard of living of the most unfortunate has been steadily improving.'[89] A generation later, his son, Jacob, would help the Conservative Party reverse the situation, famously campaigning with his nanny for a seat in Glasgow before becoming MP for North East Somerset. He was so extremely arrogant he was still seen as a 'toff' despite the divisions in English society having rapidly widened again.

A combination of high mortality among even the upper classes in the First World War and from the 1918–20 influenza pandemic, increased death duties, and loss of wealth during the Depression and later redistribution by increases in income and inheritance taxation, all helped to bring down inequalities in income and wealth from 1918 to the end of the 1970s. However, it is also not hard to see that as wealth became a little more equally spread, it became easier for people to choose who they might love, easier to tolerate a little less those they were expected to tolerate, just to maintain the family silver.

Greater social mixing occurs with the aid of 'human nature being what it is';[90] it is very hard to avoid people you are attracted to and just mix with those you are supposed to. But if that is so, then why should a large part of the story of Figure 14 be different? Why, from the late 1970s onwards, should we see individual earnings again concentrating within the best-off percentile? It was not just the progressive tax structure being dismantled after 1979 that led to this. Earnings before tax (shown as the higher line in the same figure) follow almost exactly the same trend. The rise is so quick that by 2005, the trend line suggests that we had returned to early 1930s levels of income inequality at the very top end. But by 2010, the Labour Party's increase in the top tax rate to 50 per cent led to a fall in post-tax inequality; the Conservative–Liberal

Democrat coalition reduced that rate as soon as they gained office,[91] but not quite back to 40 per cent, and the two lines in the figure diverged.

In the first edition of this book, correlations were calculated between the pre-tax income share of the richest percentile and the excess mortality of the poorest 30 per cent, the health advantage of the best-off tenth and the geographical concentration of Conservative votes over the 1918–2005 period, which were 0.57, 0.82 and 0.51 respectively (see Table 5, p 176 of that edition). Again, this is no evidence of a causal link – clearly the health advantages of the rich are most closely connected to their share of wealth. But these are also both in some way related to trends in inequalities in voting, and to the fluctuations in the rates of premature mortality suffered by the poor.

There is only a one in a hundred chance that even the lowest of the correlations between Figures 12, 13 and 14 could have occurred by chance. The correlations with the post-tax income trend shown in Figure 14 above were even stronger – 0.60, 0.86 and 0.58 respectively – and they were both larger and even more statistically robust. When the rich take even more of the national income of a country, the health of the poor suffers, and voting in general elections becomes more spatially polarised. Similar trends have been suggested in the US.[92] The UK figures are not updated here because the relevant health data for 2010 is not yet publicly available, but the one correlation we could update, between Conservative vote segregation and the rising pre-tax take of the top 1 per cent, will have strengthened.

Globally, the very richest people on earth, ultra high-net-worth individuals (UHNWIs), are now estimated by the Swiss bank and financial services company UBS's *Wealth-X* report to make up just 0.004 per cent of the planet's human population. In 2014, that bank predicted that '... in the next five years, the size of the global ultra-high net worth population will swell to more than 250,000 individuals and their combined net worth will almost surpass $40 trillion US'.[93] What the bankers describe as a 'swelling' in absolute terms is, in fact, a shrinking to 0.003 per cent for a human population approaching 8 billion in the next 10 years. Meanwhile, the bank Credit Suisse suggests that total global wealth will rise by 40 per cent, or by an additional $106 trillion, in the five years from 2014 to 2019, with almost all of that newly 'created' wealth going to the very richest people on earth.

In 2013, Credit Suisse estimated that the richest 1 per cent held 41 per cent of all wealth on the planet. By 2014, their estimate for that same group had grown to 1 per cent then holding 48 per cent of all the wealth on the planet. At that rate of increase, at some point during 2021, the 1 per cent will come to hold every last penny – some 99 per cent of the population will have nothing or be in debt, which is impossible to conceive.[94] And in fact, Oxfam's prediction in January 2015, that they will come to hold more than half of all the wealth on the planet by 2016, predicts something of a slowdown. We are living in the most remarkable and dangerous times, times when what is currently occurring is simply not sustainable, not even for just half a dozen more years.

Assortative mating

The story from the late 1970s onwards is again, one of assortative mating becoming popular in times of rising inequality, but it is now no longer simply about the sharing of the family wealth. This assortative mating became also about marrying people with similar occupational incomes. From the early 1970s onwards, more and more women were permitted to hold jobs that paid more than a pittance, and to keep working after marriage. Looks and freedom began to matter less and less, even for the poorest; what mattered more and more was class.[95]

From the late 1970s, salaries at the top end began to diverge upwards. Warped morals also began to be countenanced again in countries like Britain, morals that suggested that ruthless competition was good, cooperation bad, just a few were truly talented, and they should have their talents supposedly 'justly rewarded'. If you began to believe that, you became more careful with whom you slept. It was not just that the lives of the rich became more separated from the poor, but that the implications of mixing became more daunting.

Slowly at first, and then more quickly, the highest paid became even more highly paid. Dual-income higher-earner households moved away from all other household types most quickly. Income inequalities rose, and as they rose, the idea of mixing socially with those a little less well-off became just a little less palatable with every year that passed; there was literally more, in terms of money (much more), to lose by a 'bad marriage'. This reached such an extent in the US that by 2007, young people from affluent families were being told that on early dates they should be clear and say: 'There's something important I need to share with you. In my family we do prenups.'[96] It is difficult to think of a phrase, other than 'I have herpes, would you like to share?', as off-putting as 'in my family we do prenups', unless you already have either, in which case it doesn't matter.[97] Rates of mixing by marriage fell in the more unequal of countries from the 1970s onwards.

In the US, those falls in social mixing resulted in a slowing down of the rise, since the abolition of slavery, in the number of inter-racial marriages.[98] Until recently, white and black couples were rarely shown on television in the US, and it is partly low rates of inter-racial marriages that maintain such high poverty levels among black Americans. In the US, having great-great-grandparents who were in slavery is the legacy single-handedly most likely to result in low financial inheritance, because of the legacy of slavery, and of laws and then traditions designed to prevent non-assortative mating between what were seen as separate races (miscegenation). This has resulted in both the huge extent of inequalities in wealth found in the US, and the great reluctance of even those who own just a little wealth to work cooperatively and to sociably invest in the common good.

There is a great misconception that affluent North Americans donate monies to charity to aid the common good, but, as a former director of the Ford Foundation revealed in forensic detail, only a tiny fraction of their charitable giving is for that.[99] The rich in the US are happy to take money from the poor, but do not like to 'give' to the poor, either through charity or taxation. It is a wider kind of racism that begets a legacy that breeds the mistrust that maintains such miserliness. This mistrust is much greater than simply the self-interest of the rich, the majority of whom are ultimately rich directly as a legacy of inheritance and, in the not so distant past, of entrepreneurship such as slave owning. It is a mistrust that becomes endemic and spreads throughout almost the whole of societies, where the continued inheritance of wealth within very unequal families is so crucial to the social status quo.

It is one of the cruellest ironies of inheritance that it results in the great-great-grandchildren of slaves in the US also being so likely to have their freedom denied, as they end up living in the one country in the world where imprisonment among blacks is the most common. Incarceration in the US is predominantly applied to poor non-white Americans, whose inheritance is to be written out of that country's official picture because they have been born in a country where both their social position and skin colour make it much more likely that they will find they are routed to live through the earnings of crime. It is the extreme end of more widespread prejudice that says so many black Americans are not part of the formal economy, not part of society, and once convicted of a felony, in over a dozen states no longer part of politics, as they can no longer vote again under those states' laws.

Those in prison are not called unemployed, because it is said they are not looking for work. While it is true that they cannot look for work, it is disingenuous in the extreme to suggest, in effect by omitting them, that they would rather not have paid work. The unemployment rate in the US would be a percentage point higher if prisoners were included. The vast increase in the size of prison populations in those affluent nations that have chosen to build the most prisons has had the effect of dramatically increasing the range of possibilities on the social scale in those countries, creating a lot more over-crowded space at the very bottom, in cells, and a lot more under-occupied space at the top for a few, in mansions.

Those prison cells for people at the bottom act, in a way, as a counterweight to the great wealth of the few at the top. It is hard to find a country where the richest are so very wealthy, and where they do not also have many prisons. Racism is needed to maintain these differences – not just the inheritance of wealth, but also the inheritance of disadvantage and prejudice. People would not tolerate mass incarceration in jails in Britain or the US if so many of the inmates were not labelled as a 'race apart' through the colour of their skins. Jails in Japan and Scandinavia are few, and are individually much smaller and less punitive institutions; this is because other people in Japan and the Scandinavian countries are so much more often viewed as equals.

The colour of our skin is one of the few things we clearly physically inherit. However, we only notice that inheritance because of the time and place we were born in. Had those who first sailed to the places that became called New England, the Caribbean, the Indies and Australasia, differed most from the people they met there by height, or by the size of their noses, or the colour of their hair, then those characteristics would have become the physical features that would be used as a shorthand for social status. Because it was skin colour that most clearly and reliably differentiated Europeans from those they conquered, skin colour has the longest legacy, and is the great inheritance.

As more and more extreme life events are considered, skin colour matters more in influencing life chances. The risk of suffering rises almost everywhere as skin colour darkens. Only deaths from melanoma are the exception. This prejudice born in Europe is now most blatantly expressed in those countries on the edge of rich world empires. Thus in Brazil, nine out of ten of the suspects police shoot are black, while five times fewer black civilians (2 per cent) make it to college compared with whites (10 per cent).[100] South Africa rivals Brazil, even after the formal abolition of apartheid, in terms of income and wealth inequalities, and in India, potential brides and bridegrooms are advertised in newspapers by the lightness of their skins, to indicate a caste structure that was greatly reinforced through British rule. Countries that were not colonies tend to have far weaker so-called 'traditions' of social division. All these evils are largely at source an inheritance, or an old prejudice preserved with European assistance, from thinking that dates from what Europeans still call their 'Enlightenment' period.

5.5 The 1970s: the new racism

On a visit to the US in the 1970s, the Conservative politician and later Prime Minister Margaret Thatcher explained her thinking on equality thus: 'One of the reasons that we value individuals is not because they're all the same, but because they're all different.... I would say, let our children grow tall and some taller than others if they have the ability in them to do so. Because we must build a society in which each citizen can develop his full potential, both for his own benefit and for the community as a whole....'[101] Others endlessly repeated her thoughts and occasionally her words. Eventually the assertion that different individuals have different 'ability' within them became normalised. Ability potential was to be treated like height. Apparently, a child should be well fed intellectually only after showing potential to grow, and only well educated as a result of passing some test of their supposed inherent ability early on, or qualifying because of their parents' high earnings.[102] And thus, by the end of the

20th century, the strange notion that by acting selfishly people benefit others in some way became accepted.

The turning points in Figures 12–14 have all fallen in the 1970s. Whether we consider inequalities in health, in voting, or in wealth, in Britain people and places became less and less divided from the end of the First World War right through to the early 1970s. A similar story can be told of the US and of those other affluent nations that decided to go the way of the rich Anglophone giants (such as Singapore or Australia). The 1960s had been a decade of social achievement, not so much for what was achieved during those years as for their being the apogee of half a century of slow and steady social progress. This progress was partly won at the expense of the rest of the world, who took over much food production (freeing peasants in Europe), who began to mill textiles (freeing factory workers in Japan), and who dug coal (freeing many miners in the US from dirty dangerous work). The story told in these countries was that technology and mechanisation had made them rich, but that did not explain why, by the end of the 1960s, so much more of what they consumed came from abroad compared with the 1920s.

While the 1960s might be portrayed as the progressive era within rich nations it was hardly so for other countries. Around the world people had to fight for their independence from colonialism. They were not released from those shackles willingly, although again, this is not the story commonly now told. We easily forget that there was a point not long ago where it was only half-heartedly joked that the majority of the world's leaders had at one time or another seen the inside of a British-run prison. Today, the majority of those leaders are more likely to have seen the inside of the LSE, or one of a few similar universities, as we now co-opt and attempt to convert future national leaders to our mythologies more often than incarcerating them.

The 1960s were also the time when talk of 'development' began to become commonplace. The story was that there was a path that could be followed, and that if poorer countries were to do what richer countries' mythologies said they had done, then the poor could be rich too. All that was needed was to mechanise, industrialise and democratise, then the people of poor countries could be rich too. We still say this today. When this did not occur, the mutterings of racist reasoning began.

Racists suggested that black and brown people were simply not capable of running countries, were inherently lazy, or corrupt, or both. They could not be trusted in countries like Vietnam to make their own choices. Across Africa intervention was needed in terms of arms if not troops. Latin America was looked down on with concern from Washington, a capital city from where strings began to be pulled in earnest, most obviously in Chile in 1973. The underlying rhetoric all the time was that these people needed 'help', that providing such 'help' was the continued 'white man's burden'[103] that richer countries needed to indirectly rule those not so white, especially if they might turn to socialism or communism. As elitist thoughts were sustained in rich nations throughout the 1950s, and exclusion of the poor became tolerated again in the 1960s at home, in the 1970s, the rich began again to see their destiny as to rule, but now through intervention, co-option and conversion rather than directly through colonial mandate. And they called this leadership.

Instilling a sense of fear

Although tempting for the sake of simplicity, it would be wrong to claim everything fits neatly into decadal buckets. The antecedents of the rise of new racism in the 1970s abounded in the late 1960s, but were then mainly found between the cracks of what were otherwise progressive politics. Briefly, in 1969, rebellious students even took over running the LSE (for a day or so). Across the rich world students were becoming mistrustful of what they were being taught. Outside of the UK they were usually far more radical and effective. But not all politics was moving to the left.

It was perhaps the commissioning of the publication of the 1968 book *The population bomb* in the US that marked the beginnings of the 'new racism' most clearly. We now know that the book was commissioned by a group with the aim of using it to try to encourage the further restriction of immigration from poorer countries to rich countries. We also now know that similar groups and work spread to Europe very soon after.[104] The book was about attempting to protect the privileges of the rich, and it was not produced with much concern for the rest of the population. It was written in the midst of mass sterilisation campaigns, mostly designed to prevent people in poorer countries who were not white from having their non-white babies.

In the US internally, it was in the early 1970s that the political shift towards the right began. At first it was at grassroots level. In 1972, a young man called Karl Rove, who was later nicknamed George W. Bush's 'brain', was elected chair of the (student) college Republican movement. People like Rove capitalised on the new fears of the rich of the time, fear of the levels that equality within their rich countries had reached, fear of unions, fear of women's groups, fear of blacks and civil rights, fear of homosexuals, of communists, of almost anyone who was not like how they liked to think they were, fear of the hordes they saw massing in the poor countries of the world, fear of all those black and brown babies, fear of an end to their status. The Republican message swung to the political right to address these fears, and funding came from the scared rich to its campaigns. You could see repercussions both in votes, in Congress in 1976 and 1978, and in the nomination and election of growing numbers of far-right senators, doubling in number between 1975 and 1979, culminating in the selection and victory of Ronald Reagan in 1980.[105]

David Goldberg puts it thus: '[within the US] … from the 1970s on, the state increasingly came to be conceived as a set of institutions supporting the undeserving.… Fear of a black state is linked to worries about a black planet, of alien invasion and alien*ation*, of a loss of the sort of local and global control and privilege long associated with whiteness.'[106] Thus it was a new racism itself that was at the heart of these political swings. Fear of 'oriental hordes' who could beat American troops in the 'Far East', fear of the grandsons and daughters of slaves who would march for and win their rights at home, fear that as economic growth in the US began its long and steady slowdown from 1973 onwards (see Figure 10 in Chapter 4) the empire of the US was beginning to see the end of its time.

The fear of others at the gates was held most acutely by the elite in the late 1960s and early 1970s. By the end of that decade, these fears had been projected into the consciousness of the public at large. Inflation rose, joblessness increased, and above all, immigration was blamed and those so-called 'greedy Arabs' who were *all* becoming millionaires by making oil as expensive as gold (or so the myths went). Racism rose in the 1970s because the times were right and enough people thought they would benefit from promoting it. A long and steady progressive

Figure 15: Net immigration, England and Wales, by birth year, 1840–2080

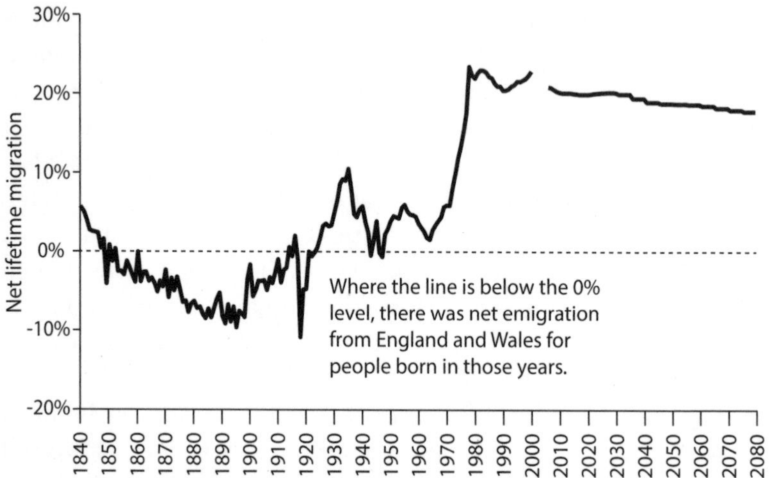

Note: The graph shows how many more people entered than left England and Wales, as a proportion of the recorded births in any year, calculated from the number of recorded deaths of people born in that year. Official projections up to 2080 are used to extrapolate forwards and include people who have not yet died and those not yet born.

Source: Dorling, D. (2009) *Migration: A long run perspective,* London: IPPR, Figure 8.

Estimates and projections for net immigration (every tenth year only)

	Births	Deaths*	Net lifetime migration	% net migration of birth cohort
1840	502,303	532,528	30,225	6%
1850	593,422	598,424	5,002	1%
1860	684,048	683,873	-175	0%
1870	792,787	775,043	-17,744	-2%
1880	882,643	829,769	-51,874	-6%
1890	869,937	803,806	-66,131	-8%
1900	927,062	912,111	-14,951	-2%
1910	896,962	888,575	-8,387	-1%
1920	957,782	914,563	-43,219	-5%
1930	648,811	682,586	33,775	5%
1940	590,120	626,421	36,301	6%
1950	697,097	725,268	28,171	4%
1960	785,005	814,493	29,488	4%

	Births	Deaths*	Net lifetime migration	% net migration of birth cohort
1970	784,486	833,726	49,240	6%
1980	656,234	842,088	185854	22%
1990	706,140	888,176	182036	20%
2000	604,441	784,451	180010	23%
2010	714,345	895,859	181,514	20%
2020	725,246	906,760	181,514	20%
2030	715,630	897,144	181,514	20%
2040	749,792	931,306	181,514	19%
2050	780,560	962,074	181,514	19%
2060	786,580	968,094	181,514	19%
2070	811,200	992,714	181,514	18%
2080	835,088	1,016,602	181,514	18%

*Deaths within England and Wales of people born this year

social trend was coming to an end, bringing uncertainty, and it is easy in uncertain times to breed yet more fear. That new trend of uncertainty also concerned fertility and the demand for more people.

Figure 15 shows the number of people who died or who are predicted to die in England and Wales as a proportion of the population who were born there (or will be born there) at their time of birth, from 1840 through to predictions made up to 2080. The trends it shows are similar to those found elsewhere in Europe, such as in Sweden, and the recent trends are also typical of the US. Of those born in the 1840s, more people came to England and Wales to live (and die) than left. Famine in Ireland helped ensure that, but there was also great demand for labour in the 19th century, more than could be met simply by fertility at home and migration from the countryside. But as economic recession hit (towards the end of the century), demand for labour fell, and emigration was commonplace for those born in 1850 onwards, rising throughout the gilded age, peaking around the 1890 to 1900 birth cohorts for people who would be sent to their deaths abroad in the First World War or in the turbulent 1920s or the Great Depression of the 1930s, when they left to find work and a new life abroad. At least a tenth of those born in 1919 in England and Wales emigrated and died elsewhere. But fertility also fell in the 1920s and 1930s; contraception became widespread; women slowly gained the power to say 'no' more often; and so, by the time of the cohort of the late 1930s, those who were born and stayed in England and Wales were joined by at least an extra 10 per cent who were born overseas or in Scotland. They came in the late 1950s, 1960s and early 1970s. They came to replace the babies who were never born, and many used their arrival to reignite racism.

Immigration and colonisation

The peak in immigration to Britain in the 1960s and early 1970s was of people born abroad in the late 1930s and early 1940s, and was clearly a response to demand for labour. It was seen as such then, and in hindsight, it is even more clearly apparent now. There was less demand in the 1980s, so the record in Figure 15 shows that later (net) immigration of people born in the late 1940s and 1950s fell rapidly as the baby boomers of 1946 onwards entered the job market, and as the 1970s and 1980s recessions reduced demand. Figure 15 also shows how net immigration rates fell again until the cohorts born abroad in the 1970s and later began to arrive in large numbers into England and Wales in the late 1990s. Racism has recently again been rekindled, as first reflected in votes for the BNP in 2009, and then in much of the voting for UKIP in 2014, at a time when 'British workers are suffering their biggest slump in real wages since economic crises in the 1860s and 1870s.'[107]

People can easily be swayed into racist thought, and with a little more persuasion, into racist action. On racist thought, opinion polls swing wildly. Ask the right question at the right time, and you can suggest that uppermost in a majority of British, or American, or German, or Japanese minds, are fears of immigration. Say the right key words enough times, and never mention countervailing views, and you can pick up a great many votes from people who have been made to fear those not as white (or light-skinned) as themselves. It took right-wing parties in the US and the UK almost the whole of the 1970s to come to fully play the race card at the end of that decade. Richard Nixon played it a little, Ronald Reagan a lot; Edward Heath did not find space for Enoch Powell in his government, but Margaret Thatcher was careful to court racist voters.

In Britain, racist murders became much more common by the late 1970s, and it took all of the 1980s and most of the 1990s and 2000s to bring levels of racism, violence, intolerance and fear back to what had been more normal in the 1960s. However, in both the US and Britain, that new racism did not really lessen after the 1970s; rather, it became transformed into a wider racism applied by those who felt superior not just to black people, but also to particular white people who they saw as a group of humanity, as a race 'by common descent', as inferior to themselves. And once you see other human beings as a group as inferior when compared with your group, as different from you and yours, then your compulsion to behave well towards them is greatly reduced.

On acting out racism, the orchestrations of massacres in Vietnam, and those later made possible in Cambodia as a result, were the most well-known set of atrocities exposed in the years immediately before and during the 1970s. Connected with the Cold War, and undertaken in the fog of that war,[108] far more again were being killed in wars both in and on the borders of India, and in atrocities within China and Cambodia, but it was on Vietnam that the world's press first focused. One particular massacre, in the village of My Lai on 16 March 1968, drew particular ire once it was revealed that it had happened, and that the authorities had subsequently covered it up in the early 1970s. Hundreds of civilians, almost all women, children or old men, were systematically murdered over the course of a day by just a handful of US soldiers.

For a time it was thought that the one soldier who blew the whistle on the My Lai massacre, Ron Ridenhour, was also one of the few hundred people tested in the famous psychological experiments conducted by Stanley Milgram in the early 1960s to find out how well people would follow orders if these were given by an authority figure. These were the experiments in which people were asked by a man in a white laboratory coat to turn a dial administering an electric shock to an unseen but screaming victim. Ron Ridenhour was one of the very few people undertaking Stanley Milgram's experiments who refused to turn the dial on the machine up high when ordered; if he was not the same man who refused to keep quiet over the My Lai massacre, they were both, nonetheless, very unusual. But their attitudes were illustrative of the shape of things that could come.[109]

Just as there were a few individuals brought up well balanced enough to risk their lives saving people persecuted by the Nazis in occupied Europe, so when the US invaded Vietnam there were a few willing to act against their orders, and conscientious objection rose rapidly following news of the My Lai massacre. Never again could the US draft men to war; instead, it had to coerce the poor to fight for money in its later wars. Men and women do not join armies by free will when the alternative is poverty, but many of the poor know how bad a deal this coercive 'offer' really is. By the 21st century the US had started bribing people from abroad with green cards to enter the country if they promised to join the army and fight in Iraq. The US military only met its 2008/09 recruitment targets because the economic crash had left so many young men jobless and desperate. Opposing a war, which was rare a century ago, became commonplace by the start of the new century, with the largest demonstrations of all time being the worldwide marches in protest at the US-orchestrated invasion of Iraq in 2003.

In the 1970s the protests were against the US, British and other affluent nations' governments' support for apartheid in South Africa. But most people did not understand what the protestors were protesting about. South Africa was a long way away, and the people the protestors appeared to be concerned about were black. In the UK overt racism by the authorities was common in the 1970s. Young white policemen beat up young black men as a matter of routine. It has taken yet another generation for it to be widely accepted now, just how abhorrent that was.[110]

Hardening of souls

In the past many individuals found it easier to follow orders. Childhoods across the rich world were often traumatic just a couple of generations ago. And traumatised individuals will more often blindly do what they are told and not question authority. Army training is deliberately traumatising. Children just two generations ago were to be seen and not heard, were often abandoned, regularly beaten and systematically terrorised to such an extent that the majority of children were what we would now consider abused – according to Lloyd DeMause, historian of childhood and psychologist.[111] Children who have been abused can, in adulthood, become formidable, sometimes racist, bullies. Now in affluent countries, far fewer children are brought up in these ways, but sadly, many still suffer trauma, not just from abuse, but also from events such as having the misfortune of experiencing the loss of a parent through divorce and separation or even death early in their childhood, with subsequently insufficient care taken over their welfare. That can harden people. When the poor are hardened, they teach their toddlers to fight, to harden them in turn, and often find ideas such as racism attractive.[112] When the powerful are hardened in these ways, they may be far less empathetic to the poor (or anyone else) later in life. And they may find it easier to behave in ways that are also racist. Upbringing of a particular type, regardless of wealth, is what later leads to racist beliefs.

Racism is the belief in the superiority of a particular race. A race is seen as a major division of humanity, a group of people connected by common descent. Traditionally racism has been targeted at a series of people who were seen to have their common descent revealed by the colour of their skin, facial features or language, but any group treated with disdain because they are seen as connected by common descent can become the subject of racism. As racism among many affluent people has evolved from its crude 1970s form to a more general detesting of the poor as inferior, so the nature of those who enact the changing racism, the treating of people as racially inferior, has changed. In 2011 Owen Jones published *Chavs: The demonization of the working class*, to illustrate class racism.

Now the wider racism is much more enacted in boardrooms by businesspeople who consider their target groups of customers – as groups – as inferior, the kind of people (they say) you need to know in order to exploit, but who you would not want to live near or mix with. One estate agent specialising in 'executive property' in London in 2007 even took out newspaper advertisements suggesting that while you needed to understand 'the customer' to do well in business, there was no need to live near 'them'. It is worth comparing the renewal of racism in the 1970s and the rise of business thinking then, to the great racism of business behaviour now, and the people who organise what can be most clearly thought of as racist ways of 'segmenting' markets of consumers. Why might they do this?

It is too much of a coincidence that successful but ruthless businesspeople have generally had traumatic early childhoods.[113] We also now know from a great deal of scientific research that people with psychopathic tendencies tend to do well in business,[114] and that the 'business ethic' requires people to behave in ways that are seen as immoral in personal life. As a counter-culture grows, as their own children ask them why they are working to try to produce more and more when the world needs fewer goods, less consumption, increasingly a few more people working towards the top of private businesses come to know, within their heart-of-hearts, that what they are doing and how they are acting is wrong. The evidence comes when people drop out and say how much they hated themselves for what they were doing; it can be seen through attempts to 'greenwash' companies, and to try to suggest they are ethical, corporately responsible, in some ways.

If businesspeople were happy with their image, they would not engage in puffery to imply they care more than they do. There are a few who proclaim that they believe wholeheartedly in unfettered free markets. These are the kinds of people who charge extra for a wheelchair on their airline's aeroplanes; or who run very large advertising agencies and truly believe that that industry is beneficial for everyone, and not just a money-spinner for them. Such individuals exist, but most free-marketers are less fundamentalist. Like all of us, businesspeople try to legitimise their lives and to find ways to defend why they do what they do, but it was becoming clear that this was becoming harder and harder to achieve before the financial crisis of 2008.

People are now trying to run businesses knowing that they are increasingly despised for how they act, how they pollute, how they hire and fire at will, how they profit from misery.[115] Although a few more than before are learning, most still rarely admit that what they do is wrong. More and more of the general public are becoming aware that bankers are not often compassionate, well-meaning people, but few realise that corporate law requires businesses to act in ways psychiatrists would diagnose as psychopathic in an individual. However, such concepts that once just appeared in academic papers and tomes are now increasingly discussed in books aimed at the general public.[116]

Defending the indefensible

Trauma in the childhood or young adulthood of men (in particular) leads them to be more likely to later act in anti-social ways. This is undisputed as concerns criminality, but it is just as true for anti-social activity that is currently legal. For instance, to be able to take orders and kill as a sniper in the army it helps to have psychopathic tendencies: how else could you line the sights up slowly on another human being's head and then, when you are ready, gently pull the trigger, or (more often today) be able to press the button to release the drone's rockets? You need to be able to imagine that the target is not really human, is not like you (or that you are a god). During the Second World War it would have been treasonable to say that of soldiers on your side of the war. Today it is common sense, but once you see sniping and bombing as psychopathic, you begin to question war more widely.

In England, school children are given books written by George Orwell as set texts for understanding literature. In one, Orwell wrote: 'In our time political speech and writing are largely the defence of the indefensible.... Political language ... is designed to make lies sound truthful and murder respectable.'[117] We now collectively both know and can say so much that could, until recently, only be said in private.

Similarly to what it takes to make killing in war appear respectable, we now recognise that those who tend to rise to the top in business and politics are more likely than their fellow men (and it is normally fellow men) to have what is described as a '... ruthless readiness to disown the obligations of regard',[118] to be willing to tread on the necks of others on the way up, make promises but not honour them, take gifts but not give something back, be self-assured to the point of megalomania. In universities just after the 2009 crash, it was said that these more selfish people are more often found among '... the kind of people we find in business schools and economics departments'.[119] However, although that may have been true then, it may well be changing now.

What we think of as racism changes over time. It has only been since the 1930s that we began to widely recognise racism as it is currently thought of, and only since the 1960s that the word 'racism' has appeared in dictionaries (including the word 'racialism'[120] and the even more recent 'racist'). Just as with poverty, exclusion and elitism, racism has not always been with us as it appears now, and, as with poverty, only recently have very large numbers of people become committed to its eradication.

The currently propagated mass prejudice, that the poor are somehow inherently inferior, will come to pass too. But its passing must be aided, and we must be vigilant for what spite will next be promoted by those who fear a world in which they and theirs are no longer supreme. Human beings are easily prone to prejudice, and can easily fall under the spell of a single charismatic individual. We have seen this often enough to learn from our collective experiences. Those with less are not a 'race apart' you should fear living near, mixing with, or your children marrying.

It is as simple and, for some, as hard to understand as that.[121]

6

'Greed is good': consumption and waste

> … the rich are way more likely to prioritize their own self-interests above the interests of other people. It makes them more likely to exhibit characteristics that we would stereotypically associate with, say, assholes.[1]

By late 2014, chief executives of UK FTSE 100 firms were paid, on average, 342 times more than their minimum wage employees. Their pay had risen by 243 per cent since the minimum wage was introduced in 1999, three times faster than the rise in the minimum wage. The price of a loaf of bread had risen twice as fast as the minimum wage, gas prices by even more, but the 'compensation' of chief executives by more again. The poor could afford less food, while the rich had more than ever before.[2]

Because 'the great and the good' know that suggesting in public that greed is good is seen as a little immoral, many of those in positions of power, who produce the news, who can use their positions to promote their opinions to us, are nowadays very careful not to be too explicit, or at least not too often explicit, about their beliefs. The majority of those who favour inequality use phrases such as preferring to be 'independent', or 'neutral', or wishing to be seen as 'considered', 'balanced' or 'reasonable' in what they say. Many of our elected politicians believe that a few deserve far more than others, but to be successful, they want to win as many votes as they can from those holding as wide a range of opinions as possible so they need to appear magnanimous and to have the common touch and to be presented in the media as reasonable people.

Those politicians who believe that most citizens are feeble and destined to be ruled by the few (like them) do not say 'you need a firm hand' to 'their' public. Similarly, many leading journalists do not want to give their readers, listeners and viewers the impression that they look down on them, so tend *not* to display their real views prominently when on air or writing for the mainstream media. We know what they really think of most people, however, from what they say in their more obscure publications, and sometimes from their affiliations. You have to look carefully for direct evidence that so many 'at the top' believe in propositions such as that, ultimately, 'greed is good'. Similarly, academics in public life who believe that most people are not as *generally* able as they are (or think they are) are usually polite enough not to say so in so few words because even egoists can predict the medium-term consequences of saying what they really think about others.

Public figures often wish to appear to be concerned about the environment, inequality, even elitism, when speaking openly. On the printed page they are occasionally more direct, especially if that printed page is an obscure pamphlet, in an elite publication, or when tucked away towards the end of a book of more than 300 pages. Take, for example, what in 2008 the British Broadcasting Corporation's (BBC's) then business editor meant when (buried deep in his book) he suggested that: 'It may not be pretty but, on the whole, greed is good.'[3] The man who said this, Robert Peston, was subsequently the most viewed face to be seen on British television news describing the anatomy of the economic crash of that year, the same year in which his book made clear that he believed greed is good, not because of what he had seen and was seeing, but because of what he had earlier been taught to believe as an economics student. His father was also an economist, and after university, before taking up journalism, Robert had been a stockbroker.[4]

The man who wrote the archetypal film about stockbrokers, 'Wall Street', who coined the phrase 'greed, for lack of a better word, is good', was talking on the radio one Saturday morning on a show to which Robert Peston frequently contributed.[5] When asked in 2009 if he could write the film today, he told the presenter that, whereas in the 1980s greed had been individual, in the early years of the current century, it had become institutional. By 2013, films such as 'The Wolf of Wall Street' were quasi-historical depictions of the 1980s, and a few who had supported greed before were changing their minds. In 2012, Robert Peston, now the BBC's economics editor, published *How do we fix this mess? The economic price of having it all and the route to lasting prosperity.* But the former economics editor, Paul Mason, left the BBC to work for Channel 4 and to publish books, including in 2009, *Meltdown – The end of the age of greed*, a book that did not have to be BBC-vetted and so could go a little further into possible explanations for our current economic dilemmas. Accepted wisdom is being questioned in economics as it has not been questioned for decades, but that questioning is not yet very evident on mainstream news outlets such as the BBC and other broadcasters in the most inequitable of affluent countries.

The BBC is an example of an institution that, for all its 'balance', subtly promotes greed as good through the style of its economic coverage. US news outlets provide even more obvious examples of such bias. However, it would be harder to create a character like Gordon Gekko from 'Wall Street' today and make him plausible as anything but an historical figure. Gekko was an unusual loner, out for himself, but he was convinced that his selfishness was for the common good. By 2008, this thinking had entered the mainstream. Today, almost all of us know what folly it is to celebrate the greedy. And it is only a small subset of the greedy who are unapologetic believers that they, the 0.01 per cent, '... create thousands of jobs and invest billions in human capital each year',[6] but the mainstream media in the US and the UK have not yet begun to hold such individuals to account or expose the unsustainable pension and other 'savings' schemes they encourage.

Anyone with a private or occupational pension (in practice, the same thing) now acts, by proxy, like Gordon Gekko. Their pension fund managers believe 'greed is good' and they have acted on those beliefs. Laws have been passed which say they must do this – they must act to maximise the return on their clients' investments regardless of the consequences, and so they have done this on a global scale, acting solely on behalf of the most affluent section of society in just a few rich countries of the world. These bankers acted a little bit more diligently to maximise returns for themselves, it must also be said. Thanks to greed, fund managers tend to be better off than most people, even those with occupational pensions. As a result people on occupational pensions are now also much better off, compared with those reliant solely on state pensions. This widening can be seen most clearly when the early 2000s are compared with the early 1980s, when we were again taught a lesson we last heard in the 1920s, a lesson about the apparent 'goodness' of greed.

At the very top of the pile of fund managers were those managing the amalgamated private funds of just a few extremely rich individuals. These were the young bankers who, until the 2008 crash, were often pictured in newspapers partying in Manhattan and Mayfair, metaphorically dripping with cash. At the dizzy temporal and spatial apex of the boom, in London's elite party land of 2007, you could spend £35,000 on a single drink. Three days after this fact was reported in a national newspaper, that same paper revealed how the British Labour government's budget decisions had resulted in a huge future transfer of wealth to the rich due to changes to the law on inheritance tax. A leading columnist wrote that the '... juxtaposition was cruel: poor children got another 48p a week, while the middle-aged middle class, whose parents leave a house worth, say, £400,000, gained another £40,000'.[7] That tax break for the rich, following even greater tax breaks occurring across the Atlantic (in the years up to and including 2007), was seen – together with the bankers' most extreme excesses – as evidence that we were back in the last years of a 'gilded age'. At the heart of all this was greed.

The £35,000 drink contained a diamond, so its true unrecoverable cost will have been much lower, but not very low. Diamond prices collapsed with the economic crash of 2008, so, unless the drinker sold his diamond quickly, the cost to him of that drink may have been around $10,000. This is almost the exact equivalent of smoking a cigarette rolled in a $100 note in the 1920s, which was a popular activity in notorious parties of the North American super-rich held over a century ago, right up to the eve of the great crash of 1929.[8] As the graphs in the last chapter made clear (especially Figure 14), it was in the early decades of a century ago that wealth inequalities were last as unequal as they became by 2007, when greed was last seen as being as great, when people were last so profligate, when consumption by those with money was last so vaunted as valuable.

This chapter describes how we have come again to see greed as good, and have erected a new great squalor of excess so quickly after having largely demolished the old squalor of the most unfit homes in the most affluent of countries. The injustice of greed has replaced the old social evil of squalor as surely as elitism has overtaken ignorance, exclusion has eclipsed want, and prejudice has transcended idleness. But in the years since the 2008 crash, more and more people have come to realise this. Now, only the most fervent believers in the old order consider the greedy to be 'wealth creators'. Most commentators who are not rich have changed their tunes, and some may have also changed their minds.

6.1 Not part of the programme: just getting by, a quarter of all households

Squalor in the 1940s was life in crowded damp accommodation with inadequate hygiene, no hot running water, and often no inside toilet. By the late 1970s, in most rich countries, most of the least hygienic dwellings had been converted or demolished, but a new form of squalor then arose. The rich began to take a greater and greater share of living space, of land, of luxury possessions, spare houses and anything else not actually needed by themselves but seen as a good investment. Local life in poor areas became downgraded despite the renewal of the worst housing.

In poorer areas local shops closed, which meant people needed a car to do the weekly shopping if they also had children to look after, or if they found walking difficult, and especially so in the US, a country with many parts largely bereft of pavements. In contrast, in urban Japan, public transport is so good that it is not necessary to drive, and many people who could afford a car choose not to own one. In Britain, statistics on car ownership are now released through surveys of wealth. Cars are seen as an asset signifying wealth or poverty because public transport is not well distributed. By 2014, the Joseph Rowntree Foundation was reporting that '... worsening public transport has necessitated more use of taxis for households without children, or cars for those with children'.[9] Cars for people with children had become a necessity.

The British Wealth and Assets Surveys, first taken in their current form in 2006/07 and released in 2008,[10] showed that almost two in every five households had goods and furniture in their home worth more than £30,000, and often worth much more, while many others could not even afford the simple things that had become necessities, such as access to a car for those looking after young children. The surveys revealed, through showing which families did not have these goods, that in Britain, it was people most likely to need goods such as cars who did not have them.

In 2007, a quarter of households in Britain had no access to a car (26 per cent). Among that quarter were almost half (48 per cent) of all lone parents, adults whose children were solely dependent on them for care. In contrast, half (51 per cent) of married couples with dependent children owned at least two cars, and more than two thirds (69 per cent) of married couples without dependent children also had at least two cars.

We allocate goods like cars almost directly in reverse proportion to need. Amazingly, some 7 per cent of all people who live on their own also have two or more cars! Clearly families with young children have more need for cars, in order not to have to carry shopping and push buggies simultaneously, for instance. And it would also make sense to bring shops back nearer to the people, and simultaneously to improve public transport. This is what happens in more equitable affluent countries (see Figure 26, Chapter 8). It may not be mostly due to planners that it happens, but due to great equity and the private market working better (driving fewer poor decisions) where there is greater overall equity. Many decisions of the elite are bad decisions in places where the 1% take the most.

In countries like Britain, where inequalities have been allowed to rise so high, many households cope with inequality by getting into debt; some 35 per cent have unsecured debts, some of many kinds; 3 per cent have store card debt; 6 per cent mail order debt; 9 per cent hire purchase debt; 13 per cent have other unsecured loans; and 20 per cent have credit card debt. The rates are higher for people in employment, who are more likely to be given and offered loans. The debt rates are highest for women aged 25–34, most of whom have unsecured debt they are trying to repay, and this is all before including student loans that are being deferred, and excluding any mortgage liabilities. All these numbers come from the Wealth and Assets Surveys. The surveys were first press released in an attempt at a triumphant January 2008 'good news' story, with the headline, 'Seven in ten adults have savings or investments'.[11]

By 2014, the latest statistics from the Wealth and Assets Survey, Wave 3, were revealing that among people in the UK aged 60–64, the best-off 20 per cent had 174 times the wealth of the 20 per cent worst-off people of their age in terms of accrued pension pots. For the worst-off 20 per cent of the population, it is not until they reach age 60 that they are likely to be just out of debt. In contrast, the best-off fifth of people mostly start to have savings, rather than debt, from their teens onwards. This is excluding the mortgages most of the best-off fifth will be able to both take out and repay. Many then find that on retirement they can often move house and receive a huge unearned windfall – inheritance tends to be greatest to those who already have the most wealth overall, and to be received at the point when they are already very wealthy in their lives. People whose need for more is least tend also to get more when they need it the least. The overall result now is that: 'Whereas a generation ago, status in society depended crucially on school and education, in future it could well depend on access to the southern property market.'[12]

Although the original Wealth and Assets Survey, based on pre-crash data, showed most households had savings, it simultaneously revealed that about a quarter were also in one kind of serious financial difficulty or another, and the assets of the rest were slowly (and in some cases rapidly) crumbling, not least as the British government was 'lending' unprecedented amounts of money it did not have to some of the largest of the same banks in which those seven in ten adults had investments (to keep the banks afloat). But most households with substantial savings in the UK were not suffering. To see who literally had least, you need to look at the distribution of simple goods that have become essential, and at who is unable to have those essentials.

Figure 16 shows how, by 2007, there were more households with two, three, four or even more cars than there were households with no car in Britain. These figures are again taken from data collected for the first Wealth and Assets Survey to be carried out in Britain for many years. The previous survey was carried out in the 1970s by a Royal Commission, after which successive British governments did not appear to believe that the distribution of wealth mattered enough to try to measure it properly. The recent survey showed clearly that there were more than enough assets to go round in the country, enough wealth and money for all to be well off, and cars provide just the simplest example of this. As the second table in Figure 16 reveals, the surveys also showed that whereas property and financial wealth was becoming more unequally distributed even in the years after the 2008 crash (as compared to immediately before it), the projected value of private pensions fell, which at least temporarily balanced out other aspects of growing wealth inequality. Overall wealth inequality did not rise between 2006 and 2012. The UK could be at a tipping point.

There are clearly enough cars for every household that needs a car to have a car. It is worth repeating that 7 per cent of single adults, who cannot physically drive more than one at a time, own two or more. The

Figure 16: Households by number of cars, and those with no cars in Britain, 2006/07; and wealth inequality trends, 2006–2012

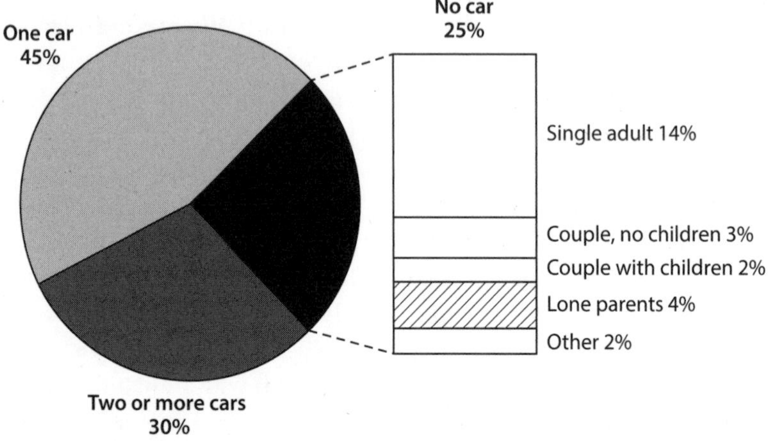

Source: ONS (2008) *Wealth and assets survey: Initial reports*, London: ONS, Table 3.

Household ownership of vehicles, by household composition, 2006–07

	% of households
Two+ cars	30.0
One car	45.0
No car:	
Single adult	13.8
Couple, no children	3.4
Couple with children	2.1
Lone parents	4.0
Other	2.1
Total	100

Note: Enumeration period: July 2006 through June 2007

Gini coefficients for aggregate total wealth, by components, Great Britain, 2006–08 to 2010–2012

	2006–08	2008–10	2010–12
Property wealth (net)	0.63	0.63	0.64
Financial wealth (net)	0.89	0.89	0.92
Possessions (including cars)	0.46	0.45	0.45
Private pension wealth	0.77	0.76	0.73
Total wealth	**0.61**	**0.61**	**0.61**

Source: Table 2.5 *Wealth in Great Britain Wave 3, 2010–2012*, Chapter 2, p.7 (ONS, 2014).
Note: The Gini coefficient is a measure of inequality, 1 being maximum inequality and 0 being complete equality.

majority of households without cars are also single-adult households. One in seven of all households are single adults without a car (the 14 per cent shown in Figure 16, or just over half of all non-car-owning households). Clearly there are many households, especially single-adult households and households with no dependent children, living in cities, which can get by relatively easily without a car. This makes it even more obvious that for those who need a car and do not have one, or for the households with families where their only car is failing, there are enough other largely unused (or unnecessarily used) cars to go round to meet their needs.

Britain need not make or import a single extra car to meet its need for cars for some time to come. A significant redistribution of the current stock of vehicles will not happen in the short term, but there is no reason other than our collective inability to see clearly (and so distribute income and wealth a little more fairly) for cars not to be slightly more fairly shared out, year after year, rather than being progressively less fairly distributed as time passes. In fact the second table in Figure 16 shows just such a slight increase in the equality of distribution of moveable material possessions, of which the most expensive are cars. Exactly the same can be said of housing, a slightly fairer system of allocation, with tax curbs on the buying of second and subsequent homes, would help house all far more efficiently than forever planning to build more homes in the south of England, and never quite building enough.

By 2014 it had became clear that some 3 per cent of households in Britain owned a second home, and 4 per cent held buy-to-let property. A further 3 per cent owned land and property overseas, 1 per cent owned other buildings in the UK, and 1 per cent owned other land in the UK.[13] But none of these proportions are immovable. Again consider the second table below Figure 16 which shows that in a very few years, between 2006 and 2012, property wealth in Britain became more unevenly distributed, financial wealth such as savings and debt became much more unevenly distributed, personal items held as wealth (goods and chattels), including cars, became a fraction more evenly distributed, and private pension wealth both fell and became more evenly distributed, so that overall wealth inequalities neither fell nor rose, the overall Gini inequality statistic being 0.61 in each wave of the survey.

The ONS suggests that inequalities in private pension wealth partly fell because: 'A large number of current pensions in 2006/08 were no longer receiving contributions in 2008/10. One possible explanation for this was the effect of the economic downturn, in terms of increases in unemployment, people moving jobs and, perhaps, pension scheme closures', and there was a 9.5 per cent fall in men holding private pensions between 2008/10 and 2010/12.[14] Because it tended to be better-off men who held private pensions, this fall in private pension holdings and worth resulted in no overall increase in wealth inequality when all wealth was estimated for 99 per cent of the population over the 2006–12 period – all these estimates specifically exclude the richest 1 per cent of UK society who are mostly not included in the Wealth and Assets Surveys.

So far we have not considered the implication of the incredibly uneven distribution of wealth from the point of view of children. Figure 16 is based on statistics that revealed that two thirds of all children living in households without a car were and are living in lone-parent households.[15] Many people can travel, do their shopping and get to work or school without the need for a car. However, a lone parent struggling to carry shopping while looking after two young children is one of the clearest examples of someone in need, having more need than two parents (with four arms between them), but there are many similarly worthy situations of others who find walking and carrying difficult.

Many of the households who need a car could get that car now, but to do so they would have to go into further debt, not only just to buy it, but to insure it, fill it with petrol, park it, repair it, service it and tax it. Many of the households that do have a car cannot really afford to run it, but it is a necessity, and so they go into debt. Individualised transport solutions are presented as some kind of panacea, giving the freedom of the road to the masses; but in reality, car manufacturers and car dealers make most of their profit out of the debt many of their customers take on when buying their product. Remarkably, it is easier to get a much larger amount of credit to buy a new car than a second-hand one, as manufacturers have such a vested interest in new sales.

Calamity was coming

In 1951, one dollar of income for every seven earned in the US was spent repaying personal debts; by 1963, that ratio had risen to one dollar in every five earned.[16] The idea that it was normal to live life with debt began in 1950s America; it was exported around the rich world, with credit cards and supposedly cheap home, car and consumer loans. By the start of the 21st century, with mortgages, extra home equity loans, credit loans, student loans, car, sofa, washing machine (and dryer) loans, to live by loans became what it meant to live normally in the US and in the most ardent of its imitators, the UK.

North American personal debts rose and rose through the 1960s and 1970s, but most rapidly in the 1980s. By 1999, the average US family held about $5,000 of credit card debt at any one time, paying about a fifth of that total a year in interest, but not paying off the balance. This debt rose dramatically as people were told they were living through boom years and, by 2002, it stood at nearly $9,000 per US family.[17] Although the near doubling of recent years may shock, it was in the 1980s that most adults received their first credit card, and then in those same brief 10 years that personal credit card debt rose fastest. Personal bankruptcies became six times more common in the US between 1980 and 2002 as a result of all these changes,[18] and US bankruptcy rates continue to be very high compared to pre-1990 norms.

In Britain by 2005, annual counts of statutory personal insolvency had risen to the record level of 70,000 individuals, double the number recorded just five years earlier. Overall amounts of debt also doubled in Britain between 2000 and 2005, rising to £1.15 trillion on mortgages, other loans and credit card debt by 2005. This was debt rising at about an extra £1 million every four minutes, and the trend was accelerating. The accountants PricewaterhouseCoopers, who, through their analysis and reports, in effect advised the finance industry that calamity was coming long before the 2008 crash, reported all these figures in 2006.[19]

A couple of years later, the Citizens' Advice Bureau reported that in Britain, between 2005 and 2008, the rate at which people's homes were being repossessed for failing to make mortgage payments had doubled.[20] Thus credit card debt doubled, and then overall debt doubled, then home repossessions doubled. During 2009, the BBC reported that personal insolvencies were expected to double again, to 140,000 a year, and company insolvencies were also expected to continue to rise.[21] By the end of 2014 total personal insolvencies were still running at over 100,000 a year, and had begun rising again as creditors saw rising property prices as an opportunity to recoup more of their monies from those who were defaulting.[22]

Apart from the very richest fraction of a percentile, the rich in North America also tend to borrow. Researchers who investigate their behaviour find that they borrow to try to keep up with those above them, to maintain what they see as basic standards, to 'invest' in multiple house purchases, to cope with what they hope are short-term stock market falls, or their diamonds declining in value. The debt of the very richest 1 per cent of North Americans more than tripled between 1989 and 2004, growing twice as fast as their wealth grew. This is partly because the wealth of some grew more slowly on paper as they normally received interest from the debt of others, and others were beginning to default.

By 2004, the very richest percentile of North Americans owed $383 billion more than they had borrowed in 1995.[23] This debt then rose, so that by 2007, the richest 5 per cent of North Americans accounted for 20 per cent of gross debt in the US. Apart from a few at the very top, from the late 1980s onwards, significant proportions of almost every group were borrowing more to try to keep up with those they saw as just above them. So debt is no longer just for the poor – it affects even the richest, and has also become normal for the middle classes. A few years ago, documenting these figures was seen as revelatory. Today, it is just the history of the long build-up to the economic crash.

In Britain around 1990, only a quarter of university students took out loans. Students tend disproportionately to be the children of the better-off, but of those who were not, many could not rely on their parents to help them out, and these poorer students took out the most loans. In 1990, that poorer quarter borrowed some £70 million. Ten years later, after the abolition of maintenance grants, almost three quarters of UK university students had to take out loans. Their annual debt was raised 25-fold in just one decade, to £1.8 billion (still a minuscule sum compared with the debts held by members of the richest 1 per cent of North Americans, but a great deal of money as far as the UK students are concerned).[24]

A decade later again, and with UK student fees rising to £9,000 a year, annual loans increased to £10 billion a year, outstanding loans being predicted to stand at £100 billion by 2018, and £330 billion by mid-century, although that is at 2014–15 prices, and they will almost certainly be far higher nominally as inflation rises. In late 2014, the UK government guaranteed a further £5.5 billion was available to ensure yet more students could take out loans as student numbers were allowed to rise rapidly during 2015.[25] Debt was spreading up the social scales and escalating in quantities to amounts never before recorded. People also began to have to borrow more often just to tide themselves over for shorter and shorter periods of time.

In Britain, the number of people taking out so-called 'payday loans' to get them through to the end of the month more than doubled in less than a year between August 2007 and May 2008; these loans charged interest rates which, when annualised, could be as high as 2,000 per cent before regulation was brought in during January 2015.[26] 'Payday loans' may be a term new to Britain, but it is now part of the common language in the US, where there are more than 22,000 payday loan shops, including some 133 cheque-cashing outfits in central Los Angeles alone (one per 3,000 people). Roughly $25 billion is loaned annually at far greater repayment costs in the US each year, and all this is just to tide people over to payday. The number of Americans taking out such loans rose threefold in the decade to 2010.[27]

Some 12 million North Americans additionally take out annual loans in anticipation that they will receive a tax refund later in the year. On top of that, by 2006, more than a third of a million extremely high interest rate sub-prime mortgages were also being sold in the US each year, at an annual servicing cost of $300 billion.[28] Lending at these rates in these conditions turned out not to be sustainable for more than 12 months longer. The 2008 crash was the end result of 30 years of debt being racked up and up and up; it was not simply a short-term event.

Money crowds out virtue

The increase in debt was planned. In both 1978 and 1996, usury laws in the US were relaxed by Supreme Court rulings. These rulings allowed far more monies to be lent far more freely than before to increase the short-term profits of the moneylenders at a disservice to borrowers, increasing the medium-term risk to all.[29] These laws were relaxed because enough right-wing judges had been appointed by various right-wing US presidents to the Supreme Court by this time to overcome the reservations of their older (wiser) colleagues, many of whom remembered the last crash.

Similarly in Britain, the Conservative government's 'big bang' for the City of London relaxed usury laws in 1986. Allowing people to borrow more meant that the price of some goods such as houses rose in supposed value, purely because more money was available to buy them. As a result of so much over-lending, negative equity (the value of a property becoming less than the mortgage secured on it due to a fall in house prices) followed in 1989–93; the proportion of buyers with negative equity then fell, and then rose again in the early years of the current century, resulting in UK negative equity spiralling up again by 2009.[30]

Usury laws are ancient religious laws banning profiteering from interest payments on debts. All human societies have found moneylending for profit to lead to great injustice. In Venice, prototype investment bankers had to claim it was at the discretion of their customers whether they paid interest in order to avoid the wrath of the church. Islamic teaching still bans simple interest payments. When people are valued by how much money they can amass, rather than by what they can contribute, disaster results. 'A great deal of evidence (both experimental and historical) has accumulated to show that money crowds out virtue. When the incentives of peer approbation are replaced by cash, the quality and quantity of performances suffer.'[31]

It is not just in Britain that one quarter of households cannot cope, have insufficient savings and often have to resort to debt. In the US, the poorest quarter of households in theory survive on about $50 a day, but many do not even see that. In 2001, over a quarter (27 per cent) of the poorest of households in the US were in severe difficulties, and it will be the same in 2015 and for some time to come, because almost all rises in living standards have been concentrated among the best-off. These were the households that were trying to live on $20,000 or less as their annual income. Severe difficulties mean having to spend at least 40 per cent if not more of your income simply on debt service payments, and not even on repaying the debt. This 27 per cent of US citizens are, in effect, trying to live on $10,000 or less a year, $20 dollars a day, in some cases just $10 dollars a day, to pay for food, rent and clothes, and all this in the US at the start of the 21st century. Unsurprisingly, some 13 per cent of this quarter were 60 days or more late in paying their bills. One adult in every 28 in the US was on the edge of defaulting on their debts during Christmas 2000, the time when most people on the North

American continent celebrated the 2,000th birthday of the man who had thrown the moneylenders out of the temple.[32] By 2014 there had been no improvement, and the overall US consumer debt had risen to $3.2 trillion.[33]

The contrast between rich and poor by the millennium in the US became so great that the small minority who had previously made money out of the poor, who were so much smaller in number than the poor, could no longer even begin to try to understand their problems. Even the merely quite affluent, people with incomes of $90,000–$100,000 a year (around $250 a day), found it difficult to comprehend life on so much less. They had mostly become rich either directly from working in the financial services industry or indirectly, through, say, teaching in universities or working in private hospitals, where the fees or bills were disproportionately paid by these very rich people, or they had a high income through sources such as investments.

It is very easy to forget the truism that *one rich man's investment income is many poor women's payday loans*. Although the rich also had debt, only some 2 per cent of them had to make debt repayments of 40 per cent or more of their income in 2001.[34] Most were not living at great risk. The rich sometimes like to suggest they are highly rewarded for astute high risk-taking, but the risks they have to take are not so high. Only 1.3 per cent of those high earners in debt were 60 days (or more) late paying their bills. The risks that the very rich really fear is that their great-grandchildren will not be as rich as they are. And to ensure their descendants might at least be a little rich, the very rich can be driven to try to amass huge fortunes.

The lives of the children of the rich can be especially complicated. F. Scott Fitzgerald first succinctly summed up their greatest problem in *The rich boys* when, in 1925, he explained: 'They think, deep in their hearts, that they are better than we are….' There are even websites that the children of the super-rich can use to meet other offspring of billionaires, and a cheaper version for less well-off multi-millionaires.[35]

It was during the 1980s that societies such as those in Britain and the US changed from being relatively cohesive to becoming collections of people where inequalities rose so greatly that it became near impossible for one group to comprehend the fears, concerns and wishes of another. By 1999, university students were being taught through their textbooks that: 'Debt for basic necessities is one of the severest manifestations of deprivation and mental anguish. Not being able to see a way out must cause constant strain and anxiety, particularly to mothers in lone parent families, as well as feelings of guilt and shame in a society where being financially independent is highly valued.'[36]

By 2009, the next cohort of textbook-reading students was facing a job market with fewer good prospects than for any previous generation of graduates. As a result, it has currently become less of a necessity to say things such as 'must cause constant strain and anxiety'. It had become easier to empathise. The stress has trickled upwards – the children of the affluent (but not the extremely affluent) have become more sensitised again: both a little more sensitised to others' lives and to the hypocrisy of many of their parents' beliefs. By late 2014, almost a quarter of all young adult Europeans were unemployed.[37] Europe has never had a smaller proportion of young people in its population, and it has never had less work for them to do. This is not the fault of the young.

The squalor of riches

> In 1985 [worldwide] there were only 13 billionaires. In 2013, Forbes put the number at 1,426, with a total net worth of $5.4 trillion – up from $1.2 trillion in 2003... So within the span of 28 years or about a generation in the world's wealthiest nations, the billionaire class increased by 10,869%.[38]

During 2014, global inequalities in wealth were soaring again to heights never before attained.[39] The best-off 1 per cent in the world owned 48 per cent of all the personal wealth in the world, up from 41 per cent a year earlier.[40] Eight more years of such an asset grab and they would own everything on the planet, and the remaining 99 per cent would all be effectively indentured. We are clearly at a tipping point – not because anyone is wishing hard enough for a transformation, but because it is mathematically impossible to sustain such an acceleration in inequality for many more years.

When worldwide inequalities rose to their last recent pinnacle, just before the crash in 2007, it began to be noted how: 'Wealth affects people's perceptions and sentiments, makes them much less sensitive to the indignities of poverty and much more likely to misperceive their own wealth as being richly deserved and in the national interest.'[41] However, it is not just between continents that empathy declines with distance; just as much insensitivity can be found within a single town in an country where the rich talk of the laziness, laxness, fecklessness and general uselessness of the poor, in contrast to their perceptions of themselves as great risk-takers and great labourers, as highly efficient, intelligent and sensitive people. What many who are rich really have is a very highly developed sense of personal self-worth. It is difficult not to think of yourself as valuable if you are that affluent, and it is how very many affluent people think; if you are rich and admit to not being that different from other people, well, how do you excuse your riches?[42]

It is necessary to get a long way above the heights of those with annual incomes of $100,000 to see the true extent of the rekindled squalor of riches. In practice, you have to get high up into the very top ranks of the exclusively rich before luxury really sets in; you have to look through the keyholes of the fine, great and old country houses, which the gilded age of the 1920s was fabled for, to see a past way of life which a few have recreated today.

Today, an *income* of two or three million dollars a year might mean you are expected to employ a staff of around six live-in servants, including a cleaner, a nanny, a cook and a couple of gardeners, but your 'household manager' will have to check with you the bills of the additional 200 tradespeople who will 'regularly come to the house.... It turns out you can't just call A1 plumbing to fix an Etoile faucet'[43] (a broken Etoile faucet is a dripping tap of a particularly expensive make).

Being very rich is not really very easy or free of care. And if you are this rich, do you trust your 'household manager'? Do you trust those accounts? Are your investments safe? Who are these strange people coming to fix that dripping tap with their ridiculous bill? Why is your spouse spending so much time with other people, in your other homes? Why didn't you sign a prenup when you married? And when did you last talk with your children?

It is only the very rich who have to question whether their children are as interested in them as they are in their money. All this might sound very personal, but a fantasy world of effortless happiness is presented alongside the idea of holding great wealth. Real life for the wealthy is often not quite as wonderful. Most wealthy people in a very unequal society would lead happier lives with far less wealth in a more equal society (see www.equalitytrust.org.uk/).

Between 1987 and 2005, mean average personal wealth in the UK rose from about four times the national average annual income to about six times that income.[44] Shared out equally, that meant that everyone in the country could have taken a four-year holiday, taken 1987–90 off, before the money ran out, and just 18 years later they could have taken an additional two years to make six in all (a national 2005–10 holiday). In practice, the money was very poorly shared out and became even more badly distributed over time, and if everyone were to take those holidays, they would have to do so abroad because the country would almost immediately become uninhabitable.

Recent increases in recorded wealth have meant that British bankers and accountants have made enough money out of people, mostly overseas, convincing enough to send money to Britain and to receive less, in effect, back, that, relative to the rest of the world, people in Britain could claim more riches and more leisure time. In practice, it was just a very few people who had these riches, but this minority could (by 2005) take entire lifetimes' worth of holidays given their apparent 'savings'. For most of these super-rich people their household managers had not stolen their ill-gotten gains, and for a small cut (called a 'fee'), their accountants ('family offices') had warned them as the economic crash played out, and they moved many assets to safer ground. Most of their money was still relatively safe by the end of 2010, despite the turbulence, and then through to 2015 they began to make yet more money. They began to buy property they did not intend to live in where it was about to become more scarce, and they can still holiday for the rest of their lives, if they choose to, because others pay them rent.

The lives of the extremely wealthy take on new forms. Most tend not to holiday forever, as holidays are not such a fulfilling activity once they become normal life. Although the wealthy still take far more holidays than anyone else, they also find other ways to feel good, ways of being valued, being seen to give money to charity, for example, or getting into expensive activities with a sense of exclusivity such as owning racehorses, playing polo or grouse shooting. Expensive horses are especially valued by the super-rich, as they can be owned and presented like slaves –

paraded as sleek and beautiful. Accounts of the lives of the super-rich include an uncanny number of references to beautiful racehorses and other extremely expensive equine endeavours.[45]

Many animals feature highly in the lives of the rich – they kill them, sit on them (ride), cuddle them. For instance, pets increasingly substitute for children in the richer parts of the globe, where the once exclusive behaviour of the rich in pampering their pets is now becoming more mainstream.[46] A pet is not really such a gratifying acquaintance as a person – the conversation is not great, for instance (although it may not be with other people) – but a pet is a substitute for human relationships when your offspring come to distrust you and they (and your spouse) have eyes mostly for the money. At least you know the pooch doesn't have a bank account. It is remarkable how frequently the super-rich are found with their appreciative little animals: think of Elizabeth Windsor's corgis, Michael Jackson's chimp, Paris Hilton's Chihuahua. The lives of the rich are *not* enviable when you think carefully about them. The poor have pets too, but not the kind that require extreme pampering.

No claim is being made here that there is some intrinsic worth in poverty, or that it is better to be average than to be rich in an unequal society. What is being suggested is that even the rich, including many of the extremely rich, do not fare well under high rates of inequality. It is obvious that the poor suffer, and fairly clear that those on average incomes do not do well when and where inequality is high, but it is far less well understood that even the very rich in unequal affluent countries, despite having so much more money than the rich in more equitable countries, suffer as a result of inequality. Compare the lives of those in the best-off 1 per cent of society in Japan or Northern Europe with those in the best-off 1 per cent in the UK or the US. Which group are actually more at ease with themselves, popping fewer pills and mixing more easily with their fellow citizens? Which group live with less fear, with more trust for others and are genuinely more respected by those around them for what they do? Greater equality is in almost everyone's interest. The majority of the richest groups in the most unequal of places remain to be convinced.

An age of excess

Expect to see fewer celebrity animals in future, because the age of excess is coming to an end. In 1915 and 1916, and again briefly in the late 1920s, the very wealthiest 1 per cent of 1 per cent of the population (0.01 per cent) in the US received more than 5 per cent of all national income. By 2008, inequalities had risen enough for that to happen again. The 15,000 US families now *each* getting by on around $9.5 million a year or more were as pampered in relative terms as their gilded age forebears.[47]

There are great problems managing when you 'earn' over $9.5 million a year – your household expands far beyond six employees, and there are the other homes, the plane and the yachts to consider. You fear the stock market falling, you fear your girlfriend discovering the extent of your second wife's alimony, and you fear yacht-docking fees escalating.

The fears of the super-rich are not even vaguely related to the kind of fears that those earning much less than $9.5 an hour have to worry about. They are quite different fears again from most of those worries that the extremely affluent people who live on $950,000 a year might face. And these are people who, again, are living in a different sphere from the merely very rich, who are earning a tenth of that, $95,000 a year – what do these affluent individuals think? They mostly cannot comprehend the lives of the poor of North America, people earning ten times less again a year ($9,500). So what do those at the very top say about their own lives and their own fears? What most frightens them? When asked, they say: ' … don't publish my name: if you publish things like that my children's lives get endangered … gun to his head … kidnappers … I'm not speculating; it does happen.'[48] Those whose children are most likely to get a gun to the head are, of course, the very poorest. Not through kidnap, but just through living in the poorer parts of America.

It is hard to admit that great wealth is not a great asset, but that it simply protects you from poverty, which is worse. Wealth does not bring wonderful benefits to your life; to suggest it does is to sustain the greatest myth of our times. If you are wealthy enough, you can see the evidence from the air. Around the world, where it is warm enough, in rich enclaves, many swimming pools were built in back gardens at huge expense during the 1980s and 1990s. Most of the world's swimming pools are for the exclusive use of the rich and most are just a decade or two old. And there is almost *never* anyone swimming in them.

A swimming pool in the garden, or a hot tub, a tennis court, or a spare car (or three), all sound like great things to have. In practice, it is more convenient, safer and more fun to use the same pools that other people use; by definition, it is far less of a lonely pursuit to use sports facilities that are communal. Parking and the upkeep of all those cars can become a bit of a drag; it's just hard to admit it. You can't admit it openly, but in private, you often say life would be a lot easier with less, although you are very afraid of having less. But what do you do with those cars if you decide not to keep them all for yourself? It takes a newly developed and finely honed lack of imagination not to be able to see the answer. Unfortunately this is the lack of imagination that gave us the idea that inequality is efficient, the warped thoughts that grew out of the modern incarnation of the academic discipline of economics, the thoughts that provide just enough justification for the rich to hold onto their riches because they are told to view them as some kind of reward.

6.2 Economics: the discipline with so much to answer for

The most serious and in the long term most deadly outcome of rising inequality is that as inequalities rise, those who argue that inequality is good become politically stronger, and their arguments gain ground. When inequality is rising, if there is a recession, market forces are allowed to operate unfettered, and the poor are the first to be laid off – the ranks of the unemployed are not swelled by too many managers. They sack themselves last. Next, they ensure that welfare benefits are cut so low that the poor will take any work going, and then they celebrate their 'job creation'.

When inequality is rising, if there is an economic boom, it is the highest paid who tend to win the highest pay rises, and inequality rises even further as a result. There are times when inequalities are allowed to rise, and there are times when inequalities are engineered to fall, and these times are independent of boom or bust. There are people advocating rises in inequality and people arguing for falls. The former have won the debate for most of the last 45 years in those rich countries that have become most socially unequal as a result. Social inequalities do not rise by unforeseen accident.

Those advocating rises in inequality see inequality as good. They see it as the quantitative expression of how they view human nature. A great many people need to be fooled by a few especially able people (they think) to ensure that the majority go on buying things they mostly do not need, and to ensure that demand for new goods remains high. Not all the advocates of inequality argue that people are rational. Those who argue for inequality most effectively foresee problems if most people acted rationally and voted in their actual interests. If most, in future, were to buy what they need, rather than purchase so often on impulse and go shopping often just for recreation, then the economy that has been built up on social pressures and obligations (made reality by inequality) would slump very badly.

A version of the academic discipline of economics, called orthodox or neoclassical economics, rose to the fore of all the social sciences in the 1980s and 1990s in terms of how it was perceived outside universities, how much funding it received from government and private business within universities, how it spread into bright new shiny schools of management there, how its acolytes preached on efficiency outside academia to the private sector, and in how a degree in economics became almost essential to becoming a policy adviser over the course of those decades in certain countries. Orthodox economists think market forces and not political action should be used to solve the problems of the economic system. Their failure to foresee the economic crash of 2008 that many others had predicted has not yet resulted in their demise, despite their sub-discipline failing its own market test.

A wide and growing range of heterodox economists oppose orthodox economics, but it is the orthodox economists that are still in almost all the positions of real power. Long before the crash, in 2005, the revolt among those just below the most powerful economists was spreading. A few economists based in business schools began to explain, apologetically, that their subject had veered so far from having an interest in human beings, that it had become '... so obscure that even orthodox economists are bemoaning its intellectual poverty'.[49] However, modern-day orthodox economists continue to produce asinine academic papers, such as the now famous paper from the *Journal of Economic Perspectives*, which argued that eating junk food was beneficial because of the amount of time people saved given how much more quickly they could eat.[50]

Orthodox economists have always had a lurid interest in junk, in desire and temptation. Academic papers that suggest junk food is good for you because it saves time are no worse than the argument put forward in the first ever essay to be written by a paid economist, Thomas Malthus, in the first edition of his treatise on population published in 1798. That essay led others to assume that to create wealth it was '... necessary to bring the urges of sexual attraction under control.'[51] Thomas, in turn, was following the concerns over sexual temptation expressed by Adam Smith in 1776, concerns that 'wealth gave rise to temptation, temptation to indulgence, and indulgence ate up the wealth'.[52]

Over the course of the 19th and 20th centuries, many economists moved away from the old orthodox economic obsession of concern with temptation. However, by the early 1980s, a group had arisen again in large numbers who saw the poor as monsters driven by '... growling stomachs, clenched fists and insatiable genitalia'.[53] The conceptualising problems of some leading economists is now well known to have resulted in the creation of the heterodox side of that discipline and of a 'post-autistic economics' movement. While unfair to autistic people who cannot help being autistic, whereas most orthodox economists did have a choice to make, the naming of the movement does hint at difficulties with social thinking among many modern-day orthodox economists. As a group, many economists appear to find it harder to think of other people as human compared with most social groups. Future studies may well find that certain types of people with particular traits and idiosyncrasies were more attracted to becoming the new orthodox economists than others.[54]

Just as Adam Smith (1723–90) influenced Thomas Malthus (1766–1834), Thomas Malthus influenced Francis Galton (1822–1911), Francis Galton influenced Karl Pearson (1857–1936), Karl Pearson influenced Joseph Schumpeter (1883–1950), and Joseph Schumpeter influenced Milton Friedman (1912–2006). The full web is more complex but not incomprehensible. In hindsight it is not surprising to find that economics, biology and statistics all borrowed from each other for those parts of the tales their advocates told, which most often turned out to be wrong or greatly misguided.

In heterodox economics, doing social good is seen as economically beneficial (see the work of Molly Scott Cato and her colleagues).[55] However, among those whom heterodox economists often cite as having been heterodox in the past are people who still held very elitist views. In 1947, economist Joseph Schumpeter, for instance, claimed that what was crucial to economic success was enough '... men of superior energy and intelligence'.[56] Joseph Schumpeter was far from the worst. At least he tried to think of the economy as if it contained people, not just as an abstract mathematical model. However, more careful historical analysis has revealed that such superiority and vigour were not so essential to becoming rich, but an advanced degree of unscrupulousness was useful.

Brains to master difficult skills?

As a discipline, almost as a whole, in the 1960s and 1970s, economics turned towards the orthodox version, towards worshipping selfishness while simultaneously criticising temptation, as typified by the writing of Milton Friedman. It attracted young acolytes who would later come to see and describe themselves as being the modern embodiment of Schumpeter's energetic super-able individuals. It is not hard to find many quotations from such then contemporary economists, in which they claim that either they or their students possess special brains, the kind able to master difficult skills, the implication being that others simply do not make the cut.

There remain mainstream economists who continue the temptation/obsession theme by writing popular books that imply that women are attracted to them because of their economic intellect. In one, in a chapter entitled 'High heels and school uniforms', under a picture of two large male moose locking horns, a popular contemporary economist (Robert H. Frank) wrote: 'Some traits, such as intelligence, not only contribute to individual reproductive success but also serve the broader interests of the species.'[57] His book was subtitled *Why economics explains almost everything*. It is surprising that orthodox economists have not recommended polygamous marriages to maximise their imagined utility, and reproduce much more quickly the armies of little orthodox economists that they clearly feel the world would benefit from. There remains only a small but highly astute minority who still realise that '… there is not usually a queue to jump into bed with economists'.[58]

Orthodox economists are not monstrous or demonic individuals, although a few are remarkable fantasists. When it comes to considering the alternatives, most simply suffer from a 'total absence of thinking … the refusal to read, to think critically or deeply, the rejection of all but one or one kind of book.'[59] Although this description applies well to followers of the faith of economic orthodoxy, it was not written of economists. It was written about an unremarkable man, Adolf Eichmann, who efficiently timetabled the railways in Germany to ensure that as many Jews and others deemed undesirable as possible could be routed to the gas chambers. He was technically accomplished, very good at what he did, but, as Hannah Arendt carefully explained, he just did not stop to think much about what it was he was doing and the effect of what he was doing. He believed the words of the one rulebook he had been taught, the one faith. Orthodox economists suffer from the same banal refusal to open their eyes.

Modern-day orthodox economists describe how they are spat at by officials in airports in Africa when they reveal that they work for bodies such as The World Bank, and argue for policies such as: 'Economic theory does give us the right answer, but it is not very attractive. The government needs to create a convincing signal of its intentions, and to do this it has to adopt reforms that are so painful that a bogus reformer is simply not prepared to adopt them. It thereby reveals its true type, to use the language of economics.'[60]

Some of the men who used to say that 'economic theory gives the right answer' are now beginning to realise how many people hold them largely responsible for evils such as 'structural adjustment',[61] and the idea that governments in poor countries should behave so callously towards their populations as to give 'the free market' the clear 'signal' that no bogus economic reformer could give. The signal that the market apparently wants to see is that officials are prepared to watch and stand aside as their citizens die, due, for instance, to lack of clean water as a Western contractor privatises the supply. Given this, it is no wonder that popular books now describe how orthodox economists behave like members of a cult, as if in '… part of their training, their brains get … reprogrammed … everything they were taught when they were young as being right and true is removed and replaced by a new understanding of the laws of the universe.'[62]

Now that great economic misfortune is hitting rich countries so hard, many orthodox economists are trying to appear reformed characters, moving towards the side of the heterodox, but it is not clear whether this is genuine; it is through their actions that we should look for the 'signal' that they now doubt the god of the market. Just as crypto-eugenists kept eugenics alive in the 1950s, someone will still be holding a torch for the wonders of the market's fictional ability to achieve equilibrium in a few years to come.

The orthodox faith

Orthodox economists are blamed for allowing the debt mountain to build in the richest of countries and, especially in the US, they are blamed for having the belief that if you leave the market alone, it somehow naturally corrects itself. By 2005, members of an average household in the US owed 124.7 per cent of their annual income in outstanding debt, more than twice the debt level of 1975 (see Figure 17). Although that debt ratio had risen every five years from 1975 onwards, before 2000 it had risen fastest, by 15 per cent, in the period 1985–90. This was not a period of recession; it was the period in which people were told for the first time since the 1920s that greed is good.

The rate of household debt growth was curtailed a little in the 1990s, as Figure 17 demonstrates, before accelerating beyond all previously recorded levels of growth in the years 2000 to 2005; in those five years alone, average US consumer debt rose by some 29 per cent. Then came the crash.

In the first edition of this book, US consumer debt in 2005 was reported as being $225 billion less than it turned out to actually be when the final revised figures emerged in time for this edition, but household disposal incomes were some $361 billion higher than it was realised at the time, and so it then looked as if debts were rising by 31 per cent rather than the current figure of 29 per cent. Although the difference of 2 per cent appears small, the hundreds of billions of dollars of error involved shows how little grasp federal authorities have of the situation in any recent

Figure 17: Outstanding consumer debt as a proportion of post-tax income, US, 1975–2013

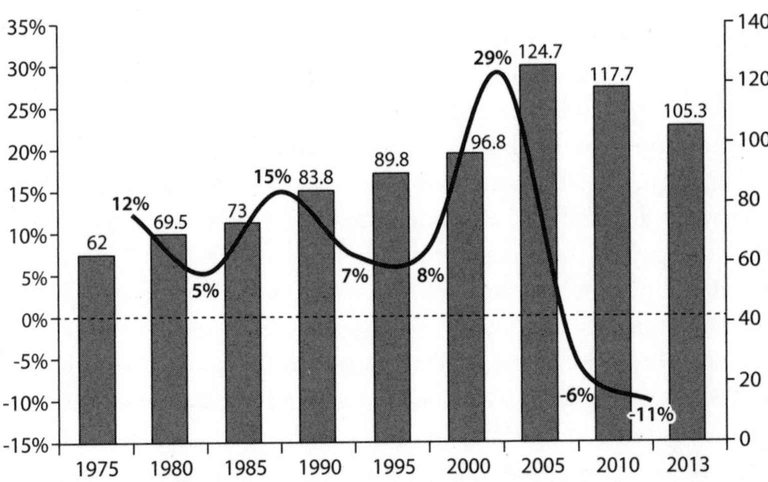

Note: The bars show the ratio (×100) of debt to annual disposable income with scale to the right. The line shows the percentage change in that ratio over the coming five years with scale to the left. The greatest increase was in the years to 2005: 29% is 100% × (124.7–96.8) ÷ 96.8 = 28.8%. Disposable income is the income left to households after paying taxes.

Source: Foster, J.B. (2006) 'The household debt bubble', *Monthly Review*, vol 58, no 1 (www.monthlyreview.org/0506jbf.htm), Table 1; and www.federalreserve.gov/releases/ Z1/ Current/. 2005 data onwards updated from the December 11, 2014 file (before revision the 2005 ratio was 127.2). Revised data located in *Historical Annual Tables 2005-2013*, tables L1 and L10.

Ratio of consumer debt to disposal income and change in that ratio in the US, 1975–2013

	Ratio (× 100)	Change	Consumer debt (£ billions)	Consumer disposable income (£ billions)
1975	62.0	12%	736	1,187
1980	69.5	5%	1,397	2,009
1985	73.0	15%	2,273	3,109
1990	83.8	7%	3,593	4,286
1995	89.8	8%	4,858	5,408
2000	96.8	29%	6,961	7,194
2005	124.7	-6%	11,721	9,401
2010	117.7	-11%	13,231	11,238
2013	105.3		13,172	12,505

year. Reporting national accounts to the nearest billion, or fraction of a billion, implies a degree of accuracy that is not available.

From 1977 onwards, mortgage debt and other consumer debts rose in tandem, rising most quickly when an additional $1.041 trillion of mortgage debt was incurred in 2005 alone. This trillion was a figure that turned negative within three years, with borrowers in 2008 probably repaying more than they borrowed for the first time since 1929. However, they repaid just $46 billion more, around 4 per cent of that extra trillion-dollar debt amassed in 2005 alone. Analysis of US borrowing trends shows that when the federal government borrowed less to spend less, households borrowed more on their credit cards.[63] That had to change with the economic crash.

As households borrowed a trillion less additional income to buy homes or otherwise spend in 2008, compared with 2005, the federal government borrowed an additional trillion just between the two years 2007 and 2008 in an attempt to keep the market-based banking system running. The financial sector in the US itself had borrowed an additional $18 trillion over the 1977–2008 period, all on the advice of their orthodox economist high priests. They were being greedy. But discovering this is hardly surprising given that they had only recently been taught, and come fully to believe, how good greed supposedly was.

High priests of gold

The danger of selfishness and greed in business and finance has been recognised since trading began. Warnings have been copied from religious book to religious book: 'Business turns human producers into commodities. Nor does it spare their employers – "For what shall it profit a man, if he shall gain the whole world, and lose his own soul?"'[64] However, words and thoughts such as those are not our religion now. Too many of us began to worship money; we created a new religion of just a small part of human knowledge – science – and, within that religion, high priests of gold were anointed: economists. According to a contemporary philosopher of social justice, while '... economists present themselves as disinterested scientists, they function today more typically as ideologists for our political and economic "elites" – much as theologians did in an earlier age.'[65]

In the orthodox church of economics, profiteering (termed 'arbitrage') is seen as price stabilising, as a public service! It is now becoming commonly accepted that the behaviour of the greedy is not at all stabilising. Most people are *not* primarily driven by greed, and do not think or behave like calculating little cogs. Because of this the world does not balance out and reach some equilibrium when a minority are allowed to be greedy. Arbitrage resulting in price stability has been termed the 'dead parrot' of utility theory. The idea that 'greed is good' no longer has any validity outside orthodox economics; it has ceased to be a concept to be treated as rational.

Despite all the evidence that has accumulated since the 2008 crash, in the self-justifying minds of too many men of money, they still tell themselves that they are of some great value; they find a way of justifying their actions and existence as good, or, much more worryingly, do not care much about what others care for. However, the orthodox economists are far from immune from being hurt, and it is mainly to preserve their sense of identity that they continue to hold onto their faith. As the economic crash of 2008 hit, suicides among bankers rose, and one observer of that rise noted that: 'The identity of these people is so tied into their career that when it's gone they don't know who they are anymore.'[66] However, the suicides reduced once people adapted to the new times – there was a fall in deaths from despair both among bankers and their customers.

People adapt very quickly to dramatically changing circumstances. At an individual level, most people are very grateful to be alive within a year of having suffered a serious accident that may involve losing limbs. At the group level, mass unemployment can become a new norm. In every year that followed 2009, Americans paid back more to their mortgage companies than they borrowed in new loans.[67] Home ownerships may be becoming a vanishing dream for most people who are now born in the US (and the UK). Future generations may have to rely on low quality landlords for their housing.

People also fight back and resist their freedoms being taken away. In 2014, one group noted that in the US, annual wage theft amounted to three times the money annually stolen in robberies. Wage theft is when an employer makes their employees work outside their allotted hours, buy their own uniforms, or carry out other costly actions in contravention of US labour laws. By 2014, it was evident that some 90 per cent of fast food workers had experienced wage theft at some point in recent years.[68] Wage theft and poor quality landlords are symptoms of an inability to accept greater frugality by the rich.

Returning to a world of frugality from a world of greed will be hard to comprehend for those whose lives have revolved around amassing money. There is growing evidence that orthodox economists have been finding it hard to understand altruism, and the fact that people have developed not to be naturally anti-social. A small group of such economists are even engaged in an endless debate about lighthouses and why we build them, arguing that the private sector could do it for profit![69] Some have even extended their models to try to build in a degree of wider social motivation, and to find some kind of communal rationality in the selfish actions of the few that limit freedom of real choice for so many.

Some economists are adapting to the changing circumstances, however, and are looking back at the history of an older economics to find that rational choice theory was only developed by an economist (Vilfredo Pareto) to explain that very narrow slice of human conduct where individual preferences were possibly best satisfied through such emotion-free 'rational' behaviour. Vilfredo (1848–1923) never meant his observations to become a general theory.[70] If people are naturally selfish, why do they pull over to let ambulances overtake them? It is not because they don't want their cars damaged as ambulances try to get past them, as would be suggested by orthodox economics. All but sociopaths understand why we pull over when an ambulance has its lights flashing.

It is calculated that at least half of the US economy is devoted purely to transactional purposes. These purposes involve monitoring who does what, accounting, logging the shipping of goods and the selling of goods, including point-of-sale work at tills. One orthodox economist, in an attempt to justify this, said it was '… in a sense, a tribute to the productivity of the market economy that it can bear costs of this magnitude and yet provide high standards of living. The cost of counting beans is [supposedly] repaid many times by the extra beans which result from careful counting.'[71] It is a tragedy that otherwise able human beings, once drawn into the culture of orthodox economic thinking, become compelled to defend the indefensible, and have to say there is an intrinsic value in so much stock taking and bar code scanning. There is an intrinsic human value in chatting to the person helping you in a shop, in being social, not in the accuracy of the stock take.

Before orthodox economic theory became established, there was a far wider range of thinking possible. However, by the 1950s, it was becoming apparent that economists were becoming dangerous. Only part joking, the celebrated biologist Lancelot Hogben summed it up in a little list published in 1950: 'I like Scandinavians, skiing, swimming and socialists who realize it is our business to promote social progress by peaceful methods. I dislike football, economists, eugenicists, Fascists, Stalinists, and Scottish conservatives. I think that sex is necessary and bankers are not.'[72] It is worth noting that only football remains popular among his list of dislikes.

When an orthodox economist begins to talk of tribute economies as being productive, like some priest who has begun to doubt the existence of a particularly fearsome and vengeful god, they, too, are beginning to doubt the proclaimed truth of the wonders of free markets. Unfortunately, like the priests of old, so much of their own status is invested in their religion that they usually see no alternative. They dare not voice their doubt in public, and they redouble their belief in preaching about the orthodox. On 16 January 2009, one anonymous member of the British government's Cabinet, with apparently a little economic savvy, was reported to announce: 'The banks are fucked, we're fucked, the country's fucked.'[73] They say such things in private to journalists, but are not yet willing to have their names put on the record.

In praise of the counting of beans!

The same group of economists who say that huge transaction costs, the inefficiency of the market, are, in fact, a tribute to its productivity, also claim that it is only orthodox economists who can truly understand these things, others having not been sufficiently trained in the way and the light of their scriptures. They attack any attempt to uncover the illogical nature of their arguments as amateur do-it-yourself economics.[74] They talk of other people as being only 'normally intelligent', by implication, mere mortals not trained in their orthodoxies, people who are unable to comprehend the arcane truths of the market.

Orthodox economists unsurprisingly react very angrily on reading even the politest of books that carefully explain how they have become so misguided.[75] Having your beliefs questioned is upsetting. Having your beliefs publicly questioned when you, too, are beginning to have doubts but have to put a brave face on things must be infuriating. Orthodox economics will not simply disappear; it has to be argued out of court. It has to give the market of public opinion the proper 'signals' that it is changing. It has to stop praising the counting of beans.[76]

When it is suggested that a tribute economy, in which most people count beans, can maintain high standards of living for a long period, it is worth asking for how long such economies have successfully operated in this way before. For whom in the US are such high living standards being maintained? Does the median North American, the woman in the middle, experience a good life compared with the median citizen of other affluent nations? The median household in Britain received an income before housing costs, but after tax, of the equivalent of €36,300; in 2012 in Germany it was €36,400; in the US it was €36,450; in France €39,000; and housing costs are lower outside of Britain although health costs are much higher in the US.[77] It is worth asking, for both the US and these European countries, from whom in the rest of the world is this physical tribute mostly extracted, and with what effect?

The example quoted above, of how the price of counting beans is supposedly repaid many times over, is continued by its protagonist to suggest that people in the US receive better 'medicine' by having more accountants in hospitals. The people making these kinds of claims do not concern themselves over whether healthcare is *actually* better in the US, and why life expectancy is lower than across all of Western Europe and Japan, for example. Also the (median) average French household might be better off than the average German household, which is better off than the average British household, which is better off than the average household in the US once healthcare costs are considered – all of these households are, to one extent or another, benefiting from unequal terms of trade with people in poorer countries. Just as inequality within a country harms the rich as well as the poor, does inequality in the world harm the rich countries as well as the poor ones?

Despite their wealth, the wealthy do not necessarily receive as good services as they might think they do. For the very few who can afford to sign up to concierge doctor schemes, those private doctors who serve only a few rich families, health appears to be good, and on average they live long, if far from unmedicated, lives. But the health of most people in the US is worse than that of many citizens in countries that are poorer. For the very rich, too, the interests of their private physicians are not in maximising their patients' health, but in maximising the cost of their health treatments, and when a doctor wants to maximise his or her income, that is not necessarily good news for the patient. Michael Jackson's death at the hands of his doctor illustrates how money does not ensure that your doctor will have your best interests at heart.[78] These realities and life expectancy figures are inconvenient truths that orthodox economists prefer to ignore, along with the millions who go hungry and sleep rough in the US, despite – or when you think about it, more likely because of – the 'efficient' accountant culture there.

The effects of living in a country where orthodox economics has been allowed to run wild have been closely studied as a natural, if unethical, mass experiment. It has been found that households in the middle of the income distribution in the US have been forced to spend higher and higher proportions of their income over time on things such as housing to maintain their social positions. This includes the housing costs that enable them to send their children to the median-quality publicly funded schools.

As inequalities in education rise, mirroring inequalities in income, schools become more and more differentiated in terms not just of average pupil exam success, but also over whether or not armed police are stationed in the school to deal with gun crime. In the childhoods of current parents in the US, the stationing of armed police in school was much further from the norm than it is now. The effect is to make geographic location ever so much more important, and this, in turn, raises house prices in all areas not seen to be at the very bottom, raising them fastest the further from the bottom they are.

The middle-income family struggles to pay its mortgage. At the top the rich see the value of their assets rise dramatically, even while a few of their number borrow greatly to keep up appearances. Simultaneously, in Britain, the proportion of young families unable even to save enough for the deposit to become first-time buyers rose from half to two thirds between the mid-1980s and 2001; four fifths of all such households in

London could no longer afford to get on the bottom of an unbelievably tall ladder by the turn of the millennium.[79]

Of the *shrinking minority* who could afford a mortgage across Britain by 2001, some 20 per cent relied on inheritance or premature inheritance from their parents to help pay the deposit. This rose to 40 per cent of first-time buyers needing such help by 2005,[80] a huge rise in a very short time, and in hindsight, one of many portents of doom. However, by 2015, we looked back on those statistics for the turn of the millennium, and laughed at how funny it was that people then could not see how much less affordable much housing would soon become. It was no longer a question of getting on the bottom rung of the ladder. The bottom rungs were missing.

In the UK, the country approached a general election in 2015 with the government's own commissioners highlighting that: 'High housing costs are dragging more children into poverty. 1.4 million more children are in relative poverty after the effect of rents and mortgages are taken into account.'[81] It is only very recently that housing has become this expensive. For most of the 20th century, however, homes have not been the greatest personal expense of median families in affluent nations, including the UK – that has been cars.[82]

6.3 Gulfs: between our lives and our worlds

The automobile and its recent history provide the pre-eminent example of how the growth of greed out of the eradication of squalor has created a new and very different kind of squalor. The old squalor was that of damp homes with earthen floors, of dirty water and of roads covered in horse manure. It was of people tramping to work, undertaking journeys that were repetitive, arduous and often, especially in poor weather, miserable. The advent of mass motorised travel offered an apparent end to such misery. It appeared to herald a brave new world of short efficient journeys, clean streets and happy upright people, not stooped, as in Lowry landscapes, not tired out as they arrived at their destination.

Largely unforeseeable when automobiles were first sold was the congestion of streets and motorways that filled up with thousands of cars, the choking of lungs with millions of tiny particles. The need to fight wars for oil to keep people moving was also then unforeseen. Perhaps hardest to foresee would be the psychological attachment people would form with their cars, especially many men in their middle age.

Cars became status symbols of rank. People began to pretend that they liked the particular clunk of how the door closed on an expensive model, and that that clunk alone was itself worth many thousands of pounds, maybe even the average annual salary of a typical worker! This was behaviour not dissimilar to house buyers explaining that they had taken out such a high mortgage because they liked the décor, rather than admitting they were paying for the area they wanted to live in, for the kinds of neighbours they wanted.

Lovers of the clunk of an expensive car door shutting had fallen in love with what they thought owning that car said about them, how it showed they were adequate men, even depicted them as highly successful if the clunk was right. The squalor of greed is a vice to be pitied. It is hard not to conclude that the rich spent so much of their money on especially expensive cars because so much more began to be missing from their lives as their riches rose. In the UK in 2014, TV presenter Jeremy Clarkson typified the banality when trying to look like a nonchalant winner in life, reciting a rhyme trying to choose between two expensive cars, and then trying to deny he said 'the n-word' in the process.[83]

From the beginnings of mass motoring, cars began to take on a value way beyond their functional utility. In 1940s rural and small town North America, where it was easier to see their practical value, people began to buy their first car before they purchased their first bathtub. The purchase of Model T Ford automobiles before bathtubs is an early example of how the old squalor of grime began to be overtaken by the new squalor of greed. Even earlier, in 1929, as the economic crash hit, social commentators could be found stating that 'People give up everything in the world but their car.'[84] Much the same was being said 70 years later, when attempts to persuade people to become more 'green' saw them agreeing to recycle, avoiding flying, turning off lights and insulating their homes, but not giving up their car or even one of their many cars. It is not simply the convenience of having a car that encourages people to hold on to them so dearly – it is the psychological attachment that forms. It is, however, cheaper to use taxis in most cases than to buy, to service, and to park your own car.

The new squalor

From the 1960s onwards, at least two thirds of the rise in the cost of cars every year was due to the cost of changing how cars looked, not due to their improving functionality.[85] This was called 'styling'. From the mid-1950s onwards, cars would be restyled, later called having a 'face lift', every single year, so that new models could constantly be offered and identified. All this styling and the marketing that went with it was aimed at getting inside potential drivers' minds and persuading them that to be complete, to be seen as adequate for their social standing, they needed a new motor. For the very rich this meant a new motor every few years.

By the end of the century, the sports utility vehicles (SUVs) that were being sold to North American men had become enormous, and were being given militaristic names such as 'The Raider', 'Trooper', 'Liberty', 'Commander' and 'Patriot'. In Britain, it was along the medieval street layouts of London (and Oxford), not on some off-road prairie, that the majority of men and a few women who had budgets large enough to waste on huge motorcars lived. They often did not realise they were being extravagant because in the heart of Mayfair, 24 year-old members of Middle Eastern royal families were driving around in £350,000 supercars by 2013.[86]

Expensive gas-guzzling SUVs were not sold in increasing numbers simply to bolster egos; they also made their occupants feel safer, driving higher in their 'Chelsea tractor' above the road. But as deaths mounted, it became apparent that when these huge cars collided with smaller, less statement-making cars, the occupants of the smaller cars were *ten times* more likely to die as a result of the collision, not to mention the appalling odds for pedestrians and cyclists.[87] This is the new squalor. Cars are now the main killers of people aged under 35 in countries like Britain. In the past, the main killers were diseases spread through the old squalor of untreated sewage. By buying cars before bathtubs, we ushered in different health hazards – lung-damaging air pollution and (until the advent of lead-free petrol) also brain damage, obesity from sitting in vehicles for so many hours and all the hazards of the abolition of much exercise, and road crashes becoming commonplace.

As rents rise almost everywhere, and house prices in the south east of England surged forward, ONS standard statistics for housing costs only very recently showed them becoming more expensive than transport costs; for decades it had been the other way round.[88] By 2014, the figure for housing was £74.40 a week per family in Britain, for transport the average cost had risen to £70.40 a week, but was still below housing. The main increase for the rise was that new cars were being purchased again. The average spent on car purchases was £20.30 a week, running costs £29.00, averaged over all households including those without vehicles. Public transport and taxi costs amounted to £15.30. The weekly averages for housing include fuel and power and rent (taking into account housing benefit), but exclude mortgage interest payments, and are spread over all families including many who don't rent.[89] Including mortgage payments, average housing costs were £147.90, but varied dramatically depending on where you lived. However, this figure would be much lower if you subtracted how much property values had gone up for those that did not rent, and deducted that saving resulting from property investment.

As recently as 2006, despite the price of housing having sky-rocketed up that year, people in Britain were spending an average £5,500 per family per year simply on buying and running their cars.[90] Purchase costs of new vehicles averaged over all households were £8.30 per week, for second-hand vehicles £12.00. This discrepancy arose because there were well over twice as many households with second-hand vehicles compared with new. These sums of money, if totalled up, were enough to buy and run an old second-hand car every year for every family in Britain; many people, however, want new or nearly new cars. Those with the most money almost all want new cars, and those with most of all want the most prestigious new cars, cars of very particular makes.

The sums of money being mentioned here are so high because they are what are called mean, or arithmetic-average, prices. They are the total spent on cars by all people divided by the number of families in a country, including those without a car. Just a few people spending inordinate amounts on cars have pulled those averages up sharply, and it takes many families to spend nothing on cars to counter-balance the effect of a single expensive purchase by a single individual.

In 2007 in the US, just before the economic crash, it was suggested that some rich men became embarrassed to be seen by their friends, rivals and acquaintances as being miserly for only spending around $55,000 on a car as a present for their girlfriend. In one case the car was a Mercedes SLK, and the report continued by saying that a year later, when this particular man spent $110,000 on a Bentley for his girlfriend, he thought he had escaped the sniggers. However, these brand-name cars, including BMWs and Jaguars, had come to be seen as '... almost common'[91] among the glitterati of the super-rich during those pre-austerity early years of the current century. The rich can still afford and still buy very expensive cars; in fact, it has only been luxury brands that have sold well since 2008. But now the rich tend not to flaunt their purchases as much, unless they are so rich and detached that they have no subtlety.

The arithmetic averages on the amount spent on cars are still inflated sharply because a few men are worried about impressing their girlfriends, their so-called friends, and particularly people who do not know them, but who look just at their car. Great wealth is no predictor of great ability or of any sense of proportion. If it were, there would be no luxury car market.

Eyeing up the talent

The super-rich have also been bamboozled by the cult of orthodox economics. When US economists try to write popular books on economics, they tell their (presumed to be male) readers that: '... one can make a crude guess about how *talented* a person is by looking at the kind of clothing he wears or the kind of car he drives'.[92] It is true that the super-rich do differ in one significant way from the rest of us – they are more likely to feel a little more insecure. For those at the top, if they can't cling on, the only way is down. Perhaps some are even a little incredulous as to the position they appear to have reached.

A few at the top step back and say, well, they were handing out all these top jobs and someone had to get one. Many say to themselves that they were specially able and deserving of their fortunes, but it is hard to keep telling that to yourself if you know in your heart of hearts that you are not superhuman.

If you dress up in expensive suits, put a watch worth thousands of dollars on your wrist, step into a car worth hundreds of thousands of dollars from a home worth millions in the morning, it can be easier to tell yourself you are worth it, that you are a big man, to maintain a delusion of grandeur. There are subtle psychological reasons why so many well paid men spend so much of their income on cars, leading to more being spent on cars than on homes nationwide. It remains '… the nature of status symbols that people are rarely aware of their motivations for acquiring them. No man buys a sports car thinking of it as a penis substitute.'[93] But it is better to joke that you bought your car to make up for the inadequacies of your penis than to admit it was for your lack of super-sized all-round talent.

Even those who have only one small car, or no car at all, cannot indulge in smugness. In the US it was found some time ago that college-educated men often bought slightly smaller cars because they gained their sense of superiority in other ways, or felt they did – a form of inverted snobbery. Rarely, however, would they live in poorer neighbourhoods or dress especially cheaply and scruffily. Much of our normal behaviour is about keeping up appearances. We do not think of how we dress, drive and live as statements we make about ourselves; but they all are.

It is also worth noting that modes of transport change more quickly than the rate at which we learn not to show off. The (now) billionaire founders of the company Google are reported to have bought cheap environmentally friendly hybrid cars to show their commitment to a better world, while at the same time purchasing a 224-seat wide-bodied aeroplane, and refitting it to take only 50 very large seats, so that they and their entourage could quickly get '… to places like Africa … that can [apparently] only be good for the world'.[94]

Other millionaires and billionaires are reported to have said that they have felt depressed in their private jets when forced to queue for take-off at airports, backed up with other private jets, with so many 'important guys' all just sitting on the tarmac behind their pilots looking at each other. And from this deep well of rich people's tales comes also the apocryphal story of the daughter of a billionaire who asked if she could have a 'normal' air ticket for her birthday so that she could see the inside of an airport, a pleasure the children of the super-rich are denied when their chauffeurs deliver them to their jets.[95] Recently the daughter of a Korean airline owner ensured a steward was taken off the plane for serving her nuts in a packet. In February 2015 that daughter was sentenced to a year in prison for her arrogant behaviour. Our collective tolerance of the extremely rich may be coming to an end.

Looking up to the heavens

Mass air travel is another example of the new squalor of our times. Although the super-rich might fly most often with the least care about their actions, many more of us in affluent countries now fly. We might fly to avoid a long train or road journey, to get to where it is sunnier because we think a holiday there will be more relaxing and do us good, or we might fly simply for a weekend 'city break', to see a place we have not been to before and be able to say 'been there, done that'. We also, of course, may choose to fly because sometimes it is cheaper than taking trains or buses, and sometimes it is the only way we get to see family abroad. But we mainly now fly so much because we can, and because we think we will lose out if we do not, because we think we might be missing out on something from which others who fly so much are gaining. But what are the frequent fliers gaining? Is it happiness, status, freedom?

Every year more and more people are born who will never fly, and a greater proportion of the world's population will look up at the heavens rather than down from the clouds. Also, every year, more and more people live lives in the world that are not centred on the petrol-driven motorcar. Most extra cars are consumed by families that already have one, and most of the extra families being formed in the world will never get to own a car – not at current production rates and given our road space – even in China where there are too many people for too few roads and far more plans to built largely car-free cities than in supposedly more developed countries. Almost everywhere, but especially in poorer countries, for those who have cars, roads become ever more clogged and dangerous to walk near and even more difficult to cross, as more and more cars congest them.

For aeroplanes, flight lanes are becoming congested, and airports are becoming even more anti-social places, with fewer seats to sit on, but more shops to walk through. The increased pollution and travel of a minority not only increases the squalor of lives in the rich world, but raises the sense of failure and pollutes the air and feelings of all those who have never got, or hardly ever get, to travel in these ways. Cheap air travel to where you might want to travel is not as cheap as the adverts suggest. If it were, the poor would fly much more – more than three quarters of air passengers in the UK are middle class, and while the number of flights being taken was growing in number between 2000 and 2004, the number taken by the poorest fifth of society simultaneously fell.[96] Mass air travel has not been some great boon to the masses, and it cannot be while flight is fuelled by hydrocarbons.

Great gulfs are created by the new squalor between our social worlds. Those looking out from a poor city neighbourhood in Britain or the US at the drivers of the cars passing their bedroom windows on the dual carriageway or freeway nearby look at the faces of those who fear them, who have paid so much not to live near them. These people drive to offices in town to receive salaries which they can spend on the suits they are required to wear, the car they need to get to that office, and to reflect their status in their own minds as well as others. When they look out from their car windows they see why they paid their mortgage, so that their children did not have to go to the schools they drive past.

Affluent commuters do not worry that in driving past poor estates or city blocks they are adversely affecting the lives of the children there. Consider the irony of it. Those children will be forced to inhale far more particles and noxious gases from car exhausts than their children will ever have to breathe, and are at far greater risk of injury or death from cars despite their families often not even having a car. The greatest daily mortality risk to children in a country like Britain or the US is of being killed by a car. That risk is seven times greater in poor neighbourhoods compared with affluent ones. Part of the reason for this is that the rich drive by and through poor inner-city areas on their way to and from work.[97] Given all this, isn't it bizarre that the rich fear the poor?

Squalor was much more widely felt in the past. It was also harder to avoid tuberculosis or cholera simply because you were affluent. To some extent, affluence did help; for example, the rich lived higher up the hill, where both the air and water were cleaner; on the other hand, smog across towns harmed almost everyone. A century ago even the most affluent of families saw one in ten of their children die before their first birthday, mostly as a result of infectious diseases, a rate only 2.5 times lower than that experienced by the very poorest of families. That gap is far wider today, as affluent families have seen the environmental conditions under which their children are brought into the world improve materially so much that they are now as much as one hundred times more likely to survive to their first birthday as were their great-grandparents. *In countries*

Figure 18: Poverty, car exhaust emissions and pollution inhaled in Britain, by area, 1999

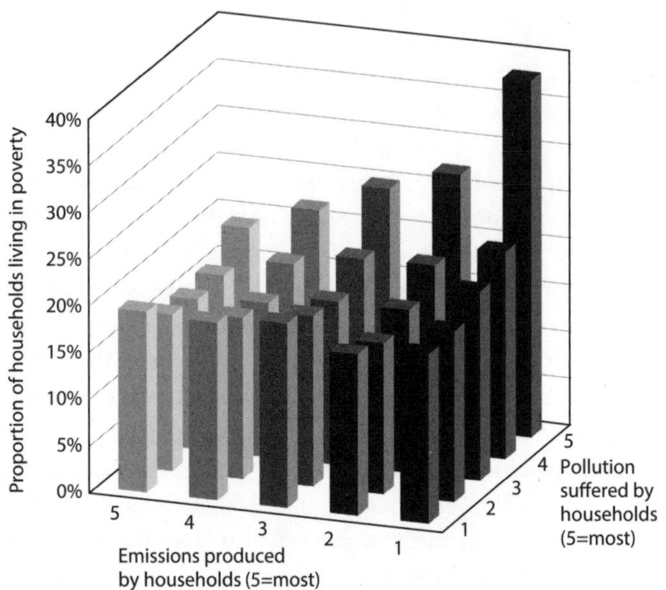

Note: The contribution of residents to emissions is estimated from the vehicles they own, and the degree of pollution they suffer from mean annual ambient NO_2 measurements. Lowest emitting and polluting quintiles are labelled 1, the highest are labelled 5. The areas used are local government wards, and these are put into 25 groups by their emission and pollution quintile positions.

Source: Mitchell, G. and Dorling, D. (2003) 'An environmental justice analysis of British air quality', *Environment and Planning A*, vol 35, pp 909-29, Figure 9: Poverty rate by NO_X emission and ambient air quality for 10,444 British wards (defined by their 1981 boundaries) in 1999.

Percentage of households living in poverty by emission and pollution rate of ward of residence, UK, 1999

		Pollution received by ward of residence (1=lowest, 5=highest quintile)				
		1	2	3	4	5
Emissions made by ward of residence (1=lowest, 5=highest quintile)	1	18.0	18.2	20.1	22.1	38.1
	2	17.2	16.1	17.4	19.8	27.3
	3	19.7	18.2	17.4	19.7	24.9
	4	19.0	17.2	16.4	18.3	21.8
	5	19.3	16.7	16.0	16.3	19.1

like Britain, and even more so in the US, the improvement experienced by poorer families in the environments into which they have to bring up their children has not been so great. Although those environments are much better than they were, the improvements to their lives and areas have come more slowly, so that poorer infants are now many more times more likely to die young than infants from affluent families.[98]

Ingesting the dirt of others

In the rich world in these times of unparalleled affluence, common goods such as clean air are much more unevenly distributed geographically in terms of quality. In affluent countries now, it is emissions from car exhausts that do most harm to air quality, not coal fires or factory chimneys. Figure 18 shows how those people living in the fifth of wards in Britain where air quality is worst are much more likely to be poor on average, with poverty rates in these areas ranging from 20 per cent up to 40 per cent of local residents. The columns on the graph rise up towards the right because those are areas where the poverty rates reach almost 40 per cent of families, and where pollution is highest. They are also the areas where local residents are responsible for producing the *least* emissions, where fewest people own and run cars. *The very poorest neighbourhoods in Britain pollute the least but suffer from the most pollution.* The tallest column in Figure 18 represents those inner-city neighbourhoods that the affluent so often drive by in their polluting cars to get to their offices.

Figure 18 shows the local distribution in Britain of the injustice of new squalor. What the figure depicts will have worsened since it was drawn, because levels of inner-city air pollution have worsened in London, and poor households are now poorer and much more overcrowded and so less able to add to pollution by having a car. The figure is in microcosm a reflection of the worldwide pattern, whereby those who pollute most currently suffer least from the results of their actions. Metaphorically, too, through their control of media outlets the rich and powerful can also disproportionately pollute the minds of others with the ideas they have come to believe, including fuelling the cult of the car and the petrol-head. A very small but ever so significant group who own newspapers, television channels or political parties employ others to promote the views that benefit the very rich.

In 2014, Robert Reich reported that the political spending of the richest 0.01 per cent in US society was increasing by more than their spending on any other item, and on average, each of the rich one in ten thousand people had over one thousand times the wealth of the average person, to spare.[99] These very richest individuals are also representative of our greatest polluters, and are often lauded as examples to be followed. It is repeatedly suggested that people should aspire to run businesses and have their own private jets; if not Boeing 767 aeroplanes capable of flying them and 49 of their friends to Africa, then just a 'small' jet, or to be able to fly first class, or business class, or even 'just' being able to fly. That, and all these other things referred to as 'the hallmarks of success'.

We are taught to aspire to car ownership, particularly of large cars. We are taught to aspire to travel huge distances around the planet to visit holiday destinations we can boast about, instead of enjoying a holiday much nearer home. One way in which we are taught this is through the actions of celebrities and how they are portrayed and how their expenditure is admired. Just as no one sat down two centuries ago at the start of the industrial revolution and planned to create enormous slums of squalor, so no secret committee met in the early 1980s under an agenda headed 'How can we persuade the masses that they should always aspire to have so much more?'.

There were no 'break-out' meetings to determine how best to try to explain to people that true happiness was not possible without high exhaust emissions. There were just people trying to sell things, lots of things. The advertising industry was not concerned with long-term consequences, only in maximising immediate profit, and doing so by engendering envy. And there were people whose faces and images sold things, which sold movies, who won in sport, people who could be portrayed as special, as inspirational, as worthy of emulating. Celebrity became part of the new squalor, a part that helps greatly to explain just what is going on.[100]

6.4 Celebrity: celebrated as a model of success

Celebrity culture is all about trying to encourage envy. Its central message is 'look at me'. There is a good case to be made that '... the phrase "politics of envy" should be wiped from the language. Its endless repetition amounts to a kind of cultural brainwashing of the 99 per cent by the 1 per cent. People who talk about envy appear to want to belittle what others feel about the unfairness of the world and our current society.'[101] We could also rename the politics of envy as the politics of celebrity, the politics of putting a few on pedestals labelled 'beautiful' or 'clever' or 'rich' and treating everybody else as unimportant nobodies.

What is the most you can spend? There are limits, and it is at those limits that true global celebrity is found. Those at the very top often keep a lower profile than the popular celebrities of television and magazines, who are still trying to work their way up. True celebrities do not sell their wedding photographs for a few million – a few million is too little to bother with.

Have you ever wondered how much money would be 'enough'? Robert and Edward Skidelsky did, and in 2013 were criticised because they had apparently failed to realise that people would get bored if they could not afford cosmetic surgery![102] Even more ridiculous, the most it was possible to spend on underwear by 2007 was $5 million on a diamond-studded bra, about seven times more than the most expensive watch on the market at that time.[103] You can get more diamonds on a bra. However, a bra studded with diamonds works less well than one you can buy for just $12. Similarly, a watch you buy for hundreds of thousands of dollars is likely to be of less use to you in telling the time accurately than a cheap digital watch, because very expensive watches have mechanical, not digital, workings. Furthermore, you won't wear the expensive timepiece as frequently for fear of losing it or breaking it, or for fear of someone robbing you for it, and I'm not sure the diamond-studded bra sounds that comfortable. Cosmetic surgery is a very dangerous and expensive cure for boredom when you have to have procedure after procedure to fill up your time. Only a minority of celebrities are stupid enough to do that – perhaps (although discounts are often offered on subsequent procedures and on the procedures to correct earlier procedures).

The cult of celebrity and of watching the super-rich is part of a wider trend that has been incorporated into and has transformed the lives of almost all people in affluent countries. Chauvinism, bigotry and racism were the human failings associated most closely with the injustices of elitism, exclusion and prejudice. With greed, the most acute new human failing to emerge is a new kind of financial narcissism born out of insecurity, spending money on ourselves and our possessions because *such spending temporarily, fleetingly, boosts how well we value ourselves in societies where we feel less valued in general.* In the early years of the current century it was reported that homeowners in Britain alone spent £150 billion on (what a magazine said were) tasteless home improvements that had actually reduced the values of their homes, but which clearly they must have felt at the moment of purchase were worthwhile. At about £7,500 per homeowner, this was a huge national outlay to achieve a series of very short-lived 'warm' feelings.[104] All that money was just the average cost over recent years of those decorations and fittings deemed to have lowered the market value of properties. Putting in a Jacuzzi and losing a bedroom as a consequence is an extreme, but sadly not uncommon, example. Homeowners were persuaded to part with their money by the 'home improvement' industry, an industry that offered to provide that instant feeling of gratification that comes by adding yet another fixture or fitting that perhaps you did not really need.

We can now spend many hundreds if not thousands of pounds on refrigerators that have designer labels on them but which, in essence, do not do a better job than one many times cheaper. We are enticed to purchase expensive televisions with screens so flat and so wide that our sitting rooms do not let us sit back far enough to view them properly. When the television breaks down, we rush out immediately to buy another because the cost of repairing it is even greater, or it is not possible to make a repair, and even a few days without television is hard to contemplate for the 99 per cent of us who regularly watch it.

Just as we can buy cars that are ever shinier and more stylish, kitchen work surfaces are now sold which, if you are affluent enough, enable you to see your reflection in highly polished granite. This could be granite shipped out of war-torn Angola, if you are willing to pay or borrow enough for the privilege of being able to say that your worktop was made of chic 'Blue in the Night' stone. It is worth pausing for a few seconds to count up the hypocrisies involved in shipping a ton of granite – a trade that in the past was limited to gravestones, a maximum one per person per lifetime – half way round the world to put your fair trade coffee cups on.

Low trade is better than fair trade; consuming less, especially less from further afield, reduces both exploitation and pollution. Trade is essential, just like food, but more is not always better, just like food. For every mile travelled, shipping burns more oil than flying because there is more friction when travelling through water than through air. However, the hypocrisy of kitchen worktops made from African granite is minimal when you consider that entire kitchens are now sold that cost more than mid-priced and comfortable terraced homes, or that some very affluent people are being encouraged to redecorate most of their home every two years or less because style changes so quickly.

When people begin to view the way they themselves chose to have their homes decorated two years ago as tasteless enough to warrant redecorating, it is fair to say that we live in a society that is suffering deeply from the afflictions of affluence.

The afflictions of affluence

At the heights of profligacy, the greed for ever more designer goods, sleek cars, flash kitchens, bathrooms that would not look out of place in a five star hotel, anything that mirrors celebrity, went way beyond people's means to pay for those goods. Those heights were reached in the early years of the 21st century. And it was in the most unequal of rich countries that debt rose fastest and became highest as a result.

Average debt in the US soared to increase consumer non-mortgage 'credit' by $121 billion in 2006, and then by a further $151 billion by 2007. There was then a dip as lending was frozen when the banks crashed before credit debt rose again by $170 billion in 2012 and $174 billion in 2013.[105] By 2013, *total* household debt in the US stood at $13.2 trillion, only 70 per cent of that being mortgages.

Across in Britain, consumers held more than half of all Western European credit card debt by 2006, some £60.8 billion by October 2014, with a further £1.25 billion added in November 2014, the highest addition for almost seven years, prompting the shadow consumer minister to state that there is clearly a '... big gaping hole at the heart of our economy being fuelled by borrowing'.[106] By 2007, as compared with residents of any other European country, Britons also held twice as many of their mortgages under rates that could be varied at the will of their lenders. The most similar country, with half as many variable mortgage holders, then, was Italy.[107] Outstanding mortgage lending in Britain had risen to £1,294 billion by October 2014.[108]

In the years leading up to 2008, the US and the UK, and to a lesser extent Singapore, New Zealand, Australia and Canada, were following more closely than most other rich countries a model that had led to doom before and was about to do so again. These are also the countries whose officials are trying their hardest to get people to return to that behaviour now, to borrow so much again and not think too carefully about how they might pay it all off. It is possible that exposure to the worldwide cult of celebrity has its worst effects on those who speak the English language in which most movies are released, that most advertising is conducted in, in which most right-wing papers are printed and so many satellite television broadcasts are made in. Although it is debatable, speaking English may not be as particularly advantageous in the age of greed (and high volume global trade in material goods), as is often suggested.

Great excesses typify times of great inequality. The world's largest home, George Vanderbilt the Second's 255-room Biltmore Mansion, was first envisaged in 1895 and built when the very richest had proportionately even more wealth than the richest have today. It has yet to be replicated in opulence or arrogance, but larger and larger 'homes' were, until very recently, being built once again in the US. The largest equivalent built today is only a third of the size of Vanderbilt's and is marketed at 'just' $135 million. It is in Aspen and is owned by Prince Bandar bin Sultan of the Al Saud Royal Family (nicknamed Bandar Bush for his close working relationship with former President George Bush the Second). It is the extreme end of the housing market, a market in which, with a brief hiatus in 2009/10, is now booming again. Larger and larger properties are again being built out of town, and former enormous townhouses are being converted back from flats to single homes, most commonly along some of the more pricey streets of the world's richest cities, such as London.[109] The effect of all this greed has been to end up housing fewer people in these larger properties, forcing those progressively further and further down the social scale to occupy relatively smaller and smaller homes.

Across cities like London, overcrowding rates have risen rapidly in recent years, as the rich and super-rich have begun to occupy more and more square feet per person. Bizarrely, rates of overcrowding and under-occupation both increase at the same time. Outside London, in the nearby English countryside, a trend in building country mansions began at a similar time, so that as the housing shortage has risen, a small group at the top have gained more space than ever before, as many rooms, home gyms, home cinemas and swimming pools as you can imagine. Because very affluent households are smaller today than in Vanderbilt's time, each extremely rich person now has even more space! Similar mansions were documented as being built, again until very recently, in and around New York. These were built to provide for celebrity lives that were last portraying such crude greed during the era of the Great Gatsby, especially in the summer of 1922.

About 100 English council-built family maisonettes could be fitted within the floor space of Bandar Bush's modern US mansion. The space ratio calculations are less dramatic within cities, but it is certainly not the poor or poor immigrants who take up most space. There is no overall lack of space to house people well in the rich world, but a huge lack of willingness. Among the quite rich in the US, and for many MPs in Britain, second home owning is now passé; the trend for the US super-rich is to maintain at least four homes, flying into your fourth home, a mountain retreat in, say, Montana, for just a few days of the year.[110]

How did we end up accepting the afflictions of affluenza? Once it became normal at a certain income bracket to own a second home and inequalities continued to rise, it was only a matter of time before it became normal for a growing minority to own a third, then a fourth home. In those countries where inequalities in income and wealth were rising most quickly, these could be: the family home, the city pad, the bach by the sea in New Zealand (a holiday home to escape from the northern winter for a few sunny weeks), and that house kept in London as an 'investment'. The bach could be rented out occasionally, and the London home might house tenants intermittently, but it would be so much better if second, third and fourth homes were available for others to live in full time as their first home.

A couple could retire to someone's second home by the sea, a family could grow up in the London home (not in fear that it might be sold from under them if they are tenants), a city pad could be the permanent home of someone who both works and lives in the city. People could commute, or retire, and instead rent a property when they went on holiday or stay in bed and breakfast accommodation, or youth hostels (which take 'oldies' now, too). However, rising inequalities, lax taxes and easy tax evasion made so many housing purchases appear to be good investments, at least until the economic crash came. People felt they deserved all those properties; they had 'worked hard' for them. If pressed, they thought, well, there are just too many people in the world, we can't house them all, so why start with my 'homes'? Once you start to think like that, saying 'why worry about others?', 'why pay taxes?', it becomes what the British call 'a mug's game' to do what the Americans call 'the right thing'.

Limits to people or to growth?

If you had a chance to avoid paying a little tax, you might well take it; after all, what minuscule difference could your contribution make? Thinking more and more like this made it acceptable from the 1980s onwards for authorities to increasingly prosecute the poor when they are found to cheat social security systems, but not others for the far greater sums stolen when people do not pay their taxes. Figure 19 shows just how clear the trends are. Data from Australia are used here, but all of the more unequal affluent countries would show similar trends. Note that the axis for taxation fraud has to be drawn with a scale magnified by a factor of ten to be able to see it. By 2014, only 45 people in all of Australia were being taken to court for serious fraud over not paying their taxes, only 34 of those cases resulted in a conviction, and only 26 people received a custodial sentence as a result, but some AU$3.36 million were recovered from those few people, or roughly AU$100,000 each. In that same year, 3,107 Australians were investigated for possible welfare fraud, or roughly 69 times as many despite far fewer Australians claiming welfare than paying (or not fully paying) tax. The investigations into social security fraud reduced in tenacity after the rapid 1990–2003 rise was revealed, but Australian politicians continue to talk of scroungers, welfare cheats, or, as they are called there, 'rorts'.[111]

The idea that there is not enough space to house people, that there cannot be enough welfare for the poor to prevent poverty, and that there are too many to feed, is an old one. The world's first salaried economist, the Reverend Thomas Malthus, was just one of many to dream up the

Figure 19: Social security and taxation prosecutions, Australia, counts, 1989–2014

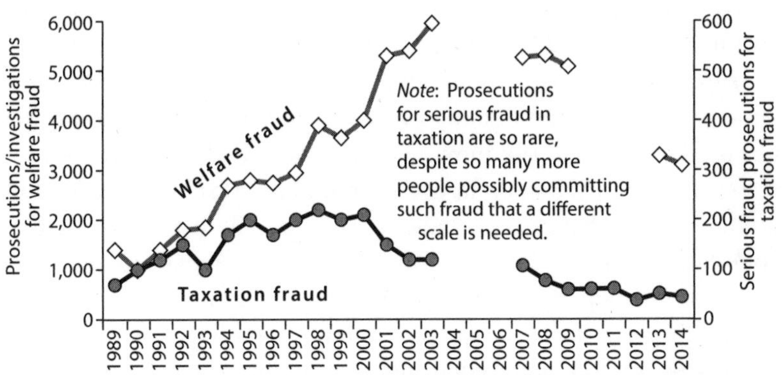

Source: *Journal of Social Policy,* and in a presentation on 'Welfare fraud, welfare fiction' by Greg Marston, Social Policy Unit, The University of Queensland. Tax figures updated after 2003 through https://www.ato.gov.au/General/The-fight-against-tax-crime/ News-and-results/Tax-crime-prosecution-results/. Welfare fraud figures updated after 2003 through: http://www.aic.gov.au/publications/current%20series/tandi/421-440/tandi421.html , and http://www.humanservices.gov.au/corporate/publications-and-resources/annual-report/resources/1314/chapter-09/fraud-investigations

Referrals to the Director of Public Prosecutions for social security fraud and serious tax fraud in Australia, 1989-2014

	Social Security	Taxation
1989	1,400	70
1990	1,000	100
1991	1,400	120
1992	1,800	150
1993	1,850	100
1994	2,700	170
1995	2,800	200
1996	2,750	170
1997	2,950	200
1998	3,900	220
1999	3,650	200
2000	4,000	210
2001	5,300	150
2002	5,400	120
2003	5,950	120
2004		
2005		
2006		
2007	5,261	108
2008	5,312	78
2009	5,082	60
2010		61
2011		62
2012		39
2013	3,294	52
2014	3,107	45

Note: Of the 15,655 people referred to the Australian Director of Public Prosecutions for social security fraud between 2007 and 2009, 60% received a conviction. The tax fraud figures do not include summary offences under the Tax Administration Act which are not referred to the Director of Public Prosecutions. Of the 505 people referred during the 2007-2014 period for serious tax fraud, 96% received a conviction. Despite this the government website giving these latter figures states: 'Australia has a strong culture of voluntary tax compliance'.

idea that there were limits to how many people there could be, rather than limits to what people in total could consume and demand of other people's time. When we treat ourselves to a bit of paid-for pampering, we rarely think 'couldn't that person do something more useful with their time?'. When we buy something we don't really need, we rarely think of the labour and resources we have just wasted, only selfishly that we may have wasted 'our' money. We also do not like our time wasted, even when having to wait at traffic lights, but don't care much about having wasted other people's time. When it is pointed out that you have done this, do you say 'sorry' or 'tough luck', or does that depend on the 'rank' (or how you perceive the rank) of the other person?

In 1927, it was declared that, on reaching 104 million people, the US had surpassed its 'optimum' population. Any more ordinary people would be worse than useless, sub-optimum. This was according to some ornate and in hindsight clearly misguided mathematics credited to one Henry Pratt Fairchild. Shortly afterwards, in 1934, Sir John Megaw said that the population of India, which had expanded despite the famines that came with colonialism, had reached its 'optimum' limit. Sir John became Director-General of Medical Services in India in 1930, and illustrated clearly how humans could be viewed as animals when he declared that the Indian population 'multiply like rabbits and die like flies.'[112] Sir John retired in 1939, and died 10 years after India secured independence. He is remembered for advocating air conditioning to be used across the subcontinent.[113]

Places rarely suffer from having too many people, but frequently suffer from a few people taking far too much. By early 2008 it became evident that preceding the economic crash, the acquisition of most of the world's remaining available land was occurring at rates never seen before. Huge swathes were being bought up by a tiny number of the super-rich. Pop stars, celebrities and former presidents had bought up almost all the large ranches in places like Santa Barbara (California), forcing the rest of the population to live at the highest of densities ever seen there. Around London and despite the crash, land prices in the South East were soaring for similar speculative reasons, increasing the most in 2014. Far away, it was principally US money that was being used to buy great tracts of land in places like New Zealand, and, according to at least one newspaper report, some 45 per cent of the land area of Cambodia was 'seized' by property speculators in 2008 alone, along with two thirds of the British Virgin Islands.[114]

Celebrities do not just want land; they want the most valuable and more rare land, riverside and shoreline, including a space to moor yachts. *The world with its billions does not have too many people, but it does have too many in their thousands who think that they are worth a million others.* Individually these people take up the space that used to house hundreds; they consume fossil fuels and other resources far less sustainably than thousands of others collectively consume, and they demand the time and labour and subservience of tens of thousands of others in supplying the resources for their needs, manufacturing them and servicing them in a way that deprives millions more of the potential benefits of that labour. And they know this is unfair. In early 2015 at Davos, reports began to emerge of '… hedge fund managers all over the world who are buying airstrips and farms in places like New Zealand because they think they need a getaway.'[115] These getaways are needed in case high and rising inequality results in insurrection closer to their main home.

Just think of all the human work required to create the materials and technology needed to furnish a grand mansion, to kit out a large yacht or to construct a private plane, and then you can begin to comprehend how just one of the world's many hundreds of billionaires, someone who can spend a couple of million dollars a day on leisure time outgoings, harms millions of other human beings *who in total* get by on less than that for *all* they need. Billionaires and multi-millionaires live in a state of luxury that could only be sustained, and can certainly only be justified, if they were a separate species. However, at the same time, the average reader of this book – who may be living what they think of as a modest life in comparison – is living the life of a king compared with most people in the world. When you read of the excesses of celebrity, it is worth considering which aspects of your more ordinary life may appear just as excessive to most other people alive today. People's concepts of what is normal, what is reasonable, covers a huge range. Because of this we find it so difficult to comprehend each other's perspectives. Each of us is living in our own small social island in an archipelago of insularity, so separated are we by income and wealth.

For the most affluent of celebrities, even cupboards and closets can become pricey items requiring home alteration. Readers of popular accounts of the lives of the 21st-century super-rich can marvel at how some have come to require dry-cleaning factory-style conveyor belts to help organise their 400ft^2 walk-in closets.[116] Before dismissing such excess and greed as simply the acts of a few with far more money than sense, consider how numbers of self-storage facilities have shot up so frequently in recent years in towns across rich countries, so that when moving home people can put their furniture and other possessions temporarily into storage. Many people now use these facilities when they simply have a little too much, or inherit stuff, or just want a little more space (but want to keep all their 'stuff').

Look at your own clothes and consider how often you are likely to wear any item before you throw it away. You may think it is many times; it is more likely to be on average just a dozen or so washes before, after languishing in your stuffed cupboards unloved for a few years, the garment is binned. If we wore our clothes until they began to wear out, then the global garment industry as currently arranged would collapse, only shortly after the demise of the fashion industry.

Clothing style has mattered for a long time. We have not suddenly become fashion conscious, but many of us have suddenly been able to satisfy our desire for quantities of apparel that could only be dreamt of before. Adam Smith talked of the need for men to have good quality shoes and linen shirts to be able to hold their heads up high. Clothing was also a constant theme in the accounts of the century that followed his pronouncements. It was used to demarcate style and respectability; dress had to be '*correct*'. There was extensive theft of clothing as a result to preserve respectability and a '… large and sophisticated trade in second-hand clothing, the development of fashion styles in adornment and ornamentation'[117] across 18th-century Europe. This, by the 20th century, became 'accessorising'. But there were no 400ft^2 walk-in wardrobes even for Marie Antoinette, no purchasing and abandoning of garments so freely, no consumption that was quite so conspicuous as was seen in the last years of our most recent gilded age.

Purchasing new cars, clothes, homes and home decorations are not the most conspicuous acts of consumption of all. That label has been reserved for the purchasing of new looks for new faces, breasts, noses, and new ourselves. By the start of the current century, the British were reshaping themselves at only a tenth of the rate they were reshaping their homes, but still undergoing 2.5 million acts of cosmetic surgery a year on a population of about 50 million adults in Britain, at a cost of about £5,000 a face lift.[118] Many more were having bits chopped off or sucked out and stuck together again in the US.

The great increase in stomach stapling as obesity increased coincided with increases in starvation and hunger elsewhere in the world as food prices also rose. The leading private plastic surgery company in Britain used to follow a model from the US and offer its customers loyalty cards whereby they receive discounts on later operations, as long as they have enough procedures carried out in a specified period.[119] Liposuction and stomach stapling, taking laxatives and all manner of other tortures are now used to shrink our bodies when the search for instant gratification settles on food, and then settles on looks, before we head off shopping again to make ourselves feel good … before the money runs out.

The fear of not being recognised

Why do we idolise celebrity? Do we fear not being rewarded? Or fear not even being recognised as human? Above all else celebrities are recognised, not just literally, but financially. Their faces adorn hundreds of magazines available in every corner shop. They are the staple ingredients of the most watched television shows. Surveys in unequal affluent countries routinely report that '… ten-year-olds think the very best thing in the world is having money and being rich, followed by being famous'.[120] When one school teacher asked her primary school children what they wanted, they too said, "to be famous"; when asked famous for what, they typically replied: "Dunno, I just want to be famous."[121] Another primary school teacher with a similar tale to tell said of her pupils and of their ambitions: "These kids don't know they're working class; they won't know that until they leave school and realise that the dreams they've nurtured through childhood can't come true."[122]

Those most damaged by living through our times of greed have yet to grow old enough to experience all of the repercussions. Already in North America, one in seven adolescent girls report enough signs of serious depression for it to be clear that an upward trend in an epidemic of anxiety is occurring at the point, past primary school, when most young people suddenly realise that they will not be famous (see Figure 21 in Chapter 7, this volume).

In a world in which celebrities are lauded, where the super-rich are so visible, where fat cat salaries are discussed as rational and lives of luxury presented as normal, it is easy to feel undervalued. When our labour is sold cheaply we rightly fear '... falling victim to the denial of human dignity which went together with such a sale....'[123] Human dignity falls to its lowest under such circumstances where labour has no price on it at all, no worth. Housework is put in that category, as is much childrearing and care for the sick within families, but at least most families recognise their relatives as human. Some of the time those who do less housework value the unpaid contributions of others, but quite often they take them for granted. If it is easy to ignore people in your own home, it is even easier to ignore them on the street.

In 2007, and again where greed has progressed furthest, in the US, researchers reported that they had scanned the brains of a sample of university students while simultaneously showing them photographs of people, including the homeless, to ascertain the degree to which the key part of their prefrontal cortex, the part which is normally active when empathy is felt, reacted at the point when each photograph was shown. The researchers were subsequently shocked to find that when the university students viewed photographs of people such as the homeless and drug addicts, this stimulated no activity in the region associated with empathy at all. The suggestion was that typical US university students had come to consider this group of their fellow citizens to be less than human. This was a coping mechanism on behalf of the students that allowed them to carry on with their lives without having to think further and deeper. Fortunately, the researchers also reported finding that if a question was asked about the homeless people in the photographs being shown, such as 'What food do you think this beggar might prefer?', then the emotional part of the cortex began to become active again on the scanner.[124] The damage that had been done to these students was thus not irreversible.

Some young children, adolescents and students can be more damaged than others. We know from empirical studies of psychological assessments at the time they made their choice, that people who in recent times have chosen to try to become economics students have tended to be both less cooperative than most, and to be more self-interested individuals.[125] Other studies have found that those who take degrees in economics usually go on to express an even greater preference for selfish beliefs at the end of their courses than they did at the beginning; they become more self-interested.[126] It is quite likely that those who were most willing to believe what they were taught were more likely to get the higher grades, the starter jobs, to become economic policy advisers, to rise high in business or government, and to accelerate the process of like picking like. And a few did become famous. Where this takeover by the newly indoctrinated occurred, it did so with most vengeance in the 1980s, and the scars can be seen in the statistical record on inequalities in income and wealth, and the terrible outcomes later seen for mental health.

6.5 The 1980s: changing the rules of trade

When it comes to the distribution of wealth, it was in the early 1980s that the tide turned, and it turned in those countries where the rich won the debate over whether to increase inequality or not. In Britain, inequality in wealth fell from the late 1920s through to 1981, when the richest 10 per cent of people reached an all-time low for their group of holding 'only' half of all the marketable wealth in that country.[127] The trend was similar in the US, with wealth slowly becoming more evenly distributed, if still grossly unfairly awarded, year by year, right through to the very early 1980s. Earlier, redistribution from rich to poor had come about because of progressive income taxation and effective inheritance tax, but also because wages for poorer people, including the US minimum wage, were higher in the past in real terms; unions had been successful in fighting for workers' rights, rights that, when well won and well defended in the long term, reduced wealth inequalities.

The famous super-rich families of the gilded age saw their riches slowly whittled away, taxed away, wasted by their offspring, and in a few cases, given away. Crucially, a new aristocracy of other newly wealthy folk did not immediately replace them. This did not occur until governments in Britain and the US changed in 1979 and 1980, and changed the very meaning of being fair. What had before been seen as cheating became reclassified as shrewd. They followed the teachings of economists such as Milton Friedman who was associated with the University of Chicago, teachings first tested in Chile, New Zealand and Britain, before being enacted in the US, with remarkable effect.

Two thirds of the wealth increases in the US in the 1980s and 1990s were in assets held by the richest single percentile of the population. By 2000, the wealthiest 1 per cent of US citizens owned 40 per cent of the wealth and the poorest 40 per cent owned 1 per cent of their country's wealth, that 1 per cent thus being shared out very thinly between them. Those in the wealthiest single percentile of the population were each *individually* 1,600 times better off, on average, than two out of every five people walking on the streets that they were chauffeured past or which their private planes flew over.[128]

Holding on to your place on the hill

In 1980, average households in the US spent 11 per cent of their disposable income simply on servicing two parts of their debts: the interest on their mortgage and the interest on their credit card debts. This does not include money spent actually paying those debts off, paying off and servicing other debts, or costs such as rent which can be seen as a debt for borrowing property. Once lease payments for cars were added, rental payments on tenant-occupied property, homeowners' insurance and property tax payments, most things that simply had to be paid (and which mostly did not pay off debts), the debt service ratio rose to almost 16 per cent of annual disposable income. It is that ratio, called the overall financial obligations ratio (FOR), which shows by how much more North Americans became indebted in the mid-to-late 1980s and mid-1990s onwards to 2008, and which is plotted in Figure 20.

For renters, the FOR in 1980 was nearer a quarter of their annual income; for mortgage holders, it was more like a seventh. It fell from 1980 through to the first quarter of 1984 as people spent less on things that might put them into further debt. But as the US and most of the rest of the rich world began to exit the mass unemployment legacy of the early 1980s recession, the ratio began to rise again, rose quickly, and peaked at almost 18 per cent in 1987. The housing market then slowed again, and there was another, smaller, recession, but the FOR did not fall back below 16 per cent until three years after the crash in 2011. Debt servicing rose again from 1994, passed 18 per cent in 2000, 19 per cent in 2006, peaked at almost a fifth of average incomes being spent solely on interest and rent payments in 2007, and then began to fall back again in 2008, as the economic crash rapidly curtailed spending coupled with interest rates plummeting.

The table in Figure 20 also shows a huge difference between the total FOR for renters compared to homeowners. It is partly due to renters earning less on average and so having to spend a higher proportion of their income on these items, including rent. However, much of this money is destined to be unearned income for the wealthiest in society who syphon off a higher proportion from the incomes of the poorest in society than from the less poor who can afford to buy their homes.

The world is now awash with debt, and those debts increased most quickly, as Figure 20 shows, in the mid-1980s, because it was then that we were told most often, most clearly and most consistently, and with the least understanding of the implications, that 'greed is good'. Although the debt appears to fall after 2008 in the figure, most of the fall is the result of interest rates falling, and only affects people with mortgages. The amount they owed didn't fall very much. Furthermore, for renters, their FOR was still in excess of 25 per cent and rising by the end of 2012.[129] Nevertheless, Figure 20 does imply that in one way a great deal of the harm done in the 1980s and 1990s in the US was unwound by the 2008 crash simply because people no longer had incomes that could support their required debt repayment – that is why interest rates had to fall.

In the first paperback edition of this book, Figure 20 was included as a warning of an unsustainable rise, and the available data ended on a high in 2008. Now, just a few years later, all the apparent growth in earnings made from that debt since 1981 has been more than cancelled out by the crash. The 1980s boom simply created the antecedents of the crash to come and the warnings were more than borne out. Seven years after 2008 we still have no idea when the aftershocks will end. No one expects stability any more.

As the debts rose in the late 1990s as a result of both 1980s deregulation and the 'greed is good' mantra spreading, something had to give. Poorer households became forced by other people's spending to have to spend more themselves just to maintain their social standing. Once others decided to rent a 'pad' in the city to reduce weekday commuting, the supply of rental property was reduced and its price increased. Once

Figure 20: Debt payments as a percentage of post-tax income, US Financial Obligations Ratio (FOR), 1980–2014

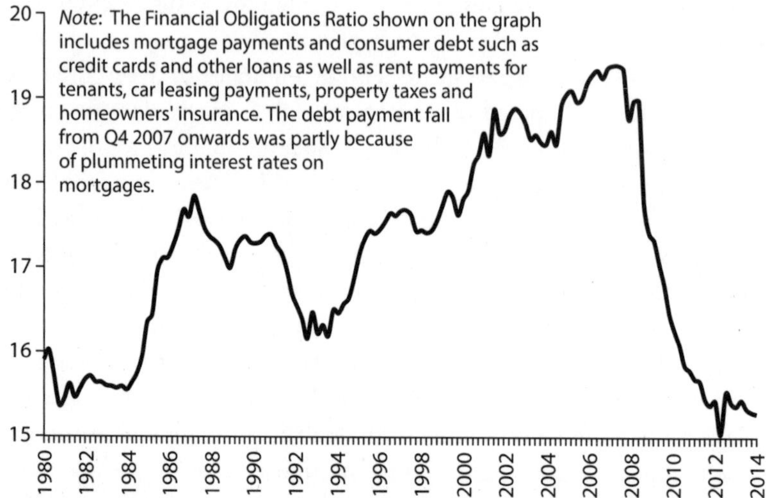

Source: Derived from data provided by the Federal Reserve Board (www.federalreserve.gov/releases/housedebt/). For a series of data just including mortgage and consumer debt see Chart 1 in Foster, J.B. (2006) 'The household debt bubble', *Monthly Review*, vol 58, no 1 (www.monthlyreview.org/0506jbf.htm). Data plotted in the figure above is the Total FOR series (see below): data for Q1 2009 to Q3 2014 downloaded on 2 January 2015 (only Total FOR comparable). Note older data may be found in Foster, 2006.

Household debt service payments and financial obligations as a percentage of disposable personal income (seasonally adjusted), 1980–2008

	DSR	Total FOR	Renter FOR	Homeowner Total	Homeowner Mortgage	Homeowner Consumer
1980	11.13	15.90	24.57	13.77	8.12	5.65
1982	10.71	15.67	23.66	13.65	8.81	4.85
1984	10.64	15.55	22.65	13.68	8.80	4.88
1986	11.87	17.11	25.71	14.95	9.44	5.51
1988	11.95	17.36	26.05	15.23	9.67	5.56
1990	11.99	17.29	24.67	15.44	10.07	5.36
1992	11.29	16.69	23.56	14.87	10.15	4.72
1994	10.96	16.50	24.55	14.44	9.63	4.81
1996	11.83	17.40	26.75	15.15	9.48	5.67
1998	11.94	17.43	27.28	15.22	9.22	6.00
2000	12.26	17.62	29.07	15.25	9.08	6.18
2002	13.24	18.59	30.52	16.18	9.51	6.67
2004	13.50	18.48	26.38	16.89	10.14	6.75
2006	14.03	19.00	25.80	17.67	11.19	6.48
2008	14.26	19.34	26.38	17.97	11.65	6.32

Note: DSR = Household Debt Service Ratio (excludes home rent, car lease, building insurance and property tax payments), FOR = Financial Obligations Ratio.

others decided to try with just a little more urgency to spend more to buy a house slightly higher up the hill, all house prices were shifted upwards. Again, a few more deciding that they 'needed' two or three or four homes more than before was crucial in ensuring that space was not opened up at the bottom due to aspiration rising so quickly at the top.

Richer university students having homes bought for them by their parents, and not living in the kinds of densities students used to live at, also added to the squeeze, as did the influx from abroad of affluent bankers and other financial and service people into buzzing world cities like London. The largest single immigrant group in the centre of London consisted of people born in the US who lived in the greatest concentration in some of the most expensive areas. In the most expensive of places in London, such as around Hyde Park, one seventh of all children living there were US-born, according to the 2001 Census.[130]

The growing greed at the top increased the cost of living for those in the middle further. It is affluent immigrants who take up most space at the top. Poor immigrants squeeze into the cheapest of rented property at the bottom of any housing market, and have many times less effect on prices and space than a single rich banking family does on its arrival in London from the US. Ever more unsecured debt was amassed in affluent countries where inequalities had been allowed to rise rapidly.

By 2008 it was reported that almost one in ten households in Britain had a mortgage for which they had agreed only to repay the interest. These households also had no other savings set up or being put away to repay the capital sum. Some 6 per cent of married couples with dependent children had an 'interest-only' mortgage by 2007.[131] These mortgage holders were not and are not buying their homes; they are, in effect, renting, with a fraction more security of tenure than renters usually enjoy. The situation in the US over mortgage lending is even worse than in Britain, and Figure 20 does not highlight this problem; it only shows interest payments and not the amounts required for the debts to eventually be run down. As debts increased in general, less and less was actually being repaid. People were not simply being feckless in amassing this debt – many have had to amass it to be able to live in an average place, and even more were being repeatedly advised to get into debt. Debt is presented as a sensible option. If you could afford to borrow more, you were said to be foolish not to. As interest rates fell, more could be paid off. But wages were also falling, and more and more people were only able to rent. They had no hope of buying.

Mis-selling, debt, exploitation and tribute

In Britain, the organisation that used to be called the Financial Services Authority (FSA) carried out mystery shopper surveys in 2005 and 2006, and found that *the majority* of financial advisers surveyed broke all eight of the basic rules laid down over mis-selling products such as those for 'equity release'. Unsurprisingly (perhaps) the majority of financial advisers were simply interested in lining their own pockets and were happy to break every single one of the rules that they were expected to follow if it boosted their income and they thought they would not be found out. Remarkably, when the Council of Mortgage Lenders reported these numbers, they suggested that as few recipients knew how to complain or thought it was worth complaining about the awful service, then: 'It is important to put these negative views and images in perspective. Complaints to the Ombudsman about equity release products are limited.'[132] In other words, the lenders admitted that mis-selling was taking place in most cases, but said it was not that bad as the customers did not appear to realise that they were being misled!

In the US, writing about the predatory and unethical mortgage and loan industry is an academic staple, providing many scholars with a livelihood. In looking for stories similar to those of mis-selling in Britain, they find an abundance of '... evidence suggesting that subprime mortgage segmentation exacerbates rather than reduces traditional inequalities of denial-based exclusion'.[133] Thus, being lent so much did not help the poor, and did not get them out of ghettos, but for a short time, it did make the rich much richer.

During the 1980s in the US, the top 1 per cent more than doubled their share of national wealth while (when calculated in constant 1995 dollars that adjust for inflation) the bottom 40 per cent of households in the US, those who by now have just one percentile of the total wealth to share among all of them, also saw their mean net wealth fall from $4,000 on average in 1983 to $900 by 1995.[134] They were robbed, and they were robbed first by being put into debt by the 1980s loan sharks who were presented as respectable bankers in suits, helping them to enjoy a trickle down of wealth, then by increased material poverty in the 1980s recession, then through falling wages in real terms at the bottom.

All the changes of the 1980s, coupled with rising inequality, led to it becoming necessary for those with even small savings to spend rather than save in the round. And all this was long before the 2008 crash. There was little point in having faith that the future would be better than the past and that meagre saving would be worthwhile; it wasn't. It turned out to be right to enjoy yourself when you could if you were not at the top. And not just for the poor in rich countries. The poor worldwide were being robbed too, just on a far grander scale.

Internationally the poor countries of the world had to produce 40 per cent more goods in 2006 compared with 1977 to buy the same amount of similar goods from rich countries at each date. Simultaneously, between 1997 and 2006, the total debt of the domestic, business, government and finance sectors of the US rose by $41.9 trillion. North Americans were not making more things to sell to afford what they purchased at ever-greater discount abroad; instead, they were borrowing more to afford it at those discounts. Given this, it is hardly surprising that poor countries progressively received less back in return for what they sent in tribute. Increased global trade has increased inequalities not just between countries but also within poorer countries as well as within rich countries. Within 90 per cent of Latin American countries (when measured between 1985 and 1995), it was the rich who benefited most from trade liberalisation.[135]

It was also during the 1980s that consumption in rich countries rose most steeply because the primary economic activity of some rich countries turned from 1970s manufacturing towards full-blooded 1990s finance. When a good is manufactured and sold at a profit, the ability to exploit others is limited in that the good has to physically exist, be physically transported to those who are to buy it, and it must work for at least a short period of time. This is if the customers are to be enticed to produce yet more agricultural crops to buy the next offer. Clearly, if the interest is in profit, then what is sold should soon break down and have obsolescence inbuilt, or be designed to be destroyed (as in the case of the arms trade) in order for many future sales to be quickly guaranteed, but something actually has to be delivered. Financial services are not like this.

When financial services are provided, people are given promises, often not even pieces of paper, but electronically transferred pieces of a promise. These are promises to insure them and to pay up if there are great natural disasters, to satisfy the desire of others who feel a need to hedge their bets, insure their lives or livelihoods. You charge them far more than the risk for these things; you transfer funds electronically to pay for those misfortunes that do occur, it is true (unless you go bankrupt), but you transfer as grudgingly as you can if you really want to get rich very quickly, and you do not have to make a single actual widget.

Nothing physical needs to move from you to those you 'serve' for you to provide them with financial services. However, a huge amount needs to move physically in the opposite direction. Because you quickly make large profits when you convince others to buy your financial protection, to invest in your schemes, or simply just to deposit their little sums of wealth in your huge coffers, you quickly amass great sums of money to spend. All manner of tributes are sent to your offices in New York, London and Tokyo.

Ensuring that the rains come

People gawped when the very first barrels of 'special' water arrived at the most prestigious of offices to be plugged into early 1980s water coolers, but soon, every top office had one. It is only recently that people have criticised the water cooler as being environmentally damaging. What will some future archaeologist make of all those plastic water barrels that have ended up in 1980s and 1990s landfill sites? Will they assume that the public water system broke down? Will they ever find out that a few countries rigged the system in their favour by establishing reserve currencies,[136] and much else? The countries in which the largest numbers of water coolers first became affordable were those with reserve currencies.

Archaeology involves a great deal of head scratching. When the city at the centre of the ancient Chaco canyon civilisation of the south-western US was being unearthed, the key question the diggers asked themselves was: what on earth had the city produced to justify its existence? It was placed in a canyon that provided insufficient space to produce food or goods to trade. There were no signs that advanced tools were manufactured in the city, or that it was a site for the exchange of goods to an extent that justified its size, its opulent buildings, and what appeared to have been a very large population. Eventually, the archaeologists looked to ancient Rome and modern-day London to find the model that could explain its existence and persistence (until its environmental collapse in the 12th century CE). The city had existed on tribute. Food and goods had been sent to its inhabitants purely because of who they were, how they were venerated and presumably because of what powers they said they possessed.

Just as London bankers at the start of the 21st century said, 'send us your chattels and we will multiply them, trust us', priests of the 12th-century city of Chaco said, 'send us food and we will ensure the rains will come.' And the rains came. But the rains were eventually insufficient to grow everything demanded by those who ruled the temples at the heart of the city in the centre of the Chaco canyon. The Anasazi civilisation (or ancient Pueblo people) centred on Chaco is now best known from the signs left in the dirt and the stories told.[137] The civilisation is thought to have ended because all tribute economies eventually result in environmental degradation too great to continue producing the tribute.

As the last of the original Anasazi who had enjoyed that culture were dying of starvation, a third of the way around the world, in Lombard Street in London, the prototypes of the first international banks were being established with the help of immigrants from Lombardy. They were established to ease the trading of wool, just as the Medicis of Venice, the city in a swamp, grew rich first by facilitating the trading of textiles, and only later through lending at supposedly discretionary interest rates, just as the Dutch did later when they became the economic centre of Europe.

In low-lying London, in the 16th century, newly established bankers also grew rich from the debts of others. Much later, by 1740, these debts were being sold through 550 coffeehouses [138] – caffeine helped create an air of opulence, and emboldened the spirit of the man about to borrow. Contemporaries such as Adam Smith (1723–90), seeing this, and with no knowledge of tales such as that of the Anasazi, wrote about how such debt-supported trade could only be for the good. It was the spirit of the times, and a forgetting of the lows, the bubbles and the crashes in between, that led in the 1980s to the rise in London and New York of a political new right that revelled in '… the rediscovery of the 18th century economics of Adam Smith'.[139] By 2006, the cost of even a modest home in the London banking borough of Westminster exceeded half a million pounds, in Kensington over £800,000 by 2010, and £1,400,000 by late 2014! That year, 2014, also saw a 40 per cent rise in homes being left empty in the Kensington borough as investors brought property purely as an investment, not even to rent.[140] It had taken just three decades, from the rediscovery of Adam Smith and the re-veneration of banking, to its demands for tribute becoming unaffordable. And London became the centre of it all. As one anonymous but very widely read source explained:

> London is one of the best locations for the super-rich to base themselves. Being no more than 12 hours from most major cities and financial centres – New York, Paris, Frankfurt, Tokyo, Moscow, Hong Kong – it is easy to do business anywhere in the world. It is also only a few hours away from the favourite super-rich holiday destinations: Monaco and Cannes for the Arabs, the Byblos in St Tropez and Courchevel for the Russians, the Hamptons and the Caribbean for the Americans, and the Maldives for the Asians, Chinese, Russians, British, French and Indians. A £10,000 holiday may sound like a lot to you or me, but for the super-rich, you can multiply that figure by 10.[141]

Entire countries have largely become tribute economies where people do very little of any real value but have to perform particularly intricate rituals to justify their existence while growing no crops, making nothing and helping no one. Being a tribute economy does not greatly benefit most citizens of these countries or even most inhabitants of the tribute cities, of which the greatest in the world are London and New York. The roads are not paved with gold as a result of all the tribute that flows in. It is only a tiny few at the top of these tribute systems who collect many more tithes than they can spend. In 2010, senior bankers at Goldman Sachs in London each received on average an income of £4 million a year, that average fell below £2 million in 2011 once it was subject to scrutiny, but by 2013, it had risen again, to around £3 million each annually.[142] Whether it falls or rises in future depends on how people react politically to the long recession and austerity as much as on future events, the inevitable, the unpredictable, and all the other currently largely unforeseen events to come.

Extremely high salaries at the very top are defended by people paid many times less, but still highly, just beneath the top. Beneath the top bankers are lackeys who are mostly consigned to undertake work that is soul-destroying in its banality. This is the kind of work that economists label as 'transaction costs' or 'bean counting'. The taking up of so much of our money and time by transaction costs is not a new phenomenon. In 1970, almost half of US 'productivity' was transaction costs, most (55 per cent) occurring between firms, while the proportion of sales workers in the US rose from 4 per cent of all employees in 1900 to 12 per cent of all by 2000.[143] If that rate of 'progress' were to carry on, a third of the US employees will be working in frontline 'sales' in a few generations time, another third will be counting the receipts, and the final third will be managing the others. This cannot possibly come to pass – *somebody somewhere has to do something of actual value*. What matters is not that it has to end, but how it unravels.

North Americans have yet to understand that most of what they think they own came about due to banking 'liberalisation' in the 1980s affecting what tribute they received from abroad. However, many are beginning to see that what is happening within their wide and bountiful land is now unsustainable. Take, for instance, that rural green idyll, the one place that should be self-sufficient, Montana: '… half the income of Montana residents doesn't come from their work within Montana ... Montana's own economy already falls far short of supporting Montana [which is] by and large dependent on the rest of the US.'[144] The half that this particular author refers to is made up partly of social security payments flowing in, but mainly of '… out-of-state pensions, earnings on real estate equity, and business income.' It is easy to see why it is now commonly understood that the entire country is in deficit if looked at in this way.

The US does not support itself by its own labour or resources, and could not possibly support its current rate of consumption and behaviour on its own; it must have 'free trade'. To those outside of the US, this is trade that is often far from freely entered into, and where much is not traded back from the free traders in return – think of the global duopoly of Apple and Microsoft. America does not freely trade computers and operating systems with the rest of the world. European computer manufacturers also independently produced machines with WIMP (windows, icons, menus and pointer) systems in the 1980s, but they did not have the monopoly advantages and the back-up of a global super-power, which makes a lie of free trade being free.

In microcosm, Montana, despite its mountains, forests, mines and grasslands, could not support the average lifestyle of its population through what it could truly freely trade. This lack of sustainability is partly because of the lavish lifestyle of a minority of its most wealthy residents, but also because many other North Americans have come to think that they can drive where they like, and many think they can fly where they like, when they have already burnt almost all the oil under the land they live on and are now quickly fracking out what is left. Those who currently consume most have most to lose. In such a situation it is easier to see how, like priests in the Chaco canyon, they try to cling on to their past beliefs to the very last.

How it all unravels

Sustainable ways of living are likely to involve much greater social changes than a massive curtailment of air travel and the demise of the petrol engine. For instance, it is only our current generation of human beings who do not, as a worldwide majority, live in villages, and it has been villages that have proved to be the most sustainable as a form of settlement over time. Traditionally, village life means multigenerational living, in households that are home to several families. When people live in large households they each consume less on average, waste less, travel less and have less need to have recourse to the inefficiencies of the market to provide care for the young and old, or simply to find someone to fix things. When people help each other out, out of obligation and for regard rather than for purely financial reward, they are more likely not to do things that are not worth doing.

There can be much to be fearful about in returning to more village-like living, places where too many know your business, where women could be made subservient more easily, and communities in which strangers are more often feared rather than being the norm. Traditional villages are the very opposite of cosmopolitan living, yet despite this, a return, in many ways, to such social units, or larger village-like small eco-towns, is being repeatedly suggested by social activists as a valid proposal for a preferable '… social unit of the 21st century has nothing to do with numbers.'[145] This is not so much a garden city movement, but one that sees cities as less of a necessity, since internet technology means that it is no longer essential to live in settlements of millions to be able to visit a theatre or to be able to read a specialist newspaper. The gross inefficiency of living in ones and twos in city apartments is now commonly calculated by mainstream scientists, and reported on in the most respected of their journals.[146] City living could be highly efficient, but not if we live too individualistic lives.

The 1980s saw the population revival of London and New York after decades of shrinking; people began to move into tiny apartments. Around the rich world the young flooded into the largest of cities again; city living and city jobs were lauded. Being single became normal for people of working age across all of London by 1991, according to the Census, then across much of the rest of Britain just a decade later. However, being single, living on your own, is expensive, and often lonely – but it became harder and harder not to live like this across the rich world. Part of even London's housing problem is that there are more single adult households in the capital and more households without children. Single adult living has become the norm across all of Japan most recently. Only excessive tribute makes such cell-like existences possible, because it is so economically inefficient to live alone. Monasteries also often survived on tribute, just as rich world cities do today. Monasteries and nunneries were a drastic form of birth control. In some ways, modern city living is also a form of limiting reproduction, aided by contraception rather than celibacy. Both a monastic and a hedonistic life can be a lonely life.

In Britain, surveys undertaken as long ago as 2006 found that, when multiplied up, some 9 million adults reported experiencing feeling lonely at weekends. Almost one in five people aged 55 and over admitted to regularly spending a full day without speaking to anyone. And although 'only' one in 50 people said they had no one to turn to in a personal crisis, the numbers of both single old and single young found to have died alone with no one claiming their bodies rose at this time.[147] The great cities we have created also happen to be places of great loneliness for many. Admitting you are lonely is only allowed in secret, in newspaper columns and websites entitled 'lonely hearts', or revealed in statistics on urban suicide,[148] but it is worth remembering loneliness when lauding cities and city living..

Cities now cover just 2 per cent of the earth's land surface, but house 50 per cent of the population, who consume 75 per cent of all resources and produce 75 per cent of all human waste.[149] Because cities are usually well served by public transport, they can appear environmentally friendly at first glance, but life within cities could simultaneously be so much less wasteful and more fulfilling. We commonly now mistake our wants for our needs, and consider our way of living to be the only possible way, whereas the bricks and mortar of our homes would not disappear if we changed the rules of our lives.

Suppose we moved away from a design for life based on amassing debt and then expecting others to finance our pensions through their debt payments. Suppose we introduced citizens' incomes: where not just our pensions, but also all our basic needs, for all of us, are met as a right from current expenditure, not from desperately hoped-for future 'capital growth'. How much of what we currently quietly despair of is simply supported by a mirage of inevitability? To what extent have:

> … we in the developed world … completely lost track of the connection between the practical need to have a home and what it communicates about our social significance to others[?] To a remarkable extent, the price we pay for our inflated borrowings is far greater than the monthly direct debit. Suppose for a moment that you had no mortgage, and no one else you know did.… You would be able to walk away from jobs or careers that had no intrinsic value to you. You would be liberated from the pressure to keep up with the Joneses by having a home in the right street, decorated in ways that will impress them.… The truth is that it is the rich who mainly benefit from so much of our capital and income being tide up in housing. They can afford to buy homes for their children and benefit far more than the rest of us from inflated property values … but they unite the size, number and grandeur of their homes with their fragile identities.[150]

Greed has benefited the rich materially, but it has not made a better world for them to live in. It has not led to their families being much happier compared with previous generations, or to their children and partners trusting them any more than anyone else would trust a person who is so greedy. Some give money to the 'good cause' they choose because they think this will benefit their children. Bill Gates puts it thus: 'Melinda and I are strong believers that dynastic wealth is bad for both society and the children involved. We want our children to make their own way in the world.'[151] By this, he and Mel mean just leaving them extremely rich rather than stupendously rich, but the fact that they recognise their problem and talk about it is telling. As riches amass, many of the rich are coming to recognise the dangers of riches, but they can see no long-term alternative other than a little philanthropy. They cannot see that a world in which fewer become so rich in the future could be so much better.

The most serious and long-term deadly outcome of rising inequality is that, as inequalities rise, the rich – who in the US and the UK still mostly argue that inequality is good – become both richer and as a consequence politically stronger, and their arguments gain ground. Seeing inequality as a necessary evil is bad enough; seeing it as the solution is worse. Seeing inequality as unnecessary for human beings to live well requires a change in core beliefs as great as that which priests who begin to doubt their own religion usually cannot stomach. It is not the greedy we should fear – we can all be greedy – but those who carry on preaching that there is good in greed. They are likely to continue doing so long after they have stopped believing it themselves, because they can see no alternative.

7

'Despair is inevitable': health and wellbeing

> There's this terrible sense of human waste. They're existing rather than living, like battery hens. Apart from the telly and the cigarettes they are living like animals.[1]

Human beings are not mentally immune to the effects of rising elitism, exclusion, prejudice and greed. They react like rats in cages to having their social environments made progressively more unpleasant.[2] Rachel Johnson, former editor of *The Lady*, when commenting on 'the poor' in the quote above described others as living like animals. Because we can now measure how humans have reacted to injustice and where that injustice has been most detrimental, many now convincingly claim that all the injustices and inequalities which underlie most rich societies are having a 'dose-related response' to the mental wellbeing of populations: the greater the dose of inequality, the higher the response in terms of poor mental health.[3]

In this chapter, the first section brings together new evidence to show how there appears to have been a marked rise in depression among children living in the most unequal of affluent countries, as recorded from the mid-1980s and throughout the 1990s, and now into the 2000s. This is yet another new finding which suggests that poor mental health among affluent nations is worst in the US and least common where social inequalities are lowest. It strongly suggests that, for children and adults, living in more unequal environments increases measurable poor mental ill health most strikingly.[4]

Part of the mechanism behind the worldwide rise in diseases of despair is suggested, with evidence provided below, to be the anxiety caused when particular forms of competition are enhanced. School children's mental health deteriorates as they are given progressively more and more examinations to undertake. The effects of the advertising industry in making both adults, and especially children, feel inadequate, are also documented here, and many of the latest calls from all quarters – from psychiatrists to psychologists to archbishops – to curtail child-targeted advertising are listed.

The powerful have little immunity from the effects of despair if they live in more unequal countries. The most detrimental damage to ill health is found near the geographical hearts of the problem – the widest health inequalities in rich countries are to be seen within the very centres of London and New York. The third section in this chapter shows this, and also illustrates the fractal geography that results from psychological damage and social inequality.

This is followed by an illustration of just what kind of 'bird-brained' thinking was required to get us into our current situation, and how such thinking has continued throughout the economic crash despite its credibility having come to an end. In 2015, scientists revealed new evidence that suggested humans count in the same way that newborn chicks count.[5] They suggested that in many ways we are not as advanced as we think we are. But our capabilities can also be reduced when we become fearful.

It is not just that the mental health of human beings is damaged, that more people justifiably become anxious and depressed as social injustices increase, but that our collective capacity to think well and work well together to do the right thing is also clearly much harmed when we become so individualistic and atomised. Under high levels of inequality, great untruths become presented as truths, and much effort, that could otherwise have been spent for good, is either used for harmful purposes, is wasted outright, or is exerted by many trying to explain that some particular rise in inequality is not some great achievement.

The final section of this chapter documents the rise in the mass medicating of populations that has resulted from increased anxiety, in the context of a very brief history of psychiatric prescribing practices. The pressure on pharmaceutical giants now to make a profit is so great that if a pill were discovered that would cure mental illness with one dose, it would almost certainly have to be destroyed. However, it is unlikely that such an effective 'happy pill' could exist.

The human condition, our drive, our questioning, our angst and our concern, means that we cannot always be happy, but learning to live better with each other is beginning to be seen as the key to learning to live better within our own minds, to be happier or at least more at ease with ourselves. Not making children anxious, tearful, fearful and stressed in the first place is the best place to start. By looking to see in which places children are most anxious, we can also begin to see what might underlie the problems of adults who grew up under different social regimes.

7.1 Anxiety: made ill through the way we live, a third of all families

There are dangers in all shapes and sizes; it is the little numbers you have to look out for. The danger of saying that a certain proportion of children or adults suffer a particular mental illness is that it sustains the fantasy that everyone else is fine. All but the psychopathic have an '... innate need for social connection and egalitarian community',[6] and it has been shown that psychosis (severe mental ill health) is a natural human reaction to being deprived of normal human contact and treated as if you are a different species, not being respected. It is not hard to understand that: 'Human beings have an innate need to bond. Healthy, happy people bond with other humans.' It is not hard unless you are one of the few who can't.[7]

Being deprived of feeling valued, being excluded, not being treated as an equal, and not being respected, makes us mentally ill. Psychiatrists now suggest that our brains have developed in a way that means we cannot cope when we are not treated as equals.[8] The effects on our psychological states of mind of living in some of the most unequal of times in the most unequal of places have recently been recorded as enormous, so great, in fact, that we have become accustomed to widespread mental ill health. In Britain: 'According to the respected Psychiatric Morbidity Survey, one in six of us would be diagnosed as having depression or chronic anxiety disorder, which means that one family in three is affected.'[9]

The 2007 Adult Psychiatric Morbidity Survey of England found that 'nearly one person in four (23.0 per cent) in England had at least one psychiatric disorder and 7.2 per cent had two or more disorders' and '5.6 per cent of people aged 16 and over reported having ever attempted suicide but were not successful.' The survey also demonstrated 'a strong association between the presence of a disorder and a low adjusted household income.' The results of the 2014 survey will not be published until 2016. However, it was revealed that 'the proportion of women (aged 16-74) reporting suicidal thoughts in the previous year increased from 4.2 per cent in 2000 to 5.5 per cent in 2007', so a further increase is to be anticipated.[10]

Mixed anxiety and depression is the most common mental disorder in Britain, with almost 9 per cent of people meeting the criteria for diagnosis. Between 8 and 12 per cent of the population in Britain experience depression in any year. Women are more likely to have been treated for a mental health problem than men (29 per cent compared with 17 per cent). A quarter of women will require treatment for depression at some time, compared with a tenth of men. Women are twice as likely to experience anxiety as men. Of people with phobias or obsessive-compulsive disorders, about three fifths are female. One in ten children between the ages of 5 and 15 have a mental health disorder. In 2014 the Royal College of General Practitioners reported that these statistics were worsening, especially among older children and young adults.[11] And the figures for the US are worse.[12]

In Britain, around a fifth of children have a mental health problem in any given year, and about a tenth at any one time. Rates of experiencing poor mental health among children increase as they reach adolescence. Disorders of all kinds combined affect 10.4 per cent of boys aged 5–10, rising to 12.8 per cent of boys aged 11–15, and 5.9 per cent of girls aged 5–10, rising to 9.7 per cent of girls aged 11–15. The first three of these statistics have stayed the same or fallen slightly in the early 2000s, but the figure for girls aged 11–15 had risen to 10.3 per cent when last measured in 2004.[13]

Not all mental disorders have their origins in the way we live, but the way we live greatly affects how we are able to help people suffering all kinds of distress or confusion, and whether we exacerbate or mitigate suffering. At the other end of the age range to children, as the number of older people increases, the total number of people with dementia in the UK was forecast in 2014 to rise to over two million by 2051.[14] When the first edition of this book was published, in 2010, that estimate had been just over one million! How will we develop the care and compassion that will be needed if most of us are not to suffer neglect and indifference in our old age? Market forces will not be our salvation.

Anxiety in adolescence

Studies undertaken since 1974 have found a rise in what are known as 'conduct problems' among British children aged 15 and 16, accelerating in the 1990s, and providing 'evidence for a recent rise in emotional problems'.[15] The conduct problems included in these studies were a propensity to be involved in fighting, bullying, stealing, lying, disobedience, fidgeting, restlessness, inattention and fearfulness of new situations. One particular study found that for both boys and girls the increase in these problems had been substantial, with faster rises since 1986 than those found in earlier years.

The proportion of British children with severe problems doubled over the period 1974–99. The increase in the number of children suffering emotional problems was even starker, with almost all the increase having occurred since 1986. An earlier study of children in Scotland found similar results, with rising levels of distress from 1987 to 1999, but concentrated among girls, and most acutely felt among the *most affluent* of girls. Overall, by the start of the 21st century, a third of adolescent girls in Scotland were reporting symptoms of being depressed compared with just over a sixth in 1987.

The fact that the Scottish figures are so high is in all probability related to the part of Scotland where the study was undertaken, a part which also had one of the highest rates of anti-depressant prescription levels for those aged 15 and over. It is not just the children of the very rich who suffer disproportionally from poor mental health,[16] but also children and their parents living in some of the poorer parts of the rich world. In Greater Glasgow, anti-depressant prescriptions were enough for the equivalent of a tenth of the population to be on the *standard daily* (typical) dose of them by 2006. High levels of distress were becoming normalised. The researchers who conducted the study of adolescents reported that a significant relationship was found between the children's distress and how near to school examinations they were. The authors of the same study concluded that it was changes in society that had harmed the mental health of so many adolescents, not any increase in sensitivity.[17] How, where, and when a child grows up matters greatly.

Some analysts suggest that concerns over the rise in poor mental health may be overblown, or that we may have reached a plateau. In 2006 research was reported which suggested that there was not a growing epidemic of increased anxiety in adolescents. Here, I use the same data from that research to suggest that, actually, there is. The original research reported on 26 studies producing some 45 data points (each point being a rate of mental illness reported for a particular group of children at a particular time). The conclusion of the authors of the study was that there was no long-term rise to be seen in the rates of depression being reported. However, the authors had taken studies from a wide range of countries.[18] By looking at geographical differences between the countries they studied, it is possible to find clues as to where the rising tide of poor mental health in children is worse.

If a subset of the original 26 studies is selected, just those studies undertaken among children living in North America, then a different trend results. In North America, rates of adolescent depression have more than doubled since 1984, one extra adolescent girl in ten suffered symptoms of depression by the start of the current century as compared with two decades earlier, and 17 per cent prevalence rates are projected for 2014 compared with rates of around 4 per cent being reported in 1988. Thus, one in six adolescent girls in North America may by now suffer mental ill health compared with possibly as few as about one in 25 of their mothers' generation at their age.[19]

By August 2012, the US National Survey on Drug Use and Health was reporting that already 12 per cent of all girls in the US between aged 12 and 17 in the years 2008–10 had experienced major depressive episodes, peaking at 15 per cent by age 15 having experienced episodes in the past year. Thus, data produced more recently than the meta-analysis described above suggests that the trend shown in North America revealed in previous data does appear to be continuing.[20] Adding that data point, based on an annual survey of 67,500 young people (of whom approximately 5,600 were girls aged 15) changes the calculated correlation from being just significant (p=0.24), to potentially much more significant (p=0.001), although to be a fair comparison, a sweep of all possible studies conducted since 2004 should be made. For boys, there

Figure 21: Adolescent girls assessed as depressed (%), as reported in various studies in North America, 1984–2010

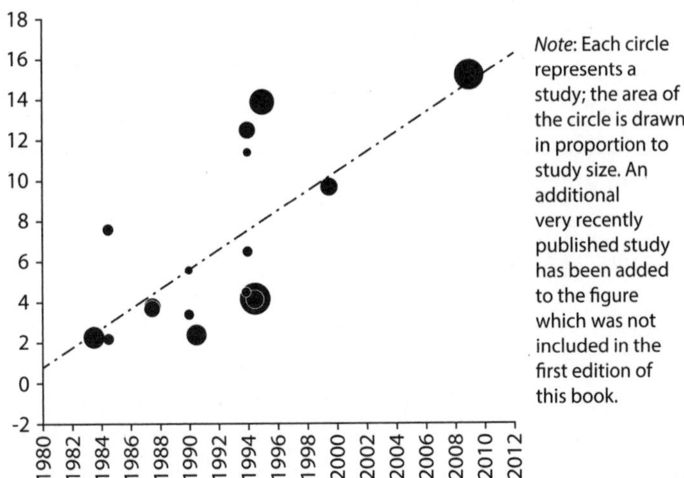

Note: Each circle represents a study; the area of the circle is drawn in proportion to study size. An additional very recently published study has been added to the figure which was not included in the first edition of this book.

Source: Re-analysis of Costello, E.J. et al (2006) 'Is there an epidemic of child or adolescent depression?', *Journal of Child Psychology and Psychiatry,* vol 47, no 12, pp 1263-71. The data shown above are for those studies where the children lived in the USA, the US territory of Puerto Rico, or Canada. The final study was published in 2012 by Substance Abuse and Mental Health Services Administration (SAMHSA) and based on combined data from the 2008 to 2010 SAMHSA National Survey on Drug Use and Health.

Studies of depression in adolescent girls in North America, 1984–2010 (see table 7, page 274 of the first edition of this book for details)

Year	Rate (%)	Observations	Born (year)	Age	Study #	Location
1984.5	7.6	776	65–74	10–20	2	USA
1983.5	2.3	2852	66–79	6–16	6	Canada
1987.5	3.8	1710	69–74	14–18	8	USA
1987.5	3.7	1710	69–74	14–18	9	USA
1984.5	2.2	792	71–72	13	10	USA
1990	5.6	336	73–81	9–17	17	USA
1990	3.4	542	73–81	9–17	18	USA
1990.5	2.4	2762	74–83	8–16	20	USA
1994	12.5	1847	75–82	12–19	22	Canada
1995	13.9	4023	78–83	12–17	26	USA
1994	4.5	558	79–82	12–15	29	USA-Anglo
1994	6.5	665	79–82	12–15	30	USA-African-American
1994	11.4	429	79–82	12–15	31	USA-Mexican-American
1994.5	4.2	4984	80–84	9–16	34	USA
1994.5	4.2	1691	80–84	9–16	35	USA
1999.5	9.7	1886	82–96	4–17	41	Puerto Rico
2009	15.2	5625	94	15	New	USA (SAMHSA)

0.56 Correlation Coefficient (ignoring last observation)
2.2600 Test Statistic; 0.024 p value
0.46 mean percentage point rise per year 1983–2000

0.7 Correlation Coefficient (including last observation)
3.2447 Test Statistic; 0.001 p value
0.48 mean percentage point rise per year 1983–2009

is only a 0.42 correlation coefficient (p=0.108), and thus 'only' an 89.2 per cent chance that the rate is rising. Studies usually require a higher chance than this to be taken seriously. So let us just talk about the girls for now. Figure 21 shows those 16 studies from the original meta-analysis that reported depression rates for girls and which were undertaken in North America, and the study of the 2012 report added to those. The date used for each study is not the date of publication, but the average year of birth for each study group plus their average ages at interview.

National context is key

The original meta-analysis of many studies that formed the basis for this repeat study came to the opposite conclusion to that shown here. Its authors suggested that there was no rise over time. From selecting that North American subset, and adding that extra data point for 2009, we can now see that it would appear that there was a very significant rise. In the first edition of this book, the rise was shown to be significant, even without the latest data being seen. The authors of the original study suggested that there wasn't a rise because they thought that it was fine to include all reasonable studies in affluent countries that they could find.

Researchers based in countries outside North America mainly studied their children in later years, and so, in the original study in later years, the authors included studies from Australia, Brazil, Finland, Germany, Japan, the Netherlands, New Zealand, Sweden and Switzerland, where, in many cases, the rates of poor mental health reported for children in these age groups were lower than those found in North America. Apart from Brazil, all these countries are also more equitable than in almost all of North America. In earlier years, most of the studies available to the original meta-analysis used samples of girls assessed in North America, because this kind of research on poor adolescent mental health began in North America (which in itself is telling).

Given that we have only recently begun to understand how crucial differences in human geographical context are to social wellbeing, it is not surprising that the authors of the original meta-analysis assumed that they could pool studies from different countries. One study they included, reporting in 2001, found that the rates of adolescents suffering major depression without (and with) impairment were: in the US 9.6

per cent (and 4.3 per cent) for Anglo-American children aged 12–15, 13.4 per cent (and 6.1 per cent) for African-American children, 16.9 per cent (and 9.0 per cent) for Mexican-American children, and for children compared in the same way living in Japan, 5.6 per cent (and 1.3 per cent) respectively. Note that the rates given in brackets in the last sentence are the proportions with the more severe symptoms and consequences.

The 2001 study suggested that these huge differences, with Mexican-American children living in the US being seven times more likely to suffer major depression with impairment than Japanese children living in Japan, all '… disappeared after sociodemographic adjustments … [concluding that] ethnicity does not have a significant impact on the risk of adolescent major depression after sociodemographic adjustments.'[21] The implication of that finding was not that it is fine to compare children living in different countries, but that the sociodemographic differences (such as levels of inequality) between the lives of children living in different countries are so great that those differences can account for such great inequalities between countries. The children living in Japan are excluded from the re-analysis above, as are all other children not living in North America.

Feeling safe and connected

The above re-analysis of data for this volume, suggesting that depression in adolescents is rising dramatically in unequal affluent countries, is itself taken from (and hence refutes) the most important study reporting no increase. Increasing levels of depression are now being reported by many other studies. For adults, it is well known that in the US, those born after 1955, compared with those born before 1915 (when tested at the same ages), are up to ten times more likely to have been found to be suffering major depression, and that similar, if less extreme, trends have been reported from studies undertaken within Sweden, New Zealand, Germany and Canada.[22] Given these rises, it would be surprising if the rates for adolescents had not been rising, but the implications of the most recent rises are clearly that worse could be to come.

We know from other studies that by the late 1980s, the average North American child was already more anxious about life than some 85 per cent of North American children in the 1950s. In fact, the *average* North American child has become more anxious than *child psychiatric patients* in the 1950s in the US. This has been attributed to the collapse of a safe society and an increase in environmental dangers as perceived by children.[23]

By 2000 it was said that economic factors had so far played only a small role in explaining the rising anxiety trends. The study that reported those findings concluded that: 'Until people feel both safe and connected to others, anxiety is likely to remain high.'[24] That was written eight years before the economic crash. All these studies either show that rates of anxiety and depression are rising in children in North America and in Britain or – in the one confounding case – they once again show that same upwards trend when that one study is re-analysed to avoid mostly comparing rates from earlier studies in North America with rates from later studies in Europe and Japan.

What is driving the increase in adolescent despair, particularly in North America, but also in Britain? In Britain, a remarkably similar proportion of around one in seven children reported in recent official government surveys that they often felt sad or tearful, were often anxious or stressed. Those receiving free school meals due to poverty were, unsurprisingly, slightly more likely to say this,[25] but not very much more likely than the rest. However, 40 per cent of all children in contact with the justice system suffer from poor mental health, 50 per cent in local authority care and 70 per cent of all children in residential care. Furthermore, some 43 per cent of those who had mental health disabilities in 2004 still had them in 2007, especially children living in families in private rented accommodation.[26] In recent years, something has been making children feel worse, especially in particularly unequal rich countries. We can collect clues as to what that something is due to by analysing who suffers most and what happens to them more often.

7.2 Competition: proposing insecurity as beneficial

Why should rates of depression be rising among children? What is it about their environments, especially in North America, which has caused not just more adults, but many more children, to become depressed? There is a mix of reasons, but it is worth looking first at those who have said that their actual aim is to make people anxious, especially to make children anxious. These groups are found in that part of commercial industry whose very purpose is to make children in rich countries insecure: advertising.

Not very long ago an advertising agency president helpfully explained that: 'Advertising at its best is making people feel that without their product, you're a loser. Kids are very sensitive to that.... You open up emotional vulnerabilities, and it's very easy to do [that] with kids because they're the most emotionally vulnerable.'[27] This particular president was no lone voice; a year after her words were published, another advertiser, in 2003, explained: 'In our business culture, children are viewed as economic resources to be exploited, just like bauxite or timber.'[28]

The fact that advertisers behave in ways that have deliberately detrimental effects on the mental health of children is not some secret knowledge of conspiracy theorists. In Britain in 2007, the BBC reported that: 'Children see some 10,000 TV adverts a year and recognize 400 brands by age 10.'[29] The most recognised symbol is the twin arches of McDonald's, which 70 per cent of British three-year-olds recognise. Less than half of these children know their own surname, but they know Mr Mac's.[30]

The head of the established church in England in 2008 explained (in his own press release) that more and more research has found that advertising on television is harming children, making them harmfully competitive, and promoting what he called 'acquisitive individualism' to such an extent that: 'Evidence both from the US and from the UK suggests that those most influenced by commercial pressures also show higher rates of mental health problems.'[31] The situation is far worse in the US where exposure to the harmful effects of commercialisation has been so much greater that the young adult population can now be described as having been *marinated* in the mentally stultifying stuff of advertising.[32]

Fostering acquisitive individualism

Advertising grew first and grew most strongly in the US out of work undertaken to study how best to produce propaganda in wartime, and later in public relations. Arguments for using propaganda to alter consciousness in peacetime can be traced to around the time of men like Walter Lippmann (1889–1974). Walter Lippmann was a colleague of Edward Bernays (1891–1995), the man credited with the creation of the industry of public relations. Lippmann worked for the US government helping to manufacture propaganda during the First World War.

Lippmann came to believe that the 'manufacture of consent' must become a '… self- conscious art and regular organ of popular government. The whole process would be managed by a "specialized class" dedicated to the "common interests" of society … the key role of the new public relations industry was to keep society in the dark.'[33] Modern-day advertising aimed at children grew out of this, and is no less sinister. The adverts never say 'This toy is no fun; you'll be bored with it in minutes, why not go play in the park.'

Very recently, a well-known philosopher and a political economist suggested that criticism of advertising was overrated, and that it '… cannot, for instance, persuade us to buy dog turd, except possibly by associating it with some already existing object of longing'.[34] What the philosopher and economist forgot is that this is how advertising has always worked. How else could it be used to encourage children to *start* smoking a particular brand of cigarette?

There are very simple reasons why those who run businesses and favour competition see advertising as essential. People cannot be allowed to be too happy, because in the most consumer-orientated societies, if they are satisfied with their lot, they might slow down their consumption. And most importantly it would be very hard to persuade them to buy things that they did not really need, things that harmed them. If people were:

> … allowed to follow old routines and stick to their habits, [it] would spell the death knell of the society of consumers, of the consumer industry, and of consumer markets.… Consumer society thrives as long as it manages to render the *non-satisfaction* of its members (and so, in its own terms, their unhappiness) *perpetual*. The explicit method of achieving such an effect is to denigrate and devalue consumer products shortly after they have been hyped into the universe of the consumers' desires.[35]

Today, archbishops preach against advertising, psychologists proselytise for an advertising-free world, philosophers ponder on its harm in their writing, and all the while it remains the bread and butter of business, especially of public relations.

It is an open secret that it is the job of many people to make us and our children feel uncomfortable, to develop a feeling of failure, of lacking. What is less well known is that, while women record the highest rates of depression (both as girls and as adults), when the results are fatal, it is men who are many times more affected. Calculated over a 140-year period, Figure 22 shows the chances of men dying as compared with women, by age and by their decade of birth. It is based on data taken from all the rich nations of the world and combined. These are all the nations rich enough to afford to have systems of recording mortality rates that were reliable at each point in time. What the figure shows is that right across the rich world, for the most recent cohort born in the 1970s, by the time they reached their twenties, men had become three times more likely to die than women of the same ages.

The manufacture of consent

Figure 22 shows that at first, the rises in mortality inequality between the sexes began in old age for men born in the 1890s compared with those born in the 1880s, those later-born men having been encouraged to take up smoking when mass-produced cigarettes became available in their twenties, and so more often dying a little earlier than women 40 years later. In this case, it was because women were not usually permitted to smoke (at first) that a difference in mortality later emerged. Similar differences occurred at young ages for those born at times that meant they would be young adults in wartime. However, it was to be born in the 1940s and 1950s, and especially later, that had the greatest relative detrimental effect on men. This was long after the birth cohorts for whom childbirth had been made much safer, but these were the birth cohorts that became able to own a car at a young age. Everyone could watch car racing on television, an advertising ploy by manufacturers, and the images suggested that the only way for a man to drive a car was fast, and so frequently fatal. They were also presented with images that smoking was 'cool' in the country that invented mass advertising, that promoted death from cancer of men in their forties, heart attacks in their fifties and strokes in their sixties, or later.

Men born in the 1940s and more especially in the 1950s were particularly likely to be affected by the worldwide recession of the mid-

Figure 22: Male/female mortality ratio by age, 1850–1999

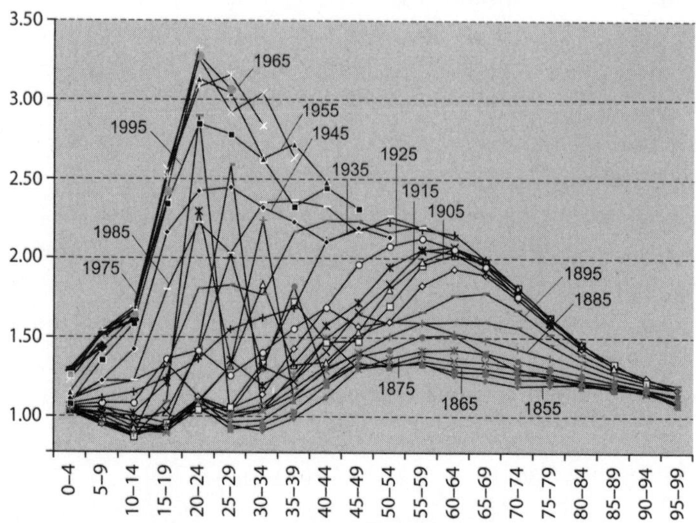

Note: Each line refers to the cohort born in the five years from the year it is labelled with. X-axis gives age of cohort members. Y axis depicts the M/F mortality ratio.

Source: Original figure given in Rigby, J.E. and Dorling, D. (2007) 'Mortality in relation to sex in the affluent world', *Journal of Epidemiology and Community Health,* vol 61, no 2, pp 159-64.

Mortality ratio of men to women by year of birth and age at death (how many men die for each woman who dies, standardised for population numbers at risk)

Year of birth	Age at death																			
	0-4	5-9	10-14	15-19	20-24	25-29	30-34	35-39	40-44	45-49	50-54	55-59	60-64	65-69	70-74	75-79	80-84	85-89	90-94	95-99
1850	1.05	1.00	0.97	0.96	1.12	0.97	0.93	0.96	1.10	1.24	1.30	1.32	1.25	1.22	1.17	1.19	1.18	1.19	1.15	1.08
1855	1.04	1.02	1.01	0.95	1.11	0.94	0.91	0.99	1.12	1.30	1.33	1.34	1.26	1.23	1.19	1.20	1.20	1.18	1.17	1.10
1860	1.05	1.06	0.96	0.93	1.07	0.92	0.94	1.03	1.20	1.33	1.33	1.33	1.28	1.28	1.23	1.23	1.21	1.18	1.16	1.08
1865	1.04	1.02	0.93	0.91	1.04	0.96	0.98	1.10	1.22	1.34	1.32	1.35	1.32	1.30	1.27	1.26	1.19	1.19	1.15	1.09
1870	1.05	1.00	0.91	0.89	1.09	0.99	1.03	1.13	1.29	1.41	1.32	1.39	1.35	1.34	1.31	1.24	1.22	1.19	1.15	1.09
1875	1.05	0.97	0.89	0.91	1.11	1.02	1.04	1.26	1.50	1.30	1.37	1.42	1.42	1.40	1.29	1.27	1.23	1.20	1.17	1.12
1880	1.04	0.95	0.88	0.93	1.11	1.02	1.30	1.82	1.22	1.38	1.42	1.51	1.51	1.41	1.36	1.30	1.27	1.22	1.17	1.14
1885	1.04	0.96	0.89	0.94	1.10	1.31	2.24	1.12	1.30	1.40	1.51	1.59	1.53	1.48	1.43	1.38	1.31	1.24	1.20	1.17
1890	1.03	0.95	0.87	0.94	1.44	2.59	1.04	1.18	1.32	1.51	1.60	1.59	1.60	1.60	1.56	1.45	1.35	1.27	1.22	1.17
1895	1.03	0.94	0.87	1.09	2.89	1.02	1.07	1.22	1.49	1.64	1.59	1.66	1.76	1.78	1.67	1.52	1.39	1.30	1.23	1.20
1900	1.04	0.95	0.88	1.33	1.12	1.04	1.14	1.43	1.69	1.57	1.60	1.83	1.93	1.89	1.74	1.58	1.43	1.32	1.24	1.18
1905	1.04	0.97	0.87	0.96	1.04	1.06	1.34	1.72	1.47	1.48	1.70	1.96	2.02	1.97	1.81	1.63	1.46	1.34	1.23	
1910	1.04	0.96	0.93	0.94	1.09	1.32	1.83	1.33	1.34	1.54	1.80	1.98	2.06	1.99	1.81	1.63	1.46	1.31		
1915	1.03	1.02	0.97	1.03	1.40	2.01	1.32	1.22	1.41	1.66	1.83	2.05	2.07	1.96	1.79	1.62	1.45			
1920	1.06	1.05	1.02	1.21	2.30	1.35	1.19	1.34	1.57	1.72	1.94	2.05	2.03	1.91	1.77	1.59				
1925	1.06	1.08	1.09	1.36	1.42	1.26	1.40	1.55	1.69	1.96	2.08	2.13	2.05	1.95	1.76					
1930	1.08	1.11	1.15	1.24	1.36	1.55	1.62	1.68	2.10	2.18	2.23	2.18	2.15	1.99						
1935	1.10	1.18	1.22	1.32	1.80	1.83	1.77	2.16	2.23	2.23	2.16	2.20	2.12							
1940	1.09	1.22	1.22	1.80	2.22	2.03	2.35	2.36	2.32	2.16	2.26	2.19								
1945	1.11	1.22	1.42	2.16	2.42	2.44	2.32	2.23	2.10	2.19	2.13									
1950	1.08	1.35	1.59	2.34	2.84	2.78	2.62	2.32	2.45	2.31										
1955	1.15	1.43	1.63	2.52	3.13	3.04	2.63	2.72	2.48											
1960	1.23	1.48	1.66	2.56	3.26	2.92	3.04	2.63												
1965	1.26	1.52	1.67	2.52	3.08	3.15	2.83													
1970	1.28	1.53	1.64	2.42	3.27	3.06														
1975	1.29	1.54	1.69	2.51	3.32															
1980	1.28	1.54	1.67	2.36																
1985	1.30	1.52	1.61																	
1990	1.28	1.43																		
1995	1.26																			

1970s, and later generations by the recessions of the early 1980s and 1990s. The source from which this diagram is drawn provides greater detail of the timings to confirm this. Being brought up in societies which increasingly labelled you as 'failing', and then being also seen to have failed in the labour market, a market that became ever more competitive, was sufficiently deadly for men to cause changes in mortality ratios greater than those seen either at the height of the smoking epidemic or during wars. New data from the US suggests that the sex ratios have recently stabilised, which might imply that both older women and younger men are now doing worse than before.[36]

There were many ways in which young men in rich countries began to die at greater rates than young women: suicide, accidental overdoses, fights, road accidents, even cirrhosis. There is also a convergence between suicide and accidents into which deaths from unnecessary risk-taking, extreme and dangerous sports, gross carelessness and other reckless behaviour fall. The health and welfare services, which in earlier years might have looked after those whose early deaths were more preventable, were also beginning to fail more often in an age of austerity. On top of that, enhanced economic competition in recent years, and a greater rate of failing, means that almost all adult men of almost all ages up to at least 70, in any given year, are now (across the rich world) twice as likely to die as are women of their age. Men react badly to competition. When they feel they are a failure, they are more prone to reckless behaviour, whether to impress or just for the hell of it, and often out of desperation. And men suffer (far more than women) from a prevailing belief that when they fail in competition, no one will be there to help.[37] Competition is greatest and care most lacking in the US where health and social care is so often found to be the worst among affluent nations. Competition and care are in many ways opposite types of behaviour, with very different outcomes as a result.

Someone there to help?

Every year, around 100,000 people die prematurely in the US simply because of a lack of basic medical care, not care they did not seek, but care they were denied. This is three times the numbers who died in the US of AIDS in the early years of this century. Those who revealed these facts found it hard to cope with the lack of interest they received. They wrote: 'Any decent person should be outraged by this situation. How can we call the United States a civilised nation when it denies the basic human right of access to medical care in time of need? No other major capitalist country faces such a horrendous situation.'[38] But no other capitalist country believes so ardently in competition. Rising competition not only causes more deaths, but it also helps prevent the efficient treatment of diseases that, if not treated, lead to early death. *Competition is inefficient.*

Some types of competition are more inefficient that others. Private medicine is found to be inefficient by every decent study carried out on it. The UN Research Institute for Social Development (based in Geneva) recently confirmed that it was the spending of a significantly higher proportion of money on state healthcare, rather than private healthcare, which marked out countries where life expectancy was high and infant mortality low. The WHO, OECD and numerous other international bodies constantly rank the UK's NHS as the most efficient health service in the affluent world. Spending on private or even charitable health services is counter-productive,[39] and it is even counter-productive for the rich.

Very wealthy people do not necessarily get good healthcare. When they are ill, people who have an interest in keeping them alive surround them, but such an interest is not the same thing as providing good healthcare. From the point of view of private medicine, the ideal patient is one who is very ill for a very long time, who requires constant treatment and the injection, inhalation and ingestion of many expensive drugs. So it makes sense for private physicians to scour the bodies of their most affluent patients particularly thoroughly in search of any malady that can be further investigated and treated, and then the side effects of those treatments can also be treated.

Ideal private patients are ones in a coma. Patients in a coma do not object to the way in which they are being used. Death is a very private thing in most of the US. If it were not, if there were better oversight and recording there would be less fear of those frequently better systems of healthcare available elsewhere. In many states, death records are not public, as they are in much of Europe, and the last years of the lives of the very rich are generally hidden from view, although they can be pieced together from their hospital receipts, which detail every needle inserted, every exploratory invasion of their bodies, every operation, even every meal they are sold.[40] Occasionally there is scandal over the death of a very rich individual, as in the case of the singer Michael Jackson, and all the details of the drugs administered by personal private doctors are revealed.

Private medicine may not improve the lives of the rich very much, but it does deprive the poor from receiving some of the most basic of services from doctors because it diverts these doctors from doing their job. The wealthy in the US are only able to receive the pampering that they get and mistake for a good health service because so many others there have no health service at all. Similarly, wealthy North Americans can only live in homes built and serviced by so many servants that they appear as palaces because so many other North Americans do not even have the right to have their rubbish collected by a government agency, so strong is the desire in the US to reduce taxes on the rich.[41] Everything is connected. A highly unequal society will not just provide poor quality and expensive healthcare, with appalling overall outcomes, but it will also fail to house its population well, to provide efficient public transport, to organise. Instead, effort concentrates on satisfying the immediate short-term interests of the very rich, in direct proportion to their wealth; one dollar, one vote.

Being surrounded by people paid to be sycophantic, to crawl or to otherwise suck up, does not add greatly to the underlying sustained wellbeing of the rich, but it does deprive others of the labour of their servants that could potentially be put to so much better use. A butler could be a teacher; a nanny could be a nurse. It is often suggested in Britain that free-market ideas brought over from the US are increasingly incorporated where they make least sense – in our much better health service, and in 2012, significant sections of the NHS were part-privatised by the UK coalition government. By 2013, it became possible for up to half the beds in an NHS hospital to be private health sector beds. Private health care is more often poor health care. In September 2014, the private health firm Optical Express was accused of using hard-sell tactics to encourage people to purchase laser eye surgery without thinking too much about it.[42] In January 2015, that same firm was investigated by regulators after claims that lens implant surgery procedures it had undertaken had harmed patients' sight, requiring them to undertake yet more treatment, which in some cases was not possible.[43]

Introducing a little competition and a market-based system into state healthcare is dangerous. It individualises the idea of health. The incoming coalition government of 2010 told public health officials that their new remit would be 'supporting the public so they can protect and improve their own health',[44] instead of furthering 'the science and art of preventing disease, prolonging life and promoting health through the organized efforts and informed choices of society, organizations, public and private, communities and individuals'.[45] Individuals are being told to act alone to help themselves while the government fails to build cycle paths or tackle fast-food marketeers. More individualistic 'competition' is being introduced into the NHS, especially its variant in England. In 2012 the Health and Social Care Act made it legal for 'any willing provider' to compete to undertake what had formerly been NHS work – the coalition was privatising provision. Privatisation had begun under the previous 1979–97 Conservative regimes, and was then accelerated by the 1997–2010 Labour government, but the most recent changes dwarf all those earlier attempts to begin to dismantle the NHS ethos.

In England, between 2002 and 2005, the number of GPs rose by an extra one for every 25,000 people. However, in the poorest fifth of areas, an extra GP was provided for only every 35,700 people, whereas in the least deprived areas, an extra GP was made available for every 18,500 people. The availability of good medical care tends to vary inversely with the needs of the population served. This inverse care law operates more completely where medical care is most exposed to market forces, and less so where such exposure is reduced. The poorest areas had the lowest number of doctors per head to begin with, and the least poor areas – often with the least need – had the most per head. Somehow, as privatisation began to gather pace, the NHS administrators managed to further widen this particular inequality, despite having more resources to share out in the shape of some 2,000 extra doctors to be deployed in just these three years. In 2008, England's Department of Health proudly published the graphs that these figures were derived from to show how well it was monitoring the situation as part of its evidence-based drive to reduce inequalities in health.[46] Then NHS funding was cut, and by 2014, there were 356 fewer GPs working across all of England than there had been in 2010, despite the population ageing.[47] It should be no surprise to find that the areas most lacking in GPs are still the ones with the greatest health needs. These figures are disputed, other sources claiming that the cuts have been far greater than this.

Even semi-privatised, the NHS remains the top-ranked health system in the world in 2014, followed closely by Switzerland's, and all this despite the second lowest spending per head of 11 affluent countries studied. The NHS also loses a significant and rising proportion of its budget each year in payments it has to make to the private sector, which now leases (rather than just builds) new hospitals, often making profits of up to 40 per cent or more in the process in particularly bountiful years.[48] Again, despite this, and because large-scale privatisation has only recently begun, the NHS in 2014 was still very recently ranked first in terms of efficiency and minimising cost-related access problems, and ranked second only to Sweden in terms of equity of provision. In contrast, the US ranked last of the 11 countries studied most recently in terms of performance, and is the most expensive per patient.[49] The pace of change towards privatisation suggests that elites in the UK are currently looking to adopt more of the US model as quickly as they can.

Over a quarter of all operations that now take place in private hospitals are funded by the NHS. Increasingly, these are not seen as safe operations. Clinicians working in private hospitals are routinely working alone, away from other medical colleagues who could help them or blow the whistle if there is a problem. Over 200 people a year die unexpectedly in private hospitals in the UK, and yet no sophisticated records are kept to monitor these hospitals that use public funds, usually just for straightforward cases. Only the most basic statistics are available – the numbers dying. The NHS knows that 6,000 patients a year are sent back to it from private hospitals because a situation arises with which the private physicians cannot cope. The number of patients who sustained serious injuries from adverse events in UK private hospitals is rising and reached 403 in 2013, three times higher than in that sector in 2011.[50] If the NHS forbade its own consultants to work privately, the UK private health sector would largely disappear.

7.3 Culture: the international gaps in societal wellbeing

Insecurity is not good. Being told you have to compete against each other rather than work together is not good. Introducing private markets into state healthcare is not good. The 'notion that market price is the only measure of value [is] "crass, offensive and contrary to human beliefs and actions". Price based on scarcity does not reflect the value of a commodity to human life, as "the low valuation of water and the high valuation of diamonds" shows.'[51] Understanding the limitations of the market mechanism is hardly rocket-science, but for those brought up in the faith of orthodox economics, it can be as hard as learning that the world isn't flat if your religion told you it is.

Today in Britain, their political masters are now telling even 'health and safety' inspectors that they must see making money as something they should encourage above safety. The 'economic progress' seen as paramount in the US has in recent years been inflicted ever more forcibly on people in the UK, to the point whereby health and safety and other regulators are now told by Her Majesty's Government that '... regulators should recognize that a key element of their activity will be to allow or even encourage economic progress'.[52] If some form of making money is detrimental to health and safety, you don't encourage it unless you are callous.

Ultimately, if you want people to compete, you have to keep them needy. Otherwise, most people in rich countries come to realise that there is enough to go around. Over two centuries ago, among those with power who thought that there was too little to go around to cater for all, it was becoming widely recognised that: '[Slavery] ... is attended with too much trouble, violence, and noise, ... whereas hunger is not only a peaceable, silent, unremitted pressure, but as the most natural motive to industry, it calls forth the most powerful exertions.... Hunger will tame the fiercest animals, it will teach decency and civility, obedience and subjugation to the most brutish, the most obstinate, and the most perverse.'[53] Just over a century ago in London, those people, again, in positions of power, had refined what kind of a wage they saw as needed: 'The ideal wage, therefore, must be sufficient to persuade a man to offer his labour, but insufficient to allow him to withdraw it for more than a few days. Capitalism thus replaces the whip of the overseer with the lash of a more terrifying slave-driver – hunger.'[54] Today we have the advertising to the well-fed of fast food that makes people feel hungry. The food is moreish, the adverts appetizing, and the results are obesity and heart disease. It is time to stop making people hungry.

Mental despair and the imagined need to consume more and more to try to avert it are greatest where politics is rendered most meaningless, where it has been captured by those with the most power and money. That sense of meaninglessness is enhanced when the news media is almost totally controlled by a small number of men, such as very rich businessmen in the US, or a few communist party bosses in China. As in both the US and China, the more advertising and other propaganda people are exposed to, the more they are told that individually they need to be wealthy and collectively they need to support economic growth. The more that public opinion and debate is almost totally controlled by a small elite (with a tiny number of carefully vetted people allowed to speak), the more it is dominated by those drawn from the 'top' couple of universities, from the dominant party or party-pair; the more 'positional competition and success are celebrated relentlessly',[55] then the greater the number of people who become losers.

The poison of capitalism

Despite the 2008 attack striking their twin beating hearts, world finance continues to be utterly dominated by London and New York. The large majority of the world's hedge funds are organised from these two cities, although some four fifths continue to be registered in tax havens like the Cayman Islands. The derivative markets in these two centres were worth $7 trillion a day by 2007; two days' trading was the equivalent of the annual US GDP.[56] By 2014, despite the crash, these markets had grown to be 20 per cent larger in volume, tottering, and still 95 per cent unregulated. Our economies had become even more unstable than before.[57] Yet hardly anyone understands derivatives and what they really achieve, not in theory, but in practice.

For over a decade now, most key commentators have agreed that derivative market excesses are harmful, and that the speculators are harming rich countries as well as poor. In 2005 the Deputy Chancellor of Germany said of the London and New York-based speculators:

'Some financial investors spare no thought for the people whose jobs they destroy. They remain anonymous, have no face, fall like a plague of locusts over our companies, devour everything, then fly on to the next one.'[58] These words appeared in a German newspaper and resulted in the response in *The Wall Street Journal* from a hedge-funded chief executive who claimed that at least the North Americans and British bankers were '... bringing a measure of capitalism to Germany'.[59] As a result of that particular little poisoned spoonful of capitalism, the GDP of Germany was reported to have fallen by 3.8 per cent in just the first three months of 2009, the fastest fall measured since modern German records began.

The US hedge fund manager had no reason to crow – even before the crash, the top one fifth of earners in Manhattan in 2000 earned 52 times more than the bottom quintile living there (existing on $7,047 a year), a gap similar to that found only in countries as desperate as Namibia.[60] An infant born on the poor side of the tracks in New York's Morningside Heights in Harlem, for example, had a 2 per cent chance of dying in his or her first year of life, 12 times greater than the chance for infants born in the nearby salubrious Upper East Side.[61]

By 2004, unemployment rates for black men in Harlem were up to 50 per cent worse than they had been even during the 1930s depression.[62] By the age of 15, all US teenagers had only a 75 per cent, a *three in four*, chance of reaching the age of 65, one of the lowest rates in the rich world. The chance is partly not higher because black teenagers in the US had only a 33 per cent, a one in three, chance of seeing their 65th birthday.[63] But by 2013, there were a few tiny signs of improvement. The poorest quintile in Manhattan now lived on $9,823 as the minimum wage had been increased, but this was still 88 times less than the incomes enjoyed by the richest 5 per cent of Manhattan residents in 2013, who had enjoyed a 9 per cent rise in their income in just that year alone, each affluent family receiving a *rise* in their income in that year equivalent to the *entire* annual incomes of more than seven of the poorest families in 2013![64]

In the heart of London, in the borough of Westminster, a woman who has made it to the age of 65 living in the Church Street Estate can expect (on average) to live roughly another 12 years. In contrast, a woman of the same age living in the opulent Little Venice enclave in the same borough can expect to live another 26 years,[65] most thus living to at least the age of 91. On the streets outside their incredibly sumptuous and expensive homes are found more rough sleepers and more people who are officially counted as suffering serious mental illness and seeking housing than anywhere else in Britain. And just down the road are the women of Church Street, who have had such different lives and whose prognosis beyond 65 is to live half as many more years as those in Little Venice.[66] London and New York are the most divided cities of the rich world.

The lines that divide

The convergence of people labelled as mentally ill on Westminster and Manhattan was an unforeseen outcome of the successful movement to close down asylums from the 1970s onwards, the failure of treatment and care in 'the community', and perhaps some strange attraction among those labelled as 'mad' towards these financial centres (Westminster borders the financial heart of the City of London).[67]

There was over-optimism in the 1970s that psychiatrists could cure all mental illness with drugs. Many of these drugs were treatments rather than cures. Severely mentally ill patients often never felt fully recovered, and were often not well motivated to continue to take medication for long. Simultaneously, as banking hours became longer and longer, the rumours that City traders could only keep going with artificial stimulants became more often the truth. It wasn't just those sleeping rough on the streets outside the trading houses who were taking drugs.

Geographical divides come with varying degrees of contortion. Just as those supposed to be taking drugs for a mental illness (but not taking them) stumbled so close to those financiers supposed not to be taking drugs (but nevertheless partaking), so too were the living quarters of the very poor and very rich in these centres closely intertwined. It is hard to find social statistics as extreme and environments as different but so close together as are found within the hearts of London and New York. The intertwining of rich and poor neighbourhoods is far greater in the centres of these two cities than anywhere else in the rich world. The line separating rich and poor in the centres of these cities is most twisted at their hearts and less and less contorted further out.

The lines that divide inner from outer London and New Jersey from Long Island are less convoluted to draw. Further out still they become straighter, or more smoothly curved. An outlying affluent suburb is surrounded by slightly less affluent suburbs, and then by average places, and only then do they touch on poorer districts. In Britain, at the far commuting boundary of London the smoothest divide is now found, that which separates the south of England from the rest of the UK.

Figure 23 shows my attempt to provide a description of where the North–South divide runs through England. Inset in the figure is the rich/poor world dividing line and the current political divide that runs through the UK capital. The world is awash with dividing lines. Each usually becomes more intricate the further in you zoom. The London divide turns into an archipelago of islands of segregation when drawn at ward level, but a clear divide still exists.[68] At a global level there are patches of affluence in the poor world and areas of abject squalor in the rich, but a virtual wall remains between the two sides despite many travelling over it (or burrowing under). Similarly, to say that the UK North/South does not exist because the Midlands has its own identity is to miss both how divided the Midlands is, and how the identity which it did have has been pared down with the repeated decimation of manufacturing employment decade after decade. There does not need to be a physical wall for a virtual wall to exist.

The North–South divide in England, drawn in Figure 23, is really the outermost boundary of London. It can be seen in how people vote, how they die, in their wealth, but even in things as mundane as how the fittings of pumps in pubs are altered so that a different head forms on pints of beer on either side of the border. You don't really leave London until you've crossed this line; you can tell that you are still in the south not just from the cost of homes, but also from the taste of the water you drink. However, places both north and south are slowly losing their identities, as what begins to matter more and more within the human geography of Britain is the exact orbit of your locality in relation to the capital. In other words, how well placed is your place to trade with that capital? It was that capital which did most to establish the current global divide, a capital city that is itself so clearly divided internally.

Figure 23: The fractal nature of geographical divides, North/South, World, Britain, London, 2012

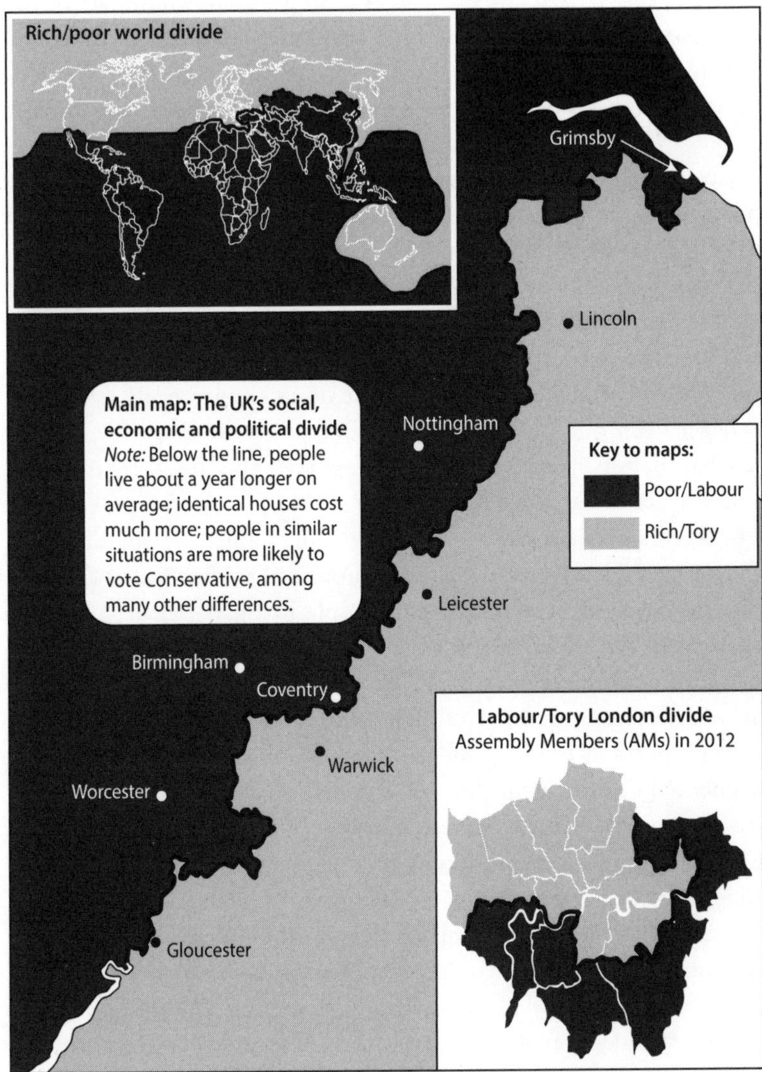

Sources: UK divide: drawn by the author with help from John Pritchard and derived from many sources. London divide: Assembly seats in 2012 (political control), from http://www.telegraph.co.uk/news/politics/local-elections/9247664/London-Assembly-elections-2012-results-map.html Global divide: Found on the Chinese version of Wikipedia by searching for "north south divide". Other versions do not bend the lines as much to include islands.

The origins of inequality

Divides are everywhere; they are the stuff of geography. They are found along country lanes in Lincolnshire, between regions in Europe, and between countries worldwide. Divides are not there because of a lack of interaction, but because over the borders things move in particular directions. Today the best health in the world is enjoyed in countries like Japan, Belgium and Norway, the worst in the Congo, where life expectancy is the lowest of any large region. There is both an indirect and a direct connection. The indirect connection is trade.

Belgium and Norway both need things that come from the Congo – industrial diamonds for machine tools, minerals that make mobile phones function – and both countries pay a pittance for these. If they did not, there would be much less of a divide. We don't know exactly how these goods get from one place to another, but we know that they do, and that what matters more and more to how well you are likely to fare is where you are to start off with, your orbit within the world trade system.

The direct connection that explains why the Congo is poor and other places are rich is less well known. From around 1885, Europeans and later people in North America, and then people in Japan, began '… to live longer partly *because* people in other parts of the world were suffering deprivation and dying young'.[69] The direct connection was that very soon after King Leopold II of Belgium took the Congo as his own private property in 1885, as well as instigating one of the first large-scale documented cases of genocide, his colonial officers ensured that there was a rapid increase in the harvest of latex rubber, a proportion of which was exported to become condoms and diaphragms, resulting in smaller families in richer countries.

Congolese villages whose inhabitants failed to meet their quota for producing rubber in a year could pay for that failure in baskets of severed hands cut from protesting fellow villagers, including children.[70] It comes as a shock when you first learn that baskets of severed hands became the symbol of the Congo 'Free' State under colonial rule. But we quickly become anaesthetised. At present, there is a worldwide death toll of over 2,000 children from diarrhoea every day.[71] This is equivalent to 15 per 1,000, a rate that matches that found in many English towns around a century ago, and death from diarrhoea is just as preventable abroad as it is in England today.[72] You probably don't think every day of these deaths as shocking. That is because they occur far away, and while it is kept at a distance, it is a shock to which we can easily become anaesthetised.

International divides make local divisions often appear paltry, but not caring about poverty within rich countries is a precursor for not caring more widely. On Sunday, 15 March 2009, the Health Select Committee of the House of Commons released its report on health inequalities within Britain. The report had been produced because the government was failing to achieve the target on health inequalities that it had set in 2003. The target was, by 2010, to reduce inequalities in health outcomes by 10 per cent as measured by infant mortality and life expectancy at birth – success in Britain is still counted in the live bodies of babies. The report described this as perhaps one of the 'toughest' health targets in the world. However, other affluent countries did not need such tough targets because, apart from the US, they tended not to have such great health inequalities, inequalities that have such an impact on the overall health of their citizens.

There was a precedent for all this 'tough' talk. In 1985, when she signed up to the WHO inequality targets, Margaret Thatcher had agreed to a tougher target of a 25 per cent reduction in health inequalities by 2000. Britain spectacularly failed then, with health inequalities increasing dramatically instead of reducing. Thatcher failed to achieve many of her goals, such as the spread of home ownership, which was declining shortly after she left office, a decline caused by her policies to liberalise finance. After the Conservatives lost power in 1997, health inequalities continued to increase under New Labour, and even the most recent statistics show little sign of the widening gap abating.

In the US in 2008, long before a single case of swine flu occurred or a few cases of Ebola in the US were even thought possible, and for completely different reasons, 'For the first time since the Spanish influenza of 1918, life expectancy is falling for a significant number of American women.... The phenomenon appears to be not only new but distinctly American.'[73] The phenomenon being discussed was absolute rises of poverty in the poorest of US counties. Two years later, in January 2010, the charity Save the Children reported absolute rises in the numbers of children living in the worst states of poverty in the poorest areas of the UK. And then, by 2014, rising mortality rates were reported among elderly women coupled with a decline in their life expectancy from the age of 65, as fmany ewer elderly people received any social care home visits due to cuts in caring budgets.[74]

7.4 Bird-brained thinking: putting profit above caring

The cost in the US alone of the 2008 bailout of banks was estimated to be greater in real terms, even in November 2008, than the combined sum of the costs of the Marshall Plan ($155 billion), the Louisiana Purchase ($217 billion), the Moonshot ($237 billion), the Savings and Loan Crisis ($256 billion), the Korean War ($454 billion), the New Deal ($500 billion), the Iraq War ($597 billion), Vietnam ($698 billion) *and* the all-time budget of NASA ($851 billion). When combined, all these nine giant expenses, at $3.9 trillion, are dwarfed by the $4.6 trillion bailout price tag, and that was just the price as first announced.[75] Three years after the crashes, figures as high as $29 trillion were being muted and disputed, disputed because at some point the cost has to be zero – it all has to be paid back.[76]

Something changed in 2008; this was not business as usual, not even crisis management as usual. It was the result of the most spectacular example of bird-brained thinking ever to have occurred in human history. This is a particular trait that humans have for not being able to think well ahead and for flocking in their behaviour in ways that can bring about catastrophe. It was bird-brained thinking, by bankers, businessmen (and a tiny number of businesswomen), politicians and consumers that led to the crash of 2008. Figure 24 shows just one of what will become thousands of similar graphs to be drawn of the crash. This one could be drawn early because the crash was initially most acute in the US.

Even early on the economic crash looked very unlike an economic recession. By August 2009, a tenth of the world's merchant shipping was reported to be just sitting at anchor.[77] Electricity and petrol (gasoline) consumption in countries like Britain fell in a year by a similar amount, by a tenth, because many industries shut down operations.[78] A recession, such as that of the early 1980s, tends to see home borrowing fall as fewer houses are sold, but then borrowing increases again afterwards, as in the 122 per cent rise in borrowing shown in Figure 24 that occurred in the US between 1983 and 1984. The recession in the early 1990s saw home borrowing slow down again, the rates of change go slightly negative, but then rise gently again in the late 1990s, then oscillate, then go higher, then peak at over a trillion dollars in 2005, and then come crashing down and down.

Change in net lending did not just go negative in 2007–08, but had fallen by over $600 billion in one year. Recessions are not depicted by the plummeting figures seen in US mortgage lending. Recessions are slowdowns, not crash landings. It takes concerted bird-brained thinking to rise so high that the only way down is to crash. But crashes can be made to disappear statistically, debts are written off and payment reduced when interest rates are brought to near zero. The black bars in the figure show that the 2007–08 household debt fell by $640 billion in that one year. Today's revised Federal Reserve statistics, which have been used to update this graph from that published in the first edition of this book, suggest that the crash was deepest in 2010, not 2008, and that we are now heading towards a new normal, such was the damage done by a few extremely greedy people. The graphic is slightly less dramatic than that produced before from the original data, but still staggering. Quantitative easing and the writing off of the debts went hand in hand with revising the tables of data to reduce its visual impact a little. But none of this should let us forget that the crash came about because of the extreme greed of a few, who came to be known as snakes,[79] and who fed off the much lower level greed of the many.

Snakes in suits

The small groups of people who run corporations in the most profit-hungry of countries act most often with a kind of bird-brained thinking that is called 'hyperbolic discounting'. That is because *culturally* they have evolved in a way that is similar to the way birds have evolved *biologically*. Corporate bosses have not literally evolved to become bird-brained. Rather, the modern corporation in unequal rich countries has evolved to favour promoting most often those individuals who demonstrate bird-brained behaviour.[80]

Whichever organisation was the greatest cheerleader for the status quo was going to look bad when the problems that were the product of believing so much in markets unravelled during 2008. Graduates of

Figure 24: The crash – US mortgage debt, 1977–2013 (% change and US$ billion)

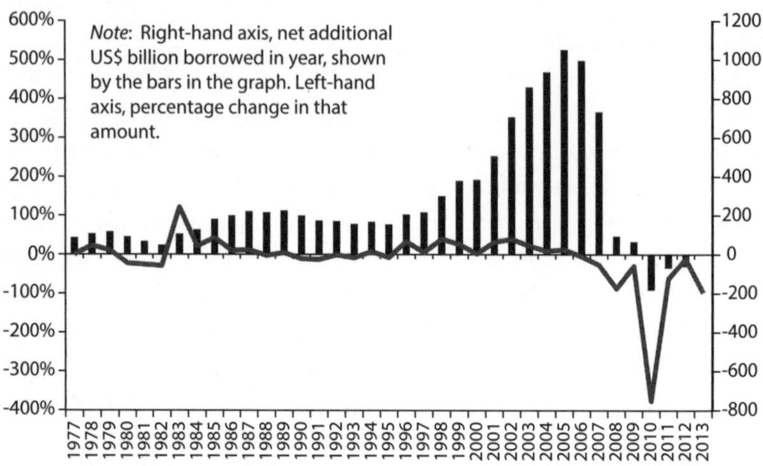

Source: Table 6 in the first edition of this book, first column of data (household home mortgage debt change); updated in January 2015 using the 'Debt growth, borrowing and debt outstanding tables' (www.federalreserve.gov/releases/Z1/Current/), updated by the *Historical Annuals, 2005–2013*, December 11, 2014; final two columns updated by the December 2014 figures for the 2005–2013 period (table F.100) including home equity loans secured by junior liens. Provisional figures for 2008 and 2009 were -46 and -370, but these had to be revised later to +94 and +66 (US$ billion). The provisional figures are shown in the first edition of this book.

Data as available in January 2015 from the Federal Reserve

	Household debt (US$ billions)	Change (%)
1977	86	-
1978	106	23%
1979	117	10%
1980	90	-23%
1981	67	-26%
1982	47	-29%
1983	105	122%
1984	127	21%
1985	182	43%
1986	199	10%
1987	222	11%
1988	216	-3%
1989	225	4%
1990	199	-11%
1991	174	-13%
1992	171	-1%
1993	157	-9%
1994	167	7%
1995	154	-8%

	Household debt (US$ billions)	Change (%)
1996	206	33%
1997	216	5%
1998	302	40%
1999	380	26%
2000	386	2%
2001	507	31%
2002	706	39%
2003	860	22%
2004	938	9%
2005	1053	12%
2006	998	-5%
2007	734	-26%
2008	94	-87%
2009	66	-29%
2010	-183	-376%
2011	-69	-62%
2012	-62	-11%
2013	-1	-98%

the Harvard Business School began to admit in 2009 that, 'There's a certain self-consciousness now that we may be part of the problem.'[81] The school's graduates, far more often than others, were running the banks that crashed, headed security exchanges that failed to spot massive fraud (such as Bernard Madoff's 'Ponzi' scheme), or had even been directly involved in fraud themselves. These stories were reported not in the obscure left-wing press, but on Bloomberg News, the television/internet channel of big business! But the greater fraud, not broadcast on Bloomberg, was the fraudulent message that the elevation of people with MBAs to such heights of reputation sent out. This was the message that bird-brained short-term thinking was somehow efficient.

Bird-brained thinking, of the kind corporate bosses recently engaged in (and still do so), was first recognised by studying pigeons. 'Hyperbolic discounting' is an accounting method that explains how birds choose to eat or store grain. Essentially, pigeons exhibit a huge appetite to consume now rather than save. Saving would allow them to be able to eat a little more evenly later. However, it is not that pigeons eat as much as they possibly can now, but they can be observed to discount the potential future value of grain according to a function that sees its value fall hyperbolically (very fast) with time.[82] Clearly behaving in this way helped pigeons survive in the past, or at least the few that evolved into those we get to study in experiments now. Pigeons that waited might wait in vain if another pigeon had eaten their grain. These were the kinds of experiments in which the pigeons get to tap on a lever and receive grain now, or on another lever and get twice as much grain in one minute's time. Which would you tap if you were a pigeon?

Currently it is still not legal to put business school MBA graduates into cages and to give them levers to tap, one which gives them a treat now, and another that makes them wait, but get more later. What we can do instead is look to the past to see how their forebears behaved in these situations. The particular economics that people who take MBA courses are traditionally taught tells them that when a good becomes scarce, its price rises, which both reduces consumption and increases the number of people trying to supply the good, so preserving its availability. But that did not happen with passenger pigeons.

Catching the pigeon

Soon after Europeans arrived in North America, they observed staggering numbers of passenger pigeons, flocks said to be a mile wide and *300 miles long*. These pigeons were hunted to extinction, the last one dying in 1914. They were killed for their meat, the price of which did not rise one blip as their numbers fell and scarcity rose.[83] People simply ate other food, and ate pigeon when they could, to the very last bird. The hunters of passenger pigeons killed them at a rate explicable only if they were applying hyperbolic discounting to their value. A dead pigeon in the hand was worth so much more to a pigeon hunter in 1900 than two in the bush, even though two would breed more, more which the hunter might be able to hunt in future. But then another hunter may kill those two first, so why not kill them now?

Stories such as the passenger pigeons' fate led those with imagination not curtailed by undertaking an MBA to worry that there is no reason why conventional economics should preserve oil supplies. Consider the following exchange that took place in December 1972 on the occasion of the parliamentary debates surrounding the manner in which UK North Sea oil and gas was to be taxed. It was between Sir Robert Marshall, who was at the time Secretary for Trade and Industry, and Martin Maddan MP. First, Mr Maddan asked: "Do we want to see a limit on the speed of exploitation of the United Kingdom Continental Shelf?" to which Marshall answered in the negative. Maddan asked whether this meant that "we do not want to do things which will make that exploitation slower", to which Marshall replied, "that is right". Maddan then asked whether "charging, whether for concessions by auction or otherwise, and ... the imposition of royalties, have any effect on the speed with which organisations wish to exploit these resources?" To which Marshall replied: "in our judgment and in the judgment to the best of my knowledge of all the western countries with which we discuss these things, very much". So, Maddan put it to Marshall that "if the United Kingdom Exchequer sought not to gain a penny from these things the exploitation would go ahead quicker?" The latter's answer was an emphatic "absolutely yes".[84]

Instead of taxing extracted oil highly, as they did in Norway, and so conserve the stock and raise far more money for public goods, even to create a Sovereign wealth fund, the British introduced the lowest oil extraction taxes in the North Sea so that businesses could make a large immediate profit, but were in fact selling it at what (in hindsight) was a low price. This is happening again – as these words are being typed in early 2015, oil prices are still falling despite the supply dwindling. The price of oil need not rise sky-high as the last marketable drops are squeezed out of the last well, 'fracked' out of rock, or dug up from the last tar sands. *Today's price does not factor in tomorrow's scarcity*. If substitutes for oil are found, such as electric cars, organic fertilisers, paper instead of plastic, then as long as they provide short-term alternatives, the last drops of oil can be sold cheaply. The price of oil plummeting during 2014 illustrated this. Corporate thinking is short-term thinking. Today, the corporate canon does not portray itself as a short-term doctrine, but it says that there is no alternative to the market, and that the market works by a kind of magic to result in the best of all possible worlds. This is make-believe magic. In 2008, just as the great crash had begun, The World Bank published its central argument on market magic. It suggested that:

> Growth is not an end in itself. But it makes it possible to achieve other important objectives of individuals and societies. It can spare people en masse from poverty and drudgery. Nothing else ever has. It also creates the resources to support health care, education.... We do not know if limits to growth exist, or how generous those limits will be. The answer will depend on our ingenuity and technology, on finding new ways to create goods and services that people value on a finite foundation of natural resources. This is likely to be the ultimate challenge of the coming century. Growth and poverty reduction in the future will depend on our ability to meet it....[85]

Economic growth is a very recent phenomenon. To portray all human life before it as poverty and drudgery requires the maintenance of a remarkable level of historical ignorance. To then see technology as our future saviour, irrespective of our current behaviour, requires another dose of that same foolishness. Technological innovation is the great trump card played in these arguments. The MBA candidate may suggest at interview that in future we will be able to genetically engineer a new passenger pigeon. But new technology unchecked benefits the rich far more than the poor. It is no great panacea.

Being able to genetically engineer old species back into existence gives you the ability to create monsters. Being able to create new sources of power allows you to burn up even more of some other resource to carry out an activity that you perhaps do not need to undertake. Worldwide it has been the very opposite of growth that has spared people from poverty and drudgery. Through curtailing growth and greed, far more people have been spared poverty and have seen their parents brought out of it. Trade unions curtailed profiteering by bosses and argued wages up. Governments nationalised health services and freed their citizens from fear by curtailing the greed of private physicians. In Britain they told those physicians that if most wanted to work, they would have to treat all those who were sick, and not just the wealthy.

The French rebelled against the excesses of a king in a revolution partly inspired to reduce poverty; the North Americans had a revolution to overcome the greed of the English; the English reduced poverty in England by exploiting others in an empire, but also partly by occasionally voting down the power of the aristocracy, especially between 1906 and 1974, to distribute wealth better within England. The world bankers are unfortunately being selected for their bird-brained attributes. They appear to remember little, and either know or accept nothing of most of the history of actual human progress. Bird-brained economic thinking requires almost no memory.

Most mammals do not undertake hyperbolic discounting; many even store food excessively. Presumably there were, at times, some particularly severe winters in the past, and those cautious few prudent savers prevailed. A few humans are not so prudent but have been found to behave in predatory reptilian ways towards others, sometimes due to being a little brain damaged. The evidence for this is found in abnormalities in the prefrontal cortex and the potentially criminal-like disregard of some psychopaths. This includes people with psychopathic tendencies who have been well educated and have found agreeable work in business.[86]

Fortunately, most humans are more normal and behave in mammalian rather than reptilian or bird-brained ways; they save and store, including for others. We are not doomed to greed or vicious selfishness. However, humans did not collectively plan the world systems they came to live in, and so these systems came about because we did not plan. Like passenger pigeons flocking across the North American plains, we mostly follow our nearest neighbours, and do what they do. The nearest neighbours of world bankers are other economists, and especially those elite Harvard MBA graduates.

One renowned Professor of Classics, History and Archaeology suggests that 'Change is caused by lazy, greedy, frightened people looking for easier, more profitable and safer ways to do things.'[87] Two other academics convincingly argue for the very opposite, concluding that: 'The image of man as a congenital idler, stirred to action only by the prospect of gain, is unique to the modern age.'[88] Perhaps a way out of these oppositions may be offered by a new feminist approach to politics suggested recently by Jacqueline Rose to '... confront the subterranean aspects of history and the human mind, both of which play their part in driving the world on its course, but which our dominant political vocabularies most often cannot bear to face'.[89] We can be both lazy and not lazy, greedy and not greedy, frightened at some times and brave at others; all of us, because we are all human, not superhuman or subhuman.

Before asking why all the passenger pigeons were wiped out, ask first why there were so many of them in the first place. Passenger pigeons expanded to such huge populations partly due to the decimation of competitors when Europeans first arrived, and so drastically altered the ecology of the North American continent. Just as we are not sure why there were so many pigeons, neither are we sure why there were suddenly so many extra humans available to come to the Americas. We do not have much of an idea as to why human populations rose rapidly when they did, to spread out around the world from Europe. We know about the enclosure of land forcing people from the fields, and the new silver from the Americas disrupting the pan-continental balance of the old world before that, but we are still putting together the pieces of the story of why capitalism emerged when it did, and for how long it is likely to last as a transformation to something else.

What we do know is that the human population rise seen only in recent centuries coincided with a new order of thinking which included a new leniency over profiteering. The two are coincident. Something did enable population growth, and that population growth may have contributed to (among much else) those French and then American revolutions. Profiteering, however, is not a magic solution, but a monster: 'Capitalism is a machine programmed to do one thing – make profit.

That is its great strength. There is no morality, no sentiment, just a never-ending quest to increase profits, locally, nationally and ultimately globally.... Enough is never enough. Capitalism always ends up eating itself. It's like a shark that has its stomach cut open and briefly feeds on itself.'[90] The last time the world saw six-fold population growth globally was during the Neolithic revolution. We have no other precedent for the rate of transformation we now see.

Ending the feeding frenzy

For 64 years, between 1926, the end of the last gilded age in the US, and 1990, the beginning of the end of our current gilded age of wealth, gross national product (GNP) in the US rose by an average of 3 per cent a year. The return rate on the shares of all corporations trading on the New York Stock Exchange over the same period rose by some 8.6 per cent a year on average. While it could be argued that technical growth and improved education may partly account for the rise in GNP, the same argument cannot be used to account for the much higher share price increase. The researchers who highlighted this discrepancy favour the suggestion that shares rose faster in price through the increased exploitation over time of people and parts of people's lives which were not part of the market system in 1926, but which had been incorporated into it by 1990, not just within the US, but also from abroad.[91]

In 2014, the mainstream economist Thomas Piketty published the English edition of his 2013 book, *Capital in the twenty-first century*, that noted similar trends. He gave a slightly different explanation for the cause of the divergence, seeing it as an inherent self-destructive flaw in capitalism. He concluded that current wealth inequality was unacceptable, and that the trend unsustainable. He proposed an annual global wealth tax of up to 2 per cent, combined with a progressive income tax reaching as high as 80 per cent. This would need policing very carefully if it were to work. In 2015, it was revealed that ex-Labour Minister Peter Mandelson, who once said he was 'intensely relaxed about people getting filthy rich as long as they pay their taxes',[92] had taken £400,000 tax-free from his company in 2014 in the form of a loan which need never be repaid, and had managed to secure enough income and (apparently legally) not to pay tax on that income to the extent that he had been able to purchase an £8 million Regent's Park townhouse with 'its own wine cellar' in 2011.[93] It will now be worth much more due to runaway London housing inflation between 2011 and 2015. Hardly any of this money has been earned by hard honest work. A wealth and income tax would repatriate these takings.

In the grand scheme of things, one former minister's footnote in history is inconsequential, but it illustrates the precarity and absurdity of the transformation we are currently living through. The rises in share prices relative to GNP was a measure of how much was being sucked out of the coffers of the rest of humanity and out of the planet's resources by those who could secure shares. This blood sucking fell for a short time after 1926, and it is falling again now, but between economic crashes it was rife. Some argue that, in the 1930s and 1940s, economic recovery began not through war kick-starting economies, but because of the marketing of consumer goods and then services to people in the poorer countries of the world. This eventually turned depression into growth. Today there is no largely untouched poor world to begin to exploit. It is because there isn't an extra planet waiting to have its surplus extracted that we have to start planning for a more frugal future now.[94] For centuries, our way of living has been metamorphosing from one steady way of life towards another. The period of transformation is called capitalism, and unsustainability is its hallmark.

Frugality is required not because we consume so much more in rich countries than is consumed in poor countries, but because we consume so much more than even our parents did just a few decades ago. We consume more mostly because we are offered so many more things, things that our parents never had, things that are made from materials that are not sustainable and, to a much lesser extent, because there are more of us. Those of us living in the rich world, the rich fifth of global society, consume on average *six times* more oil, minerals, water, food and energy than our parents.[95] It is not that we literally eat six times as much as they did, but we waste so much food and eat so much meat. We do not drink six times as much water, but more water is used in the production of many of the extra things we now consume, things that our parents did not buy and use up.

The way corporations create food today and the way in which we consume it is responsible for almost a third of carbon emissions from rich nations.[96] Far more food is created than we can healthily eat (and than we do eat), far more animals are now reared solely to be eaten than is healthy, and these animals are literally 'produced' in ways that certainly are not healthy. There were no battery chickens in our grandparents' time. Now chickens are the most common bird on earth, almost all only ever living in sheds. We throw away a huge amount of food, but it is estimated that we throw away *five times* as much food packaging in weight each day as even the food we throw out. None of this can carry on for very much longer. Our grandchildren will live very different lives to us.

In the UK and the US especially, we throw out food at the same time as the poorest mothers go to food banks as an alternative to turning to prostitution to pay the rent.[97] And why might the rent be so much harder for some to suddenly pay than it was a few years ago? It is not just the increasingly punitive and enhanced benefit sanctions. One key reason many people in the UK can no longer pay the rent is the new bedroom tax, implemented only on the poor in April 2013.[98] So the poorest people in the UK now have to purchase the cheapest, lowest quality food, or take whatever they can find if they can accept the shame of what is, in effect, begging. This is unjust and not sustainable.

Of the food that we do eat, its nutritional value has been falling as its sugar and fat content has been increased to sell it more easily. The worldwide redistribution of fat and oil production over the course of the last third of a century, coincident with the industrialisation of food production, has been staggering, as the rich in the richer countries progressively consume healthier olive oils, while most people in the poorer countries consume more of the least healthy of fats.[99] Food poisoning is becoming more common, especially as we eat out more, eating in restaurants whose core interest is not necessarily to serve good food, but to make a profit. Our food system is essentially unhealthy, both globally and locally. But there is no need for life to be like this.

The idea that economic growth is essential is based on the belief that human beings cannot escape their bird-brained tendencies, the belief that we will always be greedy and stuff our faces given the opportunity. This is a counsel of despair that fails to recognise how simple it would be to eat more healthily. The first step is to eat less or no meat and not too much fish, both because of the current levels of our pollutants in fish, and to preserve fish stocks. Meat is simply not very good for us and hugely expensive to rear, let alone dangerous in indirect ways, including creating greenhouses gases, promoting new strains of disease, and making the industrial treatment of animals a norm that is easily transferred to people. The health benefits of eating fish have luckily recently been found to be overrated. Medical reviews have found that evidence of reduction in cardiovascular events and mortality from eating fish is less conclusive than was recently thought.[100] This is lucky because fish stocks are now so depleted and polluted that we cannot substitute much fish for meat.[101]

Eating more healthily is not just good for individuals, but for social groups and the environment. Consuming both less and more healthily, and spending more time on pursuits that involve exercise rather than shopping, also has far wider social and environmental benefits. Most of the rise in pollution from poorer countries such as China has been due to the generation of the power needed to run factories to make things for people in rich countries to buy. The levels of lead in the blood of people who live in cities in China are recorded to be twice what is considered a dangerous level, and certain to harm the mental development of huge numbers of children in China.[102] Occasionally, high lead levels are found in the paint on toys made in China, but we rarely wonder why it is in the paint in the first place and what it is like to make that paint.

People in China have had to live under a regime of having far fewer children than almost anywhere else in the world partly to allow their factories to be built so quickly and staffed so fully by adults not occupied in child rearing. The policy was only introduced partly to keep population levels down. It mainly allowed a huge economic leap forward. The epidemic of lead poisoning among children in China is just one of many cruel and largely unforeseen consequences of those policies of going for growth above all else. More factories and power stations in China will not raise levels of health in China in the future. It would be a bird-brained response to continue to add to that pollution, to produce goods for others overseas just in order to have increased riches for a few in China, who then often spend much of that money travelling abroad themselves, or sending their children to expensive Western universities. Often overseas students studying for business degrees are taught that there is some merit in even more bird-brained thinking, and that there is no alternative to only ever working for a yet greater profit, when that era – along with population growth – is so clearly coming to an end.

However, it is confusing to live in a world where so much is so obviously wrong. And when most people feel something is wrong, the first thing they question is their own sanity.[103]

7.5 The 1990s: birth of mass medicating

When you are no longer in control of your life, you live in fear. The most extreme case of losing control is imprisonment. At the start of the 1990s it was reported that more sedatives, tranquillisers and other such drugs were being dispensed per inmate in British prisons than in Britain's psychiatric institutions. The highest recorded 'doping' was of an average of 941 doses per woman per year in Holloway women's prison in London.[104] In 2001, it was found that 17 per cent of women coming into Holloway prison were on psychotropic medication, but that this increased in prison to 90 per cent, mainly prisoners being prescribed benzodiazepines.[105] Since the 1970s, good prescribing guidelines have advised that benzodiazepines should only be prescribed for two to four weeks because of the risk of dependence and withdrawal symptoms. But the prison doctors were not the only ones ignoring those guidelines. Worldwide, by the 1990s, Roche was making $1 billion a year just from selling the benzodiazepine Valium.[106] By the end of the 1990s, some 11 million children in the US were being prescribed Ritalin to calm them down, and 83 million adults were being prescribed Prozac or its equivalents.[107] All this is even more worrying when you know that it is being reported more and more often that to stabilise populations '... mass treatment options are not far off.'[108] These options could include anything from over-the-counter sales of former prescription-only drugs, to more sinister suggestions that would begin with compulsory medicating for prisoners in prisons. As prescriptions of very strong legal drugs rise there is concern that we are moving towards mass medication. Between 2000 and 2013, the number of prescriptions for anti-depressants in England more than doubled, from 22 million to 53 million.[109]

In an attempt to prevent what may become seen as necessary mass treatment, governments are turning to behaviour therapies that involve talking more than doping. In Britain in 2008, an extra 3,500 cognitive behaviour therapists were supposed to be recruited, trained to talk to people and to suggest ways in which their clients could become more optimistic; the patients did at least get someone to listen to them, a government-provided substitute for having a friend, someone who is good at listening and who is upbeat. In the event, this proposed programme was one of the first victims of the cuts, often being cut before a service ever really existed in an area.[110] It had become financially unsustainable to pay people to tell other people that all will be okay when – clearly – it won't.

The original 3,500 new therapists were to be organised around 'happy centres'. At the time it did not go unnoticed that '... the idea of 250 happiness centres to promote rose-tinted bubbles of positive illusions is faintly sinister....'[111] The problem is that in many cases, the real reasons for people's mental distress are genuine and cannot be talked away that easily. An underlying reason for rising mental ill health is that much of the way we are living in the rich world is mentally unhealthy. To see what treatments for distress are now advocated and why, we need to take a short journey through the history of the medication revolution. For a longer journey, William Davies' recent book, *The happiness industry*, is well worth reading.[112]

Treating the symptoms

Governments respond to rising distress by trying to treat the symptoms. The UK government has been employing health trainers for our bodies as well as more therapists for our minds. In 2008, the Department of Health in England reported on what its 1,200 new health trainers who had actually been appointed were doing. Its assessment was undertaken by recounting the anecdotal case of Tammy and Jane (fictional names). In its report, the Department suggested it was doing well because its employees had found a 'service user' (a person) who is grateful for their help. 'Tammy' for instance, talking of her trainer 'Jane', said: 'Jane has supported me from the beginning of my referral programme. Without Jane's presence and guidance, I would have felt unable to attend to begin with because of my low self-esteem. With her help I feel able to reach my goals of improved health and fitness.'[113] Why was Tammy's esteem so low? How have human beings been able to be mentally healthy and physically fit for generations without such personalised health trainers? What could Jane be doing more usefully in a society in which people like Tammy were not so crushed? Do people really talk with such near perfect English as this, or was the conversation as fictional as the names?

At least 'Tammy' can talk of her esteem being low and 'Jane' can talk of not giving Tammy a pill (as Jane isn't allowed to give pills). Tammy and Jane's grandparents lived in a world where mental ill health was less common, the lunatic asylum was greatly feared, and there was not much that could be done about it if you did begin to show symptoms. Since then we have developed many drugs, and not all drugs are bad for us. Some work, especially for severe mental illness (psychosis) and severe depression. The first anti-psychotic drug, chlorpromazine, was marketed in Europe as Largactil and in the US as Thorazine.[114] It was synthesised in 1950, and by 1954, began to be widely used to treat schizophrenia. Chlorpromazine belongs to a group of drugs called phenothiazines, and their use was a major factor in the halving of the population in those old-fashioned lunatic asylums in Britain to stand at some 75,000 by 1975,[115] the majority by then being voluntary patients rather than being compulsorily detained. Phenothiazines suppressed hallucinations, delusions and violence, and thereby allowed so many to be released, but many were reluctant to keep taking the pills.

The first effective anti-depressant drug was imipramine (Tofranil), first licensed in 1956. It belongs to a class called tricyclic anti-depressants, the most effective probably being amitriptyline (Tryptizol), licensed in 1961. These drugs changed a situation where seriously depressed patients were admitted to psychiatric hospitals often for six to twelve months before recovering well enough to cope, to a situation where many were getting better within a month. However, partly because of the danger of overdoses from taking too many of these tricyclic anti-depressants (which had only been developed during the 1950s and 1960s), other new drugs were introduced, many of which turned out to have other harmful side effects.

Largactil, Tofranil and Tryptizol were breakthroughs that had their problems but worked well in particular situations. But both before and after them there have been other drugs that in retrospect it would have been better never to use in many of the situations for which they were prescribed. In Victorian times, Laudanum, a solution of opium in alcohol, was used to help sleeping problems as well as to relieve pain. It was, of course, a very addictive drug.

The first sleeping 'tablet' was not licensed until 1903. The barbiturate Veronal was initially used to put dogs to sleep, and was later used in Nazi Germany for the euthanasia (killing) of some psychiatric patients and mentally and physically disabled children.[116] In 1913, another barbiturate, Luminal, was licensed, a sedative used to treat tension and anxiety. It was one of the first of many that were lethal in overdose and also contributed to depression. The First World War saw demand for this and other barbiturates rise rapidly. The Second World War saw a similar explosion in the demand for another set of the newly marketed drugs, amphetamines, which were first put in tablet form in 1937. Legal use of new and very strong drugs rose when circumstances became abnormal, such as during war.

Experiments with synthetic and especially targeted drugs are a very recent affair. For millennia we have evolved symbiotically with alcohol, hallucinogenics and many other varieties of natural mind-altering substances. We have only been deliberately making, taking and testing variety after variety of synthetic drugs for a few decades, and it may be centuries before we really understand what they do. The first randomised control trial of any mind-altering drug did not take place until 1954.[117] New drugs in the 1950s and 1960s were often developed for one purpose, and then found or thought to be better for another very different condition, while all the time human life was becoming massively more bewildering as we urbanised and consumerised, as we filled our television screens with horror films and the horrors of the news and our children's minds with uncertainties.

We also learned a little as we went along, often the hard way. By 1970, barbiturates were rarely prescribed in Britain as sleeping tablets because of their dire side effects, and because a new set of drugs, benzodiazepines, were seen as preferable. Valium was licensed in 1963, Mogadon in 1965, and then Temazepam in 1969 (a later favourite of addicts). These drugs turned out to have side effects including dependency, resulting in a short-term problem being turned into a long-term one, from which the pharmaceutical companies profited more.

Our collective failure was not to realise the danger of allowing companies driven by the profit motive to research, manufacture and sell drugs that could be addictive and that may not be that effective. Often the newer drugs were no more effective than the older ones, but cost much more. Lithium was given to manic-depressives from the 1960s onwards, and reduced manic episodes, but also took the spice out of life. There were no magic pills, but given the profits that could be made through claiming to have found one, there was no slowdown in the search for that magic, nor any great profit to be made in looking for the underlying causes, rather than for potential treatments.[118]

Feeling better than ourselves?

In the 1970s, a new class of anti-depressant was developed, the selective serotonin re-uptake inhibitors (SSRIs). They were based on theories that depression was caused by a shortage of serotonin in the brain. There is still very little evidence that this is actually the case.[119] The best known SSRI is fluoxetine (Prozac), approved in 1988. It became very widely used and very widely criticised:

> Prozac is the emblematic anti-depressant, and the fact that is has become as common a household name as "aspirin" illustrates the extent of the phenomenon.... [Prozac et al] allow depressed subjects to work on their inner selves so as to "feel better", or even "better than themselves" ... [but] it is becoming difficult to tell which is the self and which is the artificially reworked self.[120]

Prozac's one great advantage is that overdosing on SSRIs is rarely fatal. Many people take it for years, but it is difficult to assess whether that is due to ongoing benefits, or just to avoid withdrawal symptoms. The longer people stay on medication, the more profit the manufacturer makes. In contrast, for children there was also the development of the amphetamine derivative methylphenidate, marketed as Ritalin, which, by 2008, turned out to be so harmful that it had a health warning circulated by the authorities against its continued use in Canada.[121]

SSRIs became the mass medication drugs of the 1990s. They had the effect of stopping people complaining, which caused speculation that this was a large part of the reason why so many GPs were willing to prescribe them so often. This was despite repeated stories such as that blazoned on the front page of *The Guardian* on 26 February 2008 that read: 'Prozac, used by 40 million people, does not work, say scientists.' A year earlier, in 2007, the BBC had reported (as a national news story) the fact that in Scotland anti-depressant use had risen more than four-fold, 85 daily doses of anti-depressant drugs being prescribed by 2006 per 1,000 people in the general population as compared with 'just' 19 doses per 1,000 in 1992. The report itself showed that it was between the ages of 25 and 44 that use peaked. What the report did not do was predict just how much worse the situation would get in the next few years.

By 2006, across the whole of Greater Glasgow sufficient anti-depressants were being prescribed for around 10 per cent of all people aged 15 or over to take a standard daily dose, every day, the implication being that in poorer parts of Glasgow rates would be far higher. Mass medication had arrived; the targets that the 2007 report had announced were simply to try to stop these high rates rising further.[122] All those targets came to nothing. This was partly because of the economic crash of 2008, and the rise in mass joblessness across Britain became most concentrated in places like Glasgow – by 2014, sufficient anti-depressants for continuous standard daily doses for some 16 per cent of all Glaswegians were being prescribed there. It also came about because the drugs were there, they were available, and someone stood to make a huge profit if so many people started taking them so regularly.

Figure 25 shows just how rapid the rise in prescriptions across all of Scotland has been. It shows how policy, and possibly market saturation, had been having the effect of a slight curtailment in that rise after 2004. In 2010, this chapter in this book ended by suggesting that for curtailment to continue, a remarkable change in Scotland would be required given the most recent rise in economic distress, and given so little curtailment of the underlying causes of mass despair. The underlying causes being that despair is often rational, given the life that so many people now find they have to live. In the event, prescriptions and use accelerated from 2006 onwards. Ironically, the new NHS source for this data is titled *Better information, better decisions, better health.*[123]

The ultimate reward

The British adults, and children aged 15, 16 and 17, being prescribed anti-depressants increasingly frequently, almost always now SSRIs (except in some cases of more severe depression, when interestingly amitriptyline

Figure 25: The rate of prescribing anti-depressants by the NHS in Scotland, 1992–2014.

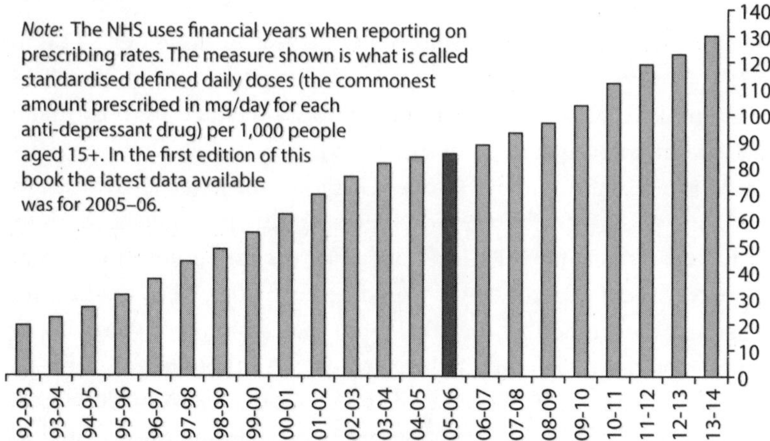

Sources: NHS Quality Improvement Scotland (2007) NHS quality improvement Scotland: Clinical indicators 2007, Glasgow: NHS Quality Improvement Scotland, Table 1.1, p. 12. Updated using: *ISD Scotland (2015) Better Information, Better Decisions, Better Health: Data Tables*, NHS Scotland (http://www.isdscotland.org/Health-Topics/Prescribing-and-medicines/Publications/data-tables.asp?id=1309#1309)

Rate of prescribing antidepressants by NHS Board: Defined Daily Doses per 1,000 population (aged 15+), Scotland, 1992–2014

	92-93	94-95	96-97	98-99	00-01	02-03	04-05	06-07	08-09	10-11	12-13	13-14
Scotland	19	26	37	48	62	76	84	88	97	112	123	130
Ayrshire & Arran	19	26	37	51	65	81	90	95	107	123	136	145
Borders	20	26	35	43	54	68	78	84	93	110	123	132
Dum. & Galloway	21	27	39	48	64	78	83	85	92	105	118	125
Fife	21	26	36	47	60	74	80	84	93	109	121	129
Forth Valley	22	29	42	53	65	81	88	91	98	114	125	132
Grampian	15	20	28	37	48	59	67	71	78	92	103	108
Greater Glasgow	19	27	39	53	68	84	94	103	113	129	139	157
Highland	15	22	31	41	54	66	71	75	80	93	103	107
Lanarkshire	19	27	37	49	63	80	88	95	105	123	137	128
Lothian	20	27	37	46	57	70	75	78	85	99	110	115
Orkney	22	26	34	39	45	58	64	65	73	86	99	109
Shetland	14	20	29	40	52	53	55	61	70	81	96	104
Tayside	20	26	37	49	65	79	87	91	98	113	121	128
Western Isles	18	25	33	43	54	63	69	73	82	96	105	108

Note: In 2006/07, NHS Argyll & Clyde was dissolved as an NHS Board and its Community Health Partnerships (CHPs) were absorbed into NHS Greater Glasgow and NHS Highland. From 2006/07 onwards 'Inverclyde and Renfrewshire' CHP became part of NHS Greater Glasgow & Clyde, and 'Argyll & Bute' CHP became part of NHS Highland.

is still useful), include the parents of the girls who had recorded such sharp increases in depression in the study undertaken around Glasgow with which this chapter began. This rise in anxiety will also include some of the girls themselves. There are many reasons for expecting to see despair and the treatment of its symptoms rising in years to come. But it is hard to imagine a world in which an apparently continuously rising proportion of people are being medicated. At some point, the rise shown in Figure 25 will have to end. At some point, the future will begin to look less uncertain and hopefully less unsustainable,.

Almost all the legalised medical drugs with which we have to treat despair were inventions of the last century. We are only now beginning to fully discover the long-term detrimental side effects of many prescription drugs. This is because they are such recent inventions, because of the reluctance to accept that there is not a pill for every problem, and because of the manufacturers' wish to suppress any information that might have a bad effect on sales (although there are now more and more campaigns demanding full disclosure).

There are also those drugs for which you do not need a prescription. We still turn to alcohol more than to any other drug to try to deal with our despair, with hugely detrimental results for both our physical and our mental health. Despair reaches across social classes and areas, but some of the most comprehensive studies have been undertaken in Scotland where a long-established Medical Research Council funded centre is based. Rates of diagnosed despair were a little higher in Glasgow by 2006, at 10 per cent, than in the least affected part of Scotland, Grampian, where the Royal Family goes on holiday, and where 'just' enough for 7 per cent of adults to take anti-depressants daily was prescribed in 2006. By 2014, the proportion in Grampian had almost doubled, to 13 per cent, higher than Glasgow in 2006. But in Glasgow, the proportion had passed 13 per cent in 2011, and was still climbing rapidly when measured most recently. Grampian's future can be seen in Glasgow today, unless we do something about the things that are driving people to despair.

For children, rates of anxiety and depression are now found to be higher in the higher social classes in Scotland. In 2014 in the *Telegraph* newspaper it was revealed that the children of the much-lauded aspirational-for-their-children parents have often not got enough emotional resilience to cope with failure.[124] Wealth does not shelter you or those you love from despair. Should you be rich and live in a rich unequal country, your children are far more likely to suffer from mental illness than you were, as you will have grown up in more equitable, less competitive, less brutal times. Should they escape the worst effects, around them huge proportions of other people will be zoned out, behaving in placid ways, artificially 'enhanced' or otherwise medicated not to complain. In 1970s Britain and America the economic gaps between the social classes were narrow and falling. Today they are greater and widening. There is more to fear.

For parents today and parents to be, unless we change the current trajectory, the next generation of children will grow up in a world where they will repeatedly listen to others talk about their therapists, their anxieties and their pills. At the extreme, just prior to the 2008 presidential election in the US, those suggesting new ways to imprison people more effectively in maximum security jails were quietly implying that inducing a coma in inmates might be an option. Mass medication is no cure for society's problems. If any reason were needed as to why injustice is harmful, it is the effects that we now know the resulting inequalities have on our mental health. Material wealth offers no protection, when, after all and ultimately, '… all rewards are in the mind'.[125] We need a more stable world simply to stay sane. And our social world can become more stable only when it becomes more equitable. Humans have evolved to respond well when treated with respect.

8

Conspiracy, consensus, conclusion

> The 0.1% have abandoned any sense of restraint. They now appear incapable of even enlightened self-interest; it's all naked self-interest. They want everything, they want it now and they want it from you.[1]

Chapters 3–7 each began with a statistic of injustice:

- a seventh of children being labelled today the equivalent of 'delinquents';
- a sixth of households excluded from social norms;
- a fifth of people finding it difficult or very difficult to get by;
- a quarter not having the essentials to play a normal role in society;
- a third now living in families where someone is suffering from mental ill health.

The statistic that ends this series of statistics concerns people's ability to choose alternative ways of living, and how limited those choices are: *half are disenfranchised*. In the UK half of the electorate don't vote or if they vote then under the first-past-the-post system it matters not. In the US, almost half of all those old enough to vote either choose not to vote or are actually barred from voting.[2]

8.1 No great conspiracy

The greatest indictment of unequal affluent societies is for their people to be, in effect, disenfranchised, to think they can make no difference, to feel that they are powerless. Apathy has risen as we have to put in more effort applying for numerous jobs and working longer hours and indeed years to make our livings, lulled into a false comfort through consuming to maintain the 'norms' of modern living. We have become so busy just trying to get by, and so apathetic about change, that most of us no longer think we can alter our collective futures.

In the space of about 100 years we've gone from fighting for the right for women to vote, to a situation where half of the population in the most unequal of affluent countries are not effectively exercising their right to vote. However, give people a proper choice, a voting system where your vote will matter, or a decision that it is important to make, and seven out of eight will routinely vote.

When the Scottish people were offered a more interesting choice in 2014 – between rejecting London-centred politics or voting not to take the risk – 85 per cent voted in their independence referendum. Had 5 per cent more voted 'Yes' instead of 'No', by 2016 Scotland would have been an independent country, no longer just a part of the 'United' Kingdom. A remarkable number were voting 'Yes' for greater equality, both greater equality with England and within Scotland. By the end of the 2014 referendum campaign they were promised that, and even greater devolution, even if they voted 'No'.

Greater equality was becoming popular. Apathy grows unless people think their vote is going to make a difference. The Scottish people turned out to vote in large numbers because it was a vote for greater equality, not simply for a nationalistic name-change of the nation-state. In contrast, although there has been coordinated action, and many advocates of inequality, there has been no great, well-orchestrated conspiracy of the rich, just a few schools of free market thought, a few think-tanks preaching ludicrous libertarianism occasionally verging on race hate, but no secret all-powerful committees. It is true that there are occasional meetings of mostly old men in dinner jackets trying to feel important, but they are not that important.

Suppose there was, in fact, a conspiracy of the rich, a grand plan coordinated to preserve our current state of inequality. Conspiracy theorists often suggest such easy explanations, as suddenly everything can be made to fit; and many actual conspiracies are often revealed long after events. However, these are almost all relatively simple conspiracies, the assassination of a leader, the covering up of evidence, a plan to ensure a friend's election to be party leader through apparently legal but devious means. Grand conspiracies, however, require a degree of organisation and secrecy that humans are rarely capable of. Suddenly introduce 'free market' reforms to the Soviet Union and societal collapse eventually results in a dictatorial president, but that was the outcome of a naïve miscalculation, not careful conspiracy.

I would argue that there is no great conspiracy. This was first realised in the aftermath of the First World War, when it became clear that no one '… planned for this sort of an abattoir, for a mutual massacre four years long'.[3] Those in charge, the generals, planned for a short war. Similarly, there is no orchestrated conspiracy to prolong injustice, that would be easier to identify and to defeat. Instead, unjust thoughts have seeped into everyday thinking out of the practices that exist to ensure a profit is made. Ideologies of inequality have trickled down. Once only a few argued that hunger should be used as a weapon against the poor (see Section 7.3 above). Now it has become a little more common to grumble when inconvenienced by a strike, to talk of those requiring benefits as 'scroungers', and to hope to make or inherit money or to become famous.[4]

As the nature of injustice has evolved from the former 'five giant evils' to the new five modern evils of elitism, exclusion, prejudice, greed and despair, injustice begins to propagate itself more strongly. And because they do not recognise this transformed injustice for what it is, too many people unwittingly favour arguments that actually bolster contemporary injustices in rich nations. They suggest identifying a 'deserving poor' rather than reducing inequality, or clearing the streets of the homeless rather than ensuring there are good homes, treating the symptoms of injustice rather than the causes. However, unlike them, many others now recognise that the nature of injustice has changed, that in Britain and the US 'Beveridge's Five Giants – Disease, Idleness, Ignorance, Squalor and Want – are different now….'[5]

Books of this kind usually struggle in their conclusion to make suggestions as to what could and should be done. Some say that it is easy to criticise but hard to find solutions. The central argument of this book is that it is beliefs that matter most – the beliefs that enough of us still hold – the beliefs that underlie most injustice in the world today. To ask what you should do after you dispel enough of those beliefs to overcome injustice is rather like asking how to run plantations after abolishing slavery, or how to run society after giving women the vote, or how to run factories without child labour. The answers have tended to be: not very differently than before in most ways, but vitally different in others.

Dispelling the untruths that underlie the injustices we currently live with will not suddenly usher in a utopia.[6] A world where far more people genuinely disapprove of elitism will still have much elitism, and something else unjust will surely arise in place of what we currently see as unfair. We cannot know what it will be, just as no one could have been expected in the 1910s to have predicted the world a century on. But what we currently view as 'normal' will soon appear as crude, old-fashioned snobbery, which has happened many times before.

There is a great metamorphosis under way in all our societies today. Few people in an affluent Western or Eastern country now so obviously bow and scrape, or otherwise tug their forelocks in the presence of their 'betters'. What do you do today that will appear so quaint and yet so unnecessary in a hundred years' time? How do you currently treat others, how are you yourself treated, and do you think those and other current customs will be tolerated or remembered with affection in the future?

The limits of humanity

Elitism, exclusion, prejudice, greed and despair will not end just by being recognised more clearly as unjust. Slavery did not actually end even when it was formally abolished, women were not emancipated simply by being allowed the vote, and dangerous labour for children did not end with the Factory Acts. It is, however, *in our minds* that injustice continues most strongly, in what we think is permissible, in how we think we exist, in whether we think we have the right to use others in ways we would not wish to be used ourselves. We have yet to add the poor to the list of groups who should not be treated so badly simply because they are not in a powerful position.

All the five faces of social inequality that currently contribute to injustice are clearly and closely linked. Elitism suggests that educational divisions are natural. Educational divisions are reflected both in the misfortunes of those usually poorer children who are excluded from life choices because they are seen as not having enough qualifications, and through the supposed achievements of those able to exclude themselves, often by opting into private or otherwise segregated education. Elitism is the incubation chamber within which prejudice is fostered. It provides a defence for greed. It increases anxiety and despair as endless examinations are taken, as people are ranked, ordered and sorted. It perpetuates an enforced and inefficient hierarchy in our societies. Elitism is a profound injustice.

Just as elitism is integral to all the other forms of injustice, so is exclusion. The exclusion that rises with elitism makes 'the poor' appear different, exacerbates inequalities between ethnic groups, and literally, causes the racial differences we identify so easily and don't realise are so temporary – racism and wider prejudice always shifts to new targets over time but a minority are often excluded simply because they are said to be racially different. Similarly, rising greed could not be satisfied without the exclusion of so many, and so many would not now be excluded were it not for extreme greed. But the damaging consequences of exclusion caused by the greed of the rich spread upwards to the rich. They even reach up to those who appear most successfully greedy: rates of despair might be highest for those who are most excluded, but even the wealthy in rich countries are now showing many more signs of despair, as are their children.

Growing despair has become symptomatic of our more unequal affluent societies as a whole. The prejudice that rises with exclusion allows the successfully greedy to try to justify their greed as apparent reward for some superiority, and makes many others think they deserve little. The divisions and ostracism that such prejudice engenders further raise depression and anxiety in those made to look different, the apparent failures, 'the losers'. When inequalities rise, those who feel that they have succeeded in life begin to behave more callously to others. As elitism incubates exclusion, exclusion exacerbates prejudice, prejudice fosters greed, and greed – because wealth is simultaneously no ultimate reward and makes many without wealth feel more worthless – causes despair. In turn, despair brings us into a state of apathy and prevents us from effectively tackling injustice.

Removing one symptom of the disease of inequality is no cure, but recognising inequality as the disease behind injustice, and seeing how all the manifestations of injustice which it creates, and which continuously recreate it, are intertwined is the first step that is so often advocated in the search for a solution to injustice.[7] Each route to that solution only differs in how the twine is wrapped around different descriptions of the object we are trying to describe. Think of injustice in these ways and you can begin to distinguish between suggestions that will increase it and those that will be more likely to promote more fairness and greater equality.

The situation is aggravated 'by introducing an inequality that renders one or more persons better off and no one [apparently] worse off.'[8] The awarding of more elite qualifications to an already well-titled minority reduces the social standing of the majority. Allowing those with more to have yet more raises social norms and reduces people on the margins of those norms to poverty through exclusion. To imagine that others are, apparently, no worse off when you introduce inequality requires a prejudicial view of others, to see them as 'not like you'. And this argument legitimises greed.

In 2009, the US government introduced policies to tackle some injustices, the first designed to be effective for 30 years. With some progressive changes taking places in the US, it is possible that Britain may appear more clearly as a backwater of social progress; this is certainly the case when social security changes are considered, and where human rights are rapidly being curtailed, but there are exceptions in other areas. For instance, there is a great deal of work being undertaken to help us move away from elitism – people explaining to those 'above them' just how stupid they sound when they pontificate in an elitist manner. Comics now readily mock politicians who appear condescending, while calling a police officer a 'pleb' effectively became a sackable offence for one government minister.

A great deal of elitism goes unrecognised. A minister still treats his underlings as plebs but does not use the word; the right-wing newspaper may sneer, but only between the lines. It is usually very embarrassing to have your elitism revealed. While fewer people are so contrarian today as to say in public that they are 'unashamedly elitist', one infamous former English Education Secretary, Michael Gove, even managed to get an approving headline in *The Telegraph* newspaper saying he was, although illustrated with a photograph in which he looks a dunce squatting on a tiny chair.[9]

Official rhetoric changes, and despite the odd setback, tends to improve over the decades, reflecting what we have come to appreciate and value more. The 2007 *Children's plan*, the British government's official guidance for schools, suggested that schools should aim for children to better understand others, value diversity, apply and defend human rights. It suggested that schools should help ensure that their teachers and other staff were skilled in ensuring participation for all, and should work towards the elimination of inequality. There should be '… no barriers to access and participation in learning and to wider activities, and no variation between *outcomes* for different groups; and … [children should] have real and positive relationships with people from different backgrounds, and feel part of a community, at a local, national and international level'.[10]

Less bound by elitism, the Welsh administration had earlier decreed that: 'For young children – when they play – it is their work.'[11] The Welsh government's advice to schools is that they should encourage more play, as learning benefits greatly from play and the encouragement of imagination. In Wales it is now officially recognised that children can be stretched rather than being seen as having a fixed potential; the Welsh government says that if children play to the full extent of their capabilities, they then feel their capabilities extend further as a result. The 2010 General Election did not change how education in Wales is organised, and a very different ethos is now dominant in Wales compared to England. The English right-wing Conservative Party try to talk down the Welsh education system, as they also do its health service, and its higher council tax band for the most expensive housing, because they see prioritising the collective good as a threat.

In Scotland, the educational curriculum is similarly being re-designed. It is no longer to be based on learning for children to become 'factory fodder', or 'competition careerists', but instead, there should be learning to ensure the development of '… wisdom, justice, compassion and integrity.'[12] All this for Britain is very new, and for England much of it has yet to come, but it may be a tipping point in the long-term trend of what people are willing to tolerate for their children's futures. As one young father from Northern Ireland in 2008 commented, on living through troubled times, '… when you've got kids you don't want them to live what you've lived.'[13] Times can change abruptly, as often for the better as for the worse. It is worth looking back not only to see what we have lost, but also how much we have gained. Corporal punishment was only outlawed in all UK state schools in 1987, and between 1999 and 2003 in all other schools. To now be talking about teaching compassion – so shortly after such lack of compassion – is remarkable.

Our changing circumstances

Change can happen fast in the most unlikely of places. The pendulum of public opinion was swinging in the US even before President Obama was elected. That was why he was elected. The US has historically been a place of remarkable bigotry and intolerance. Barack Obama's selection as a candidate was initially a shock. In 1987, a majority of adults in the US believed that schools should be able to sack teachers if it was discovered that they were homosexual, and more than two thirds agreed with (or did not strongly dispute) the idea that women should return to their traditional roles. By 2007, only a quarter still held the former view and a narrow majority completely disagreed with the latter.[14]

In 2014, Janet Yellen, the new chair of the US Federal Reserve, described growing inequality as *un-American.*[15] Public surveys, however, show how far US public opinion still has to go. There was a great swing back towards believing again that government should ensure that all were fed and also sheltered after the 2008 economic crash, but these are only the most basic of human rights. Growing numbers of people in the US now know that inequality has been rising and don't blame themselves. This slow progress is welcome but, in 2009, a Texan politician said: 'Where did this idea come from that everybody deserves free education? Free medical care? Free whatever? It comes from Moscow. From Russia. It comes straight out of the pit of hell.'[16]

It can be hard for someone from Texas to understand the rest of the world, because the rest of the world is just so different. Figure 26 and the table of data within it shows a great deal of information including how extremely economically unequal the US currently is, and how few people ever walk or cycle to work – just 3.5 per cent of the entire population. The high degree of correlation in the figure's graph suggests that there may well be an underlying connection, and also with obesity and life expectancy (but not with smoking or drinking). It is no wonder that 35 per cent of Americans are clinically obese. Contrast this with the Netherlands, where the proportion who are clinically obese is only 12 per cent – more than half the population walk or cycle to work, and the best-off 1 per cent take less than 7 per cent of all income.

In the 17th century, the Netherlands contained the richest, most powerful and most unequal province on earth, the County of Holland, centred on old Amsterdam. The Dutch have not always been as well organised and relatively equitable as they are now; but today they show what is possible for a former major world power. The Dutch demonstrate one version of what the British and Americans could aspire to be.

It is far easier to organise a country well, to build bike lanes and organise public transport, when those at the top are not so intent on just becoming richer. But clearly change is possible. Where the top 1 per cent aren't so engrossed in getting richer, more time and more public money tends to be spent on public transport including providing bike lanes and that is one of many factors in reducing obesity rates. You can chose to smoke or drink less as an individual but you cannot paint a bike lane as an individual or create a decent train system all by yourself.

Their absurd reactions are not entirely the fault of the kind of Texans who talk of 'hell' when they hear the word 'equality'. Many in the US still think in this way and don't realise that great equality does not mean uniformity or communism. Thinking that any move towards greater equality was bad began long before European immigrants, immigrants with the profit motives of Protestant ethics,[17] overran Texas. This kind of thinking got its first foothold around four centuries ago, on the other side of the Atlantic, in old Amsterdam in the County of Holland. In 1631, a young man named René Descartes noticed that all around him people had stopped thinking about much more than earning money. He said: 'In this great city where I am living, with no man apart from myself not being involved in trade, everyone is so intent on his profits that I could spend my whole life without being seen by anyone.'[18]

In the same year that Descartes died, 1650, a Dutch prince, William of Orange, was born, who, in 1688, landed in England with an army, causing King James II to flee to France. Despite the fact that William was then a king (not a revolutionary), and because he ended up on the side of history's victors, the event became recorded as a 'glorious revolution' rather than as the beginnings of a new mindset of mercantile and militaristic misery. Within a dozen years William had increased the national debt of England from £1 million to £15 million, and set in

Figure 26: Healthy behaviour and income inequality, walking and cycling, 2006–10, affluent countries

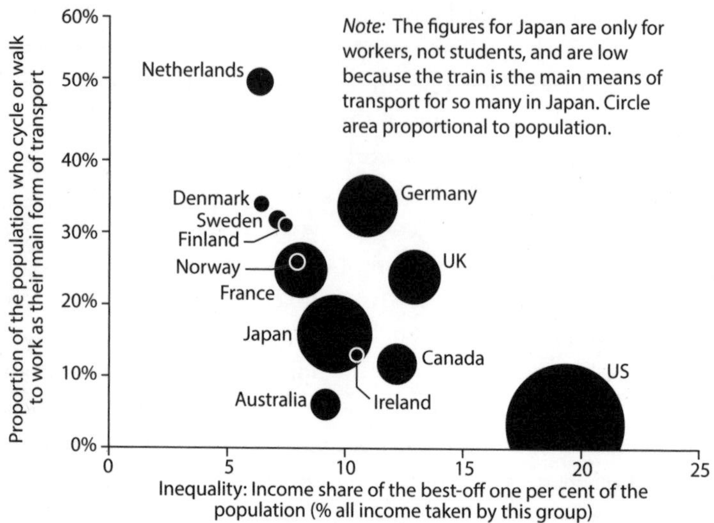

Source: http://www.dannydorling.org/?page_id=4350 as accessed in January 2015; cycling and walking for Japan: http://www.tokyobybike.com/2013/10/how-many-japanese-cycle-to-work.html

Selected measures of inequality and healthy behaviour – all countries for which data exists on all measures, latest comparable data

	Top 1% income share	Cycle/ Walk (%)	Population (mil)	Cycle (%)	Walk (%)	Obesity (%)	Alcohol (litres)	Cigarettes	Life expectancy in 2008
Australia	9.2	6	22	1	5	28	10	1,034	81.5
Netherlands	6.3	51	17	26	25	12	9	801	80.3
Sweden	7.1	32	9	9	23	12	7	715	81.4
Norway	7.9	26	5	4	22	10	7	534	80.6
France	8.1	25	63	3	22	15	13	854	81.2
Canada	12.1	12	34	1	11	25	8	809	80.7
Finland	7.5	31	5	9	22	16	10	671	79.9
Ireland	10.5	13	5	2	11	23	12	1,006	79.9
Germany	10.9	34	82	10	24	15	12	1,045	80.2
UK	12.9	24	62	2	22	25	10	750	79.7
Denmark	6.4	34	6	18	16	13	11	1,413	78.8
US	19.3	3.5	310	0.5	3	35	9	1,028	77.9
Japan	9.5	16	127	9	7	4	7	1,841	82.7

Note: Data sources as above except obesity data, which is % of population obese aged 15 years and over in 2012 (Source: http://www.oecd.org/els/health-systems/Obesity-Update-2014.pdf). Cigarettes is number of cigarettes smoked per adult per year in 2007 (Source: http://en.wikipedia.org/wiki/List_of_countries_by_cigarette_consumption_per_capita) Alcohol consumption measured in equivalent litres of pure ethanol per capita per year 2008 –2012 (Source: http://en.wikipedia.org/wiki/List_of_countries_by_alcohol_consumption_per_capita). Life expectancy source is: http://www.oecd.org/berlin/47570143.pdf

place the idea that a nation-state should permanently borrow in order to fight wars and expand trade.[19]

All of William of Orange's wars and killings cost money. National debt rose and rose, to £78 million by 1750 and £244 million by 1790: 'The trend was remarkable and indeed exceptional, by European standards.... What did the government do with all the new resources, tax and loan money at its disposal? It conducted wars.'[20] These were wars with Spain, Austria, France, and lastly, with North America, which the British lost. As a result, the mantle of 'defender of the free world' began to move across the Atlantic. In 1791 Thomas Paine wrote that, for the English government, '... taxes were not raised to carry on wars, but ... wars were raised to carry on taxes'.[21] He could have added, '... and debts rose greatly', and he could have been writing about what his own country was to become, the world power that replaced the British Empire in global supremacy and almost bankrupted itself fighting a cold war that included real wars with Russia and Communism by proxy, most obviously in Vietnam.

The Texan politician's idea of fraternity and cooperation as hell was first fermented in the commercial imperatives that had swept Amsterdam by 1631; the idea was further brewed in the militarist megalomania of 18th-century England, and the gilded greed of the US that was apparent to Mark Twain, who coined the phrase 'the gilded age' in the 1870s. All these transformations, in one way or another, involved debt dressed up as wealth, debt dispensed in order to gain wealth.

Depending on how you count money (and it is a slippery business), the US current account was in surplus until 1977, in deficit but balanced by overseas 'investments' until 2002, and after that the US truly became a debtor nation in any sense of accounting. In 2004, the writer, Richard Du Boff, who pointed this out (like many others at the time), warned that a dollar rout could result, which '... could cause skittish investors to dump US stocks and bonds, sending Wall Street into a dive'.[22] In the event, much more than a rout took place. And that Texan legislator's political party, the Republicans, were routed from office. What replaced them was a little different from the Democrats of old, and not just because of the President's skin colour, or what that colour revealed about how people in the US could now vote.

Signs of hope

President Obama's proposals for the 2010 Federal Budget were released in March 2009. The proposals appeared designed to reverse the growing levels of economic inequality in the US. This was seen as a significant development given that inequality had been rapidly increasing in the US for 30 years, mostly as the inevitable result of previous government policy. Commentators initially said it was difficult to predict exactly what the effect of the hundreds of proposed Obama budget measures would be, but they included approximately $100 billion a year in tax increases for the rich, and $50 billion a year in net tax cuts for those less wealthy.

The *New York Times* predicted that the proposed budget changes would result in an increase in the take-home pay of the median household of roughly $800 a year, and tax increases on the 'top 1 per cent' of $100,000 a year.[23] Some of the budget policy proposals that appeared to be aimed directly at helping the poor included: $20 billion to increase food stamp benefits for desperate families; $15 billion to increase pensions and benefits for nearly 60 million retired Americans and Americans with disabilities; the increasing of weekly unemployment benefits by $25; and the expansion of the child tax credit programme.

The introductory text to the 2009 US budget proposals was entitled '*Inheriting a legacy of misplaced priorities*' and was widely welcomed as a remarkable document by recent historical standards. It stated that: 'By 2004, the wealthiest 10 percent of households held 70 percent of total wealth and the combined net worth of the top 1 percent of families was larger than that of the bottom 90 percent.'[24] Figures in the report also showed how the top 1 per cent of earners had increased their share of the total income from 10 per cent in 1980, to 22 per cent by 2006, and how the cost of health insurance had increased by 58 per cent since 2000, while average wages had only increased by 3 per cent.

By spring 2009 it had become clear to those in power that business as usual would no longer suffice.[25] By spring 2010 it was becoming obvious that curtailing business as usual, the lobbyists that its billions of spare dollars paid for and their protests over any proposed reform, was going to be far from easy. The Republicans in both the Senate and Congress fought hard to prevent President Obama's budgets from becoming law. It took until 2013 for higher taxes on the wealthy to be implemented, with the introduction of increased taxes on people earning over $400,000 a year, which were designed to raise some $600 billion over 10 years.[26]

By 2014, it became apparent that the government had raised taxes, mainly from the rich, to collect $3 trillion, or 9.2 per cent more than in the year before.[27] By 2015, the US authorities were intensifying their search for tax avoidance by American citizens who were living overseas. This search included the opening up of Swiss bank accounts and even demanding that the Mayor of London, American-born Boris Johnson, pay capital gains tax on property he has profited from selling. Boris's reaction: 'They're trying to hit me with some bill, can you believe it?'[28] But in the end he paid his bill, in full. The Americans have an expatriation tax (exit tax) for people as rich as Boris – they can tax their rich even when they are overseas.

Contrast the US budget proposals of 2009 and the tax rises of 2013, 2014 and the evasion-prevention action of 2015 with the criticism made by more maverick (although, as it turns out, largely correct) academics writing just seven years earlier on how global problems were being faced up to by leading politicians: 'All these and other problems of global or more local magnitude are … the icebergs threatening the Titanic that contemporary world society has become. The icebergs are financial (currency speculation and over-valued stocks), nuclear, ecological (global warming), and social (billions of people with no prospects for gainful employment or decent living standards). There is no captain and the officers (the world's politicians) mill around disclaiming authority and denying responsibility.'[29] Responsibility is, of course, still denied, but what was impossible one year became possible the next. What was solid economic certainty in 2007 melted into the air of social reality of 2009, and then re-crystallised in a new political battle when the consequences for the rich became clearer in 2010, and for the poor in 2015.

The very richest people of all, like the Mayor of London, and those even wealthier than him, are able to evade and avoid many taxes if they are British, but those not quite as rich are beginning to have to pay their way again. Inequalities are falling among the 99% in the UK. However, for the richest 1 per cent, incomes continued to soar, and for a few, their wealth appeared to balloon in value. By 2015, the houses and flats of just the borough of Westminster were valued at £120.5 billion, while those of neighbouring Kensington and Chelsea were said to be worth

£110.5 billion, according to the estate agent Savills, which pointed out that, when combined, these two London boroughs appeared to be worth more than the entire annual product of the 35th largest economy in the world, Denmark, the GDP of which was 'just' £222 billion at that point in time.[30] Such extraordinarily high housing prices could only be sustained by extremely high incomes, and even then, not for long.

In autumn 2014, the Irish statistician Michael Mernagh wrote a letter to a national newspaper. He called for a wage cap at the top: for the cap that had already been applied to the entire Irish public sector to also be applied to the entire private sector. He explained to the newspaper's readers that by then, in Ireland, due to austerity:

> Two-thirds of all taxpayers earned only the average wage of €37,500 or less. The top 1%, who earned €200,000 or more, took 9% of all gross income. They were in the private sector. The pay cap of €200,000 should also apply to the private sector. The top 1% would still receive 5% of the national pay cake. The 4% saved would equal €3.25 bn. The Government could channel that into the Exchequer. Alternatively, they could distribute it to the 99% of us who are less fortunate. Each of us would be better off by an extra €1,600 annually. That may not seem much, but, coming up to the centenary of 1916, it would be a start on the road towards a fairer society.[31]

1916 was the date of the Irish Revolution. Its anniversary is almost upon us. Just a few weeks later, in very early 2015, the French economist Thomas Piketty explained in an interview that:

> All the big revolutions engendered a big tax reform. Take the French Revolution, the American Revolution, or World War One … we need a big fight and sometimes violent shocks to make progressive tax accepted. It would be a big mistake to think of progressive taxation as a technocratic process that comes quietly from a minister and experts. This is not at all the history of taxation.[32]

Taxes are the best way we know of curtailing the behaviour of those who are most greedy. High marginal taxation on very high incomes deters those who have enough from working even harder to get even more. When marginal taxes are high, incomes tend to be more equitably distributed because of this, and because those at the top have less of an interest in the wages of the poor being lowered. Raised taxation is always violently opposed and then very quickly accepted and adapted to; but without a shock, taxes tend not to be increased. Fortunately the shock need not be war. It can be a banking meltdown, an ecological disaster, an education revolution, or a demographic shift. All of which in one way or another are happening now.

8.2 Using the vote

In the British budget of spring 2009 taxes were raised so the rich would, if they earned over a certain limit, again pay 50% tax on that component of earned income. Sadly most of the sources of income that the very rich enjoy were taxed at a much lower rate. Nevertheless the House of Lords proposed an amendment that all companies should, by law, publish the ratio of the wages of their highest paid director or executive to the wages of the lowest paid tenth of their workforce.[33] Then government minister Harriet Harman introduced the new Equality Bill to Parliament, stating that it was now the British government's understanding that inequality hurt everyone.[34]

In the spring of 2010, inequality, bankers' bonuses and greed all featured strongly in UK pre-election debates. They have featured even more strongly in the run-up to the 2015 General Election, where cuts to NHS budgets were also high on the agenda, following tax cuts for the rich. The incoming 2010 coalition government had reduced the top tax rate to 45 per cent, but did not lower it further; they did introduce capital gains tax on property bought by non-domiciled purchasers, but only on gains made after 2015. Because the tax take fell, funding for services such as the NHS also fell in comparison to the growing needs of an ageing population. The Conservatives planned for real terms cuts in state school funding after 2014 and to shrink the size of the state back to its 1930s proportions. The coalition as a whole did as little as they could to try to reduce inequalities, but they could not ignore the growing clamour against the excesses of the rich, and could not reduce the top rate of income tax to 40 per cent, the rate it had come down to in 1988 and had stayed at until 2009.

Greater equality is easily possible – we have had it so recently before. In 1951 the communist hating, soon-to-be consumer society, nuclear-powered US taxed the rich at 51.6 per cent of their margin earnings, at earnings just above what the vast majority managed to live well on. It has been estimated that returning to that tax rate for just the richest percentile of a percentile of North Americans (0.01 per cent) would raise $200 billion a year, three times all that the US government spent on education and the environment combined in a year, or more than half of the (initial) 2008 Federal Budget deficit.[35]

By 2010, following the economic crash, the super-rich did not appear to be as opulent as they recently had been. Their investment earnings certainly suffered during 2009. Nevertheless, President Obama's tax proposals were initially set to net roughly half that $200 billion sum, but in the end, netted only 30 per cent of it, $60 billion annually.[36] It is well worth remembering that Barack Obama won the nomination of the Democratic Party in 2008 largely due to millions of small campaign donations from ordinary voters making him a credible candidate. Only after that did the corporate money also start rolling in to his campaign coffers. Had he not secured a second victory in 2012, taxes would not have been raised on the rich as they have now been. It may not have been enough, but it was a start.

The power of crowds

Almost every time there is a victory for humanity against greed, it has been the result of millions of small actions mostly undertaken by people not in government. Examples include: votes for women, Indian independence, civil rights in America, or that earlier freedom won just to be able to say that the earth goes around the sun, a victory against the power of those holding most of the riches of those times and their prejudices.[37] People can choose between falling into line, becoming both creatures and victims of markets, or they can resist and look back for other ways, other arguments, different thinking. When they have resisted in the past, resistance has been most effective if exercised by those thought to be the most powerless. But we quickly forget this. We need to be constantly reminded.

Almost anyone who gets near the top of any institution is self-selected by a desire for superiority – unless there is evidence of some other strong and intrinsic motivation. That is part of the reason why the harmful effects of inequality go all the way to the top. More inequality means we are all more obsessed with status, and those who get furthest up are the most obsessed; the main exception is those who are born to assume superiority.[38] The antidote to being dominated is to act collectively, otherwise all that results is a new aristocracy. It is true that some people genuinely want to get to the top to help others. The quote 'Never underestimate the power of persistence' is usually attributed to Nelson Mandela, but Mandela's power was a movement outside of his prison. It was a movement of millions.

It is often said that: 'The struggle of people against power is the struggle of memory against forgetting.'[39] Thinking that you have to do all your thinking anew and alone is the wrong place to start. To remember earlier times, times before you were born, you need stories, stories that tell you it need not be like this, because it has not always been like this.

In 2008, adults in the US remembered that they had power in their vote, and were repeatedly reminded of this by a grass-roots political campaign. As a result, more of those who were allowed to vote exercised their vote than at any time since the pivotal 1968 election, which Richard Nixon won, partly with George Wallace's help, and partly on a racist ticket. That 1968 vote was the last election that changed the trend but, like me, you probably don't remember it.

In the US it is only necessary to go back to the early 1960s, before many civil rights were won, to see terrible inequality, some of a kind that has now been eradicated. Hundreds of thousands of black Americans still do not get to vote because they have died prematurely due to poverty and discrimination.[40] Millions of poor Americans get to vote in fewer elections than rich Americans because their lives are foreshortened through the effects of destitution and a callous health system. But despite all this, there is still progress.

By 2014, US research was being published, revealing that Americans supported an unequal society, but much less unequal than the one they currently had: 'For example, the actual pay ratio of CEOs to unskilled workers in the United States is 354:1, but Americans report an ideal ratio of 7:1 – unequal, but more equal.'[41] A widening of inequality is bad for the economy, because '… being both too high and too low in a distribution can impair decision-making'.[42] Those at the top make worse decisions when the top is in the clouds because they are so keen to try to stay at the top. Those at the bottom are also more likely to cheat when the gap is at its widest, get caught and then do badly.[43]

Think of all those debtors, pickpockets and fraudsters locked up in Dickens' novels. And think of how bad Scrooge's decisions were. Now think of all those US bankers found to have broken financial law, and the far higher rate of suffering crime among the poor in the US compared to the poor in any other rich country on earth. The US prison population is 707 per 100,000 people. In England and Wales it has doubled in the past 20 years, and is the highest rate in Western Europe, at 'just' 148,[44] which is more than four times lower than in the US. In Sweden, where in 2012 they decided to close four jails because of a shortage of prisoners, the rate of imprisonment is 12 times lower than in the US, at 57.[45]

In countries such as Britain, people last lived lives as unequal as today, if measured by wage inequality, in 1854, when Charles Dickens was writing *Hard times*. Of course, things are much better now because we have benefits that we did not have then. Wage inequalities after those hard 1850s times fell, but then rose in the gilded age, peaking in 1906 before falling for 70 years, then rising in just 10 years to be as great again in 1986 as in 1906. Next, they rose again to unprecedented levels by 1996.[46] By 2003, British researchers were writing in their careful prose that wage inequalities were '… higher than at any point since the Second World War and probably since representative statistics were first collected at the end of the nineteenth century….'[47] People in Britain thought little of this at the time; they were told it did not matter because great inequalities had become portrayed as natural.

The brink of despair

A key member of the New Labour 1997–2010 government said they were 'seriously relaxed' about the situation, that inequality was not a key issue for them.[48] That key member was found, in 2015, to have been avoiding paying tax by making extremely large loans – to himself![49] The British had forgotten that for most of their recent history they had not lived like this. By 2014, it was becoming necessary to explain again and again that the '... deepest threat Britain faces comes not from migration. It comes from the relentless transfer of wealth and opportunity from the poor and middle class to the wealthy....'[50] Part of that wealth grab had been achieved by the group of New Labour government ministers who had become so rich during and after holding office. They were replaced by a coalition government, stuffed full of even richer multi-millionaire ministers.

Despair grew, greed spiralled, prejudice seeped in, more were excluded, the elite preached that there was no alternative, that their experts were so able, that the 'little people' were safe in their hands, and that greed, greed of all things, really was good. Even when the economic crash came, they said recovery would come and that things would soon be back to normal. And many were still saying this when these words were first typed in the autumn of 2009 for the first edition of this book. However, far fewer were suggesting the same recipe for success by spring 2015 when worrying about 'lost decades'. The world has changed greatly in just five years, but in other ways, we have been here before.

In 1929 the stock market rallied several times. In the early 1930s unemployment rates in the US exceeded 14 million. This was just before the statisticians who did the counting were sacked. In Britain there were real falls in prices – deflation. Prices fell again 80 years later in 2009, and general deflation began to be noticed across the entire Euro-zone by 2015.[51] The UK government cut wages across the public sector by 10 per cent in the 1930s, and by a similar amount in the 2010s. Although we began to become more equal in wealth during those depression years, inequalities in health peaked as the poorest died young in the greatest numbers in that same 1930s decade.[52] In many other newly rich countries, but especially Germany, it was far worse. Ten years after the 1929 crash, the turmoil ended in catastrophe. W.H. Auden's poem '1 September 1939' ends:

> I and the public know
> What all schoolchildren learn
> Those to whom evil is done
> Do evil in return.

The most unequal of rich countries were those most willing to go to war in Iraq 64 years after 1939. More equitable nations find it easier to refuse to join, or make only paltry contributions to any supposed 'coalition of the willing'. It is when injustice is promoted at home to maintain inequality within a country that it also becomes easier to contemplate perpetrating wrongs abroad. At home in the UK and US, politicians sought to plaster over the wounds caused by inequality by building more prisons, hiring more police and prescribing more drugs. But by 2007, it was becoming widely recognised that rich countries could not simply employ palliative treatment for the symptoms and outcomes of extreme inequality.

The realisation that change had to come dawned on many even before the money suddenly ran out. Time and again articles were written explaining that: 'Extreme social inequality is associated with higher levels of mental ill health, drugs use, crime and family breakdown. Even high levels of public service investment, alone, cannot cope with the strain that places on our social fabric.'[53] After the economic crash, after the troops had been pulled out of Iraq and Afghanistan, after achieving so little in a decade, after soup kitchens spread from the US to across Europe, no one was surprised any more when they heard claims that change had to come. They just wanted to know how, and when.

Overcoming the power of kings

The latest era of growing inequalities is coming to an end. It is something that cannot go on forever, and so it won't. But it will not end without the millions of tiny acts required to no longer tolerate the greed, prejudice, exclusion and elitism that foster inequality and despair. Above all else, these acts will require teaching and understanding, remembering what is fundamental about being human, remembering compassion: 'The human condition is fundamentally social – every aspect of human function and behaviour is rooted in social life. The modern preoccupation with individuality – individual expression, individual achievement and individual freedom – is really just a fantasy, a form of self-delusion....'[54]

Accept that individuality is an illusion – we all have and are both kith and kin. Start to behave differently, and even the most apocalyptic of writers will agree that every act of defiance, no matter how small, makes a difference; whatever '… we do or desist from doing *will* make a difference….'[55] We can never know precisely what difference, and have no reason to expect our influence to be disproportionately large, but nor should we expect it to be especially small.

It is equally vital to recognise that none of us are superhuman.[56] Seeing yourself as special can lead to loathing others you see as lazy or feeble and below you. This contempt can often be hard to disguise, and is clear to see in the expressions of some right-wing politicians when they talk of 'the poor'; they appear to feel dirty just talking about 'them'. At its extreme, for those who hold this disgust for others, social cleansing is attractive – removing the poor because you think they are dirty. This is how fascism begins, and it always ends in death. A fascist is someone who believes it is right to kill. Fascists differ in how dirty they get their hands. They range from the small town doctor slowly dispatching his elderly female patients, to the planner creating the new clean city designed only to hold the chosen few.

Because none of us are that special, trusting a small coterie is dangerous. It makes no sense to expect others to do great deeds and lead us to promised lands, at least not with any reliability. We are slowly, collectively, recognising this, learning not to forget that although we can learn without limits, we may not get that far when we each try to learn on our own; our minds were not made to live as we now live: 'The world is indeed a strange and mysterious place, but not because of any hidden causal order or deeper purpose. The mystery is largely in the operations of the human mind, a strange organ capable of creating its own vision of reality with little regard to how the world really is.'[57] We need each other because we have evolved not to be loners. Without tolerance and understanding of each other we are all capable of causing great harm through persecution.

In our minds we can either despair or celebrate our stories. Sometimes we can see absolute immiseration as food prices soar and barbarism takes place in wars on terrorism that repeat older histories of persecution. From other moments of our histories we can tell numerous celebratory stories where injustices have been progressively defeated, the power of kings overcome, principles of equality in law secured, slavery abolished, voting franchises extended, free education introduced, health services or health insurance nationalised, minimum incomes guaranteed (including for unemployment, sickness, old age and childcare). In these celebratory tales, legislation is won to:

> … protect the rights of employees and tenants, and … to prevent racial discrimination. It includes the decline of forms of class deference. The abolition of capital and corporal punishment is also part of it. So too is the growing agitation for greater equality of opportunity – regardless of race, class, gender, sexual orientation, and religion. We see it also in the increasing attention paid by lobby groups, social research and government statistical agencies to poverty and inequality over the last 50 years; and most recently we see it in the attempt to create a culture of mutual respect for each other.[58]

And we see it in a redistributive budget in the US that could not have easily been imagined as possible a year earlier than it was created. We see it in the contempt in which many of those who have taken most are now held, the tax avoiders and art hoarders; but we can also see the danger of a return to business and misery as usual. 'The tradition of all dead generations weighs like a nightmare on the brains of the living.'[59] We see our history, our future, our nightmares and our dreams first in our fickle imaginations. That is where we first make our present, in minds which each mix the same ingredients so differently. How we come to live is not predetermined. Across Europe we see change. Political parties that once would never have made it near the sidelines came to power in Greece in 2015, and are now contenders for power elsewhere. They threaten the power of modern political kings and dynasties.

Geographically all it takes is a little imagination, a little 'wishful thinking', to see that a collection of movements will achieve the change so many wish to see in the world; these are movements that need only to exist in our imaginations in order to work. If we have and spread enough faith that they will work, then they will work. These are movements to '… make our own world from below [where we] are the people we have been waiting for'.[60] These are the opposite of movements towards world government: too many of those have been proposed '… in which the best stocks could rule the earth'.[61] These are, instead, movements where it is proclaimed that '… the future will be amazing, and after that the whole world will become a better place. [Because] if we cannot make that happen, then no one can.'[62] And these are movements about which people who advocate them repeatedly tell us that: 'It can happen – so long as everyone does not leave it for somebody else to do....'[63]

The words above were written before the most recent wave of protests; before the Arab spring that began with the death of Tarek al-Tayeb Mohamed Bouazizi in Tunisia on 17 December 2010; before Los Indignados was created in Spain in 2011;[64] before Syriza became the second largest party in the Greek Parliament in 2012; before the Occupy movement swept around the world, reaching Australia in 2013;[65] before the Podemos Party was formed in Spain in 2014; before all the events of 2015, 2016 and 2017 which – whatever they are – are unlikely to be predictable, minor, or unrelated to the change that is now upon us, the dawning of a fairer world as the old order that René Descartes saw take form on the dockside in Amsterdam in 1631 abates.[66]

8.3 Coming to the end

Great transformations are always turbulent. It is easy to see events that will soon be footnotes in history as more important at the time, or even as a great step backwards, when, in fact, they are just part of a wider turmoil. The first edition of this book was widely reviewed in the UK because its publication happened to coincide with the final few weeks of the UK 2010 General Election contest, and because issues of fairness rose to the fore immediately after the Conservative and Liberal Democrat Parties formed their coalition government. This coalition revealed itself to include a large majority who appeared to prefer to see the injustices outlined here maintained, a majority who offered lip service compassion for the 'deserving' poor, but who also suggested that this 'deserving' group comprised a very small set of people.

The second edition of this book was prepared as the coalition government came to the end of its time in office in early 2015. The election of the 2010 government provided a clear set of examples of how the beliefs of many in power maintain injustice. Many coalition MPs, sitting behind their Chancellor, George Osborne, cheered on the cuts as he announced them, budget after budget. It was as if he was their actual spiritual leader. However, the UK was in a great mess before coalition ministers came to power and became the poster boys and girls of injustice.

Not the economic mess Osborne liked to suggest, but a mess that arose from being ruled by a small group of people who viewed so many as being inferior to them.

Accepting criticism

I have read several of the reviews of the first edition of this book. Reviews tell you to write more clearly in future, to be blunt; they reveal when you are wrong (for when you rewrite); they explain how some can misunderstand you; and in a few cases, they demonstrate how some people choose to misrepresent your work when they fundamentally disagree with you but do not want to say so – perhaps for fear of revealing their prejudices. Reviews are also very occasionally flattering to read, because they describe the book you have written as being much better than it actually is.

I wish I could be more succinct and arrange my arguments better. In revising this volume it kept on changing. In many cases I was modifying what I believed as I wrote the first draft and have modified again many things for this 2015 edition. I am constantly reconsidering what I believe. If you do not constantly question what you believe, you can become inclined to lay down principles as being undeniably true, without seeing how, in doing so, you become more and more like those you most disagree with. I also wish I could have written a shorter book, and this revised and updated edition is even longer than the first. However, one reviewer kindly suggested that on the subject of rising selfishness, the sheer weight of evidence provided in this book makes it clear that I am:

> … crystal clear in believing that this came about because the powerful were anxious about losing their privileges in a more equal society. Implicitly and explicitly, the powerful recognised that the elevation of the market to be the arbiter of good policy was likely to consolidate their hold on power. So instead of actions being for the public good, they had only to be for the market's good. Over the next 50 years the huntsmen of the apocalypse regrouped, added a fifth steed, and came galloping into our society in the guise of elitism, exclusion, prejudice, greed, and despair.[66]

I wish I could have been as clear as that about such things, and (having almost finished this text) you may think the same, but I still don't credit the powerful with being so well organised. I have sat opposite enough 'business leaders' talking about how their increased wealth would trickle down – if only they were allowed to be even more selfish – to have come to realise that many of these people came to believe this nonsense in the same way that hundreds of thousands came to believe that Elvis still lives among us, or in the way in which millions of others have faith in the existence of alien life forms who frequently visit this planet.

I don't want to upset anyone waiting for the second coming of Elvis, or for the mother-ship to descend, and I have to admit that I don't have much evidence that you are wrong if you are hoping for these occurrences (just no evidence that you are right), but when it comes to 'trickle-down economics', we now have decades of proof of the fallacy of this claim. The very affluent who say that by being so rich they somehow benefit others can now only point to the additional servants they employ as evidence for the so-called beneficiaries. In the last five years those same trickle-down economists captured thinking in the UK Liberal Democrat Party and made that coalition government possible.[67]

National politics in the UK had swung far to the right just as people were beginning to question our widespread acceptance of the breadth of inequality in the UK, and to ask if inequality in and of itself was damaging. In 2009, *The spirit level* by Richard Wilkinson and Kate Pickett had the greatest effect in directing the media spotlight onto these crucial questions. If their book had been published a few year earlier, it may have had even more of an impact, including on the general election. In 2014 it certainly helped the Scottish Independence campaign come so close to winning its arguments for a fairer society north of the border. *Injustice* was greatly influenced by *The spirit level*, and was often reviewed or referred to alongside Tony Judt's far better constructed and considered *Ill fares the land*, also published in 2010.

> In making it clear that they aren't offering solutions Dorling and Judt are staying true to the intuitively attractive Australian Aboriginal saying, "Traveller, there is no path, paths are made by walking." But surely we now know enough to put an occasional signpost in the

> sand? Our collective inability to act on the good information that we have, made reading these books unsettling.[68]

Similarly, when the first edition of *Injustice* was reviewed in one leading social science journal, the main criticism was the lack of what could be termed a *messiah moment* in its conclusion. True, I have been unable to take that tiny fraction of all that is known which I have read and produce a new testament. Many people want a new testament, but in the midst of our current turmoil what we believe is going to change again and again, as it has changed so much in each of the last five generations. In response to my final line of the first edition: 'So what matters most is how we think', came one reply:

> This is rather like the pacifist's pledge, that wars will stop when men refuse to fight. It is clearly true that beliefs lie in the mind, but it doesn't quite identify what will change beliefs sufficiently to change practice in substantial and long-lasting ways.[69]

My view is that no one can truly know what will be sufficient to change deeply held and institutionally transmitted beliefs. Over time a few have deluded themselves that they did have the answer, and many others have wished to follow those few. Even more have wished to find something to follow. There is even an elegant argument that there is a need for occasional mad leaders to get us out of social ruts.[70]

Anger and passion

Many of the early reviews of *Injustice* described the book using terms such as 'powerful and passionate',[71] expressing 'righteous anger',[72] or even '… fuming with barely suppressed anger'.[73] These comments are what most took me aback: there are things I am very angry about, but I didn't think I had mentioned them much in this book. I had thought that the draft I wrote originally was quite bland. Furthermore, the very diligent copy-editor deleted everything from that draft that sounded even slightly angry to me. However, she deleted hardly anything from the revised manuscript for this edition, so either I have become more placid, she is now angrier, or what appeared angry in 2010 appears reasonable five years on.

We, in the UK and the US, have become so used to the extremely unfair state of our societies that it can sound angry if you write about injustices and inequalities as they are. I am used to injustice: this is how we live, this is how it is, and of course, there has to be a mechanism whereby unjust inequalities are maintained in affluent countries, otherwise our efforts to reduce them would have had far more effect.

One day, when I am much older,[74] I hope to write a book about what really upsets and angers me. This, honestly, is not that book. Injustices are wrong, but I have become acclimatised to these wrongs, just like so many others around me. In fact, they are the source of my livelihood, what I teach about, what I am paid to write about. I don't think it is possible to write about something that is wrong without sounding at least a little angry – unless you do not have normal human emotions – but the injustices described in the pages above are simply the worldview I gain from studying inequalities.

On the book's overall approach, reviewers ranged between saying that the book was 'unashamedly partisan … preaching (albeit convincingly) to the converted …',[75] to saying that the work was 'no ivory tower exhorter to revolution … not allow[ing] us the comfort blanket of just blaming the rich, or some powerful world elite.'[76] One reviewer's 'preaching' is another's 'authoritative description'. One's complaint that the text is too 'strident'[77] is compensated for by a reviewer of an opposing political persuasion saying the same text is too 'downbeat'.[78]

The reviewers of *Injustice* were not being inconsistent; they were simply as divided as the distinct readerships of the publications they wrote for, they were divided in their beliefs. Although we read to learn, individually we hold a narrow picture of how the world is. It is a very uncomfortable feeling to have that view upended. We enjoy much more having our prejudices confirmed. So please indulge me if I bring this book to its end by confirming and enhancing what will probably be a few of your prejudices, because if they were not at least partly your prejudices, you would probably not have read this far.[79]

Precarity and riot

What has happened since the economic crash, and especially in the years since the hardback version of this book was published, to change what we might say about the persistence of inequalities and injustice? In many ways the worldwide story is still a tale of the prevalence of William Beveridge's five social evils of ignorance, want, idleness, squalor and disease, as most people in the world do not live in affluent countries. But Figure 10 in Chapter 4 of this revised edition shows how richer countries became (on average) so much poorer, and poorer countries became (on average) richer after the crash, while still within most countries and continents inequalities were growing.

Worldwide, *ignorance* continued to fall as access to the internet spread and more children learned to read each year than could read the year before. In contrast, *want* rose in many places as food prices spiked again to their highest ever levels in 2011, and absolute misery threatened billions.[80] As a result of such an obvious crisis in January 2014, the 'Masters of the Universe' (business 'leaders' who met in Davos) announced that growing inequality had become the most important world issue, alongside climate change.

Our masters have short memories. Just 12 months after their 2014 meeting, in their global risk report of 2015, the same world business leaders collecting again at Davos suggested 28 alternative threats now mattered most, including *adapting* to climate change rather than trying to reduce it. Severe income disparity, which had actually been identified as a great risk to the world in all of their 2012, 2013 and 2014 reports, was removed from the rankings in 2015 as the wealthiest of businessmen became bored of pretending they actually either cared about the harm they did by fostering it, or that they were concerned about the risks their selfish behaviour might impose on others.[81]

Increases in mass idleness, and the poverty and boredom that result from human labour being discarded in the name of efficiency by those seeking to maximise profit, resulted in increased rioting, not just in affluent nations, where it received most attention, but in many poorer countries too. From December 2009, when the Greek police shot a 16-year-old dead for throwing a stone, through to the rioting over corruption and joblessness in Tunisia, which caused the president to flee the country to take up exile in Saudi Arabia in January 2011, and around much of the globe both in between and afterwards, idleness has been rising, and rioting is one response.

By February 2011, the president of Egypt was forced to resign and failed to flee to Saudi Arabia in time to join his fellow despots. The Americans were again reconciled to watching regime change take place that was not of their making although they intervened in Egypt a few years later. By August 2011, riots spread across London and reached beyond the poor enclaves, a shock to Londoners but normal elsewhere, where riots had become a way of life – some 5,077 cases of rioting were reported in the Indian state of Assam in 2012 alone.[82] In December 2013 hundreds of foreign migrants rioted in Singapore,[83] and in November 2014 riots that began in Ferguson, Missouri, then spread to other poor US cities.

Everywhere large groups of people are dissatisfied with their lot in life because what they have been allocated is not enough and there are no great signs of a better future being planned. Many believe that the next generation will have harder lives. Even in affluent Britain, home building, which had already slumped to a record low by the end of 2008,[84] declined further, despite immigration rising. The annual total numbers of homes built continued to decline through 2009 and 2010.[85] By 2015, despite the most acute need for homes there, London investors were building luxury flats to leave empty as they thought they could profit simply by selling them on to other very rich buyers, as a secure form of savings; and anxiety spread.[86] London was not made safer by growing inequality.

Worldwide, rising disease and despair was an inevitable consequence where poverty rose. Across India, an epidemic of suicides began among the poor, which a BBC correspondent suggested was a direct result of the financial crisis that began in the richest of Western banks in summer 2007.[87] It took 30 months for the wrong financial decisions by traders in the City and on Wall Street to result in poison being swallowed by the financially desperate in so many of the back streets of the villages in Andhra Pradesh.

It would be possible to produce a list of hopeful stories at this point, bringing together a few of the positive signs that people are learning from the collective errors of our society. Such stories are vital to keep hopes high, and to show that change is possible. However, this is a book on injustice, and the period 2010–14 was a terrible period for injustice, not just worldwide, but also in the country that this book is mostly concerned with, the UK, and depressingly, so much of what happened could have been foreseen in 2010.

8.4 Injustice deepens

Between 2010 and 2015 in the UK there was a revival of old social evils. Want returned as hunger reared up again, and thousands of food banks were opened and hundreds of thousands of people began to rely on them as benefit payments were repeatedly sanctioned and wages fell; squalor increased as more people became homeless, and destitution rose; and disease became an issue again as the life expectancy of elderly women fell.[88] But these extreme deprivations only had an impact on a minority of the population, although fear spread among the majority. For most people it was the rise in the new social evils that took the greatest toll. Elitism, exclusion, prejudice, greed and despair were on the rise. And it could have been so different.

In May 2010, during the negotiation process that formed the coalition, if just a single key Liberal Democrat MP had wavered, the UK might have had a different combination of politicians in power and far less austerity. Had civil servants not frightened the politicians so much into forming a government so quickly, then new splinter groups might have emerged from what had previously appeared rock-solid parties. Had a second election been held that 2010 year, then the public sector cuts in the UK could have been similar to those in most other European countries, far slower and less deep. Instead, 2010 became the year in which so much changed.

Market rule

In January 2010, the New Year began with good news; it was announced that for the first time in British history, a majority of additional university places had been awarded to young adults from working-class areas.[89] Elitists, however, cannot tolerate this expansion, what they see as the 'dilution' of the 'value' of a university education. For them, if greater numbers of the poor have to go to university at all it should be to 'lesser institutions' that they go.

In October 2010, the Browne review on university funding[90] recommended limitless 'market' fees for higher education, which was used as an excuse by ministers to announce the tripling of annual fees to as much as £9,000 a year. The actual cost to students was much higher than £9,000 when (as was usual) it was financed using a loan that had to be paid back with interest. In the event, almost all universities charged the maximum £9,000 by 2015, but there was no fall in the numbers or proportion of students from poorer backgrounds going to university.

More and more young people realised that a university education had become their only chance of not having to take a servile job for life, and in 2015, the student numbers cap was removed so that any university could take – and charge – as many students as it could attract through marketing. UK universities collectively spent more than £36 million on student marketing in 2012–13, a rise of 14.7 per cent on 2011–12, and a 33 per cent rise on 2010–11.[91] Nationally a sum of money equivalent to the full fees of more than 4,000 university students a year are now being spent not on funding their teaching, but on advertising to secure the next set of bums for their seats. That sum of money is rapidly rising.

Higher education in Britain has become the most expensive and hence most elitist in Europe. Only a quarter of the state funding for university teaching in 2010 remained by 2012. The Deputy Prime Minister, Nick Clegg, liked to talk of the government in 2012 still spending £2 billion a year on higher education, while never mentioning the much higher amount that was spent before he came to office. Teaching in the social sciences in England has now been fully privatised, with no government 'subsidy' remaining, as if there was no longer any value in understanding society. The coalition also largely abolished the Educational Maintenance Allowance (EMA), resulting in some poor younger people not staying on at school, and further impoverishing many others who did stay on.

Reflecting a few months after the shock of the EMA announcements, Albert Aynsley Green, the former Children's Commissioner for England, said: 'The Coalition's "savage" cuts risk robbing a generation of the chance to improve their lives and risk crushing social mobility.'[92] Some suggested keeping fees low if a youngster went to a local university, but they might as well have been whistling in the wind.[93] In 2014, it was reported that social mobility had begun to fall, even when it was measured in the most old-fashioned of ways, using flawed statistics that had not revealed the subtler falls before.[94] At the upper reaches of qualifications, mobility became even rarer. More than 200 PhD graduates were applying for a single junior level temporary academic post in some universities.[95] It felt like survival of the fittest, but getting through was almost always simply down to luck and 'connections', not to being the most fit for the post.

Government ministers became boring as they repeatedly claimed there was 'no alternative'. They refused to address the possibilities of saving money by cutting those expensive activities we engage in which many of us already think are shameful, such as conducting overseas wars and buying American nuclear weapons. Neither would they recognise that having greatly expanded the national debt when bailing out the banks, the group to look to first for payments should not be the poor, but those who hold most of the national wealth. They should be suggesting solutions such as introducing the kind of land value tax which already exists in many states of the US, and now in Ireland and elsewhere in Europe: if it is possible in Ireland, why not in the UK?

George Osborne, who was appointed Chancellor of the Exchequer in 2010, would probably consider a wealth tax affecting his affluent family to be unjust, and especially the taxing of their inherited land holdings. He would avoid being interviewed on the subject at all: if interviewed he would try to move the conversation away from the subject but, if pressed, would claim there had already been increased taxation of rich families such as the one he was born into. Since elections became open to all, no British government has had so many millionaires in Cabinet so effectively representing the interests of such a tiny proportion of society.

Three of the five Liberal Democrat MPs appointed to the new 2010 Cabinet were drawn from among that party's tiny number of millionaires. These were Nick Clegg, Chris Huhne and David Laws; one had to resign within weeks of being appointed after an expenses scandal, another resigned in February 2013 after pleading guilty to perverting the course of justice, and the third just managed to hold onto his job through to 2015, despite having promised no rise in university tuition fees prior to the 2010 General Election, but later that year voting the highest ever rises through.[96] It is not just the voters who have been conned into letting swindling and lying millionaires rule them; the majority of less affluent MPs (including MPs actually in the governing parties but not in government) have also been duped by their much richer brethren.

Before the May General Election, the first (Labour) budget of 2010 was progressive, but George Osborne's (Conservative) June 2010 budget-in-all-but-name was highly regressive, and then announcements on taking away money from local authorities showed that it was people governed by Labour authorities that would lose the most. But it was the October 2010 Comprehensive Spending Review that most clearly revealed the intentions of the new UK government ministers. It was the most wide-ranging attack on the livelihoods and wellbeing of poor people and those on average incomes that can be recalled in a lifetime. In the event, even more was subsequently cut than that and yet deeper cuts were planned for the period 2015–20. Even Thatcher in her darkest hour was less cruel.[97] The elite were determined that only those below them should suffer.

Administering truth

The language of Orwell's *Nineteen Eighty-Four*[98] is vital for introducing new injustices. Cuts are presented as 'savings' or 'reforms', and increased elitism as more opportunity for the aspirational poor. Charity for a few became 'bursaries for the deserving'. As the government put it: 'Poverty is about more than income', and eradicating 'child poverty in the UK will [they say] not be achieved by simply throwing money at the symptoms.... Worse, it has exacerbated the problem by weakening incentives to work for some groups and preserving cycles of entrenched deprivation.'[99] Poor people are apparently poor because they have an inadequate aspiration to be better off, and need incentives such as greater poverty. That, at least, is how Osborne and those around him think.

At the time of the April 2011 government report *A new approach to child poverty*, within which these beliefs were most clearly presented, 58 per cent of children in poverty had a parent who was working, doing a job that an employer wanted done, but usually by a class of person that the employer apparently thought didn't warrant receiving a living wage. Following that April 2011 report, the overall rate of child poverty rose to 23 per cent for families with two parents, and 42 per cent in families with a single parent. If that single parent was working full time, the rate of child poverty even for them had risen from 17 to 22 per cent of that group within a year.[100] Soon the majority of the extremely poor were in low-paid work.

Just as a pretence was made that many working-class students were still *very* welcome in universities, even when the proportion at the most elite universities fell, so too did the government pretend that they were not driving the poor from those cities where jobs could still be more easily found. When speaking publicly, Boris Johnson, Conservative Mayor of London, said his party had gone too far in what he termed their 'Kosovo-style social cleansing' of the poor from cities.[101] One Conservative minister admitted in *The Telegraph* newspaper that they were planning the equivalent of the Highland Clearances, but now in central London.[102] And then the evictions in London began.

In January 2015, the Joseph Rowntree Foundation reported that nearly 4 out of 10 British households with children now relied on a level of income lower than that which was regarded by the public as the minimum needed to participate in society; for lone parents the figure had risen to 71 per cent.[103] At the global scale, Oxfam reported that 'The combined wealth of the richest 1 percent [worldwide] will overtake that of the other 99 percent of people next year [2016] unless the current trend of rising inequality is checked.'[104] The global 1 per cent were now attracted in numbers never before imagined to London and towards the policies of the coalition government, and the poor who were not their servants had to be moved out of their way.

How has this happened? How can we explain it? One City businessman published a book in 2014 arguing that: 'If we demonstrate that the system allows people effectively to take purchasing power from others and give it to themselves without creating anything of value others will see that unfairness is at the root of the problem. That does not mean that people will automatically decide that they oppose a demonstrably unfair system. Self interest will lead many, possibly most, to conclude that they could be the gainers from such a system and will favour it.'[105] In his career this one businessman has been 'responsible for cross border tax based leasing, off balance sheet financing structures and various bespoke structured finance arrangements … a pioneer in the UK government's Private Finance Initiative … [and] responsible for or involved in the financing of more than £2 Billion [of Private Finance Initiatives]'. His book helps explain how unsustainable the City of London and our wider economy now is. People on the inside are beginning to speak out.[106]

Our unjust society

The wider public can be taught to accept injustice. Around the time of the autumn 2010 Spending Review I went on a tour of different schools, universities and colleges, telling some of the stories of this book, and gathering reactions. I have given over 300 public lectures in the years since then on issues relating to injustice and inequality. The impression I gained when school students questioned me was that we teach young people conflicting versions of the truth depending on their particular institutions, versions that help them to *fit in* to their allotted places in our unjust society. The reactions to the same talk I received from those different groups of students suggested that those most likely to get to the top are the ones most likely to think it fair that they got there.[107] And I was reminded of the more precocious of those students when I had to listen to a collection of the men appointed to 'advise' the new coalition government.

Frank Field was appointed in June 2010 to lead an independent review on child poverty. He welcomed the announcement of his position by casting aspersions on the European-wide definition of child poverty and by suggesting he would 'redefine away' rather than try to solve the problem.[108] He announced it was impossible for there ever to be no children living in households with below 60 per cent of median income. This meant that either he did not understand the concept of a median, or he was being disingenuous.[109]

Will Hutton was appointed to lead an independent review of the pay divide and – in essence – he recommended maintaining the status quo, the 20:1 average inequality ratio, in public sector pay. Initially he ignored more progressive suggestions, such as that the public sector should include in their prospective contracts with private sector firms a clause excluding as ineligible those who break that 20:1 income ratio. Such threats would be an extension of the policies whereby local government refuses to subcontract to private sector companies that pay some workers below the living wage.[110] Five years later, he was reporting how that pay divide was widening as the incomes of the bottom 90 per cent fell in the UK and the US.[111]

With regard to greed, the super-rich saw their greatest ever annual gains in wealth being reported in early 2010. *The Sunday Times* revealed that the wealth of the super-rich in Britain had risen by 29.9 per cent in the year to 2010, to stand at £335.5 billion held by the best-off 1,000 people combined (or £335.5 million *each* if shared out evenly among them).[112] By December 2010 it was Bob Diamond of Barclay's Capital who had become most closely associated with the unacceptable face of capitalism.[113] He resigned in 2012 in the midst of the Libor banking scandal.

By 2014, the combined wealth of the 1,000 richest people on the *Sunday Times* rich list had risen to £519 billion – a 55 per cent rise in their wealth in just another four years, in the same four years in which most other people in the UK became poorer. Had that rise been spread over every family living in the UK, each would have become more than £6,000 better off.[114] The rich were becoming much richer, everyone else was becoming poorer and the poorest were facing absolute immiseration. As a result despair and anxiety rose. We should have known it would rise. We should have been better prepared and more concerned before this great robbery of wealth occurred. It was because we were not that we did not act to prevent it. On despair, Professor Sir Michael Marmot, the President of the British Medical Association, delivered the review that carried his name in February 2010. While his report and the efforts of hundreds who contributed provided a series of useful summaries of the evidence, it failed to deal adequately with the growing evidence of the overarching and most urgent need to reduce inequality in wealth and income, of the need to focus on excesses at the top end of the social hierarchy, and not simply to concentrate on the harm of material deprivation at the bottom.[115] The incoming coalition government took note of the report, but rather like their New Labour predecessor (who had commissioned it), they were less interested in action. In many ways, the coalition government was New Labour continued, just as we slowly learned that much of New Labour had been Thatcherism continued.[116] At some point this continuum will end.

8.5 What to do

When you start to write, there is, at first, just you. And any individual cannot know that much. Then others clean up the typescript before it is printed, so it reads far more clearly. Others, again, take what you have written and use parts of it for better things, ignoring the majority of what you typed. What is most interesting, however, is what unsettles.

As to the way forward, perhaps we are stuck ever wishing for all the answers? For the far-right in the 1970s who last broke the continuity they actually thought they had found all the answers when they came to believe that 'Inequality was not some moral injustice, but an accurate representation of differences in desire and power.'[117] In great contrast, some contemporary feminists convincingly suggest that attempting to master all the answers is a 'doomed attempt to bring the uncertainty of the world to heel'.[118] But suggesting everything is too complex makes it hard to oppose those who say the world is simple, those supporters of injustice who say winners deserve their prizes, and that you are a lightweight.

How to do it

People on both the left and the right construct their stories, testaments and beliefs as to the way to behave. On the right, what is key is survival of the fittest (the most selfish?) and apparent market efficiency (blindness?), not being held back by the weakest (the feckless?), not believing that humans are capable of organising themselves (leave it to the 'price mechanism'?).

On the left there is too much faith in the ability of all of us to see sense and to rationally organise ourselves, too much faith that the majority will succumb to good argument when they hear it. There is too much harking back to defend previous success, defending council housing estates, comprehensive school uniformity, or clinical authority over patient inclusion. The left needs to regain the imagination it once had – it needs a metamorphosis.

The left still underestimates the extent to which the minds of many in power have been closeted by upbringing, and the huge disadvantage caused by each generation having to learn the world anew.[119] But there are a few certainties. One certainty we can be quite sure of is that the near future really will be very different, because, for at least the last five human generations, the near future has changed radically with each one.[120]

Don't despair that there won't be change. Don't assume it will be for the better, nor necessarily for the worse; it may simply just be different.

The very least we can do is describe clearly the crux of our present predicament; namely, that much that is currently wrong is widely seen as either inevitable or justifiable – despite not even being sustainable.

Where to do it

As 2014 drew to a close, a protest took place in Mayfair at the London headquarters of the landlord Westbrook Partners. Some 60 tenants of the New Era housing estate took to the streets outside Westbrook's plush offices to complain that they would soon be evicted because the rents were to be raised. One mother brought her two children, Angel, then aged 10 and Alfie, aged 11.[121] The public mood had changed. There was no way that this eviction was going to be permitted. Within 20 days a deal had been done, and the tenants could stay. The news was announced on 19 December and spread around the world.[122]

You can no longer evict children at Christmas, not in front of the cameras, not if the world is watching, and not when people have stopped being so afraid to act. In Britain, the vast majority think it is obvious that the NHS, state education and benefits matched to needs are good things; that ignorance, want, idleness, squalor and disease are bad things needing to be tackled, not accepted as inevitable. However, there is still a small, but rich and powerful, minority who are appalled at the amount of taxpayers' money that goes into the NHS and push for more privatisation in the name of efficiency, the end result of such false efficiency often meaning that they can make a personal profit out of the NHS. They also think that as little as possible should be spent on welfare, state education and social services. They aim to shrink the state, and some of them will go to extraordinary lengths to avoid paying taxes at all.

It is obvious that elitism, exclusion, prejudice, greed, despair and the inequality that binds them all are harmful and need to be tackled. We need to beware the small, but rich and powerful minority who feel that they personally benefit from inequality, and who preposterously try to claim that in the end everyone else benefits, or who say that rising inequality is inevitable because of market forces and globalisation, or that the 'riff-raff' do not deserve any more whereas they are so very deserving. We only have to look around the world to see that many other affluent countries are not behaving like Britain and the US are behaving today. Injustice is not inevitable. What is important is not getting to some arbitrary goal, but the direction in which we are travelling. The current levels of inequality in the US and the UK would have been unimaginable a few decades ago. We do not know by how much it will be possible to reduce inequality, but we will easily know if we are heading in the right direction, which will be when the share of the richest 1 per cent falls.

When to do it

When I started to work on this new edition, I was expecting to just update the facts and figures with more recent statistics. What I found in the numbers surprised me. Following the 2008 economic crash, the US Federal Reserve Board was floundering over financial statistics that it had been updating quarterly since 1980, and in retrospect they had to revise their recent statistics substantially. What had been published was fiction. The UK government preferred to avoid producing statistics where possible, even proposing to stop the national census that had been undertaken every 10 years since 1801 (other than in wartime). Statistics from non-government sources showed that the poorest were getting poorer and the richest much richer.

In the US and across Europe, we moved from an atmosphere of 'the bankers should suffer for this' to 'we are all in this together'. We then began to realise that the richest, including the bankers and financial institutions that had created the crash, were actually not in it with us, but were making a bonanza for themselves, and the bottom 99 per cent were paying for it. The poorest were suffering the most gratuitous hardship, gratuitous because the cuts to their standards of living hardly dented the deficit but destroyed so many lives. There was an element of sadism in the new UK government policies. Many of the unemployed accepted zero hours contracts, low wage (below living wage) employment or registered as self-employed, despite little prospect of financial benefit but so as to avoid the ritual humiliations of the 'job' centres.

While inequalities have increased within most nations in the last five years, there was some evidence of increasing equality between nations, but between individuals worldwide there was still rapidly increasing inequality. Those in power were being more careful over how they chose their words, but their actions showed no change in their attitudes to the very rich and how many they thought were undeserving.

The elite are reluctant to do anything about that which is morally wrong, but still technically legal, while they are happy to pillory 'benefit cheats'. The UK MPs' expenses scandal,[123] first publicised by *The Telegraph* newspaper in May 2009, revealed just how upright and honourable many of our political leaders actually were. The wealth of those in government and of their friends revealed their probable allegiances: 'All great political action consists of and begins with, speaking out about that which is. All political petty-mindedness consists of being silent and covering up that which is.'[124] To that we should add: 'To be truly radical is to make hope possible, rather than despair convincing.'[125] Now is the time when we most need hope.

All the endings have already been written, all the enthusiasm and eulogies have been penned, posies of men's and women's flowers have been offered, future students are exhorted to work with joy, humour or at least irony, and with an expansive love, to keep honest, humble, honourable, and '… on the side of the proverbial angels'.[126] And all writers end in one way or another, similarly saying, although rarely with as much humility as this:

> Having come to the end of this book, the reader now knows what I know. It is up to the reader, then, to decide whether there is any validity and utility to what is presented here and then to decide what, if anything, to do about the developments and problems discussed. While I would like to see the reader choose a particular course of action, I do not think that other choices are indications that those making them are judgmental dopes.[127]

And slowly, collectively, with one step back for every two taken forward, we inch onwards to progress; we gradually undo the mistakes of the past, and recognise new forms of injustice arising out of what we once thought were solutions. We collect together posies, all tied a little differently, and we realise that, although none of us is superhuman, neither are any of us without significance. Everything it takes to defeat injustice lies in the mind. What matters most is how we think. And how we think is metamorphosing because – everywhere – there are signs of hope.

> We live in a world that is not changing or transforming, but "metamorphosing".[128]

Notes and sources

Chapter 1

[1] Jones, O. (2014) 'The year the grassroots took on the powerful – and won', *The Guardian*, 29 December (www.theguardian.com/commentisfree/2014/dec/28/year-grassroots-powerful-elites-democracy).

[2] Rosling, H. (2011) Hans Rosling Tweet, 12 July, reported 5 August 2011, documented with estimates (http://liveatthewitchtrials.blogspot.co.uk/2011/08/peak-baby.html), and demonstrated by Hans himself using boxes representing a billion people each on video, 4 July 2012 (http://blogd.com/wp/index.php/archives/9542).

[3] Dorling, D. (2013) *Population 10 billion: The coming demographic crisis and how to survive it*, London: Constable.

[4] Klein, N. (2013) 'How science is telling us all to revolt', *The New Statesman*, 29 October (www.newstatesman.com/2013/10/science-says-revolt).

[5] In revising this book, I have been shocked to find how often the sources I had used in the first edition have altered the wording of their documents if such documents were placed on the web. The authors most likely did this because they received so many other criticisms, but they have not often changed their underlying methods. For an example, see the discussion on the language and labels used by the Programme for International Student Assessment (PISA) in education, Chapter 3, this volume.

[6] The affluent or rich world consists of those countries where the best-off billion people live, that is, almost all of the countries in Europe, North America and Japan.

[7] On the categorisation of injustices, see Wolff, J. and de-Shalit, A. (2007) *Disadvantage*, Oxford: Oxford University Press, pp 38, 39, 106 and 191, who, in turn, refer to Amartya Sen's listings; and for similar categorisations, see Watts, B., Lloyd, C., Mowlam, A. and Creegan, C. (2008) *What are today's social evils? Summary*, York: Joseph Rowntree Foundation (www.jrf.org.uk/publications/what-are-today's-social-evils). Both of these tend to produce lists of around 10 modern evils, or sources of injustice and disadvantage, but many are easily paired and so are collapsible to five (as shown in the first edition of this book in Chapter 2, Table 2, p 17).

[8] Dorling, D. (2012) *The visualisation of spatial social structure*, Chichester: Wiley.

[9] Cartography and utopia have a long and connected history. Maps often included the heavens. 'A map of the world that does not include Utopia is not worth even glancing at, for it leaves out the one country at which Humanity is always landing. And when Humanity lands there, it looks out, and, seeing a better country, sets sail. Progress is the realisation of Utopias' (Wilde, O., 1891, *The soul of man under socialism*, London: privately printed).

[10] Observant readers may notice the debt owed here to the concluding paragraph of Mrs Thatcher's 1981 interview with Ronald Butt, which ended with her saying: 'What's irritated me about the whole direction of politics in the last 30 years is that

it's always been towards the collectivist society. People have forgotten about the personal society. And they say: do I count, do I matter? To which the short answer is, yes. And therefore, it isn't that I set out on economic policies; it's that I set out really to change the approach, and changing the economics is the means of changing that approach. If you change the approach you really are after the heart and soul of the nation. Economics are the method; the object is to change the heart and soul' (Interview, *Sunday Times*, 3 May 1981, www.margaretthatcher.org/docment/104475).

[11] A mantra exposed very clearly in Lawson, N. (2009) *All consuming*, London: Penguin.

[12] Health budgets are raided (top-sliced) to fund armies of counsellors to tell us that all is not so bad. See Davies, W. (2015) *The happiness industry*, London: Verso. Family doctors spend most of their working hours dealing with people whose problems are not physical, and the World Health Organization (WHO) ranks mental ill health higher and higher with every assessment it makes of the leading causes of death and debility worldwide, specifically showing that the rates of prevalence of mental ill health are almost perfectly correlated with income inequality in rich countries. See WHO-comparable psychiatric surveys, as reported in Wilkinson, R.G. and Pickett, K. (2009) *The spirit level: Why more equal societies almost always do better*, London: Allen Lane, p 67.

[13] With a group of colleagues I helped produce www.worldmapper.org, which shows over 1,000 of these. See Dorling, D., Newman, M. and Barford, A. (2010, 2nd edn) *The atlas of the real world: Mapping the way we live*, London: Thames & Hudson.

[14] See Krugman, P. (2007) *The conscience of a liberal*, New York: W.W. Norton, p 18. The height of excess in the last gilded age was seen in the 'Great Gatsby' summer of 1922. Money moved more slowly then, and the financial crash came seven years later. The height of excess in the current gilded age was recorded in the autumn of 2007, as City bankers partied on their bonuses right up to Christmas. The hangover in 2008 was unparalleled: see Chakrabortty, A. (2007) 'If I had a little money ...', *The Guardian*, 8 December. For the origin of the term 'new gilded age', see also Bartels, L.M. (2008) *Unequal democracy: The political economy of the new gilded age*, Princeton, NJ: Princeton University Press.

[15] See Section 3.1 in Chapter 3, this volume. The proportion is designed so as not to change over time.

[16] Pearson, K. (1895) 'Contributions to the mathematical theory of evolution – II. Skew variation in homogeneous material', *Philosophical Transactions of the Royal Society of London, Series A, Mathematical*, vol 186, pp 343-414. This paper may have contained the first histogram of human subjects by area.

[17] For the cycles to exist, enough people had to be given the opportunity to cycle up the social scales to then be available to fall back down in sufficient numbers, and that circumstance first occurred only in the 1960s, which is why the term 'cycle of deprivation' first came into widespread use in the 1970s. With the prejudice of those times, it was more often, and erroneously, used to suggest 'family pathology' as a mechanism whereby poverty was passed down the generations. This was simply a rehashing of the old claim that paupers mainly bred more paupers. The phrase 'cycles of exclusion' here means those shown in Figure 8 (Chapter 4).

[18] As made so clear so recently in Piketty, T. (2014) *Capital in the twenty-first century*, Cambridge, MA: Harvard University Press. This is the most significant book to have been written in the last five years on this subject in terms of influencing the global debate.

[19] The figure varies between times and countries. This particular fraction was first derived for Britain in 1999 as an estimate of the proportion of households found to be poor by at least two definitions. It would very probably be a little higher if the

same measurement were made in 2015, and a little lower across most of Europe. See Chapter 4 for updates, and Bradshaw, J. and Finch, N. (2003) 'Overlaps in dimensions of poverty', *Journal of Social Policy*, vol 32, no 4, pp 513-25.

[20] For the statistics, see Dorling, D. (2014) 'Class segregation', in C. Lloyd, I. Shuttleworth and D.W. Wong (eds) *Social-spatial segregation: Concepts, processes and outcomes,* Bristol: Policy Press, pp 363-88, and for the mechanism, read Bauman, Z. (2006) *Liquid fear*, Cambridge: Polity Press, which provides a very succinct description of the process by which the social distancing between rich and poor occurs as inequalities rise.

[21] See Hayter, T. (2004) *Open borders: The case against immigration controls*, London: Pluto Press, p 151, for examples of what then results, ranging from the building of the Cutteslowe Wall between neighbourhoods within Oxford, to the widespread toleration of an intolerance of international immigration.

[22] Bauman, Z. (2007) *Consuming life*, Cambridge: Polity Press, p 147, quoting Neil Lawson on consumption.

[23] See Section 6.1, in Chapter 6, this volume, and Offer, A. (2006) *The challenge of affluence: Self-control and well-being in the United States and Britain since 1950*, Oxford: Oxford University Press, pp 190-6.

[24] See Bauman, Z. (2008) *The art of life*, Cambridge: Polity Press, pp 57, 120, 132.

[25] See Figure 21 in Chapter 7, this volume.

[26] CEPMHPG (Centre for Economic Performance's Mental Health Policy Group) (2006) *The depression report: A New Deal for depression and anxiety disorders*, London: CEPMHPG, London School of Economics and Political Science.

[27] See Figure 25 in Chapter 7, this volume.

[28] Kay, J. (2004) *The truth about markets: Why some nations are rich but most remain poor* (2nd edn), London: Penguin, p 323.

[29] The coalition has accelerated privatisation, aiming to cut the state to pre-war dimensions, most significantly with an Act allowing more of the NHS to be privatised in 2012. See Dorling, D. (2013) *Unequal health: The scandal of our times*, Bristol: Policy Press.

[30] O'Hara, M (2015) *Austerity bites: A journey to the sharp end of the cuts in the UK*, Bristol@ Policy Press.

[31] See Clarkson, T. (2001 [1785]) 'An essay on the impolicy of the African slave trade', in G. Davey Smith, D. Dorling and M. Shaw (eds) *Poverty, inequality and health in Britain: 1800–2000 – A reader*, Bristol: Policy Press, pp 2-6.

[32] 'Throughout the era of slavery the Negro was treated in a very inhuman fashion. He was considered a thing to be used, not a person to be respected. He was merely a depersonalized cog in a vast plantation machine' (Washington, J.M. King, 1956 [2003], *A testament of hope: The essential writings of Martin Luther King, Jr*, London: HarperCollins, and as quoted at the start of Cooke, B., 2002, *The denial of slavery in management studies*, IDPM Discussion Paper Series Paper No 62, Manchester: Institute for Development Policy and Management, www.seed.manchester.ac.uk/medialibrary/IDPM/working_papers/depp/dp_wp68.pdf).

[33] For an early example of the debunking of those who were supposedly especially great and good, see Strachey, L. (1918) *Eminent Victorians*, New York: G.P. Putnam & Sons.

[34] We have traditions of telling fairy stories that do not state the mundane truth that all inventions were of discoveries about to be made because it had just become possible to make them, and who exactly made them is largely inconsequential. We also rarely point out how constrained people are by their circumstances, and that '… the average newspaper boy in Pittsburgh knows more about the universe than did Galileo, Aristotle, Leonardo or any of those other guys who were so smart they only needed one name' (Gilbert, D., 2006, *Stumbling on happiness*, London: HarperCollins, p 213).

You can argue that most of the now forgotten toilers who were just beaten to the winning post of invention were also equally exceptional people, but that argument fails to hold recursively, as for every one of them, there is another. Elvis Presley is a good example of the right (white) man being in the right place at the right time to become seen as so special later.

[35] Mason, P. (2014) 'Economic recovery in Greece, but will it mean "Mad Max" in government?', Channel 4 News Blog, 16 December (http://blogs.channel4.com/paul-mason-blog/signs-economic-recovery-greece-mad-max-government/2715).

[36] According to www.geog.ubc.ca/~ewyly/acknowledgments.html, Elvin Wyly's home page.

[37] According to John Bartlett (1820-1905) in his book of *Familiar quotations* (10th edn, published in 1919), quotation number 9327, this was attributed to Michel Eyquem de Montaigne (1533-92). It is attributed to *Of physiognomy* (Book, 3, Chapter 12) (see www.bartleby.com/100/731.58.html).

[38] See Cohen, G.A. (2008) *Rescuing justice and equality*, Cambridge, MA: Harvard University Press.

Chapter 2

[1] Piketty, T. and Saez, E. (2014) 'Inequality in the long run', *Science*, vol 344, pp 838-43. Quoted in turn in Norton, M. (2014) 'Unequality: who gets what and why it matters', *Policy Insights from the Behavioral and Brain Sciences*, vol 1, no 1, pp 151-5.

[2] Dorling, D. (2012) *The no-nonsense guide to equality*, Oxford: New Internationalist.

[3] The Reverend Fredrick D. Robinson (2014) 'What God is screaming in Ferguson, Missouri', CNN, 23 August (http://religion.blogs.cnn.com/2014/08/23/what-god-is-screaming-in-ferguson-missouri/).

[4] Professor Robert Beckford (2014) 'Thought for the day', 'Today Programme', BBC Radio 4, 30 December, edited by Lenny Henry.

[5] Miller, G. (2000) *On fairness and efficiency: The privatisation of the public income during the past millennium*, Bristol: Policy Press; see pp 53-7 on rent.

[6] Irvin, G. (2008) *Super rich: The rise of inequality in Britain and the United States*, Cambridge: Polity Press; see pp 37-61 on 'Do we need fat cats?'

[7] Shah, H. and Goss, S. (2007) *Democracy and the public realm: Compass Programme for Renewal*, London: Lawrence & Wishart, p 83.

[8] The phrase is best known from its appearance in the American Declaration of Independence. Thomas Jefferson is thought to have heard an Italian neighbour, the physician and Virginian arms runner Philip Mazzei, use it (http://en.wikipedia.org/wiki/All_men_are_created_equal). For a collection of many wider thoughts about fairness and inherent equality, see Dorling, D. (2011) *Fair play: A reader on social justice*, Bristol: Policy Press.

[9] Kasser, T. (2002) *The high price of materialism*, Cambridge, MA: The MIT Press, pp 110-15.

[10] Skidelsky, R. and Skidelsky, E. (2013) *How much is enough? Money and the good life*, London: Penguin.

[11] See the projections for the years 2050 and 2300 mapped in Dorling, D., Newman, M. and Barford, A. (2008) *Atlas of the real world: Mapping the way we live*, London: Thames & Hudson, maps 7 and 8.

[12] Dorling, D. (2013) 'A global population of 10 billion is nothing to worry about', *The Guardian*, 14 June (www.dannydorling.org/?page_id=3737).

[13] For a good example, see Lawson, N. (2009) *All consuming*, London: Penguin.

[14] Ballas, D., Dorling, D. and Hennig, B. (2014) *The social atlas of Europe*, Bristol: Policy Press.

[15] Diamond, J. (1992) *The rise and fall of the third chimpanzee* (2nd edn), London: Random House, p 168.

[16] Neolithic farming life appears now to have often been taken up out of necessity rather than choice as it began to develop around the world. We first farmed when we were forced to due to there being too many of us in one area simply to hunt and gather, or due to some change in the climate reducing the supply of what there was to hunt or gather. The story archaeologists tell is that we became a little shorter following our first forays into farming, at first, because farming was not very efficient, and later, especially outside the North China plain, as farmers became peasants who became subject to taxes, tolls and population pressures that caused food to be often insufficient. See Davis, M. (2000) 'The origin of the third world', *Antipode*, vol 32, no 1, pp 48-89.

[17] Modern women remaining an inch shorter than their distant ancestors may be modern biology faithfully marking the cumulative effects of our remaining gender insults.

[18] Greek news report, kindly translated by Dimitris Ballas in 2007. The report was from 19 November 2004 (www.in.gr/news/article.asp?lngEntityID=581606).

[19] Dorling, D. (2006) 'Infant mortality and social progress in Britain, 1905-2005', in E. Garrett, C. Galley, N. Shelton and R. Woods (eds) *Infant mortality: A continuing social problem*, Aldershot: Ashgate, pp 213-28.

[20] The speed of the rise in internet access suggests that majority access is possible in a lifetime when that rise is coupled with projections of how many fewer children there soon will be worldwide. The deciding factor is currently the date when the manufacturers of silicon wafers decide it is profitable for them to double the diameter of the discs they produce, discs from which the silicon chips are made. To decide that, they, too, look at the same rise in access, the spread of money worldwide and projections on population falls. It is currently only global inequality in incomes that deters them (according to the author's personal communication with someone who advises the manufacturers of silicon wafers).

[21] Of the more than one hundred million university students in the world, a narrow majority are female; see Dorling, D., Newman, M. and Barford, A. (2008) *Atlas of the real world: Mapping the way we live*, London: Thames & Hudson, maps 221 and 228 on the growth in tertiary education, map 229 on youth literacy, and maps 241 and 242 on changing internet access.

[22] Table 2, 'Injustices, social evils, political, philosophical and public labels combined' (www.dannydorling.org – see publications/books/injustice).

[23] The title headed *The Guardian* newspaper's report of the publication of Wilkinson, R.G. and Pickett, K. (2009) *The spirit level: Why more equal societies almost always do better*, London: Allen Lane.

[24] For a recent literature review of work on the harm caused by inequality, see Wilkinson, R.G. and Pickett, K. (2015: forthcoming) 'Income inequality and health: a causal review', *Social Science & Medicine*, doi:10.1016/j.socscimed.2014.12.031.

[25] Hennessy, P. (2014) *Establishment and meritocracy*, London: Haus Publishing.

[26] Smith, R. (2007) *Being human: Historical knowledge and the creation of human nature*, Manchester: Manchester University Press, p 89.

[27] See Table 2, p 17, in the first edition of this volume.

[28] Wolff, J. and de-Shalit, A. (2007) *Disadvantage*, Oxford: Oxford University Press, p 7.

[29] Watts, B. (2008) *What are today's social evils? The results of a web consultation*, York: Joseph Rowntree Foundation; see p 3 on reciprocity, empathy and compassion.

[30] Leech, K. (2005) *Race*, London: SPCK; and see Leech's pamphlet on Brick Lane referenced within.

[31] Dorling, D. (2013) *The population of the UK*, London: Sage. See especially the maps in Chapter 6 (www.dannydorling.org/books/ukpopulation/Maps_%26_Figures/Pages/Chapter_6.html).

[32] See the first edition of this volume, and column 5 of Table 2, p 17, for the evidence for these claims.

[33] Gordon, D. (2009) 'Global inequality, death, and disease', *Environment and Planning A*, vol 41, no 6, pp 1271-2.

[34] Amin, S. (2004) 'World poverty, pauperization and capital accumulation', *Monthly Review*, vol 55, no 5.

[35] Kelsey, J. (1997) *The New Zealand experiment: A world model for structural adjustment?*, Auckland: Auckland University Press, p 256.

[36] Richard Tawney, in his book *Equality*, published in 1931 (p 57 of the 4th edn), quoted in George, V. and Wilding, P. (1999) *British society and social welfare: Towards a sustainable society*, London: Macmillan, p 130.

[37] Rose, S., Lewontin, R.C. and Kamin, L.J. (1990) *Not in our genes: Biology, ideology and human nature*, London: Penguin, p 145.

[38] Baggini, J. (2008) *Welcome to Everytown: A journey into the English mind* (2nd edn), London: Granta, p 195.

[39] Marmot, M. (2004) *Status syndrome: How your social standing directly affects your health and life expectancy*, London: Bloomsbury.

[40] Monbiot, G. (2014) 'Naked mole rats and eusociality', D. Dorling, Oxford, personal communication. Note 'eusociality' is the highest level of organization of animal sociality, is defined by cooperative brood care, including brood care of offspring from other individuals and similar characteristics.

[41] Wilkinson, R.G. (2009) 'Rank', D. Dorling, York, personal communication.

[42] Although it is implied that the snake lost it legs in the Garden of Eden, suggesting that a few thoughts about evolution or adaptation existed, even in the oldest books of Abrahamic and other religions.

[43] According to the present-day holy text of our times: 'Some of the earliest known condemnations of usury come from the Vedic texts of India. Similar condemnations are found in religious texts from Buddhism, Judaism, Christianity, and Islam.... At times, many nations from ancient China to ancient Greece to ancient Rome have outlawed loans with any interest. Although the Roman Empire eventually allowed loans with carefully restricted interest rates, the Christian church in medieval Europe banned the charging of interest at any rate....' Like all holy texts, this one (known today as Wikipedia) is constantly changing and being updated and corrected by many people. The version shown here was retrieved on 13 January 2015 (https://en.wikipedia.org/wiki/Usury).

[44] Or, put properly: 'Men make their own history, but they do not make it as they please; they do not make it under self-selected circumstances, but under circumstances existing already, given and transmitted from the past. The tradition of all dead generations weighs like a nightmare on the brains of the living' (*The eighteenth brumaire of Louis Bonaparte, Karl Marx, 1852*, www.marxists.org/archive/marx/works/1852/18th-brumaire/ch01.htm).

[45] Michael Douglas, playing Gordon Gekko in the 1987 film 'Wall Street', first coined this mantra.

[46] As the counter-mantra of a generation later relayed: 'Choose life. Choose a job. Choose a career. Choose a family. Choose a fucking big television, Choose washing machines, cars, compact disc players, and electrical tin openers. Choose good health, low cholesterol and dental insurance. Choose fixed-interest mortgage repayments.

Choose a starter home. Choose your friends. Choose leisure wear and matching luggage. Choose a three-piece suite on hire purchase in a range of fucking fabrics. Choose DIY and wondering who you are on a Sunday morning. Choose sitting on that couch watching mind-numbing spirit-crushing game shows, stuffing fucking junk food into your mouth. Choose rotting away at the end of it all, pishing your last in a miserable home, nothing more than an embarrassment to the selfish, fucked-up brats you have spawned to replace yourself. Choose your future. Choose life ...', from the 1996 film of the book *Trainspotting* (www.generationterrorists.com/quotes/trainspotting.html).

[47] James, O. (2008) *The selfish capitalist: Origins of affluenza*, London:Vermilion, p 1.

[48] Dorling, D. (2007) 'Guest editorial: the real mental health bill', *Journal of Public Mental Health*, vol 6, no 3, pp 6-13.

[49] Dorling, D., Mitchell, R. and Pearce, J. (2008) 'The global impact of income inequality on health by age: an observational study', *British Medical Journal*, vol 335, pp 873-7.

[50] Dorling, D. and Thomas, B. (2011) *Bankrupt Britain: An atlas of social change*, Bristol: Policy Press.

[51] The labelling of a seventh of children as, in effect, modern-day delinquents, is true even in the more equitable of these affluent countries. By the same criteria, a sixth of children in the UK and a quarter of all children in the US qualify as modern-day delinquents – see Figure 2, this volume. These education statistics are derived from OECD publications and are discussed in Chapter 3. The statistics on poverty and exclusion mentioned in Chapter 2 are discussed further, and sources are given in Chapter 4. The claims of current levels of debt and prejudice are given in detail in Chapter 5. Chapter 6 provides a breakdown of wealth, housing and automobile statistics. And Chapter 7 is concerned with statistics on rising mental ill health and general despair.

[52] Excluding wealth hidden offshore, they held 21.5 per cent of all wealth. That 2 per cent extra (23.5-21.5) shared among 0.1 per cent of the population is 20 times arithmetic mean wealth holding. The rest of the 1 per cent hold about 13.5 per cent of all wealth, some 13.5 times the mean average wealth, but 16 times less than the 0.1 per cent hold. Because wealth is so skewed, 9 out of 10 Americans don't even have the mean average wealth. And as one wealthy US citizen put it: 'The more money that you have, the easier it becomes to hide that and avoid taxes' (Smialek, J., 2014, 'The 1% may be richer than you think, research shows', *Bloomberg*, 7 August, www.bloomberg.com/news/2014-08-06/the-1-may-be-richer-than-you-think-research-shows.html, reporting on work by Philip Vermeulen and Gabriel Zucman, and quoting Jeffrey Hollender).

[53] Dorling, D., Rigby, J., Wheeler, B., Ballas, D., Thomas, B., Fahmy, E., Gordon, D. and Lupton, R. (2007) *Poverty, wealth and place in Britain, 1968 to 2005*, Bristol: Policy Press.

[54] Those who labour hardest in the world have the least wealth. Those who have most wealth need to (and usually do) labour least. The most cursory observation of the lives of the poor in poor countries and comparison with the lives of the rich in affluent nations reveals this.

[55] Sabel, C., Dorling, D. and Hiscock, R. (2007) 'Sources of income, wealth and the length of life: an individual level study of mortality', *Critical Public Health*, vol 17, no 4, pp 293-310.

[56] Of the 25 richest countries in the world, the US and the UK ranked as second and fourth most unequal respectively, when the annual income of the best-off tenth of their population was last consistently compared with that of the poorest tenth. In descending order of inequality the 10 per cent richest/10 per cent poorest income

ratios are: 17.7 Singapore, 15.9 US, 15 Portugal, 13.8 UK, 13.4 Israel, 12.5 Australia, 12.5 New Zealand, 11.6 Italy, 10.3 Spain, 10.2 Greece, 9.4 Canada, 9.4 Ireland, 9.2 Netherlands, 9.1 France, 9 Switzerland, 8.2 Belgium, 8.1 Denmark, 7.8 Korea (Republic of), 7.3 Slovenia, 6.9 Austria, 6.9 Germany, 6.2 Sweden, 6.1 Norway, 5.6 Finland, and 4.5 Japan. This is excluding very small states, and is derived from the UN 2009 *Human Development Report*, Statistical Annex, Table M (http://hdr.undp.org/en/media/HDR_2009_EN_Indicators.pdf).

[57] For instance, in countries with less greed, more people can spend more time doing more useful things than working to try to overcome the outcomes of greed.

[58] The questions begin: 'Been able to concentrate on whatever you are doing?' and end 'Been feeling reasonably happy, all things considered?'

[59] Shaw, M., Dorling, D. and Mitchell, R. (2002) *Health, place and society*, Harlow: Pearson, p 59. This book is now available on creative commons general open-access copyright (http://www.dannydorling.org/?page_id=984)

[60] Dorling, D. and Barford, A. (2009) 'The inequality hypothesis: thesis, antithesis, and a synthesis?', *Health and Place*, vol 15, no 4, pp 1166-9.

Chapter 3

[1] Debrett's advertising suggests that Britain is a meritocracy run by those with the ability to lead. Michael Young's nightmare comes true (Young, M., 1959, *The rise of meritocracy,* London: Thames & Hudson; see www.debretts.com/shop/books/people-of-today-2117.html). The full quote continues: 'Debrett's People of Today recognises the achievements of over 25,000 people drawn from every sector of society, providing the widest possible coverage of any biographical reference book in the UK. Leading figures include: chairmen, chief executives & managing directors of leading companies; members of the medical profession; directors of banks and financial institutions; architects, designers and engineers; artists, composers & musicians; members of the legal profession; directors of marketing & advertising agencies; film, theatre & television actors; editors, publishers and journalists; scientists, academics & educationalists; leading literary figures; sportsmen & sportswomen; bishops and church leaders; MPs, MEPs, MSPs, MLAs and AMs.'

[2] Furness, H. (2013) 'Teenagers from aspirational families suffering "executive stress burnout"', *The Telegraph*, 4 October (www.telegraph.co.uk/health/children_shealth/11140659/Teenagers-from-aspirational-families-suffering-executive-stress-burnout.html).

[3] For one of the clearest explanations of why so much is not so complex, see the work of David Gordon on child poverty. For example: 'The absence of any useful economic theory of child poverty is not a result of the complex nature of this subject. In fact, the economics of child poverty are very simple and are entirely concerned with redistribution – where sufficient resources are redistributed from adults to children there is no child poverty; where insufficient resources are redistributed from adults to children child poverty is inevitable' (Gordon, D., 2008, 'Children, policy and social justice', in G. Craig, T. Burchardt and D. Gordon [eds] *Social justice and public policy: Seeking fairness in diverse societies*, Bristol: Policy Press, pp 157-79, at p 166).

[4] Dorling, D. (2013) *The 32 stops: The central line*, London: Particular Books.

[5] Using data released in 2014, collected in 2012 that is available here (although tables M1, S1 and R1 have to be summed) (http://nces.ed.gov/pubs2014/2014024_tables.pdf), and described in detail here (and already summed): OECD (Organisation for Economic Co-operation and Development) (2007) *The Programme for International*

Student Assessment (PISA), OECD's latest PISA study of learning skills among 15-year-olds, Paris: OECD, p 20.

[6] As above; OECD (Organisation for Economic Co-operation and Development) (2009) *PISA 2006 technical report, OECD's technical report on the latest PISA study of learning skills among 15-year-olds*, Paris: OECD.

[7] For all of these phrases, see OECD (Organisation for Economic Co-operation and Development) (2007) *PISA, OECD's latest PISA study of learning skills among 15-year-olds*, Paris: OECD, pp 7 and 14.

[8] Published in 2014, the 2012 proportions of children achieving the top level 6 in the UK in mathematics, science and literature respectively were 2.9, 1.8 and 1.3 per cent. The average of these is 2.0 per cent, which compares to the published average 2006 figure of 2.9 per cent or almost a third less. The OECD no longer publish a combined average, just as they no longer use the same labels, but none of their methodology has changed. Of course the number of students who excel in all three areas of mathematics, science and literacy is low. In the December 2013 publication of the *New Zealand PISA 2012* results, it was estimated to be just 8.0 per cent out of 21 per cent of candidates; in the OECD as a whole, just 4.4 per cent out of 16.2 per cent. See p 14 of www.minedu.govt.nz/~/media/MinEdu/Files/EducationSectors/InternationalEducation/ForInternationalStudentsAndParents/PISA2012PresentationPDF.pdf

[9] Wilby, P. (2013) 'The OECD's Pisa delivery man', *The Guardian*, 26 November (www.theguardian.com/education/2013/nov/26/pisa-international-student-tests-oecd), and Ripley, A. (2011) 'The world's schoolmaster', *The Atlantic*, 7 June (www.theatlantic.com/magazine/archive/2011/07/the-worlds-schoolmaster/308532/).

[10] OECD (2007), as above.

[11] Many of the key OECD advisers appear to have vested interests. For example, Andreas Schleicher, Director for Education and Skills and Special Adviser on Education Policy to the Secretary-General at OECD, Paris, is also listed as an adviser to the private education organisation of India, XSEED (see www.schooloftomorrow.in/about-sotx/ last accessed 9 February 2015).

[12] As in the UK in 2009, when 10,000 'extra' places were made available in universities for science, technology, engineering and mathematics students, but in the small print, universities were told that they could also provide more places in business studies and economics. This small print appears to have been kept from the public. Given the huge increase in demand for places that year, and a small increase in cohort size, these 'extra places' were, in practice, a cut in opportunity to study. The newly elected 2010 coalition government then introduced £9,000-a-year fees.

[13] Howell, J. (2014) '"Pull up the drawbridge" say graduates: graduates are more likely than non-graduates to want the amount of people who can study at university to be reduced, a study has found', *Graduate Jobs News*, 7 September (www.graduate-jobs.com/news/12898/_Pull_up_the_drawbridge__say_graduates).

[14] Gerhardt, S. (2004) *Why love matters*, Hove: Brunner-Routledge, p 127.

[15] Glover, J. (2001) *Humanity: A moral history of the twentieth century*, London: Pimlico, p 382; referring, in turn, to the works of Samuel and Pearl Oliner, and of Emilie Guth.

[16] Bauman, Z. (2008) *The art of life*, Cambridge: Polity Press, p 97.

[17] The way in which collaboration occurred in the Channel Island offshoots of the UK that were occupied by Germany during the Second World War is only just being acknowledged today. Similarly, the fact that the high command in Britain, the US and the Soviet Union were not overly concerned about genocide in Europe is a tale also only just beginning to be told.

[18] Goldberg, D.T. (2009) *The threat of race: Reflections on racial neoliberalism*, Oxford: Blackwell, p 155.

[19] Ball, S.J. (2008) *The education debate*, Bristol: Policy Press, p 33; referring, in turn, to a description of the OECD posted on the web by others in May 2002. As a provider of data the OECD does have some uses, and it does, of course, have many supporters, but you have to be so careful in looking for the assumptions made in any data it 'models' that those uses are limited.

[20] OECD (Organisation for Economic Co-operation and Development) (2009) 'History of the OECD' (www.oecd.org/general/historyoftheoecd.htm).

[21] Such as: 'What are all the possible factors that could influence global temperature change apart from carbon dioxide emissions?' The OECD testers give naming one of these as an example of the kind of 'harder questions' they set to be awarded a high score, but they do not give a list of what would be considered suitable answers, although they must have given such a list to their markers (see OECD, 2007, *PISA, OECD's latest PISA study of learning skills among 15-year-olds*, Paris: OECD, p 17).

[22] At least since a century ago: see Tuddenham, R.D. (1948) 'Soldier intelligence in World Wars I and II', *American Psychologist*, vol 3, pp 54-6; and the arguments of Flynn, J.R. (1984) 'The mean IQ of Americans: massive gains 1932 to 1978', *Psychological Bulletin*, vol 95, pp 29-51.

[23] Flynn, J.R. (1987) 'Massive IQ gains in 14 nations', *Psychological Bulletin*, vol 101, pp 171-91.

[24] Two standard deviations below the current mean, according to the Psychological Corporation (2003) *Wechsler Individual Intelligence Test for Children* (4th ed.) WISC-IV, San Antonio, Texus: The Psychological Corporation, p 229), as reported in Flynn, J.R. (2007) *What is intelligence? Beyond the Flynn effect*, Cambridge: Cambridge University Press.

[25] Wilkinson, R.G. (2009) 'Intelligence', D. Dorling, York, personal communication.

[26] Wilkinson, R.G. (2014) 'Eugenists', D. Dorling, Oxford, personal communication.

[27] That country with the maximum of 4 per cent of children at level 6 (genius status) being New Zealand (OECD, 2007, *PISA, OECD's latest PISA study of learning skills among 15-year-olds*, Paris: OECD, p 20), the unsaid implication being that, given this international distribution, even in the best of all possible worlds we should not expect more than, say, 5 per cent of children in rich countries to ever reach level 6. If it were possible for more to do so, then (the testers might argue) that should have occurred somewhere by now. It would not be hard to counter such an argument by pointing to how very high average test scores can easily be achieved for a large group of children simply through hot-housing them in the most expensive of private boarding schools. The outcome often produces children who can pass tests and who have also been led to believe that they should be leaders. By 2014, the OECD was no longer producing average scores across all three subject areas. Its individual results did include some cities and regions in China with higher proportions of the supposedly most able in mathematics: 12.3 per cent in Taipei, 17.7 per cent in Shanghai. But it became obvious that many, if not most, children in such areas were not included in the tests because they were not officially resident, and the rest were being so hot-housed by the authorities that they considered dropping out of the programme: Strauss, V. (2014) 'No 1 Shanghai may drop out of PISA', *The Washington Post*, 26 May.

[28] OECD (Organisation for Economic Co-operation and Development) (2014) *PISA 2012 data tables, figures, and exhibits*, Paris: OECD (http://nces.ed.gov/pubs2014/2014024_tables.pdf).

[29] Note that the technical report was released three years after the survey: OECD (Organisation for Economic Co-operation and Development) (2009) *PISA 2006 technical report, OECD's technical report on the latest PISA study of learning skills among 15-year-olds*, Paris: OECD, p 145.

[30] White, J. (2002) *The child's mind*, London: RoutledgeFalmer, p 76.

[31] Anderson, E.S. (2009) *Schumpeter's evolutionary economics: A theoretical, historical and statistical analysis of the engine of capitalism*, London: Anthem Press, p 87.

[32] You can search the internet and easily find such examples, but it is far more rewarding to be diverted by insights such as that it is: '... factors in modernized societies that have made music a specialty – individuality, competitiveness, compartmentalization, and institutionalization [are not found].... In small-scale pre-modern societies (and in any large modern sub-Saharan African city, as well as in children anywhere who are customarily exposed to frequent communal musical activity), everyone participates in music – regularly, spontaneously, and wholeheartedly' (Dissanayake, E., 2005, 'A review of *The singing Neanderthals: The origins of music, language, mind and body* by Steven Mithen', *Evolutionary Psychology*, vol 3, pp 375-80, at p 379).

[33] Jolly, R. (2007) 'Early childhood development: the global challenge', *The Lancet*, vol 369, no 9555, 6 January, pp 1-78, at p 8.

[34] The idea of innate intelligence is the idea that human brains are wired so that people who are good at some things are more often good at others, and that correlation cannot be greatly influenced by society. James Flynn has recently explained (while discussing Clancy Blair's findings) that: 'The only thing that could prevent society from unravelling the correlational matrix would be brain physiology: a human brain so structured that no single cognitive ability could be enhanced without enhancing all of them. As Blair triumphantly shows, the brain is not like that' (Flynn, J.R., 2006, 'Towards a theory of intelligence beyond g', *Behavioral and Brain Sciences*, vol 29, no 2, pp 132-4, at p 132).

[35] Kamin, L.J. (1981) 'Some historical facts about IQ testing', in S. Raby (ed) *Intelligence: The battle for the mind*, London: Pan Books, pp 90-7.

[36] Howe, M.J.A., Davidson, J.W. and Sloboda, J.A. (1999) 'Innate talents: reality or myth?', in S.J. Ceci and W.M. Williams (eds) *The nature–nurture debate: The essential readings*, Oxford: Blackwell, pp 258-90, at p 279.

[37] Clark, L. (2009) 'Middle-class children have better genes, says former schools chief ... and we just have to accept it', *The Daily Mail*, 13 May.

[38] Wilkinson, R.G. and Pickett, K. (2009) *The spirit level: Why more equal societies almost always do better*, London: Allen Lane; see Chapter 8 on education and comments on ethnicity on pp 177-9.

[39] Since the first edition of this book was published, genome-wide effects have been found that suggest possible tiny influences of particular inherent (but not inherited) dispositions to be good at particular tests. For example, in measured English ability for children aged 11-14, the genome-wide association is very small. As the authors of the study who discovered this put it: 'Put another way, these differences approximate to a tenth of that seen across the sexes for performance in English at this age' (Ward, M., McMahon, G., St Pourcain, B., Evans, D., Rietfeld, C., Benjamin, D., Koellinger, P., Cesarini, D., The Social Science Genetic Association Consortium, Davey Smith, G. and Timpson, N.J., 2014, 'Genetic variation associated with differential educational attainment in adults has anticipated associations with school performance in children', *PLOS One*, 17 July).

[40] For more recent criticisms of twin studies see Wrigley, T. (2014) 'The zombie theory of innate IQ', *Education for Liberation*, no 8, April; see also http://changingschools.

org.uk/E4L%20zombie%20IQ.pdf which points out that in sibling studies that suggest all siblings have a similarly shared environment, '... identical twins are often persuaded into dressing the same and doing things together. They are likely to be in the same class, have the same maths teachers, work together on homework and so on.' See also Wrigley, T. (2014) 'Bad science, worse politics', *Education for Liberation*, no 8 (http://changingschools.org.uk/E4L%20Bad%20science%20worse%20politics.pdf), and Rose, S. (2014) 'Is genius in the genes?', *Times Educational Supplement*, 23 January (www.tes.co.uk/article.aspx?storycode=6395677).

41 Some people suggest that it could be genetic similarities in the structure of the brains of identical twins that may cause them to behave slightly differently to other pupils in class, and that difference could then be greatly magnified by environmental factors. There is, however, no evidence for this, whereas there is a great deal of evidence to suggest that teachers and other key individuals treat children slightly differently according to their appearance, and, of course, the one thing we know about identical twins is that they tend to look very much like each other. You might think this point is obvious, but it is remarkable how well those involved in twin studies have ignored it. For one of the most insightful discussions, which does not discount the genetic possibilities, but which says they are so tiny that by implicit implication appearance could be as important, see the open-access copy of James Flynn's December 2006 lecture at Trinity College Cambridge (www.psychometrics.cam.ac.uk/about-us/directory/beyond-the-flynn-effect); the full-length version of the argument is in Flynn, J.R. (2007) *What is intelligence? Beyond the Flynn effect*, Cambridge: Cambridge University Press.

42 Gladwell, M. (2007) 'What IQ doesn't tell you about race', *The New Yorker*, 17 December.

43 Goldberg, D.T. (2009) *The threat of race: Reflections on racial neoliberalism*, Oxford: Blackwell, p vi. The US prison population actually peaked in 1939 and fell then to a low in 1968, when incarceration rates were much less than 10 times below contemporary rates; see Vogel, R.D. (2004) 'Silencing the cells: mass incarceration and legal repression in US prisons', *Monthly Review*, vol 56, no 1.

44 Literally as well as metaphorically, as entertainment and sport were the two fields in which black Americans were allowed to partake. With Ronald Reagan's election, politics and entertainment merged, and as well as B-movie appearances, political bit parts too became possible for a miniscule minority of the black minority. President Obama himself was no great break from elitism. He was educated in the most prestigious private school in Honolulu as a child. See Elliot Major, L. (2008) 'A British Obama would need an elite education', *The Independent*, 27 November.

45 Corver, M. (2014) 'What happens when you change fees and number controls? Some answers from UCAS' analysis', Cheltenham: UCAS, 1 October.

46 Ball, S.J. (2008) *The education debate*, Bristol: Policy Press, p 70.

47 Timmins, N. (2001) *The five giants: A biography of the welfare state* (new edn), London: HarperCollins, p 380.

48 Downes, T.A. and Greenstein, S.M. (2002) 'Entry into the schooling market: how is the behaviour of private suppliers influenced by public sector decisions?', *Bulletin of Economic Research*, vol 54, no 4, pp 341-71, at p 349.

49 Downes and Greenstein (2002), as above, p 342.

50 Dorling, D., Shaw, M. and Davey Smith, G. (2006) 'Global inequality of life expectancy due to AIDS', *British Medical Journal*, vol 332, no 7542, pp 662-4, at p 664, figure 4.

51 Dorling, D. (2006) 'Class alignment', *Renewal: The Journal of Labour Politics*, vol 14, no 1, pp 8-19.

[52] George, S. (2008) *Hijacking America: How the religious and secular right changed what Americans think*, Cambridge: Polity Press, p 213.

[53] OECD (Organisation for Economic Co-operation and Development) (2014) *Education statistics at a glance*, Paris: OECD, Chart B3.3 (www.oecd-ilibrary.org/education/education-at-a-glance-2014_eag-2014-en).

[54] To see the end result of what happens with educational corruption, it is worth looking at India where it is more explicit: 'Cheating happens at every level. Students bribe to get admission and good results. Research students get professors to write their dissertations. And the professors cheat too, publishing articles in bogus journals' (Jeffrey, C., 2014, 'The students who feel they have the right to cheat', *BBC News Magazine*, 9 November, www.bbc.co.uk/news/magazine-29950843).

[55] Until 2008, spending in the US was always greater for incumbent Republicans compared to Democrats, and higher in years of rising incomes. The two parties only came close when postwar spending was lowest in 1952. See Bartels, L.M. (2008) *Unequal democracy: The political economy of the new gilded age*, Princeton, NJ: Princeton University Press, p 119.

[56] Goldberg, D.T. (2009) *The threat of race: Reflections on racial neoliberalism*, Oxford: Blackwell, p 70.

[57] Perelman, M. (2006) 'Privatizing education', *Monthly Review*, vol 57, no 10.

[58] Mihalyfy, D.F. (2014) 'Higher education's aristocrats', *Jacobin Magazine*, 27 September (www.jacobinmag.com/2014/09/higher-educations-aristocrats/).

[59] Irvin, G. (2008) *Super rich: The rise of inequality in Britain and the United States*, Cambridge: Polity Press, p 158; quoting Jonathan Kozol in *Harpers Magazine*, September 2005, pp 48-9, in turn, quoting from the headteacher who called the pupils he created 'robots'.

[60] See Giroux, H.A. and Saltman, K. (2008) 'Obama's betrayal of public education? Arne Duncan and the corporate model of schooling', Truthout (www.truthout.org/121708R).

[61] Petrill, M.J. (2014) 'Arne Duncan's office of civil rights: six years of meddling', *The National Review*, 10 October (www.nationalreview.com/education-week/389992/arne-duncans-office-civil-rights-six-years-meddling-michael-j-petrilli).

[62] Tomlinson, S. (2007) 'Learning to compete', *Renewal: A Journal of Social Democracy*, vol 15, nos 2/3, pp 117-22, at p 120. The 57 varieties include numerous types of specialist school, 'beacons', 'academies' and many other flavours of division.

[63] Goldberg, D.T. (2009) *The threat of race: Reflections on racial neoliberalism*, Oxford: Blackwell, p 78.

[64] Seton-Rogers, S. (2003) 'Watson, Crick, and who?', *Web Weekly: News from the Harvard Medical Community*, 7 April.

[65] BBC News (2007) 'Lab suspends DNA pioneer Watson', 19 October (http://news.bbc.co.uk/2/hi/science/nature/7052416.stm).

[66] Connelly, M. (2008) *Fatal misconception: The struggle to control world population*, Cambridge, MA: Harvard University Press, p 272; Shockley's prize was given to him and two others for the invention of the transistor, the key to early computing.

[67] 'Francis Crick's controversial archive on first public display', see www.wellcome.ac.uk/News/Media-office/Press-release-archive/WTD002850.htm

[68] Not simply as a result of having no great prizes, but perhaps also as a product of a little more understanding and acceptance of humanity, is the arrangement of prestige in academic journals and departments in the social sciences, arts and humanities, which is far less hierarchical than is often found in other academic disciplines. Of course, generalisations such as this are not rules. The longest-lived person to have received two Nobel Prizes, Fred Sanger (1918–2013), appears a remarkably humane biochemist

despite leading quite a closeted life. Linus Pauling (1901–94) similarly showed it was possible to be more than just a chemist, and won two prizes. These were for such different things that he is the only person counted twice in Figure 4 (this volume).

[69] The Post-Autistic Economics Network and the Association of Heterodox Economists have pointed out how ridiculous traditional economics has become. Orthodox economists produce 'dictionaries' of their subject where almost 90 per cent of the 'great economists' listed are men from just eight US Ivy League universities. Just as it is a little unfair on those with autism to link them to those who have chosen to be economists, so, too, it is a little unfair on the 'mad' (who are often far more sane) to repeat the oft-told retort that only the mad and traditional economists believe that growth is forever possible; even prizewinners such as Joe Stiglitz now criticise economics as it is traditionally taught. For these stories and more, see Scott Cato, M. (2009) *Green economics: An introduction to theory, policy and practice*, London: Earthscan, pp 25 and 31.

[70] Rogoff, K. (2002) 'An open letter to Joseph Stiglitz', International Monetary Fund (www.imf.org/external/np/vc/2002/070202.htm); see also Kay, J. (2004) *The truth about markets: Why some nations are rich but most remain poor* (2nd edn), London: Penguin, p 381 for references to economists slandering one another. And on the errors later found in Rogoff's work, see Cassidy, J. (2013) 'The Reinhart and Rogoff controversy: a summing up', *The New Yorker*, 26 April.

[71] Irvin, G. (2008) *Super rich: The rise of inequality in Britain and the United States*, Cambridge: Polity Press, p 157.

[72] McDermott, K. (2013) 'Sending a child to nursery is now "more expensive than paying for private school", after cost of a full-time place doubles in a decade', *The Daily Mail*, 6 March (www.dailymail.co.uk/news/article-2288839/Sending-child-nursery-expensive-private-school-cost-time-place-doubles-decade.html).

[73] Mayer, S.E. (2001) 'How did the increase in economic inequality between 1970 and 1990 affect children's educational attainment?', *American Journal of Sociology*, vol 107, no 1, pp 1-32.

[74] Even as late as 1982, a child such a Nigel Farage could leave the prestigious Dulwich College public school in London and get a job in the City of London at age 18, bypassing university.

[75] In Britain in 1997, Gordon Marshall, the then head of the nation's Economic and Social Research Council (ESRC), and his colleagues suggested that there was the possibility: '... that children born to working-class parents simply have less natural ability than those born to higher-class parents' (documented in White, S., 2007, *Equality*, Cambridge: Polity Press, at p 66). It may be a tad cruel to the facially disfigured, but it is now often stated that the lie that the upper classes have better genes is simply propagated by ignorant chinless wonders whose only valid claim to special genetic inheritance is their lack of chin. Faced with increasing vocal and sustained opposition to their claims to be innately superior, those who have been told they are superior often retreat into self-supporting social bubbles for security. Within such comfort bubbles it is easier to believe statements such as that children born to working-class parents simply have less natural ability than children born to upper-class parents.

[76] Di Muzio, T. (2015) *The 1% and the rest of us: A political economy of dominate ownership*, London, Zed Books, p 153, quoting as examples: Frank on 'Richistan', Freeland on 'Plutocrats', and Jim Taylor, Doug Harrison and Stephen Kraus (2009) *The new elite: Inside the minds of the truly wealthy*, New York: Amacom.

[77] '... children of different class backgrounds tend to do better or worse in school – on account, one may suppose, of a complex interplay of sociocultural and genetic factors'

(Goldthorpe, J. and Jackson, M., 2007, 'Education-based meritocracy: the barriers to its realization', *Economic Change, Quality of Life and Social Cohesion*, 6th Framework Network, www.readbag.com/equalsoc-uploaded-files-regular-goldthorpe-jackson).

[78] Ellis, L., Hershberger, S., Field, E. et al (2008) *Sex differences: Summarizing more than a century of scientific research*, New York: Psychology Press; see p 405 on autism, p 321 on mathematics, p 324 on science, and p 355 on males rating their abilities highly during adolescence.

[79] Ward, M., McMahon, G., St Pourcain, B., Evans, D., Rietfeld, C., Benjamin, D., Koellinger, P., Cesarini, D., The Social Science Genetic Association Consortium, Davey Smith, G. and Timpson, N.J. (2014) 'Genetic variation associated with differential educational attainment in adults has anticipated associations with school performance in children', *PLOS One*, 17 July.

[80] Rose, S.P.R. (2006) 'Commentary: Heritability estimates – long past their sell-by date', *International Journal of Epidemiology*, vol 35, no 3, pp 525-7.

[81] Identifying potential 'Oxbridge material' was an old term used in England for such practices before they became institutionalised. The idea that different people are made of different mental 'material' was most commonly espoused in the era of 1920s and 1930s eugenics, when those who advocated the inheritability of intelligence wrote that it '… is seen with especial clearness in these numerous cases – like the Cecils, or the Darwins – where intellectual ability runs in families' (Wells, H.G., Huxley, J. and Wells, G.P., 1931, *The science of life*, London: Cassell and Company Limited, p 823). That the offspring of such families do not now dominate intellectual life provides an extra spoonful of evidence to add to the great pile built up since the 1930s that now discredits eugenics and other such '… foolish analogies between biology and society [whereby the world's richest man] … Rockefeller was acclaimed the highest form of human being that evolution had produced, a use denounced even by William Graham Sumner, the great "Social Darwinist"' (Flynn, J.R., 2007, *What is intelligence? Beyond the Flynn effect*, Cambridge: Cambridge University Press, pp 147-8).

[82] Asbury, K. (2014) 'Better at reading than maths? Don't blame it all on your genes', *The Conversation*, 14 July (https://theconversation.com/better-at-reading-than-maths-dont-blame-it-all-on-your-genes-28947).

[83] The number of women expected to be awarded prizes in every decade from 1901 onwards has always been less than five, so the statistical test that is taught to novice students of probability cannot be applied. However, in an exact test, if the process is random, and on average 4.9 per cent of prizes were awarded to women each year before 1950, then over the 15 years 1948–62 (inclusive) and the five prizes then available, the chance that not a single woman would be awarded a prize in any year is $(1-0.049)^{(15*5)}=0.023$ or 2.3% (if all prize giving is independent).

[84] Currently, 1901-63 for peace, physics, chemistry or literature, or 1901-53 for physiology or medicine (www.nobelprize.org/nomination/archive/). The names of the nominees cannot be revealed until 50 years later. Note that the Women's International League for Peace and Freedom (WILPF) was nominated every year in the late 1950s, albeit mostly by women (www.nobelprize.org/nomination/archive/show_people.php?id=10295).

[85] Walter Lippmann, who was also an early critic of IQ testing, quoted in Kamin, L.J. (1981) 'Some historical facts about IQ testing', in S. Raby (ed) *Intelligence: The battle for the mind*, London: Pan Books, pp, 90-7, at p 90. Just as Albert Einstein came to regret the work he had done that was later used to develop the nuclear bomb, so Walter Lippmann regretted that which his early work was later used to produce.

[86] Howe, M.J.A., Davidson, J.W. and Sloboda, J.A. (1999) 'Innate talents: reality or myth?', in S.J. Ceci and W. M. Williams (eds) *The nature–nurture debate: The essential readings*, Oxford: Blackwell, pp 258-90.

[87] Timmins, N. (2001) *The five giants: A biography of the welfare state* (new edn), London: HarperCollins, p 380. Note that there were also a few technical schools, but they never caught on so are not mentioned further here, apart from saying that they were early evidence of beliefs in a continuum.

[88] A significant few had been deemed not educable until the Education Act of 1981 decreed that none were to be obviously warehoused (or 'garaged') any longer, all having a right to some kind of education.

[89] Wilkinson, R.G. and Pickett, K. (2009) *The spirit level: Why more equal societies almost always do better*, London: Allen Lane, p 238.

[90] Ministry of Education (2013) *PISA 2012: Summary of results*, Wellington: New Zealand Government (www.minedu.govt.nz/~/media/MinEdu/Files/EducationSectors/InternationalEducation/ForInternationalStudentsAndParents/PISA2012PresentationPDF.pdf).

[91] Gillborn, D. and Youdell, D. (2000) *Rationing education: Policy practice, reform and equity*, Buckingham: Open University Press.

[92] Hirschfield, P.J. (2008) 'Preparing for prison? The criminalization of school discipline in the USA', *Theoretical Criminology*, vol 12, no 1, pp 79-101, at pp 79, 82.

[93] Orr, D. (2008) 'Proof that we fail too many children', *The Independent*, 19 March.

[94] Rwanda only ranks similarly to the US if those awaiting trial for war crimes are included; for the ranking by civilian crimes see the Worldmapper website, in particular, www.worldmapper.org/posters/worldmapper_map293_ver5.pdf

[95] This figure is for Canada, but there is no reason to presume it does not follow more widely: O'Brien, M. (2014) 'Poor kids who do everything right don't do better than rich kids who do everything wrong', *The Washington Post*, 18 October (www.washingtonpost.com/blogs/wonkblog/wp/2014/10/18/poor-kids-who-do-everything-right-dont-do-better-than-rich-kids-who-do-everything-wrong/).

[96] The most expensive course in the country as of early 2014: Kyprianou, A.E. (2014) 'The UK financial mathematics MSc', 29 May, p 10 (http://arxiv.org/abs/1405.6739).

[97] The likelihood of children from different areas getting to university and to different types of university is mapped in Thomas, B. and Dorling, D. (2007) *Identity in Britain: A cradle-to-grave atlas*, Bristol: Policy Press, which uses data from studies that show that in absolute terms, almost all the extra places went to children resident in the already most 'privileged' areas. In January 2010 the Higher Education Funding Council for England published research showing a reverse in the trend. See Dorling, D. (2010) 'Expert opinion', *The Guardian*, 28 January, p 10. But by late 2014, UCAS was showing that this brief reversal had itself been reversed (in press, see note 45 above).

[98] Ball, S.J. (2008) *The education debate*, Bristol: Policy Press, p 180, criticising and quoting from p 20, para 1.28 of the 2005 White Paper *Higher standards: Better schools for all*, Department for Education and Skills, emphasis added.

[99] Dorling, D. (2014) *Inequality and the 1%*, London: Verso, p 40.

[100] Stanton, A. (2007) *Mr Gum and the biscuit billionaire*, London: Egmont, p 66. Incidentally, it has been convincingly argued that J.K. Rowling, author of *Harry Potter*, based her main character on Tony Blair, and that Harry's fortunes mirrored his, so all is still far from utopia in the world of children's stories. 'Rowling is Blair's triumph (single mum becomes billionaire) and dark mirror' (Kelly, S., 2008. 'Novelising New Labour', *Renewal*, vol 16, no 2, pp 52-9, at p 58).

[101] Gillborn, D. and Youdell, D. (2000) *Rationing education: Policy practice, reform and equity*, Buckingham: Open University Press, p 221.

[102] Ball, S.J. (2008) *The education debate*, Bristol: Policy Press, p 173, referring to *The Independent on Sunday*'s release of an unpublished Department for Education and Skills report, during December 2006.

[103] Higgins, S., Katsipataki, M., Kokotsaki D., Coleman, E., Major, L.E. and Coe, R. (2014) *The Sutton Trust Education Endowment Foundation teaching and learning toolkit*, Education Endowment Foundation (educationendowmentfoundation.org.uk).

[104] Wilkinson, R.G. and Pickett, K. (2009) *The spirit level: Why more equal societies almost always do better*, London: Allen Lane, p 115.

[105] McCarthy, M. (2008) 'The big question: is it time the world forgot about cannabis in its war against drugs?', *The Independent*, 3 October. Jonathan Adair Turner, who also goes by the title of Baron Turner of Ecchinswell, was a banker who was a Conservative student, but joined the British Social Democratic Party when it was formed, and then became a favourite of the Labour government. This was all possible without the need for him to alter a single conviction, such was the shift in British politics from 1979 to 1997.

[106] Crim, K. (2005) 'Notes on the intelligence of women', *The Atlantic*, 18 May. Although Larry was taken to task, within just four years he was appointed to advise President Obama on economics. It is reported that in April 2009 he fell asleep on the job (http://thinkprogress.org/2009/04/23/summerssleep/). Apparently he uses diet coke to try to stay awake. For some advice Larry was given of how to stay awake and be smarter, see www.huffingtonpost.com/2009/04/23/larry-summers-falls-aslee_n_190659.html

[107] Clarida, M.Q. (2014) 'Professor Summers', *The Harvard Crimson*, 23 October (www.thecrimson.com/article/2014/10/23/larry-summers-profile/).

[108] Dorling, D. (2013) *Population 10 billion: The coming demographic crisis and how to survive it*, London: Constable.

[109] In the first edition of this book the date given was 2052. Since then, the UN has raised its projection slightly and delayed the date, and so I have altered the text, but I have also published a book suggesting that it may now have over-estimated through failing to recognise a temporary baby boom as temporary (see note 108 above for details of the book in which these claims are made). Here is what I wrote in 2010, which I think still holds: It is now largely accepted that fertility decline in the world is approaching replacement levels, according to UN central population projections (see www.worldmapper.org on the 2050 projection and technical notes available there). The driving force in this has not been the availability of contraceptives; these have been necessary but are not sufficient. Fertility falls when elitism is overcome enough for women to be allowed to learn and to gain just enough personal power to decide more for themselves. As a result we are now some way past the point where 'Nearly half of the world's population … lives in countries with fertility at or below replacement levels' (Morgan, S.P. and Taylor, M.G., 2006, 'Low fertility at the turn of the twenty-first century', *Annual Review of Sociology*, vol 32, no 1, pp 375-99, at p 375). And, as fertility falls faster during economic slumps, we may be even further past that point than we currently realise. The date of 2052 is given as this article suggests that it will be just after the mid-century when, worldwide, human population stops rising. It may be earlier. It is unlikely to be later.

[110] Fertility in China fell from 6.4 children per woman to 2.7 in just that one decade immediately preceding the introduction of the one child policy: Connelly, M. (2008) *Fatal misconception: The struggle to control world population*, Cambridge, MA: Harvard University Press, p 570.

[111] Wilkinson, R.G. (2009) 'Rank', D. Dorling, York, personal communication.

Chapter 4

[1] A petition was started calling for the Conservative Party councillor to resign. She then claimed her comment had been taken out of context: Grafton-Green, P. (2014) 'Bromley councillor denies making insensitive comments about suicide', *This is London*, 5 June (www.thisislocallondon.co.uk/news/11258899.Bromley_councillor_denies_making_insensitive_comments_about_suicide/).

[2] Morris, N. (2013) 'Majority of British children will soon be growing up in families struggling "below the breadline", Government warned', *The Independent*, 13 March (www.independent.co.uk/news/uk/politics/majority-of-british-children-will-soon-be-growing-up-in-families-struggling-below-the-breadline-government-warned-8531584.html).

[3] Laverne, L. (2014) 'How come we can't fix child poverty but we can spend billions replacing Trident?', *The Observer*, 12 October (www.theguardian.com/lifeandstyle/2014/oct/12/cant-fix-child-poverty-but-spend-billions-replacing-trident-lauren-laverne).

[4] Quoted in Purdam, K., Garratt, E. and Esmail, A. (2014) *Hungry? Food insecurity, social stigma and embarrassment in the UK*, Manchester: University of Manchester Institute for Collaborative Research on Ageing and Manchester City Council. Personal correspondence with Kingsley Purdam.

[5] Adams, A. and Levell, P. (2014) *Measuring poverty when inflation varies across households*, York: Joseph Rowntree Foundation (www.jrf.org.uk/publications/measuring-poverty-inflation).

[6] Wilkinson, R.G. and Pickett, K. (2009) *The spirit level: Why more equal societies almost always do better*, London: Allen Lane, p 143.

[7] Worstall, T. (2013) 'Astonishing numbers: America's poor still live better than most of the rest of humanity', *Forbes Magazine*, 1 June (www.forbes.com/sites/timworstall/2013/06/01/astonishing-numbers-americas-poor-still-live-better-than-most-of-the-rest-of-humanity/).

[8] Hickel, J. (2014) 'Exposing the great "poverty reduction" lie', *Al Jazeera News*, 21 August (www.aljazeera.com/indepth/opinion/2014/08/exposing-great-poverty-reductio-201481211590729809.html).

[9] Hardoon, D. (2014) 'The devil is in the data', Mind the gap: Discussion and debate about social justice issues, *Oxfam Blog*, 15 October (http://oxfamblogs.org/mindthegap/2014/10/15/the-devil-is-in-the-data-2/).

[10] Alesina, A., Tella, R.D. and MacCulloch, R. (2004) 'Inequality and happiness: are Europeans and Americans different?', *Journal of Public Economics*, vol 88, pp 2009-42.

[11] Wolff, J. and de-Shalit, A. (2007) *Disadvantage*, Oxford: Oxford University Press, p 110, using arguments from Bradshaw, J. and Finch, N. (2003) 'Overlaps in dimensions of poverty', *Journal of Social Policy*, vol 32, no 4, pp 513-25.

[12] UNICEF (2014) *Guide to estimating child poverty*, Regional Office for Latin America and the Caribbean: United Nations (http://dds.cepal.org/infancia/guide-to-estimating-child-poverty/presentation.php), which also includes the words 'achieving their full potential' as it was, in turn, drawn from *The state of the world's children* report of 2005, which used the phrase many times (www.unicef.org/sowc05/english/sowc05.pdf). In contrast, the 2014 report hardly uses it at all, referring to Article 6 of the 1989 Convention on the Rights of the Child: 'All children have a right to life, and to survive and develop – physically, mentally, spiritually, morally, psychologically and socially – to

their full potential.' Few drafting that right will have realised that the phrase 'potential' could be turned around to imply that these rights were largely attained because so many are now said to have such low potential. On the 25th anniversary of the 1989 Declaration of the Rights of the Child, the UN emphasised that the rights were for all children, and did not mention 'potential' once. See 'On the occasion of the 25th anniversary of the Convention on The Rights of the Child: Stepping up the global effort to advance the rights of every child', 20 November 2014 (www.childhood.org/2014/11/20/25th-anniversary-of-the-convention-on-the-rights-of-the-child/).

[13] See www.poverty.ac.uk/editorial/pse-team-calls-government-tackle-rising-deprivation: 'Almost 18 million people cannot afford adequate housing conditions; 12 million people are too poor to engage in common social activities; one in three people cannot afford to heat their homes adequately in the winter and four million children and adults aren't properly fed by today's standards. One in every six (17 per cent) adults in paid work are poor', and from www2.rgu.ac.uk/publicpolicy/introduction/needf.htm: 'Poverty, like all need, is defined in terms of the society where it takes place: what people can eat, and where they can live, depend on the society they live in. That does not mean that it is based on a comparison with others in the same society; there are some countries where most people are poor.'

[14] Dorling, D., Rigby, J., Wheeler, B., Ballas, D., Thomas, B., Fahmy, E., Gordon, D. and Lupton, R. (2007) *Poverty, wealth and place in Britain, 1968 to 2005*, Bristol: Policy Press.

[15] Lucchino, P. and Morelli, S. (2012) *Inequality, debt and growth*, London: Resolution Foundation. Summarised at www.poverty.ac.uk/report-low-income-households-debt-housing/poorest-households-%E2%80%98borrowed-spend%E2%80%99-prior-crisis

[16] Bradshaw, J. and Main, G. (2014) *Impact of the recession on child poverty and deprivation in the UK*, Poverty and Social Exclusion Reports, Table 3 (www.poverty.ac.uk/editorial/impact-recession-child-poverty-and-deprivation-uk).

[17] Irvin, G. (2008) *Super rich: The rise of inequality in Britain and the United States*, Cambridge: Polity Press, p 189. A fifth of the entire population had outstanding debt on credit cards by 2007; they were no longer a middle-class-only niche: ONS (Office for National Statistics) (2008) *Wealth and Assets Survey: Initial report*, London: ONS.

[18] Hyde, D. (2013) 'Britain has "third worst credit addiction" in Europe: only Romanians and Turks are more likely than Britons to put increased Christmas spending on credit cards this year', *The Telegraph*, 18 December (www.telegraph.co.uk/finance/personalfinance/borrowing/creditcards/10525354/Britain-has-third-worst-credit-addiction-in-Europe.html).

[19] The 1968/69 Poverty Survey of Britain showed this to be the case. See Dorling, D., Rigby, J., Wheeler, B., Ballas, D., Thomas, B., Fahmy, E., Gordon, D. and Lupton, R (2007) *Poverty, wealth and place in Britain*, 1968 to 2005, Bristol: Policy Press.

[20] ONS (Office for National Statistics) (2013) *Poverty and social exclusion in the UK and EU, 2005-2011*, London: ONS, 16 January (www.ons.gov.uk/ons/dcp171776_295020.pdf).

[21] Ballas, D. and Dorling, D. (2007) 'Measuring the impact of major life events upon happiness', *International Journal of Epidemiology*, vol 36, no 6, pp 1244-52, table 3, which suggests that in essence, bad and good holiday experiences tend to balance out, and that holidays not taken with family tend to be associated with a slightly more positive outcome.

[22] In 1759, Adam Smith wrote about the linen shirt and shoes and has been endlessly quoted thereafter. In 1847, Karl Marx wrote on how homes would appear as hovels

if a castle was built nearby. In 1901, Seebohm Rowntree wrote on the necessity of being able to afford a stamp to write a letter to a loved one.

23 Karl Polanyi's writing of 1944, quoted in Magdoff, H. and Magdoff, F. (2005) 'Approaching socialism', *Monthly Review*, vol 57, no 3.

24 Bobak, M., Jha, P., Hguyen, S. and Jarvis, M. (2000) 'Poverty and smoking', in P. Jha and F. Chaloupka (eds) *Tobacco control in developing countries*, Oxford University Press for The World Bank and World Health Organization, pp 41-61 (http://siteresources.worldbank.org/INTETC/Resources/375990-1089904539172/041TO062.PDF).

25 Almond, S. and Kendall, J. (2001) 'Low pay in the UK: the case for a three sector comparative approach', *Annals of Public and Cooperative Economics*, vol 72, no 1, pp 45-76, at p 45.

26 Offer, A. (2006) *The challenge of affluence: Self-control and well-being in the United States and Britain since 1950*, Oxford: Oxford University Press, pp 234, 292.

27 Frank, R.H. (2007) *Falling behind: How rising inequality harms the middle class*, Berkeley, CA: University of California Press, p 4.

28 Burns, J. (2007) *The descent of madness: Evolutionary origins of psychosis and the social brain*, Hove: Routledge, pp 99, 136, 184-5.

29 Aldridge, H., Bushe, S., Kenway, P., MacInnes, T. and Tinson, A. (2013) *London's poverty profile 2013*, London: Trust for London, Figure 2.6 (www.londonspovertyprofile.org.uk/LPP_2013_Report_Web.pdf).

30 GLA (Greater London Authority) (2002) *London divided: Income inequality and poverty in the capital*, London: GLA; p 11 of the summary reported that some 20 per cent of children were living in families that could not save £10 a month or afford to take a holiday other than by visiting and staying with family.

31 O'Hara, M. (2014) *Austerity bites*, Bristol: Policy Press.

32 For 2001, see p 64 of GLA (above). For 2012, see Gordon, D., Mack, J. et al (2013) *The impoverishment of the UK: PSE UK first results: Living standards*, Swindon: Economic and Social Research Council (www.poverty.ac.uk/system/files/attachments/The_Impoverishment_of_the_UK_PSE_UK_first_results_summary_report_March_28.pdf).

33 Raymond Baker, Director of Global Financial Integrity, and a respected authority on money laundering and corruption, quoted in Mathiason, N. (2007) 'Tax evasion taskforce to probe UK: international group will track $1 trillion of illicit funds', *The Observer*, 1 July.

34 Shah, H. and McIvor, M. (2006) *A new political economy: Compass Programme for Renewal*, London: Lawrence & Wishart, p 110.

35 Merrill, J. (2014) 'Number of global billionaires has doubled since the financial crisis', *The Independent*, 29 October (www.independent.co.uk/news/world/politics/number-of-global-billionaires-has-doubled-since-the-financial-crisis-9826345.html).

36 Take, for instance, the Enlightenment taste for ranking races: 'Immanuel Kant could wedge "the Arab", "possessed of an inflamed imagination", between the basest of (Southern) Europeans and the far East, but significantly above "the Negroes of Africa"' (Goldberg, D.T., 2009, *The threat of race: Reflections on racial neoliberalism*, Oxford: Blackwell, p 163).

37 Karl Pearson, the man who gave it that name, apparently thought of calling it 'normal' to try to end the dispute between those who termed it 'Gaussian' and those who called it 'Laplacian'. Ending that dispute would in hindsight not appear to have been his only motive in choosing such a loaded term.

38 Over time, the curve tends to move up the grades. Students perform better at tests when teachers can teach better to the test, which they can with each year that passes and,

as there are always pressures on those who mark to be more generous as compared with the previous year, especially if their students are supposed to be especially able, markers have a tendency to become more lenient over time. A department in an elitist university in Britain may now award many more first-class degrees compared with lower second-class degrees. In general, as we learn and know more, we have become cleverer, but we still have huge difficulty in trying not to constantly claim that within any generation some of us are much cleverer than others.

[39] Unemployment is only possible in countries that have chosen to afford unemployment benefit. Unemployment rates fall when benefit levels are so low that they are very hard to live on. People will then do any work, no matter how demeaning, and will more often turn to crime. The rates of unemployment in a country, and who is unemployed, are thus the results of choices made as to how many jobs to provide for whom, and how punitive a rate of benefit to set. Often fewer jobs are provided for younger adults, who consequently experience higher unemployment and crime rates (Gordon, D., 2008, 'Unemployment', D. Dorling, Bristol, personal communication).

[40] The chances are at least 10 times less likely than the chance of tossing a coin 100 times and counting exactly 50 heads and 50 tails. The chance of that is about 8 per cent (not to be confused with the chance of counting exactly 50 heads then exactly 50 tails, which is extremely small). I'm unsure how many times precisely as my computer dislikes calculating factorials over 170. The figure of 8 per cent is calculated as $100!/50!/50!/2^{100}$.

[41] MacKenzie, D. (1999) 'Eugenics and the rise of mathematical statistics in Britain', in D. Dorling and S. Simpson (eds) *Statistics in society*, London: Arnold, pp 55-61.

[42] Pearson, K. (1902) 'On the fundamental conceptions of biology', *Biometrika*, vol 1, no 3, pp 320-44, at p 334.

[43] Tomlinson, S. (2013) *Ignorant yobs? Low attainers in a global knowledge economy*, Abingdon: Routledge, p 87, quoting Sadler, M. (1916) 'Need we imitate the German system?', *The Times*, 14 January.

[44] Cot, A.L. (2005) '"Breed out the unfit and breed in the fit". Irving Fisher, economics, and the science of heredity', *American Journal of Economics and Sociology*, vol 64, no 3, pp 793-826. There have been too few female economists for a test to be undertaken as to whether they would have been drawn to eugenics had they been greater in number. What is important to remember is that some people were more resistant to eugenicists' ideas than others, and that presumably remains the case today. See Section 6.2 for how orthodox economics and eugenics are so closely related.

[45] Ellis, L., Hershberger, S., Field, E. et al (2008) *Sex differences: Summarizing more than a century of scientific research*, New York: Psychology Press; see p 405 on autism, p 321 on mathematics, p 324 on science, and p 355 on males rating their abilities highly during adolescence.

[46] Livesey, R. (2007) *Socialism, sex, and the culture of aestheticism in Britain, 1880-1914*, Oxford: Oxford University Press, pp 75, 80, 81, referring explicitly to Karl's doubts over women's 'capacity' and his arguments of 1894 with Emma Brook. Note that Karl was not the worse of the eugenicists. For that mantle, Sir Francis Galton, Charles Darwin's cousin, is widely regarded as a more 'able' contender. Charles Darwin's son (Leonard Darwin) and grandson (Charles Galton Darwin) are also contenders.

[47] Livesey (2007, as above, p 188, quoting from writers in *The new age* editions published in 1911. In this case, the so-called 'race' being discussed was the 'British race', a thing we hear little of today, thankfully, as Scots and Welsh and Irish balk at being racially incorporated so crudely (and those three five-letter labels are also now very rarely discussed as if they described 'races').

[48] Whereas just as the things that matter with ethnicity are not 'race' differences but the difference that 'race' makes, what matters with sex '... is not the gender difference; it is the difference gender makes' (MacKinnon, C.A., 2006, *Are women human? And other international dialogues*, Boston, MA: Harvard University Press, p 74).

[49] The war made planning for a National Health Service in Britain possible far earlier than might otherwise have been the case, planning that was not simply a theoretical pipedream. See, for example, Morris, J.N. (2001 [1944]) 'Health, no 6, Handbooks for discussion groups, Association for Education in Citizenship', in G. Davey Smith, D. Dorling and M. Shaw (eds) *Poverty, inequality and health in Britain*, Bristol: Policy Press, pp 245-62.

[50] Connelly, M. (2008) *Fatal misconception: The struggle to control world population*, Cambridge, MA: Harvard University Press, p 163. Because it was largely used in secret (and in the past), you won't find many mentions of the term 'crypto-eugenics' using Google, but there are some.

[51] Kamin, L.J. (1974) *The science and politics of IQ*, New York, NY: John Wiley & Sons.

[52] Kamin, L.J. (1981) 'Some historical facts about IQ testing', in S. Raby (ed) *Intelligence: The battle for the mind*, London: Pan Books, pp 90-7.

[53] Smith, R. (2007) *Being human: Historical knowledge and the creation of human nature*, Manchester: Manchester University Press, p 89. For an example, see Rushton, J.P. (1992) 'Life-history comparisons between orientals and whites at a Canadian university', *Personality and Individual Differences*, vol 13, no 4, pp 439-42 (Sally Tomlinson, personal communication, 2014).

[54] 'Questions of nature versus nurture are meaningless.... For human behavioural disorders such as schizophrenia and autism, the inherent plasticity of the nervous system requires a systems approach to incorporate all of the myriad epigenetic factors that can influence such outcomes' (Gottesman, I.I. and Hanson, D.R., 2005, 'Human development: biological and genetic processes', *Annual Review of Psychology*, vol 56, no 1, pp 263-86, at p 263).

[55] Miller, D. (2005) 'What is social justice', in N. Pearce and W. Paxton (eds) *Social justice: Building a fairer Britain*, London, Politico's, pp 3-20, at pp 14-15.

[56] Staff reporter (2014) 'Last German state to do away with university tuition fees', *The Australian*, 23 September (www.theaustralian.com.au/higher-education/last-german-state-to-do-away-with-university-tuition-fees/story-e6frgcjx-1227066213629?nk=f3837cb02490f4ab6a7787ecde4d7f1d).

[57] See Chapter 3, this volume, and also Dorling, D. (2014) 'Review of G is for genes', *International Journal of Epidemiology*, doi: 10.1093/ije/dyu232 http://www.dannydorling.org/?page_id=4319

[58] A few people have pointed out to me that it is ironic that I am now based in this university, and I usually reply that it is, but that things are slowly changing. Some changes are faster than others. On one colleague's university website in 2015 it read, 'She is keenly interested in widening access to higher education and is always delighted to receive applications from students from non-selective state schools and colleges.' If you Google the phrase, you'll find out if it is still there.

[59] As quoted in White, S. (2007) *Equality*, Cambridge: Polity Press, p 66, which gives the details of who these people were, and the wider context. Stuart White's book is also itself an example of welcome evidence that exceptions to this contemporary prejudice exist, even within the hallowed halls. Of the halls themselves there is change and a little progress, it is just usually much slower change than is found elsewhere, and small victories may be over-celebrated.

[60] Goldthorpe, J. and Jackson, M. (2007) 'Education-based meritocracy: the barriers to its realization', Economic Change, Quality of Life and Social Cohesion, 6th Framework Network, p S3 (www.equalsoc.org/uploaded_files/regular/goldthorpe_jackson.pdf). See also Chapter 3, note 56, this volume.

[61] Tony Blair disguised his geneticist beliefs by talking of them as the 'God-given potential' of children, but it is clear from the policies he promoted, his 'scientific Christianity', and the way he talked about what he thought of his own children's special potential, that his God dealt out potential through genes. For the full wording of his text about children's abilities delivered in 2005, see Ball, S.J. (2008) *The education debate*, Bristol: Policy Press, p 12.

[62] Dixon, M. (2005) *Brave new choices? Behavioural genetics and public policy: A discussion document*, London: Institute of Public Policy Research.

[63] Joseph Rowntree Foundation (2014) *A UK without poverty: The case for tackling poverty and suggested policy options available to governments*, York: Joseph Rowntree Foundation, Section 5 (www.jrf.org.uk/a-uk-without-poverty#section-5).

[64] Bourdieu, P. (2007) *Sketch for a self-analysis* (English edn), Cambridge: Polity Press, pp 8, 9. Pierre Bourdieu does admittedly go on to criticise French colleagues too, particularly over how the support of some for Stalinism and Maoism was only made possible due to their geographical exclusion from more usual places and people.

[65] Gordon, D. (2007) 'Want 1999–2005', D. Dorling, Bristol, personal communication; comparison made between the 1999 Joseph Rowntree Foundation Poverty and Social Exclusion Survey and the 2004–05 equivalent questions asked in the official Office for National Statistics Family Resources Survey.

[66] Dorling, D. (2008) 'Worlds apart: how inequality breeds fear and prejudice in Britain through the eyes of two very different teenage girls', *The Guardian*, 12 November.

[67] Gordon, D., Mack, J. et al (2013) *Living standards in the UK: PSE UK first summary report*, Swindon: ESRC, p 16 (www.poverty.ac.uk/sites/default/files/attachments/The_Impoverishment_of_the_UK_PSE_UK_first_results_summary_report_March_28.pdf).

[68] Hills, J. and Stewart, K. (2009) *Towards a more equal society? Poverty, inequality and policy since 1997*, Bristol: Policy Press.

[69] The graph was due to appear first in Gordon, D. (2000) 'The scientific measurement of poverty: recent theoretical advances', in J. Bradshaw and R. Sainsbury (eds) *Researching poverty*, Aldershot: Ashgate, pp 37-58, but was not reproduced correctly. Later, a full description was provided in Gordon, D. (2006) 'The concept and measurement of poverty', in C. Pantazis, D. Gordon and R. Levitas (eds) *Poverty and social exclusion in Britain: The Millennium Survey*, Bristol: Policy Press, pp 29-70.

[70] These are taken from the categories used in Dorling, D., Rigby, J., Wheeler, B., Ballas, D., Thomas, B., Fahmy, E., Gordon, D. and Lupton, R. (2007) *Poverty, wealth and place in Britain, 1968 to 2005*, Bristol: Policy Press.

[71] Abdallah, S. (2008) 'Family Resources Survey', London: New Economics Foundation, personal communication. His analysis of the Family Resources Survey showed that what is called the 'mean average net unequivalised for household structure weekly income' for the five quintile groups in Britain in 2005/06 were: £150.69, £270.31, £398.13, £576.09 and £1,104.09, not that the nine pence matters at that point. Equivalised for household composition, there is no meaningful difference in the resulting ratios. In 2005 the national arithmetic mean income was £499.15 a week, which was so much higher than median income that more than 60 per cent of households lived on *less than* that sum.

[72] High Pay Centre (2014) *What would the neighbours say? How inequality means the UK is poorer than we think*, London: High Pay Centre, 16 June (http://highpaycentre.org/blog/what-would-the-neighbours-say-how-inequality-means-the-uk-is-poorer-than-we).

[73] WageMark (2014) 'A brief history of wage ratios' (www.wagemark.org/about/history/).

[74] Gabaix, X. and Landier, A. (2008) 'Why has CEO pay increased so much?', *The Quarterly Journal of Economics*, vol 123, no 1.

[75] Lopez, L. (2014) 'The problem is not that PIMCO founder Bill Gross made a $290 million bonus', *Business Insider*, 14 November (http://uk.businessinsider.com/gross-bonus-did-not-mirror-performance-2014-11?r=US).

[76] George, S. (2008) *Hijacking America: How the religious and secular right changed what Americans think*, Cambridge: Polity Press, pp 209-12.

[77] Oskarsson, S., Cesarini, D., Dawes, C.T., Fowler, J.H., Johannesson, M. and Teorell, J. (2014) 'Linking genes and political orientations: testing the cognitive ability as mediator hypothesis', *Political Psychology*, First published August 18th, DOI: 10.1111/pops.12230

[78] The Equality Trust (2009) 'About inequality' (www.equalitytrust.org.uk/about-inequality/effects).

[79] Kraemer, S. (1999) 'Promoting resilience: changing concepts of parenting and child care', *International Journal of Child and Family Welfare*, vol 3, pp 273-87.

[80] Dorling, D. (2008) 'Cash and the class system', *New Statesman*, 24 July.

[81] Rosewell, B. (2013) *Reinventing London*, London: London Publishing Partnership, pp 46 and 62.

[82] Private cars were commandeered. They had only recently become one of the key symbols of status. For a précis of Orwell's account, see Harman, C. (2002) *A people's history of the world* (2nd edn), London: Bookmarks, p 500.

[83] Piketty, T. (2014) *Capital in the twenty-first century*, Cambridge, MA: Harvard University Press.

[84] 'The Price is Right' had over 300 episodes between 1984 to 2001, and 124 episodes between May 2006 and January 2007 when it was cancelled because of poor audiences. It lasted so long possibly because of the comedy element. See https://en.wikipedia.org/wiki/The_Price_Is_Right_(UK_game_show)

[85] Peter Jones, talking on the BBC show 'Top Gear' during 2008. For information on the man and his views of his offspring, see "Meet the Joneses" at www.bbc.co.uk/dragonsden/dragons/peterjones.shtml (this page has now been deleted but internet archive services, such as the wayback machine, will find copies for you saved in 2010 and 2011, see: https://archive.org/web/

[86] Some 13.4 per cent of Americans had no health insurance by the summer of 2014, and that was after the rate had fallen sharply due to policy changes: see Levy, J. (2014) 'In US, uninsured rate sinks to 13.4% in second quarter', Gallop polling, 10 July (www.gallup.com/poll/172403/uninsured-rate-sinks-second-quarter.aspx).

[87] Beck, U. (2000) *World risk society* (2nd edn), Cambridge: Polity Press, p 6, on how the richest fifth of people on the planet consume six times more than their parents did.

[88] UN (United Nations) (2014) *World economic and social survey 2014: Reducing inequality for sustainable development*, New York: UN, p 11 (www.un.org/en/development/desa/policy/wess/wess_archive/2014wess_overview_en.pdf).

[89] Wade, R.H. (2007) 'Should we worry about income inequality?', in D. Held and A. Kaya (eds) *Global inequality: Patterns and explanations*, Cambridge: Polity Press, pp 104-31, at p 109.

[90] Dorling, D. (2014) *Inequality and the 1%*, London: Verso.

[91] Frank, R.H. (2007) *Falling behind: How rising inequality harms the middle class*, Berkeley, CA: University of California Press, annual figures derived from graphs on pp 17 and 19.
[92] Between 2000 and 2005, according to George, S. (2008) *Hijacking America: How the religious and secular right changed what Americans think*, Cambridge: Polity Press, p 211.
[93] Dickens, R., Gregg, P. and Wadsworth, J. (2003) 'Introduction', in R. Dickens, P. Gregg and J. Wadsworth (eds) *The labour market under New Labour: The state of working Britain 2003*, Basingstoke: Palgrave Macmillan, pp 1-13, derived from figure 1.2, p 11.
[94] Dickens et al (2003), as above.
[95] Dickens et al (2003, as above.
[96] BBC (2008) 'UK income gap "same as in 1991"', 16 December (http://news.bbc.co.uk/2/hi/business/7786149.stm).
[97] Hills, J. (2014) *Good times, bad times: The welfare myth of them and us,* Bristol: Policy Press, p 43 (42-27 = 15).
[98] Hirst, K. (2007) *Working welfare: Welfare recommendations for the UK based on the US reforms of the 1990s*, London: Adam Smith Institute (www.adamsmith.org/wp-content/uploads/working_welfare_final.pdf).
[99] George, V. and Wilding, P. (1999) *British society and social welfare: Towards a sustainable society*, London: Macmillan, p 37.
[100] Elliott, L. and Curtis, P. (2009) 'UK's income gap widest since 60s: Labour admits child poverty failure, incomes of poorest fall', *The Guardian*, 8 May.
[101] Corlett, A. and Whittaker, M. (2014) *Low pay Britain 2014*, London: Resolution Foundation, p 19 (www.resolutionfoundation.org/wp-content/uploads/2014/10/Low-Pay-Britain-20141.pdf).
[102] George, V. and Wilding, P. (1999) *British society and social welfare: Towards a sustainable society*, London: Macmillan, p 110.
[103] SNP (Scottish National Party) (2014) 'UK cooks the books on aid spending', 16 September, Edinburgh: SNP (www.snp.org/media-centre/news/2014/sep/uk-cooks-books-aid-spending).
[104] Kelsey, J. (1997) *The New Zealand experiment: A world model for structural adjustment?*, Auckland: Auckland University Press, p 333, far from agreeing with, but quoting the views of Alan Gibbs from 1994.
[105] Swinford, S. (2013) 'Mothers in problem families should be given contraception, government adviser says', *The Telegraph*, 10 September (www.telegraph.co.uk/news/10297486/Mothers-in-problem-families-should-be-given-contraception-government-adviser-says.html).
[106] Casey, L. (2104) 'The national Troubled Families programme', *Social Work and Social Sciences Review*, vol 71, no 2, pp 57-62.
[107] Dorling, D. (2013) *Population 10 billion: The coming demographic crisis and how to survive it*, London: Constable.
[108] And even that man, Alan Gibbs, in New Zealand! See Kelsey, as above.
[109] Somers, M.R. and Block, F. (2005) 'From poverty to perversity: ideas, markets, and institutions over 200 years of welfare debate', *American Sociological Review*, vol 70, pp 260-87.
[110] Sabin, L. (2014) 'Ninety-year-old man faces jail for giving food to homeless people', *The Independent*, 4 November (www.independent.co.uk/news/world/americas/ninetyyearold-man-faces-jail-for-giving-food-to-homeless-people-9838728.html).
[111] Wolf, M. (2014) 'Why inequality is such a drag on economies', *The Financial Times*, 30 September (www.ft.com/cms/s/0/8b41dfc8-47c1-11e4-ac9f-00144feab7de.html).

Chapter 5

[1] The Council of Economic Advisors to President Obama (2014) *The war on poverty 50 year later: A progress report*, Washington, DC: Executive Office of the President of the United States.

[2] Garner, R. (2014) 'More than half of children born in the year 2000 have faced poverty', *The Independent*, 17 December (www.independent.co.uk/news/uk/home-news/more-than-half-of-children-born-in-the-year-2000-have-faced-poverty-9888430.html).

[3] Sweeny, E. (2014) *Making work better: An agenda for government*, London: The Smith Institute, p 8; and p 16 quoting Yeoman, R. (2014) *Meaningful work: A philosophy of work and a politics of meaningfulness*, Basingstoke: Palgrave Macmillan.

[4] Gilroy, P. (2012) '"My Britain is fuck all": zombie multiculturalism and the race politics of citizenship', *Identities, Global Studies in Culture and Power*, vol 19, no 4, p 382.

[5] People who were seen as having the wrong colour skin were more frequently stabbed; see Leech, K. (2005) *Race*, London: SPCK, pp 79-84, 141-5.

[6] Krugman, P. (2007) *The conscience of a liberal*, New York: W.W. Norton, p 160.

[7] So soon after dictatorships were overthrown in Greece (1974), Portugal (1974) and Spain (1975).

[8] Dorling, D. (2001) 'Anecdote is the singular of data', *Environment and Planning A*, vol 33, pp 1335-40, at pp 1336-9, in which mention how it felt to be attacked by the National Front, as viewed by a child.

[9] The National Front vote collapsed in 1979 as far-right voters voted with the Conservative Party.

[10] Ballescas, R.P. (2003) 'Filipino migration to Japan, 1970s to 1990s', in S. Ikehata and L.N. Yu-Jose (eds) *Philippines–Japan relations*, Manila: Ateneo de Manila University Press, chapter 15, at p 563. Indirectly related is Adolf Hitler's description of women's work as *kinder, küche* and *kirche* (children, kitchen and church) from an earlier time of prejudice. Incidentally, in Britain, in more recent years, the work for which migrant labour has been most needed has been described as 'picking, plucking and packing'.

[11] Originally published in Moxley, D. and Finch, J. (eds) (2003) *Sourcebook of rehabilitation and mental health practice*, New York: Plenum Books and reprinted in Tomlinson, S. (2013) *Ignorant yobs? Low attainers in a global knowledge economy*, London: Routledge, p 78.

[12] See Hayter, T. (2004) *Open borders: The case against immigration controls*, London: Pluto Press, p 49, on how the 1960s immigration controls inadvertently encouraged immigration. The rise in prejudice ensured that it was soon forgotten that these immigrants were also deliberately brought to Europe to work night shifts in mills and car plants, to drive buses and to be nurses. By 1989, MORI polls in Britain found over 60 per cent of respondents saying there were too many immigrants. By 2007 that had risen to 68 per cent, and by 2013, over 75 per cent wanted levels of immigration reduced (www.migrationobservatory.ox.ac.uk/briefings/uk-public-opinion-toward-immigration-overall-attitudes-and-level-concern). It is easy to stoke up prejudices about numbers of people; see Finney, N. and Simpson, L. (2009) *'Sleepwalking to segregation'? Challenging myths of race and migration*, Bristol: Policy Press – these particular statistics are from p 53.

[13] Krugman, P. (2007) *The conscience of a liberal*, New York: W.W. Norton, p 133. The quote begins 'But for reasons that remain somewhat unclear….' Migration replacement of fertility decline is a possible reason to explain the trend across most of the rich world; the pull of money and huge demand for service labour are other reasons.

[14] Very few of us know their ancestry back more than a few generations. We may not even correctly know the ancestry of some English monarchs, including Henry VIII,

Elizabeth I and some more recent royals too: see Hartmann, M. (2014) 'Richard III's bones provide evidence of royal family adultery', *New York Magazine*, 3 December (http://nymag.com/daily/intelligencer/2014/12/richard-iiis-bones-point-to-royal-adultery.html).

[15] That particular claim, it is suggested on Wikipedia, is made in the biography by Simon Heffer (1999) *Like the Roman: The life of Enoch Powell*, London: Weidenfeld & Nicolson.

[16] Junankar, P.N. (1987) *Costs of unemployment: Programme of research and actions on the development of the labour market*, Luxembourg: Office for Official Publications of the European Communities.

[17] Krugman, P. (2007) *The conscience of a liberal*, New York: W.W. Norton, p 210.

[18] Dorling, D. (2013) 'It is necessarily so', *Significance Magazine*, vol 10, no 2, pp 37-9.

[19] Dorling, D. (2007) 'The soul searching within new Labour', *Local Economy*, vol 22, no 4, pp 317-24.

[20] Carrera, S. and Beaumont, J. (2011) 'Income and wealth', *Social Trends*, No 41, Table 1: Perceptions of the current economic climate by income grouping, 2009 (www.ons.gov.uk/ons/rel/social-trends-rd/social-trends/social-trends-41/index.html).

[21] MacInnes, T., Aldridge, H., Bushe, S., Tinson, A. and Born, T.B. (2014) *Monitoring poverty and social exclusion 2014*, York: Joseph Rowntree Foundation, p 7 (www.jrf.org.uk/sites/files/jrf/MPSE-2014-FULL.pdf).

[22] MacInnes et al (2014), as above, p 23.

[23] Goody, J. (2006) *The theft of history*, Cambridge: Cambridge University Press, p 15.

[24] Agence-France Presse (2014) 'Inequality worst in decades in range of countries: OECD', *The Indian Express*, 9 December (http://indianexpress.com/article/business/economy/inequality-worst-in-decades-in-range-of-countries-oecd/).

[25] Wilkinson, R.G. and Pickett, K. (2009) *The spirit level: Why more equal societies almost always do better*, London: Allen Lane; see Chapter 9 on teenage pregnancies.

[26] Thoburn, J. (2000) *A comparative study of adoption*, Norwich: University of East Anglia, p 5; the number of children placed in non-family care doubled in the US between 1987 and 1999, was higher than in other affluent nations, and more children were consequently adopted. More are also given up for adoption in the US without being placed in care than in Western Europe or Australasia.

[27] On teenage pregnancy rates see: www.equalitytrust.org.uk/resources/spirit-level/teenage-births (the rate is highest in the US and UK, and up to 10 times lower in Japan and Sweden), while on degrees varying in value in unequal countries, see 'The UK may offer particularly high economic rewards for going to a "good" university, whereas, in other countries, "a degree is a degree"' (Havergal, C., 2014, 'Parents' education "has greater effect" in unequal countries', *Times Higher*, 31 October, www.timeshighereducation.co.uk/news/parents-education-has-greater-effect-in-unequal-countries/2016701.article). It is not that other countries do not have elite universities but some, such as the University of Tokyo, are less exclusive, not taking up to a third of their intake from just 100 schools, mostly private (as happens at the top of the UK system), and also confer less of an unearned advantage later.

[28] See *Basic Income Earth Network* (www.basicincome.org/bien/) on how all could be paid a living income.

[29] In the few cases where this was not the case, it is remarked on as a problem. As the Public Broadcast Service in the US explains to its browsers: 'Slaves were the lowest class in Athenian society, but according to many contemporary accounts they were far less harshly treated than in most other Greek cities. Indeed, one of the criticisms of Athens was that its slaves and freemen were difficult to tell apart' (www.pbs.org/empires/thegreeks/background/32b.html).

[30] James, O. (2009) *Contented dementia*, London:Vermilion, p 23.

[31] Presumably this was also the view of his wife, or she was not strongly enough opposed to prevent the school choice, but that has not been documented. Blair's comments about the work that would be beneath his children are recorded in Steel, M. (2008) *What's going on*, London: Simon & Schuster, p 8. It is now often repeated on the web: 'There's a great quote in Robin Cook's memoir. He was talking to Blair about [Blair's] son's selective school and Roy Hattersley was there and they said Harold Wilson had sent his children to a comprehensive and one became a headmaster and the other was a professor in the Open University and Blair said, "I rather hope my sons do better than that!"', as recorded by John Paul Flintoff (www.flintoff.org/what-happened-to-meritocracy). Flintoff repeats online Mark Steel's now widely spreading comment: 'For Blair, status and wealth are everything. It's beyond him to think that education might be worthwhile for itself. He can't possibly think along those lines.'

[32] Robber barons were businessmen who had amassed huge fortunes immorally, unethically and unjustly.

[33] Irvin, G. (2008) *Super rich: The rise of inequality in Britain and the United States*, Cambridge: Polity Press, p 64.

[34] For a few years in the 1970s, it was touch and go. Across the Atlantic, the population centre of Britain oscillated between moving north or south at this time, and voting became much more unpredictable. Thousands of individual decisions swung one way and another in that decade 1968–78. The most equitable year was probably 1976, but even by then, the underlying trajectory on inequality had almost certainly shifted direction. It was within those years in the 1970s that the direction of long-term social change turned. See the argument in Section 4.5 of this book as to why 1971 is a key date in the US; many other years can also be singled out. In Britain, the discussion of Figure 13 in this volume suggests the choice was made in 1974. Worldwide, the year 1973 is the year nearest to the knife-edge, to the point when the pendulum was hovering appearing to be almost still, pulled almost equally in all directions, and the future was most shrouded.

[35] Irvin, G. (2008) *Super rich: The rise of inequality in Britain and the United States*, Cambridge: Polity Press, p 65.

[36] Offer, A. (2006) *The challenge of affluence: Self-control and well-being in the United States and Britain since 1950*, Oxford: Oxford University Press, p 325.

[37] James, O. (2008) *The selfish capitalist: Origins of affluenza*, London:Vermilion, p 152.

[38] Rose, M. (2005) 'The cost of a career in minutes and morbidity', in D. Housten (ed) *Work–life balance*, London: Macmillan, pp 29-54, at p 42.

[39] Rutherford, J. and Shah, H. (2006) *The good society: Compass Programme for Renewal*, London: Lawrence & Wishart, p 37.

[40] TUC (Trades Union Congress) (2014) *Only one in every forty net jobs since the recession is for a full-time employee*, London: TUC, 12 November (www.tuc.org.uk/economic-issues/labour-market-and-economic-reports/only-one-every-forty-net-jobs-recession-full-time).

[41] Irvin, G. (2008) *Super rich: The rise of inequality in Britain and the United States*, Cambridge: Polity Press, p 87, Figure 4.2; and p 118.

[42] It may be an apocryphal proportion, but if you include not just security guards and caretakers, but all those who monitor credit card theft and so on, to reduce the costs to banks and hence to the rich, this could easily be true. Matt Stoller, quoted in Brand, R. (2014) 'What monkeys and the Queen taught me about inequality', *The Guardian*, 13 October.

[43] UNESCO (1950) 'The race question', 18 July, Statement 14, on p 8, Paris: UNESCO House, Publication 791 (http://unesdoc.unesco.org/images/0012/001282/128291eo.pdf).

[44] In her television interview for Granada's 'World in Action' ('rather swamped') on 27 January 1978 (www.margaretthatcher.org/speeches/displaydocument.asp?docid=103485). Unlike Enoch Powell she did not even suggest allowing in just enough others to meet what she saw as the country's needs.

[45] James, O. (2007) *Affluenza: How to be successful and stay sane*, London:Vermilion, p 72.

[46] Creese, B. and Lader, D. (2014) *Hate crimes, England and Wales, 2013/14*, London: Home Office (www.gov.uk/government/uploads/system/uploads/attachment_data/file/364198/hosb0214.pdf).

[47] Dearden, L. (2015) 'David Cameron says anyone criticizing Eric Pickles' letter to Muslims "really has a problem"', *The Independent*, 19 January (www.independent.co.uk/news/uk/politics/david-cameron-says-anyone-criticising-eric-pickles-letter-to-muslims-really-has-a-problem-9987397.html).

[48] Bauman, Z. (2007) *Consuming life*, Cambridge: Polity Press, p 142. This wording was often used by Goran Persson, Prime Minister of Sweden (1996-2006).

[49] According to Gøsta Esping-Andersen, as described in Irvin, G. (2008) *Super rich: The rise of inequality in Britain and the United States*, Cambridge: Polity Press, p 103.

[50] Lindley, J. and Machin, S. (2013) *The postgraduate premium: Revisiting trends in social mobility and educational inequalities in Britain and America*, London: The Sutton Trust (www.kent.ac.uk/graduateschool/Postgraduate%20premium%20Sutton%20Trust%20report.pdf).

[51] The suggestion that UK postgraduate students will be able to pay back their loans in future is misguided, unless we are planning to have an even more divided future society: see Britton, J., Crawford, C. and Dearden, L. (2014) *The government's proposed new postgraduate loan scheme: Will the RAB charge really be zero*? London: Institute for Fiscal Studies (www.ifs.org.uk/publications/7472).

[52] Many could describe themselves as English in London, but do not because of the connotations in such a mixed city. In cities where people mix less well, such as in some of the towns and cities of Yorkshire, people often do not describe themselves with a single word that says they are from a particular city, but as a 'Yorkshire man', for instance. Levels of tolerance are particularly high in London and are a little lower than average in some parts of Yorkshire. See the survey studied in Kaur-Ballagan, K., Mortimore, R. and Sapsed, E. (2007) *Public attitudes towards cohesion and integration, Ipsos MORI Report for the Commission on Integration and Cohesion*, London: Commission on Integration and Cohesion, p 50. This survey predated the rise in BNP and then UKIP votes in Yorkshire.

[53] Pálsson, G. (2002) 'The life of family trees and the book of Icelanders', *Medical Anthropology*, vol 21, pp 337-67, at p 345.

[54] The figures for Japan are now widely known following the publication of Wilkinson, R.G. and Pickett, K. (2009) *The spirit level: Why more equal societies almost always do better*, London: Allen Lane. This book also includes the original argument that equality reduces ethnicity (p 178). Similarly, statistics of a 3.5:1 inequality ratio for Iceland can be derived from Statistics Iceland (2007) 'Risk of poverty and income distribution 2003-2004' (www.statice.is/Pages/444?NewsID=2600). And those ratios have not worsened since the crisis. Similarly, Japan continues to be the most equitable of affluent nations, although misleading statistics are often referred to, suggesting it is not as equitable: see Ballas, D., Dorling, D., Nakaya, T., Tunstall, H. and Hanaoka, K. (2013) 'Income inequalities in Japan and the UK: a comparative study of two island economies', *Journal of Social Policy and Society*, vol 13, no 1, pp 103-17.

55 Mazumdar, P.M.H. (2003) 'Review of Elof Axel Carlson. The unfit: a history of a bad idea', *Bulletin of the History of Medicine*, vol 77, no 4, pp 971-2.

56 Connelly, M. (2008) *Fatal misconception: The struggle to control world population*, Cambridge, MA: Harvard University Press, pp 347-8.

57 BBC News (2014) 'Kenyan women with HIV sue over sterilization', 10 December (www.bbc.co.uk/news/world-africa-30417266), and Suresh, A. (2014) 'Forced sterilization in Peru: did modern eugenic practices slow population growth?', *Genetic Literacy Project*, 11 December (www.geneticliteracyproject.org/2014/12/11/forced-sterilization-in-peru-did-modern-eugenic-practices-slow-population-growth/).

58 It is possible that this policy, coupled with poorer mothers having to have their babies outside of the island, and thousands of maids being pregnancy tested every few months, has resulted in Singapore having one of the lowest recorded rates of infant mortality ever found in the world. This argument is expanded in Dorling, D. (2013) *Unequal health: The scandal of our times*, Bristol: Policy Press.

59 Goldberg, D.T. (2009) *The threat of race: Reflections on racial neoliberalism*, Oxford: Blackwell, p 26, referring to the work of Ruthie Gilmore on racism as premature mortality. Her definition can even be extended to patterns in murder. See Dorling, D. (2005) 'Prime suspect: murder in Britain', in P. Hillyard, C. Pantazis, S. Tombs, D. Gordon and D. Dorling (eds) *Criminal obsessions: Why harm matters more than crime*, London, Crime and Society Foundation, pp 23-38, on how supposedly individually motivated murder reflects wider changes in prejudice over time, with rates reducing for women and rising for the poor, as the status of both groups changes.

60 Including unemployment, where today the threat of it can increase suicide levels. When losing your job was rarer, there was an even stronger relationship: see Junankar, P.N. (1991) 'Unemployment and mortality in England and Wales: a preliminary analysis', *Oxford Economic Papers*, New Series, vol 43, no 2, pp 305-20.

61 Hayter, T. (2004) *Open borders: The case against immigration controls*, London: Pluto Press, p 103.

62 According to the 2001 Census; see Thomas, B. and Dorling, D. (2007) *Identity in Britain: A cradle-to-grave atlas*, Bristol: Policy Press, p 46.

63 Green, R. (2007) 'Managing migration impacts', Presentation to the Migration Impacts Forum, 17 October, on 'Community cohesion' by Rodney Green, Chief Executive, Leicester City Council, London: Home Office, p 6. Last found (11/10/09) at www.communities.gov.uk/documents/communities/pdf/communitycohesion (now removed but accessible via the wayback machine: http://archive.org/web/ where 332 web pages from 2008 are held

64 Brinded, L. (2015) 'Britons claiming benefits across EU "outnumber immigrants getting welfare in the UK"', *International Business Times*, 19 January (www.ibtimes.co.uk/britons-claiming-benefits-across-eu-outnumber-immigrants-getting-welfare-uk-1484091).

65 Cohen, S. (2006) *Standing on the shoulders of fascism: From immigration control to the strong state*, Stoke-on-Trent: Trentham Books, p 114.

66 Cohen, N. (2004) *Pretty straight guys*, London: Faber & Faber, p 74.

67 ONS (Office for National Statistics) (2013) 'Health inequalities: trends in all-cause mortality by NS-SEC for English regions and Wales, 2001-03 to 2008-10', Health Inequalities release, 24 May (www.ons.gov.uk/ons/rel/health-ineq/health-inequalities/trends-in-all-cause-mortality-by-ns-sec-for-english-regions-and-wales--2001-03-to-2008-10/index.html).

68 Dorling, D. (2015) *All that is solid*, London: Allen Lane.

[69] Dorling, D. (2008) 'London and the English desert: the grain of truth in a stereotype', *Geocarrefour*, vol 83, no 2, pp 87-98.

[70] Obama, B. (2015) State of the Union address, *Time Magazine*, 20 January (http://time.com/3675705/full-text-state-union-2015/).

[71] Figures from Krugman, P. (2007) *The conscience of a liberal*, New York: W.W. Norton, p 16; extra math(s) is derived: 17/(44-17)×(10-1).

[72] Dorling, D. (2006) 'Commentary: the fading of the dream: widening inequalities in life expectancy in America', *International Journal of Epidemiology*, vol 35, no 4, pp 979-80; Dorling, D. (2006) 'Inequalities in Britain 1997-2006: the dream that turned pear-shaped', *Local Economy*, vol 21, no 4, pp 353-61.

[73] In the early 1950s in the US, 80 per cent of income growth went to the bottom 90 per cent of society, just 20 per cent to the top 10 per cent. Fifty years later, all the growth went to just a few within the top 10 per cent, and the bottom 90 per cent saw their average incomes falling by nearly 20 per cent in the worse period. In contrast, in Sweden until 2007, there was redistribution from the richer to the poorer most years: see Weissmann, J. (2014) 'How the rich conquered the economy, in one chart', Money Box blog, 25 September (www.slate.com/blogs/moneybox/2014/09/25/how_the_rich_conquered_the_economy_in_one_chart.html). (Accessible as of February 10th 2015)

[74] Galbraith, J.K. (1992 [1954]) *The great crash 1929*, London: Penguin, p 194 on the unsoundness of the economy.

[75] Standing, G. (2014) 'Why the precariat is not a "bogus concept"', *Open Democracy*, 4 March (www.opendemocracy.net/guy-standing/why-precariat-is-not-"bogus-concept").

[76] Short, J.R., Hanlon, B. and Vicino, T.J. (2007) 'The decline of inner suburbs: the new suburban gothic in the United States', *Geography Compass*, vol 1, no 3, pp 641-56, at p 653.

[77] Buehler, R. and Pucher, J. (2012) 'Walking and cycling in Western, Europe and the United States, trends, policies, and lessons', *TR News* 280, May-June (http://policy.rutgers.edu/faculty/pucher/TRNWesternEurope.pdf).

[78] Kesteloot, C. (2005) 'Urban socio-spatial configurations and the future of European cities', in Y. Kazepov (ed) *Cities of Europe: Changing contexts, local arrangements, and the challenge to urban cohesion*, Oxford: Blackwell, pp 123-48, at p 141.

[79] For John McCain, it was at least seven, but may have been as many as 11. All 11 'family' properties were listed by the *New York Times* (www.nytimes.com/ref/us/politics/mccain-properties.html) on 23 August 2008 (by reporter David M. Halbfinger). David Cameron and his wife owned at least four in 2009, maybe more. David asked the reporter who revealed this, 'please … not to make me sound like a prat for not knowing how many houses I've got.' Yes 'please' was part of the original quote. David tries to be polite, even when pleading. *The Times* newspaper revealed this in 2009 (www.timesonline.co.uk/tol/news/politics/article6267193.ece?token=null&offset=84&page=8).

[80] Frank, R.H. (2007) *Falling behind: How rising inequality harms the middle class*, Berkeley, CA: University of California Press, p 136.

[81] Even if you say you believe in inheritance because you believe that your offspring are somehow inferior, incapable of surviving without your help, they would do far better under such circumstances to live in a society that was more equal, where inheritance of wealth was less tolerated. This would be one of those societies that already exist, where the living look out for each other more, rather than just for themselves or their families. Such societies are found in most rich countries such as Finland, Sweden,

Austria, Korea, Belgium, France, Ireland and Greece. In more unequal societies, those few fortunate 'inferior' ones who have to rely on the generosity of their dead relatives live hoping not to be duped out of their inheritance by their unscrupulous and not so financially fortunate neighbours. If you believe in inheritance, even though you do not see your offspring as superior, you still help create division, and maintain suspicion, mistrust and racism.

[82] The story is well known, but usually still told as a valiant feat of exploration. The exact date is debated as the date line was not in existence at this time, and Cook had travelled from the East.

[83] James I also ruled over Wales, which had been overrun by the English conquest in 1282–83, was treated as a principality from 1301, but was, in effect, a colony, and had its law replaced by English law in 1536. The idea of Britishness would not even begin to become popular until another century had passed and the Kingdom of Great Britain was created in 1707. Britishness as an identity was not widespread until a century later again, when its rise in popularity was brought about to help with wars against France. The 'British race' is, in fact, a very recent invention. The Britons originally all spoke Welsh.

[84] Taken from an assessment by three Harvard economists that more calmly says 'a major reason', but which does think of race as widely defined. The quotation is from Krugman, P. (2007) *The conscience of a liberal*, New York: W.W. Norton, p 178. It is worth noting that it could similarly be argued that race is the reason for much of the absence of a Japanese welfare state because pay is so equal due to assumptions of racial unity.

[85] Gordon, D. (2009) 'Global inequality, death, and disease', *Environment and Planning A*, vol 41, no 6, pp 1271-2.

[86] Their report did not receive the attention it should have: UN (United Nations) (2014) *World economic and social survey: Reducing inequality for sustainable development*. The 2014 survey can be found at www.un.org/en/development/desa/policy/wess/index.shtml

[87] Many were from Central America. Note that the US Border Force counts children it catches by financial year; see Castillo, M. (2014) 'Immigration: more Central Americans apprehended than Mexicans', *CNN*, 19 December (http://edition.cnn.com/2014/12/19/us/dhs-immigration-statistics-2014/).

[88] Jerrim, J. and Macmillan, L. (2014) *Income inequality, intergenerational mobility and the Great Gatsby Curve: is education the key?*, Working Paper No 14-18, London: Department of Quantitative Social Science, Institute for Education, University of London, October (https://ideas.repec.org/p/qss/dqsswp/1418.html).

[89] Quoted in Jarvis, F. (2014) *You never know your luck: Reflections of a cockney campaigner for education*, Guildford: Grosvenor House Publishing.

[90] As the medical geographer, Peter Haggett, touchingly described to undergraduates the process whereby sexual diseases were spread (Haggett, P., 1996, 'Sex', D. Dorling, Bristol, personal communication).

[91] The precise share that the 1 per cent takes depends very much on whether individuals or households are measured, and whether an estimate for tax evasion is included: Dorling, D. (2014) *Inequality and the 1%*, London: Verso.

[92] Krugman, P. (2007) *The conscience of a liberal*, New York: W.W. Norton.

[93] CBC News (2014) 'Richest of the rich gain ground in Canada', *Canadian Broadcasting Corporation*, 21 November (www.cbc.ca/news/business/richest-of-the-rich-gain-ground-in-canada-1.2844712).

[94] Dorling, D. (2014) 'Growing wealth inequality in the UK is a ticking time-bomb', *The Guardian*, 15 October (www.theguardian.com/commentisfree/2014/oct/15/wealth-inequality-uk-ticking-timebomb-credit-suisse-crash).

[95] The rich have always known this. However, when three decades later even the poorest were recorded as saying they looked 'for the image not the face', the brands of clothes each other wore, it caused some shock; see Lawson, N. (2009) *All consuming*, London: Penguin, p 56.

[96] Frank, R. (2007) *Richi$tan*, New York: Random House, p 231. A prenuptial agreement, or prenup, is a contract drawn up prior to marriage to prevent the sharing of wealth if the marriage is dissolved.

[97] In Britain, prenuptial agreements were described as a 'valuable weapon in the armoury of the wealthy' by one lawyer on Valentine's Day 2009 (http://business.timesonline.co.uk/tol/business/law/columnists/article3368933.ece, as reported in *The Times*, 14 February 2009), and it was later announced, on 5 July 2009, in the case of one woman, Katrin, who had married a banker, that the agreements were binding under British law: 'Nicolas was then a banker at JP Morgan, earning about $500,000 a year. As Katrin has argued during her legal battle, he too stands to inherit a substantial amount of money. His father is a former vice-president of IBM. She has said his parents are worth £30m; he says £6m.' In this particular relationship, it was Nicolas who was the 'poor' one; she was said to be 'worth' between £55 million and £100 million (http://business.timesonline.co.uk/tol/business/law/article6634106.ece). Despite her wealth, she is reported to have ended up sleeping on a mattress on the floor of her flat at one point, when Nicolas would not move out of the bedroom. It does not sound as if she was particularly happy. The point of recounting this tale is to remember how little great riches actually increase happiness.

[98] Acceptance of inter-racial marriage in the US and UK continued to increase. See Dorling, D. (2014) 'When racism stopped being normal, but no one noticed: generational value change', in Cowley, P. and Ford, R. (eds) *Sex, lies, and the ballot box*, London: Biteback, pp 39-42.

[99] Only one dollar in twenty that North Americans give to charity goes to charities that carry out work for 'public and societal benefit'; see Edwards, M. (2008) *Just another emperor? The myths and realities of philanthrocapitalism*, London: Demos and The Young Foundation.

[100] Goldberg, D.T. (2009) *The threat of race: Reflections on racial neoliberalism*, Oxford: Blackwell, p 238.

[101] This version of her words is taken from the *Daily Mail* and was printed just a few days before the 30th anniversary of her first general election victory; see Phibbs, H. (2007) 'Harman's crazy class war will make us all poorer', *Daily Mail*, 27 April.

[102] Margaret Thatcher first became well known as the government minister who took free milk away from all British school children in 1971; presumably she thought most were not destined to grow tall, and hence all did not need to be given milk – that milk should be only for those whose parents could afford it. An argument was put forward that parents should be responsible for the nutrition of their own children – it was not the state's responsibility. But the state continued to provide free school meals to those deemed poor enough, and religious instruction to all who did not opt out. The British state provides mostly free healthcare, just as it once gave children free milk. Where the line is drawn depends on what is thought to be fine for some to go without. Free fruit might have been better than free milk, however. It went off less quickly.

[103] 'The white man's burden' was originally a poem by Rudyard Kipling, which extols the duty of colonial powers to instill Western ideas and rule over the supposedly more brutish and barbaric parts of the world. See https://en.wikipedia.org/wiki/The_White_Man's_Burden

[104] Connelly, M. (2008) *Fatal misconception: The struggle to control world population*, Cambridge, MA: Harvard University Press, pp 258-61.

[105] Krugman, P. (2007) *The conscience of a liberal*, New York: W.W. Norton, p 170.

[106] Goldberg, D.T. (2009) *The threat of race: Reflections on racial neoliberalism*, Oxford: Blackwell, p 337; original emphasis.

[107] Doward, J. and Bissett, G. (2014) 'Pay squeeze worst since Victorian age, study finds', *The Observer*, 11 October (http://www.theguardian.com/politics/2014/oct/11/british-pay-squeeze-worst-150-years-tuc-study)

[108] Wars provide a fog that allows other atrocities to take place. Among the many reasons to try to avoid war, this one is not often stated. Even if a war may appear just, in taking part in that war the smokescreen in which genocide is possible is created. In 1935, Adolf Hitler explained that 'if war came, he would take up and carry out this question of euthanasia, because it was easier to do so in wartime' (Glover, J., 2001, *Humanity: A moral history of the twentieth century*, London: Pimlico, p 352).

[109] Glover (2001), as above, p 333. Recent reports suggest that this Ron was a different man with the same name (see the Ron Ridenhour entry in Wikipedia as of 16 August 2009, in which the doubts are highlighted). If it was two different men, then the cause for optimism is ratcheted up a fraction higher, as it would suggest that such behaviour, even at that time, was less rare than we thought.

[110] Abhorrent enough for those in power to do something to curb it, which they did, by passing the Police and Criminal Evidence Act 1984 and installing CCTV in police stations and vans.

[111] Wilkinson, R.G. (2007) 'Commentary: the changing relation between mortality and income', *International Journal of Epidemiology*, vol 36, no 3, pp 492-4, 502-3, at p 493, referring to the evidence collected by an historian of childhood, DeMause, L. (ed) (1974) *The history of childhood*, London: Condor.

[112] Both the examples of racism being attractive in circumstances of inequality, and of a poor family where the parents were jailed when video evidence was found of their teaching their toddlers to fight each other to harden them, are discussed in detail in Wilkinson, R.G. and Pickett, K. (2009) *The spirit level: Why more equal societies almost always do better*, London: Allen Lane.

[113] The sad personal details of the lives of many men at the head of British industry are described in Peston, R. (2008) *Who runs Britain? How the super-rich are changing our lives*, London: Hodder & Stoughton, pp 46, 82-3, 129, 201-2.

[114] Spinney, L. (2004) 'Snakes in suits', *New Scientist*, 21 August.

[115] Moran, M. (2008) 'Representing the corporate elite in Britain: capitalist solidarity and capitalist legacy', in M. Savage and K. Williams (eds) *Remembering elites*, Oxford: Blackwell, pp 64-79, at p 74.

[116] Reiner, R. (2007) *Law and order: An honest citizen's guide to crime and control*, Cambridge: Polity Press, p 6.

[117] Bauman, Z. (2007) *Consuming life*, Cambridge: Polity Press, p 118, quoting from Orwell's 1953 collection of essays.

[118] Offer, A. (2006) *The challenge of affluence: Self-control and well-being in the United States and Britain since 1950*, Oxford: Oxford University Press, p 95.

[119] Pogge, T.W. (2007) 'Why inequality matters', in D. Held and A. Kaya (eds) *Global inequality: Patterns and explanations*, Cambridge: Polity Press, pp 132-47.

[120] Leech, K. (2005) *Race*, London: SPCK. See the introductory pages.

[121] Anonymous (2014) 'Congress passes Bill to add armed patrol to US poverty line', *The Onion*, Issue 50/45, 12 November (www.theonion.com/articles/congress-passes-bill-to-add-armed-patrol-to-us-pov,37431/).

Chapter 6

[1] Paul Piff, quoted in Miller, L. (2012) 'The money-empathy gap: new research suggests that more money makes people act less human. Or at least less humane', *New York Magazine*, 1 July (http://nymag.com/news/features/money-brain-2012-7/).

[2] The Equality Trust (2104) '342 years for National Minimum Wage worker to earn pay of FTSE 100 CEO', Press Release, 30 September (www.equalitytrust.org.uk/news/342-years-national-minimum-wage-worker-earn-pay-ftse-100-ceo).

[3] Peston, R. (2008) *Who runs Britain? How the super-rich are changing our lives*, London: Hodder & Stoughton, p 336.

[4] It was said that he had himself become 'a market force' through his pronouncements that year: see Treneman, A. (2009) 'Appalling delivery, rambling replies but the Robert Peston show is a masterclass', *The Times*, 5 February.

[5] 'Today Programme', 2 May 2009, BBC Radio 4.

[6] As Martin Sorrell suggested while presenting himself as a member of the 1 per cent, when he is far richer than that. See Brinded, L. (2015) 'World wealth inequality: WPP's Sir Martin Sorrell "makes no apology" for the 1% club', *International Business Times*, 23 January (www.ibtimes.co.uk/world-wealth-inequality-wpps-sir-martin-sorrell-makes-no-apology-1-club-1484791).

[7] Quote from a poorly titled article: Toynbee, P. (2007) 'Balls's bold plan to end child poverty could revive Labour', *The Guardian*, 11 December. And on the most expensive of drinks, see Chakrabortty, A. (2007) 'If I had a little money...', *The Guardian*, 8 December.

[8] The chief vice of the affluent has switched from smoking to drinking because of health concerns, and more now avoid cocaine. It was during Herbert Spenser's tour of the US that the cigarette story was first told; see James, O. (2008) *The selfish capitalist: Origins of affluenza*, London: Vermilion, p 193.

[9] Davies, A., Hirsh, D. and Padley, M. (2014) *A minimum income standard for the UK in 2014*, York: Joseph Rowntree Foundation (www.jrf.org.uk/publications/minimum-income-standard-2014).

[10] ONS (Office for National Statistics) (2008) *Wealth and Assets Survey: Initial report*, London: ONS.

[11] ONS (2008), as above. It is worth speculating on why the ONS chose this particular headline at this time. Later, on 10 December 2009, when the full results were released, their headline was 'Household wealth in GB £9 trillion in 2006/08'.

[12] Kumar, A., Ussher, K. and Hunter, P. (2014) *Wealth of our nation: Rethinking policies for wealth distribution*, London: Smith Institute, p 24.

[13] ONS (Office for National Statistics) (2014) *Wealth in Great Britain, Wave 3, 2010-2012*, London: ONS, Chapter 3, table 3.2, p 3. These groups may well overlap, so will not sum to constitute 11 per cent of all households in total, and are likely to represent a smaller proportion of people than households, as they will more often be affluent older people. Note that the charity Shelter estimate that only 2 per cent of all people are landlords.

[14] ONS (2014), as above, Chapter 6, text under table 6.7, p 20. The 9.5 per cent fall is the decline in the proportion of men holding private pensions, from 21 to 19 per cent (2/21=9.5 per cent).

[15] This is calculated as 4 per cent divided by (4+2), and assumes equal numbers of children in each household type with children. The latest survey reports do not break down the numbers, but there has been no decline in lone-parent families and a very large increase in austerity, so a conservative estimate is that this inequality continues.

[16] Foster, J.B. (2006) 'The optimism of the heart: Harry Magdoff (1913-2006)', *Monthly Review*, vol 57, no 8 (www.monthlyreview.org/mrzine/foster020106.html), quoting figures revealed by Harry Magdoff, chief statistician of the New Deal Works Progress Administration in the 1940s, and an American socialist.

[17] Frank, R.H. (2007) *Falling behind: How rising inequality harms the middle class*, Berkeley, CA: University of California Press, p 90.

[18] James, O. (2008) *The selfish capitalist: Origins of affluenza*, London: Vermilion, p 153.

[19] PwC (PricewaterhouseCoopers) (2006) *Living on tick: The 21st century debtor*, London: PwC.

[20] Edwards, S. (2008) 'Citizens' Advice response to latest repossession figures', Creditman.biz report on remarks of Citizens' Advice Head of Consumer Policy, Sue Edwards, London: Citizens' Advice Bureau.

[21] BBC News (2009) 'Personal insolvency at new record', 7 August, (http://news.bbc.co.uk/1/hi/business/8189053.stm).

[22] Tovey, A. (2014) 'Personal insolvencies on the increase despite economic recovery', *The Telegraph*, 29 July (www.telegraph.co.uk/finance/economics/10997622/Personal-insolvencies-on-the-increase-despite-economic-recovery.html).

[23] Frank, R. (2007) *Richi$tan*, New York: Random House, p 153.

[24] The figures for British university students are given in GLA (Greater London Authority) (2002) *London divided: Income inequality and poverty in the capital*, London: GLA, p 80.

[25] Bolton, P. (2014) *Student loan statistics*, Standard Note SN/SG/1079, London: House of Commons Library, 28 November (www.parliament.uk/briefing-papers/sn01079.pdf).

[26] Press Association (2008) 'Watchdog to investigate "payday" loans', *The Guardian*, 28 July. Attempts have been made to slow down the growth of these loans in the UK with legislation taking effect from 2 January 2015 to curb the interest that could be charged.

[27] Dayden, D. (2014) 'Payday lending: the loans with 350% interest and a grip on America', *The Guardian*, 23 March (www.theguardian.com/money/2014/mar/23/payday-lending-interest-banks-advantage-congress).

[28] Yates, M.D. (2006) 'Capitalism is rotten to the core', *Monthly Review*, vol 58, no 1.

[29] Irvin, G. (2008) *Super rich: The rise of inequality in Britain and the United States*, Cambridge: Polity Press, p 183.

[30] The cover of the May/June 2009 issue of the journal in which these claims were made had the byline: 'One repossession claim every half hour: non-high street lenders only want to get their money back'. See *Roof*, vol 34, no 3, and for more details of the wider losses, Dorling, D. (2009) 'Daylight robbery', p 11 of that issue.

[31] Offer, A. (2006) *The challenge of affluence: Self-control and well-being in the United States and Britain since 1950*, Oxford: Oxford University Press, p 90.

[32] Foster, J.B. (2006) 'The household debt bubble', *Monthly Review*, vol 58, no 1 (www.monthlyreview.org/0506jbf.htm), reporting on data released in the biennial *The state of working America*, written by economists at the Economic Policy Institute (www.epinet.org) in Washington, DC: Mishel, L., Bernstein, J. and Allegretto, S. (2005) *The state of working America: 2004/005*, Ithaca, NY: Cornell University Press.

[33] Moore, H. (2014) 'Americans, with record consumer debt of $3.2 trillion, are taking out more credit card and auto loans', *The Guardian*, 19 November.

[34] See the Economic Policy Institute report, *The state of working America: 2004/05*, referred to in Foster (2006), above.

[35] See www.billionairefish.com and West, D.M. (2014) *Billionaires: Reflections on the upper crust*, Washington, DC: Brookings Institution Press, pp 199-203.

[36] George, V. and Wilding, P. (1999) *British society and social welfare: Towards a sustainable society*, London: Macmillan, p 147.

[37] Vollman, C. (2014) 'The IMF's lack of vision on youth unemployment', *Equal Times*, 17 December (www.equaltimes.org/the-imf-s-lack-of-vision-on-youth).

[38] Di Muzio, T. (2015) *The 1% and the rest of us: A political economy of dominate ownership*, London, Zed Books, p 43.

[39] An alternative UBS-sourced estimate put the number of billionaires not at the Forbes 1,426, or even 1,645 by 2014, but at 2,325 (also by 2014), holding $7.3 trillion or 4 per cent of all the world's wealth: see Anonymous/RIA Novosti (2014) 'Number of billionaires worldwide rises again this year: report', *Sputnik International*, 18 September (http://sputniknews.com/world/20140918/193055525/Report-Number-of-Billionaires-Worldwide-Rises-Again-This-Year.html).

[40] Roberts, M. (2014) 'Global wealth: 1% own 48%; 10% own 87% and bottom 50% own less than 1%', Blog on the 2014 Credit Suisse report, 14 October (http://thenextrecession.wordpress.com/2014/10/15/global-wealth-1-own-48-10-own-87-and-bottom-50-own-less-than-1/).

[41] Pogge, T.W. (2007) 'Why inequality matters', in D. Held and A. Kaya (eds) *Global inequality: Patterns and explanations*, Cambridge: Polity Press, pp 132-47, at p 143.

[42] Cohen, G.A. (2002) *If you're an egalitarian how come you're so rich?*, Cambridge, MA: Harvard University Press.

[43] Frank, R. (2007) *Richi$tan*, New York: Random House, p 34.

[44] Blastland, M. and Dilnot, A. (2007) *The tiger that isn't: Seeing through a world of numbers*, London: Profile Books, p 17.

[45] Hay, I. (ed) (2014) *Geographies of the super-rich*, Cheltenham: Edward Elgar.

[46] Nast, H.J. (2006) 'Critical pet studies?', *Antipode*, vol 38, no 5, pp 894-906, at p 900 and p 903, note 1. Pets also rose to the fore in their importance to the rich during the last gilded age. For this, and for how pet cemeteries arose, see the work of Howell, P. (2002) 'A place for the animal dead: pets, pet cemeteries and animal ethics in late Victorian England', *Ethics, Place and Environment*, vol 5, pp 5-22.

[47] Edwards, M. (2008) *Just another emperor? The myths and realities of philanthrocapitalism*, London: Demos and The Young Foundation, p 91, using as his source the work of Kevin Philips.

[48] A hedge fund manager interviewed in November 2005 and reported in Peston, R. (2008) *Who runs Britain? How the super-rich are changing our lives*, London: Hodder & Stoughton, p 205.

[49] Kitson, M. (2005) 'Economics for the future', *Cambridge Journal of Economics*, vol 29, no 6, pp 827-35, at p 827.

[50] The paper is referred to and discussed further in Irvin, G. (2008) *Super rich: The rise of inequality in Britain and the United States*, Cambridge: Polity Press, p 127.

[51] Offer, A. (2006) *The challenge of affluence: Self-control and well-being in the United States and Britain since 1950*, Oxford: Oxford University Press, paraphrasing and quoting both Thomas Malthus and Adam Smith on p 53.

[52] Offer (2006), as above. It has been suggested that the population rise that caused Thomas Malthus such consternation was partly created by the greed that drove the enclosures of the commons. Personal communication with Molly Scot Cato, referring to Neeson, J.M. (1996) *Commoners: Common right, enclosure and social change in England, 1700-1820*, Cambridge: Cambridge University Press.

[53] Patel, R. (2008) *Stuffed and starved: From farm to fork, the hidden battle for the world food system*, London: Portobello, p 85; see also his note 34 on p 334 for a short essay on Thomas Malthus's mistakes, including how they were partly an English reaction to the French Revolution, reflecting an old English fear of, and fascination with, 'the untamed and fecund flesh of the destitute' French revolutionaries.

[54] There are already studies showing that economics students find moral behaviour hard, and that less morally inhibited students perform better in learning the subject. The popular TV series 'The Apprentice' illustrates this well without its main characters appearing to realise it. For some evidence of the extent of the problem see Zsolnai, L. (2003) 'Honesty versus cooperation: a reinterpretation of the moral behavior of economics students', *American Journal of Economics and Sociology*, vol 62, no 4, pp 707-12, and Frank, R.H., Gilovich, T. and Regan, D.T. (1993) 'Does studying economics inhibit coöperation?', *Journal of Economic Perspectives*, vol 7, no 2, pp 159-71.

[55] Reardon, J., Madi, M.A.C. and Scott-Cato, M. (2015) *Introducing a new economics: Pluralist, sustainable and progressive*, London: Pluto Press.

[56] Prendergast, R. (2006) 'Schumpeter, Hegel and the vision of development', *Cambridge Journal of Economics*, vol 30, no 2, pp 253-75, at p 254, note 1. In this context it is also worth noting that from 1937 to 1945 John Maynard Keynes was director of the British Eugenics Society, now known as the Galton Institute.

[57] Frank, R.H. (2008) *The economic naturalist: Why economics explains almost everything*, London: Virgin Books, p 101. Contrast this book with Frank's masterpiece of a year earlier (*Falling behind: How rising inequality harms the middle class*, Berkeley, CA: University of California Press, cited in notes 10 above and 52 below) for a good example of great variance within a single person's capabilities.

[58] Harford, T. (2009) *Dear undercover economist: The very best letters from the 'Dear Economist' column*, London: Little Brown, p 15, letter to Cecilia.

[59] Goldberg, D.T. (2009) *The threat of race: Reflections on racial neoliberalism*, Oxford: Blackwell, p 373, referring to Hannah Arendt's description of the thoughtless man, that 'greatest danger to humankind'.

[60] Collier, P. (2007) *The bottom billion: Why the poorest countries are failing and what can be done about it*, Oxford: Oxford University Press, p 90.

[61] This refers to the conditions often attached to World Bank and International Monetary Fund loans to countries in economic crisis. These are the implementation of unfettered free market policies, including the privatisation of state-owned resources and austerity programmes. Even in purely economic terms, such programmes do not often work.

[62] Magnason, A. S. (2008) *Dreamland: A self-help manual for a frightened nation*, London: Citizen Press Ltd, p 53. The 'dreamland' in the title of this book refers to Iceland. Note that Milton Friedman's influence on Icelandic politics following his 1984 visit is now seen as pivotal among the antecedents of the 2008 financial crash there.

[63] The analysis and the figures these statements are made from were reported in Table 6, on pp 231 and 232 of the first edition of this book, where correlation coefficients were also presented. The year 2008 is probably the first since 1929 that borrowers have paid back more than they have borrowed, but we do not have records before 1977.

[64] Cohen, G.A. (2002) *If you're an egalitarian how come you're so rich?*, Cambridge, MA: Harvard University Press, p 181, quoting from the New Testament (Mark 8:36).

[65] Pogge, T.W. (2007) 'Why inequality matters', in D. Held and A. Kaya (eds) *Global inequality: Patterns and explanations*, Cambridge: Polity Press, pp 132-47, at pp 139-40.

[66] Prentice, C. (2009) '"Econocide" to surge as recession bites', BBC News, 11 March (http://news.bbc.co.uk/2/hi/business/7912056.stm), quoting Manhattan psychotherapist, Jonathan Alpert.

[67] US Federal Reserve (2015) Debt growth, borrowing and debt outstanding tables, especially table F100.1 (www.federalreserve.gov/releases/Z1/Current/), including home equity loans secured by junior liens … net payback was $183 billion in 2010, $69 billion in 2011, $62 billion in 2012, and $1 billion in 2013.

[68] Covert, B. (2014) 'The biggest robbers in America are employers', *Think Progress*, 12 September (http://thinkprogress.org/economy/2014/09/12/3566891/wage-theft-robberies/).

[69] Bertrand, E. (2006) 'The Coasean analysis of lighthouse financing: myths and realities', *Cambridge Journal of Economics*, vol 30, no 3, pp 389-402.

[70] Bruni, L. (2000) 'Ego facing alter: how economists have depicted human interactions', *Annals of Public and Cooperative Economics*, vol 71, no 2, pp 285-313.

[71] Kay, J. (2004) *The truth about markets: Why some nations are rich but most remain poor* (2nd edn), London: Penguin, p 361.

[72] Kunitz, S.J. and Haycraft, H. (1950) *Twentieth century authors: A biographical dictionary of modern literature* (3rd edn), New York: The H.W. Wilson Company, pp 658-9, as referenced here: http://en.wikipedia.org/wiki/Lancelot_Hogben#cite_note-k.26h-10

[73] Wintour, P. (2009) 'Labour stakes its reputation on second gamble', *The Guardian*, 19 January (www.theguardian.com/politics/2009/jan/19/economy-banking (reporting on the Monday about the Friday).

[74] Kay, J. (2004) *The truth about markets: Why some nations are rich but most remain poor* (2nd edn), London: Penguin, p 162. The argument presented is that you should only go to an economist to learn about the economy because you would not go to a DIY dentist to have your teeth fixed. As most people in the world, and increasing numbers even in rich countries, cannot afford to go to dentists due to the inequalities created by free market economics, and as so many dentists, following their accountant's advice, are concentrating now on cosmetic work rather than ending pain, this is hardly a convincing analogy. Worldwide most people who want their teeth fixed have to go to a DIY dentist. Orthodox economists have not improved that situation.

[75] John Kay is the author of a book that explicitly says it is aimed downmarket (of John) at the supposedly 'normally intelligent people': see Kay, J. (2009) *The long and the short of it: Financial investment for normally intelligent people who are not in the industry*, London: Erasmus Press. He also provides a good example of how orthodox economists, when they have their arguments upset, complain in aggrieved tones in public; see Kay, J. (2009) 'The spirit level (review)', *The Financial Times*, 23 March.

[76] Some economists will cling on into their dotages trying to argue for the old-school thinking. Take an example from John Kay, and see the two notes immediately above for context. Here John is trying to explain Christmas and what we make of presents, why we give presents, and what he thinks are other people's limitations: 'Our judgment of what the recipient will value is a means of demonstrating intimacy (or failing to do so). Those who discern irrationality in such behaviour display only the limits of their own conception of rationality' (Kay, J., 2014, 'Rationality will be at work this Christmas', Personal blog from personal website, 24 December, www.johnkay.com/2014/12/24/rationality-will-be-at-work-this-christmas).

[77] European figures derived from the EU Statistics on Income and Living Standards (EU-SILC) survey by the author, using sample weights. It is possible that French households are, on average, larger than in Germany, the UK, Spain and Italy, that more people live with an elderly relative or grown-up children, and so the figure is higher because it is a household and not an individual adults' figure (although individual French adult median incomes in 2011 were €19,550 – personal communication, Laurent Chalard, 2 January 2015). For the US, an equivalent post-tax household median of €36,450 can be roughly estimated by combining several sources. This figure was derived from a published figure of $49,486 for 2012, or roughly €40,500, less 10 per cent after subtracting average median taxes (see www.davemanuel.com/

median-household-income.php). The methodology used by the US Census Bureau is at www.census.gov/prod/techdoc/cps/cpsmar13.pdf and the US median household tax rates are given at www.voxeu.org/article/income-taxation-us-households-facts-and-parametric-estimates

78 BBC News (2014) 'Michael Jackson's doctor Conrad Murray loses appeal', 16 January (www.bbc.co.uk/news/entertainment-arts-25755822).

79 Offer, A. (2006) *The challenge of affluence: Self-control and well-being in the United States and Britain since 1950*, Oxford: Oxford University Press, pp 284, 285. See also Frank, R.H. (2007) *Falling behind: How rising inequality harms the middle class*, Berkeley, CA: University of California Press, who explains 'The price of the median house has escalated not just because houses have gotten bigger, but also because of the higher premium that desirable locations now command' (p 56).

80 Tatch, J. (2007) 'Affordability – are parents helping?', *Housing Finance*, no 3, pp 1-11, at p 6, chart 6.

81 Social Mobility and Child Poverty Commission (2014) *State of the nation 2014: Social mobility and child poverty in Great Britain*, London: The Stationery Office, p xxv.

82 Dorling, D. (2015) *All that is solid: The great housing disaster defines our times and what we can do about it*, London: Allen Lane.

83 There were even accusations of trying to fix international polls over whether he said it! Cliverton (2014) 'Top Gear's Jeremy Clarkson: "Catch a Nigger by the toe, when he squeals…"', *Barbados Free Press*, 2 May (https://barbadosfreepress.wordpress.com/2014/05/02/top-gears-jeremy-clarkson-catch-a-nigger-by-the-toe-when-he-squeals/).

84 Offer, A. (2006) *The challenge of affluence: Self-control and well-being in the United States and Britain since 1950*, Oxford: Oxford University Press; see p 190 on bathtubs and p 196 on Robert and Helen Lynd's quote from 1929.

85 I am grateful to Bob Hughes for this argument. He draws on articles including: Fisher, F.M., Grilliches, Z. and Kaysen, C. (1962) 'The cost of automobile model changes since 1949', *Journal of Political Economy*, vol 70, no 5, October, discussed in Baran, P. and Sweezy, P.M. (1966) 'Monopoly capital: an essay on the American economic and social order', *Monthly Review*, pp 138-41.

86 Tomlinson, S. (2013) 'First it was carted off on the back of a truck, then it faced the crusher, now glow-in-the dark Lamborghini is ticketed in Mayfair', *The Daily Mail*, 5 July (www.dailymail.co.uk/news/article-2356689/Glow-dark-Lamborghini-Aventador-ticketed-Mayfair.html).

87 Crawford, E. (2007) *Beyond 2010 – A holistic approach to road safety in Great Britain*, London: Parliamentary Advisory Council for Transport Safety, p 80.

88 ONS (Office for National Statistics) (2014) *Family spending*, December 2014 online edition, especially chapters 1 and 2 (www.ons.gov.uk/ons/rel/family-spending/family-spending/2014-edition/index.html).

89 Holehouse, M. (2014) 'Cars, televisions and computers get Britons spending again', *The Telegraph*, 2 December (www.telegraph.co.uk/news/shopping-and-consumer-news/11269483/Cars-televisions-and-computers-get-Britons-spending-again.html).

90 Baggini, J. (2008) *Welcome to Everytown: A journey into the English mind* (2nd edn), London: Granta, p 98; £5,539 to be exact, £427 more than average housing costs. These are mean averages; the median would be lower, the mode lower still.

91 Frank, R. (2007) *Richi$tan*, New York: Random House, p 137 (prices given on p 123).

92 Frank, R.H. (2008) *The economic naturalist: Why economics explains almost everything*, London: Virgin Books, p 145 (emphasis added).

[93] Baggini, J. (2008) *Welcome to Everytown: A journey into the English mind* (2nd edn), London: Granta, p 107.

[94] According to one multi-billionaire quoted in Frank, R. (2007) *Richi$tan*, New York: Random House, p 134.

[95] Frank (2007), as above.

[96] Shah, H. and McIvor, M. (2006) *A new political economy: Compass Programme for Renewal*, London: Lawrence & Wishart, p 48.

[97] That seven-fold ratio is found in Sheffield, where it is partly also caused by almost all affluent children under the age of 10 no longer being allowed to play on pavements or walk to neighbours' homes. A similar ratio was reported nationally in evidence given in 2008 to the House of Commons Transport Committee (2009) *Ending the scandal of complacency: Road safety beyond 2010: Further government response to the Committee's Eleventh Report of Session 2007–08*, London: The Stationery Office. In this report, MPs said 'We urge the Government to renew its focus on tackling the appalling level of child road traffic deaths associated with deprivation.' In April 2009 the government responded that, 'We are proposing to amend our guidance on speed limits, recommending that local highway authorities over time, introduce 20 mph zones or limits into streets which are primarily residential in nature' (see pp 2 and 14 for the Committee's concerns and the government response in www.publications.parliament.uk/pa/cm200809/cmselect/cmtran/422/422.pdf). Evidence that the major single cause of mortality in Britain for those under the age of 35 is road traffic accidents was given in Dorling, D. (2008) 'Supplementary memorandum, ending the scandal of complacency', House of Commons Transport Committee, *Ending the scandal of complacency: Road safety beyond 2010*, Eleventh Report of Session 2007-08, pp EV 323-4. For more of the underlying studies see Graham, D., Glaister, S. and Anderson, R. (2005) 'The effects of area deprivation on the incidence of child and adult pedestrian casualties in England', *Accident Analysis & Prevention*, vol 37, no 1, pp 125-35.

[98] Dorling, D. (2006) 'Infant mortality and social progress in Britain, 1905–2005', in E. Garrett, C. Galley, N. Shelton and R. Woods (eds) *Infant mortality: A continuing social problem*, Aldershot: Ashgate, pp 213-28.

[99] The best-off 0.01 per cent have 11 per cent of all wealth, or 1,120 times average wealth, more than the same group had just prior to the 1929 crash as a share, and five times more than they had in 1978 as a proportion; see Reich, R. (2014) 'The 1 percent is gutting America's middle class', *Salon On-line Magazine*, 19 November (www.salon.com/2014/11/19/robert_reich_the_1_percent_is_gutting_americas_middle_class_partner/?utm_source=facebook&utm_medium=socialflow).

[100] 'What's going on' is one of the favourite lyrics of celebrity, from Marvin Gaye asking 'why there's so many of you dying (brother)', to the 4 Non-Blondes 'praying for a revolution'. It has always been a popular question to ask why social inequality persists and what might be done to increase justice. The question is most often asked in the lyrics of popular tunes played on commercial radio to gain an audience for radio advertisements.

[101] Allan, V. (2015) 'We're not envious, Mr Blunt – we're raging mad', *The Sunday Herald*, 25 January (www.heraldscotland.com/comment/columnists/were-not-envious-mr-blunt-were-raging-mad.116846207).

[102] Skidelsky, E. and Skidelsky, R. (2013) *How much is enough? Money and the good life*, London: Penguin (by Richard Posner in his *New York Times* review of the first edition of their book on which they comment on p xv).

[103] Frank, R. (2007) *Richi$tan*, New York: Random House, pp 49, 143.

[104] Blastland, M. and Dilnot, A. (2007) *The tiger that isn't: Seeing through a world of numbers*, London: Profile Books, p 112; £7,500 is derived by dividing £150 billion by the authors' 20 million homeowner estimate.

[105] In the first edition of this book, this sentence read: 'to raise consumer "credit" in total by $104 billion in 2006, and then a further $134 billion was borrowed in 2007'. Since that edition was published, the US Federal Reserve have raised their estimates for unsecured borrowing in those two years, by $17 billion each year! Although they might well have changed substantially yet again if you look now; for the official guesses on US lending, see www.federalreserve.gov/releases/Z1/Current/ for the UK figures; see pp 92-6 of the first edition of this volume on how rising social inequalities had fuelled that borrowing, and where the estimates came from.

[106] Osborne, H. (2015) 'New consumer debt reaches seven-year high in UK', *The Guardian*, 3 January (www.theguardian.com/money/2015/jan/03/new-consumer-debt-reaches-7-year-high).

[107] Smith, S.J. (2007) 'Banking on housing? Speculating on the role and relevance of housing wealth in Britain', Paper prepared for the Joseph Rowntree Foundation 'Inquiry into home ownership 2010 and beyond', Durham: University of Durham, p 22.

[108] The latest statistics are on UK debt reported at http://themoneycharity.org.uk/money-statistics/

[109] Frank, R. (2007) *Richi$tan*, New York: Random House, p 132; and Dorling, D. (2015) *All that is solid*, London: Allen Lane.

[110] Diamond, J. (2006) *Collapse: How societies choose to fail or survive* (2nd edn), London: Penguin, p 61.

[111] Wilcock, S. (2104) 'Official discourses of the Australian "welfare cheat"', *Current Issues in Criminal Justice*, vol 26, no 2 (www.austlii.edu.au/au/journals/CICrimJust/2014/20.html).

[112] Connelly, M. (2008) *Fatal misconception: The struggle to control world population*, Cambridge, MA: Harvard University Press, pp 70, 90, 411.

[113] Although only for a certain elite, according to Major-General Hugh Stott of the Indian Medical Service in a letter to the *British Medical Journal*, published on 13 December 1958 (vol 2, p 1480).

[114] Hughes, B. (2008) 'Land', D. Dorling, Oxford, personal communication; see 'Country for sale', *Guardian Weekend*, 26 April 2008 (www.theguardian.com/world/2008/apr/26/cambodia), and on the Virgin Islands: www.thepetitionsite.com/takeaction/119884382?z00m=15374441

[115] According to former hedge fund director, Robert Johnson – see Hogg, A. (2015) 'As inequality soars, the nervous super rich are already planning their escapes', *The Guardian*, 23 January (www.theguardian.com/public-leaders-network/2015/jan/23/nervous-super-rich-planning-escapes-davos-2015).

[116] Frank, R. (2007) *Richi$tan*, New York: Random House, p 131. When a wardrobe is this large, it becomes potentially so much more than a receptacle for the storage of clothing. Most wardrobes do not have many other uses, but these monster closets could each be a very large sitting room, 20ft by 20ft, four decent-sized bedrooms, and much more besides.

[117] Berg, M. (2004) 'Consumption in eighteenth- and early nineteenth-century Britain', in R. Floud and P. Johnson (eds) *The Cambridge economic history of modern Britain: Volume 1: Industrialisation, 1700–1860*, Cambridge: Cambridge University Press, pp 357-87, at pp 377-9.

[118] James, O. (2007) *Affluenza: How to be successful and stay sane*, London: Vermilion, p 35.

[119] Bauman, Z. (2007) *Consuming life*, Cambridge: Polity Press, p 101.

[120] Baggini, J. (2008) *Welcome to Everytown: A journey into the English mind* (2nd edn), London: Granta, p 225.

[121] Bauman, Z. (2007) *Consuming life*, Cambridge: Polity Press, p 13, reporting a teacher's description.

[122] Wilkinson, R.G. and Pickett, K. (2009) *The spirit level: Why more equal societies almost always do better*, London: Allen Lane, p 117, quoting Gillian Evans, in turn quoting an anonymous teacher.

[123] Bauman, Z. (2006) *Liquid fear*, Cambridge: Polity Press, p 162.

[124] George, S. (2008) *Hijacking America: How the religious and secular right changed what Americans think*, Cambridge: Polity Press, p 248 and the footnote on that page referring to Mark Buchanan's 2007 article, 'Are we born prejudiced?', *New Scientist*, 17 March.

[125] Zsolnai, L. (2003) 'Honesty versus cooperation: a reinterpretation of the moral behavior of economics students', *American Journal of Economics and Sociology*, vol 62, no 4, pp 707-12.

[126] Frank, R.H., Gilovich, T. and Regan, D.T. (1993) 'Does studying economics inhibit cooperation?', *Journal of Economic Perspectives*, vol 7, no 2, pp 159-71.

[127] George, V. and Wilding, P. (1999) *British society and social welfare: Towards a sustainable society*, London: Macmillan, p 132; the fraction is derived from table 5.1.

[128] Keister, L.A. and Moller, S. (2000) 'Wealth inequality in the United States', *Annual Review of Sociology*, vol 26, no 1, pp 63-81. The ratio of 1,600:1 is derived from calculating the fraction 40/(1/40).

[129] See "Sober Look's" anonymous article entitled 'Financial obligations rising for renters, falling for homeowners' in the 'Credit Writedowns' blog as of 5 November 2013, last accessed on 2 January 2015, lasted accessed in February 2015 (www.creditwritedowns.com/2013/11/financial-obligations-rising-for-renters-falling-for-homeowners.html).

[130] According to the 2001 Census: see Thomas, B. and Dorling, D. (2007) *Identity in Britain: A cradle-to-grave atlas*, Bristol: Policy Press, p 46.

[131] ONS (Office for National Statistics) (2008) *Wealth and Assets Survey: Initial report*, London: ONS, Table 2 and p 3 of press release.

[132] Williams, P. (2008) *Please release me! A review of the equity release market in the UK, its potential and consumer expectations*, London: Council of Mortgage Lenders, p 26.

[133] Wyly, E.K., Pearce, T., Moos, M. et al (2009) 'Subprime mortgage segmentation in the American urban system', *Tijdschrift voor Economische en Sociale Geografie*, vol 99, no 1, pp 3-23, at p 3. Denial-based exclusion refers to, for example, not being offered accommodation in an area, or not being offered a mortgage because of the colour of your skin. For those interested, see also Wyly, E.K., Atia, M. and Hammel, D.J. (2004) 'Has mortgage capital found an inner-city spatial fix?', *Housing Policy Debate*, vol 15,no 3, pp 623-85; Wyly, E.K., Atia, M., Foxcroft, H., Hammel, D.J. and Phillips-Watts, K. (2006) 'American home: predatory mortgage capital and spaces of race and class exploitation in the United States', *Geografiska Annaler B*, vol 88, no 1, pp 105-32; and Wyly, E.K., Atia, M., Lee, E. and Mendez, P. (2007) 'Race, gender, and statistical representation: predatory mortgage lending and the US community reinvestment movement', *Environment and Planning A*, vol 39, pp 2139-66.

[134] Kloby, J. (2002) 'Wealth gap woes', *Monthly Review*, vol 53, no 8.

[135] Scott Cato, M. (2009) *Green economics: An introduction to theory, policy and practice*, London: Earthscan, pp 126-7. The $41.9 trillion US debt estimate is derived from Table 6, pp 231-2, first edition of this volume.

[136] Scott Cato (2009), as above, which provides an excellent introduction to how the majority have been deceived about how reserve currencies are manipulative.

[137] Diamond, J. (2006) *Collapse: How societies choose to fail or survive* (2nd edn), London: Penguin, p 150. The term 'Pueblo people' is also used and continues to be used today by some groups as, although civilisations die out, whole peoples rarely do in their entirety.

[138] Berg, M. (2004) 'Consumption in eighteenth- and early nineteenth-century Britain', in R. Floud and P. Johnson (eds) *The Cambridge economic history of modern Britain: Volume 1: Industrialisation, 1700–1860*, Cambridge: Cambridge University Press, pp 357-87, at p 366.

[139] Cockshott, W.P. and Cottrell, A. (1983) *Towards a new socialism*, Nottingham: Spokesman, p 23.

[140] Cumming, E. (2015) '"It's like a ghost town": lights go out as foreign owners desert London homes', *The Observer*, 25 January (www.theguardian.com/uk-news/2015/jan/25/its-like-a-ghost-town-lights-go-out-as-foreign-owners-desert-london-homes).

[141] Rich banker's wife, quoted in Anonymous (2014) 'I'm rich. But not rich enough', *The Times*, 12 October (www.thetimes.co.uk/tto/magazine/article4229469.ece).

[142] Treanor, J. (2014) 'Senior City bankers paid an average of £1.3m, data shows', *The Guardian*, 31 December (www.theguardian.com/business/2014/dec/31/city-of-london-bankers-paid-1300000-average).

[143] Offer, A. (2006) *The challenge of affluence: Self-control and well-being in the United States and Britain since 1950*, Oxford: Oxford University Press, p 94.

[144] Diamond, J. (2006) *Collapse: How societies choose to fail or survive* (2nd edn), London: Penguin, p 75.

[145] Magnason, A.S. (2008) *Dreamland: A self-help manual for a frightened nation*, London: Citizen Press Ltd, p 274.

[146] Liu, J., Daily, G.C., Ehrlich, P.R. et al (2003) 'Effects of household dynamics on resource consumption and biodiversity', *Nature*, vol 421, 30 January, pp 530-3.

[147] Buonfino, A. and Thomson, L. (2007) *Belonging in contemporary Britain*, Report for the Commission on Integration and Cohesion, London: Commission on Integration and Cohesion, p 5; unclaimed bodies information from personal communication, John Mohan, University of Southampton, work in progress; finding mortality rates to be especially high for young men with few friends living in bedsits in the largest cities, exactly how high is yet to be determined.

[148] Dorling, D. and Gunnell, D. (2003) 'Suicide: the spatial and social components of despair in Britain 1980-2000', *Transactions of the Institute of British Geographers*, vol 28, no 4, pp 442-60.

[149] Calcott, A. and Bull, J. (2007) *Ecological footprint of British city residents*, CarbonPlan, Godalming: World Wildlife Fund UK (www.wwf.org.uk/filelibrary/pdf/city_footprint2.pdf), p 8.

[150] James, O. (2007) *Affluenza: How to be successful and stay sane*, London: Vermilion; a remix of pp 158-9, with the final sentence from p 148 (having consulted the author about taking such liberties – or 'making posies', see the end of the introduction to this volume).

[151] Gates, B. (2014) 'Why inequality matters', *Gatesnotes*, 13 October (www.gatesnotes.com/Books/Why-Inequality-Matters-Capital-in-21st-Century-Review).

Chapter 7

[1] Buerk, M. (2014) 'Boris Johnson's sister Rachel: I was so precious, so spoilt', *The Radio Times*, 12 March (www.radiotimes.com/news/2014-03-12/boris-johnsons-sister-rachel-i-was-so-precious-so-spoilt).

[2] We now know that the way rats behave in cages tells us more about the cage than the rats. Psychologist Bruce Alexander created experiments with rats that suggested that: 'Addiction is an adaptation to your environment. It's not you; it's the cage you live in.' Quoted in Aitkenhead, D. (2015) 'Lair, addict … reformed man?', *The Guardian*, 3 January (www.theguardian.com/media/2015/jan/02/johann-hari-interview-drugs-book-independent).

[3] The strongest evidence comes from the US, where, using data from 2002-06, and having taken into account absolute income, it was found that for the odds of reporting poor health, '… regardless of how the reference group was defined, there was a "dose–response" relationship; with individuals in the highest quintile of relative deprivation more likely to report poor health than individuals in the next highest quintile and so on' (Subramanyam, M., Kawachi, I., Berkman, L. et al, 2009, 'Relative deprivation in income and self-rated health in the United States', *Social Science & Medicine*, vol 69, pp 327-34, at p 329). This study concerns reporting ill health of all kinds. Among younger adults in affluent countries, the majority of serious poor health is poor mental health.

[4] Since the first edition of this volume was published, a great deal of new evidence has emerged adding support to these theories: Layte, R. (2012) 'The association between income inequality and mental health: testing status anxiety, social capital, and neo-materialist explanations', *European Sociological Review*, vol 28, pp 498-511, and Pickett, K. and Wilkinson, R. (2015) 'Income inequality and health: a causal review', *Social Science & Medicine*.

[5] Rugani, R., Vallortigara, G., Priftis, K. and Regolin, L. (2015) 'Number-space mapping in the newborn chick resembles humans' mental number line', *Science*, vol 347, no 6221, pp 534-6 (www.sciencemag.org/content/347/6221/534).

[6] Burns, J. (2007) *The descent of madness: Evolutionary origins of psychosis and the social brain*, Hove: Routledge, p 74. The reference here is to Erich Fromm's *In fear of freedom* (1942), and ends with the suggestion that following industrialisation and individualisation, we are now '…witnessing the psychological consequences of human isolation and dislocation.'

[7] Johann Harri, as quoted by Aitkenhead (2015), as above. The quote continues: 'But if you can't do that because you're so traumatised by your childhood that you can't trust people, you may well bond with a drug instead.'

[8] Burns (2007), as above, p 197.

[9] CEPMHPG (Centre for Economic Performance's Mental Health Policy Group) (2006) *The depression report: A New Deal for depression and anxiety disorders*, London: CEPMHPG, London School of Economics and Political Science. The figure is derived by doubling 16.4 per cent given in a table at the end of that source based on a survey undertaken in the year 2000. If this appears too crude a method, as in some families more than one adult will be suffering poor mental health, and in others there will be only one adult, then take Oliver James' estimate of 23 per cent of individuals suffering emotional distress in Britain, based, in turn, on WHO estimates, and then, clearly, at least a third of families are affected (James, O., 2008, *The selfish capitalist: Origins of affluenza*, London: Vermilion, p 1; James, O., 2009, 'Distress', D. Dorling, Oxfordshire, personal communication). Just under a quarter, 23 per cent, is the figure also reported by The Equality Trust in January 2015 (www.equalitytrust.org.uk/research/mental-health).

[10] National Centre for Social Research and the University of Leicester (2009) *Adult psychiatric morbidity in England, 2007: Results of a household survey*, London: Nation Archives Web Archive, 27 January (http://webarchive.nationalarchives.gov.uk/20090204140018/ic.nhs.uk/statistics-and-data-collections/mental-health/

other-related-publications/adult-psychiatric-morbidity-in-england-2007-results-of-a-household-survey).

[11] CEPMHPG (2006), as above, is the source for the statistics in this paragraph except for here, which is: Whitworth, D. (2014) 'Mental health issues rising says Royal College of GPs', BBC News, 15 January (www.bbc.co.uk/news/health-25740866).

[12] As revealed by the most comparable WHO psychiatric surveys reported in Wilkinson, R.G. and Pickett, K. (2009) *The spirit level: Why more equal societies almost always do better*, London: Allen Lane, p 67.

[13] The statistics for Britain in this paragraph up to this point and in the previous one were derived from ONS (Office for National Statistics) (2001) *Psychiatric morbidity*; ONS (2003) *Better or worse: National statistics*, London; ONS (2005) *Mental health in children and young people in Great Britain*; MIND (2009) *Statistics 1: How common is mental distress?* (www.mind.org.uk/help/research_and_policy/statistics_1_how_common_is_mental_distress); National Statistics Online (2004) *Mental disorder more common in boys*, London: National Statistics Online; and MHF (Mental Health Foundation) (2005) *Lifetime impacts: Childhood and adolescent mental health, Understanding the lifetime impacts*, London: MHF. They were kindly made available by Dan Vale (2008) 'Mapping needs', Project seminar presentation, The Young Foundation, 24 June, D. Dorling, London, personal communication. They could be updated, but only by a few years, and would differ only very slightly from those early reports. According to *Social Trends* No 36 (2006), by then they altered slightly to be 10.2 per cent, 12.6 per cent, 5.1 per cent and 10.3 per cent. See Chapter 7, Table 7, based on the ONS Mental Health of Children and Young People Survey (2004). More recent data for the UK is lacking due to coalition government cuts, especially of the 'Tell Us' surveys. Note that all these percentage estimates will have sampling error margins.

[14] Alzheimer's Society (2015) *Demography, based on estimates made for the year 2013* (www.alzheimers.org.uk/site/scripts/documents_info.php?documentID=412). If current trends continue and no action is taken, the number of people with dementia in the UK is forecast to increase to 1,142,677 by 2025 and 2,092,945 by 2051 (from 1.1 million to 2.1 million people).

[15] Collishaw, S., Maughan, B., Goodman, R. et al (2004) 'Time trends in adolescent mental health', *Journal of Child Psychology and Psychiatry*, vol 45, no 8, pp 1350-62.

[16] West, D.M. (2014) *Billionaires: Reflections on the upper crust*, Washington, DC: Brookings Institution Press (see pp 199-201).

[17] West, P. and Sweeting, H. (2003) 'Fifteen, female and stressed: changing patterns of psychological distress over time', *Journal of Child Psychology and Psychiatry*, vol 44, no 3, pp 399-411, at pp 406, 409.

[18] The full set is shown in Table 7 in the first edition of this book. See Costello, E.J., Erkanli, A. and Angold, A. (2006) 'Is there an epidemic of child or adolescent depression?', *Journal of Child Psychology and Psychiatry*, vol 47, no 12, pp 1263-71.

[19] The one in 25 estimate can be reached either by extrapolating backwards or by taking the lowest rates recorded in the past, which both produce similar results as the extrapolation is based on those rates.

[20] See SAMHSA (Substance Abuse and Mental Health Services Administration) (2012) *Data spotlight: Depression triples between the ages of 12 and 15 among adolescent girls*, 2 August, a report based on combined data from the 2008-10 SAMHSA National Survey on Drug Use and Health (NSDUH). NSDUH is a scientifically conducted annual survey of approximately 67,500 people throughout the country, aged 12 and older. SAMHSA is a public health agency within the Department of Health and Human Services (for more details see www.medscape.com/viewarticle/768584, 2012). The

number of major depressive episodes (MDEs) increases dramatically as adolescent girls enter puberty, according to this new report, which did not make comparisons over time. Approximately 12 per cent of all girls in the US between 12 and 17 years of age experienced an MDE in the past year compared with only 4.5 per cent of boys between the same ages. In addition, 5.1 per cent of the girls experienced past-year MDEs at the age of 12, compared to 15.2 per cent who experienced the episodes at the age of 15.

[21] In fact, they found that 'Only fathers' educational attainment and family financial status remained significant (odds ratios: 3.28-5.30 for grade school of fathers and 2.62-2.78 for being worse off economically)' (Doi, Y., Roberts, R., Takeuchi, K. et al, 2001, 'Multiethnic comparison of adolescent major depression based on the DSM-IV criteria in a US–Japan study', *Journal of the American Academy of Child and Adolescent Psychiatry*, vol 40, pp 1308-15, at p 1308).

[22] Offer, A. (2006) *The challenge of affluence: Self-control and well-being in the United States and Britain since 1950*, Oxford: Oxford University Press, p 348.

[23] Twenge, J.M. (2000) 'The age of anxiety? Birth cohort change in anxiety and neuroticism, 1952-1993', *Journal of Personality and Social Psychology*, vol 79, no 6, pp 1007-21.

[24] Twenge (2000), as above, p 1018.

[25] ONS (Office for National Statistics) (2008) *Sustainable development indicators in your pocket 2008: An update of the UK government strategy indicators*, London: Department for Environment, Food and Rural Affairs, p 130. The equivalent ONS publication of a year earlier had broken down these statistics by social grade AB, C, D and E (p 125), but not by age, the publication of a year later reported the responses to different questions (p 137), and so comparisons over time for children from this source are not yet possible (in the 2008 study, children could say it was 'a bit true' that they were happy, but that option was removed from the later survey and apparent happiness rose by 10 per cent!). For adults by social grade in England, stark differences in wellbeing were reported in 2007. Only those in the best-paid work, grades AB, reported much net happiness and feeling engaged with what they were doing. Those in the worst paid work, grade E, most often felt unhappy, not engaged, unsafe, depressed, lonely, and that everything was an effort – most probably because they were, and it was.

[26] These figures are from data collected in 2007, released in the report by Davidson, J. et al (2008) *Children and young people in mind: The final report of the National CAMHS Review*, pp 19-21, which also explains that '*Children who face three or more stressful life events, such as family bereavement, divorce or serious illness, are three times more likely than other children to develop emotional and behavioural disorders.*' Published in the year of the economic crash, few of the report's recommendations were acted on. The report's foreword ends tellingly: '*Anyone in contact with a child has an impact on that child's mental health and psychological well-being.*' In other words, everyone and everything matters, including those we determine who can have contact with children, which children's centres are to be cut and which youth workers are to be sacked first. (http://webarchive.nationalarchives.gov.uk/20081230004520/publications.dcsf.gov.uk/eorderingdownload/camhs-review.pdf).

[27] Nancy Shalek, President of Shalek Advertising Agency, as quoted in Kasser, T. (2002) *The high price of materialism*, Cambridge, MA: The MIT Press, p 91.

[28] McChesney, R.W. and Foster, J.B. (2003) 'The commercial tidal wave', *Monthly Review*, vol 54, no 10.

[29] In comments reported in association with the publication of DCSF (Department for Children, Schools and Families) (2007) *The children's plan: Building brighter futures*,

London: The Stationery Office. Ed Balls, who was quoted as the source, was the relevant government minister in charge of this department at the time. In subsequent years he did nothing to reduce the exposure of children to advertising.

[30] Baggini, J. (2008) *Welcome to Everytown: A journey into the English mind* (2nd edn), London: Granta, p 224, relying, in turn, on a National Consumer Council survey of 2005. The same consumer council report revealed that some 78 per cent of children in Britain say they 'love shopping'.

[31] Rowan Williams was elected Archbishop of Canterbury in 2002 and retired from that office at the end of 2012. These words are from the press release to a report from the Children's Society written in his name: Williams, R. (2008) 'Good childhood inquiry reveals mounting concern over commercialisation of childhood' (www.childrenssociety.org.uk/whats_happening/media_office/latest_news/6486_pr.html), referencing, in turn, Schor, J. (2004) *Born to buy: The commercialized child and the new consumer culture*, New York: Scribner; and NCC (National Consumer Council) (2007) *Watching, wanting, wellbeing*, London: NCC.

[32] Or, to quote verbatim, 'marinated in the most aggressive advertising and marketing environment ever known', according to Anya Kamenetz, author of *Generation debt*, one of many popular books about the evil of advertising, quoted in Harris, J. (2007) 'The anxious affluent: middle class insecurity and social democracy', *Renewal: A Journal of Social Democracy*, vol 15, no 4, pp 72-9, at p 75.

[33] Trotter, C. (2007) *No left turn: The distortion of New Zealand's history by greed, bigotry and right-wing politics*, Auckland: Random House, p 124, noting that the observation was made first by John Dewey.

[34] Skidelsky, R. and Skidelsky, E. (2013) *How much is enough? Money and the good life*, London: Penguin, p 33.

[35] Bauman, Z. (2007) *Consuming life*, Cambridge: Polity Press, pp 46-7; original emphasis.

[36] Hoyert, D.L. (2012) '75 years of mortality in the United States, 1935-2010', NCHS Data Brief No 88, Atlanta: Centre for Disease Control, Figure 4 (www.cdc.gov/nchs/data/databriefs/db88.pdf).

[37] As explained by Sebastian Kraemer, and as clearly evident in the current economic recession/depression. For a summary of the odds of unemployment making you ill, the efficiency of the various alternatives, and Kraemer's explanation, see Dorling, D. (2009) 'Unemployment and health (editorial)', *British Medical Journal*, vol 338, p b829.

[38] Navarro, V. (2003) 'The inhuman state of US health care', *Monthly Review*, vol 55, no 4.

[39] Research reported in Edwards, M. (2008) *Just another emperor? The myths and realities of philanthrocapitalism*, London: Demos and The Young Foundation, p 51.

[40] The dissection of meaning of the private hospital receipt is one of the most striking and memorable of illustrations included in Edward Tufte's book, *Envisioning information* (published by the Graphics Press in 1990). It is not hard to understand that a medical system that aims to give the best care at the lowest cost, and one in which profit is not allowed, is both likely to do the least harm, and most likely to treat you quickly and appropriately when you actually most need treatment. There are no private accident and emergency wards in the UK; it is not in the interest of private hospitals to provide such facilities, ones where the need is so clear, and the scope for profiteering so low.

[41] Goldberg, D.T. (2009) *The threat of race: Reflections on racial neoliberalism*, Oxford: Blackwell, p 88.

[42] Jones, S. (2014) 'Optical Express accused of using hard sell techniques', *The Optician*, 23 September (www.opticianonline.net/optical-expess-accused-using-hard-sell-techniques/).

[43] Boffey, D. (2015) 'Top eye clinic faces claims over "faulty" model of lens: doctors' complaints prompt inquiry after claims that implants have caused loss of vision', *The Observer*, Sunday 4 January (www.theguardian.com/society/2015/jan/03/top-eye-clinic-faces-claims).

[44] One of the professed remits of the new body Public Health England, as described in January 2015 on its own website, as part of its limited responsibilities (www.gov.uk/government/organisations/public-health-england/about).

[45] What is generally understood as public health, as reported on Wikipedia (http://en.wikipedia.org/wiki/Public_health), using the definition of Winslow, C.E.A. (1920) 'The untilled fields of public health', *Science*, vol 51, no 1306, pp 23-33.

[46] DH (Department of Health) (2008) *Tackling health inequalities: 2007 status report on the programme for action*, London: DH, Health Inequalities Unit, p 46, and with Professor Michael Marmot, Chair of the Scientific Reference Group on Health Inequalities, suggesting on p 5 that, 'action on inequalities in health in England conforms rather well to evidence-based policy making.'

[47] Campbell, D. (2015) 'New doctors offered NHS fund "golden hello" to become GPs', *The Guardian*, 26 January (www.theguardian.com/society/2015/jan/26/new-doctors-offered-golden-hello-become-gps-nhs-fund).

[48] Hellowell, M. (2014) *The future of PFI: Will the NHS pay a higher price for new hospitals?*, Centre for Health in the Public Interest (CHPI), November (data concerning private finance 2 [PF2] on p 5 and profits to be made on p 8). The total cost is currently around 2 per cent of a shrinking budget and rising. The government forces the NHS to use private finance initiative (PFI) deals because it can pretend this does not add to national debt, and because MPs' friends in the private sector get rich as a result (including many peers in the House of Lords). Why else would almost all MPs vote to support PFI? And why else did the coalition ensure even more NHS money would go to PFI in its PF2 'reforms'?

[49] Davis, K., Stremikis, K., Squires, D. and Schoen, C. (2014) *Mirror, mirror on the wall: How the performance of the US health care system compares internationally*, New York: The Commonwealth Fund.

[50] Leys, C. and Toft, B. (2014) *Patient safety in private hospitals – The known and unknown risks*, Centre for Health in the Public Interest (CHPI), August (serious injury data on p 14).

[51] Kelsey, J. (1997) *The New Zealand experiment: A world model for structural adjustment?*, Auckland: Auckland University Press, p 359, quoting, in turn, and in part, from Prue Hyman.

[52] Whyte, D. (2007) 'Gordon Brown's charter for corporate criminals', *Criminal Justice Matters*, vol 70, pp 31-2. Original source was HM Government (2007) *Regulators' compliance code: Draft code of practice laid before Parliament under section 23(4) of the Legislative and Regulatory Reform Act 2006 for approval by resolution of each House of Parliament*, London: Better Regulation Executive, Cabinet Office.

[53] Robert Townsend Farquhar, in the 19th century, arguing in favour of wages in place of slavery for islanders in the Caribbean and Indian Ocean, and quoted in Hudson, M. (2004) 'Scarcity of what and for whom?', *Monthly Review*, vol 56, no 7.

[54] Trotter, C. (2007) *No left turn: The distortion of New Zealand's history by greed, bigotry and right-wing politics*, Auckland: Random House, p 57, quoting a director of the London Docks speaking during the 1889 strike.

[55] Offer, A. (2006) *The challenge of affluence: Self-control and well-being in the United States and Britain since 1950*, Oxford: Oxford University Press, p 295, where it is interesting to think how different Britain might be if it were not so dominated by just a few intuitions. Avner Offer also makes all these points in regard to the US but not China,

although the connections are clear, and that is without mentioning how frequently the death penalty is applied in both countries, including for executing (in clear language, murdering) children. On a light note, a year later, Avner was involved in an academic argument over the book concerning how often people might have sex, which is very telling (www.nybooks.com/articles/archives/2007/nov/22/theyd-much-rather-be-rich/).

[56] Elliot, L. and Atkinson, D. (2007) *Fantasy Island: Waking up to the incredible economic, political and social illusions of the Blair legacy*, London: Constable and Robinson, p 229.

[57] Rodríguez Valladares, M. (2014) 'Derivatives markets growing again, with few new protections', *New York Times*, 13 May (http://dealbook.nytimes.com/2014/05/13/derivatives-markets-growing-again-with-few-new-protections/).

[58] Franz Münterfering, SPD (*Sozialdemokratische Partei Deutschlands*, Social Democrat Party) chair, as quoted in *Bild* and reported in Peston (2008) *Who runs Britain? How the super-rich are changing our lives*, London: Hodder & Stoughton, p 210.

[59] Daniel Loeb, chief executive of the hedge fund Third Point, as reported in Peston (2008), as above, p 211.

[60] DeVerteuil, G. (2007) 'Book review: *Fragments of inequality: Social, spatial, and evolutionary analyses of income distribution*. Sanjoy Chakravorty', *Annals of the Association of American Geographers*, vol 97, no 1, pp 219-20, at p 219, according, in turn, to a recent study by Andrew Beveridge, published in the *New York Times* and referenced by Roberts, S. (2005) 'In Manhattan, poor make 2 cents for every dollar of the rich', 4 September. Note that following the widely reported success of the Namibian basic income project in Otjivero, conditions are becoming slightly less desperate there.

[61] Jackson, T. (2001) 'Website of the week: health inequalities', *British Medical Journal*, vol 322, no 7286, p 622.

[62] Cole, M. (2007) 'Learning without limits: a Marxist assessment', *Policy Futures in Education*, vol 6, no 4, pp 453-63.

[63] Offer, A. (2006) *The challenge of affluence: Self-control and well-being in the United States and Britain since 1950*, Oxford: Oxford University Press, p 287.

[64] Roberts, S. (2014) 'Gap between Manhattan's rich and poor is greatest in US, Census finds', *New York Times*, 17 September (www.nytimes.com/2014/09/18/nyregion/gap-between-manhattans-rich-and-poor-is-greatest-in-us-census-finds.html).

[65] Guy, M. (2007) *Public health annual report 2005/06: Focusing on the health of older people*, London: Westminster Primary Care Trust (figures given in an accompanying press release).

[66] Guy (2007), as above, p 22.

[67] The NHS reports for Westminster do suggest such a concentration, although for a wider view, see Parr, H. (2008) *Mental health and social space: Towards inclusionary geographies?*, Oxford: Blackwell, p 9. It is also partly the story of Largactil, as told later in this chapter.

[68] Donovan, T. (2014) 'How will the vote change the colour of the capital?', BBC News London, 16 May (www.bbc.co.uk/news/uk-england-london-27395620).

[69] Connelly, M. (2008) *Fatal misconception: The struggle to control world population*, Cambridge, MA: Harvard University Press, p 29; original emphasis on the word 'because'.

[70] Connelly (2008), as above, p 32. A photograph of the mutilated children of the Congo, with their severed hands, was one of the first photographs of genocide survivors to be distributed worldwide. That circulation continues today (http://en.wikipedia.org/wiki/File:MutilatedChildrenFromCongo.jpg).

[71] CDC (Centers for Disease Control and Prevention) (2014) *Global diarrhea burden*, Atlanta, GA: CDC, 24 January (www.cdc.gov/healthywater/global/diarrhea-burden.html).

[72] Hall, E. and Drake, M. (2006) 'Diarrhoea: the central issue', in E. Garrett, C. Galley, N. Shelton and R. Woods (eds) *Infant mortality: A continuing social problem*, Aldershot: Ashgate, pp 149-68, at p 149.
[73] Brown, D. (2008) 'Life expectancy drops for some US women', *Washington Post*, 22 April.
[74] Dorling, D. (2014) 'Why are the old dying before their time? How austerity has affected mortality rates', *New Statesman*, 7 February (www.dannydorling.org/?page_id=3970).
[75] Mesoy, E. (2008) "Bailout costs more than Marshall Plan, Louisiana Purchase, moonshot, S&L bailout, Korean War, New Deal, Iraq war, Vietnam war, and NASA's lifetime budget – combined", *Civilization Fanatics Centre*, 26 November 26 (http://forums.civfanatics.com/showthread.php?t=300384), with thanks to ideas merchant Molly Scott Cato for passing on this example.
[76] Carney, J. (2011) 'The size of the bank bailout: $29 trillion', *CNBC News*, 14 December (www.cnbc.com/id/45674390#).
[77] According to *The Economist* (2009) 'Sea of troubles', 1 August, pp 51-2, which predicted that worldwide shipping supply would soon exceed market need by 50 to 70 per cent.
[78] Seager, A. (2009) 'Industry shows unprecedented fall in demand for power, says Drax', *The Guardian*, 5 August, p 22.
[79] Babiak, P. and Hare, R.D. (2006) *Snakes in suits: When psychopaths go to work*, New York: Harper Business Press.
[80] Master's courses in Business Administration (MBAs) became successful because they nurtured short-term bird-brained arguments. 'Profit matters more than anything else, especially in the short term', is one such argument. These were the kinds of arguments that those hiring business graduates wanted to hear, and so such arguments had to be generated with the greatest ferocity by business schools trying to place themselves on the very highest perches in the aviary.
[81] Staley, O. (2009) 'Harvard begins case study as tainted MBAs reveal damaged brand', *Bloomberg News*, 2 April. This report was, in turn, quoting the words of Louis Lataif, reported to be a 1964 graduate of Harvard Business School.
[82] Offer, A. (2006) *The challenge of affluence: Self-control and well-being in the United States and Britain since 1950*, Oxford: Oxford University Press, p 47. On p 53, Avner Offer explains how recently more and more people have also come to behave like those who run corporations: 'Consumption surveys indicate much higher levels of "hand to mouth" consumption than either exponential or hyperbolic models suggest, but the hyperbolic model comes closer to reality, and reality is much less prudent even than the hyperbolic model.'
[83] According to the *New York Times* of 16 January 1910. See also Hudson, M. (2004) 'Scarcity of what and for whom?', *Monthly Review*, vol 56, no 7. In this article, Michael Perelman is quoted with reference to the price of passenger pigeons not rising at all as supply fell.
[84] Committee of Public Accounts, First report from the Committee of Public Accounts, together with the Proceedings of the Minutes of Evidence, Part of the Minutes of Evidence of Session 1971-72 and Appendices thereto, *Session 1972-73, North Sea Oil and Gas*, London: HMSO (1973), p 74. Kindly supplied by Juan Boué of the Oxford Institute for Energy Studies, personal communication, October 2014. In January 2015 legislation went through Parliament demanding even more oil was extracted more quickly from the North Sea: see Monbiot, G. (2015) 'Why leaving fossil fuels in the ground is good for everyone', *The Guardian*, 7 January (www.theguardian.com/environment/georgemonbiot/2015/jan/07/why-leaving-fossil-fuels-in-ground-good-for-everyone).

[85] CGD (Commission on Growth and Development) (2008) *The growth report: Strategies for sustained growth and inclusive development*, Washington, DC: The International Bank for Reconstruction and Development and The World Bank, on behalf of CGD, pp 1, 12. The one concession made to their critics here is the admission that resources are, eventually, finite, although a few still talk of mining the moon!

[86] Abnormalities of the prefrontal cortex are usually referred to among other features causing some people who do well in business to prosper partly because they behave psychopathically. See Spinney, L. (2004) 'Snakes in suits', *New Scientist*, 21 August. The article also reports the 1977 work of Cathy Spatz Widom, which discovered that for psychopaths in everyday life, the kind who can be found in boardrooms, the '… main difference she noted between her respondents and convicted criminals who were typically studied at that time was that they were better educated.'

[87] Morris, I. (2011) *Why the West rules for now*, London: Profile, p 28.

[88] Skidelsky, R. and Skidelsky, E. (2013) *How much is enough? Money and the good life*, London: Penguin, p 10.

[89] Rose, J. (2014) *Women in dark times*, London: Bloomsbury, p ix; many thanks to Karen Whitfield for the reference.

[90] Shah, H. and McIvor, M. (2006) *A new political economy: Compass Programme for Renewal*, London: Lawrence & Wishart, p 143. Note that the enclosure of the commons may have caused the population rise, but what caused the enclosures to start when they did?

[91] Gordon, M.J. and Rosenthal, J.S. (2003) 'Capitalism's growth imperative', *Cambridge Journal of Economics*, vol 27, pp 25-48, at pp 33, 43; they do mention that this was initially Rosa Luxemburg's suggestion, made long before the events she foretold.

[92] Or words to that effect; this version is quoted here: http://forums.digitalspy.co.uk/showthread.php?p=76701399

[93] Davies, H. and Ball, J. (2015) 'Peter Mandelson gets £400,000 tax-free loan from company he owns', *The Guardian*, 27 January (www.theguardian.com/politics/2015/jan/27/peter-mandelson-400000-pound-tax-free-loan).

[94] Elliot, L. and Atkinson, D. (2007) *Fantasy Island: Waking up to the incredible economic, political and social illusions of the Blair legacy*, London: Constable and Robinson, p 235

[95] Beck, U. (2000) *World risk society* (2nd edn), Cambridge: Polity Press, p 6.

[96] Rutherford, J. and Shah, H. (2006) *The good society: Compass Programme for Renewal*, London: Lawrence & Wishart, p 85.

[97] Purden, K. (2014) 'Food poverty: experts say foodbanks are inevitable in the UK', University of Manchester press release, 1 October (www.manchester.ac.uk/discover/news/article/?id=12916), based on the unpublished paper by Purdam, K., Garratt, E. and Esmail, A. titled: *Hungry? Food insecurity, social stigma and embarrassment in the UK.*

[98] Edwards, P., Jarvis, A., Crow, R., Crawshaw, P., Shaw, K., Irving, A. and Whisker, A. (2013) *The impact of welfare reform in the North East*, A research report for the Association of North East Councils by the Universities of Durham (Institute for Local Governance), Northumbria and Teesside and the North East region of Citizens' Advice (www.northeastcouncils.gov.uk/downloaddoc.asp?id=598).

[99] Pitts, M., Dorling, D. and Pattie, C. (2007) 'Oil for food: the global story of edible lipids', *Journal of World-Systems Research*, vol 13, no 1, pp 12-32, at p 28.

[100] Brunner, E. (2006) 'Oily fish and omega 3 fat supplements', *British Medical Journal*, vol 332, pp 739-40.

[101] We have known this for over 20 years now: see Safina, C. (1995) 'The world's imperilled fish', *Scientific American*, 00368733, November, vol 273, issue 5 (http://blueocean.org/files/Safina1995SciAm.pdf).

[102] Diamond, J. (2006) *Collapse: How societies choose to fail or survive* (2nd edn), London: Penguin, p 368.

[103] Popular culture is replete with references to it not being your sanity that should be questioned. Most popular is this quote: 'What you know you can't explain, but you feel it. You've felt it your entire life, that there's something wrong with the world. You don't know what it is, but it's there, like a splinter in your mind, driving you mad' (Morpheus, a character from *The Matrix*, 1999, a film written and directed by Lana and Andy Wachowski, two gamers with vivid imaginations). Morpheus continues with an offer: 'You take the blue pill, the story ends. You wake up in your bed and believe whatever you want to believe. You take the red pill, you stay in wonderland, and I show you how deep the rabbit hole goes.'

[104] Rose, S., Lewontin, R.C. and Kamin, L.J. (1990) *Not in our genes: Biology, ideology and human nature*, London: Penguin, p 174.

[105] Rickford, D. (2003) *Troubled inside: Responding to the mental health needs of women in prison*, London: Prison Reform Trust (www.prisonreformtrust.org.uk/Portals/0/Documents/TROUBLED%20INSI%20-%20WOMEN%20.pdf).

[106] The proprietary form in which Diazepam was first marketed by the (now) pharmaceutical giant, Roche; see James, O. (2007) *Affluenza: How to be successful and stay sane*, London: Vermilion, p 204. Although not mentioned in any of Oliver James' books as his mother-in-law (Penny) taught him a great deal about old age care and may well be the least annoying known, other sources reveal that the first tests of Valium on humans were done on the mothers-in-law of a few Roche executives. The executives were reported to have thought that it rendered their mothers-in-law significantly less annoying; see http://pharmakon.me/2012/10/04/the-magic-drug-developed-by-roche-and-how-it-revolutionized-the-pharmaceutical-industry/ as posted in October 2012, and retrieved in January 2015.

[107] Masters, R.D. (2001) 'Biology and politics: linking nature and nurture', *Annual Review of Political Science*, vol 4, no 1, pp 345-69, at p 346. Often children are prescribed Ritalin because schools will not include them if they are not 'dosed up'.

[108] Dumit, J. (2005) 'The depsychiatrisation of mental illness', *Journal of Public Mental Health*, vol 4, no 3, pp 8-13, at p 11.

[109] Johnston, L. (2014) 'Hooked on happy pills as antidepressant prescriptions soar to 50m a year', *The Express*, 16 November (www.express.co.uk/news/uk/535893/NHS-spends-billions-antidepressants-prescriptions-soar-50m).

[110] A 'wellbeing' centre is being planned to be opened in 2015, but it has no therapists: see NHS (2014) 'Minister aims to boost nation's happiness with new wellbeing centre', Public Health Wales press release, 31 October (www.wales.nhs.uk/sitesplus/888/news/34649).

[111] James, O. (2008) *The selfish capitalist: Origins of affluenza*, London: Vermilion, p 205.

[112] Davies, W. (2015) *The happiness industry*, London: Verso. See p 162 onwards on the history of Prozac.

[113] DH (Department of Health) (2008) *Tackling health inequalities: 2007 status report on the programme for action*, London, Health Inequalities Unit, p 80.

[114] The standard format is capital letter for propriety (trade) names but not for generic (chemical) names.

[115] About the number that the non-psychiatric prison population reached by 2005. For earlier figures, see Timmins, N. (2001) *The five giants: A biography of the welfare state* (new edn), London: HarperCollins, pp 210-11.

[116] Baumslag, N. (2005) *Murderous medicine: Nazi doctors, human experimentation, and typhus*, Westport, CT: Praeger, p 42.

[117] Davies, W. (2015) *The happiness industry*, London: Verso, p 162.

[118] I am very grateful to my father, who was a GP prescribing in Britain in these years, for parts of this history. He suggests that so many mistakes were made over the use of medication because doctors often assumed that if patients kept asking for a drug, it was because it was doing good, rather than because the drug was causing dependence and addiction. The staff in prisons, old people's homes, hospitals, children's units and certain schools found it easier to cope with doped-up 'inmates'. Often in research the wrong questions were asked, or even the wrong people. Relatives and friends were often not asked if the medication had done any good; even the patients themselves were often not asked if they felt that they were back to normal. For other sources of background information see Dorling, D. (2007) 'Guest editorial: the real mental health bill', *Journal of Public Mental Health*, vol 6, no 3, pp 6-13.

[119] Swanson, J. (2013) 'Serotonin deficiency may not cause depression after all', *Salon* (via *Scientific American*), 13 December (www.salon.com/2013/12/13/new_developments_may_help_those_with_depression_partner/).

[120] Dufour, D.-R. (2008) *The art of shrinking heads: On the new servitude of the liberated in the age of total capitalism* (translation), Cambridge: Polity Press, p 72.

[121] Reported by the Canadian Broadcasting Corporation: CBC (2008) 'Use Ritalin only as last resort for kids with ADHD, guidelines say', 24 September (www.cbc.ca/news/technology/use-ritalin-only-as-last-resort-for-kids-with-adhd-guidelines-say-1.712451).

[122] NHS Quality Improvement Scotland (2007) *Clinical indicators 2007*, Glasgow: NHS Quality Improvement Scotland, pp 6, 10, 12, 24.

[123] ISD Scotland (2015) *Better information, better decisions, better health*, Data tables, NHS Scotland (www.isdscotland.org/Health-Topics/Prescribing-and-medicines/Publications/data-tables.asp?id=1309#1309).

[124] Furness, H. (2014) 'Teenagers from aspirational families suffering "executive stress burnout"', *The Telegraph*, 4 October (www.telegraph.co.uk/health/children_shealth/11140659/Teenagers-from-aspirational-families-suffering-executive-stress-burnout.html).

[125] Offer, A. (2006) *The challenge of affluence: Self-control and well-being in the United States and Britain since 1950*, Oxford: Oxford University Press, p 9.

Chapter 8

[1] Proud, A. (2014) 'Why aren't the British middle-classes staging a revolution?', *The Telegraph*, 22 September (www.telegraph.co.uk/men/thinking-man/11109845/Why-arent-the-British-middle-classes-staging-a-revolution.html). The text includes: 'Also, vain fools that we were, identified upwards. We thought the elite had our interests at heart. The 0.1% must have found this pretty cute.'

[2] For the latest (2012) US presidential election, there were '235,248,000 people of voting age in the United States, resulting in a voting age population (VAP) turnout of 54.9%', according to the fount of knowledge that is Wikipedia (http://en.wikipedia.org/wiki/Voter_turnout_in_the_United_States_presidential_elections).

[3] Bauman, Z. (2008) *The art of life*, Cambridge: Polity Press, p 6.

[4] In place of this conspiracy of the rich, and for a neat two-page recipe, should you wish to know what's going on see Wallerstein, I. (2005) 'The actor and world-systems analysis: comments on Blau and Wieviorka', *Contemporary Sociology*, vol 34, no 1, pp 9-10.

[5] Stephens, L., Ryan-Collins, J. and Boyle, D. (2008) *Co-production: A manifesto for growing the core economy*, London: New Economics Foundation, pp 7-8.

[6] There are many versions of utopia still being painted. See, for example, Marshall, A. (2014) 'Eco-utopia 2121: future car-free cities across the world' (www.ennrjournal.com/ENRIC/Data/2014/ENRIC2014%20Session%204%20Climate%20Change%20Vulnerbility.pdf).

[7] Dorling, D. (2015) 'The mother of underlying causes – economic ranking and health inequality', *Social Science & Medicine* (http://dx.doi.org/10.1016/j.socscimed.2015.01.008); see also www.dannydorling.org/?page_id=4350

[8] The insertion of the word 'apparently' is all that is needed to begin the process of dismantling the logic of this well-known argument attributed originally to John Rawls. The quotation is taken from Arneson, R.J. (2009) 'Justice is not equality', in B. Feltham (ed) *Justice, equality and constructivism: Essays on G.A. Cohen's 'Rescuing justice and equality'*, Chichester: Wiley-Blackwell, pp 5-25, at p 25.

[9] A telling photograph of Michael Gove (who even a man as pompous as David Cameron demoted from being Education Secretary for being too much of a 'pompous traditionalist') is to be found here: Bloxham, A. (2011) 'Michael Gove promises to push "unashamedly elitist" approach in state sector', *The Telegraph*, 24 November (www.telegraph.co.uk/education/educationnews/8914499/Michael-Gove-promises-to-push-unashamedly-elitist-approach-in-state-sector.html).

[10] DCSF (Department for Children, Schools and Families) (2007) *The children's plan: Building brighter futures*, London: The Stationery Office, pp 73-4 (emphasis added); they did not mean 'opportunities' when they wrote 'outcomes'. They were saying that there was no excuse for one group of children, say, black or poor children, to consistently be told they were worse than other children, to be treated worse, and to learn less.

[11] Rutherford, J. and Shah, H. (2006) *The good society: Compass Programme for Renewal*, London: Lawrence & Wishart, p 51, referring in turn to the Welsh government statement.

[12] Shuayb, M. and O'Donnell, S. (2008) *Aims and values in primary education: England and other countries*, Primary Review Research Survey 1/2, Cambridge: Faculty of Education, University of Cambridge, p 22.

[13] Haydon, D. and Scraton, P. (2008) 'Conflict, regulation and marginalisation in the North of Ireland: the experiences of children and young people', *Current Issues in Criminal Justice*, vol 20, no 1, pp 59-78, quoted in the last sentence of the article.

[14] Krugman, P. (2007) *The conscience of a liberal*, New York: W.W. Norton, p 211.

[15] Da Costa, P.N. (2014) 'Janet Yellen decries widening income inequality', *The Wall Street Journal*, 17 October (http://online.wsj.com/articles/feds-yellen-says-extreme-inequality-could-be-un-american-1413549684).

[16] Krugman (2007), as above, p 215, on an unnamed Texas legislator (identified on the web as Debbie Riddle); poll figures are given on p 202. On 7 September 2009, Debbie gave instructions to her friends and neighbours on how to avoid their children ever having to hear President Obama speaking, and claimed that '100% of this president's agenda is not to be trusted' The original blog appeared here: http://debbieriddle.org/2009/09/your-children-do-not-have-to-hear-obamas-speach/. And is now archived here: http://web.archive.org/web/20091221093944/http://debbieriddle.org/issues/

[17] *The Protestant ethic and the spirit of capitalism* is a book by Max Weber, a German sociologist, first published in German in 1905, and in English 1930. It is available online (http://en.wikipedia.org/wiki/The_Protestant_Ethic_and_the_Spirit_of_Capitalism).

[18] Dufour, D.-R. (2008) *The art of shrinking heads: On the new servitude of the liberated in the age of total capitalism* (translation), Cambridge: Polity Press, pp 168-9. The quotation continues: 'Descartes's capitalist Amsterdam has now conquered the world. It is not

just that everyone in this planetary city is now involved in trade; trade is now involved in everyone in the sense that it shapes us all.'

[19] William ordered the massacre of Catholics in Ireland, where he is remembered by some the Protestant section of the population as 'King Billy'.

[20] Harris, R. (2004) 'Government and the economy, 1688-1850', in R. Floud and P. Johnson (eds) *The Cambridge economic history of modern Britain: Volume 1: Industrialisation, 1700-1860*, Cambridge: Cambridge University Press, pp 204-37, at p 217.

[21] Dixon, T. (2005) *The invention of altruism: Making moral meanings in Victorian Britain*, Oxford: Oxford University Press, p 213, quoting Thomas Paine's *Rights of man*, part I, p 94.

[22] Du Boff, R.B. (2004) 'US hegemony: continuing decline, enduring danger', *Monthly Review*, vol 55, no 7 (www.monthlyreview.org/1203duboff.htm).

[23] Leonhardt, D. (2009) 'A bold plan sweeps away Reagan ideas', *New York Times*, 27 February. Note that as the year 2009 progressed, the plan began to look a little less bold when the President began to associate himself more closely with those associated with bankers and their ideology. In October 2009 he was awarded the Nobel Peace prize, not for what he had done, but in a move widely reported as being encouragement to be more progressive in future, both at home and abroad.

[24] OMB (Office of Management and Budget) (2009) *A new era of responsibility: Renewing America's promise*, Washington, DC: The White House (www.whitehouse.gov/sites/default/files/omb/assets/fy2010_new_era/A_New_Era_of_Responsibility2.pdf), p 9.

[25] Thanks to Dave Gordon for passing on a version of this summary; see Figures 9 and 11 at www.whitehouse.gov/omb/assets/fy2010_new_era/Inheriting_a_Legacy1.pdf

[26] Wiseman, P. and Rugaber, C.S. (2013) '2013 tax rates to rise, even with fiscal cliff deal', *The Huffington Post*, 1 January (www.huffingtonpost.com/2013/01/01/higher-taxes-in-2013-even_n_2392693.html).

[27] Rubin, R. (2014) 'Wealthiest pay higher taxes with scant US economic harm', *Bloomberg Businessweek*, 11 April (www.businessweek.com/news/2014-04-11/wealthiest-pay-bigger-bills-with-scant-u-dot-s-dot-economic-harm-taxes).

[28] The full sentence is: 'The United States comes after me, would you believe it, for capital gains tax on the sale of your first residence which is not taxable in Britain. They're trying to hit me with some bill, can you believe it?' Quoted in McSmith, A. (2014) 'American-born Boris Johnson refuses to pay hefty US tax bill', *The Daily Mail*, 20 November (www.independent.co.uk/news/uk/politics/americanborn-boris-johnson-refuses-to-pay-hefty-us-tax-bill-9874022.html). Yes, we can believe it. Yes, he paid it. Yes, we could introduce the same wealth taxes here.

[29] Grimshaw, A.D. (2002) 'A review essay on "In search of politics"', *Contemporary Sociology*, vol 31, no 3, pp 257-61, at p 259. The text missing from the quote is '(and here Bauman adopts Jacques Attali's metaphor).'

[30] Prynn, J. (2015) 'Homes in top boroughs worth more than GDP of Denmark', *London Evening Standard*, 12 January, p 9.

[31] Mernagh, M. (2014) 'Why are ordinary workers still being made to pay?', *The Irish Examiner*, 11 October (www.irishexaminer.com/viewpoints/yourview/why-are-ordinary-workers-still-being-made-to-pay-290827.html).

[32] Dolcerocca, A. and Terzioglu, G. (2015) 'Interview with Thomas Piketty: Piketty responds to criticisms from the Left', *Potemkin Review*, 6 January (http://potemkinreview.com/pikettyinterview/). He also explained: '... most of the time the kind of math that economists do would not impress a mathematician, but it is enough to impress people around them in the school of social sciences'.

[33] The Companies and Remuneration Bill had its third reading in the House of Lords on 13 July 2009, and then went for consideration to the Commons. In the strange world of immediate post-crash 2009 politics, many of their Lordships were more opposed to high rates of inequality than the Party that once represented the interests of the poorest commoners (Labour). There was little expectation that the Commons would accept the Bill and make it law, but then these were the strangest of times, and that strangeness was changing the nature of the art of the possible. When Britain was last bankrupt, in 1945, the only secure and cheap way to provide security for all, including many of the affluent, and a health service for all, was to introduce a welfare state and national health service. Being less rich can often create more possibilities.

[34] The key person proposing the amendment was Lord Taverne. The Chancellor who delivered the budget was Alistair Darling. On the amendment see http://www.equalitytrust.org.uk/news/spirit-level-cited-lords-debate and on the Bill see www.mirror.co.uk/news/columnists/maguire/2009/04/29/harriet-harman-s-equality-bill-points-to-the-route-for-a-better-britain-115875-21316506/

[35] Irvin, G. (2008) *Super rich: The rise of inequality in Britain and the United States*, Cambridge: Polity Press, p 209.

[36] Wiseman and Rugaber (2013), as above, note 26.

[37] This list is taken from Steel, M. (2008) *What's going on*, London: Simon & Schuster, p 247, and Kelsey, J. (1997) *The New Zealand experiment: A world model for structural adjustment?*, Auckland: Auckland University Press, pp 370-1.

[38] Richard Wilkinson and Kate Pickett, personal communication, 31 January 2015.

[39] This itself is, of course, just another of those lessons so easily forgotten by humans, given that our brains have not evolved to cope with having to remember so much. The original quote replaced 'people' by 'man', but that has now changed in the telling. For four versions of the chant being remembered and repeated see Field, P. (1999) 'The anti-roads movement: the struggle of memory against forgetting', in T. Jordan and A. Lent (eds) *Storming the millennium: The new politics of change*, London: Lawrence & Wishart, pp 68-79, at p 74. Patrick Field quotes Milan Kundera, as recorded in turn by Neil Goodwin in *Life in the fast lane* on the M11 road protests. And see also Bauman, Z. (2007) *Consuming life*, Cambridge: Polity Press, p 84, also referring to Milan Kundera's novel *Slowness*. Milan Kundera originally wrote these words in *The book of laughter and forgetting* in 1979. For a much fuller quote and explanation, see http://vannevar.blogspot.co.uk/2009/03/struggle-man-power-memory-forgetting.html

[40] Rodriguez, J.M., Geronimus, A.T., Bound, J. and Dorling, D. (2015) 'Black lives matter: differential mortality and the racial composition of the US electorate, 1970-2004', Paper submitted for possible publication in an academic journal. If you search for its title on the web, you'll find out if it was accepted for publication and published by the time you read this.

[41] Norton, M. (2014) 'Inequality: who gets what and why it matters', *Insights from the Behavioral and Brain Sciences*, vol 1, no 1, pp 151-5 (http://bbs.sagepub.com/content/1/1/151.full.pdf+html).

[42] Norton (2014), as above, citing, among others: Kuziemko, I., Buell, R.W., Reich, T. and Norton, M.I. (2014) 'Last-place aversion: evidence and redistributive implications', *Quarterly Journal of Economics*, vol 129, pp 105-49.

[43] John, S.K., Loewenstein, G. and Rick, S.I. (2014) 'Cheating more for less: upward social comparisons motivate the poorly compensated to cheat', *Organizational Behavior and Human Decision Processes*, vol 123, no 2, pp 101-9.

[44] Proud, A. (2014) 'Could Britain's prisons soon be as bad as America's?', *The Telegraph*, 6 October (www.telegraph.co.uk/men/thinking-man/11139520/Could-Britains-prisons-soon-be-as-bad-as-Americas.html).

[45] The most comprehensive list (as of January 2015) is available at www.prisonstudies.org/highest-to-lowest/prison_population_rate?field_region_taxonomy_tid=14

[46] When the best-off tenth of skilled manual men earned 2.55 times the amount earned by the worst-off tenth; see Section 4.5 of this volume for the ratio series. Overall wage inequality rates are, and were, much higher, with mostly men in managerial positions at the top, and mostly women in care work at the bottom by 1996.

[47] Machin, S. (2003) 'Wage inequality since 1975', in R. Dickens, P. Gregg and J. Wadsworth (eds) *The labour market under New Labour: The state of working Britain 2003*, Basingstoke: Palgrave Macmillan, chapter 12, at p 191.

[48] In 1997, Lord Peter Mandelson, then an MP, told Oliver James, who subsequently quoted this in *Affluenza* (p 471), that 'we [New Labour] are seriously relaxed about people becoming very very rich.' In 2009 he suggested that 'anti-elitism of some parts of the left on education policy has often been a dead end', presumably to cause more annoyance, as almost everyone is anti-elitist today; see BBC News (2009) 'Fee rise "must aid poor students"', 27 July (http://news.bbc.co.uk/2/hi/uk_news/education/8169838.stm). On the same day, a key government adviser, Sir Jonathon Porritt, working on a completely different area of policy, resigned, citing Mandelson as the problem: 'Lord Mandelson had been particularly hostile to the concept of sustainable development' (BBC News, 2009, 'Porritt parting shot at ministers', 27 July, http://news.bbc.co.uk/1/hi/uk/8169627.stm). One week later it was revealed that Mandelson was trying to find a job for a friend of his (Trevor Phillips) who might otherwise become a Conservative Party adviser, given how easy it was to switch sides by 2009 (according to the *Daily Mail*, www.dailymail.co.uk/news/article-1203653/Mandelson-tried-persuade-Trevor-Phillips-quit-promising-Ministerial-post.html). Neither Lord Mandelson, Sir Jonathan Porritt, or Mr Phillips held any elected post, but all were in government in one way or another, and this series of spats typified the dying days of New Labour. In January 2015 Peter Mandelson hit the headlines again, but now over his tax payments and his own growing wealth; see Davies and Ball (2015), directly below.

[49] Davies, H. and Ball, J. (2015) 'Peter Mandelson gets £400,000 tax-free loan from company he owns', *The Guardian*, 27 January (www.theguardian.com/politics/2015/jan/27/peter-mandelson-400000-pound-tax-free-loan).

[50] Which continues '… a transfer masked and rendered temporarily palatable by the chest-thumping of resurgent nationalism and the paper gains of credit-fuelled property prices' (Hamid, M., 2014, 'Why migration is a fundamental human right', *The Guardian*, 21 November, www.theguardian.com/books/2014/nov/21/mohsin-hamid-why-migration-is-a-fundamental-human-right).

[51] Even as unemployment in Germany fell to a 23-year low of 5 per cent: see Evans-Pritchard, A. (2015) 'EMU deflation is the final betrayal of southern Europe', *The Telegraph*, 7 January (www.telegraph.co.uk/finance/comment/ambroseevans_pritchard/11331694/EMU-deflation-is-the-final-betrayal-of-southern-Europe.html).

[52] For the effects of an economic crash within a period of such inequality reduction, see Figure 12, Chapter 5, this volume. I am grateful to my grandfather, Eric Charlesworth, for telling me these stories in 2009. He was born in 1916 and died in 2013, at the age of 97.

[53] O'Grady, F. (2007) 'Economic citizenship and the new capitalism', *Renewal: A Journal of Social Democracy*, vol 15, nos 2/3, pp 58-66, at pp 62-3.

[54] Burns, J. (2007) *The descent of madness: Evolutionary origins of psychosis and the social brain*, Hove: Routledge, p 182.
[55] Bauman, Z. (2008) *The art of life*, Cambridge: Polity Press, p 39; original emphasis is as Zygmunt meant it to be.
[56] Dorling, D. (2012) *The no-nonsense guide to equality*, Oxford: New Internationalist.
[57] Baggini, J. (2008) *Welcome to Everytown: A journey into the English mind* (2nd edn), London: Granta, p 181.
[58] Wilkinson, R.G. and Pickett, K. (2009) *The spirit level: Why more equal societies almost always do better*, London: Allen Lane, pp 260-1.
[59] Marx, K. (1907 [1852]) *The Eighteenth Brumaire of Louis Bonaparte*, Chicago, IL: Charles H. Kerr.
[60] Shah, H. and Goss, S. (2007) *Democracy and the public realm: Compass Programme for Renewal*, London: Lawrence & Wishart, p 17; Mohandas Gandhi's words used in the sentence before are quoted on p 11.
[61] Connelly, M. (2008) *Fatal misconception: The struggle to control world population*, Cambridge, MA: Harvard University Press, p 380.
[62] Magnason, A.S. (2008) *Dreamland: A self-help manual for a frightened nation*, London: Citizen Press Ltd, p 279.
[63] Kelsey, J. (1997) *The New Zealand experiment: A world model for structural adjustment?*, Auckland: Auckland University Press, p 393; and see pp 394-8 for just one set of ideas on the way to do the right thing.
[64] BBC News Europe (2012) 'Spain's Indignados protest here to stay', 15 May (www.bbc.co.uk/news/world-europe-18070246).
[65] And the site was dismantled twice in a week by the authorities – they just keep on coming back: Yahoo News Australia, 5 July 2013 (https://au.news.yahoo.com/a/17879013/sydney-occupy-site-dismantled-again/).
[66] Stott, R. (2010) 'Review of "Injustice" and Tony Judt's "Ill fares the land": a treatise on our present discontents: how can we rediscover the magic of more equal societies?', *British Medical Journal*, 4 August.
[67] As one *Guardian* editorial put it: 'Without the Orange Book, there may have been no coalition at all.' In Editorial (2014) 'The Guardian view on the Lib Dem Orange Book', *The Guardian*, 27 June (www.theguardian.com/commentisfree/2014/jun/27/guardian-view-liberal-democrats-orange-book).
[68] Stott (2010), as above.
[69] Simpson, L. (2011) 'Injustice: why social inequality persists', *Environment and Planning B*, vol 38, no 1, pp 191-4.
[70] Burns, J. (2007) *The descent of madness: Evolutionary origins of psychosis and the social brain*, Hove: Routledge.
[71] Coyle, D. (2010) Blog comment on *Injustice*, posted 2 May 2010 (http://blog.enlightenmenteconomics.com/blog/_archives/2010/5/2/4519257.html).
[72] Wright, J. (2010) 'Book of the month: more equal than others', *Geographical Magazine*, July, p 63.
[73] Clark, P. (2010) 'Fiery Dorling preaches to the converted', *Public Health Today*, September, p 15.
[74] If I get to be much older – it is careless to take longevity for granted, and you can take too long carefully working out exactly what you want to say. For what makes me angry, however, see Shook, K. (2014) 'Danny Dorling – Times Higher Education biography', *Times Higher*, 20 February. http://www.dannydorling.org/wp-content/files/THESBio2014.pdf
[75] Clark (2010), as above.

[76] Harkins, E. (2010) 'Review, *Injustice: Why social inequality persists*', *Scotregen*, no 50, p 20.
[77] Clark (2010), as above.
[78] Harkins (2010), as above.
[79] The fact that those who do not agree with the kinds of arguments made in a book like this rarely read through to the end helps explain why social inequality still persists. A few are convinced inequality is good, and they work hard to avoid having their views dislodged.
[80] Meyer, G., Blas, J. and Farchy, J. (2011) 'World moves closer to food price shock', *Financial Times*, 12 January.
[81] World Economic Forum (2015) *Global risks 2015: 10th edition*, Insight Report, Geneva: World Economic Forum, Table 1.1.1, p 14 (www3.weforum.org/docs/WEF_Global_Risks_2015_Report.pdf).
[82] TNN (2015) 'Assam police register 10,000 riot cases since 2012', *The Times of India*, 7 January (http://timesofindia.indiatimes.com/city/guwahati/Assam-Police-register-10000-riot-cases-since-2012/articleshow/45782883.cms).
[83] BBC News Asia (2013) 'Singapore bus death triggers riot', 9 December (www.bbc.co.uk/news/world-asia-25294918).
[84] Butterworth, M. (2008) 'House building slumps to a record low', *The Telegraph*, 20 November.
[85] DCLG (Department for Communities and Local Government) (2014) Live tables on house building, 3 December (www.communities.gov.uk/housing/housingresearch/housingstatistics/housingstatisticsby/housebuilding/livetables/).
[86] Dorling, D. (2015) *All that is solid: How the great housing disaster defines our times and what we can do about*, London: Allen Lane (see the Afterword to the paperback edition).
[87] Biswas, S. (2010) 'India's micro-finance suicide epidemic', BBC correspondent, BBC online, 16 December (www.bbc.co.uk/news/world-south-asia-11997571), who reported that: 'India's micro-finance crisis mirrors the 2008 subprime mortgage meltdown in the US, where finance companies threw cheap and easy loans at homebuyers until prices crashed and borrowers were unable to sell their homes or pay their debts.'
[88] Dorling, D. (2014) 'Why are the old dying before their time? How austerity has affected mortality rates', *New Statesman*, 7 February.
[89] Dorling, D. (2010) 'One of Labour's great successes', *The Guardian*, 28 January, p 10.
[90] Browne, J. et al (2010) *Securing a sustainable future for higher education: An independent review of higher education funding and student finance* (www.bis.gov.uk/assets/biscore/corporate/docs/s/10-1208es-securing-sustainable-higher-education-browne-report-summary.pdf) (note that the 'independent review' is a document held within the government's Department for Business, Innovation and Skills under the assets/biscore/corporate directories!).
[91] Dorling, D. (2015) 'Money changes everything', *Times Higher*, 12 February.
[92] Williams, R. (2011) '"Savage" cuts to youth spending could rob a generation of chances', *The Guardian*, 5 January.
[93] Dorling, D. (2010) 'The Browne review moves us further away from a system in which the majority can get the benefits of higher education', *Adults Learning*, November, vol 22, no 3, p 25.
[94] A high level of social mobility in a highly unequal society becoming more unequal is not a pretty sight (Russia after 1989, for instance). The study that suggested mobility rates were declining used an old-fashioned definition of class that saw job titles as more important than income. Its scheme was created in an Oxford University College, where academic staff had grand job titles but not necessarily grand incomes.

It concluded: 'Insofar, then, as a mobility problem could be thought in this respect to exist, it concerns not the overall level of mobility but rather the extent to which the experience of upward mobility is becoming less common, and that of downward mobility more common in the lives of members of successive cohorts' (Bukodi, E. et al, 2014, 'The mobility problem in Britain: new findings from the analysis of birth cohort data', *British Journal of Sociology*, 22 October, reported in the press as Butler, P., 2014, 'Decline in professional jobs fuels increase in downward mobility', *The Guardian*, 6 November, www.theguardian.com/society/2014/nov/06/downward-mobility-graduates-parents-jobs-careers).

[95] Grove, J. (2014) 'Hundreds of PhD students chasing every early career post', *The Times Higher*, 6 November (www.timeshighereducation.co.uk/news/hundreds-of-phd-students-chasing-every-early-career-post/2016799.article).

[96] See the wonderful world of Wikipedia wisdom: http://en.wikipedia.org/wiki/Vote_for_Students_pledge

[97] Dorling, D. (2011) 'Clearing the poor away', in N. Yeates, T. Haux, R. Jawad and M. Kilkey (eds) *In defence of welfare: The impacts of the Comprehensive Spending Review*, London: Social Policy Association, pp 14-16.

[98] Orwell, G. (1949) *Nineteen Eighty-Four*, London: Secker and Warburg.

[99] DfE (Department for Education) (2011) *A new approach to child poverty: Tackling the causes of disadvantage and transforming families' lives*, April, London: HM Government (www.gov.uk/government/publications/a-new-approach-to-child-poverty-tackling-the-causes-of-disadvantage-and-transforming-families-lives).

[100] Bennett, A. (2014) 'Child poverty soars in UK as charities lament "lack of progress"', *Huffington Post*, 1 July (www.huffingtonpost.co.uk/2014/07/01/uk-child-poverty-iain-duncan-smith_n_5547084.html).

[101] Dorling, D. (2010) 'Letter: Boris is right to fight housing cuts', *London Evening Standard*, 1 November, p 47.

[102] 'A political storm broke today after a government minister claimed that plans to cap welfare benefits would prompt an exodus of Labour voters from London. The unnamed Conservative minister was quoted as describing the policy as "the Highland Clearances" – the eviction of farmers from the Scottish highlands and islands in the 18th and 19th centuries', as reported by Murphy, J. (2010) 'Welfare cuts "will be like the Highland Clearances"', *Evening Standard* (quoting in turn from *The Telegraph*, 7 October, www.thisislondon.co.uk/standard/article-23885725-welfare-cuts-will-be-like-the-highland-clearances.do).

[103] Wintour, P. (2015) '40% of British families "too poor to play a part in society"', *The Guardian*, 19 January (www.theguardian.com/society/2015/jan/19/british-families-poor-society-income-level-cost-of-living-benefit-cuts).

[104] Oxfam (2015) 'Richest 1% will own more than all the rest by 2016', Press release, 19 January (www.oxfam.org/en/pressroom/pressreleases/2015-01-19/richest-1-will-own-more-all-rest-2016).

[105] Peter Kralj, personal communication, 22 January 2015. Peter is the author of *Wealth creation or redistribution: How a select group profit at the expense of the rest* (CreateSpace Independent Publishing Platform, latest edition 2015).

[106] See Kralj (2015), as above. Peter Kralj is Head of Chambers, Griffin Capital (www.thearbitrationchambers.com/sample-page/peter-kralj-griffin-capital).

[107] Dorling, D. (2010) 'Are students pre-programmed to live with inequality?', *The Guardian (Education)*, 26 October.

108 Frank Field suggested redefining the child poverty measure rather than reducing child poverty in the style in which Margaret Thatcher had attempted to redefine away unemployment 30 years earlier.

109 Dorling, D. (2010) 'Axing the child poverty measure is wrong', *The Guardian Society*, 16 June, p 4. A mention should also be made of Frank Field's Labour Party (but coalition-commissioned) sidekick, Graham Allen MP, who suggested that city investors could make a profit out of sponsoring schemes to reduce child poverty, and so turned the clock back a few more years again towards Victorian values of profit motives and paternalism: see Gentleman, A. (2011) 'Making the case for early intervention', *The Guardian*, 19 January.

110 Dorling, D. (2010) 'Britain must close the great pay divide', *The Observer*, 28 November.

111 Hutton, W. (2015) 'A too powerful financial elite threatens wider prosperity', *The Observer*, 25 January.

112 Dorling, D. (2010) 'The super-rich are still soaring away', *New Statesman*, 27 April (www.newstatesman.com/blogs/the-staggers/2010/04/super-rich-rise-inequality).

113 Dorling, D. (2011) *So you think you know about Britain?*, London: Constable and Robinson, ch 7.

114 Some £183,500 million (£519 billion less £335.5 billion) spread over approximately 30 million families (http://en.wikipedia.org/wiki/Sunday_Times_Rich_List_2014).

115 Pickett, K. and Dorling, D. (2010) 'Against the organization of misery? The Marmot review of health inequalities', *Social Science & Medicine*, vol 71, pp 1231-3.

116 Dorling, D. (2010) 'New Labour and inequality: Thatcherism continued?', *Local Economy*, vol 25, nos 5–6, August-September, pp 397-413.

117 Davies, W. (2015) *The happiness industry*, London: Verso, p 61 (of proofs).

118 Rose, J. (2014) *Women in dark times*, London: Bloomsbury, p 268 (writing of Rosa Luxemburg and her arrival in Berlin).

119 Dorling, D. (2010) 'Mean machine: structural inequality makes social inequality seem natural', *New Internationalist*, no 433, pp 20-1 (www.sasi.group.shef.ac.uk/publications/2010/Dorling_2010_New_Internationalist_2010.pdf).

120 It is worth remembering in conclusion that '… with the roughly 300,000 generations that humans spent as hunter-gatherers and the 500 generations they spent as agrarians, the 9 generations passed in the industrial era and the 1 generation so far spent in the emerging post-industrial era … a drop in the bucket of time. As organisms, we cannot possibly have adapted to the environment in which we now find ourselves' (Massey, D.S., 2002, 'A brief history of human society: the origin and role of emotion in social life: 2001 Presidential Address', *American Sociological Review*, vol 67, no 1, p 15). Note that 300,000 is probably an over-estimate, as it gives modern hunter-gatherers a six-million-year history. Humans, in our current state as evolved social animals with sophisticated language, have possibly only experienced around 3,000 generations. We really are all still learning and trying to understand exactly where fate has placed us. My parents grew up without computers, my grandparents without television, my great-grandparents without radio, and not all of their parents were able to read. Only very recently have we, the majority of humanity, been given access to enough information to be able to discover so much for ourselves. No wonder we are confused, do not agree, and often continue to preach the unjust thinking of the tiny minority who used to hold such a monopoly on knowledge.

121 Booth, R. (2014) 'New Era estate protest: "We are asking for the moral thing – leave our homes"', *The Guardian*, 1 December (www.theguardian.com/society/2014/dec/01/new-era-housing-estate-protest-mayfair).

[122] Staff reporter (2014) 'Londoners toast victory over "greedy" US rent-hikers, stave off eviction', *Aljazeera News America*, 19 December (http://america.aljazeera.com/articles/2014/12/19/new-era-housing.html).

[123] Martin, I. (2014) 'MPs' expenses: a scandal that will not die', *The Telegraph*, 13 April (www.telegraph.co.uk/news/newstopics/mps-expenses/10761548/MPs-expenses-A-scandal-that-will-not-die.html).

[124] Ferdinand Lassalle, 1862, who was paraphrased by Rosa Luxemburg in 1906 as: 'The most revolutionary thing one can do is always to proclaim loudly what is happening' (http://permalink.gmane.org/gmane.politics.marxism.marxmail/175220).

[125] Williams, R.H. (1989) *Resources of hope*, London: Verso, p 118. Raymond Henry Williams was a Welsh socialist academic, and this book was published posthumously.

[126] Krieger, N. (2000) 'Passionate epistemology, critical advocacy, and public health: doing our profession proud', *Critical Public Health*, vol 10, no 3, pp 287-94, at p 292, who does, indeed, provide a very good guide to being on the side of the angels.

[127] Ritzer, G. (2004) *The globalization of nothing*, London: Sage Publications, p 216.

[128] As quoted in one of Ulrich Beck's obituaries: Kaldo, M. and Selchow, S. (2015) 'Ulrich Beck obituary, German sociologist who pointed to the risks that come from technological change', *The Guardian*, 6 January (www.theguardian.com/education/2015/jan/06/ulrich-beck). Ulrich Beck dedicated his life to trying to understand uncontrollability, ignorance and uncertainty in the here and now. He was born a week after the Second World War ended, and died on the first day of 2015. He knew that the human world was not just changing but becoming something completely new, something utterly unpredictable was coming. He found a way to give others hope despite so much uncertainty, and perhaps because there was so much uncertainty, so much to play for and so much that could still be won.

NAME INDEX

Page references for notes are followed by note numbers (in italics), eg 395*n9*

SUBJECT INDEX

Page references for notes are followed by note numbers, eg 395*n9*

C

D

E

H

I

J

K

L

S

T

V

W

Y